Green Infrastructure for Sustainable Urban Development in Africa

This book shows for the first time how green infrastructure can work in an African urban context. On one level it provides a major rethinking of the role of infrastructure in urban society since the creation of networked infrastructure in the early 20th Century. On another, it explores the changing paradigms of urban development through the fundamental question of how decisions are made.

With a focus on Africa's fast-growing secondary towns, where 70% of the urban population live, the book explains how urban infrastructure provides the key to the relationship between economic development and social equity, through the mediation of natural resources. Adopting this view enables investment to be channelled more effectively to provide the engine for economic growth, while providing equitable services for all residents. At the same time, the management of resource flows integrates the metabolism of the city into the wider ecosystem. This vision leads to a new way of thinking about infrastructure, giving clear definition to the concept of Green Infrastructure.

Indigenous solutions are needed to address the failure of urban development in Africa, which is due, in large measure, to the use of inappropriate Western development models. The history of control over Africa's intellectual space by Western countries and external agencies continues through current planning methodologies and the influence of international organisations. Addressing the issue of how Africans regain control is a prerequisite to tackling the decisions that define the continent's long-term development.

On the basis of research gathered throughout an extensive career, John Abbott draws in particular from his experience in Ethiopia to demonstrate the ways in which infrastructure needs to respond to the economies, societies and natural environments of 21st Century urban Africa.

John Abbott is an international consultant specialising in the management of urban infrastructure, most recently with the government of Ethiopia. Over his career he has worked in local government, NGOs, the private sector and academia, where he was Professor of Urban Engineering at the University of Cape Town, South Africa.

Green Infrastructure for Sustainable Urban Development in Africa

John Abbott

publishing for a sustainable future

First published 2012
by Earthscan
2 Park Square, Milton Park, Abingdon, Oxon OX14 4RN

Simultaneously published in the USA and Canada
by Earthscan
711 Third Avenue, New York, NY 10017

Earthscan is an imprint of the Taylor & Francis Group, an informa business

British Library Cataloguing in Publication Data
A catalogue record for this book is available from the British
Library

Library of Congress Cataloging in Publication Data
Abbott, John, 1947–
   Green infrastructure for sustainable urban design in Africa/John
   Abbott.
   p. cm.
   Includes bibliographical references and index.
   1. Sustainable urban development–Africa. 2. Sustainable urban
   development–Government policy–Africa. 3. Urban ecology
   (Sociology)–Africa. 4. City planning–Africa. I. Title.
   HT169.A3A23 2012
   307.1416096–dc23

                                                    2011034155

ISBN: 978-1-849-71472-3 (hbk)
ISBN: 978-0-203-13822-9 (ebk)

Typeset in Baskerville
by Wearset Ltd, Boldon, Tyne and Wear

MIX
Paper from
responsible sources
FSC
www.fsc.org   FSC® C004839

Printed and bound in Great Britain by
CPI Antony Rowe, Chippenham, Wiltshire

Contents

     Notes   454
     References   465
     Index   477

Figures

Tables

Acknowledgements

This book draws on experience that covers several decades and has bene-fited from interactions with many people over that time. With each inter-action I have learned something new and would like to offer my thanks and appreciation to everyone, recognising that the list is too great to cover every individual by name. At the same time, there have been a number of specific experiences that have had a major impact on the way I see this world of urban development, particularly in the smaller towns. These fall into three stages. First there was my community-based infrastructure work of the 1980s that began after the South African government changed its forced removals policy. The experience of working with civic associations, both through and after the State of Emergency that was imposed in the mid-1980s, was transforming. In particular, I would like to acknowledge here Mr Zwane, chair of the Kwa Thandeka civic, and his committee; the residents' committee of Ramakodi in the Winterveld; the civic association of Langa, Uitenhage informal settlement near Port Elizabeth, and col-leagues at PLANACT, an inspirational development NGO during difficult political times.

The second period was in the 1990s working on informal settlement upgrading in Cape Town. Here I would like to thank Mr Mvumvu, the chair of the New Rest informal settlement Civic Association, for all our work together on upgrading; Siviwe Matika, in memoriam, without whose political influence, support and involvement the work would never have advanced to create a new methodology for informal settlement upgrading; my students of the time Iuma Martinez, David Douglas and Nic Graham; and my friend and colleague Ivo Imperato, currently with the World Bank in Mozambique, who facilitated and supported the linkage between Cape Town and Belo Horizonte in Brazil and the transfer of upgrading practices.

The third phase was in the 2000s working in Ethiopia. This provided the catalyst to finally write this book. My thanks go first to my close col-league and friend Ato Fikreyohanes Yadessa, for his hard work, unfailing support and immense insight; to all in the Ministry of Works and Urban

Development (now the Ministry of Urban Development and Construction), in particular Dr Abraham Tekeste and Ato Abuye Aneley; to colleagues in GTZ IS, the Urban Institute and the GIZ Urban Good Governance and Decentralisation Programme; and to the mayors, city managers and staff in the project cities.

Cutting across time, a special word of thanks goes to my good friend and colleague Barry Jackson. Throughout the 1980s and 1990s, whenever I argued against different development approaches, be it variable levels of services, privatisation of urban water supply or the fragmentation of the urban infrastructure base, it was Barry who pushed me to provide a workable alternative. Well, Barry, it may have taken longer than expected, but here it is!

As regards my writing of this book, the greatest tribute is to my wife, Ania Grobicki, who has been my inspiration and pillar of support, providing discussion, input, feedback and ideas of her own that have contributed significantly to the final outcome. Whenever I was blocked or could not see a way forward she was always there to help me over the hurdle; I could not have written the book without her. My thanks also go to Ania, daughter Stephanie and son James for being so patient and supportive over what often appeared to them to be a never-ending saga.

Finally, I would like to thank my editor, Nicki Dennis of Earthscan, for taking on the book and providing me with support and the benefit of her knowledge and expertise to make it happen.

Chapter 1

The failure of western intervention in Africa

Introduction

This book is written on two levels, which will be explored interactively. On one level this is a book about urban infrastructure, and its potential to support a sustainable urban future in the rapidly urbanising countries of sub-Saharan Africa. On a broader level, though, it is a book about the nature of decision-making in development, and ultimately an exploration of how much 'freedom' African countries really have when taking decisions that affect their own development. That African cities (and countries) are underdeveloped is not in question; the real question, which has still not been answered almost fifty years after the majority of African countries achieved independence, is why.

In the first thirty years or so, it was primarily Marxist academics and practitioners who sought to explore this question, and they had a relatively easy task, since the spectre of imperialist hegemony still loomed large in Africa, as did the spectres of both neo-liberalism and neo-colonialism. However, twenty years further on, these arguments about physical and economic domination become ever more difficult to sustain. The condition can no longer be defined solely in terms of a construct based upon the overwhelming power of a dominant economic system. Social concerns are higher up the agenda and the world is more concerned with how to achieve the Millennium Development Goals (MDGs).

And yet the niggling doubt persists. Are we really living in a world where African governments are the masters of their own decisions? Is the answer really as simple as abandoning aid in favour of direct foreign investment? On the other hand, if there is some truth in this belief that sub-Saharan Africa has never fully escaped from colonialism, how can this possibly be justified after so long a period? The problem with the Marxist analysis is that it constantly sought to rationalise events primarily within an economic framework, even if this meant adjusting what it saw to fit with what it believed. This is understandable, since it would not be Marxist otherwise; but it can be limiting. But even after Marxism lost its power to question, it is still economic analysis that dominates the debate, as the book *Dead Aid* by Dambisa Moyo (2009) shows.

There is an alternative view, though. None of us can claim to be totally free from a value system; that is an integral part of what it means to be human. In this case – and it is important to say this upfront – the ideas and beliefs that underpin this book derive from a value system embedded in the teaching of Keir Hardie, the great Scottish social reformer, whose work provided the moral framework and the social bedrock of our household when I was a child.

That does not imply a socialist perspective, as many might immediately conclude. Such a term is, in any case, fairly meaningless in the world of the twenty-first century, regardless of whether one regrets, or rejoices in, its passing. What it does imply is that the focus of the analysis lies within the social sphere, rather than the economic arena. So while this background does carry its own 'baggage', it at least allows an exploration of the wider development arena outside the confines of a dominating economic construct, and this has enabled an intellectual freedom of thought which, it is hoped, will enable this book to take a different approach to African urban development from those written previously.

Why infrastructure?

The subtext of the book, as is reflected in its title, is urban governance, with a specific focus on infrastructure governance. But governance cannot be separated from the development process (though it often is); hence, it is that process which is central to the study. Ultimately, the objective, as indicated at the beginning, is the creation of a sustainable urban infrastructure base that can provide the foundation for ongoing development, and a basis for sound and effective governance.

At first glance, while urban infrastructure may appear to be an unusual perspective from which to explore wider socio-political issues, it does have its own rationality. First, the failure to provide urban infrastructure is one of the great development failures of the twentieth century, not only in sub-Saharan Africa but in many other developing countries. And yet to date, none of the arguments for this failure, be they rapid urban growth, low income levels or high costs, are fully convincing. So, there has to be another answer, which then begs the question as to whether we are looking at infrastructure in the right way.

Obviously this is not a simple issue. Management and operational capacity constraints are clearly critical issues, and have a role to play, but they are not the core issue. It has then been proposed that what we are dealing with here is a lack of political will on the part of African leaders, a view that UN-Habitat (2008) puts forward when discussing the failure of countries in Africa to decentralise. Again perhaps a possibility; but this too is questionable, given that the failure is widespread across so many diverse countries.

There is, however, another option, namely that the failure is linked to external interventions. This argument has been discredited to some degree by the ideological dimension of this position, which has generally been situated within an economic discourse. Yet there is a need to look at the role of external actors much more critically than has been done to date. In doing this, however, we need to start from a clearly stated position, which is a recognition that we are no longer dealing with an exploitative development scenario here, regardless of whether or not this was the case under colonialism. On the contrary, it has to be assumed that the majority of those working in the field of development (speaking now specifically of external actors) are well intentioned, knowledgeable, at least within their own specialisations, and genuinely believe they have something to contribute to the development process in Africa.

Finally, we have a third option, which asks the question: what if there is simply too much external input? This debate, to the extent that it exists, tends to focus on the oppressive impact of aid. This has been a recurring theme in the literature on development, going back to the early 1970s,[1] when the focus was primarily political and linked to aid as a tool of imperialism, and continuing to the present time,[2] sometimes with the same focus, sometimes with a different one, yet always strongly passionate – as, of course, are those in the opposite camp who argue the benefits of aid. This polarised, and again often ideological, to and fro sees aid in a direct causal relationship with an outcome, which is either negative or positive depending upon the author you read; yet the debate is still no nearer to a solution now than it was when it began forty years earlier.

So, perhaps the time has come to start looking at this question of external involvement from a different perspective. In keeping with the social reference framework used here, the idea is that, instead of discussing aid per se, we should rather explore the potential for oppression (interpreted here in the sense of suffocation, not exploitation) caused through the sheer weight of external cultural and intellectual involvement.

This last point is the least explored of the three perspectives, yet perhaps the most important, though I would suggest that what we are looking at in practice is some combination of all of them. The challenge is to understand the interplay between them, and in this context infrastructure provides an ideal framework within which to explore the issue. And we do need new ideas. For if there is one thing that we can say, and this is as good a point to begin the discussion as any, is while the past fifty years have seen a continuous shift in external approaches to urban development practice, in an attempt to address this failure, none of them has, to date, proved blindingly successful.

Throughout all this time, though, there has been one inexorable trend in urban infrastructure, which is the steady, but continuous, decline in the 'level of service' provided to urban residents – and in particular to the politically weak group in society known as the 'urban poor'. This has now reached a point, with the 'basic needs' approach to service delivery, epitomised by the MDGs, where the level of infrastructure service aimed for has reached the bottom – the absolute minimum – and can go no lower; yet even this minimum target cannot be achieved. Why? Nobody actually knows. However, we can question the external response, which is to throw ever greater sums of money towards paying ever greater numbers of external western 'consultants' and new specialist 'delivery agencies' in order to meet moving targets. Surely the time has come to recognise that there is a much more fundamental malaise involved here, and the only way to address this issue in any meaningful way is to stop throwing money at 'solutions' aimed at addressing the symptoms, and instead return to the root of the problem and find the real cause.

What is needed here is a complete rethink of the way in which urban society functions, particularly a society where the majority of the residents are poor. In that context a rethink about the role of urban infrastructure in sub-Saharan Africa, and associated delivery processes, is not only essential, but central to the discussion. Unfortunately, we still live with a mindset about urban infrastructure that was created in the nineteenth century for a world that was completely different from the one we now live in. Sub-Saharan Africa of the twenty-first century is a quite different place as compared with Britain in the nineteenth.

A second reason why infrastructure should be seen as a basis for African development relates to the symbiotic relationship that exists between infrastructure, the social construct of an urban society, and the physical environment. Before the Reagan–Thatcher economic reforms of the 1980s, urban infrastructure was grounded largely in a social development construct. The degree may have differed, with America, not surprisingly, having a more dominant economic focus; yet even there the social context existed, as embodied by the American concept of 'public works'. This means that underpinning the provision of urban infrastructure to the rich countries of the world in the twentieth century was the principle not simply of social improvement but also of social equity – a principle that is far more crucial to political and social stability in Africa than the economic principle that has replaced it: affordability.

Thus, infrastructure is about far more than technology; that is only the physical manifestation. Rather, infrastructure is an integral part of the social and cultural framework of an urban society. So, it is to that framework that we must look first to initiate change and develop a new approach. Such a rethink would need to be broad in scope, involving not only a new approach to the social, economic and political framework that underpins urban development, but also, and perhaps more importantly, an exploration of the external intellectual forces that shape that framework. It is to this last issue that we must turn first, to begin our analysis, if we are to reach an understanding of the wider canvas upon which urban development plays itself out.

Who really controls African development?

On a superficial level, the determinants that have led to the current urban conditions which prevail throughout most of sub-Saharan Africa are relatively straightforward: inappropriate policies and ineffective implementation strategies result in poor decision-making which leads to failed outcomes. How easy it is, for those looking in from the outside, particularly in the western countries, to blame this on weak leadership, or corruption, or simply mismanagement by African governments. This book will argue that not only is this far too simplistic an answer but, more worryingly, it is grossly unfair and inaccurate. To get to the heart of this failure we need to delve much deeper, and explore one central, albeit quite complex, question, which is: *who really made the decisions that led to the current urban condition?* Or, phrased slightly differently, *where did the ideas come from that failed repeatedly, time after time?* And the heart of this central question is not: who makes the decisions; but rather: who decides who makes the decisions; and who actually decides what decisions will be made, where they will be made, and how they will be made? The real issue is not who decides – the answer to that is fairly straightforward; the real question is who decides who decides, and that is far more complex. Whatever the answer, this book would argue that one thing is clear: wherever the location for the decisions about exactly what decisions African countries can take may be situated, it is certainly not in the capital cities of sub-Saharan Africa.

Those Marxist analysts of old, looking at colonial history, highlighted a critically important issue, namely that colonial oppression was as much an oppression of the culture as it was military dominance and economic exploitation; yet they failed to follow the exploration of this strand of colonial oppression through to its logical outcome. The reason for that failure, of course, is that Marxism, while recognising the greater oppression, always returns to its (perceived) roots in economic oppression, and in doing so misses the deeper and more insidious oppression of the colonised countries, which is, on the one hand, not simply the oppression of the cultural space, but also, on the other hand, and less well documented, the domination of the wider intellectual space.

The nineteenth century was the industrial age, when mechanics ruled and the perceived future was one driven by technology for the benefit of society. And we have to acknowledge that many Africans also bought into the technological dream. Now, though, as we view it only 150 years later, we can see that this advance came at a huge cost. It was not only an accumulation of wealth that was occurring through industrialisation; it was a theft of resources, perhaps unintended but no less a theft for that, coupled with a transfer of the true exploitation cost of industrialisation elsewhere, in the form of an ever-growing debt burden. And the bank that had to carry this burden of debt was the biosphere. That of course is the core of the climate change debate with regard to carbon output. The real issue is not how much carbon different countries discharge to the atmosphere now; the question is how do we allocate a cost to the benefit gained from adding all that carbon to the atmosphere previously?

This issue of carbon discharge was not, of course, recognised at the time. The technologies developed in the nineteenth and early twentieth centuries were based upon an open-ended supply of resources and, equally important, a boundless space in which to discharge the waste. That model is now coming up against the reality of the earth as a closed system. Yet we cannot simply blame technology for our present impasse, though we will need to seriously change our view of, and approach towards, technology. The first step is to go broader, to assess the nature of the system that operates the technology.

In an article entitled 'All Cultures Are Not Equal', Kenan Malik[3] (2002) quotes a statement by the Marxist writer and theorist C. L. R. James as follows: 'I denounce European colonialism.... But I respect the learning and profound discoveries of Western civilisation' (James, 1980, p. 179). Malik then goes on to say:

> James was one of the great radicals of the twentieth century, an anti-imperialist, a superb historian of black struggles, a Marxist who remained one even when it was no longer fashionable to be so. But today, James' defence of 'Western civilisation' would probably be dismissed as Eurocentric, even racist.

This analysis by Malik provides the key, with the use of the word 'civilisation', but previously we have tried it in the wrong locks. As a result, we have been forced back on clichés, such as neo-colonialism or neo-liberalism, to try to explain what lay behind the unopened door. Much more telling, when it comes to exploring how a colonising race first obtains, and then retains, dominance over other societies, is the exploration by the historian Peter Berresford Ellis of how the Romans defined their relationship with the least well known of their serious antagonists in their early development phase: the Celts. Speaking about this relationship in the context of the Druids – the 'Celtic intelligentsia' – he writes:

> The early surviving sources about the Druids are written in support of Rome and its conquest of the Celts and suppression of the Druids. In

AD 54 the Roman Emperor Claudius officially prohibited the Druids by law. It was an obvious move for Rome to make: in order to conquer any people and absorb them, you first have to get rid of their intellectuals and destroy their cultural knowledge.

(1998, p. 63)

Here we see two elements at play that define all forms of oppressions: control over the intellectual debate and the suppression of the intellectual base of the oppressed. It is to these aspects of oppression that we must look to understand the current development scenario in Africa.

The words of Berresford Ellis quoted above are timeless, and could just as easily describe the oppression of the indigenous African population in South Africa under apartheid, but are they valid elsewhere? After all, apartheid was a special case, was it not? In addition, there is the valid point that Africa was not the only continent to suffer colonial oppression. Many other countries found themselves in the same situation; and the majority have found mechanisms to deal with the consequences more effectively than is the case across generally in sub-Saharan Africa.

To understand the wider (sub-Saharan) African canvas, we need to understand more fully the way in which external dominance shifted over time, and the forces that drove this shift. In the sections that follow, I will argue that the way in which the colonial relationship evolved in the subcontinent (sub-Saharan Africa) is quite different from how it did so in other countries, and that Africa, because of its history, was not capable of emerging from colonial control in the way that countries in other parts of the world were able to do. The focus in the book is concerned primarily with anglophone Africa, since it is an exploration in English, and here the locus of external control was Britain. This was therefore a critical relationship. This book will argue that it remains critical to this day, and that British influence is much more deeply ingrained than has been assumed previously, with unintended, yet fairly catastrophic, consequences for Africa. The use of the word 'unintended' is intentional and critical. This book acknowledges that the British government and the British people have, by and large, the best of intentions towards Africa. What is being explored is the nature of cultural and intellectual domination in a modern context, a context dominated increasingly by global, English-language media, with the term 'media' being used here in its widest sense to reflect all forms of communication. This domination by the English-language media leads to the question: to what extent does the use of one specific language as a global communication vehicle enable, or facilitate, cultural domination by those, in this case primarily the American and the British, who have it as their home language?

Of worldviews, paradigms and *Weltanschauungen*

Worldviews

Berresford Ellis's book on Celtic history in Europe,[4] quoted earlier, provides an interesting analogy that is surprisingly relevant to the present
context. For the author shows how there were two, quite diverse, views of
this important civilisation, but that the vast majority of people who read
history know only one: that written by the Celts' conquerors, the Romans,
who clearly had their own specific perspective and agenda. It is said that
the victors define history, but there is a more subtle, and relevant, point
here, namely that it is those who write the books (or who generate the
websites) who define the perceived reality; and it is this perception that
matters.

The problem is: how do we penetrate the perception to arrive at a
deeper truth, or even an alternative view? Berresford Ellis's book on the
Celts of course deals with history, and describes the problems of trying to
get beyond the interpretation of events provided by a historical dominant
culture (Roman) that no longer exists. That is a minor problem compared
to the one we face here. For seeking to explore the impact of a dominant
culture from within its own time, while that dominance is still in force, is
even more difficult. What we are looking at in the exploration of anglophone Africa is a dominant culture, and that dominant culture is referred
to as Anglo-Saxon.[5]

The first problem we encounter when we seek to understand the nature
of a dominant culture is related to the way in which we communicate,
using a verbal language, which in turn requires a vocabulary. Those
belonging to a dominant culture, by the very nature of a culture, have
little need for words or phrases that describe how they control cultural
and intellectual space; after all, their view is the accepted reality. So, we
come up against a conundrum: those whose language dominates define
the ideas, not only through their ability to define the common usage of
words and phrases, but also through the absence, or at least the paucity, of
words to describe how the subservient cultures view the dominant one.

To the extent that we can speak of this phenomenon of cultural and
intellectual domination at all, we do have the term 'worldview', as being
something that reflects '[t]he overall perspective from which one sees and
interprets the world' (*Free Dictionary*, 2010). Yet while this may express the
condition at a very broad level, it is also very imprecise, not least because it
is itself a translation of a German word, *Weltanschauung*, a term that will be
returned to later.

This term 'worldview' has also been described as '[a] collection of
beliefs about life and the universe held by an individual or a group' (*Free
Dictionary*, 2010). Yet this interpretation does not sit easily with the

previous one. How, for example, does one go down to the level of those individual beliefs conceptually? The fact is that we have taken a term that has real meaning in another language, in this case German. When we translate it into English we may be able to use it up to a point; but we are not able to take it to a level of detail, because for a dominant culture there is simply no need to do so. That is the paradox we face when we seek to explore dominant cultures: we simply lack the terms that might help us in that task.

Paradigms

But we do have a term: 'paradigm' – isn't that appropriate? Well, actually, no it isn't. The word 'paradigm' was created, in its modern form, by the historian of science Thomas Kuhn in the 1960s. Prior to that, it had been used in its Greek derivative form to describe distinct concepts in linguistics and science (Kuhn, 1996). Kuhn 'gave *paradigm* its contemporary meaning when he adopted the word to refer to the set of practices that define a scientific discipline at any particular period of time' (Wikipedia, 2010e). His own preference, and the translation in the *Oxford English Dictionary*, interprets the word as a pattern or model, but mainly an 'exemplar'. In this context, then, if we seek to use this word in the context of a dominant culture, then the impact is to reinforce that culture rather than question or challenge it.

This problem is compounded when we look at the second element of Kuhn's exposition of the word, which is that paradigms are incommensurable, meaning that 'two paradigms cannot be reconciled with each other because they cannot be subjected to the same common standard of comparison' (Kuhn, 1996). And the whole purpose of an exploration of a dominant culture and its impact is constructed around a presupposition of different 'standards', since culture is itself linked to a value system.

Thus, the word 'paradigm' is used quite easily by those already within the dominant culture, since the very definition of the term acts to reinforce the dominance of that culture, or at best to question it gently and safely from the inside; but it is totally inappropriate for use in exploring the dominant culture from the outside. To say so is not being pedantic; if we use words that mean something else, then we risk misdirecting the debate and blocking meaningful analysis. We are left with only one solution. If we are serious about unbundling the worldview of the dominant culture, then we have to integrate the word *Weltanschauung*[6] into the English language; for only then can we really begin to understand the full cultural and intellectual implications of domination.

At this point, you, as a reader, have just undergone your first test. If, in reading this, you fail to see the point of the discussion, then this means that you most likely belong to the dominant culture; that is, you are comfortable with an Anglo-Saxon worldview. If, on the other hand, you find the discussion intriguing and are interested in seeing where it is going, then you are probably someone who is situated outside the dominant culture; that is, there are aspects of the Anglo-Saxon worldview that you experience as oppressive, or at least constraining.

Weltanschauungen[7]

There are several components to the term '*Weltanschauung*', as we would expect from such a complex idea. In the first instance, a *Weltanschauung* 'describes a consistent (to a varying degree) and integral sense of existence and provides a framework for generating, sustaining, and applying knowledge' (Wikipedia, 2010c). That is exactly what we are talking of here. And if we see the existing Anglo-Saxon worldview as a dominant *Weltanschauung*, then we also can see how any challenge to that view is extremely threatening, calling into question not only the value base of the dominant culture, but also the knowledge structure that it uses to underpin that dominance.

The second aspect relates to language, which is described as follows: 'The linguistic relativity hypothesis ... describes how the syntactic-semantic structure of a language becomes an underlying structure for the *Weltanschauung* of a people through the organization of the causal perception of the world and the linguistic categorization of entities.' Further, 'The language of a people reflects the *Weltanschauung* of that people in the form of its syntactic structures and untranslatable connotations and its denotations' (Wikipedia, 2010c).

In linguistics, the exploration of this side of the *Weltanschauung* is often used to better understand different peoples, in the way that Whorf in the United States used it to contribute to an understanding of different Native American minorities (Wikipedia, 2010d). In terms of the current dominant Anglo-Saxon *Weltanschauung*, however, we can see how the overwhelming use of English as a global language contributes to, and partially explains, the extent of the dominance of the current Anglo-Saxon world order.

The third aspect of the *Weltanschauung*, which is actually the one of greatest relevance to this book and its topic, picks up on the aspect described above as 'the linguistic categorization of entities'. In this context, Kay and Kempton (1984) made the observation that '[a]s linguistic categorization emerges as a representation of worldview and causality, it further modifies social perception and thereby leads to a continual interaction between language and perception' (Wikipedia, 2010c). This sentence is absolutely crucial to an understanding of what is driving urban development in Africa today. It is not that the current all-pervading dominance of economics (whether it is the capitalism decried by Marxists, or the value of foreign direct investment beloved by capitalists) is unimportant. It is rather that economics is only one of several elements that comprise the greater Anglo-Saxon *Weltanschauung*, or worldview. In its use of this expression (Anglo-Saxon) the book differs from the French interpretation, arguing that the original (French) definition of the term, which the authors perceived as being grounded primarily in economics, failed to see the wider intellectual and cultural domination that is implicit in a global hegemony. This is, of course, because the French always refused to accept the reality of global cultural domination (at least by anyone other than themselves) – but that is a separate debate.

It is on this wider stage, then, that the notion of an Anglo-Saxon *Weltanschauung*, described previously as 'a collection of beliefs', becomes critically important. I will show how these beliefs extend into every aspect of development thinking, and in doing so how they predefine the development path, particularly in urban development, and so constrain African freedom of action. That is the basis for intellectual domination which constitutes, in an African sense, a continuation of colonisation, the only distinction being that we have moved from physical occupation to the colonisation of Africa's intellectual space. Before we can move on to explore these issues further, though, we first need to explore how we came to be there in the first place.

The rise of Anglo-Saxon hegemony, 1815–2009

There is a broad recognition, evident in numerous books and newspaper articles, that the world is changing, and the changes that are coming will bring about a new world order. A much more interesting question is what lies at the heart of the change. In a book on the rise of American power in the Pacific region, Bruce Cumings argued that the dominating American role in the world emerged out of Cold War necessities, 'ow[ing] more to NATO than to Plato' (Cumings, 2010, p. 5, quoting David Armitage). In writing this, the author follows the commonly accepted view that dominance is linked to a combination of military force (alternatively viewed as a military-industrial complex) and economic power.

In 2002, O'Brien and Clesse published a collection of essays on the nature of British and American hegemony in the nineteenth and twentieth centuries. While this may have generated a great deal of angst and soul-searching around specific terms, such as 'empire', for example, the broad gist of the evolutionary process was clear. Britain rose to military dominance in the period after the Napoleonic Wars, but slowly lost this over time as other powers, including the United States, Germany and, in the Far East, Japan increased their military power. In economic terms, Gilpin (2002) argues that

[t]he world has known only two eras of economic liberalism based on a hegemonic power. From the late nineteenth century to the outbreak of World War I [1914], Great Britain led the efforts for trade liberalisation and monetary stability. Similarly, the United States led the world economy following World War II [1945].

Regarding what happened between 1914 and 1945, Gilpin (2002) goes on to state that '[t]he United States emerged from World War I with a clear vision of the new international order that it wished to create'. However, linked strongly to the fact that the United States went through a strongly isolationist period between 1918 and 1941, it was only able to initiate this new order after the Second World War (1939–45). In what Gilpin terms this 'Rooseveltian vision', the United Nations, and particularly the Security Council, would guarantee world peace, and the IMF, World Bank and International Trade Organisation 'should be responsible for promotion and administration of an open and multilateral world economy'. Most importantly,

The postwar international order was to be based on the Atlantic Charter and its Four Freedoms (today's 'human rights') in whose name the United States and its allies had fought the war. Within this structure, the victors would build the peaceful, prosperous, and humane world that had eluded mankind after World War I.

(ibid.)

This idealised model of course failed to materialise in the form originally envisaged, primarily because of the rise of the Soviet Union and the creation in its place of a duopolistic view of how the world order should develop. The result was a return to a situation where military power became increasingly important in the struggle to protect western security against a perceived Soviet threat.

Such a brief summary cannot do justice either to Gilpin's paper or to the wider debate if the objective is to discuss either military or economic hegemony, but it does give a representative snapshot; and a detailed discussion of Anglo-Saxon hegemony, important as it may be, is not the primary objective. Rather, the objective is, first, to illustrate the extent to which the discussion on British and American hegemony is defined almost exclusively in terms of economic and military power; and then, following from this, to show how a critically important facet of hegemony, namely social hegemony, interpreted here to mean external domination of another people's cultural and intellectual space, is defined primarily by its absence from the debate. Once this gap is highlighted, and the importance of social hegemony recognised as a critical issue, then it becomes possible to see why the real cause of African underdevelopment has been so misunderstood, and subsequently misrepresented, in the West, and particularly in Anglo-Saxon countries.

Africa, like many of the poorer parts of the world (termed the 'Third World' at that time), was buffeted by the dualistic power struggle between the Soviet Union and the United States, but the majority of African countries were merely pawns in a game between the Great Powers, rather than players in their own right. In this situation, the sheer economic power of the western institutions, led by the World Bank, was clearly of critical importance in shaping development policy, as the structural adjustment programme of the 1980s so clearly illustrated. On the other hand, though, I shall argue here that this has created something of a smokescreen, hiding what is, in the longer term, a much more intrusive and pervasive form of intervention: that of social hegemony. As a result, it was actually in the social arena, and particularly that of its intellectual space, where much of Africa was most deeply impacted upon, if not subsumed, by Anglo-Saxon hegemony. That is Africa's missing debate and that is the issue which is explored here.

Control over cultural and intellectual space takes two forms, destruction or co-option, generally acting in tandem, with the choice being linked to the military potential of the opposition. Again it is useful to look at history first, since we can view history more easily outside of the emotional influence that exists when viewing these topics in the present. Using the Romans again, we can see that they destroyed the Celts' intellectual base, since the Celts posed an ongoing military threat, but they co-opted the Greek intellectual base because by that time the Greeks no longer posed a military threat.

These references to the Romans, which may appear at first glance to be totally irrelevant in a book intended to focus on Africa, are extremely valuable in aiding our understanding of the current domination scenario, as I will show a little later. Equally, though, there are many other applications of the suppression–co-option model from more recent times, which demonstrate the fact that this is a standard approach for groups seeking to dominate others. Thus, the apartheid regime destroyed the African intellectual base centred on the University of Fort Hare in the 1950s, before seeking to co-opt a more malleable black South African 'leadership' in the 1970s. And the British Empire, of course, has many examples of this, not least of them being Ghana, Tanzania and Zimbabwe (then Southern Rhodesia), particularly when those cultural models challenged Anglo-American economic hegemony.

The growth of the Roman civilisation is also helpful to an understanding of America today, particularly the way Americans have viewed this 'culture of the intellect'. The two nations (Rome and the United States) both came from a weak indigenous cultural base, but they reacted to culture quite differently. The Romans saw this lack of culture as a weakness and realised the need to create one rapidly if they were to become a dominant world power. They did this by first co-opting, and then integrating and adapting, the Greek cultural heritage. This recognition was also a reason why they perceived both the Carthaginians and the Celts as such a threat, because both of these competing societies combined military strength with an indigenous cultural heritage that could be perceived as more advanced than that of Rome, certainly in its early period of development.

Americans did not see culture in the same way, nor did they attach the same importance to it. That is not to say that the United States was totally without a cultural base. It had learned from European history, rejecting much that it saw, for example the monarchical system, but integrating aspects it considered important. From this, and its own experience, it developed three 'big ideas' that were to stand the test of time: capitalism as an economic model of development; democratic government; and the centrality (and rights) of the individual in society – all of which we see coming through in the 'Rooseveltian vision' described earlier. The United States also had its academic base, which was becoming ever more powerful and respected, in institutions such as Yale, Harvard and MIT. At the same time, though, it also had a strong element in its society that could be described as 'anti-intellectual', creating a body of opinion that retains an important influence in the Republican Party to this day. One important outcome of this anti-intellectual outlook was that during the period when cultural hegemony was being imposed most strongly on Africa, between the two great wars of the twentieth century (1914–1939), America was in an isolationist phase, with its main intellectual input into global development still in the future.

That is a particularly important point when it comes to shaping the international institutions. Thus, it could be argued that the United States could shape the IMF and the World Bank, since both of these institutions operated primarily in the economic sphere where America sought to impose its own capitalist model of development. However, this did not apply elsewhere; it was the social and cultural heritage, for example, that was most influential in shaping the various UN development institutions, and the United States could not shape these alone. Rather, the influence that shaped the United Nations, at least in respect of its socio-cultural perspective, came from elsewhere, mainly from Britain and its Dominions, and only to a lesser extent from the United States and France. Britain and the United States may have shared the 'big ideas' of democracy and individual human rights, but the way these translated into practice on the ground – that is, the mechanisms through which other countries would meet these outcomes – was based to a large degree on British practices at the time.

As a result, when the focus is specifically directed towards Africa, we have to adapt the way that we see Anglo-Saxon hegemony, because we have to be able to view American global cultural and intellectual domination in a way that incorporates the British role more directly. Because we live in the present, we do tend to see the world purely in terms of American hegemony. Yet to understand the African situation we have to expand our outlook and view it in the context of a continuum of dominant Anglo-Saxon culture that began with Britain's defeat of Napoleon at the Battle of Waterloo in 1815, was shared with the United States during the second half of the nineteenth and the first half of the twentieth centuries, and then taken over progressively by the United States after 1945.

What makes this period in history so important is the way in which global domination was transferred from one power (Great Britain) to another power (the United States of America) in a way that ensured the continuation of a common cultural value system, made easier of course by the use of a shared language. For without British support, particularly in the enforced intellectual domination of the Empire, it is questionable whether America, for all of its military and economic power, could have achieved broader cultural dominance of the global institutions that was necessary to shape the world in its own image. Conversely, and equally relevant to this discussion, it was only by being able to operate within the same cultural framework with the United States that Britain was able to continue to exert its authority, and impose its own version of the Anglo-Saxon worldview (*Weltanschauung*) on Africa.

The impact of the Anglo-Saxon *Weltanschauung* on Africa: the urban experience

It is the contention of this book that the imposition of ideas that are grounded in the Anglo-Saxon *Weltanschauung* has been extremely damaging, not only to Africa's development per se but also to Africa's ability to develop for itself. During the colonial period the way in which the *Weltanschauung* was imposed was obvious, since it was linked directly to physical occupation. The assumption, at least among the general public in the West, is that, with independence, African countries increasingly took responsibility for their own destinies.[8] This book will argue that the opposite is in fact the case, certainly with regard to urban development. Far from there being a lessening of control, the power exerted over urban development in Africa today is stronger than it has ever been before; yet because external actors are so deeply embedded in the dominant Anglo-Saxon *Weltanschauung*, they are simply unable to see the extent to which this is the reality.

Urban infrastructure has been at the heart of international debate on urban development in Africa, in one form or another, from the beginning. The provision of infrastructure (primarily for the white colonial elite) was the basis for the colonial city, and it was the inability to expand this system to the wider population that drove the debate in its initial post-colonial phase. As a result, much of Africa's urban development practice, as constructed by external agencies, has been a direct outcome of the inability of those same agencies to address infrastructure delivery in Africa effectively.

While their response to this failure may have taken different forms at different times, these nonetheless tend to coalesce around three distinct strands of development, the full extent of which only began to emerge from the global social, economic and political upheavals of the 1980s. The first of these was the rise to prominence of urban spatial planning as a major force in urban development, which resulted in the current situation whereby spatial and economic development are perceived as the basis for new urban growth and regeneration strategies. In this strand, urban infrastructure is defined as a supporting service for planned land development. The second strand, which was linked to the privatisation drive of the 1980s, resulted in the commodification of certain public services, which were defined as utilities – a term that speaks for itself. The third strand, to some extent a response to this, was a recognition that the 'urban poor' were being left behind by the wider development process and marginalised by privatisation. Abandoning key principles of social equity, which had driven urban development in Europe and America, and underpinned the United Nations, external agencies, acting more out of despair than good sense, chose the lowest common denominator option of seeking to provide only basic services to the poor. Thus, rather than seeking inclusion of the poor into urban society, this strand reinforced social exclusion and institutionalised a two-tier society in Africa – a recipe for ongoing political instability.

The failure to create a viable and sustainable infrastructure model for African cities was situated, of course, within a context of rapid urban growth, which saw the collapse of the colonial urban model of government, and a breakdown of urban structures of control. These developments led initially to greater centralised government control, followed by a gradual reversal and a widespread acceptance, among African governments, of the principle of decentralisation as the basis for urban governance. All these changes provide an ideal justification for the western argument that the ensuing urban development failure was the fault of African governments.

What I will show in this book is that the real failure lies with the choice of infrastructure models, both then and now. Initially this was no one's fault; the British infrastructure model was considered the ideal and proved itself so over a period of a hundred years, certainly in Western Europe and the United States, to the extent that it provided the framework for the success of western urbanisation. It is only recently that the weaknesses of this system have started to emerge, when we see its fundamental incompatibility with a world that requires models constructed around environmental sustainability. To address this incompatibility, the western countries have to deal with their massive installed infrastructure base, which requires an emphasis to be placed on measures of mitigation. Africa presents a completely different scenario. There, the need is for a new infrastructure model grounded in the principles of environmental sustainability. The irony is that sub-Saharan Africa, with its low level of urbanisation, and African towns and cities generally, with their low installed infrastructure base, are ideally suited to lead the way in creating this new model. Yet we are locked into an Anglo-Saxon *Weltanschauung* that is incapable of seeing outside of its own historical development trajectory, and still seeks to impose a modified version of its own urban system on other countries.

The converse of this failure to create an infrastructure model is the over-reliance on urban planning, again played out within an Anglo-Saxon *Weltanschauung* that built on the (totally inappropriate) British urban planning model. The collapse of African urban government, in the colonial aftermath initiated a period of reflection, led primarily by the World Bank but also involving UN and western donor government agencies, about how cities could best be managed. The outcome was a new discipline of Urban Management, formally established as a programme by UN-Habitat and the United Nations Development Programme (UNDP) in 1986.[9] The most important point to note about this discipline was the way in which it accepted, and incorporated, the three strands of the urban development construct outlined earlier, and the way in which it is intimately linked to a dominant urban planning paradigm (using the term 'paradigm' in its scientific sense, as described previously). This paradigm – that is, the urban development model that currently dominates international thinking – is grounded in the concept of a universal (and, of course, Anglo-Saxon) planning model, applied with regional variations.

The paradigm is based on the following logic flow, described in simplistic terms. First, the West has developed an extensive understanding of how to plan and develop cities. Second, this model is driven by private-sector investment, and the role of urban planning is to facilitate that. Third, this experience can be extrapolated to become a global model, tested by experience and analysis in the major cities around the world. Finally, the model, which is clearly the only option on the table (is it not?) can then be extended to all urban areas in all countries; and we can all sleep safely in our beds at night. That the paradigm takes as its benchmark the mature cities of the western countries, all of which just happen to have a fully installed infrastructure base, is not even an issue for discussion. Similarly, the fact that this British planning model emerged in a quite specific geographical context (the United Kingdom), where it too only came to prominence after the cities had completed the construction of their infrastructure base, and where its success even on its home territory is seriously questioned, is considered immaterial.

When we move outside of Britain, the primary focus of exploration (and case-study material) for this urban planning development paradigm is the large conurbation, as is clearly evident from all recent UN-Habitat work on urbanisation over the past twenty years. It is based upon two lines of reasoning: first, that the areas in question operate in an open global economy; and second, that all cities in the developing world are on trajectory towards maturity, as defined by the model of western cities. On this (still unproven) hypothesis, the British-based urban planning paradigm has been bought into by virtually every single international development agency that has any involvement with urban development; and it is sold as a reality to non-western governments. There is just one major problem[10] with this idealised view when we look at Africa: almost 70 per cent of urban residents live in small towns, and they are neither moving towards the state of a western mature city nor engaged in the global economy! This book will show that, specifically when the urban areas in question are the secondary towns and cities of Africa, this paradigm is invalid, and this logic path fatally flawed. African small towns present a development pattern that is quite unlike anything experienced previously, certainly in the past 400 years, and require unique solutions tailored to their condition.

In addition, the paradigm is itself grounded in a *Weltanschauung* that is specifically Anglo-Saxon, the symptoms of which have already been discussed. The outcome is an assumption that the (primarily British) urban planning model is the only valid basis for urban development; that is, it is a global development model. This is simply a false assumption, situated wholly within an Anglo-Saxon worldview. There are other, quite different models of urbanism – the Brazilian 'Plano Global' used as a basis for favela[11] upgrading is one such – and several of these have a far better track record than does the British model. Their only problem, of course, is that they exist outside of the dominant Anglo-Saxon *Weltanschauung*, and the experiences are written up in a 'foreign' language, immediately downgrading their relevance and importance.

This Anglo-Saxon-based 'international' model of urban development is challenged here, and the book will demonstrate that it is totally unsuited to addressing the needs of Africa's secondary towns and cities in the twenty-first century. The basis for the model is the mature city of the West, while the history too is that of the West; and such is the lens through which Africa is ultimately viewed. That is not to deny that many of those writing about African urban development have direct experience of African cities. What I am saying, though, is that those researchers operate within a specific *Weltanschauung*, and use a specific planning paradigm, both of which are grounded in a specific way of seeing, and thinking about, the world; and that this approach is totally inappropriate to the needs of towns and cities in sub-Saharan Africa at this point in time.

Exploring the symptoms: the major pathways for western control over African urban development

In the book *Dead Aid*, mentioned earlier, Dambisa Moyo (2009) argues the case against aid in the form that it currently takes. Her arguments are focused on the broader social, political and economic implications of aid at a country level, where she asks the question, '[W]hat kind of African society are we building when virtually all public goods – education, health-care, infrastructure and even security – are paid for by Western taxpayers?'[12] The debate about aid is extremely important in discussing African development. However, this is only one aspect of western influence. What is of equal, and possibly greater, importance is the way in which operating within an Anglo-Saxon *Weltanschauung* exerts control over Africa's intellectual space and constrains African countries in their ability to make the key decisions that affect the lives of their citizens.

The power of the Anglo-Saxon *Weltanschauung* to dominate anglophone (and other) African countries' intellectual space will vary from sector to sector, as well as from country to country. The debate here is about urban development and, within that, urban infrastructure management. This is a particularly useful base for an exploration of intellectual control, since it is arguably the arena of development where the external influence is greatest – the arena of development where Anglo-Saxon influence is most dominant and most deeply entrenched. As a result, we have a totally nonsensical scenario where, on the one hand, it is external actors that, to all intents and purpose, decide Africa's urban development path while, at the same time, it is African leaders who are blamed for the failures that result from implementing these flawed ideas.

There is an interesting consensus, from a range of people who come from quite different political perspectives, that Africa suffers from aid dependency and that Africa's problems would be solved if aid were reduced. These arguments are well made, and slowly countries are coming together, both donors and recipients, and starting to discuss alternative funding mechanisms, for example donor harmonisation.[13] At the same time, there is also a need to be realistic: not only is aid entrenched, but a number of key western countries are actually increasing the amounts of aid they provide. Even if all aid were stopped with immediate effect; the impact of aid would take years to reverse.

This book argues that the relationship between western and African countries is actually far more complex than simply a debate about development aid, and that in order to reverse the current situation of aid dependency we first need to understand more fully the nature of that relationship, and the full extent of that dependency; for it extends far beyond a simple economic relationship. And if we are to go deeper, to the heart of the relationship, then we need, above all else, to understand the full impact of Anglo-Saxon control over the intellectual space; only then can solutions be developed to manage the internal–external relationships more effectively. This section defines the nature of western influence in a different way from that used previously, using as a frame of reference this concept of intellectual control and looking at how it plays itself out. At this stage, we are looking, if you like, at the symptoms – or, phrased in development terminology, at the development imperatives accepted and used by external agencies. Later chapters will take this exploration deeper to look at the underlying core issue, which is actually about who decides on roles and relationships in a society – hence the important linkage within this book between development and governance.

If we look at the specific area of development that relates to urban infrastructure delivery and management, the range of external influences can be grouped into four thematic areas, termed here 'forces of influence', whose interaction results in the complex structure shown in Figure 1.1. Arguably, each one of these forces of influence could be countered relatively easily if it were the only external 'intellectual idea' impacting on African development. What makes external control so powerful, and so dominant, is the combination of all four together, which is then further underpinned by the western academic research and knowledge base. To change the situation and begin to provide African countries with greater intellectual space, it is necessary to understand how each of these thematic forces of influence work. At this point we are looking primarily at the symptoms; that is, the way in which external dominance and control is exerted. These symptoms will then be explored in greater detail in

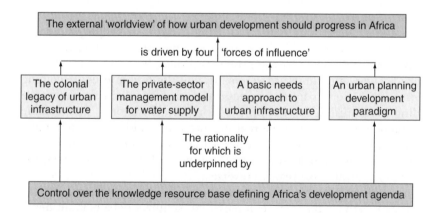

Figure 1.1 The four 'forces of influence' directing urban development in sub-Saharan Africa.

Chapters 2 to 5, taking the exploration to the next level and looking at the deeper malaise that underlies the symptoms.

External force 1: the colonial legacy of urban infrastructure

The era of colonialism may have ended, but its legacy lingers on, and in many ways continues to grow. While occupying what is now anglophone Africa, Britain set up a framework of government. Some form of government was clearly necessary, but the form adopted was one situated within Britain's quite specific political, socio-economic and philosophical construct, which together comprised the original Anglo-Saxon *Weltanschauung*. This legacy will be shown to influence each of the remaining three thematic forces of influence. At the broader level, though, the two most important elements are the inherited political process (in particular, the relationship between the legislature and the executive) and the specific nature of the policy formulation process. Regarding the first of these, the full impact has never really been explored fully in a development context; yet it is a crucial element of the decentralisation debate in particular. As such, it will be discussed in detail in Chapter 5.

Regarding the second, Britain has a quite specific approach to policy that differs significantly from that of many other countries, both within Europe and elsewhere in the world. Its approach is grounded in an empiricist philosophy that places an emphasis on output-orientated planning. It also operates a system within which the relationship between policy, strategy and practice is particularly obscure and where the lines are extremely blurred. This approach to policy has been adopted by many African countries, yet the book will provide strong reasons to believe that this may not be the most appropriate policy construct for Africa to adopt; on the contrary, its adoption is more likely to impede the development process.

This expectation that African countries use the Anglo-Saxon approach to policy exposes Africa to extensive, and often unwarranted, criticism and intrusion into areas of national sovereignty, especially when policies fail to set out explicitly how they will be followed through into an action plan. This criticism extends across every group of actors in the development field. From academics, through development NGOs, to emergency relief organisations, Africa provides an open house for any group that wishes to critique what African countries are doing. And the irony is that much of this criticism comes from academics and NGOs whose own country (Britain) has a questionable track record when it comes to measuring the success of infrastructure policy, as Chapters 3 and 4 will indicate. What we are dealing with here is not objective analysis. Those carrying out the critique are judging Africa subjectively from within their own *Weltanschauung*.

Yet when African governments object to the actions of western NGOs, for example on the grounds that they are interfering in the internal affairs of another country, their actions are often criticised as an attack on human rights, and an indication that the countries concerned are oppressive. There is too little understanding of the reverse scenario: that the attitude of many external, non-government groups is intrusive and does impinge on national sovereignty. Rarely do these external groups even try to situate this criticism within the specific social, cultural and intellectual framework of the host country; instead, they expect that country to be judged solely in terms of the *Weltanschauung* of their own society and their own value system. The impact of this continuous stream of criticism, and the way in which it exerts dominance over the intellectual space, plays a major role in preventing African academics, researchers and practitioners from developing their own indigenous policies and indigenous models of development.

External force 2: the private-sector model for water supply

The failure to match infrastructure to urban growth in the post-independence period led the World Bank to argue that infrastructure should be broken down into sectors, which would then be managed separately. This separation would enable the private sector to become more active, and thereby improve the level of service 'delivery', particularly in the sectors termed utilities (covering water, power, telecommunications and mass transport). Private-sector activity has proved particularly contentious in the water sector, where management of water supplies by the private sector has led to a strong backlash, particularly from public-sector unions and many in the NGO movement.

This has now become a debate that is primarily ideological, on both sides, with African governments often being caught in the middle. But at least this ideological perspective has brought this specific thematic issue into the public arena of debate. In addition, the arguments in favour of private-sector management of infrastructure are also being reconsidered, even in western countries, following the 2008 financial crisis, and influenced by the debate on climate change. Even in Britain, which was one of the major ideological proponents of private-sector management of infrastructure, the government began, for the first time in over twenty years, to discuss the role of the state in setting infrastructure policy, discussing openly whether it should take back control over energy (see Chapter 5).

Unfortunately, this whole debate is actually distracting African countries from a deeper exploration of the core issue, which is how to build an effective working relationship between the public and the private sectors. The issue here is not primarily one around privatisation; it is, rather, a debate around the dominance of a specific *Weltanschauung*. In Anglo-Saxon countries, free-market capitalism is probably recognised by outsiders as the main expression of the Anglo-Saxon *Weltanschauung*: a model that sees private companies having a significant control over the economy, with a minimum of regulation. There is absolutely nothing wrong with countries taking this approach; the problem arises when this *Weltanschauung* becomes dominant and is then imposed on others regardless of whether or not they share that view, as has been done in Africa.

Yet it is almost impossible to persuade those situated within this dominant economic *Weltanschauung* that other forms of relationship between the public and private sector can and do exist, and even work effectively. This is ironic given that three of the countries to emerge strengthened from the 2008 financial crisis, China, Germany and Brazil, all follow their own models as regards how the relationship between the public and the private sector functions, none of which can be even remotely described as free-market capitalism.

Nevertheless, those situated within the free-market capitalist *Weltanschauung* refuse to recognise any failings within their own model. To them the historical argument is irrefutable; after all, surely capitalism would never have become dominant in the first place had it not been the best – would it? Essentially this is an application of Darwin's biological theory of natural selection to the field of economics, a questionable transposition. An alternative interpretation is simply that capitalism is more ruthless and more effective in exploiting resources than other systems, thereby transferring wealth from the global commons to the individual more quickly and easily. Does this transfer of wealth represent value added, or is it simply asset-stripping under a different guise? There is no clear answer; it all depends on your *Weltanschauung*. What matters, though, and what is really needed in Africa, is the intellectual space for governments to develop their own management models and build their understanding of the relationship between their public and private sectors from within their own *Weltanschauung*, not an imposed Anglo-Saxon one.

External force 3: a basic needs model for urban infrastructure

The expansion of internet access and global visual coverage gives an immediacy to human events that tends to take crises out of perspective. An aeroplane crash that kills everyone on board is a tragic accident, with a deeply personal impact that evokes an emotional response among those seeing scenes of the aftermath. Yet there is also an alternative perspective, which is that air travel is in fact far safer, in terms of the ratio of fatalities per kilometre travelled, than is travel by car. But facts are not the issue here; it is the visual and emotional impact of several hundred people killed in a single event that carries the day.

Africa has more than its fair share of crises, and many of these, such as HIV/AIDS, the impact of drought or the impact of diseases such as malaria, also evoke a response on a deeply emotional level. And because they often need funding to ameliorate the impact, and the bulk of this funding comes from the West, they are presented in a way that is most likely to provoke an emotional response. Yet humanitarian aid per se constitutes only a small fraction of the total aid budget – 'small beer when compared with the billions transferred each year directly to poor countries' governments' (Moyo, 2009, p. 9). The risk with this approach is that, over time, the humanitarian response begins to define the development agenda, and the boundaries between humanitarian relief and long-term development become blurred. This is now happening with the rapidly increasing use of 'targets' to define goals, as illustrated for example with the MDGs. In this evolving scenario, development outputs are becoming of far greater importance than systems and structures.

This variant of the product versus process debate is driven almost exclusively by Britain and its Department for International Development (DFID), although it has been adopted increasingly by other donors. And of course it reflects the extent to which the UN development agencies follow what is essentially a British social development model.

Measuring output through quantitative indicators has always been an element of assessing the effectiveness of development programmes. What has changed is the conversion of indicators to development drivers, a far more controversial shift. If we ignore for the moment whether the use of targets in this way is effective (and this book will seek to demonstrate that it is not), the use of a target-based approach has major implications for government. First, its implementation requires a centralised state, and in this context it is contrary to the principle of decentralisation. In addition, it undermines the role of local government in society and has the result of making local government ineffectual as a development agent in its own right (as the example of South Africa used in Chapter 5 will indicate), turning local government into a delivery agent of central government. Finally, it provides donor agencies with immense leverage over African governments, to the extent that their national sovereignty is seriously undermined – all, of course, in the name of development, and often of poverty alleviation. When this is combined with the emotive nature of aid, any African government choosing to oppose this approach is perceived, in the donor country, as obviously being insensitive to the needs of its own citizens. After all, who can object to every family having a toilet? The reality is that one can't, and perhaps shouldn't, object; but is that the only issue? Isn't it equally important to ask who will clean up the mess when the pit latrines are overflowing, because delivery-driven targets did not consider the need for an effective long-term institutional framework?

Thus, we have to be extremely careful when we begin to allow humanitarian responses to drive development. When we work with people to address a crisis, we can deal with them directly. When we begin to apply these social interventions within a development framework, then we have to realise that they are no longer value-free; instead, they operate within the value system of the dominant *Weltanschauung.*

Development is not only about targets; it involves systems of government, and reflects specific views on the role of government, the nature of community, the role of the individual in society, on the role of the state in society, on the role of the private sector in society – and the list goes on. When a crisis occurs, it is possible for those on the outside to become subsumed by the immediacy of the event, and the need to save lives. As the nature of the intervention changes from a humanitarian response to one concerned primarily with long-term development, however, the thinking needs to change, from one that simply defines targets to one that supports the development of operational systems and institutional structures. Unfortunately, this transition occurs less and less frequently, as target-based approaches suited to a humanitarian response come to dominate the longer-term development agenda. DFID, and the British government, as the major proponents of this approach, have to show their own electorate that the aid they provide is producing immediate 'results'.

External force 4: the (British) urban planning paradigm

The fourth thematic force of external influence, the urban planning paradigm, is possibly the least expected, yet in many ways the one with the greatest negative impact. This is not to imply that planning is in any way 'wrong' or 'bad'; simply that it is based upon an external model that has failed, over the period of more than thirty years since it became the dominant urban development paradigm in Africa, to demonstrate any ability to provide a sustainable urban development framework. That it has failed, in a historical context, is fairly widely recognised; that it continues to be seen as the basis for urban development is due primarily to the absence of a credible alternative.

The urban planning model used, certainly in anglophone Africa, is based upon the British system of urban planning. Unfortunately, this particular urban planning model has two fundamental flaws that convert to destructive forces when transferred to an Africa development scenario. The first is its basic rationality. Historically, urban planning was a paper-based discipline that sought to create a land-use map prior to settlement taking place. As a result, when applied in an African context, it always lagged behind the urban growth curve, and failed to demonstrate how it can move ahead of this process to create a formal plan that leads, rather than lags, the urbanisation process itself. Africa needs a different model:

its own model; to define the relationship between the people and the land, which is much more interactive.

The second flaw revolves around the relationship between urban planning, urban infrastructure and urban economic development. In its evolution in Britain, urban planning emerged from a development model that perceived infrastructure first as a support service for social development and second as an engineering function. In this worldview, economic development is driven by externalities, such as private-sector investment, that can be facilitated by a planning process. However, as Chapter 2 will illustrate, there is actually an alternative view, which was prevalent in the United States: that infrastructure is itself a development driver. Unfortunately, by the time that urban planning in Britain emerged from the dominant engineering paradigm in the 1970s, the bulk of the urban infrastructure base had been completed and there was no evidence to support this alternative view. Instead, the initial perception was actually entrenched by the neo-liberal approach of successive British governments. As a result, this has become the de facto urban planning model for sub-Saharan Africa.

Viewed in this context, urban planning provides a classic example of how dominant cultures control the intellectual space of others. It is epitomised by the saying 'think global, act local'. This reflects a worldview that could only emanate from a hegemonic, culturally dominant group: for who actually defines what is meant by global in a developmental context? Who defines the 'global' value system that underpins the development model? What we see is the power of a small, self-selecting group who dominate the intellectual debate, creating 'models' of planning and urban management for developing countries, and then defining their rationality through a process of self-affirmation. A model of this kind is then 'verified' as being a global development model by using comparative research that is based, almost exclusively, in the megacities and large urban conurbations. Once accepted as a global model, it can then be extrapolated to cover all urban areas, with local researchers expected to 'adapt' it to local conditions. How is it possible, under these conditions, to create an African urban spatial model?

Control over the intellectual space by western agencies and academics

In any given developmental scenario it is natural to expect that the perception from the outside will be different from that from within. These different ways of seeing a development construct derive partly from the different perspective (e.g. the global and the local) and partly from the fact that people come from within different *Weltanschauungen*. In an ideal world these internal and external views should be able to interact to mutual benefit, creating a symbiotic relationship. However, when it comes to development, the benefit accruing to the host country from that relationship depends to a large extent upon the balance of resources and the nature of the interaction across the resource divide.

Thus, China, for example, is quite willing to listen to international experiences, and sends many students to Europe and the United States. At the same time, though, China has both the power and the political will to define the boundaries of influence in this external thinking, and develop its own solutions.

Brazil is another example of where the interaction between the external and the internal is broadly successful. Like China, Brazil also has a strong indigenous base of academics and professionals. At the same time, it is less powerful and therefore potentially more vulnerable to external influence. In this case, though, the major safeguard against external domination stems from the fact that Brazil is protected by its language. Because relatively few people in Anglo-Saxon countries speak Portuguese, and only limited numbers of Brazilians speak English, the language barrier acts as a filter, allowing information flow but ensuring that it does not turn into a one-way flood.

Of all the countries, or regions, of the world, there is one where this balance between the internal and the external does not apply, and that is sub-Saharan Africa. There are many reasons why that is the case; and while each in itself may not appear particularly problematic, it is the combination of factors that creates the imbalance. On the African side there is the weak intellectual and human resource base, coupled with the continued leakage of graduates, and the high level of dependence on external donor funding. On the other side there is the colonial heritage (particularly the institutional heritage), the high level of ongoing patronage in the relationship, the large number of professionals from Anglo-Saxon countries working on 'Africa' (relative to the number of African professionals), and the power of donor funding to influence both development policy and implementation strategies.

These are all different ways of controlling knowledge generation and knowledge flows. The huge imbalance between internal and external access to, and control over, Africa's intellectual space represents a continuation of western colonialism. Perhaps those in the West do not realise this; they may not intend it, and they may not even wish it to be so. Yet the condition that exists in the relationship between the West (both as individual countries and as de facto controllers of the international development agenda) amounts to nothing less than the colonisation of Africa's intellectual space.

This book will argue, and seek to demonstrate, the sheer power of Anglo-Saxon concepts and ideas to direct and control the direction of development in Africa. The Anglo-Saxon research community is the most powerful in the world, currently dominating much of the research and controlling the academic journals that are the lifeblood of the wider global research community, providing its members with intellectual credibility and building and sustaining their reputation. African development issues provide only a minute fraction of the output from this research community, and the topic as a whole has a low profile. Partly as a result, those who research and write on the subject are small in number and are concentrated in just a few institutions. The result is that they have a high degree of control over the material that is written and the ideas that are generated.

The nature of the academic discourse varies from one research area to another. In the political sciences, for example, there may be a degree of open debate, owing to the nature of the subject, giving greater access to indigenous input and alternative views of African political development. In other areas, though, particularly those associated with urban development, the debate is more closed. There are a number of reasons why that is the case. On a purely academic level, any paper on Africa struggles to achieve the level of academic rating necessary to sustain the points required by the more prestigious universities for their staff, points that are vital if the university is to maintain its 'ranking' as a top university. There is simply a far wider audience interested in experiences in Europe, the United States or, increasingly, China. Africa is not a mainstream issue in the research community.

As a result, the limited size of the academic 'pool' of Africa specialists then creates a group where the specialists engage with each other and expound to the rest. It is analogous to some of the aristocratic families of old, where a limited gene pool leads naturally to inbreeding. The limited numbers lead to a stifling of creativity. Coupled with this, the power of bilateral donors in particular to guide and shape the research agenda is increasing dramatically as these agencies consolidate their control over the funding for applied research in the area of African urban development. Finally, this condition is reinforced by the fact that this very limited group of specialists is responsible for the majority of publications generated by the international institutions, particularly the World Bank and the United Nations organisations. The result is an unhealthy and incestuous relationship between the international and the bilateral agencies on the one hand, and the university and wider research groups on the other.

I am not implying that this is a racially exclusive group. On the contrary, researchers from low- and medium-income countries are welcomed as part of the group, and it is becoming more international. However, instead of expanding the debate, the newcomers are drawn into the Anglo-Saxon *Weltanschauung*, for two mutually reinforcing reasons. First, the large majority of these new members, from whatever background, attended university in either Europe or the United States, and the large majority live and work in one of those two geographical areas. Hence, new members coming in may bring some new insights from personal experience but are nonetheless soon drawn into the group in what is a classic example of the three phases of group-forming in group dynamics: inclusion, influence and intimacy (Srivastva *et al.*, 1997). Second, of course there is the nature of the post-graduate resource system itself. Based as it is upon the use of precedent and empirical analysis, the new studies have to be situated within the framework of existing literature, which is itself part of this same body of knowledge and existing developmental *Weltanschauung*. Taken together, the result is intellectual hegemony, and it is this hegemonic grouping that provides the knowledge base for the Anglo-Saxon *Weltanschauung*.

The collective impact of external influence on Africa

The view of western, and particularly British, involvement in Africa is completely polarised, depending on whether you are an African living on the inside, or a Westerner, particularly a British person, viewing the situation from the outside. Let's take the latter perception first.

The majority of African countries gained their independence in the 1960s, meaning that the impact of colonialism, viewed from the present, is moving from a personal experience into a more historical perspective of events. As a result, there is often a genuine puzzlement among many people in Britain, particularly among the younger generation, who were not even alive in the colonial era, as to why African countries continue (or so it seems to them) to mistrust the West, and still blame the West for what appear to be their own failings. This perception was neatly summed up in an article in a British newspaper in the context of President Obama's inaugural visit to Africa in July 2009. The correspondent phrased it as follows:

> He [the American president, Barack Obama] can do something no other Western leader can do. He can pick up the phone to an African president and talk to him straight – as an African, without fear that he can be accused of neo-colonialism or racism, the weak but poisonous defence against Western pressure by many African rulers.
>
> (Dowden, 2009)

On the other hand, there is the African perspective, which was neatly summarised in an interview that Graça Machel[14] gave to the British newspaper the *Guardian* (Machel, 2010). In this discussion, focusing primarily on Zimbabwe but also covering the issues of climate change and carbon dioxide emissions, 'she indicated that the crisis in Zimbabwe has revealed the shortcomings of a persistent imperialist mindset', and her interview included the following statements:

'Can I be a little bit provocative?' Machel said. 'I think this should be an opportunity for Britain to re-examine its relationship with its colonies. To acknowledge that with independence those nations will want to have a relationship with Britain which is of shoulder to shoulder, and they will not expect Britain to continue to be the big brother....

'The more the British shout, the worse the situation will be in terms of relationship with Zimbabwe. That's why sometimes I really question, when something happens in Zimbabwe and Britain shouts immediately. Can't they just keep quiet? Sometimes you need just to keep quiet. Let them do their own things, let SADC (Southern African Development Community) deal with them, but keep quiet, because the more you shout, the worse [it is].'

Asked if Britain's attitude is patronising to its former colonies, Machel replied: 'I'm afraid so. And what I'm saying is they have expectations which do not always coincide with what are the aspirations and expectations of those who are their former colony.'

The greatest single challenge in Africa today is for the external countries, and the agencies they control, to understand the nature of *Weltanschauung* – to understand how much of what they do and how they act reflects their own understanding of the way in which they see the world; and that this is not necessarily the way that others see it. The problem is that when yours is the dominant *Weltanschauung*, it is almost impossible to achieve an objective perspective. And there is anyway no reason for such introspective exploration, simply because yours is the dominant view.

The implications of external control over Africa's intellectual space

There are two characteristics that are necessary for development ideas to flourish. The first is an internal research capacity, which creates ideas, and the second is the freedom to debate, which nurtures and improves ideas. UNESCO saw the critical importance of building research capacity in higher education in developing countries and ran a programme to support this development for a number of years. Unfortunately, it was phased out in 2008. This programme dealt with core research, and even this cannot be sustained. There are now western donor programmes (the European Union runs a major one) in which western universities have to collaborate with universities in low-income countries. While such collaboration may have a (limited) impact in building individual research capacity in Africa, it does little to further original thought or indigenous analysis. Because of the way in which it is structured, the outcome is simply that more African researchers are drawn into the dominant western *Weltanschauung*.

The combination of the four sources of thematic influence outlined above, underpinned by control over the knowledge and research base, is having a devastating effect in stifling African development. It totally dominates Africa's intellectual space and, because it is imposed from the outside, it is a form of colonisation. For this reason, what is happening here can be described as a colonisation of Africa's intellectual space. There is little scope here for Africa to break free of this colonisation, yet this is what it must do if it is to develop its own future.

Yet in spite of the odds against it, it is possible for Africa as a whole to take back its intellectual space. The key lies in two actions. The first is for Africans to take back control of their own governance, and to control the governance agenda. The second is to empower the collective organisations emerging from Africa (the African Union, the African Development Bank, the Southern African Development Community, the African Ministers' Council on Water) to take the lead in managing this governance agenda.

This discussion is about the relationship between knowledge, power and responsibility. Anecdotally, this recalls a personal comment that a community leader, recently out of detention, made about the apartheid regime in the 1980s, which was along the following lines:

> The greatest oppression of the apartheid regime was not what the police did to us, and it was not the forced removals policy, evil as those were. It was the way they prevented us from gaining knowledge. They saw that knowledge was the real source of power, and by preventing us from gaining knowledge, they sought to keep control over us.[15]

There are different ways of controlling knowledge. The huge imbalance between internal and external access to, and control over, Africa's intellectual space, is one of them, whether intended or as the outcome of history or circumstance. To deal with this imbalance, though, it must first be recognised; only then can the real question be asked as to how to change this situation. To a large degree, external institutions, and governments, take an ostrich-like 'head-in-the-sand' approach to this issue. And one of the ways in which this attitude plays itself out is through what I term here the Newtonian physics approach to development. This concept will be described in greater detail in Chapter 2, but briefly it is based upon the Newtonian view that the observer in a scientific experiment is independent of the process being observed. Quantum mechanics demonstrates the fallacy of this concept when it comes to the level of sub-atomic particles;

it shows quite clearly that the observer is also an integral part of the experiment.

And so it is with external actors in African development, particularly, though not solely, in the field of urban development. These external actors control the intellectual space almost entirely, and they are involved not only in defining the output, but also in the minutiae of processes. Any western website of an organisation involved in African development will talk proudly of its achievements – and this is across the development spectrum, from national departments for international development, through NGOs and academics, to the private sector. Rarely, though, will you find examples of their failures on these organisations' websites: those are all the responsibility of African governments.

This control of intellectual space is the real failing of aid, and responsible for the failings of current western approaches. If you control the intellectual space, and development is built on ideas that emerge from that space, then you have to accept responsibility for the failures. Of course African governments must accept some responsibility, but the western countries must accept a great deal more. The world of ideas, and the reality of the dominant *Weltanschauung*, place African development on a par with particle physics: there are no independent external observers – everyone involved is a player, and they all influence, and help to shape, the outcome.

The importance of secondary towns and cities in sub-Saharan Africa

Sub-Saharan Africa is in the midst of an exponential growth curve that will see its population increase from approximately 800 million in 2007 to over 1,400 million in 2030, and perhaps as many as 2 billion people by 2050 (UN-Habitat, 2008, p. 4). Even on their own, these growth figures are huge; however, they are also being accompanied by a demographic shift which means that urban centres will be accounting for an increasing share of this growing population.

The urban population[16] of sub-Saharan Africa was approximately 70 million people in 1970, a figure that represented less than 10 per cent of the total population. By 2030 this figure is projected to be approximately 760 million, at which point urban settlements will account for approximately 54 per cent of the total population. And on current trends, by 2050 the urban population could be in excess of 1,200 million, at which point Africa would be 60 per cent urbanised. The impact of these changes is encapsulated in Figure 1.2. In 2007 the urban population was estimated to be around 373 million.

Of equal significance to the rural–urban demographic shift is the internal urban settlement pattern. UN-Habitat, the United Nations agency

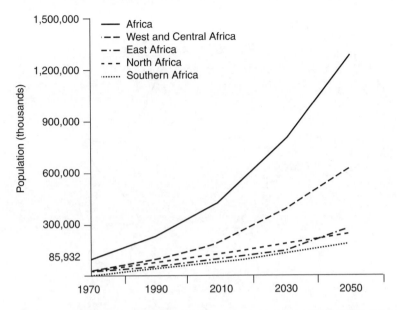

Figure 1.2 Projected urban population growth in Africa 1970–2050 (UN-Habitat, 2008, p. 6).

with responsibility for urbanisation, focuses almost all of its attention on large cities (those with over 1 million inhabitants). Clearly, this is an important sector of the urban population. In 1970 there were no cities with a population of more than 1 million inhabitants in sub-Saharan Africa. By 2008 the number of cities exceeding this population had reached 41. Figure 1.3 shows a map of Africa with the cities of over 1 million people indicated, as of 2007. This map illustrates the extent to which sub-Saharan Africa is essentially a continent of primate cities,[17] particularly if Nigeria and South Africa are excluded, while UN-Habitat (2008) also highlights the growth of a number of regional development 'corridors'.

Major cities are critically important, particularly in terms of their wealth generation capability, as a second UN-Habitat report, detailing the state of world cities in 2009, indicates. However, from an African perspective this rapid growth of major cities, and the subsequent international focus that follows this, is also seriously problematic. For as UN-Habitat's own report highlights, there is another urban world out there, which is that of the secondary towns and cities. These smaller urban centres hardly feature in the international literature, and yet

[t]he rapid urban population growth in Africa is, contrary to common wisdom, not absorbed by its largest cities. In the foreseeable future,

Figure 1.3 Map showing cities in Africa with populations greater than 1 million people (UN-Habitat, 2008, p. x).

the intermediate cities (towns with less than 500,000 inhabitants) will be the localities where two-thirds of all African urban growth is occurring.

(UN-Habitat, 2008)

So, it is in the small towns and cities that the real crisis of urbanisation exists, yet this is where human and financial resources are most limited. In this regard, UN-Habitat has failed Africa. While it may be able to produce important and valuable work on the megacities, as its 2010 global cities report on this topic indicates, its *State of African Cities* report (2008) focused on this area of megacities totally to the exclusion of these secondary towns and cities. More than anything else (although its report on slums comes a close second), this report demonstrates just how deeply UN-Habitat has been absorbed, as an international organisation, into the Anglo-Saxon intellectual ambit, as well as the dominant Anglo-Saxon *Weltanschauung*. While the megacities and major development corridors clearly have an important role in any urban analysis, if only because of the secondary towns and cities. More than anything else (although its report on slums comes a close second), this report demonstrates just how deeply UN-Habitat has been absorbed, as an international organisation, into the Anglo-Saxon intellectual ambit, as well as the dominant Anglo-Saxon *Weltanschauung*. While the megacities and major development corridors clearly have an important role in any urban analysis, if only because of the economic impact of these regions, they still account for less than one-third of the urban population.

At least UN-Habitat was honest in admitting knowing virtually nothing of the secondary cities and small towns; yet this admission is not enough. Africa's future urban sustainability depends on how these secondary urban areas cope with urbanisation. Large cities have the financial resources and create their own urban dynamic; and they do interact with the world outside. Small towns lack access to this level of resources and their sphere of engagement is much smaller and more localised. As a result, they require a different approach. It is to these secondary cities and towns that this book is addressed. And as the book will show as it evolves, the developmental approach needed will be completely different from any currently available.

Outline of the book

This book argues that existing approaches to urban development in Africa have failed, and that the primary reason for this failure lies in the use of western development models. If African countries are to develop alternatives, though, then a radical shift in thinking about the nature of development will be required. For such a shift to take place, change is required on two levels. On the higher level the imperative is to liberate Africa's intellectual space from external control, in order to enable indigenous thinking to drive the development process. On a practical level there is a need to break free of the constraints of the traditional western model of urban development that was created almost two hundred years ago to deal with urbanisation under conditions that were fundamentally different from those that exist today.

Successful approaches to urban development depend, ultimately, upon successful approaches to infrastructure delivery and management, and that underlying construct provides the rationale for this book. We urgently require a new model, and a new way of thinking about infrastructure and its role in society, both of which will be provided here. To achieve these outcomes the analysis and discussion have been divided broadly into three parts: history, practice and future direction.

The first part, running from Chapter 2 through to Chapter 5, will explore the evolution of urban development from its colonial past to the present time, looking at the forces that influence and guide the way that decisions are made, as well as the nature of the decisions themselves. Chapter 2 will look at the broad urban development trajectory of the later decades of the twentieth century and the growth of external control over Africa's urban development process, showing how this represented a slow but persistent imposition of external intellectual control.

Chapter 3 will explore the evolution of infrastructure, following the thread from its origins in England and comparing its development there to the way that infrastructure planning evolved in the United States, with the objective being to understand not only how this development happened but also the nature of the relationship between urban infrastructure and broader views of development. Chapter 4 will then take the British experience and look at how it was transferred across to anglophone Africa under colonialism; as well as the way in which it developed subsequently. This examination will provide a wider canvass from which to explore the impact of the Anglo-Saxon *Weltanschauung* on African urban development.

Chapter 5 will move the focus from the technical and managerial aspects of urban development to the institutional structures associated with decentralisation. This chapter will highlight the extent to which the failure of African governments to decentralise has been caused by external forces. Furthermore, the outcome of this failure was not only the growth in power of external agencies but, equally importantly, the undermining of local government in Africa, brought about primarily by the policies and practices of those same external agencies.

The second part of the book, dealing with practice, is made up of two chapters, 6 and 7, both concerned with events in Ethiopia. From an African perspective this is a critical component of the book, since it illustrates the full extent to which African countries would be fully capable of generating their own solutions if western countries and agencies would simply withdraw from their current domination of African intellectual space. The first of the two chapters will describe Ethiopian development in a broad context, divided into three phases. The first will explore Ethiopia's early history and lays the foundation for understanding the country, while the second will look at Ethiopia's modern history, from 1991 to the present time. The third phase will comprise events that took place during a five-year study of eighteen secondary towns in the country. The initial findings of this study will be carried forward into Chapter 7, where the outcome will be explored in greater detail. The chapter will provide both a (brief) technical and strategic analysis showing how the country moved from a condition where infrastructure was viewed as comprising purely a supportive role in an urban planning process to one where it became recognised by government as the major driver of social and economic development in the secondary towns. It is this transformation in thinking that lays the foundation for a completely new way of approaching urban development in sub-Saharan Africa, the outcome of which is to demand a radical rethinking of the role of both urban infrastructure and urban planning in African development.

The third part of the book will deal with the future direction of urban development in Africa. To do this it will take the lessons from all of this diverse history and use it to create a new approach to urban development, using as its context the secondary towns – an approach that, for the first time, is grounded in African experience. This third part comprises four chapters, which together will provide a comprehensive framework for sustainable urban development in the secondary towns of sub-Saharan Africa. Chapter 8 will begin this process by setting out a new methodological approach that can explore the current urban condition free of external bias and external influence. Using this approach, it then makes the case for a new policy process to be founded on a deeper understanding of the extent to which urban infrastructure is the major driver of development in the secondary towns of sub-Saharan Africa. In addition, it will show how urban infrastructure is the main driver of economic, social and environmental development in the secondary towns.

Chapter 9 will build on this concept of infrastructure as the main development driver to create a new urban development model. Combining the concepts of a city metabolism and an urban ecology, the chapter will show how the use of infrastructure to mediate resource flows in and around the city can integrate economic, social and environmental goals and objectives. This new relationship between urban infrastructure and the flow of urban resources then provides the framework for the new sustainability model that can be applied to the secondary towns and cities. This new model is the foundation for Africa's green urban infrastructure revolution.

Building on these principles, Chapter 10 will develop this concept of green infrastructure through a new approach to the delivery of infrastructure services, linking these back to different resource systems that together constitute the wider global ecology. For each of these systems, which include all infrastructure services, from water through energy, spatial management and sanitation to the digital surround, the chapter will develop a new technological and management framework.

Once this technological and management framework has been created, it becomes possible to create a new institutional structure with a framework linking green infrastructure and urban governance in a single integrated relationship. This is the basis for Chapter 11. Again this requires a new way of thinking about urban social systems, and particularly about the nature of good governance when applied in an African urban context. The chapter will show how the needs of urban good governance differ significantly from the good governance requirements at a national level, being linked much more directly to the services provided by local

This discussion will lead to a new urban good governance model that would enable local government to play a key role in the delivery and management of green infrastructure across the full range of infrastructure services, while at the same time redefining the concepts of public–private and public–community partnerships in a new way that is free of western ideological preconceptions.

Chapter 12, the concluding chapter, will draw together the findings from the different part of the book. In doing so, it will complete the circle initiated at the beginning of Chapter 1, by returning to the two levels of exploration. At the local level the conclusions will summarise the new approach to urban infrastructure that provides the basis for the sustainable development of the secondary cities, showing how it is the correct choice of approach if we wish to integrate economic development with social equity and environmental sustainability in the context of fast-growing, low-income towns and cities in Africa. At the higher level the book sets out how African countries can break out of the currently self-perpetuating cycle of external dominance of the subcontinent's urban development agenda to reclaim control over their intellectual space, and thereby provide their own indigenous capability to ensure long-term, sustainable urban development that is geared to the needs of Africa in the twenty-first century.

Chapter 2

The evolution of urban development

Introduction

There is by now a fairly strong international consensus in the West that people in the 'developing' world, including those in sub-Saharan Africa, should be able to make the critical decisions that affect their lives for themselves, and should be able to shape their own future. While I accept that this is a genuinely held belief, it remains pertinent to ask the question: to what extent does this belief translate into practice? That is clearly a difficult question to answer, exploring as it does the balance between opportunities and constraints on the one hand, and the mechanisms of decision-making on the other. Perhaps it is too complex, or perhaps it is a question best left alone; but whatever the reason, it is a question that is given insufficient attention in the urban development discourse.

With colonial rule more than half a century in the past, the international view would appear to be that the onus now lies with Africans themselves to take responsibility for the current situation in their countries. Some political scientists question the validity of this assumption, arguing that the impact of colonial rule still runs deep; but the majority would probably disagree. UN-Habitat (2008), for example, explicitly places the failure of African governments to decentralise squarely on the shoulders of African politicians, blaming them for a lack of political will; while studies of urban development, as well as of both decentralisation and governance, continually emphasise that the major cause is linked directly to decisions taken in the African political arena. Certainly, political leaders have to take some of the responsibility; but is this really a debate situated only in the political arena, or for that matter only in Africa?

Are the failings of African urban development political, or are they systemic?

The issue of where the responsibility lies for the current situation in Africa raises a fundamental question about how political decisions are made around development issues. In the policy arena, for example, national politicians may approve the policy, but who actually writes it? And where does the research come from that underpins the policy and defines its direction? If the entire academic or intellectual construct for a policy is assembled outside of a country, is the minister who signs the preface really the person to blame if that policy fails? Before we explore this concept in greater detail, let us look at a very simple analogy to describe this potential paradox: that of baking cakes on a commercial scale in a new African market.

In this analogy, a new commercial bakery is being set up in a particular country. Although this is to be a large-scale operation, the bakery does not have its own cake-mix designer and is reliant on an external group to provide both the design and the key ingredients. This means there are two different groups of people involved in this process. The first group is responsible for the recipe; the second group manages the mixing and baking operation. Now, this first group specialises in the creation of recipes, and has had great success in its country of origin. Spurred by this success, it would like to help bakeries in other countries to produce what are, in the opinion of its clients, delicious cakes. And so it offers the recipe, albeit with some conditions attached, and even sends out materials and advisers, to the new bakery. The second group – that is, the group carrying out the baking – has the responsibility for mixing the ingredients, preparing the cake, placing the mix in the baking tin, and finally taking the prepared baking tins and placing them in the oven, all simple steps clearly defined by the external advisers.

The cakes are baked, removed from the oven, and found to be ... a total catastrophe; they have not risen; they have not set properly; and they taste absolutely terrible! So now we are faced with a dilemma! Who is responsible for this failure? Is it the first group, who created the recipe and provided both the experts and the ingredients? Or is it the second group, that mixed the cakes, ran the ovens and baked the cakes?

The recipe specialist can provide excellent references to show how the recipe was successful in its home country. And, after all, is it not the baker's responsibility to check that the recipe is suitable? But, plead the bakers, we don't have the specialist knowledge in this area and used your recipe, and your advisers, in good faith! And what is more, we can't even take over this responsibility because you keep changing the recipe before we have time to fully understand it. I am sorry, replies the recipe specialist, but you own the bakery and, in the end, the responsibility for the end product lies with you.

Such is the development dilemma in sub-Saharan Africa. The ownership of the bakery is clearly identified; however, the work that goes on prior to baking is not quite so straightforward. In the real world of urban development, the key question is – who develops the recipe?

This analogy is intended to illustrate that there are two components that shape the direction of development. The first is the political component; and here African governments are clearly responsible for implementation. The second component, though, relates to the wider system that defines how the ideas that underpin the development process are conceptualised and translated into practice. Political decisions generally evolve from policy, but policy itself is a part of a wider decision-making process that involves a complex interaction with analysis, research and previous practice. Furthermore, political decisions are also made within a context of existing structures, be they institutional or operational, and within the framework of existing knowledge. Most developed countries have had the space to build the relationships that inform policy, and work with existing structure, over a long period of time, adapting them to suit their changing needs; African countries have never had this same opportunity.

In this chapter I will show the extent to which the major strands of urban development, from planning and infrastructure management, through social development, to urban governance, all have their origins in western development and western constructs, and that the application of these ideas, even though applied to African urban society, are based on western interpretations of urban development. As a result, these western ideas are responsible for almost every facet of current thinking pertaining to urban development policy and implementation strategy. And in anglophone Africa at least, many of these ideas are specifically Anglo-Saxon.

If we are to change this situation and open up the intellectual space to African ideas and solutions, then we need to understand where the external ideas come from and how they are applied. We need to be able to differentiate between a world trend – that is, a global event that requires a response – and a *Weltanschauung*, which interprets the trend in a specific way and provides the intellectual framework within which the response is generated. Global development trends do exist: in health, in climate change, in water resources, in urban governance, to name just a few. All countries have to respond to these trends, but different countries may develop different responses. This is because the way in which they internalise and rationalise the global trend is linked to the way in which they see and interpret events; that is, their worldview or *Weltanschauung*. In this way the response to a global trend will be firmly situated within a country's own specific value system.

The chapters that follow will explore the way in which the majority of the developmental concepts applied to African urban development, while portrayed by Anglo-Saxon practitioners, academics and development agencies as global responses, are actually their own specific interpretative response, created within their own *Weltanschauung*; they are not global at all. Now, there is nothing inherently wrong with situating a response in this way; all countries do it. Where doing so becomes problematic is in situations where a dominant culture seeks to define its response as the only conceivable, or politically acceptable, one. By understanding this, African countries can better understand the extent to which they are controlled and manipulated through being forced into one specific interpretation of events and an associated, externally defined, 'solution'. They will then be free to apply developmental concepts in a way that is better suited to their own situation; that is, create their own development frameworks within their own *Weltanschauung* – their own interpretation that their citizens can better relate to. To do this, though, African leaders, and African development professionals, need to be able to differentiate the political from the systemic; and to do so they need to have control of the recipe, which in turn requires the capacity to create the recipe. That is what is meant when we talk of control over the intellectual space; for only when they control the recipe will African leaders be able to make meaningful and effective political decisions that place the onus for success or failure where it belongs: on their own shoulders.

Urban development in a historical context

In exploring the impact of western oppression on Africa, Walter Rodney stated that '[t]his book derives from a concern with the contemporary African situation. It delves into the past only because otherwise it would be impossible to understand how the present came into being and what the trends are for the near future' (1973, p. vii). This statement is as valid today as it was when written, in 1973. There is, and should be, a concern for the contemporary African situation, both inside and outside the subcontinent. And again we need to look at the past and re-evaluate the present, in order to move into the future with confidence and belief. The question is, though: from whose perspective are we exploring the past and evaluating the present? That was the dilemma that Berresford Ellis talks of in his exploration of the Celts described in Chapter 1.

Rodney's task was relatively straightforward, in that he could build a much clearer relationship between cause (western exploitation) and effect (the destructive social impact on Africa). Fifty years after the independence era, the lines have become more blurred. Now the external influences are far more nuanced, and come from many different points. And the world is becoming more interactive, and complex, making it more difficult to identify the strands of external influence. None the less, it remains possible to do so.

This chapter will explore the nature of the forces that impact on the structure of the evolving African urban society, with a view to understanding how these forces affect the form and structure of both government, and governance, at a local level. My objectives in looking at the way which these forces play themselves out are threefold.

The first objective is simply to gain acknowledgement from all external actors, be they international agencies, western governments, NGOs or academics, that they are an integral part of the development process. Any notion that they are there simply to provide assistance, support or advice, and as such are external to the development process in the countries where they work, is disingenuous and simply not true; wherever they work, they carry their own *Weltanschauungen* with them. Britain, for example, has an approach to numerous development issues, covering the role of local government, utilities management, development planning and systems of decentralisation, that are quite distinct from those of other countries, and in several cases unique. While these *Weltanschauungen* may be perfectly valid as a basis for development in Britain, they become problematic when carried through to, and embedded in, the British aid programmes. Hence, we need to recognise that simply by being involved, and importing their own *Weltanschauungen*, external agencies become actors in Africa's development process to a much greater degree than is currently either recognised or accepted. This is a reality of development, whether the western countries wish it or not.

The second objective is to define these *Weltanschauungen* that shape urban development. All development decisions are linked to value-based *Weltanschauungen*, and they apply to every country; defining them in an objective way will assist in identifying where external interpretations of the *Weltanschauungen* are being imposed, and open the way to the creation of internal solutions.

The third objective is to show how the urban development trajectory since structural adjustment in the 1980s has been shaped almost entirely by a response to global change that has its origins in the mature cities of the West. Those in Britain and the United States particularly who write about African development from within a framework of Anglo-Saxon *Weltanschauungen* impose their own interpretation of the impact of global trends, while their *Weltanschauungen* also define their response. In this way the external involvement goes beyond influence; it creates powerful forces that drive and shape African intellectual development, in much the same way, and often with the same detrimental impact, as the western colonial forces shaped Africa's physical and social development in previous centuries.

The nature of external influence

Chapter 1 illustrated how the current African urban development construct is shaped by four thematic forces of influence (Figure 1.1), which are themselves underpinned by control over the global research agenda as it pertains to development; and that when all of these come together, they take control over Africa's intellectual space. What is interesting is that only one of these four forces is linked directly to the colonial past; the other three forces derive from externalities that are linked to more recent global change. At the same time, though, there is also an indirect causal linkage between the first one, the impact of colonialism, and the remaining three, through the Anglo-Saxon development *Weltanschauungen* that link all of them together.

So, what is happening in Africa today is linked back directly to what happened in Africa under colonialism; and time alone will not change that reality. If we really want to break that link, then what we need to do is explore and unravel the thread that links the past to the present. At the heart of the current African urban development model is the urban planning paradigm; that is, a comprehensive model that seeks to guide African urban development through the use of planning theory, applied at both a regional and a city level. All the literature on urban development in Africa – and the UN-Habitat *State of African Cities* report (2008) provides a good summary of this – is situated within this paradigm. This, then, is the recipe for the African urban development cake. If we wish to understand why African towns and cities remain underdeveloped, then the place to begin is here.

At the same time, though, any exploration of the recent (i.e. post-1945) history of African urban development has to go beyond just African history, particularly in the period after 1990. To fully understand the way in which these forces play themselves out, we have to look at the wider landscape and the global forces at play, not just in economics but in politics, the environment and social change. In this wider context I would argue that we need to see the forces of change from three different perspectives: the perspectives of the African countries themselves, those of the international agencies that play a major role in African development, and those of the western countries that have shaped Africa's recent urban development agenda. This whole relationship is illustrated in Figure 2.1. In looking at how this relational framework evolves, I would argue that the freedom of African countries to take responsibility for their own urban development is actually weakening rather than strengthening.

The diagram in Figure 2.1 divides the evolution of urban development, from the second half of the twentieth century to the present, into three phases. Rather than viewing this evolution chronologically, however, the figure constructs the evolving development process around what can be termed the transition phase of development. What came before is described as the pre-transition phase. This began in the aftermath of the Second World War (1939–45) and lasted until the late 1970s. At a local level it is a phase that situates urban development (in anglophone Africa) within a context of what has been termed 'the British colonial local government model'.

Following on from that is a zone of transition, in the sense that it has no clear start and end points, and its extent will vary depending on the nature

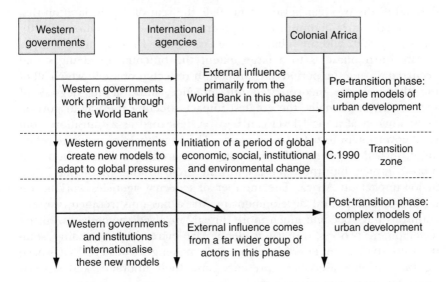

Figure 2.1 The changing nature of the external forces impacting on African urban development.

of the changes being discussed (e.g. economic, social, political). In this analysis I have used the year 1990 as the centre point of the transition, this being the year in which the Soviet Union collapsed and the global political order changed. In the wider global sense one logical starting point would be the oil crisis of 1973, while a possible end point would be 2008–9, which saw (at least the beginning of) a change in the financial world order, with the first serious questioning of the Anglo-Saxon free-market capitalist economic model, as well as environmental change with the Copenhagen meeting on climate change (COP15), notwithstanding its limited outcomes and perceived failings.

Given that the world is continuing to change rapidly, it is difficult to say that we have emerged from transition; however, when we look specifically at urban development we can be more specific in our dates, and be much clearer about the nature of the transition. For anglophone countries, one starting point for the transition is linked to the return to Anglo-Saxon economic orthodoxy under Reagan and Thatcher and, for Africa, the structural adjustment programme of the IMF and the World Bank. Viewed from this perspective, the transition began in the mid-1980s. However, the broader transition that changed local government was not only about economics. Over a period of fifteen to twenty years, changes occurred across all areas of development, alterations that in addition to the economic change encompassed social, environmental, political and institutional change. In this wider context, the end of the transition period could be defined by the two-year period from 2000, the year of the declaration that established the Millennium Development Goals (United Nations, 2000), through to 2002 and the Johannesburg Sustainable Development Summit.

The third phase is to a large extent the outcome of changes that occurred during the period of transition. It reflects a phase in which all of the changes were incorporated into practice, with varying degrees of success. Internationally, the greatest impact affecting the way in government worked at a local level can best be described as a transition from local government to urban governance. This new phase of urban development, in which the models of management are recognised to be much more complex than those required in the pre-transition phase, has had a major impact on Africa. The number of external agencies working on both urban and rural development in Africa has mushroomed; western countries have become much more directly involved themselves with the development process; western academics are increasingly providing 'solutions' to Africa's perceived problems and 'challenges'; western NGOs have significantly increased their presence, and their numbers; and western media attention is much greater.

It is this vast increase in the nature and extent of external involvement that leads us to ask the question 'Whose *Weltanschauung* is defining Africa's urban future?' In this complex international environment, with increasing numbers of western agencies becoming involved, with information flows expanding almost exponentially and with western control over the academic and research agenda, whose interpretation of the problems, and whose 'solutions', are driving Africa's urban development agenda? The next three sections will explore the three phases of urban development as a prelude to answering those questions.

The pre-transition phase of urban development

The French call the period 1945–74 'les trente glorieuses' – the wonderful thirty-year period. This was the period when Western Europe recovered from a devastating war and achieved a rate of growth that transformed the living standards of the majority of its population. It was also a period of significant importance in urban development. This period saw Western Europe complete its transition to an urbanised society; there were massive housing construction programmes; the major urban infrastructure networks were completed and in Britain all towns were fully serviced; and car ownership expanded rapidly, requiring a rethinking of transportation after eighty years during which roads had dominated the transport debate.

To a large degree, then, the mid-1970s represented an end point in an urban development process that had begun in the nineteenth century. Europe's towns and cities, many rebuilt after the war of 1939–45, were maturing, and began to face challenges that required a different way of thinking about both their organisational structures and their wider institutional frameworks of government.

The situation in Africa during that period is well documented in any text on urban development. The colonial period saw the establishment of the first urban areas based upon racial discrimination and the formation of a dualistic urban development model. This was a model where the political elite lived in areas that were laid out according to an urban plan, and fully serviced, while the indigenous majority lived, for the most part, outside of this formal city, be it in simply planned, 'traditional' or perhaps even unplanned settlements. Within the boundary, the British colonial system created a functional (though not sustainable) financial model for local government, and a political operating system that involved a degree of delegation of powers and duties. Since these were coupled with a strong infrastructure base, some have referred to the period as the 'golden age of local government in Africa' (Olowu, 2001, p. 5); however, when revisited with the knowledge of hindsight, and when compared to what was happening in Europe, this period can be seen in a very different light. A society reaching a point of maturity in its urban development exported a model of government to societies just beginning to embark upon an exponential phase of urban growth; this was a system imported from a totally different developmental context and carried within it the seeds of its own destruction.

Politically, the post-independence era witnessed a strong movement of power back to the centre, at the expense of local government. At the same time, these '[s]tate structures were generally weak ... [and] political autonomy was often eroded by superpower interests' (Rakodi, 1997a, p. 58). Economically, after a relatively healthy start there was an increasing trend towards a deficit in the external balance of trade, caused by an eroding agricultural surplus and an imbalance between the income from agricultural products and the cost of imported goods. At an urban level most countries were simply not able either to process land for urban development or to invest in housing and infrastructure at the rate required to keep pace with increasing urbanisation, which by that time was running at twice the national rate of population increase; that is, between 4 per cent and 6 per cent per annum, depending on the geographical region. The response from the World Bank was to seek alternative technical solutions, in the form of alternative sanitation options, for example, or a move to site and service schemes, while trying to streamline planning and land acquisition.

The urban development failures of that time did much to turn many agencies and donor countries away from infrastructure as a basis for addressing development issues, seeing this as the cause of the failure. The irony is that the real, though at the time unrecognised, failure of the pre-transition phase of urban development in Africa was actually something quite different. It was not a failure of the technology (i.e. of infrastructure) per se; instead, this failure was revealing of the intrinsic weakness of the western infrastructure model, as this book will later demonstrate. To return to the cake analogy: we had a recipe – the infrastructure model – that had worked in its home country, and so could not be at fault; instead, the fault had to lie in a failure to apply it effectively. That, at least, was the western agency interpretation, and as a result the next twenty years were wasted trying to address the wrong problem.

Because the majority of the analysis of development in Africa is carried out by western researchers and western agencies, this creates its own interpretative 'bias'. This is quite natural. Researchers and agencies seek objectivity through the application of academic method, which is intended to eliminate bias. The problem with that approach is that development is value driven, so the perspective a person takes in asking a question is influenced by that person's own value system. The outcome is first of all to phrase the question in a way that situates it within a value system, and then to interpret the answer within that same value-based framework.

For example, because those working for the World Bank at the time existed within an Anglo-Saxon *Weltanschauung*, they automatically assumed that the cause of the economic and institutional decline lay with African governments. Thus, their question asked about the major structural failings of those governments. If we were to assume, on the other hand, that the failings were those of the West, then we would probably still recognise that we were dealing with structural issues, but would either phrase the question differently or ask another question. This could be, for example: what was there about the systems African governments inherited, or adopted, during that period, that was totally inappropriate and might lead to systemic failure?

I would argue that such a question would reveal three outcomes from that time, none of which has received sufficient attention, yet which, when taken together, form the first strand of external influence shown in Figure 1.1; that is, the real colonial legacy of urban development. These three outcomes are:

- An implicit acceptance that certain core western development concepts, e.g. urban planning theory; water supply networks, are 'generic', which means that they apply to all countries provided they are adapted to local conditions. This has had a long-term impact, providing the legitimacy for western influence and contributing to western control over the intellectual space.
- An executive structure of government (with its line ministries) that was developed at a time when the primary focus was rural development and which reflected that focus; this is structure that is poorly suited to supporting either strong local government or effective urban governance.

- An acceptance of the principle of inequity in service delivery (i.e. the rich and the poor have different levels of service). While this was racist in origin, it is so deeply embedded in both internal and external thinking about the structure of African urban development that it is now accepted as a norm, when in fact it is an aberration.

These were the real structural failures of the time; yet all three of these outcomes continue to be accepted by international agencies, and continue to play a significant role in shaping urban development thinking and practice, through to the present time. In other words, referring back to the quotation by Walter Rodney, the ongoing failings of the present remain grounded in the inherited mistakes of the past.

The transition phase in urban development

There are elements to all processes involved in this transition phase that are critical to an understanding of the difference between a 'global response' and a response situated within a *Weltanschauung*. Invariably, the process begins with a major event; that is, one that has a global impact, or at least a widespread regional impact. One good example would be, say, the oil embargo of 1973. In October 1973 the Organization of Arab Petroleum Exporting Countries blocked oil supplies to the West 'in response to the U.S. decision to re-supply the Israeli military' (US Department of State, undated) during the Yom Kippur War of that year. There were global responses to this crisis, such as the search for alternative energy sources; but there were also individual responses. Thus, a number of countries in Western Europe were spurred to increase their investment in, and commitment to, public transport systems in the cities. The United States, on the other hand, with its greater focus on the individual in society, placed its main emphasis on both internal and external oil exploration to increase and diversify supplies.

There was then the economic transformation of the 1980s. This is an extremely interesting example of the way this term, 'global', is linked to a specific worldview. This was self-evidently considered a global event of major significance in the Anglo-Saxon world, and reflects the dominance of economics in shaping events within this particular *Weltanschauung*. In mainland Europe on the other hand the transition hinged around the fall of communism, described by one Hungarian writer as the 'end of World War 2 in Europe' (Glatz, 2000) and, perhaps even more dramatically, by Fukuyama (1992) as 'the end of history'. This was a much broader socio-political event which impacted directly on the countries of Western Europe; as such, it was perceived to be the dominant feature of the transition. The earlier economic transition did have a major impact on Europe eventually, but it was diffused over a longer period.

The point here is that the way a country (or an organisation) sees events, and the importance it attaches to them, is directly bound up with its own internal *Weltanschauung*; that is, a society will interpret major events of a transforming nature from within its own socio-cultural and economic value system. In this case the Anglo-Saxons and Europeans saw the world from within different *Weltanschauungen*, and responded accordingly. For other countries, though, and particularly those in Africa, the greatest impact came from the first shift, reflecting once again the power of hegemony and social domination to influence global perceptions and priorities.

What we are looking at here is the balance of intellectual capacity and resources. For any country to create its own response to global events and trends, there is a need for a high level of intellectual absorptive and processing capacity within its society – the knowledge base required to internalise external events effectively and create a response. African countries, among others, generally do not have this capacity; hence their response to global (or even regional) events cannot be internalised in the same way, or at the same rate, as occurs in western countries. The result is that they are particularly vulnerable to external influence, enabling a dominant culture (in this case the Anglo-Saxon hegemony) to impose its own interpretation, which they have little option but to accept. This, then, is the mechanism through which the Anglo-Saxon hegemony transforms its own specific interpretation of events into perceived 'global models'.

This transformation leads on naturally to the next stage in the process, which is adapting a society to the changes that are the outcome of major events. Again this process would normally be carried out primarily through internal mechanisms of research, evaluation and feedback, while at the same time the society would be interacting with other countries. Once again, in western countries these mechanisms and interactions are internalised and focused on the country's own perceptions and own needs, as seen through the interpretative mechanism of the *Weltanschauung*. But in African countries the process is again externally driven, since by far the greater part of the research capacity and academic input is based outside of Africa. The outcome is to further reinforce the external interpretation of the hegemony and embed this in policies and implementation strategies.

When we apply this analysis to urban development in Africa we can identify five 'global' changes that defined the future direction of African urban areas. The first three were interpreted from within a specifically Anglo-Saxon *Weltanschauung*, while the last two were interpreted within a more general western *Weltanschauung*. These five events were:

1   the neo-liberal revolution, leading to the privatisation programmes of the 1980s[1] and the return to economic orthodoxy, driven by Britain and the United States in the so-called Reagan–Thatcher reforms;

2   the structural adjustment programmes (SAPs) of the World Bank, which had the same ideological economic roots as the first, being targeted at developing countries that had a strong financial dependency on the Bank;
3   the creation of the Millennium Development Goals (MDGs), which were targeted specifically at less developed countries;
4   the fall of the Soviet Union, and the subsequent economic policy shift in China, which together changed the world political and economic order;
5   the UN Environmental Summit in Rio de Janeiro in 1992, the formation of ICLEI (the International Council for Local Environmental Initiatives) and the creation of Agenda 21.

As we move on to the next stage, these events initiated four global development trends, which can be classified as falling within the broad definition of economic development, social development, the physical environment and institutional reform. These were driven by the following factors:

1   The changing economic order opened the way for a global market in goods and services, including financial services. It also reinforced the power of the Anglo-Saxon capitalist model as the dominant model defining the relationship between the public and private sectors. Urban and regional planning became intimately aligned with facilitating this process.
2   The negative impact of structural adjustment on the urban poor, and the increased vulnerability of the poor in the light of the global economic restructuring. This led to a more interventionist approach to social development at a global level, specifically targeting the poor, both urban and rural, which was institutionalised through the MDGs.
3   A range of services were identified as 'environmental' services, and new urban models began to emerge based on a repositioning of cities within an environmental paradigm.
4   The political, economic and environmental trends led to a change in the perception of the public sector, and its role in society. This in turn led to a re-evaluation of the relationship between the public and private sectors on the one hand, and between different tiers of government on the other.

Finally, the third stage defines the response. Four such responses are given below, the first three emanating from the World Bank (1990) and the fourth from the United Nations Development Programme (UNDP, 1991). These are:

1   to improve urban productivity by remedying infrastructure deficiencies, rationalising regulatory frameworks, strengthening local government and improving the financing of urban development;

2   to alleviate urban poverty by increasing demand for the labour of the poor, investing in health and education, and supporting safety nets and compensatory measures to deal with the transitional problems caused by SAPs;

3   to protect the urban environment by raising awareness, improving strategies and programs of action;

4   to strengthen local government to help it plan, finance and manage urban programmes and improve systems for land management and information.

This, then, was the series of events that took place during the process of global transition, which impacted directly on urban development in Africa. The next section looks at how these translated into practice in the post-transition phase of development.

The post-transition phase of urban development: the emerging urban governance construct

Obviously, Africa was as strongly influenced by these global changes as any other part of the world, particularly in its larger cities. The factor that differentiates African urban development from urban development elsewhere is that much of Africa (South Africa being to some degree the exception) did not have the internal capacity to create its own response. Hence, the policies, strategies and practices that were initiated to manage the transition came from outside. The impact of this external drive was twofold. First, it created a lag response in the development debate. The seventeen-year period I chose as the core period for the global transition (1985–2002) is extremely short in development terms. Hence, the opportunity for an indigenous African response, given the internal capacity and the accelerated rate of urbanisation, was limited. As a result, a large part of the debate on solutions (in water and sanitation for example) was actually part of a delayed response to the Phase 1 development scenario.

At the same time, the internal response of western countries to this global shift is based solely on their own needs, which reflect the requirements of mature and established cities. These provide the models that have emerged and which define the response. And it is these models that are being imposed on African urban areas, which have a totally different development context and a different set of needs, as is illustrated in Figure 2.2.

The forces that impacted on development, and that resulted in the series of transfers indicated in Figure 2.2, come from different sources, as we saw earlier. Some, such as the environmental response, are international,

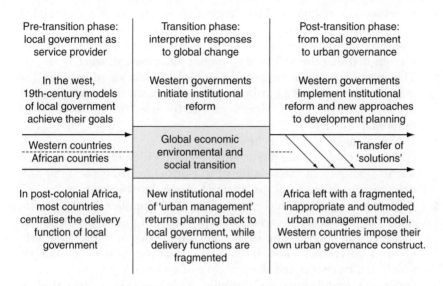

Pre-transition phase: local government as service provider	Transition phase: interpretive responses to global change	Post-transition phase: from local government to urban governance
In the west, 19th-century models of local government achieve their goals	Western governments initiate institutional reform	Western governments implement institutional reform and new approaches to development planning
Western countries / African countries	Global economic environmental and social transition	Transfer of 'solutions'
In post-colonial Africa, most countries centralise the delivery function of local government	New institutional model of 'urban management' returns planning back to local government, while delivery functions are fragmented	Africa left with a fragmented, inappropriate and outmoded urban management model. Western countries impose their own urban governance construct.

Figure 2.2 Impact of global change on urban governance in Africa.

which means that African governments were fully involved in, and supported, the outcomes. Others are termed international (or, more correctly perhaps, global) because the power and domination of the Anglo-Saxon *Weltanschauung* and hegemony have made them so. To some extent we have to accept this, as it represents the global reality. What we need to do, though, even if we are forced to accept this specific globally dominant view, is differentiate between principles and practice. In this context we are faced with a situation where all governments and actors broadly agree, or at least accept, a set of principles. However, this still leaves space for countries to create their own implementation strategies. In most of sub-Saharan Africa, though, the external influence of the Anglo-Saxon hegemony extended through to the imposition of practice (the implementation strategy).

It is these externally derived, and externally imposed, strategies that have shaped the urban development process, not only in anglophone Africa but in other parts of the subcontinent, though perhaps with a slightly ameliorated impact, in the post-transition phase of development. In the field of urban development, we can identify at least eight major strategic areas that are externally driven, emerging from the external drivers of the World Bank and UN development agencies described in the previous section, and supported by the western bilateral agencies. Each one of these had unintended consequences across several other areas of urban development practice. These eight areas of external intellectual control relate to:

1   Development planning. This Anglo-Saxon interpretation of global change places the private sector as the primary driver of economic planning and development at the apex of the urban planning process, thereby defining the wider development planning construct.

2   The environmental management strategy, which was developed for mature cities, created an artificial tension between the developmental needs of poor people in urban areas and the need for improved environmental practice.

3   Urban management. The new spatial planning/urban management approach redefined the management role of cities. One consequence was to reinforce the separation of infrastructure from planning and define urban planning as the driver of urban development.

4   Utilities management, including urban water supplies, by the private sector. This imposed a specific interpretation of public–private-sector partnerships, impacted on decentralisation policy, weakened the role of local government and formalised a dualistic system of delivery, which in turn challenged the principle of social equity.

5   Services as an individual responsibility. This impacted on decentralisation policy, weakened local government and had a negative impact on urban environmental sustainability. It also led to a centralisation of authority in urban governance.

6   The basic needs approach to water and sanitation imposed a specific interpretation of policy, which introduced a conceptually Anglo-Saxon policy process based on outcomes and targets.

7   The definition of community. The approach to urban planning, water supply and sanitation, which again uses an Anglo-Saxon interpretation of community, moved the focus of development down to sub-municipal level and carried with it a specific interpretation of local government.

8   Decentralisation. The overall impact of these changes on government resulted in a fragmentation of responsibility, both horizontally and vertically, with an impact on decentralisation and local government. This fragmentation also had an impact in terms of the indigenous capacity to respond to change.

The scaling up of external interventions in the post-transition phase of urban development has led to a rapid increase in the number of external actors, including academics and charities as well as international agencies; and a growing involvement of western government bilateral programmes. These changes also resulted in a significant increase in the use of western consultants, all supporting western government approaches. Following from this, the heavy dependence on external actors to implement the post-transition phase of the urban development process opened the way for western academics to critique, and to criticise, African policy and strategy in a way that would normally be reserved solely for internal review. This flow of advice, criticism and critique goes well beyond what in western countries would be considered interference in the internal affairs of a nation-state, and provides the justification for the statement that this degree of external interference is a form of colonisation, in this case through control over Africa's intellectual space.

The model: translating the areas of intervention into an Anglo-Saxon construct for urban development in Africa

The strategic interventions were initiated by different external agencies, at different times during the transition, to address specific components of global transformation. Thus, they represent a mechanistic response to change, and as such they are neither cohesive nor integrated. Instead, they are fragmented and competing in their demands for attention and priority. None the less, they can be 'assembled' to create an overall picture of how the sum of these external interventions links to a wider urban development agenda. This picture is shown in Figure 2.3, where the result could be described as the western 'construct' of urban development, as it is applied to anglophone countries, and influences non-anglophone countries, in sub-Saharan Africa.

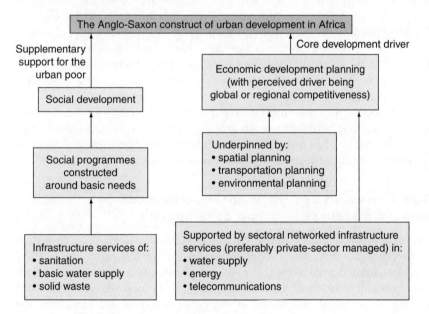

Figure 2.3 The western (predominantly Anglo-Saxon) construct of urban development in sub-Saharan Africa.

It is important to stress that although these interventions are shown collectively as a single construct, this is more for ease of understanding the different elements. In practice the individual elements are treated by international agencies and organisations as discrete initiatives within urban development. In this respect they are in direct contrast to the approaches to development policy and strategy adopted by many western countries, which tend, on the whole, to be more integrated.

The various elements of this construct represent the western interpretation of what constitutes a set of appropriate responses to the series of global events that characterised the transition. If we exclude South Africa from this discussion for the present, then none of these responses were initiated by African countries; they are all outcomes of external forces and international initiatives. While acknowledging that the management of cities in a post-transition phase world is complex, I would nonetheless argue that the way in which the responses have been imposed on African countries is detrimental to, rather than being supportive of, long-term sustainable development.

If this model was representative of an integrated approach, then that would at least provide a basis for creating a comprehensive framework for urban development in Africa, but this is not the case; instead, it is mechanistic. The multiplicity of external initiatives has resulted in a fragmented approach to urban development that is unnecessarily complex. As was mentioned in the previous section, this has vastly increased the number of external actors, from both international agencies and individual countries, that have become involved in helping to 'solve' Africa's urban 'problems'.

However, it is not only the complexity that is an issue here. Because of the way in which external agencies have structured their various interventions, the western urban development construct produces a condition where the majority of the interventions are detrimental to the achievement of effective decentralisation. Hence, the western development model results in a set of conflicting goals and objectives. To understand why this is the case, we need to link the various external interventions back to their origins in the different streams of western academic discourse.

Going forward: five fragmented streams of western discourse in urban development

At a broad regional level, to use the term 'regional' in a global rather than a sub-national sense, the model shown in Figure 2.3 provides an ideal construct for external actors. It provides a neat and simple explanation, and shows all concerned that we can have a planned regional economy that supports the private sector as the generator of wealth, and that the African natural resource base is now both available and accessible for the world to share. Excuse me, cries a small voice, drowned out by the wider excitement, but has anyone thought of the secondary towns and cities where 70 per cent of the urban population actually live? Where do they fit into all of this?

The increasing focus, since 1990, on global regional development and the megacities has left the secondary towns completely out of the picture, and in a deteriorating downward spiral. And the changes that have been initiated by external agencies have simply worsened that condition. When we consider the way in which the external changes have impacted on the secondary towns, then what we see is a completely different scenario from the one outlined above.

The global and regional changes that took place through the post-transition phase had the effect of breaking up the infrastructure base. What remained after that was a fragmented approach to urban development that proved incapable of addressing the real needs of the secondary towns and cities. Academics in Europe or the United States build their reputation on what they do best, which in international development revolves around global comparative studies, whether of cities or regions, and the analysis of global and regional trends. Small towns do not fit into this process: they can only be explored at a local or regional level; that is, by local actors. And since that is not happening, then the outcome that fills the void is an extrapolation downwards, from the large cities to the small towns. But small towns are not miniature versions of large megacities, though some may later morph into that latter state; instead, they constitute a completely different urban form.

So what we have now, in the emerging African urban construct, is a fragmented approach to development that has five distinct streams of (as usual) western discourse. These comprise:

1   a spatial and economic development planning discourse;
2   a discourse around the provision of basic needs to the urban poor;
3   a discourse around private-sector management of utilities;
4   an environmental discourse, centred on Agenda 21;
5   A decentralisation discourse.[2]

The first three of these link directly to three of the four strands of external influence described in Chapter 1. The environmental discourse represents an acknowledgement of the negative impact of these on development, and an attempt to reconcile the three. Unfortunately, its potential has been diminished by its being co-opted into the wider urban planning paradigm. Finally, the decentralisation discourse can be linked directly to the first thematic force of influence: the colonial impact. Each of these will be discussed briefly in the following paragraphs, where the objective is to demonstrate the important distinction, following from the exploration of global trends and responses discussed previously, between a development principle (or global trend), on the one hand, and the response on the other. So, while the first might be applicable globally, and therefore accepted by all countries in principle, its application – that is, the response – has to be developed locally, to suit local conditions. At present the response for Africa is being generated externally, and it is this external generation that is primarily responsible for the failure of African towns and cities to move towards a more effective, and sustainable, urban condition.

The first strand is the planning discourse. Based on a British urbanisation construct, it has three fundamental flaws when applied in an African context. The first is its underlying rationality: the need to create formal relationships in spatial development prior to that development taking place. The second is its view of infrastructure, which is seen as some form of supporting process. Here the result has been a gradual but consistent stripping out of the infrastructure function from the control of the city, as planning grapples with its primary concern of land management. At this point in time, urban planning in Africa has been reduced to what is now euphemistically termed 'ordered land management'; that is, seeking to provide at least an outline of a structured cadastre layout ahead of informal or illegal occupation of land. The third stems from its ideological alignment with external drivers of economic development, where its task is primarily to facilitate access to land driven by the need to support a free-market capitalist interpretation of land ownership.

The second stream of discourse is that which deals specifically with the urban poor. This discourse is situated in a more general social sciences arena, with the focus revolving, increasingly, around the provision of 'basic needs' and the Millennium Development Goals. Although the term 'basic needs' was conceived originally by the International Labour Organization, the approach as it applies to water and sanitation owes more to rural development policy. The critical distinction that has been lost here is that rural policy focuses on the needs of the individual farmer, or family, while urban policy is dealing with the collective. The reason why an urban policy for water and sanitation remains focused on the individual user can be traced directly to the Anglo-Saxon concept of the individual as the target of service delivery, at the expense of the collective. The outcome is self-evident in the failure to achieve the targets of the MDGs in water and sanitation in Africa.

The third strand of the discourse is related to the management of infrastructure utility services. This has a particular impact on the relationship between water supply and the city. The current western approach to utilities management is built around western contractual concepts that have been transposed without due consideration being given to the social and cultural context that made them successful in their countries of origin. In making this transformation, external actors have lost sight of the original goal, which is to create more effective working partnerships between the public and the private sector for the benefit of the whole, and replaced this with the imposition of one specific form of private-sector involvement, based upon the capitalist free-market system.

The fourth strand of the international urban development discourse is the environmental one, which is based upon a move towards urban sustainability and set out clearly by Agenda 21. Here the principle is sound, and many cities in the West are creating successful local Agenda 21 plans. The whole concept of a local Agenda 21 plan, though, was developed primarily to cater for the physical environment of a mature city; it has never been adapted to the needs of rapidly growing cities. Instead, external actors have sought to work with environmental agencies in national governments in Africa to 'adapt' the concepts applied successfully in mature cities to their own situation. And one mechanism for adapting them has been to classify specific infrastructure services, such as solid waste management, as environmental services.

The final strand of the discourse is that around decentralisation. Here the focus of the debate lies primarily within the ambit of social sciences, and has centred around the concept of cooperative local government; that is, the allocation of powers, duties and functions between the different tiers of government. Chapter 5 will deal specifically with this issue, and will show the degree to which this discourse has been separated from the others. The result has been that, even as the drive towards decentralisation continued as a goal, the reality was an ever-increasing centralisation of authority. UN-Habitat (2008), in its *State of African Cities 2008* report, blames this on a lack of political will on the part of African leaders, not recognising that it is the policies and practices endorsed by itself that are the primary cause of centralisation. Given the fragmentation described above, decentralisation and strong local government are simply unattainable.

The failure of this mechanistic approach is clear for all to see, yet the only response from western agencies is to call for even more urban planning.[3] The reality is a fragmented mechanistic approach in which the different strands create conflictual outcomes. Thus, there is tension between physical development for the urban poor and environmental needs; the inability of any of these models to create equitable development; and increased centralisation. Much of this can be traced to external control over Africa's intellectual space, and in particular the attempts to use the experience of mature cities as a role model. The conditions are totally different. Western countries as a whole have passed their peak development phase and are now in a phase of consolidation, a condition that applies especially to their urban areas. There is a high standard of living compared to the global average, and a high level of education, which means more people in tertiary education. Those interested in topics that can be classified, in the broadest sense, as developmental, including for example the issue of climate and climate change, are not faced any longer with the major development programmes of the nineteenth and twentieth centuries. Instead, their real need is to redress the negative impacts of what is already there (mitigation), or adopt new technologies (adaptation). The best way to do this is through an increase in academic specialisation, going down to increasing levels of detailed analysis. So, where at one time there may have been just one degree programme, there are now many sub-specialisations, all addressing different aspects of that activity.

When bilateral agencies explore issues in Africa, they draw on this entire range of skills, and have no problem in breaking a sector down into many parts. This has a huge impact on African countries in two ways. First, African graduate student numbers remain low and it remains a major challenge to maintain and enhance existing standards. Yet African countries are expected to be able to match the West in providing sub-sector specialists in a variety of fields; but the numbers are simply not there. Second, the sub-sector specialisation is driven by the needs of mature economies and mature cities. To respond effectively, Africa needs to mirror this set of skills. It does not follow, though, that the skills needed to manage rapidly growing cities, for example, are the same as the skills required to manage fully developed and mature cities. The urban planning system was used earlier as one example of this. In this externally controlled, multifaceted and highly specialised yet fragmented development agenda there is simply no way in which African countries can even begin to take control over the intellectual space that would enable them to provide local solutions to local problems.

Urban infrastructure: the lost urban development discourse

There is a common element that runs through the different phases of urban development in Africa, as perceived and driven by the external agencies: the outcomes at each stage are always reactive; they are never proactive. Common to all of them also is the degree to which they all need to incorporate some aspect of urban infrastructure. And in each case what we are seeing is a mechanistic response that in some reacts to the failure to manage urban infrastructure effectively. As the history of urban development unfolded, different components of the infrastructure have been cast off and relegated to a series of support services addressing other, broader developmental needs. This is illustrated in Table 2.1, linking the 'lost' infrastructure services to the post-transition development arenas.

The reasons for the loss of confidence in infrastructure as a development driver are understandable, given the history, as is the perception of the need to focus on other arenas of development activity. However, when

Table 2.1 The transfer of urban infrastructure to alternative arenas of development

Issue No	The core issue	The mechanism	The outcome	Infrastructure service transferred
1	Functional urban areas	Make spatial planning the basis for urban development	Guided land development	Roads Transport
2	Integrate the urban poor into the city	The Millennium Development Goals	Provide pit latrines and standpipes to the poor	On-site sanitation
3	Build effective public-private partnerships	Use of the private sector for delivery of services	Imposition of the Anglo-Saxon free-market capitalist model	Water supply Electricity Sewerage
4	Environmentally sustainable development	Agenda 21	Classification of some infrastructure services as 'environmental services'	Solid waste Some storm water
5	Decentralisation	No clear mechanism	Increased centralisation	The end-user component of a range of services

we look back at this historical development, which will be explored fully in the next chapter, we see two disturbing issues. First, we have a system, developed in the West, which was exported to colonial Africa as a support system for the colonial elite. It then failed to meet the needs of the indigenous majority – but that was never its intent. Thus, it was a failed western model. One could say it was up to the West, and primarily Britain, as the colonial power, to fix it; but by then the countries of Africa were mostly independent. Yet it was still external agents that defined the fixes, and each time they got it wrong. Under these circumstances it is obvious that African governments would have to take the blame; otherwise the credibility of external agencies would have been destroyed. At some point, though, we have to move away from always blaming the baker, and ask the question: who actually created the recipe for this rather tired and unsavoury development cake?

The second issue is of even greater concern, since it raises deeper and much more fundamental ethical and moral concerns. In pursuing their development agenda, these same external actors, with their constantly changing solutions, imposed a set of infrastructure services on Africa that were inferior to the services provided in their own countries. Yet there is simply no way that they would ever have been allowed to impose such a dual system on their own citizens. The result is to create in Africa a sub-continent of second-class global citizens and in doing so create a develop-mental framework that induces a fundamentally unstable political condition across all urban areas – a recipe for ongoing strife.

Not only is this action morally indefensible (though many in the West would no doubt argue that it is ethically defensible when viewed from a humanitarian standpoint), it is totally unnecessary. It is a classic example of what happens when the locus of decision-making is moved outside of the place where it is to be operationalised. When people address develop-ment issues from the inside, their perspective is fundamentally different; after all, they have to live with the consequences of their actions. It is the objective of this book to demonstrate that there is an alternative way of providing infrastructure that is socially equitable, environmentally sustain-able, and affordable. And furthermore, this alternative system builds upon a number of initiatives that are driven from inside the subcontinent, if only anyone outside would be prepared to listen.

The removal of infrastructure as an integrated system driving urban development in Africa has a second unintended consequence, linked to the one above: it has undermined local government to the point where that system of government is not only unstable but also dysfunctional. Essentially it is the outcome of these external initiatives, rather than any lack of political will on the part of African leaders, that is primarily responsible for the failure of decentralisation in Africa.

The position that we are in now, with respect to the urban discourse on Africa, particularly as it affects the secondary towns, is that urban infra-structure is effectively the 'lost discourse', airbrushed out of the wider urban development landscape. If African governments are to achieve sus-tainable urban development, then the first step is to reintegrate urban infrastructure into the development discourse.

Reintegrating urban infrastructure into the development discourse

This discussion has sought to demonstrate that infrastructure is central to any meaningful discourse on urban development. This does not imply, though, that infrastructure alone will provide all of the answers; for that infrastructure has to be situated within some form of broader develop-ment construct, incorporating what is described here as developmental urban governance. In this context there are two important examples that have been drawn on here. The first is South Africa, which sought to define a developmental role for local government in its new constitution. This took place in the mid-1990s, during the transitional phase of global change. Hence, there are important lessons to be learned about how the concept of developmental local government could function in this post-transitional phase. The second is Ethiopia, which recently carried out a major exercise in decentralisation and capacity-building. This book draws heavily upon this Ethiopian experience in developing the ideas put forward here, a number of which will be explored in the second part of the book.

Good urban governance is an essential prerequisite for sustainable urban development. Unfortunately, the current western approach to good governance, while it may express valid principles at a global level, is falling into the same trap as have so many other western-based urban initiatives in Africa: constructing an applications model on the basis of a conceptual framework developed in the mature cities of the West. This book sets out an alternative approach, one that has been developed specifically for Africa's secondary cities. Urban development in the secondary towns will only be successful if we can find a way to integrate urban infrastructure back into the development process. To do so, we have to take the existing, but currently fragmented, strands of the urban discourse and link them back conceptually to urban infrastructure. Developmental urban governance provides the mechanism through which that outcome can be achieved, as is illustrated by the conceptual shown in Figure 2.4.

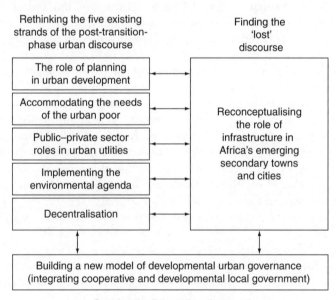

Figure 2.4 Creating a new integrated urban governance model for secondary cities in Africa.

The impact of external forces on Africa's ability to define its own set of roles and relationships

The model shown in Figure 2.4 is dependent for its successful implementation on indigenous interpretations of responses. Currently, the elements on the left-hand side of the diagram, those which presently drive the urban discourse, all reflect western *Weltanschauungen* of one form or another. The challenge is to move beyond these by going back to the core issues and building a new development discourse locally.

The starting point for this discussion is the recognition that application of approaches to urban development can never be 'value-free' – that is, every society operates within its own *Weltanschauung*; yet nor can it be based solely on a set of international values. Urban development is a process that operates within a dualistic value system. On the one level it is a process that seeks to accept and integrate a set of universal human values. At the same time, there is a second level of operation, where urban development is a process that reflects specific cultural and social relationships, which play themselves out at a local level. And different countries have the right to translate values into practice in their own way.

In an urban context the way in which they can best do so is through the establishment of a set of roles and relationships that specifically reflect the indigenous value system. This set of roles and relationships will then provide the building blocks of urban society. Ultimately, these building blocks are more important, and critical to long-term sustainability, than are actions and outcomes, which only reflect specific mechanisms used to meet targets. The way in which we can measure the freedom of individual countries to make their own decisions can, then, be defined by the extent to which these countries are free to define their own set of roles and relationships.

Within the context of African urban development, I would suggest that there are seven areas, covering the establishment of fundamental values, roles and relationships, which are the prerogative of individual countries when creating their own urban development construct, and which therefore define the degree of sovereignty and freedom that individual countries have in practice. These then provide an important set of indicators against which to measure the extent to which external actors impose their own agenda on African countries. These seven sets of key roles and/or relationships are:

1   the role of local government and the relationship between different tiers of government (cooperative local government – decentralisation);

2   the role of the private sector and the relationship between the public and the private sectors, with particular reference to the role of the private sector in the provision of public goods;

3   the role of the sub-municipal groups, both inside and outside the local
     authority, and the relationship between local government and resi-
     dents (developmental local government), particularly the application
     of this relationship to service delivery;
4   the role of social development (including social equity) and the rela-
     tionship between social and economic development;
5   the role (and nature) of environmental management and the relation-
     ship between economic and social development and environmental
     sustainability;
6   the role of the different components of the urban development (eco-
     nomic, environmental, spatial) and the relationship with the political
     decentralisation process;
7   the role of infrastructure in urban development and its relationship
     with planning and the decentralisation process.

The last two differ from the first five in that they are not core determinants of sovereignty. However, they play a major role in operationalising
the other five, and in this context they can be used to control the direction of the core roles and relationships described previously.

These seven sets of roles and relationships come together when a
country creates a development policy. This in turn highlights a further
dimension to sovereignty, which is the ability of a country to set policy.
This is the real litmus test of a country's freedom. Thus, it is the freedom
to define policy (which in this specific case means urban policy, together
with all of the subsidiary policies that accompany it), and the freedom to
be able to do this independently of external influence, that is the ultimate
definition of sovereignty over internal affairs, and thus is the basis for any
partnership formed between a country and an external agency.

This is the broad analysis of the urban development trajectory in sub-
Saharan Africa, and it ends with the proposition that urban infrastructure
and effective decentralisation provide the key to sustainable urban development, particularly in the secondary towns and cities. The next three
chapters will be concerned, then, with an exploration of these two areas of
developmental activity. Later, in Chapter 11, the book will return to these
seven sets of roles and relationships, and use them to develop a new model
of urban governance that addresses the integrative needs illustrated by
Figure 2.4.

Chapter 3

How modern urban infrastructure evolved

Is there life beyond urban network infrastructure?

The creation of centralised network infrastructure – that physical web of pipes, pathways and cables that provides the spatial framework of the modern city – has been so successful that it is difficult to imagine infrastructure in any other way. Unfortunately, though, we have now reached a point, particularly in Africa, where we have to find another way. This is because, when viewed from a global perspective, our system of network infrastructure is only available to a small fraction of the world's population; and there are many countries that are unlikely ever to be able to afford this level of service. This is not simply a financial issue, though. Increasingly, there are looming resources and environmental constraints that would prevent this system from being rolled out to 3 billion or more urban residents who would require it over the next fifty years, even if the money was there. This is a system that was developed in a different era, under vastly different circumstances, and which has now passed its expiry date. Unfortunately, there is a dearth of alternatives; and so we appear to be intellectually adrift, not knowing quite what to do.

So why are we caught in such a conundrum? Primarily because we have never stopped to think about what we are doing; instead, we have spent the past fifty years in crisis management mode. Having decided that centralised network systems were unaffordable, we have progressively reduced the level of service provided by that model in the hope that we could find a point of equilibrium between cost and affordability; but we never did. Now we have reached rock bottom with basic needs, and can go no lower. Yet still we cannot meet the demand. We have failed, and the time has come to reconsider our entire approach.

Where do we begin? An analogy might help us here. Imagine we are on a path in the forest. At some point we realise that we are going in the wrong direction; somewhere along the way we took a wrong turning. In this situation the best solution is simply to go back to the point where we went wrong and take the correct path. It is exactly the same here: we need to retrace our steps through the development process and go back to the beginning. By that I do not mean just the past fifty years, but the past two hundred years – back to where it all began.

There is actually a great deal that can be learned from that first 150 years of western development: knowledge that can help us to understand how infrastructure evolved and how people saw the role of infrastructure in urban society during that time. That is the purpose of this chapter: to explore the evolution of urban infrastructure in the two countries that drove the modernisation of western towns and cities during the nineteenth and twentieth centuries: the United Kingdom and the United States. What is most interesting about these two countries is not actually their commonalities; it is their differences – the extent to which they saw the role of infrastructure in urban society in quite different ways. By understanding these differences we can be guided back to the right path. By understanding these differences, we can move beyond centralised urban networks to see the real nature of infrastructure, and thereby lay the framework for a new urban infrastructure model in Africa. First, though, we have to understand the rationale that drove this early development, and then, in the next chapter, seek to understand why it went so badly wrong when transposed to this newly formed continent of nation-states that was emerging in sub-Saharan Africa.

Our current perception of infrastructure

A useful starting point might be to describe what exactly is meant by this term, 'infrastructure'; but that, unfortunately, is easier said than done! For while there have been many attempts to create definitions, these remain quite diverse and unhelpful. As a result, there is no single widely accepted definition of the term. Part of the reason for this is that interpretations of infrastructure change with time, as well as reflecting different perspectives of development. They are also influenced by the level of infrastructure – that is, whether it is national, regional or local – as well as the context within which they are explored, e.g. economic or technical. All of this is linked, sadly though understandably, to national *Weltanschauungen*. As a result, if we wish to at least understand how infrastructure is perceived, then we have to look across a range of 'definitions'.

Here is one that reflects an economic perspective: infrastructure defined as '[t]he facilities that must be in place in order for a country or area to function as an economy and as a state, including the capital needed for transportation, communication, and provision of water and power, and the institutions needed for security, health, and education' (Deardorf, 2009). Here we see the strong linkage between infrastructure and economic development that is central to many American interpretations of infrastructure.

A second definition, which seeks to incorporate a social context, at least broadly, states that infrastructure comprises '[t]he basic facilities, services, and installations needed for the functioning of the community, such as transportation and communications systems, water and power lines, and public institutions including schools, post office, and prisons' (*Free Dictionary*, 2011). This is an important definition because it draws attention to the linkage between infrastructure and the functioning of the community. At the same time, though, it is also very broad, with its inclusion of such a wide range of public institutions.

A third definition describes infrastructure as 'the basic physical and organizational structures and facilities (e.g. buildings, roads, power supplies) needed for the operation of a society or enterprise' (Oxford Dictionaries, 2011). This definition has two interesting implications. First, it extends to concepts beyond the physical to the organisational, yet the implications of this extension are rarely followed up. Second, it suggests that infrastructure is needed for the operation of society but does not describe the nature of this need; that is, is it a social or an economic need?

Overall, an internet search for definitions will indicate that economic and technical interpretations dominate, particularly in the United States. There we see that '[t]he term *infrastructure* has been used since 1927 to refer collectively to the roads, bridges, rail lines, and similar public works that are required for an industrial economy, or a portion of it, to function' (*American Heritage Dictionary*, 2006). This suggests two things. The first is the idea that infrastructure is actually a driver of economic development, rather than simply being linked in some general way to economic development. Second, we have a date, 1927, being linked to the early definitions. By that time there was a much clearer understanding of the technological components of infrastructure, and this in turn influenced the definition. As a result, we do not have any real understanding of how infrastructure was perceived before that time (i.e. during the eighteenth and nineteenth centuries), particularly in Anglo-Saxon countries.[1]

The confusion around the term is then further complicated by the use of three, quite distinct, key words – 'function', 'facility' and 'service' – with no attempt being made to differentiate between them. Rather, the facilities are perceived to underpin the function. This viewpoint reflects a mechanistic paradigm that is at the heart of much development thinking in the Anglo-Saxon world; that is, the world in which America and Britain play a dominant role, and the world that dominates the international development arena.

This Anglo-Saxon approach, with its focus on functionality, enables each infrastructure component, or service, to be separated out, and the whole replaced by a series of individual, functional (i.e. operational) definitions pertaining to individual services. As an example, using the service of water supply, we then move to a specific functional definition for this service, which states that it is 'a facility that provides a source of water' (*Free Dictionary*, 2008), with a facility in turn being defined as a building or place that provides a particular service. There is no social context involved here. For many technical water specialists, this definition has not changed significantly since the beginning of the twentieth century, when water supply was first defined as '[a] supply of water; specifically water collected, as in reservoirs, and conveyed, as by pipes, for use in a city, mill, or the like' (*Webster's Dictionary*, 1913). Then, having been broken down into its component parts, it can be reassembled in different combinations, thereby providing a good example of a classical Anglo-Saxon mechanistic analysis, wherein the whole is perceived as the sum of the parts.

In this logic framework, infrastructure becomes an outcome, with the focus on the individual; it is no longer either a delivery process or a communal service. The result is two tiers of definition, the combination of which is tautological, because it creates a condition whereby each infrastructure 'service', when treated individually, adopts a meaning that is quite different from the generic definition of infrastructure as a whole; that is, as a collective and communal service. This result is the intellectual flaw in the British interpretation of infrastructure.

The European approach is quite different from that found in Anglo-Saxon culture. In continental Europe, at a local government level the function of infrastructure is much more deeply rooted in the concept of supporting the 'functioning of the community'. This difference can be seen in the French interpretation that follows, which remains holistic in its conceptualisation.

Table A

French definition (Sogreah, undated)[a]	English translation
Le bon fonctionnement d'une ville, et la réussite de tout projet d'aménagement urbain, repose sur la capacité de la collectivité à planifier son développement, en s'appuyant sur un ensemble d'infrastructures de qualité, modernes et adaptées aux besoins (voies de circulation, réseaux d'assainissement, d'eau, d'énergie et d'électricité, infrastructures de télécommunications et de traitement de l'information...).	The well-functioning town, and the success of all urban planning projects, rests on the capacity of the collective to plan their development and rests upon an integrated infrastructure base that is modern and adapted to their needs (circulation routes, sewerage networks, water, energy and electricity, telecommunications infrastructure and the effective use of information...).

Note
a While this definition comes from a private consultant in France, it can be seen to reflect also the client base of that consultant, which is to be found in the urban municipalities.

This is an important discussion from an African perspective because if there is no single recognised definition, then the question becomes: whose interpretation is used in Africa? Whichever definition we choose, they all suffer from the same flaw: regardless of where they come from, they have all been developed within specific, value-based *Weltanschauungen*. This flaw simply illustrates the extent to which African countries, individually and collectively, require a new interpretation of urban infrastructure, one that is grounded in the needs and the urban realities of sub-Saharan Africa in the twenty-first century. Furthermore, while sector specialists view urban needs from within their own sectoral perspective, this book will argue that the relationship between the different infrastructure services and the city is actually a complex and interconnected one; and that fragmentation has played a major role in making African towns and cities dysfunctional. One objective of this book, then, is to explore the nature of this complex inter-action, creating a new urban infrastructure model and, ultimately, a new definition.

As part of such an exercise the final chapter of the book will seek to create a new definition of the term 'urban infrastructure' in a twenty-first-century African context, based upon what has emerged from the study that unfolds in the ensuing chapters. Clearly, though, in order for the book to be written in the first place, some assumptions need to be made now, if only to identify what exactly it is about urban infrastructure that needs to be rethought!

Defining the components of urban infrastructure

The starting point is to identify all the relevant activity areas (i.e. services and facilities) that provide components of urban infrastructure, interpret them in their widest sense, and then consider these as the core 'components' of infrastructure. It should be stressed that producing a list of components is simply a starting point that will enable a dialogue to begin; it does not indicate support for this concept, nor even recognition that such a list is a valid interpretation of urban infrastructure. It is simply that the discussion has to begin somewhere.

Using somewhat outmoded nineteenth- and twentieth-century terminology as our point of departure, then, the infrastructure 'components' generally considered to constitute urban infrastructure comprise the following:

- water provision and supply;
- sanitation, including on-site and off-site disposal systems, the latter incorporating liquid waste management and collective waste treatment systems on public property;
- urban movement for all vehicular and non-vehicular modes of transport (e.g. roads, pathways, rail and other networks);

- rainfall run-off within the municipal boundary and urban storm-water drainage systems;
- solid waste management and treatment;
- industrial and hazardous waste management and treatment;
- street lighting;
- energy, including electrical transmission networks;
- telecommunications and communications.

This is a baseline, and the terms used are intentionally conventional (i.e. from the nineteenth and twentieth centuries). The list specifically excludes the physical element of social infrastructure services such as schools (in education) and clinics (in health care), as well as buildings used for administrative purposes that are not directly associated with the above components. Armed with this list, we can now move on to begin the historical analysis.

Why explore the western history of infrastructure?

When these components of urban infrastructure are translated into operational systems, the way in which those systems evolve depends upon three variables. The first is the *technology*, and here the majority of countries developed their urban infrastructure in the nineteenth and twentieth centuries, leading to adopted technologies that were broadly similar. The second variable is the *social context*; that is, the 'value system' of the wider society. This covers issues as diverse as the cultural perception of faeces, the perceived role of local government vis-à-vis the individual, or the societal perception of the balance between economic and social objectives – all of which can vary quite significantly between countries. The third variable, which is strongly influenced by the first two, is the system of operational *management*. Today this is often reduced to a simple duality that contrasts public- and private-sector management. In practice, however, the choices are more complex, even within the public sector itself, and different countries can use quite different management systems as well as viewing the relationship between the public and private sectors differently.

This means that there is no one 'correct' way of structuring an urban infrastructure system; yet the whole thrust of external actors is to force a specific (albeit fragmented and ill-conceived) model of infrastructure management on African governments. The argument often used to defend such a model is that it is a global trend, when in fact it is simply a quite specific, value-based interpretation. The objective of this section and the one that follows is to show that the infrastructure management models being imposed on African countries today are not there because they are the best, or even the most effective, models for African countries to adopt. Rather, they are there because they are an outcome of history, and the end point in a clearly defined historical trajectory of infrastructure evolution. Thus, while the current approach is to some degree empiricist, to the extent that it takes direct experience of events in Africa to arrive at the present condition, it actually draws, often subliminally, on a historical model based on Anglo-Saxon values. This is British in its origins, although it does reflect an important American influence in selected areas. This is the model that provides the cauldron within which the various 'solutions' to Africa's urban problems have emerged.

The historical evolution of infrastructure in England

The evolutionary path that initiated the urban infrastructure trajectory in Africa (which is where we want to end up) began in the United Kingdom – more specifically, in England.[2] Infrastructure as we know it today had its origins in England and the United States, but the two did not follow exactly the same development trajectory. Both have been influential in different ways, but it is the British approach that is more relevant here, simply because it was Britain that was the colonial power in, and therefore provided the practical model for, anglophone Africa. America played some part, particularly in influencing the later economic and privatisation agenda, but the main evolutionary path passes through England and then into Africa.

In looking at this trajectory the objective is to explore the extent to which the present is an outcome of the past. To what extent are the practices that we follow today, and which drive almost all of our thinking about urban infrastructure, based on this British precedent? It is evident that they do not provide a particularly effective outcome, which should not be too surprising given that they were never conceptualised to address the current African reality. So, what we have are a range of practices and approaches that have simply adapted what has gone before. In this context, what is happening in Africa today is to a large extent an accident of (British) history. These systems were born in a different time and under different circumstances; the times and circumstances today require new, often quite different, approaches and solutions. In order to be able to view infrastructure through a new lens, though, we need to escape from this falsely scented trail: to revisit the past, seek to learn the real lessons of history and understand where it all went wrong.

Urban infrastructure in England from 1835 to 1929

There is a tendency, when discussing urban infrastructure, to focus on the development of technology, for example the use of steam engines to pump water, which led to the first water supply schemes of the late eighteenth century. Yet this focus can overlook other aspects of infrastructure that are of equal importance in shaping the future of cities. This chapter is concerned with these 'other' aspects of infrastructure, and seeks to demonstrate the full extent to which it was the interrelationship between them and the technology that shaped, and ultimately defined, the way that external actors view infrastructure in Africa today.

Prior to the 1830s, towns in England were controlled by a numerically small mercantile class, who ran them (generally through their professional guilds) for their own financial benefit; thus, towns were centres of economic activity. Social responsibility was of little concern and had to be imposed by statute originating with central government, with the statutory vehicle being the Poor Laws. These laws had first been introduced as early as the thirteenth century and continued to provide the framework for social legislation until the second half of the nineteenth century. Every aspect of urban development in Britain during that period, including infrastructure, was situated within that framework. As a result, the development of urban infrastructure was set almost entirely within a developmental goal of social improvement that was embedded in this wider conceptual and practical framework of the Poor Laws.

The entire evolutionary path of urban infrastructure in England can be traced back to two events that occurred in the middle of the nineteenth century, the one in 1842 and the other in 1854, and the ensuing practical interpretation of these two events. This was completely different from the way in which the urban infrastructure evolved in the United States, as the later analysis of that country will demonstrate.

To contextualise these two events we need to go back a little earlier, to the 1830s. It had long been recognised (experientially at least) that the construction of urban areas impacted on the natural drainage pattern; that is, that developing a town brought with it increased problems with flooding. This needed to be managed in some way; and the easiest solution was to build drains along the roads to take the water away. Unfortunately, there were no public mechanisms to pay for these drainage improvements, and the private ownership of the borough meant that those with the power and responsibility would have had to invest their own money, which they were not prepared to do. This situation persisted through to the Municipal Corporations Act of 1835, at which point the government sought to formally allocate responsibility for drainage to the boroughs, albeit feebly. In terms of this Act, local councils could, if they wished, take over responsibility for drainage and street cleaning, which were perceived to be social improvements. However, the Act did not compel them to make these social improvements. 'Consequently, by 1848 only twenty-nine boroughs had taken any action in terms of public health' (Bloy, 2011).

By that time it was becoming evident that unsanitary conditions were the norm, and that these conditions were rapidly deteriorating. The time-frame coincided with the cholera epidemics, and there was clearly a linkage. However, the real driver of change came not from any understanding of this linkage (which was still twelve years into the future), but from an entirely different source. It was the outcome of a separate, and unrelated, investigation into the Poor Laws that first provided (empirically) an incontrovertible link between disease and the urban environment: this was Chadwick's study that resulted in the *Report on the Sanitary Condition of the Labouring Population of Great Britain* of 1842 (Fraser, 1973, p. 58).

Edwin Chadwick was a barrister by profession who became increasingly concerned about the state of London's slums and subsequently about the relationship between poverty, poor hygienic conditions and disease. He was a member of the commission that produced the Poor Law Report of 1834, and was subsequently secretary to the commission, in which role he prepared the 1842 report.

Chadwick was a visionary, seeing water supply and drainage as part of an integrated environmental network that would carry water into homes and then carry the waste away, together with the storm water, depositing it on the fields, where it would provide fertiliser to the crops. This integrated approach was referred to as an arterial system. At the same time, he was also a firm believer in an activist central government (Melosi, 2008, p. 29), a belief that strongly influenced his proposed solutions to the sanitary crisis of the cities. For Chadwick the two perspectives were inseparable; thus, he argued that the (technical) solution could only be achieved if this 'improved sanitation' – that is, the integrated water supply and drainage system – was controlled by a central authority (Fraser, 1973, pp. 58–75), a belief that he converted into a formal recommendation.

We know, from subsequent developments, that this recommendation was almost universally rejected; however, different researchers offer different reasons for that rejection. Melosi, writing from the perspective of an American urban historian, situates it within a technical rationality, putting forward Hamlin's argument that it was 'an affirmation of the flexible, client-driven practices that characterized British engineering' at that time. This is on the grounds that 'it was the practice of British engineers to deal with the problems defined by their clients – not to advocate their own technical visions – and to operate in a setting where there was no single technical solution' (Hamlin, 1992, quoted in Melosi, 2008, p. 33).

Fraser, on the other hand, situated the rejection in a political and institutional context, suggesting that it was this concept of central control that was the determining factor in bringing infrastructure under local government control, highlighting that '[t]his [recommendation] mobilised local authorities who, whilst baulking at the cost of service provision, were not prepared to have centralised [i.e. central government] control for fear that this would mean the loss of local government' (1973, p. 65). Certainly the legal outcome, which was embedded in the Public Health Act of 1875, resulted in local government retaining responsibility for the management of water supply and sanitation, though central government took legislative responsibility.

While recognising the merits of both these arguments, I suggest that the institutional response was the more influential in determining the final outcome, since this better reflects the political reality of the time. At the same time, though, there was a third factor shaping this debate and supporting the argument in favour of separation of these infrastructure services (i.e. water supply and drainage), one that has not been recognised previously. This third factor is actually critical to an understanding of how urban infrastructure evolved later, as well as having a major impact on British colonial infrastructure policy: this is the whole question of water quality. This in turn leads us to the second major event of that time, in 1854. Here again, though, this event requires a context, because it was the way in which water quality was perceived, at that specific time in history, and in that small island of which England is a part, that laid the real foundation for the entire global water supply industry that exists today.

The technology of water distribution can be traced back through millennia, and across different parts of the world, and includes, for example, the tanks and channels of Sri Lanka and the *qanats* of ancient Persia. The primary objective of much of this early engineering work, though, was to provide irrigation for crops. The origin for urban water supply per se, certainly in the West, emerged elsewhere, with the growth of the Roman Empire. The Romans had an extensive water distribution system, not only in Rome but in many of the cities across Europe. However, these all operated under gravity, and this concept of distribution under gravity was to remain the only viable technical option until the eighteenth century. More relevant to this discussion was the indicator of how water was measured, which was a quantitative one.

The development of the steam engine was the catalyst for change, providing the technology that allowed water to be pumped from a source to a point of use. In this context, 'Nottingham was well ahead of its time in Victorian water technologies. By 1831, the Trent Waterworks Company's engineer, Thomas Hawksley, had designed the first constant high pressure supply, which prevented contamination from entering the mains' (Severn Trent Water, 2009), and from that point onwards the technology spread to become the dominant mechanism for delivering water to urban residents. Water delivery was still all about volume (quantity), and this remained the focus for water supply in the United States. In Britain, though, the focus changed almost overnight; and the reason for this change can be summarised in one word: cholera.

If there is a well-known name in British public health it is most likely to be Dr John Snow, who demonstrated, scientifically, the relationship between cholera and polluted water in 1854. Yet the subsequent approach to public health was shaped, to a large extent, by the lesser-known Edwin Chadwick. The evolution of urban infrastructure, on the other hand, was shaped by the interplay between the two, not in terms of their personal interaction but rather in terms of how different groups of professionals and politicians interpreted their findings within an urban development context.

The early water reticulation systems used water that was, visually at least, considered 'clean'. It came from country areas or from underground aquifers. And there was really no incentive to think differently. The publication of the findings of John Snow's linkage between polluted water and cholera changed all that. Not only was it a defining moment in the evolution of public health and epidemiology, but it also changed the nature of water-supply practice in Britain, through the introduction of water quality as a basis for water-supply practice.

Central to Snow's study was proof that cesspits situated too close to wells were leaking contamination and that this was polluting the water, with the bacterial pollutants being the direct cause of cholera. The outcome was an almost pathological obsession, if you will excuse the pun, with ensuring that water supply systems could not be contaminated. This obsession was hugely influential in shaping the thinking of water scientists and engineers, defining British water supply practice[3] for the next hundred years and embedding a way of thinking about urban water that dominates to the present time, to the extent that we are still unable to explore urban water systems in any other way than that defined by epidemiology, nor to conceive of integrating urban water supply directly with other aspects of urban water resources management. From that point on, the most important need in water supply became the need to preserve water quality; and to this end, the entire water supply system had to be separated from other infrastructure services and managed separately – not for commercial reasons, though there was a parallel public–private debate going on, but in order to ensure that water supplies would never again be contaminated.

In summary, then, if we look at the broader social context, and at the system of management that was to emerge, there is no doubt that the basis for the new framework for urban infrastructure, which was to last in Britain until 1974, was essentially a response to a perceived public health crisis in the overcrowded industrial cities. The process was initiated through a study of social conditions and health, which can be traced back to the Chadwick report mentioned earlier. The Royal Sanitary Commission was established in 1869, with a remit of investigating the manner in which laws relating to public health and sanitation were being implemented across the country. It reported its findings in 1871, which were considered by the government and resulted in further legislation being introduced relating to sanitation, sewage and housing (Stewart, 1871).

The findings were converted into legislation by the Public Health Act of 1872 and then further defined by public health and local government legislation over the next twenty-two years, culminating in the Local Government Act of 1894. Clearly, this Act was not intended to build an urban infrastructure base! That was an outcome, not an objective – another major distinction when compared to the United States, and one that was later to influence the external approach to infrastructure in post-independence Africa. Instead, the infrastructure management system emerged primarily because

> [t]he 1871 report of the Royal Sanitary Commission listed those requirements 'necessary for a civilised social life'; they were a 'wholesome water supply, proper drainage, the prevention and removal of nuisances, healthy houses in lit and well-ordered streets, inspection of food, proper provision for burial [and] suppression of the causes of disease'.
>
> (Cornwall Council, 2011)

As a result, 'Under the Public Health Act of 1872 the local health boards were incorporated into urban and rural sanitary authorities' (Archives Wales, 2009), following which the subsequent Public Health Act of 1875 gave local authorities responsibility for street lighting, water supply, sewage disposal, parks, toilets and housing (National Archives, 2011a). The 1875 Act also established aims and standards, and made compulsory the appointment of Medical Officers of Health.

These changes laid the framework. The Medical Officer of Health was charged with ensuring that sanitary conditions were improved, in essence a regulatory function. However, some entity had to take charge of providing the physical improvements that were necessary to produce the result. The Local Government Act of 1888 gave responsibility for the care and construction of roads to the reconstituted counties and county boroughs, while the second local government reform act of 1894 incorporated the urban and rural sanitary authorities into the newly constituted district councils.

At this point we need to move back in time once more, to see how roads were integrated into this local government process, since they were also included in the Local Government Act of 1888. Because England is a relatively small country, and towns were growing organically rather than being established on raw land, as they were in the United States, the primary focus was on national transportation, with a major emphasis on the development of the railways. Roads at that time were generally in a poor state of repair across the country as a whole. It was only in 1816, when John Macadam was made surveyor of the Bristol Turnpike Trust (Gregory, 1938, pp. 220–3), that road design changed, from the system developed by the

Romans over two millennia earlier, to the new, flexible pavement structure that bore the name of its inventor. This system would last until the development of the pneumatic tyre and the growth in motorised transport at the beginning of the twentieth century.

By that time the urban landscape of Britain was changing rapidly under the pressures of industrialisation and urban growth. In Britain the development of the road network lagged that of the United States, partly because the railway network was so much more extensive, relative to the geographical spread of the towns and cities, and partly because there was no national political or institutional framework capable of coordinating activities. This last point was critical, since the economic success of the railways was leading to the widespread collapse of toll roads. As a result, the late nineteenth century saw a transfer of responsibility to public authorities and away from the previous toll road management system that had evolved over the past 150 years. Yet because there was no centralised control, this took place in a piecemeal way. The result was a system of road management that was hugely fragmented, to the extent that at the beginning of the twentieth century there were no fewer than 1,900 local authorities concerned with highways, yet no single national policy for roads (Neath Port Talbot, 2009).

By the 1920s the situation had become untenable. The growth of private transport was starting to have a significant impact on urban structure, and intra-urban transport was becoming increasingly important. Traffic loads were increasing as well as traffic volumes, requiring improved engineering and more effective planning. Through the 1920s the government commissioned a series of reports on local government reform, covering the period 1925–9.[4] And though the Reform of Local Government Act of 1929 dealt with only some of the issues raised, it had a major impact on the organisation of urban infrastructure, one that was to last for sixty-five years.

The Act of 1929 strengthened the borough councils enormously. They retained control over the road network in their areas, whereas the responsibility of districts to manage roads was ceded to the counties. It also brought Poor Law infirmaries and fever hospitals under consolidated borough control, and fixed grants from central government to manage them. Overall, this Act confirmed the status of the major (county) boroughs as being on a par with that of the counties.

With regard to infrastructure, the earlier reports had identified that it was really only the county councils and the county boroughs that were involved heavily in physical infrastructure (the term at this point being used to describe primarily roads and drainage) (Onslow, 1925, pp. 81–8). Yet the growth of an engineering component to public health services was also recognised as increasingly important. And so the integration and rationalisation of all physical infrastructure services were finally addressed, in the final report on local government reform, and three broad technical functions of the large authorities were recognised: Roads and Bridges, Public Health, and Housing (National Archives, 2011b).

Water supply was not included in this reconsideration. The debate about whether water was a public or a private responsibility had continued, but eventually the public option was confirmed. At the same time, though, those joint-stock (i.e. private) water companies that had already been formed were granted a licence to continue. The financial arrangements for water supply management were codified by the second report on the reform of local government (Onslow, 1928). The major implication of this decision was the separation of the source of income (rates) from the sources of expenditure. Thus, the responsibility for water supply, while now also predominantly a local government responsibility, was separated from the other infrastructure services in its management and set up with its own, internal institutional framework.

The practical result of these local government reforms was to establish the concept that the management of local government should be based upon professional expertise, and three areas of core expertise were defined. The first was that of administration and social services (the Town Clerk), in which capacity this person was also the legal representative of the borough. The second was that of municipal finance (the Town/Borough/City Treasurer), responsible for all financial matters pertaining to council actions. And this left the third.

Here it was decided to group all urban matters of a technical nature under one 'head', who would be a civil engineer, although of a specific nature, termed a municipal engineer. It was not obvious at the time when the Royal Sanitary Commission report was published in 1871 that civil engineers would be the ones managing this urban development process. What happened was that the nature of the solutions which were proposed by the Local Government Act was closely interlinked with physical improvement; and so it was logical that these improvements should be driven by the profession most concerned with this activity. On the other hand, the field of civil engineering was more closely aligned to the design and construction phase of the project cycle,[5] whereas what was required here was a much greater involvement in both the 'front end' of the cycle (conceptualisation and planning of services) and the 'back end' (ongoing management).

As a result, there was a need for a specialised field of civil engineering to manage this urban activity. To this end, 'the Association of Municipal Engineers (subsequently named the Institution of Municipal Engineers), was established in 1874 under the encouragement of the Institution of Civil Engineers, [primarily] to address the issue of the application of sanitary science' (ICE, undated). Accepting this outcome, the boroughs then created a municipal engineering department. This was led by the Borough

Engineer, who then became responsible, over time, for all aspects of physical infrastructure and spatial organisation. These three leaders (the Town
Clerk, Treasurer and Engineer) were then joined by the Medical Officer
of Health. Although an extremely powerful and important position in the
borough hierarchy, the latter was not considered a line management function in the same way as the other three. And so what could be termed the
'3 + 1 model' was created, which would provide an urban governance structure not only for Britain but also for its colonies.

Infrastructure management in England, 1929–1974

It is difficult to imagine, looking back from the twenty-first century, the
full extent of the powers and responsibilities of the Borough Engineers in
Britain during the period from 1929 to 1974. Seeley, writing in 1967 at
what was probably the high point of municipal engineering,[6] was able to
list, quite definitively, the responsibilities of the 'Municipal Engineer',
broken down under thirteen different headings and comprising every
technical function imaginable. To give a sense of just how extensive these
responsibilities were, the list that follows provides the categories of management responsibility.[7] Thus, the Town or City Engineer in a county
borough was at that time responsible for the following:

1 Surveying, Setting Out and Site Investigation
2 Highway Engineering
3 Building and Civil Engineering Construction
4 Sewerage
5 Sewage Disposal
6 Public Cleansing
7 Water Supply
8 Traffic Engineering
9 Town and Country Planning
10 Housing Development
11 Other Physical Services
12 Contract Organisation
13 Administration.

This list covered by far the largest portion of a borough's capital expenditure and operating budget, and gave the Engineer immense influence,
enhanced because of the unique features associated with this British
model of local government. This was a model based on a committee structure for municipal government, which differed quite fundamentally from
most European systems, for example,[8] the majority of which had executive
political leadership. The committee structure allows ordinary (i.e. non-
specialist) members of the community to control the local authority.

However, in order for it to function effectively, specialist expertise is required. The outcome was the establishment of what can best be described as a 'municipal civil service', with three clearly defined career paths, of which municipal engineering was one (the others being legal and administrative, and finance).

If we look back at the growth of municipal engineering in Britain, it could be argued, justifiably, that its evolution was an accident of history – that there was no inherent reason for an integrated technical function that covered all infrastructure services. It came about because Britain at that time was driven, developmentally, by an engineering paradigm. At the same time, while it may have originated in this way, its ability to create an economically dynamic and socially viable urban structure was demonstrated by its success. The infrastructure management system set up in the 1920s delivered a full range of services equitably and, on the whole, efficiently to every home in England. By 1974, however, the original objectives had been achieved, and the country had attained a quite remarkable level of user convenience for the vast majority of its citizens. It was at that point that, with just the stroke of a pen, this system, which had built the urban framework of the country, was suddenly, and almost completely, dismantled.

The 1974 local government reform and its impact on urban infrastructure management

It can be argued that the reform of British local government that took place in 1974 was the first truly radical overhaul of local government in England since the granting of urban privileges, and the first formation of the boroughs, in the eighth century.

> The aim of the act was to establish a uniform two tier system across the country. Onto the blank canvas, new counties were created to cover the entire country; many of these were obviously based on the historic counties, but there were some major changes, especially in the north.... The act also created six new 'metropolitan' counties, modelled on Greater London, to specifically address the problems of administering large conurbations...
>
> Each of the new counties was then endowed with a county council, to generally administer the county, and provide certain county-wide services, such as policing, social services and public transport. The Act substituted the new counties 'for counties of any other description' for purposes of law. The new counties therefore replaced the statutory counties created in 1888 for judicial and ceremonial purposes...
>
> The second tier of the local government varied between the metropolitan and non-metropolitan counties. The metropolitan counties

were divided into metropolitan boroughs, whilst the non-metropolitan counties were divided into districts. The metropolitan boroughs had greater powers than the districts, sharing some of the county council responsibilities with the metropolitan county councils, and having control of others that districts did not.

(Wikipedia, 2009a)

To understand the English approach to local government at this point, it is important to recognise the extent to which the system is constructed around social infrastructure (including health in this general classification). The importance of the Poor Laws has already been discussed. In addition, prior to the Royal Commission of 1925–9 the majority of the functions of local government in Britain had related to social infrastructure such as education, watch committees, smallholdings, care of the mentally defective, and so on. The great reform of public health, beginning in 1872, started the process of integrating health into this wider social sphere. And much of the urban infrastructure that subsequently developed simply provided a mechanism for the systematic improvement of social conditions and public health.

When this situation was reviewed in the Royal Commissions of the 1920s, a new urban infrastructure management system was set out, which was subsequently adopted by the boroughs. But this was never codified in English law, unlike, for example, the incorporation of poor infirmaries in the health sphere. Thus, the entire municipal engineering function was established solely within the framework of incorporated local government, operating under delegated powers. Powerful as it was in practice, it was never legally recognised as part of the framework of government, where the 'doctrine of *ultra vires*' is the legal basis for local powers and duties (Bennett, 2000, p. 68). Thus, it was a simple matter, in legal terms, to unbundle the system; the question is, why was it unbundled? And here there are a number of contributory factors.

To a large extent, municipal engineering was a victim of its own success. On the one hand it had, within a relatively short space of time, transformed cities into healthy and generally well-functioning urban areas. In doing so, however, it had become quite rigid in its interpretation of infrastructure needs, failing to see the extent to which the role of infrastructure was changing in the society and failing to adapt to a rapidly changing urban environment. There was a need for a new urban vision to replace the old one; and that vision was not to be found in municipal engineering. This was particularly the case in urban road design. The rapid increase in vehicles and urban congestion required new approaches to transport planning, approaches that were not easily accommodated by the existing technocratic system.

Concurrently, town planning, which had been something of a poor relation previously, was gaining increasing recognition as an urban profession in its own right, and was seen to be better able to address the needs of modern cities once the major infrastructure had been installed. Housing too had become increasingly independent of municipal engineering and shared a greater commonality with town planning as the latter gained power and influence. And in the end, municipal engineers were seen as, well, engineers! In this context, urban infrastructure as a whole was seen, quite rightly, as an engineering function. Now engineers had served their purpose and new interpretations of these services were required. The outcome was that municipal engineering entered a period of rapid decline. The training of municipal engineers was halted in 1971, while the professional body to which engineers working in local government belonged, the Institution of Municipal Engineers, ceased to be an independent body in 1984 when it merged with the larger, and more powerful, Institution of Civil Engineers. In this way, whatever social aspects of engineering may have remained from that earlier period had slowly been subsumed by new technocratic goals.

The second contributory factor was political. Physical infrastructure and housing provided cities with a power base. And too many of these cities were under the control of the Labour Party, with many of them, particularly in the north of England, grounded in what could best be described as a system of municipal socialism. The 1974 reform of local government (implemented by a Conservative government) was an exercise in centralising the power of national government and removing the competitive power base situated within local government, a move that was to be taken even further in the mid 1980s under Margaret Thatcher. In taking away the historical powers, duties and functions of the powerful boroughs, central government was able to create a new structure of local government that enabled it to reallocate powers, duties and functions, and transfer power back to the centre. So while the generic names – counties, boroughs, districts – remained the same after the reform, the nature of the political relationship had changed completely.

The third, and to some extent most important, contributory factor can only be seen from within a specifically English lens. Almost every internal development in England during the eighteenth and nineteenth centuries can be traced back to an attempt by central government to tread the difficult path between revolution and reform. Governments were (speaking now of internal affairs) essentially responsive to social pressures, but committed primarily to 'orderly change', which in essence meant incremental change. This approach was captured brilliantly by Henry Kissinger in his book on Castlereagh and Metternich, respectively the British and Austrian Foreign Ministers at the end of the Napoleonic Wars, when he highlighted how '[t]o the British conservative, the [English] social problem was one of adjustment: to protect the social sphere by timely political concession' (1957, p. 195).

In the cities this approach translated into a social policy that was always linked, in some way, to the Poor Laws. And again the changes tended to be reactive, as was evidenced by the way in which both water supply and of sanitation evolved. And where additional duties and functions were added, they were added as much to prevent them from being taken over by central government as because the cities (initially at least) believed them necessary.

In this way, infrastructure grew incrementally, and was always perceived primarily in this social context. As a result, and influenced by the quite specific relationship between the central government and the boroughs (i.e. the feudal model of delegation), there was always an implicit interpretation that services delivered to residents were equally the responsibility of central government, though they were performed by local government. As such, they could be given to whoever might perform them most effectively, or most efficiently. This is the British interpretation of *ultra vires*, and is crucial to an understanding of everything that comes later.

In pursuance of this objective, and the need to bring power back to the centre, the government in Britain took direct control over many of the local government functions, keeping some, allocating others to the private sector, giving yet others to a non-democratic proxy management structure called a quango (an acronym for 'quasi-non-government organisation). In the twenty years following 1974, local government in England became an implementing agent of central government, and England was transformed from a country that had, on paper at least, the strongest and most powerful local government in the world, to the most centralised country in Western Europe.[9]

The practical outcome of this combination of circumstances and events was that the entire function of municipal engineering disappeared virtually overnight, dispersed among different sectors. Of the wide range of infrastructure services that had existed previously under borough control, only solid waste management remained, and that was limited to removal only in all but the largest authorities. Urban local authorities retained some functions associated with roads and storm-water drainage, but these were significantly reduced. In this way Britain became the first, and the only, state to remove so much urban infrastructure from the control of local government, almost returning it to its pre-1871 condition where its primary focus was on the core social services of health, education and social support. Even the role of planning was curtailed, to be reconstituted in the 2000s as a strongly deterministic function whose primary role was to support local economic development (i.e. the private sector).

The change from local government ownership to utilities management, 1974–1990

The next major change that impacted on urban infrastructure in Britain took place in the 1980s with the change to private-sector management of those infrastructure services known as utilities. The 1980s is viewed, in Anglo-Saxon countries at least, as defining a major shift in thinking about the role of the state in service delivery across all sectors of the economy. Led by Ronald Reagan, President of the United States, and Margaret Thatcher, Prime Minister of the United Kingdom, the two countries initiated a massive transfer of ownership from the public to the private sector, in a move described as privatisation.

Infrastructure, both national and local, was strongly affected by this change, with an impact on energy, transportation, water supply, sewerage and telecommunications. However, it was only the United Kingdom that viewed infrastructure management solely in terms of a public–private, all or nothing, duality. Elsewhere there was a wider debate on private-sector involvement in infrastructure that explored a range of options, situated along a continuum that reflected a range of relational interactions. In this wider debate, Britain was alone among all the western countries in choosing to place its infrastructure management on one extreme on this continuum, where the private sector had total control over both assets and resources. This arrangement has had a huge impact on western thinking about infrastructure management in Africa, which is discussed in the next chapter. The question to ask is why Britain chose this route.

In looking back at the history of Britain's transformation, considering here specifically the water supply and sanitation sectors, it is often overlooked that there were actually two phases of transition, and that the objectives behind the two changes were quite different. The first change took place as part of the wider reform of local government in 1974, and created ten regional water authorities for England and Wales, retained in public ownership. This was not without its own rationality. England, taken as a geographical entity, is a densely populated country[10] and the distance between urban centres is relatively small. Hence, the concept of regional services, in health-service delivery for example, is economically attractive. The Labour (centre-left) government, which initiated the Commission on Local Government in 1970, had intended to create larger unitary local authorities, which had an inherent logic from the perspective of regional development but was unpopular with the majority of the population, since this system was perceived as divorcing people from their historical roots. At the same time, though, it would have retained a direct linkage between infrastructure and local government. But there was an election before the reforms were implemented, and the Conservative (centre-right) Party gained power.

The Conservatives' agenda was different and they wished to retain a mixed two-tier system of county, metropolitan and local government. However, they accepted one of the principles of the earlier Commission report, which was that water and sewerage services should be regionalised. This argument had a logical basis. By dividing England into nine geographical areas (with a tenth for Wales), the country would be able to take advantage of the economies of scale that regionalisation could bring to make the management system more effective and efficient. At the same time, we can also see the thinking that underpins both major political parties in Britain: that the power to decide, to allocate and to redistribute should always rest with central government.

Even at that stage the regional concept had a number of serious flaws, the most critical of which was the way in which the creation of water authorities separated functional responsibility for sewerage from that of drainage. The distinction between water supply and water resources management is particularly strong in Britain, primarily for ideological reasons. As was mentioned previously, these date back to the cholera epidemic of the 1850s and John Snow's research, the response to which was to ensure water quality was safeguarded in the future by creating a rigorously protected, self-contained system for delivering water.

Clearly, it is essential in any water supply network to ensure that water quality standards are maintained, for health reasons; however, technology has evolved over the past 160 years, and there are now many different ways of achieving this goal. The British view of the time was that water quality could only be guaranteed by literally ring-fencing water supply, using this term in a technical rather than an economic sense, and this became the basis for all future thinking. What this regionalisation policy failed to do was to create any form of interactive overlay between the water supply, sewerage, urban drainage and natural drainage systems within the urban areas, a weakness that resulted in the loss of effective urban drainage management capacity in Britain, as described in the later Pitt Review that was set up to respond to the major flooding that took place in Britain in 2007 (Pitt, 2008).

The election of Margaret Thatcher as the British Prime Minister in 1979 brought to power someone whose 'political philosophy and economic policies emphasised deregulation, particularly of the financial sector, flexible labour markets, and the selling off of state owned companies' (Wikipedia, 2009b). By their actions in ring-fencing water supply so strongly, and refusing to accept the wider linkage between water supply and water resources, particularly urban drainage, the managers of the water authorities effectively sealed their own fate. The water authorities were sold, in their entirety, to private-sector companies (in 1989).

Britain is unusual, if not unique, in its water resources. Viewed historically, with year-round rainfall and a temperate climate, it had never really suffered major drought or extensive disruption to its water supply in the way that many other countries have (though this is changing now, with climate change and a growing population density). Neither did it have a national government minister for water. Water quality may have been a major issue, as indicated, but water quantity was never too great a concern, having been addressed effectively in the nineteenth century, when the great industrial cities were able to draw water from the high-rainfall rural catchments of Wales (for Birmingham) and the Lake District (for Manchester), and from an underground aquifer for Greater London.

It is perhaps understandable, then, that when it decided to privatise the country's regional water authorities, national government considered water as a commodity as much as, if not more than, it considered it a resource. There were of course important resource-related factors to take into account: water quality standards needed to be maintained and health protected; river pollution should be controlled; treatment of customers should be equitable; and the cost to customers 'reasonable'. Provided these safeguards could be put in place, so the thinking went, then the service could be better managed by the private sector, whose strength lies in providing a commodity to a consumer more efficiently than the public sector. And since all the concerns could be addressed by regulation, the industry was duly privatised, and a new form of regulatory system set up to act as a government 'watchdog'.

This is actually a seriously flawed model of water management (Hall and Lobena, 2007), as the discussion about South Africa in Chapter 5 will demonstrate. It is only the very specific combination of geography, typology, demography and rainfall pattern in the United Kingdom that makes it viable at all. This explains why no other country in the world has followed this particular model of privatisation. If we were to consider replicability as the sole indicator of success, the British model would be the most unsuccessful model of water supply management in the world. Of course, there are other indicators, but the point is nonetheless valid. That the model works for Britain is due solely to the country's unique geopolitical history and its unique geographical circumstances; the possibility that it would work anywhere else is extremely remote. Yet this seriously flawed model continues to exert a major influence on external thinking about water management in Africa.

Urban infrastructure development in the United States

The distinguishing features of urban infrastructure in America

Cities develop because technology, in coordination with other social, cultural, political, and economic factors, makes possible the production of surpluses.... Over time, city growth and the evolution of

> urbanized areas were closely related to a process of technological
> innovation that produced strong multiplier effects throughout the
> society.... [and] [c]apital infrastructure played a vital role in these
> major societal changes.
>
> (Joel Tarr, 1984, p. 5)

In just a few lines this quotation shows the full extent to which the United
States saw the role of urban infrastructure in a completely different way as
compared with Britain. Not only is the view of the role of technology different, so too is the wider social and economic context. In terms of finance
and affordability also, the infrastructure base was seen to represent a significant beneficial asset for the city. Thus, when we look at the way in which
infrastructure was perceived in the United States we see the emergence of
a clear trinitarian[11] construct as described at the beginning of the chapter,
which comprised a framework of economic and social values; a technology
that was highly regarded; and a management system that coordinated
these other two features operationally.

This broader perspective was only partially evident in the British case,
because social improvement was grounded in an existing framework (the
Poor Laws), while the powerful role of local government was enabled by
the absence of line ministries at central level. It is much more evident in
the United States, where systems and structures were evolving within a
wider context of an emerging economy and new urban settlements. All of
this is encapsulated by the Tarr quotation, enabling us to see, at least in
outline, the emergence of all three attributes in a way that reflects a society
emerging into a new land of space and opportunities.

If we take the three components of the infrastructure construct in turn,
the first and most important is the value system. Here we can see what is
effectively a symbiotic relationship between infrastructure and economic
development, demonstrating the extent to which infrastructure is embedded in the American vision of development itself; and it would be this economic relationship that provided the thread of continuity in the evolution
of infrastructure over time. As a result, urban infrastructure, like its
national counterpart, was perceived to be an important driver of local economic development. This is in contrast to Britain where that role was
reserved solely for national infrastructure. The primary role of urban
infrastructure in Britain was linked to a social process, supporting urban
improvement. There was also a social role for infrastructure in the United
States, which again had its origins in the perceived need for social
improvement; yet it also had significant differences, being seen much
more as a social driver in a wider process that has been termed 'moral
environmentalism'.[12]

The second important feature of infrastructure in the United States was
technology; for not only was there an overtly recognised technological

base, but the way in which technology was embraced demonstrated the extent to which it was valued as a critical component of economic development. As a result, urban development in the United States was grounded in technology; and this in turn provided the framework for the American understanding of public works,[13] which are defined as '[t]he physical structures and facilities that are developed or acquired by public agencies to house governmental functions and provide water, power, waste disposal, transportation, and similar services to facilitate the achievement of common social and economic objectives' (City of Redding, 1997).

This definition, created by the American Public Works Association,[14] was accompanied by an extensive and detailed list of environmental and technical functions, together with a list of responsibilities and competencies required for those who sought to specialise in this field.[15] It is interesting, and perhaps ironic, that this definitive interpretation of public works was published in 1974, the year when Britain dismantled its integrated urban infrastructure management system.

The third aspect of the construct that defined urban infrastructure in the United States revolved around the management system. The management of urban infrastructure has always been something of a paradox in the United States. On the one hand there was a strong interrelationship that would emerge between infrastructure and local government; that is, urban infrastructure was closely aligned with the specific municipal areas in an overt relationship, albeit one encouraged by a federal system of government. This did not imply that the local authority had to be the managing authority for the infrastructure, though many local authorities were. On the contrary – and this was the other side of the paradox – there was a never-ending debate about the role of the private sector in the management process. Generally, though, urban infrastructure was recognised to have a clear spatial and political linkage with the town it served. Again this is in contrast to the situation in England, where the spatial linkage was more an accident of history, part of the struggle local government was having with central government to retain its autonomy.

The evolution of local government

Municipal government[16] in the United States is a broad and complex topic in its own right, and one not readily suited to summary analysis. It is also confusing, since the term 'local government' applies to all units of government below the state level (*Gale Encyclopedia of US History*, 2008) – and there are over 85,000 of these across the country, from counties and school districts to municipalities and special districts (*Encyclopedia of the Nations*, 2007). To avoid confusion, this discussion will use the terms 'municipality' or 'municipal government' to describe that unit of local government responsible for the management of urban areas, recognising that this is a wide ambit covering cities, towns, boroughs and villages, and that there are variants in the way each of these is governed, not to mention interpretative variations across different states. That caveat having been provided, it is possible to draw out the key elements relating to the way in which urban infrastructure (termed public works) is managed in that country through the use of these terms 'municipality' and 'municipal government'.

Sarah Elkind (1999) has identified two distinct historical roots that shaped the urban system prior to the War of Independence (the American Revolutionary War, 1775–1783). In the original thirteen states of the East Coast, which were under British rule, the system followed closely that of England at the time; though even within these states there were significant local differences. In New England, for example, 'the town was the principal unit of local rule, responsible for poor relief, schooling, and roads' (*Gale Encyclopedia of US History*, 2008). In contrast, in the southern states, which were influenced by French rule, 'county courts were the chief elements of local government. Appointed by the royal governor, the members of the county court exercised both administrative and judicial powers, supervising road construction as well as presiding over trials' (ibid.).

As the population grew and the towns developed, the British system of 'municipal incorporation' was introduced, whereby citizens of a town could apply to the Crown representative for the rights of incorporation. This system of incorporation was retained after the revolution, but with important changes that laid the foundation for the municipal system in use today. These changes were as follows:

- The system of incorporation was codified, and changed from individual application to a generic statute, with the powers and duties defined by the individual states.
- The system was democratised, with citizens voting in the management body, together with which the system of government changed from one of committee (the English system) to one of an elected executive authority.
- Concerns about corruption and vested interests led to calls for a municipal civil service, i.e. a politically independent authority. The form this took varied, but in the twentieth century the concept of a City Manager came to dominate, so that by the end of that century the system was used by over 50 per cent of municipal governments.
- The responsibility for managing schools was taken away from local government and given to separate 'school boards'.

This last change is particularly relevant, given that health care in the United States is also predominantly a private function, because it means that responsibility for two of the key components of local government in

Britain, health and education, lay outside the jurisdiction of municipal government in the United States. However, rather than weakening local government by removing two major management and cost centres, municipal government in the United States was in many ways strengthened, and remained extremely powerful. The reason for this stemmed from, and could be directly attributable to, local control over public works spending, which gave municipal government control over a major source of inward investment and capital flows.

The evolution of urban infrastructure over time

When one is seeking to identify phases in the development of urban infrastructure in the United States, there are different approaches and a distinct categorisation stemming mainly from whether the focus of historical exploration is primarily economic or social. The first would tend to prioritise transportation, which is easier to relate directly to economic development, while the latter would tend to have a focus on health-related infrastructure. Table 3.1 provides three interpretations of changes over time, defined by American historians who have written about urban infrastructure.

The major transition corresponds to the period of the American Civil War (1861–5) and represents a shift from experimentation to large-scale delivery. In the early, pre-war period, experimentation covered every aspect of development, from exploring the role and nature of local government, through financing mechanisms and operational structures, to evaluating which technology to adopt. This era is then divided into two parts, which reflects an emerging consensus, particularly in the cities of the East Coast, that there was a linkage between poverty, sanitary conditions, crime and disease – the basis of moral environmentalism. The post-war period was the age of implementation, and again there is a subdivision. Here we see public health infrastructure dominating to a large extent (water supply, drainage, sewerage), whereas the later period reflects the massive adaptation that had to be made by municipal government to accommodate the automobile, as well as the need to revisit major concepts such as public works and municipal financing in the post-war period and during the Great Depression. In each phase there was an impact on the value system, the technology and the management system, as will be described below.

The period of foundation, 1790 to c.1860–80

There were three important characteristics of this early period that were to play an influential role in shaping both urban infrastructure and local government in the United States.

Table 3.1 The major influences on the development of urban infrastructure over time

Tarr (1984, pp. 5–6)	Adapted from Melosi (2008)[a]		Adapted from Elkind (1999)[b] (specific to Boston)
1790–1860 Urban networks and walking cities: a period of foundation	**Colonial Times–1880** The age of miasmas	**Pre-1830** Pre-Chadwickian America	**Pre 1923** Private sanitation prior to municipal incorporation
		1830–1880 From protosystems to modern waterworks; subterranean networks	**1823–1880** The age of moral environmentalism
1855–1910 Constructing the core infrastructure in the central cities	**1880–1945** The bacterial revolution	**1880–1920** On the cusp of the new public health; water supply as a municipal enterprise	**1880–1920** Public works and public health
1910–1956 Domination of the automobile and the enlargement of the federal role		**1920–1945** The Great Depression, World War II and public works; water supply as a national issue	

Notes
a This list has been extracted from the list of section and chapter headings.
b Dates have been extracted from different parts of the paper.

1   the ability of local authorities to raise capital on their own behalf, which provided the financial base from which they could grow;
2   the emerging developmental role of municipal government in a federal system;
3   the emerging role of technology as a development driver for both economic and social development.

While the first of these was quite explicit, and derived from the mandates provided to the cities by the state governments through their city charters, the remaining two were outcomes of an exploratory process that took place over an extended period. Yet it was the interaction of the three together – financing, political and institutional formation, and technology – that wove the urban construct of nineteenth-century America.

If this interplay can be said to represent the internal dynamic of cities, there were also three externalities that influenced it, all of which further differentiated the United States from Britain. The first was the urbanisation process itself, where new towns and cities were being built. The 1790 census showed an urban population comprising just 4 per cent of the country's total, with just 24 'urban places', the largest of which had a population of 42,500 (Melosi, 2008, p. 11). By 1820 the ratio had increased to close to 30 per cent, but overall numbers were still low. However, there was a significant difference between the East Coast towns, which were reaching critical densities, and those opening up in the Midwest, where densities remained low. This in turn was to lead to different perceptions later of the role of the private sector and its relationship with local government.

The second, whose impact was greatest in the eastern cities, was the spread of disease, with the high densities of the urban areas turning these outbreaks into major epidemics. Interestingly, and in contrast to Britain, the major health concern in the early period of settlement formation was not cholera, though that was to become a serious problem later, but yellow fever. As a result, disease was perceived as a miasma.[17]

This concept of a miasma is defined here as an 'externality' because it transformed the notion of disease from being something that affected individuals to something that affected the society as a whole. This was a major shift for a country whose constitution was built around the centrality of the individual, and it provided the rationality for a move towards technologies that served the collective rather than relying on technologies (such as wells and cesspits) which served individual families. The outcome was that 'American cities underwent their first major sanitary awakening between 1830 and 1880, a change so profound as to establish a blueprint for environmental services for years to come' (Melosi, 2008, p. 40).

This outcome in turn helped to define the third externality: the concept of moral environmentalism, which was concerned specifically with the linkage between crime, poverty and disease, and which created a new moral imperative that Sarah Elkind describes in the following way:

> At the beginning of this period of municipal activism, many scientists, reformers and members of the general public believed that physical conditions in the city caused epidemic disease and contributed to immoral and criminal behavior. These beliefs, termed 'moral environmentalism,' attracted popular support for extensive public works and encouraged city residents to expect their public works investments to transform urban society. The connections between sanitation, disease and crime made urban services a public responsibility.
>
> (1999, p. 7)

These were all major forces driving change; yet change itself was slow to arrive. There were a number of reasons, but the root cause was the inability to clarify the extent of municipal involvement; that is, where does municipal responsibility begin and end when addressing community needs (Melosi, 2008, p. 13)?

The conceptual shift that municipalities and their residents had to make over this period was huge. In the early formative period it was recognised and accepted that 'the city was to be an environment for private money-making and its government was to encourage private business' (Warner, 1987, p. 99, quoted in Melosi, 2008, p. 13), where the

> first priority was given to the provision of improved services to the central business districts. This reflected the concern of the downtown business interests with enhancing property values and remaining competitive with other towns as well as the technological requirements of the new office structures.
>
> (Tarr, 1984, p. 24)

As the number of services grew, cities grappled with a range of 'halfway options' that could match the management system to emerging technologies, while staying true to their original brief, an approach that was patently unsuccessful, as Elkind (1999) illustrates when she describes how

> Boston built drains to take the storm water flow and these were seen as a potential solution to the transporting of excess human waste. In line with the early role of local government to support the private sector (including residential groupings) Boston permitted suburbs to construct their own sewers. However these were often blocked and it soon became clear that the City Council had seriously miscalculated in its waste disposal policy.... Furthermore this policy did nothing to address the public health needs in the poorer areas, and a study in 1848 showed little sanitary improvement in these areas.

Given this situation, it was clear that meaningful change would require a major political shift, and this could only come about through the removal of the linkage between the vote and income, which would allow the poor a greater degree of influence over the decision-making process.

The second constraint was that of resources. The construction of infrastructure on the scale necessary to address the growing challenges required new forms of financing, a problem that was only partially addressed by the creation of a municipal bond market, but this in turn highlighted the full extent of the skills shortage. The technology, and the expertise that drove it, came primarily from Europe in these early stages of development, but the rate of diffusion was relatively slow, since 'the basic agents of technology transfer ... were individuals' (Tarr, 1984, p. 19), and these experts were in short supply, one estimate giving the number of people who were active as 'something like engineers' being limited to just thirty individuals in 1816 (ibid., p. 18).

The third constraint revolved around how far upstream municipal responsibility should extend. Philadelphia had constructed the country's first major waterworks in 1796, and opened up new ways of thinking about technology, thereby spearheading a growing awareness of the potential for technology to do so much more to benefit the city. Yet many cities had been overstretched financially by their early involvement in national infrastructure financing and were reluctant to repeat the mistake. To take just one example, 'Boston's public debate over the building of a municipal waterworks lasted from 1823 to 1846' (Elkind, 1999, p. 5); and Elkind suggests that '[f]or most of those years, public water proposals and concerns about expanding municipal authority dominated Boston's politics' (ibid., p. 5).

This example goes directly to the core issue, as valid in Africa today as it was in the United States almost two hundred years ago: who should be responsible for urban infrastructure, why, and to what degree? And for those who criticise African governments for a slow response to the need for infrastructure delivery, it is perhaps useful, from a contextual perspective, to note that Boston took twenty-three years to build its first waterworks. Similarly, but on a larger scale, the wider debate in the United States about the nature and the role of infrastructure in urban society lasted for forty years – and even then, although a degree of consensus had been reached, the debate never disappeared completely, but continued to rumble on, in a low-key way, through to the present time.

Constructing the core infrastructure and the move to public works, c.1860–80 through to c.1910–20

By 1865, the year marking the end of the Civil War, the basic systems of urban government were in place and there was broad agreement on what should be done. This was none too soon, given that the country was about to enter a period of rapid, exponential urban growth which would see the urban population rise from approximately 6 million in 1860 to 42 million fifty years later; by which time it would comprise 46 per cent of the total population of the country (Tarr, 1984, p. 21). In looking at what made this possible, there are four major elements that can be shown to underpin the success of the coming years. These were:

1   the concept of public works;
2   the effective use of technology;

3   the creation of effective management systems;
4   practical and effective financing mechanisms.

Each of these aspects will be discussed briefly in what follows.

The big idea: public works

From their earliest days in post-independence America, the towns and cities that were emerging into a new land saw infrastructure as a driver of economic development, in the same way that state and federal governments saw the role of national infrastructure. Initially this was perceived as meaning roads, whereas other services were seen as an individual responsibility; over time, though, this perception changed, first with the growth of water distribution and then with the emerging public health crisis.

When America's first waterworks was constructed, in Philadelphia in 1796, it completely transformed the perceived role of water in urban society. Water provided through pipes into the house provided new levels of user convenience, while this extended availability enabled the large-scale expansion of industry. In 1830 there were 35 waterworks in America; by 1880 there were 599; and by 1924 the total had risen to 9,850 (Melosi, 2008, pp. 50, 82).

While roads and water were seen as important development drivers, the greatest change in the perception of the city, particularly on the East Coast, was linked to theories of disease. The concept of disease as caused by a miasma, and the linkages (in the period before the emergence of germ theory) between poverty, crime and disease, made every citizen, whether rich or poor, vulnerable to epidemics. In this way, moral environmentalism transformed thinking by fostering a holistic view of the city (Elkind, 1999, p. 2).

The concept of public works was also something that emerged over time. In this case it grew out of a 'pincer movement', which can be summarised by what happened in Boston. On the one side were user expectations, where '[n]ineteenth century Boston exemplifies the community in which voters expected a wide range of public services' (Elkind, 1999, p. 2). On the other side was political opportunity, in which

> [t]he connection between the environment, public health, and moral behavior gave Boston leaders broad authority over public works. The city claimed authority to build water and sewer systems, and to inspect housing, schools and taverns, based on officials' responsibilities to protect public health.
>
> (ibid., p. 2)

Slowly but surely, the different infrastructure services were coalescing and becoming ever more interactive. Roads increased urban run-off, which then required a drainage system to carry away the surplus storm water. These drains, though, carried not only storm water but also sewage, together with the excess water from homes (which was overloading and flooding cesspits), businesses and industry. The use of water supplies expanded to provide new services such as fire-fighting. Initially, certain services, particularly those linked to the management of waste, were linked to social goals through moral environmentalism. However, with the growing acceptance of germ theory this perceived social role began to diminish. By the time this shift in thinking took place, though, the sanitary waste management infrastructure was increasingly recognised as being an important contributor to economic growth and development: effective water and sanitary waste management had become a prerequisite for a modern city. Thus, public works as a whole became an integral part of the economic fabric of the city.

A belief in the transforming power of technology

This urban expansion was driven by technology, the nature of which was neatly captured by Sarah Elkind:

> America's cities saw an explosion of public works projects in the late nineteenth and early twentieth centuries. Major cities built sewer, water and park systems, constructed public hospitals, libraries and bathhouses, and reformed their prisons. They subsidized interurban and local rail systems, roads and bridges, and invested in municipal light and power grids. Even when they judged public construction inappropriate or unpopular, city leaders extended their authority. They did so in order to address the fundamental disjunction between the natural resources and political boundaries.
>
> (1999, p. 1)

Faced with the challenge of developing a huge country, Americans were quick to see the potential benefits of technology, but it took time to build the knowledge base that would match the potential. During the early part of the nineteenth century, while different concepts and management structures were being experimented with and developed, the number of engineers grew rapidly. From just thirty in 1816, by 1880 the number of schools (i.e. universities) had risen to sixty-five, graduating 3,800 civil engineers a year (Tarr, 1984, p. 32). At the same time, the technology itself was evolving. The period after the Civil War saw new, greatly improved pipe technologies introduced and new, more efficient steam engines, together with new indigenous bridge designs, to name just three out of what were a large number of technological innovations.

Finally, new concepts of infrastructure management were emerging, though generally driven by force of circumstance rather than choice.

One example was that of sewage disposal. The ongoing use of storm-water drains to carry sewage, following the British practice, was becoming increasingly problematic from both a financial and an environmental point of view. Yet it took a major public health crisis in Memphis, Tennessee, where one-sixth of the entire population of the town died in 1878 in a yellow fever epidemic, to force a change. A member of the inspection team sent by the National Board of Health to review the situation in Memphis, Colonel Waring, proposed that the town should install small-bore drainage pipes that would transport only domestic waste and exclude storm water (Melosi, 2008, pp. 99–101). Initially controversial, this concept slowly became conventional practice across the country.

The ongoing debate: who should manage public works?

Any belief that America, as the bastion of free-market capitalism, might have unilaterally supported the private provision of public services would be a myth. For over a hundred years the debate about the relative merits and disadvantages of public- versus private-sector ownership raged across the towns and cities, as well as across states; and the debate is ongoing.[18] As late as 2003 only 5 per cent of the water systems in the United States were privately owned, while approximately 15 per cent of the population was served by corporate water providers (Melosi, 2008, p. 227).

The reality is that both the public and the private sectors have always been, and remain, involved in the delivery and management of infrastructure in the United States. And while there may be political differences of opinion about the relative roles, and merits, of public or private ownership, almost everyone subscribed to the idea that the services in question are all part of the wider concept of 'public works'. This meant that even where the private sector provided 'public works' services, it had to be accountable, whether directly (by means of a legally binding contract or agreement) or indirectly (through some form of regulation), to users living in a specific geographical area. The fact is that the choice of whether infrastructure services are managed by the public sector or by the private sector was a local one, and would depend, to a large extent, upon the dominant cultural inclination of the resident population in that particular area.

Financing

American cities had three mechanisms for funding infrastructure: their own internal budget, private-sector investment or the creation of special utility districts able to raise their own finance. Often, all three of these could be found within a single region or group of cities. The extent of the finance required to fund the burgeoning infrastructure base was generally

beyond the capacity of normal recurrent income, which led to the creation of a municipal bond market that enabled cities to borrow against
future income. This in turn led to a build-up of municipal debt, resulting
in a wave of defaults during the 1870s, to be followed by the imposition of
state controls, before the market recovered and bond financing resumed
in the 1880s.

Corruption was a major issue associated with public spending during
this latter period, often linked either to Mafia control over the construction companies or to patronage politics, in which

> [q]uestions of patronage and spoils became interwoven with the
> process of infrastructure construction. Machine politicians often
> owned the construction companies that built the infrastructure and
> delivered municipal services. In addition, large numbers of the party
> faithful secured employment on the city payroll, helping to construct
> and maintain infrastructure projects.
>
> (Tarr, 1984, p. 27)

The second funding source was private-sector investment, and here the
input was less than might be expected, primarily because it was limited
almost entirely to water supply, as the only infrastructure service[19] where
the principle of direct cost recovery could be applied. For the period
through to 1880 the private sector provided between 40 per cent and 50
per cent of waterworks, but this number tends to overstate the impact. The
major cities of the East Coast (New York being an important exception)
generally preferred to manage their own systems, leaving the private sector
to concentrate on smaller areas where the level of investment was lower
and the political climate more favourable. It was also the case that in the
larger cities such as Baltimore, private-sector delivery was class-structured
(Tarr, 1984, p. 14), at least in the early phase of development, so that
while the business district and more affluent areas received piped water,
the poorer areas had to continue to rely on shallow wells.

After 1890 there was a clear shift from private to public ownership,
driven by a number of diverse factors. Public sentiment was turning
against the private sector as criticism mounted (Melosi, 2008, p. 84); there
was a growing sense of civic pride; and the increased cost and complexity
of the newly emerging centralised systems again began to favour municipal financing. As a result, by 1914 private ownership of waterworks had
fallen to approximately 30 per cent of the total (Tarr, 1984, p. 28).

The third mechanism for funding, used particularly for water and sewerage, was the special utility district. Depending on the state, municipal
governments could come together and create a combined utilities district;
or alternatively residents could vote to remove municipal control over
these services and establish a special district. Elkind provides an example

of the former in Oakland, California, where (in terms of state legislation) '[t]he new Municipal Utility District Act [of 1921] permitted cities in California to form regional utility districts with broad authority to issue bonds, take lands and build public works' (1999, p. 42), though these powers were not unlimited. This change led to a now well-accepted option in the management of large public works, particularly in the major urban centres, where metropolitan boards would manage the service across a wide geographical area. In the case of water management, the existence of a metropolitan board could also mean an integration of water supply and water resources management for the catchments affected.

So what can we learn from the early history of urban infrastructure?

The role of infrastructure

The previous chapter illustrated the extent to which urban development in Africa is trapped in a cul-de-sac, a development path that has reached an impasse. This was clearly illustrated by an international event at World Water Day 2011, held in Cape Town, South Africa, an event that took 'Water and Urbanization' as its theme. While recognising the need to 'throw out old models', delegates to the event felt that the solution lay in 'adopting a new, multi-disciplinary, collaborative approach ... [wherein] [t]echnological innovation and public–private partnerships can provide solutions to the challenges of water and sanitation in an environment of rapid urbanization' (IRIN, 2011). This 'UN-speak' sounds impressive, but below the surface there is nothing that is fundamentally different from the current approach; it is simply reshuffling the way in which things are done, like moving deckchairs around the *Titanic* while it sinks; there is the talk, but underneath it there is no significant change to any of the underlying concepts that underpin these 'old models'.

If we really want to change the approach, then we need to understand how the existing approach came into being in the first place; and providing such an understanding is the role of history. There is much in this comparative study of infrastructure development in the United States that explains how we arrived where we are and how we arrived at this point. We can also see the origins of the British *Weltanschauung* in particular, and, in doing so, come to recognise how little relevance it has for Africa in the twenty-first century.

The first, and perhaps most important, lesson is that of relating three of the four thematic forces of influence described in Chapter 1 back to decisions that were taken in Britain in the middle of the nineteenth century. When we look at the existing planning paradigm, for example, we can see the extent to which the social improvement model that provided the basis for the British urban infrastructure model was grounded in the concept of infrastructure as a support service for social development, thereby enabling it to transmute later into a perceived support service for urban planning. In the United States, matters were quite radically different. There, infrastructure was recognised as a critically important driver, primarily of economic development but also of social development.

The British social improvement model, with its roots in the Poor Laws, can also be seen to have laid the foundation for the third thematic force of influence: the basic needs approach, which differentiates the level of infrastructure services provided to the rich from that provided to the poor. In both Britain and the United States this was later transformed into a more equitable delivery model. While this shift was aided by the move towards network infrastructure, the primary driver of this shift was the opening up of the vote to the poor. The lesson of history is clear: when the poor have a choice, they vote for equity in service delivery. This makes a mockery of current interpretations of community participation, which prescribe a differentiated level of service based upon socio-economic levels and leave the participatory process to choices such as whether a poor family will have a rectangular or a circular wall for their pit latrine.

In looking at the second thematic force of influence, the private-sector management model for water supply, we can see that this is not actually the core issue, notwithstanding that it is an important debate. Underlying this is another, more fundamental issue – the real issue. This derives from the technical ring-fencing of urban water supply due to a specific British epidemiological concern about cross-contamination, which led to the creation of a sector-based industry and the separation of water supply from water resources.

All of these are specifically British concepts created at a specific point in time to address the needs of a specific society that had to address a specific set of issues grounded in a specific value system. Yet they continue to form the basis for almost all current thinking about the way that we deliver services to this day. The next chapter will show how this strangely anomalous situation came about – how these concepts, which should have remained within British shores, were transferred across to anglophone Africa (and other countries) under British colonial rule, where they were superimposed on the newly emerging towns and became entrenched.

The nature of infrastructure

The second lesson relates to the nature of infrastructure; that is, the understanding of what it is. Current definitions, discussed in the early part of the chapter, tend to list a range of services that together somehow constitute infrastructure. In fact, these definitions only make sense within the wider conceptual framework of public works, as the term is used and interpreted in the United States; outside of that context they simply constitute a list of individual services that can be broken up and managed separately, as happened in Britain after 1974. As a result, we are in a situation where, for the majority of countries, these definitions make little sense, since they are not contextualised by a value system in the way that the term 'public works' contextualises infrastructure in the United States.

So what is the real nature of infrastructure? Well, this question will only be answered definitively in the final chapter of the book. For now, though, and to guide the discussion as the book progresses, it may be useful to lay down some pointers. The first is that infrastructure, regardless of exactly how it is defined in practice, can only exist in the context of a group of people who interact with each other. So, a single family living alone in an isolated location and cut off from the rest of society does not have infrastructure. When people come together, the first thing they do is define a common value system that provides the social basis for their society. This means that infrastructure will always be linked to a *value system* of some description. The addition of the prefix 'urban' provides a specific geospatial context to this relationship, where people choose to come together and live as a mutually interdependent society in a certain location, which we describe most commonly as a town or a city.

The second point is that the type of infrastructure being discussed here is based upon *technology*, and cannot exist without it. Infrastructure therefore implies technology, but obviously not all technology is infrastructure. A mobile phone (cellphone) is a piece of technology, with many standalone features, but these features do not make it infrastructure. It becomes part of the wider infrastructure network only when it is connected in some way, either through electromagnetic waves or via a fixed line of communication.

The third point is that infrastructure cannot exist without some form of *management* system. A dam that sits on a river is not, of itself, infrastructure. Left to itself, it is no more than a piece of concrete or a mound of earth blocking the river. Again it only becomes part of the infrastructure if it is used for a purpose. So, not only does using it for a purpose mean connecting it to some form of technology system, as with the mobile phone, but it also means managing its operation so that it is able to interact with the other parts of the system.

And so we have come full circle and we are back at our starting point, with our three components – except that we have now added another pointer. Infrastructure cannot exist outside of a flow of financial resources, at least in the formal economy, which is the context for almost all urban dwellers. So, the infrastructure has to be paid for, and the money recovered in some way from those who make use of it.

At this point you might say: but we know that, so what's new? You might highlight, or even write a paper on, how many engineers in Africa situate their approach to water supply, or to sanitation, in a value-based context (Robbins, 2007). Or you might point to the fact that the basis for the private-sector management of water supplies is grounded in the need to link effective delivery and management to investment opportunities and cost recovery. Alternatively, you could perhaps show the linkage between the need to adopt a basic needs approach and affordability.

Fair enough; but if we actually look carefully at the two studies of the United Kingdom and the United States, we will see that they are quite distinct in the way they approach these relationships. The importance of the American analysis is the extent to which all of these different components are explicit and interactive in the evolutionary process. In contrast, the evolution of infrastructure in England was quite different and the three main components were actually addressed separately and independently. In situations where they did come together, we see that they did so more by accident than design.

It is suggested here that the American experience actually leads to a greater inherent rationality, though ironically it was less stable than the British system, specifically because it embraced all the components. So, to define an infrastructure model implies that all four components are embedded in our construct. Furthermore, there is an interrelationship between these four components which is symbiotic; in other words, if we remove just one of them, then infrastructure has somehow lost a critical part of itself and our infrastructure model collapses. The nature of that relationship is described graphically in Figure 3.1.[20]

There is just one weakness with this model, which does not quite fit the reality; and that relates to the system of management. If we look at the British system, this emerged from a power struggle between national and

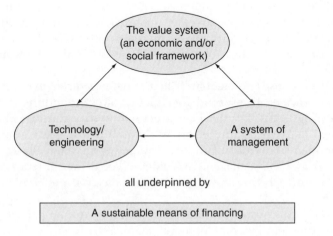

Figure 3.1 The three components of urban infrastructure.

local government. The system in the United States, on the other hand, was more complex, with different models in different places. Clearly, then, this component of 'management' is more complex than it might appear. We can see strong linkages to the political arena in both cases, but I will leave it to later chapters to draw out the nature of that linkage more fully. At this point we have a working model from which to move forward. And the key lesson to learn at this point is that we somehow require all four to be in place for urban infrastructure to be successful. If not – if we do not have that symbiotic interconnectivity – then the infrastructure model will not function effectively.

Two development rationalities behind urban infrastructure

The development of urban infrastructure in Britain and the United States during the nineteenth and early twentieth centuries followed different paths, which reflected different developmental rationalities. These became less obvious as networked urban infrastructure became the dominant infrastructure model for western cities in the mid twentieth century, so that we have lost sight of these differences now. During the twentieth century there was a convergence of urban infrastructure models in the West and that, coupled with the growing maturity of the infrastructure base, made these differences less relevant. Yet they are critically important for any analysis of how infrastructure evolves in the early stages of urbanisation, such as Africa is experiencing at the present time – because Africa will not be following this same trajectory in the evolution of its urban infrastructure. This is why the experiences of these two countries in that early period are so important.

These two developmental rationalities can be defined in terms of three distinct characteristics, specific perceptive constructs if you like, that together summarise the rationality and define the approach to the development of urban infrastructure over time. These two rationalities are shown in Table 3.2.

The first of these constructs emerges from the perceived role that infrastructure plays in society. The second construct revolves around the technology–engineering nexus. The third construct then revolves around what has been termed here 'the nature of infrastructure'; that is, the way that the three components of infrastructure – the value system, the technology (or engineering) and the management – interact, or do not interact, as the case may be. In each case the two countries perceived the construct quite differently.

Expanding on these constructs a little, the first relates to the perceived role of infrastructure in urban development: defining urban infrastructure either as a driver of development or as a support service for development.

Table 3.2 The two developmental rationalities underpinning urban infrastructure

The perceptive constructs behind infrastructure	United States	United Kingdom
Its primary role in society	As a driver of development	As a support service in a wider urban development model
The vehicle	Technology	Engineering
The nature or form	Interactive (trinitarian)	Disaggregated

In the American case it was very clearly a driver, primarily of economic development but also, albeit to a lesser degree, but nonetheless importantly, of social development. In Britain, urban infrastructure was seen as a support service, primarily for social improvement: improving the well-being of the working class, and then later in support of a system of land allocation and regularisation.

The second characteristic relates to technology. The United States had a tremendous belief in the power of technology to transform society, and this drove not only local development but also regional and federal development. The British, on the other hand, saw engineering as the transformative function. It is worth recalling the story of George and Robert Stephenson, the father-and-son team credited with building the first railway in Britain. Robert was the younger, educated one, who went on to become President of the British Institution of Civil Engineers. George was the artisan responsible for the technology: the engine itself. He was considered unsuited to membership of that same venerable institution and his application was rejected, though he went on to become a founder member of the Institution of Mechanical Engineers. Robert's main interest was in the wider engineering work; George's in the technology.

The third characteristic relates to the nature of urban infrastructure. This situates infrastructure within a framework of three core components: a value system, technology and a management system, all of which are underpinned by a comprehensive financing mechanism. In the United States these components were forever interacting and playing off each other, so that a relationship existed between them even if it was not always explicit. In Britain, on the other hand, the relationship between the components was more fragmented. There, it was more often the case, certainly in the early stages of urban development, that each of these components was being explored in isolation from the others.

This, then, is the main outcome of the comparative study of how infrastructure evolved in the United Kingdom and the United States. It is suggested here that the American developmental rationality actually provides an infrastructure model that is better suited to the African situation than the British one. Ultimately, the reason why that is the case is because the American experience is more representative of a new and expanding country.

Britain, on the other hand, provides an example of a country that is unique in its historical developmental context – a country with a developmental rationality that derives from a specific set of circumstances that came together at a particular point in time in a particular place. As such, it does not provide a replicable model. Yet circumstances dictated that this was the developmental rationality that was exported to Africa. It is the contention here that this cause of Africa's urban problems – everything that came later; all that we see now in the underdeveloped state of African towns and cities – can be traced back to that one outcome, that choice of fate. Is this a reasonable contention? The next chapter starts to develop the case by looking at how this British developmental rationality model was transferred across to Africa.

Chapter 4

Transferring the British infrastructure model to Africa

Introduction

This chapter describes how the British model of urban infrastructure mutated as it changed its social surround and moved to Africa. From a situation in the 1960s where infrastructure was the priority urban development focus in Africa, the perception slowly shifted over time to one where urban planning was now seen as the basis for urban development, with the role of infrastructure reduced to a supporting function and the services themselves broken up and scattered. Those not incorporated into the urban planning process, such as water supply, sanitation or solid waste management, were taken up by other groups: in the private sector, the environmental sector or the health sector; to name just three. Infrastructure as a component of urban development in its own right was fragmented and effectively excluded from the wider urban discourse, while knowledge of its developmental role in urban society was lost.

The objective in this chapter is to analyse how this major shift in focus occurred, illustrating how its origins can be traced back to responses and approaches that were formulated in Britain and America in the nineteenth century. Everything that happened subsequently, particularly in Africa, can then be recognised as a series of responses, each one part of an ongoing reactive process that is situated almost wholly within that early Anglo-Saxon *Weltanschauung*.

Without question, urban infrastructure played a critical economic and social role in the development of European and American cities in the nineteenth and twentieth centuries, which is why it had such a major impact. It also provides a logical starting point for this wider analysis. Chapter 3 explored the role played by, and the perception of, urban infrastructure in that early development process. This chapter will take that exploration forward by looking first of all at how this perception was transferred to the colonies under British imperial rule and then at how it evolved subsequently in the post-colonial era. By tracking the history of infrastructure in this way we can see exactly how the four external drivers of influence, described in Chapter 1, emerged. We can also see the full extent to which urban infrastructure remains critical to successful urban development. In turn, we can then see just how much the current urban crisis in sub-Saharan Africa is due to a fundamental lack of understanding of the role and nature of urban infrastructure on the part of the external agencies that control the wider development discourse. As a result, the western urban strategy in Africa remains embedded in the past, totally unable to provide the solutions needed for the delivery and management of urban infrastructure in the emerging urban societies of the twenty-first century.

So where did we go wrong? When we consider the immediate post-colonial period, there is no doubt that the approach to infrastructure at that time was totally inappropriate to the need. In transferring from its origins in Britain to a colonial setting, urban infrastructure transmuted from a system grounded in a social framework to a predominantly techno-cratic engineering function, serving first a colonial and then a slightly wider, yet still privileged, economic elite. At that point, infrastructure clearly needed to adapt rapidly to a different type of urbanisation process, but it faced three problems. In the first place, the system of urban infra-structure delivery had been so successful in the West that there were no identifiable alternatives available. Second, when external agencies finally recognised that there was a problem and began to seek alternatives, the locus of intellectual exploration, which defined the space where solutions were generated, was situated outside of Africa, even though the locus for implementation was within Africa. Third, the solutions that started to emerge gave a lower level of service than the original, generating an internal reaction from African leaders against having a 'second-class service' imposed on them.

At that point, African countries had no urban solutions of their own, while their professional, academic and research bases were all extremely weak. In combination, these factors left Africa not only vulnerable to, but dependent on, external agencies to shape their destiny. Unfortunately, reliance on external agencies has one major drawback: when something goes wrong with their ideas, they do not have to live with the con-sequences, but can simply move on to the new 'big idea', leaving African governments to carry the responsibility for the failure; and so it was here. Infrastructure had failed to develop African urban areas and so external agencies turned to urban planning to provide the solution. Unfortunately, because the locus of development thinking remained externally situated, this was equally unsuccessful. What it did, though, was create a logic flow that was powerful yet seriously flawed. Underpinning this logic flow were two assumptions. The first was that the way in which cities evolve could be explored from within a global urban paradigm, common to all countries irrespective of their location. This just happened to be built on a British

planning model, which fortuitously enabled the use of a single urban planning programme to teach the same planning programme across the entire
developing world. The second assumption was that we could take the
experience of planning and managing mature cities of the West and apply
these directly to the newly emerging and fast-growing cities of sub-Saharan
Africa.

The western pool of specialists who work on Africa is finite, so the
organisations involved need to be strategic about how they build their
information base; that is, where their experiential knowledge comes from.
Here there are three primary sources, all of which play to the strengths of
external research institutions. The first is their own internal experience,
based upon decades of western history and practice. This creates the
underlying *Weltanschauungen* within which the next two are then situated.
The second moves out to other countries and is based upon the practice
of comparative analysis, deriving data from different cities and urban
studies around the world. This works best with the large megacities,
because we can define a limited range of variables that we can compare.
The third is to focus on the needs of the individual, because here we can
draw upon sociological and anthropological theory to underpin our analyses. Unfortunately, when we combine all of these together, particularly in
Africa, we arrive at a result that is intellectually contradictory. On the one
hand there is the assumption that Africa is part of the new global movement of urban convergence in development approaches, based solely
upon megacity experience, often elsewhere in the world. On the other
hand there is the assumption that for poor people, rural 'solutions', which
provide the bulk of our experience of individual needs, are equally applicable in an urban environment.

The result, which is clearly evident in the UN-Habitat biennial reports
on the state of African cities, is that these two conceptual constructs form
a pincer movement around thinking about urban development in Africa.
On the one side, then, we have urban development thinking being driven
by a debate about megacities, in a continent where 75 per cent of the
urban population actually live in the secondary towns. On the other side
we have a view of the individual that has reduced development to its most
basic level, aptly named 'basic needs'. The outcome is exactly that feared
by African leaders in the 1970s: sub-Saharan Africa is slowly but inevitably
being reduced to a second-class global society. The external agencies
driving this process may be well-meaning, but this does not change the
outcome. What we see emerging in Africa is a model of paternalistic
charity that has clear roots in the Victorian era, reflecting an approach to
society that divides people into different social classes. This is clearly a situation that is socially and politically unsustainable.

What is required is a new approach to urban development that breaks
away from western *Weltanschauungen* and situates itself firmly in modern

African urban society. To be able to make that transition, though, we have to repeat the historical analysis carried out in Chapter 3, but this time in an African context.

In the beginning...

The complexity of British colonisation

Virtually all books on urban development in Africa will include at least a brief description of the colonial period, usually as a lead-in to post-colonial events. In discussing this period, however, they will rarely distinguish the different forms of colonial occupation, instead grouping the countries together under one generic heading of 'colonial'. This is an oversimplification as well as a serious oversight. There were quite different forms of colonial occupation, and these differences did have a significant impact, particularly on urban development policy and strategy, and even more on the development of urban infrastructure. Table 4.1 shows the four types of legislative status within those countries in Africa occupied by the British, termed respectively dominion, colony, protectorate and mandated territory.

In sub-Saharan Africa only South Africa had dominion status,[1] which made it similar to Canada and Australia, all of which enjoyed a high degree of autonomy. Next were the colonies, which meant, as the name implies, that the land could be purchased (colonised) by white settlers. There were then the protectorates, which allowed only limited access to land by non-indigenous people. And finally there were the mandated territories, German colonies that the League of Nations gave Britain and South Africa a mandate to rule after the Great War of 1914–18.

When the British government, or the settlers themselves, began to develop urban centres in Africa, the British used the municipal engineering model described in Chapter 3 as the basis for infrastructure delivery and management. From a technical perspective the approach taken to the development of the urban infrastructure base is similar for all the occupied territories, regardless of their status. However, as Chapter 3 sought to demonstrate, infrastructure is about more than technology. Bearing in mind that this 'British model' did not have a clear developmental role in its home country (where it was seen to support a social improvement process), we can see that the way was left open for the model to be interpreted quite differently in the different territories, adapting itself to the wider social and political framework of time and place. As a result, there were significant differences in the approach. It is those differences that form the basis for the current analysis, because it is only by exploring these differences that we can understand why urban infrastructure evolved in the way that it did in post-independence Africa, and why the outcome was such a catastrophic failure.

Table 4.1 List of British occupied territories in Africa[a]

Dominion[b]	Colony[c]	Protectorate[d]	Mandated Territory[e]
[Egypt-N. Africa]	Eritrea	Basutoland (Lesotho)	Tanganyika (Tanzania)
	Kenya	Bechuanaland (Botswana)	South-West Africa (Namibia) (to South Africa)
Nigeria (1954)	Nigeria	British Somaliland	
	Northern Rhodesia (Zambia)	Gambia	
	Sierra Leone	Nyasaland (Malawi)	
South Africa	Southern Rhodesia (Zimbabwe)	Swaziland	
	Sudan (Jointly with Egypt)	Uganda	
	Gold Coast (Ghana)	Zanzibar	

a This table has been summarised from a more comprehensive table taken from Stephen Luscombe (undated) 'The British Empire: Entering and Exiting the Empire': www.british empire.co.uk/timeline/colonies.htm (accessed 04 October 2009).
b It is more useful to talk of dominion status, which could be described as 'the achieve ment of internal self-rule in the form of 'responsible government'' (Wikipedia (2009) 'Dominion': http://en.wikipedia.org/wiki/Dominion (accessed 28 October 2009)).
c A colony was a potential dominion. It is a country that is controlled by a distant power and remains a dependency. However, the emigrants who settle there, while remaining subject to, or closely associated with, the parent country, have the right to settle the land (Free Dictionary (2009) 'Colony': www.thefreedictionary.com/colony (accessed 28 October 2009)). This system does not exclude indigenous peoples. However, the basis of land allocation is determined under the laws of the occupying power, which may or may not take into account indigenous rights of ownership.
d A protectorate can be described as '[a] state under the protection of an imperialist power without being directly ruled as a colony' (Answers.com (2009) 'Protectorate' www.answers.com/topic/protectorate (accessed 28 October 2009)).
e The Mandated Territories were the previous German colonies, captured from Germany during the 1914–18 war and given, respectively, to Britain and South Africa to manage by the League of Nations.

Urban infrastructure delivery in the Dominion of South Africa

The starting point lies with an understanding of the evolution of urban infrastructure in the dominions, since this is the only form of government that can explore infrastructure 'from within'; that is, in a situation where the residents of the territory had the internal freedom to interpret the role of infrastructure contextually. In many ways there were similarities here to the United States following independence. When we explore the way in which powers, duties and functions were transferred to the dominions, the mechanism for decentralisation remained delegation (as compared to devolution); yet this was no longer situated within its historical British context, with its feudal roots. As a result, different countries interpreted the extent of the powers in a different way and perceived differently the development role of infrastructure within local government.

Across the board, local governments in the dominions, including South Africa, retained a high level of control over their own development, particularly in the larger centres; and this extended to control over all the infrastructure services described in Chapter 3. Stripped of its specific historical context, though, most national governments and local governments saw infrastructure as a core function, for three reasons. First, infrastructure represented by far the largest component of the municipal budget. Second, the responsibility for health and education, which were core municipal functions in Britain, was transferred upwards, to either regional or national government level. Third, the major dominions (Canada, Australia, South Africa) all adopted federal systems of government, which acted to further strengthen the role of municipal government, since it significantly reduced the potential for central government micro-management. Given too that all of these countries were developing their urban areas from raw land, this brought the developmental role of infrastructure back to the fore. Unlike the United States, though, where this was grounded in economic development, the dominions also carried over from their British heritage the view that infrastructure was part of a social development construct. In spite of this inherited perspective, however, the wider geopolitical and spatial circumstances forced a change in thinking about the role and nature of urban infrastructure. The outcome was a major shift in the way infrastructure was perceived, moving from the British model, where infrastructure supported social improvement, to one where infrastructure was perceived not so much as a driver of development per se, but rather as a primary, core function of local government. The result was a strange hybrid: a strong engineering model operating within a wider socio-political construct of urban society. Interestingly, this enabled the British local government model, with its powerful triumvirate of Town Clerk, Treasurer and Engineer, to achieve its greatest power in the dominions.

This idea of a social underpinning to urban infrastructure may sound strange, if not ridiculous, in the context of South Africa, given that country's apartheid history, yet it was indeed the case. South Africa, like all British possessions in Africa, was structured along racial lines, yet this was a different model as compared with that of the later apartheid government – a model that could best be described as paternalistic racism. In this context, infrastructure did provide a socially equitable development framework for all in a way that housing and urban planning did not. Even after the rise of the National Party in 1947 and the introduction of apartheid, this remained the case in the major cities controlled by the opposition. It is the post-apartheid period that forms the context for this discussion.

In Johannesburg the apartheid government sought to segregate people on the basis of race. Yet while people were located in separate locations, the City of Johannesburg considered that it had a legal obligation to provide services to all its residents, regardless of race or location. In 1989 a development NGO called PLANACT was developing a comprehensive rational argument for the spatial reintegration of Johannesburg and Soweto (the political arguments being more self-evident). As a member of that team, with the area of responsibility being to explore the history and status of physical infrastructure, the author carried out a survey of infrastructure conditions in Soweto and also explored some of the history. Reviewing the research notes from that time uncovered the following analysis:

> When the services were installed originally [in Soweto] a relatively high level [of infrastructure] was decided upon. Whilst one reason for this was a lack of knowledge of low cost service provision in urban areas a second (and the major) reason was because Soweto was considered a part of Johannesburg (in spite of its geographical isolation) and *the clear intention of the Johannesburg City Council was that all residents should ultimately have the same level of service provision* [my emphasis for the purposes of this discussion]. That this was not done immediately was due primarily to the high demand for services over a short time frame and the associated capital cost of such a crash programme. At the time that this decision was taken it was recognized by the City Council that the services would not be viable if viewed from a 'stand alone' perspective and that cross subsidies [from 'white' Johannesburg to 'black' Soweto] would be required. Although not accepted by all councillors this concept was official Council policy.
>
> With the advent of the WRAB [West Rand Administration board] this policy changed to one of 'self-sufficiency' although it was recognized that this could not be achieved by conventional means (i.e. rates and service charges levied against individual tenants). Instead revenue was generated by taking a profit on the sale of liquor within Soweto. However there were insufficient funds, even with this income, so that capital works virtually stopped, maintenance declined and technical quality deteriorated.[2]

A similar situation existed in Cape Town with regard to infrastructure service delivery to the apartheid-segregated 'coloured' communities, where all residents were considered to have the right to the same levels of infrastructure service. There the system of municipal infrastructure management followed the early British model, with the city being directly responsible for all infrastructure services except telecommunications. Thus, the city was also the provider of electricity, buying this in bulk for the parastatal generator (ESKOM) but also owning its own coal-fired power station, which continued to provide a percentage of the electricity until the 1980s. This system of infrastructure management continued until the installation of democratic government in 2004.

This is clearly a politically sensitive issue, not only in South Africa but across the whole of sub-Saharan Africa, yet it is an important issue to discuss. White South Africa was responsible for apartheid, and even though it may have been an Afrikaner government there were many white people of Anglo-Saxon origin who were content to support that process, just as there were Afrikaner people who opposed apartheid. The point being made here is that, within an apartheid structure, there was a system of infrastructure delivery in place, particularly in the large cities, that sought for many years to deliver the same level of service to all residents, irrespective of their racial origins, or of the political dictates of central government. The only way that the apartheid government could prevent this from happening was to take away the responsibility for infrastructure delivery in Soweto and the other 'black' urban townships from those 'white' city councils and place it under central government control.

This makes South Africa an important case study for urban infrastructure. On the one hand there was a wider social and institutional system, extending across housing, employment and social access, that was hugely inequitable, with a system that highlighted, and was founded on, the principle of social exclusion for the majority of its population. At the same time there existed, within the area of urban infrastructure delivery, a system that sought to retain a principle of social equity for many years, in the face of strong opposition from central government, and which was able to provide a foundation for the belief that such a system (of equitable infrastructure delivery) could be extended to everyone.

The transfer of responsibility for infrastructure delivery and management in 'black' areas from the local authorities to administration boards was a disaster for residents of those areas. The study of Soweto, quoted earlier, found that 'between 1969 and 1979, not only was there negligible development of services, but the technical quality of the services actually diminished'. This deteriorating situation, which extended to all 'black' urban areas, led to a new, more technocratic approach to infrastructure service delivery. Faced with a situation that was perceived by many in the 'white' elite to be unaffordable, engineers began to develop the concept of 'variable levels of service' based upon affordability criteria, and the principle of social equity was slowly but steadily removed.

Urban infrastructure delivery in the colonies

Technically, the infrastructure model used in the colonies was similar to that of the dominions, bringing an engineering culture and creating strong technical departments; thus, a municipal engineer trained in Britain could move interchangeably between home, colonies and protectorates and perform a similar role. Climatic conditions may have necessitated modifications to some of the technical solutions, but the broad approach was similar. Again the role of infrastructure was more dominant than in Britain, but the way this played itself out was quite distinct from what occurred in the dominions. The larger towns, such as Nairobi (Kenya) and Harare[3] (Zimbabwe), did have a high level of delegated powers, but these were situated within a much more centralised system of government. Second, urban planning played a much greater role in creating the colonial city, creating a more homogeneous socio-economic and spatial framework, since it did not cater for the indigenous population, who were excluded from residence, except as servants within the 'servants' quarters' of the privileged class. From the beginning, therefore, the social basis for infrastructure in the colonial town was fundamentally different, with the urban infrastructure being constructed specifically to serve an elite.

That outcome was easy to achieve inside the formal boundary of the city; the real dilemma arose when cities were faced with having to address the 'other side' of the boundary. In the early colonial period there was a widespread assumption that Africans would come to the city to sell their labour and then go home; there was no plan B, no ideas about what to do if they chose not to return home.

What differentiated the colonies from the protectorates was that in the former, the government had to take responsibility for providing for the physical well-being of the Africans who were coming to the city to work. In his book *Verandahs of Power*, Garth Myers (2003) describes the establishment of Pumwani, the first African 'township' in Nairobi, which was constructed in 1922. This was a planned settlement and 'the project included roads, drains, public toilets and washing blocks, along with a layout of plots in a regular, rectangular grid'. So, there was planning, engineering and an installed infrastructure; but this was not to the same 'level' of service as that provided within the city boundary. Responsibility for the provision of services lay with the colonial government and was provided by the Engineering Department of the City of Nairobi, taking the form of communal standpipes and latrines, together with roads of a lower standard (because natives, not having cars, did not require roads to the same technical standard).

There was clearly a social context involved here, and it was the professional ethos of the engineers to provide services, particularly the health-related services of water supply and sanitation. However, the more dominant social ethos of racial differentiation, incorporating as it did both physical and linguistic separation, meant that those in power perceived the needs of Africans as being in a different social milieu from that which applied to Europeans. What we are seeing is a return to the British perception of infrastructure being provided for the social improvement of a lower class, with the objective being the prevention of disease. The result was a two-tier model of infrastructure delivery based upon a principle of social classification. This had happened in Britain with the original concept of social improvement for the working classes; there, however, the adoption of centralised network infrastructure created its own equity, albeit unintentionally. In the colonies there was a clearly defined two-tier system.

There is absolutely no doubt that such was the case. Thanks to Myers' study we can see that the provision of basic services in Pumwani and other African settlements was not the first step on an incremental ladder; it was 'the' service. This enables us to identify the continuity of the British model in which a social construct, founded on social improvement for the poor in Britain, transformed to a model of social improvement in Africa that reflected a 'paternalistic concern' for the health of an indigenous population. The phrasing used to justify this approach at the time was that 'they (Africans) are different and do not have the same needs (or expectations) that we (Europeans) have'.

Urban infrastructure delivery in the protectorates

The situation in the protectorates was slightly different from that in the colonies, influenced at least partly by the difference in the wider political relationship. David Nilsson (2006) provides a comprehensive analysis of the origins of the water supply and sanitation systems for Kampala, the capital of Uganda, in the colonial era. This illustrates quite clearly a carry-over of the British infrastructure model described in Chapter 3, with three key features. First, the systems followed British design practice and a technical (engineering) approach was used: 'Designing the service systems was left to experts' (ibid., p. 382). Second, 'The main, clearly stated, motive for the introduction of the water supply and the sewerage and drainage systems in Kampala was to safeguard public health' (ibid., p. 381). Here we see the British approach to infrastructure as supporting a social goal (public health). Third, the service was primarily for the more affluent. As Nilsson describes it, 'The public systems established for this purpose were, however, designed to cater primarily for the needs and preferences of the economically strong minority groups, although poorer Africans were not explicitly denied service' (ibid., pp. 381–2).

This, then, was the situation within the urban boundary; outside the boundary was another story. If the framework for infrastructure delivery outside the European town boundary had been reduced to a minimum in the colonies, it was non-existent in the protectorates. It was part of the protectorate agreement between the British governments and the political leaders that foreigners, be they European settlers or Indian or Arab traders, could not own land outside of the areas designated within the urban zones, which were defined, essentially, by the British government. In the colonies, most of the land surrounding the European town was owned by a settler (i.e. a non-indigenous person) and the government would generally rent the land in order to build an African 'township', as is the case for Kibera in Nairobi, for example.[4]

In the protectorates the boundary between town and country was much more rigidly defined, being literally a physical dividing line. Inside the boundary was a serviced town, while outside the boundary there were indigenous rural or peri-urban, and later urban, settlements. There was formal infrastructure inside but none outside. This stark difference served to highlight the clear distinction between those living on serviced land within the boundary and those living on unserviced land outside, and the racial distinction that accompanied it. The local authority had neither rights nor obligations outside of its boundary. At this point the social context for urban infrastructure provision was lost completely, since there were clearly no poor people around to provide infrastructure for; only the privileged elite. Infrastructure services had become simply a group of engineering-based, technically managed support services for the urban area. There was no specific approach to infrastructure for those living outside the boundary in areas that were subsequently termed 'peri-urban'. As a result, solutions were only developed for a 'rural' condition. This stark differentiation between 'urban' and 'rural' was to have immense consequences later in defining infrastructure 'solutions'.

Post-colonial infrastructure failure: the 1960s

This was the situation when African countries gained their independence, over a period stretching from the late 1950s into the early 1960s. At that point we can identify three distinct models for urban infrastructure. In South Africa (a dominion) there was a model that retained, at least in part, a base in social equity. It did so for reasons that were not totally altruistic and owed a great deal to the non-discriminatory nature of the centralised networked infrastructure delivery system. However, it could never provide a wider development model for Africa because it was already being overshadowed by the wider policy of apartheid, from which it could not be separated.

In the colonies we find a dualistic model. Again in the core urban areas there is a growing network infrastructure which, by the time it was built, was established practice across Europe and America, to the extent that it was generating its own rationality based upon the perceived benefit of increasing user convenience. In tandem, though, were the townships that were being built outside of the city boundary, which operated within a totally different rationality. Here the goal had reverted to the original British one of social improvement; that is, constructing a level of infrastructure support that would satisfy the public health needs of the lower classes and prevent the outbreak of waterborne or water-related diseases.

These, then, were the four infrastructure 'models' of British colonialism. First came the combined engineering/social equity model (in the dominions). In second place was what can only be described as a straight engineering model (for the colonies within the city boundary), which by that time was becoming rooted in user convenience. Third was a social improvement model (for the colonies outside the city boundary), which most closely resembled the original British model of the nineteenth century. Fourth was the rural model, which centred primarily on sanitation and the provision of individual latrines. We can see the results of this evolutionary process to this day. Networked infrastructure is perceived to be about engineering. For the poor there is the same social improvement model used as the basis for international development thinking. And then there is the individual latrine toilet, which remains the basis of thinking about both rural and urban sanitation in Africa.

When post-colonial history is reviewed by external academics, they tend to blame African governments exclusively for the ensuing collapse of infrastructure, to the point that this is now the accepted interpretation of events; yet they are wrong when they do so. There is no doubt that the dualistic model of both the colonies (all versus some) and the protectorates (all versus nothing) created immense expectations: to have any levels of service lower than those provided for Europeans would have been a continuation of racist practices. The African governments' inability to supply such levels of service was not simply because the cost was too high and urbanisation too rapid, though these were clearly contributory factors; the failure was also due to flaws in the underlying models of urban infrastructure delivery and management, with their confusing and irrational use.

This, then, allows us to see how the failings of the British infrastructure model, highlighted at the end of Chapter 3, followed through to Africa. It is clear, for example, that urban infrastructure in the colonies and protectorates was seen either as a supporting mechanism for other social development processes, or simply as an engineering service; but never as a driver of urban development in its own right. This mistake would continue to have major ongoing repercussions in Africa; at this stage, though, its greatest impact was more in terms of how this void was filled. The dominant approach that emerged from the colonial era was an engineering model where the technology had been separated from the original value system and implanted in a new value system based upon social injustice. Had infrastructure been perceived as a development driver, it is possible, though by no means certain, that this would not have happened. And even in the circumstances that existed at the time, there remained a possibility, albeit a very small one, that this flaw could have been overcome. Unfortunately, it was at this point that a new variable emerged which sealed Africa's urban decline: the specific British colonial interpretation of what constituted 'public works'.

This was a flaw in the wider infrastructure management model, which caused management (of physical development) to be perceived as an independent variable. The British colonial system was driven by a need to control expenditure in the Colonial Office (in London). To do this, the British colonies and protectorates created a Public Works Department for each country that would be responsible for the construction of capital works and the provision of goods and services that used public expenditure. However, this notion of 'public works' was something completely different from that used in the United States and described in the previous chapter. This use of the same term for two quite distinct concepts, with quite different meanings, has completely confused our understanding of urban infrastructure in Africa.

The American definition was based upon a collective outcome, i.e. the infrastructure; though this could extend beyond the categories described in Chapter 3 to include the physical fabric of social infrastructure such as schools or clinics, for example. The British colonial definition, on the other hand, is related to activities. The Public Works Department was a centralised procurement and construction department for all physical aspects of development, from school desks, through all forms of building, to large roads and bridges. In that context it was situated within the project cycle. When African countries gained independence, the department dealing with urban areas, the Public Works Department (PWD), became the main government department responsible for urban development. However, this was actually a general technical department employing engineers and architects who were responsible for building works of all kinds; the infrastructure was simply a part of what they built. Seeley's description of the responsibilities of a municipal engineer, set out in Chapter 3, defined the urban component of these public works to a large degree; and this in turn provides an understanding of final demise of the urban infrastructure model, demonstrating clearly how the management of infrastructure was transposed from a wider model to become a series of defined engineering tasks. Public works, then, was about construction; and this served to reinforce the already established belief that urban infrastructure was all about engineering.

The result was the last nail in the coffin, as it were. By eliminating the last remnants of a social infrastructure model, this transposition took away any possibility that Africa could successfully develop an urban infrastructure base. If this was not sufficient, there was a further, equally damaging, outcome; because when African governments then centralised power, it was not so much the responsibility for the infrastructure per se that they centralised. Of much greater significance was the centralised control over the budget that accompanied the shift. This was a political battle for control over the procurement process, because at that time infrastructure represented one of the biggest areas of government expenditure and hence an important power base in what was still a group of fragile, newly emerging nation-states.

Fragmenting the urban infrastructure base: the 1970s

Here we reach the final turning point: moving away from the old, failed engineering model but with no clear direction forward. It is evident with hindsight that the system of urban infrastructure management established in the British-occupied territories in Africa was impossible to sustain from the beginning. It was socially exclusive, capital-intensive and driven by engineering: designed to provide a high level of personal convenience to a small elite. The systems that were in place to manage their infrastructure were focused as much on the procurement process as they were on the end product, and had been stripped of any inherent rationality. With the demographic explosion that was about to come, the infrastructure system installed under the colonial regime was doomed to failure; the only question was how that failure would be managed.

This is the point at which the two lessons of Anglo-American history really become most important, with the flaws in the British model being the primary catalyst for everything that followed beyond this point. The first issue relates to the perceived role of infrastructure. We have already seen how the British colonial system was a paternalistic autocracy operating a command economy, which only served to reinforce the belief that infrastructure was simply a support service, as opposed to being a development driver. The growing influence of urban planning on African development, which mirrored a similar change taking place in Britain, coupled with increasing external disillusionment around the failure of what was increasingly perceived as an engineering model of urban infrastructure, led to the emergence of a new planning paradigm. Unfortunately, this was based upon the British planning model, which already interpreted infrastructure as a support service. Reinforced by what was happening in Africa itself, this new paradigm served only to reinforced and entrench that perception.

At the same time, the three-component model of infrastructure illustrated in Figure 3.1 had broken down completely and there was no longer any correlation between the three components. Instead, each operated as a completely independent entity, with its logic being defined almost exclusively by external agencies, of which at the time the World Bank was the most influential. When it became clear that alternatives were needed, the first responses were to seek to modify the individual parts of the infrastructure system, as well as the broader approach to delivery. This is neatly illustrated by the World Bank's research into alternative sanitation, developed in the 1970s, which produced a comprehensive and valuable, albeit technocratic, description of all the potential options for managing sanitation (situated within the technology component).

Under the pressure of ever-increasing urban population growth, African governments found themselves in a catch-22 situation. On the one hand there was a need to lower costs; on the other hand, though, there was still the spectre of the racially dualistic model of the colonial era fresh in their minds. The site-and-service schemes of the late 1970s were one example of how they sought to square the circle, trying to reduce costs while keeping alive the hope of a high level of service. Some governments, such as those of Tanzania and Ghana, did try indigenous solutions, such as the nationalisation of land, but none of them succeeded in delivering infrastructure effectively at a rate that could match the increase in population. At that point in history it is probably fair to say that engineering, which unfortunately (and in fact incorrectly) was also interpreted to include technology, had failed Africa.

'Privatising' the urban water supply: the 1980s

There are actually two quite distinct threads weaving through this stage of development, which have become conflated over time in the wider international debate. The first centres around a wider general debate on the role of the private sector, which operates primarily at the national level but then extends down to lower tiers of government. The second thread is more specific and relates to an exploration of what is the most effective way to manage local utilities, and in particular the urban water supply.

Let us begin with the first thread. Running in parallel with the wider technology and management failures described previously, but on a much wider scale, was a deterioration in institutional governance, with the social and political structures themselves coming under increasing strain and starting to collapse.[5] Coupled with this, on the world stage the political order was beginning to change. South Africa was forced to introduce a State of Emergency to control growing dissent. In the Soviet Union, President Gorbachev had introduced the social concept of perestroika. And across Africa, economies were in a state of almost terminal decline. At this point, the IMF and the World Bank, as the lenders of last resort, imposed structural adjustment programmes (SAPs) on African countries as a precondition to providing finance.

Depending upon the political standpoint of the observer, structural adjustment has been viewed as economic turning point for Africa or as a social disaster. That remains an open-ended debate; at this point, what is more important is simply to understand its rationale, which the World Health Organization describes in the following way:

> SAPs policies reflect the neo-liberal ideology that drives globalization. They aim to achieve long-term or accelerated economic growth in poorer countries by restructuring the economy and reducing government intervention. SAPs policies include currency devaluation, managed balance of payments, reduction of government services through public spending cuts/budget deficit cuts, reducing tax on high earners, reducing inflation, wage suppression, privatization, lower tariffs on imports and tighter monetary policy, increased free trade, cuts in social spending, and business deregulation. Governments are also encouraged or forced to reduce their role in the economy by privatizing state-owned industries, including the health sector, and opening up their economies to foreign competition.
>
> (WHO, 2011)

This, then, is a wide and diverse panorama aimed at changing the way in which a national economy is managed.

Now we can move on to the second thread. The privatisation drive that was an integral part of structural adjustment extended to public utilities, including within this urban water supply. The result has been some confusion about the way the way in which the World Bank's approach to urban water supply delivery was formulated. The common perception links the changes in water supply policy to the neo-liberal argument for a shift from public to private ownership embodied in the so-called Washington Consensus (Bakker, 2010), a range of policies adopted by the multilateral agencies to bring the world into alignment with the Anglo-Saxon free-market capitalist *Weltanschauung*. This was attributed to the growing influence of neo-liberal American academics in the early 1980s, which led to the privatisation policies of the mid-1980s. Here we have a much more specific issue, yet we are conflating it with the broader neo-liberal construct that underpinned structural adjustment.

Doing so is too simplistic; yet because it is an argument that is so widely accepted, we are unable to see the contradictions that it throws up. For example, it was pointed out in Chapter 3 that in the United States as late as 2003 only 5 per cent of the water systems were privately owned, while approximately 15 per cent of the population was served by corporate water providers (Melosi, 2008, p. 227). This is not exactly a mass takeover by the private sector! In France too, which is the conceptual home of the private-sector management model for urban water supply (described as *affermage*), the model is much more fluid and flexible than most people perhaps realise. At the end of a contract period the majority of communes review whether they wish to continue with private-sector management or take management control back under a public body; and they have every right to adopt the second option if they demonstrate its viability.

The only way we can really understand the water supply debate is to move the first thread (the wider privatisation debate) into the background and focus specifically on the second thread of the discourse: the water supply system itself. In this context, Karen Bakker, in her book *Privatizing Water*, points out, rightly, that the key lies in understanding the failings of what she refers to as the 'municipal hydraulic' paradigm (2010, p. 76). The question is: how do we do this? Here interpretations diverge. Underlying the confusion is a conflicting intellectual duality within the World Bank. On the one hand it may be valid to say, as Bakker does, that '[t]he weakness of the Bank's water supply portfolio ... made it ripe for realignment with the Bank's emerging private sector development (PSD) strategy' – and that is certainly a convenient perspective. In practice, though, it is argued here that there was a second rationality in play in the Bank at that time, which was actually based on a much more pragmatic rationality.

This second rationality was in fact very clearly outlined, and in addition expressed a valid concern. Given that the primary concern of the Bank was operational efficiency, its underlying rationale was that there are two distinct components to water supply management, the one relating to developing (and overseeing) an implementation strategy, the other relating to the management of the water supply service itself. It called the groups carrying out these two functions, respectively, the 'water service authority' (WSA) and the 'water service provider' (WSP). The argument was that when the two are combined, politics interferes with good management practice, resulting in poor decision-making that hinders effective investment in water supply. The outcomes can include inappropriate subsidies, a failure to charge tariffs that ensure cost recovery for reinvestment, and service levels that are too high to be affordable. The solution, therefore, was to separate the people who decide on how the water supply network will function, setting policy and implementation strategy, from the people who will be responsible for delivering the water, who are managers of an operational system. This was the position in the beginning, though it was lost in the early 1990s; but it was restated in the World Development Report of 2004 (World Bank, 2004). It is true that the Bank saw operational efficiency as best achieved if the WSP was in the private sector, and this was its default position; at the same time, though (in theory), it had no problems with the WSA being within government, though clearly it was extremely ambivalent on this point. It is suggested here that this ambivalence actually reflects different power bases inside the Bank itself, each with its own agenda. Whatever the case, the outcome is confusion.

We can return to this later, when the chapter looks at the way in which the Bank directed African policy in this area. At this stage there is one final aspect of urban water supply to understand, which is the mechanism proposed to manage the urban water supply network.

Once the operational framework, with the WSA and the WSP, had been created, it had to be operationalised. The process of operationalisation drew upon research conducted primarily in the United States (and originally for indigenous use), though drawing heavily on French experience, the outcome of which was to define the relationship primarily as a contractual one. Because the Bank wished to enable alternatives and a flexible working relationship, it created a range of contractual options, as described in Table 4.2. Then, because the WSP was in effect a monopoly provider, the relationship had to be managed, which required a regulatory function. Everything appeared to be so clear and straightforward at the time, but of course it all went terribly wrong.

The whole topic of water privatisation has probably been the most divisive and damaging ever to have taken place within the urban development agenda, while the level of rhetoric generated has been unprecedented. By the 1990s the Bank had retreated from its earlier position, at least publicly, though it did not change its underlying belief. All that really happened was that the debate was taken out of the water sector per se; and hidden within a new (low-profile) cross-sectoral group set up by the World Bank, called the Public-Private Infrastructure Advisory Facility (PPIAF).

The four external forces of influence: how the Anglo-Saxon approach to infrastructure shaped urban policy in Africa

Chapter 1 argued that it is predominantly external *Weltanschauungen* – that is, specific external interpretations of African needs and realities – that drive the development process in sub-Saharan Africa. The process is driven primarily through four distinct 'forces of influence', which are underpinned by external control over the knowledge resource base. These forces were summarised briefly in Chapter 1. The chapters that have followed have explored different aspects of the development process. Chapter 2 provided an overview of the evolution of urban development in Africa, situated within the context of global change. Chapter 3 then moved the focus to urban infrastructure, tracing the growth and development back to its origins in Britain and the United States. This chapter then took over from the point where concepts of urban infrastructure were applied in an African context, focusing on anglophone Africa.

This second part of Chapter 4 draws upon that broad historical canvas to demonstrate the full extent to which the western past has shaped the African present, and continues to do so, with the western thinking at all

Table 4.2 A hierarchy of management options for urban water supply

Delivery option	Description	Typical duration
Service contract	A municipality pays a fee to a private company to provide specific operational services, e.g. meter reading; billing and collection.	1–3 years
Management contract	A municipality pays a fee to a private company to assume overall responsibility for operation and maintenance of the delivery system, with the freedom to make day-to-day management decisions.	5 years
Lease – *affermage*	A private company rents facilities from the municipality and assumes responsibility for operation and maintenance. The company finances working capital and replacement of capital components with limited economic life, but not fixed assets, which remain the responsibility of the municipality.	10 years
Concession	A private company operates and maintains the system and finances investments (fixed assets) in addition to working capital. Assets may be owned by the company for the period of the concession, in which case they will be transferred to the municipality at the end of the concession period. The project is designed to generate sufficient revenues to cover the private company's investment and operating costs, plus an acceptable rate of return.	15+ years (often 25–30 years)
Build-operate-transfer (BOT)	A form of concession, with an emphasis on construction of new stand-alone systems. The municipality may or may not receive a fee or share of profits.	15+ years (often 25–30 years)
Full privatisation	A municipality sells off an asset to the private sector.	

Source: AquaMundo (German Water Alliance) GmbH: www.vik-ruse.com/document/ S_Eyd2O5.DOC (accessed 28 April 2011).

times being shaped by, and trapped within, these four forces of influence, all of which continue to be interpreted through a western, primarily Anglo-Saxon, framework of analysis.

External force 1: the colonial legacy: why the ghost of the past refuses to fade away

Africa's present was shaped by its colonial past to a much greater extent than people are willing to either recognise or accept – a reality that is clearly demonstrated by this analysis. For urban infrastructure the basis for the relationship between past and present is as shown in Figure 4.1.

There are essentially two ways of viewing the role of infrastructure in urban development: as a driver, whether of social or economic development, or as a support service. These are concepts that in the 1980s and 90s initiated a rather futile debate about whether infrastructure leads or lags development – futile because the difference is to be found not in economics but in the broader value-based surround: the *Weltanschauungen* of a society. Thus, (historically) the United States viewed urban infrastructure as a driver of (primarily) economic development, whereas in the United Kingdom the perception was quite different. There the urban infrastructure system developed out of a response to a social crisis, and while it later evolved into a large and complex technical system, it never lost its base in health and the wider social framework. Furthermore, this technical management of urban infrastructure services grew by accretion (as opposed to being a part of a larger public works construct, as was the case in the United States), as is evidenced by the following description:

> In the U.K, the Association of Municipal Engineers, (subsequently named Institution of Municipal Engineers), was established in 1874 under the encouragement of the Institution of Civil Engineers, to address the issue of the application of sanitary science. By the early 20th century, Municipal Engineering had become a broad discipline embracing many of the responsibilities undertaken by local authorities, including roads, drainage, flood control, coastal engineering, public health, waste management, street cleaning, water supply, sewers, waste water treatment, crematoria, public baths, slum clearance, town planning, public housing, energy supply, parks, leisure facilities, libraries, town halls and other municipal buildings.
>
> (Wikipedia, 2010a)

What began as a contributor to a policy of social improvement for the poor may have grown into a large technical function, but its basis as a

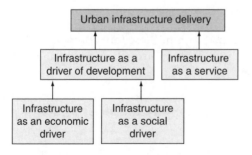

Figure 4.1 Historical perception of the role of infrastructure.

support service for a wider social policy never really changed. That was the role it played in municipal socialism; and that was why it was so easy to dismantle in the reform of local government in Britain in 1974. Its role as a driver of development was neither understood nor acknowledged in a society that viewed the provision of social services as the primary role of local government.

When the model of urban infrastructure was exported, the dominions could have provided an alternative model. Sadly, though, the only dominion model in Africa was South Africa, where the greater evil of apartheid prevented any serious exploration of the positive contribution provided by urban infrastructure. Instead, it was the colonies and the protectorates that provided the role models; and both were seriously flawed. In the colonies the development of the African 'townships' saw a return to the use of infrastructure for social improvement of the lower classes, while the towns and cities used it to provide lifestyle support for an elite. The role of urban infrastructure in the protectorates was similar to that in the colonies; outside the boundary, though, the city abrogated all responsibility. Creating an all-or-nothing scenario, this initiated the concept of an urban–rural duality, with a collective service being used to provide a high standard, and a high level of user convenience, for the middle class, while the poor were given individual responsibility for providing themselves with a basic level of service. Overall, there was nothing in any of these experiences to contradict the idea that infrastructure was simply a support service in a broader urban development process. On the contrary, the transformation of the collective service to a point where it was perceived to be a predominantly technical function only served to reinforce this view of infrastructure as being simply a collection of engineering-driven support services.

The second part of the picture is completed by an exploration of Figure 3.1, which is reproduced here.

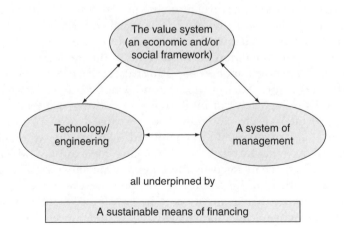

The history of urban infrastructure evolution in the United States illustrated an ongoing interplay between all four of the components shown in Figure 3.1. It is not suggested that this was always explicit; on the contrary, the interaction was rarely recognised explicitly for what it was. None the less, it was ever-present. In Britain, on the other hand, the relationship was poorly defined. There was undoubtedly a very strong value system at play, defined by the improvement to the health and physical wellbeing of the poor (social improvement). Technology was given less recognition, though it clearly existed, particularly in water supply, while much greater recognition was given to the wider concept of engineered physical improvements. The major shortcoming lay with the system of management.

From a political perspective, urban infrastructure in Britain was built around a very weak conceptual model. Local governments took over the responsibilities initially more to prevent control moving back to central government than from a specific drive to manage the services, a situation that was completely different from that in the United States. The status of the Borough Engineer too, was different. Although he (they were always male) was part of the management troika, together with the Town Clerk and the Treasurer, the Borough Engineer never had the same formal legal status, a status that had been defined for the latter two in the Local Government Reform Acts of the 1930s. In this context the legal status of the Borough Engineer was linked to his professional role, since he was designated 'the Engineer'; that is, the person responsible for the technical integrity of all civil and building works.

For a while, the rationality for urban infrastructure to be viewed as a core function of local government did exist in Britain, particularly in the northern industrial towns, where the role of infrastructure was integrated into a local government model of municipal socialism, since it was the mechanism used to provide equitable services to the working class. In this context the extension of the infrastructure base provided the foundation, together with council (i.e. social) housing, for a social equity model of the British city that remained influential until the end of the 1960s.

By that point, though, the different components of the model shown in Figure 4.2 were all coming under stress. Infrastructure had achieved its social goals defined eighty years previously, and a new value system was emerging around the high level of individual user convenience that the infrastructure provided. Technologically, the centralised network infrastructure system that had emerged was completed. This left the system of management and its relationship to the financing mechanisms, which were being increasingly challenged by the emerging neo-liberal political agenda. Given this situation, infrastructure was perceived as a primarily technical function whose management could be transferred to those best able to provide finance and operational skills. All of this was enabled by the overarching view of infrastructure as a support service in the wider urban development process.

This too was the perception of the external agencies driving urban development policy in Africa. The technical function had been relegated to a position on the project cycle defined by design and construction, in keeping with the British colonial interpretation of 'public works'. Infrastructure per se continued to be seen as a support function, or increasingly as a range of independent support services, thereby opening the way for the rise of urban planning as the dominant urban development discipline. And finally the breakdown of the linkage between the different components shown in Figure 4.2 provided the rationale for the individual infrastructure services to be explored from within just a single component of the whole. The full consequences of this quite specific historical trajectory then emerged through the three remaining forces of influence described in what follows.

External force 2: the private-sector management model for water supply. Just whose development model is this?

So why did the World Bank's urban water supply model fail? The first resort, as always, is to blame African governments. In 2009 the PPIAF,[6] a World Bank proxy organisation,[7] revisited this whole question of public–private-sector partnerships for urban water utilities. It carried out a wide-ranging review of experiences in developing countries (Marin, 2009), and had this to say:

> Although the general perception is that water PPPs in developing countries are on the decline, the situation is more nuanced. The population served by private water operators in developing and emerging countries has continued to increase steadily, from 94 million in 2000 to more than 160 million by the end of 2007. Large countries such as Algeria, China, Malaysia, and the Russian Federation have started to rely on private water operators on a large scale. Out of the more than 260 contracts awarded since 1990, 84 percent were still active at the end of 2007 and only 9 percent had been terminated early. Most cancellations were in Sub-Saharan Africa, a challenging region for reform, and in Latin America, among concession schemes.
>
> (ibid., p. 2)

So there we have it: yet again the failure lies with African governments, whose only crime is to challenge the relevance and applicability of a western model to their own country. This is truly unfortunate. Once more the World Bank had an opportunity to really understand why the private-sector management model has failed in Africa; and once more it missed the opportunity, falling back instead on old clichés. The problem with this report is the way it is situated within a particular *Weltanschauung* which then predefines the way it will interpret what constitutes a successful outcome. This is evident in its statement that sub-Saharan Africa represents a 'challenging region for reform'. Here the concept of what would constitute acceptable reform has already been predefined; it is immaterial whether or not African governments agree with that interpretation of the term 'reform' or not.

At the same time, though, the debate is also telling us something important about the three-component model, and particularly the component labelled 'management system'. Because the World Bank wanted a model for public–private-sector partnerships that would be applicable globally, it could not link the management framework to the value system of any one country. What it did was to create a new overarching concept that was perceived to be 'value-free': the contractual relationship. This would then allow the public–private partnership (PPP) to be tailored to a specific country's needs by (1) allowing a country to choose the form of partnership that was best suited to its own needs; and (2) providing a regulatory framework that was also defined in-country. In this way it can be seen as a regulatory model. Yet the fact that it provoked such a strong reaction shows a response that has its origins in the wider value system (with NGOs, for example), but also in the political system, with the objection of governments.

The political dimension links back to the early British model, with its struggle for control between national and local government; the American system, with the patronage politics of the East Coast politicians; and the clash between local and central governments in post-colonial Africa. What we are dealing with here is political regulation much more than simply management options. Recognising this allows us to modify Figure 3.1 to take this into account. The resulting outcome is shown in Figure 4.2.

This becomes very interesting, because this new relationship between the components, and in particular the type of disagreements that we see in this water-supply debate, begins to correlate with an important paper that was produced in the 1980s by the American sociologist Denis Goulet that sought to define three distinct rationalities of development: the technological, the political and the ethical. Goulet (1986) argued that

> [p]roblems arise because each rationality approaches the other two in reductionist fashion, seeking to impose its view of goals and procedures on the decision-making process. The result is technically sound decisions which are politically unfeasible or morally unacceptable or, in other cases, ethically sound choices which are technically inefficient or politically impossible.

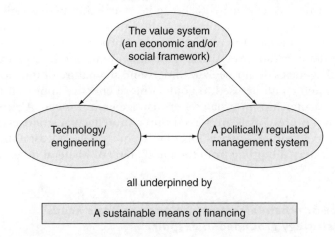

Figure 4.2 The modified three-component model of urban infrastructure.

In development, nothing is value-free, particularly in such a contentious area as public–private-sector partnerships. The World Bank sought to create a 'value-free' condition, but of course it was never that. This concept of neutrality is simply a belief that one particular system, in this case the Anglo-Saxon interpretation of private enterprise, is a global model. The World Bank operates within its own *Weltanschauungen*.

At the same time as there was a debate at this more conceptual level, there were also serious practical problems. African local government authorities rarely have the capacity to engage with water service providers from the international private sector. As a result, the exploration of PPPs takes place at a national level, centralising power and disempowering local government. The concept of regulation reinforces this further, since regulation is only required to manage a monopoly supplier. Thus, the use of regulation, which is strongly associated with the full privatisation model used in Britain, simply reinforces the view of those opposing PPPs that there is a hidden agenda that that is pushing for full privatisation. This is evident in all the South African literature on the subject, where the term 'privatisation' is used inclusively to describe all contractual relationships from *affermage* upwards.

In this analysis it is evident that in translating the private management of urban water supplies to sub-Saharan Africa has been not so much a disaster as a mess. There is a sensible rationality underpinning it: the separation of a WSA from a WSP; but no coherent underlying logic to the way it has been implemented. Local government rarely has the capacity to manage the complex contractual relationship, so the responsibility moves to central government; and the impact of this is to move power back to the centre and reverse decentralisation, as the next chapter will illustrate.

Ironically, governments can actually be quite successful in managing urban water supplies when they are given the intellectual space, as the experience of the National Water and Sewerage Corporation (NWSC) in Uganda amply demonstrates. Yet African governments are rarely given this space. External agencies do not seek to understand the nature of the local value system, which could be used to guide a more effective approach to public–private partnerships in urban water management. Instead, African governments and professionals are forced into an intellectual straitjacket, being required to adopt this illogical mix of western models, at least if they wish to receive external funding from the multilateral or bilateral development agencies.

External force 3: urban infrastructure and the basic needs approach: a strategy grounded in despair

The application of a basic needs approach to urban infrastructure services, and the creation of the Millennium Development Goals (MDGs) related to water supply and sanitation, can be seen as an evolutionary outcome of the history of urban infrastructure in Africa that was described earlier in the chapter. With the rejection of a centralised network model for urban infrastructure, primarily on the grounds of cost, the response falls back on the social improvement model of infrastructure. This is applied to those services linked to public health but now defined more generically as 'environmental' services.

The basic needs approach and the MDGs should never have been applied to urban infrastructure services. That they have been simply reflects the full extent of external control and illustrates how such control leads inevitably to a 'solution' based upon the lowest common denominator approach – truly a strategy grounded in despair that would never have been adopted if there was internal control over the intellectual space. Such an approach can be shown, through this discussion, to have its roots in Victorian paternalistic charity in a socially stratified class-based society.

Yet this was not the only push factor involved; there was also the rejection of a model of infrastructure management that was perceived as being engineering driven. Table 3.2 in the previous chapter shows the full extent to which the basic needs approach to infrastructure services is grounded in the British model. The first two characteristics, infrastructure as a support service in social improvement and infrastructure driven by engineering, become self-evident from the above discussion. When we move on to the third characteristic, which revolves around the top half of Figure 3.1, then we see the same failings as existed with the original British model, where each of the three components is treated in isolation. We have a clear value system that is the same as it was over 150 years ago. We have a rejection of technology through a falsely assumed conflation of technology with engineering. And we have a confused debate about management, with a focus on community management.

At the same time, the rural sanitation perspective (i.e. individual latrines) that was a feature of life in the duality of the protectorates lives on and continues to dominate thinking in the arena of urban sanitation. In the rural context, of course, sanitation is very much an individual responsibility. In western countries too, the transformations brought about by centralised network infrastructure moved the focus of infrastructure down to the level of the individual. All development paths, then, appear to lead down to this level, a fact that leads to one of the most unfortunate non sequiturs in the history of development thinking. If everything operates at the level of the individual, then surely this is also where we need to situate the debate about financing, and in particular affordability.

At this point we go back to the range of technical options for sanitation developed by the World Bank in the 1970s. What we have here, surely, is a simple choice: a trade-off between cost and user convenience? At this point our globalist thinking comes into play. For here we have an idea that was tried and shown to work in urban areas in India. This means that the same principle could be applied to urban areas in sub-Saharan Africa, does it not? After all, poor people are the same everywhere. So we now have truly individual choice available to the urban poor, where people are able to trade user convenience against a lower cost, thereby enabling more (financially) affordable options to be explored. When applied to sanitation, this created, in its simplest form, three 'levels' of service, as indicated in the diagram by van Ryneveld, illustrated in Figure 4.3, which

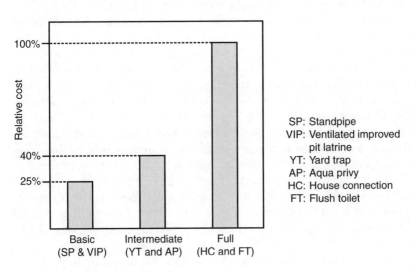

Figure 4.3 Total monthly costs for water supply and sanitation option (adapted from van Ryneveld, 1995).

shows how three levels of sanitation service might be costed for affordability analysis.

Quod erat demonstrandum.[8] What more need be said? Pit latrines are clearly the answer to the urban sanitation needs of the urban poor. What we see here is a complete mishmash of concepts and ideas taken from historical precedent and applied without any coherent integrative rationality (which is not to deny they might have their own internal rationality). As was mentioned earlier, the application of the basic needs approach and the application of the Millennium Development Goals to urban infrastructure are both part of a perception of development that is driven by Victorian paternalistic humanitarian charity grounded in a strategy of despair. Its outcome can only be to entrench a social differential in African towns that not only creates inherent political instability but also defines the majority of residents in those towns as second-class global citizens.

External force 4: applying the British urban planning model in Africa: the serpent chases its tail

Urban planning cannot of itself drive development; that would be a contradiction in terms. What planning can do is facilitate development through a manipulation of land use.[9] Simply adding the term 'integrated' in front of the term 'urban planning' does not change that, since integrated land-use planning is an oxymoron. Urban planning, like urban infrastructure, is grounded in a value system; and the value system used for the British model is individual ownership of land. So one can only 'integrate' the needs of competing users within the chosen value system.

UN-Habitat, the major international agency dealing with 'cities' in Africa, adopted a British planning paradigm as the conceptual basis for urban development. It then commissioned a report (UN-Habitat, 2009) intended to provide academic support for the continuation of this belief, something that has been necessitated by the clear failure of urban planning to create formal towns and cities in Africa. This report fully acknowledged those failures before going on to argue that they could be addressed by a new and changing approach to urban planning. However, it falls back on the same weakness that has been discussed in earlier chapters: the western experience (for its theoretical base); the globalisation principle of development (think global, act local); and the focus on megacities, where it argues that '[urban planning] also needs to recognize the changing institutional structure of cities and the emerging spatial configurations of large, multiple-nuclei or polycentric, city-regions' (ibid., p. xxii).

This report is written by people who believe that urban planning is the driver of urban development, a statement that is clearly supported by the list of background papers listed in the report. As such, it falls into the trap of being the product of a group of like-minded people, a trap that was described in Chapter 1 as being the ultimate weakness of the academic and intellectual rationality that underpins the four forces of influence generally. There are no dissenting voices and as a result it becomes a self-reinforcing document – a case of the already converted writing the gospel.

From the analysis carried out in the book to date there are five fundamental issues that emerge which highlight fundamental weaknesses in the current urban planning paradigm as it applies in sub-Saharan Africa. The first is the nature of planning as what might be termed a 'paper-based process'; that is, it requires some graphical representation of the future physical framework of the town or city. The report highlights how urban planning has been the basis of development for 7,000 years, which appears to be a fairly strong endorsement. However, it does not address the change that took place in the 1980s, which changed the first principle that under-pinned the planning process throughout that entire period: the ability to plan land use on a greenfield site. In the 1980s it finally became (almost) universally accepted that people who already occupied land could not be moved as a matter of course. The implication here is not simply that we need to manage informal settlements; the implication is that the entire rationality underpinning the concept of urban planning has changed. Yet there is no discussion of what this means on a conceptual level.

The second issue relates to the interpretation of infrastructure. The report acknowledges that '[s]ince the late 1970s, the "unbundling" of infrastructure development – through forms of corporatization or privati-zation of urban infrastructure development and provision, and developer-driven urban development – has tended to drive patterns of urban fragmentation and spatial inequality in many countries' (UN-Habitat, 2009, p. xxvi). Yet it is unable to see the extent to which planning has itself been a contributory cause of this phenomenon through its own view of infrastructure. Helen Meller, a respected urban historian in England, has produced a number of books on the development of towns, both in Britain and elsewhere in Europe, in the nineteenth and twentieth centu-ries. Acknowledging that the focus is on planning, this book nonetheless manages to discuss the development of towns in Britain (Meller, 1997) with no more than a passing mention of the role of infrastructure. The earlier chapters have shown how the British model of urban planning practised in Africa has adopted the British interpretation of infrastructure as a support service. Fragmentation is a natural outcome of this interpretation.

The third issue revolves around the relationship between urban plan-ning and the wider value system within which that planning operates. The UN-Habitat report reflects a strong altruistic belief that urban planning operates within an idealised framework of social values. While many plan-ners may well aspire to these on a personal level, the reality today is that the practice of urban planning is defined primarily by economic values. Since the 1980s this has meant an economic planning model that is a product of the same neo-liberal school that so influenced the water supply discourse described earlier. There are two implications. The first links across to the unbalanced planning focus on the megacities and the large regional conurbations. In this combination, economic drivers are (1) external; and (2) linked to (generally large-scale) private-sector involvement. In the secondary towns, certainly in Africa, the situation is quite different. There the main economic drivers are going to be internal and linked to infrastructure. The British planning paradigm has no way of integrating this process because it is only able to work with infrastructure as a support service; not as a development driver.

The second implication is that in this economic model planning actually reinforces the spatial inequity between rich and poor in Africa. Situating land within a framework of individual ownership in a free market limits the formal city to the rich; while using land regulation as the basis for informal settlement upgrading merely perpetuates the differentiation in levels of infrastructure service described previously, which leaves the poor with only basic services. Urban design on the other hand has the capacity to integrate poor informal settlements into the formal city, as the experiences of Brazilian favela upgrading have shown. In the British planning model, though, urban planning and urban design are two separate degree programmes. This is the fourth issue, creating a further weakness in the British urban planning model.

The final issue is that of internal accountability. In an era where good governance dominates the development debate, urban planning remains the only professional discipline where its practitioners have no clear accountability. This lack of accountability is evident in the UN-Habitat report discussed previously. There is recognition that urban planning has failed in the past, but it was always the failing of others: master planning was inappropriate; there was a lack of political will on the part of politicians; people moved into the city at too fast a rate – the list is endless. At what point do urban planners accept responsibility for their actions and become accountable? The reality is that they cannot, because the 'plan' is always changing.

The result of all of these flaws, when combined, is to situate planning within something of a self-delusional condition. We know that urban planning has failed to address Africa's development needs. However, this failure cannot be addressed until there is a recognition of the real weaknesses of the current model. The UN-Habitat report outlines a range of potential interventions and changes, but nowhere does it engage with reality. African secondary towns do not fit within the globalisation model that underpins that report, or within its philosophical rationality of 'think global, act local'. The time really has come for UN-Habitat to recognise the developmental needs of secondary towns as existing within a framework of development that is quite distinct from that of the megacities and large regional centres.

Underpinning the four forces of influence: a flawed western rationality

Africa does not have an urban tradition. Several countries have a history of past urban civilisation, but there is little evidence that this provided a continuity of urban traditions through into the present. In contrast to countries in Asia, for example, urban development in Africa is almost wholly a colonial construct. As a result, the nature of that colonisation makes urbanisation in the subcontinent a process that is unique, and quite distinct from that of any other continent. It is this unique situation, which is reinforced in anglophone countries by the use of English as the primary medium of communication, that allows external influences to play such a major role in defining urban development in the subcontinent. The argument evolving here is that the externally driven urban development models are grounded in fundamental assumptions about the nature of the urban development process itself, the most critical of which is a misinterpretation of the role that infrastructure plays in a society. This flawed construct then plays itself out through four thematic forces of influence.

The book has demonstrated that there is a rational consistency to this argument that explains the current state of underdevelopment in Africa's urban areas. Yet it does not really answer the question of why, if the external model is really so flawed, it continues to exist; surely it should have been questioned by now? The answer to this question is to be found in an exploration of the intellectual space that underpins the thinking that shapes not only the development process but also development practice.

There are two parts to this debate. The first lies with the debate around the role of urban planning. This has been discussed in the previous section and will be discussed further in later chapters. It is the second part that is of particular relevance, because it is a more recent phenomenon; this is the impact of the increased western specialisation within the skills and knowledge base.

The starting point is the end of the colonial era. When African countries achieved their independence they had barely any graduate professionals, and certainly no urban development professionals, be they urban planners, civil engineers, architects or land surveyors. It is true that, following independence, anglophone African countries established (or, in that very limited number of cases where they already existed, expanded) their departments of engineering, planning, architecture and other development-related specialisations. In each and every case, though, these professional programmes were modelled on the British core curriculum pertaining to that professional specialisation at that time. And this academic dependence has been self-perpetuating. At first it was through a lack of confidence and pressure from their students. African universities were afraid that if they developed their own curricula, these would be considered by their students as second-rate, because they did not follow a western model. Later, independent thought became virtually impossible as the best African students were drawn into the western (Anglo-Saxon-dominated) postgraduate system and accepted the models that they were taught, as well as the *Weltanschauungen* in which these models were situated. The result has been that the entire focus of professional development in Africa is based on how to adapt western development constructs to Africa, rather than on how to develop indigenous development constructs that are designed specifically to address the evolving urban condition in the countries concerned.

Since the post-transitional shift in global development practices, coming into force increasingly since 2000, the problems outlined above have been made much worse by the fragmentation of the urban development arena. With the move to target-based development, and the individualisation of services, the number of external agencies and individual consultants working on urban development issues in Africa has increased enormously. These consultants in particular are all operating in narrower and more specific specialisations, all defined by western interpretations of need – added to which, if that condition alone was not enough, the reports that these consultants produce are becoming longer, more numerous and more complex. Compounding this further, different agencies often commission similar studies in the same area, which can often produce conflicting and contradictory conclusions and recommendations. Throughout this process the external agencies all expect that the African governments they work with will produce specialists, on demand, to match the area of expertise defined by this externally driven process. The result, of course, is obvious: these matching African experts, who are already limited in number and under enormous pressure, must now spend valuable time, which could have been used on internal development, pairing with an external consultant. Doing so is useful for them personally, of course, since the rate of remuneration is higher than they would receive locally, but it contributes very little to building local capacity. It is this ever-increasing fragmentation of specialised inputs by external agencies that, when coupled with already existing internal skills shortages, is driving the intellectual colonisation that already existed, but is now becoming even more dominant, in sub-Saharan Africa. Moreover, as well as dominating the sectors, this vast web of external 'expertise' is also undermining the political decentralisation process in Africa, as the next chapter will show.

We can then apply these considerations to urban infrastructure development, where the range of subdivisional interests is huge. There are water specialists, sanitation specialists, storm-water specialists, urban governance specialists, environmental science professionals, road engineers, transport specialists, community activists, specialists in hygiene promotion … the list is endless. What is interesting about all of these diverse specialists, though, is that they all share a similar trait when it comes to how they see the role of their particular specialisation in relation to the urban area. This shared perception will be defined here as the *Aristotle syndrome*. Although it is the Egyptian astronomer and geographer Ptolemy who is most commonly credited with first stating that the Sun revolves around the Earth, this belief was also shared by the Greek philosopher Aristotle, a much more widely respected character. Thus, brilliance does not always equate with truth.

Aristotle's earthly parallel in modern urban development is to be found in the way that each sector specialist, regardless of their area of expertise, sees their particular specialisation or sector as being at the centre of all development activity, with the city simply providing the geospatial and physical framework for the application of their work. This is illustrated by the upper portion of Figure 4.4.

The reality that the Earth revolves around the Sun is now universally accepted, of course. In that specific case, while Copernicus was the person who proved this mathematically, a number of Greek philosophers living over 1,500 years previously had already proposed this as the only logical

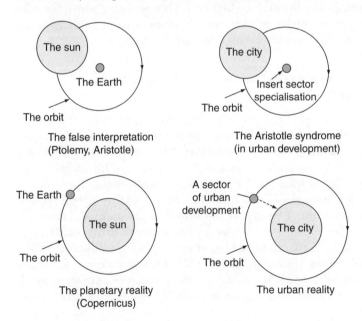

Figure 4.4 Alternative views of the relationship between the city and specific sector-based activities.

reality. What is interesting here is not so much that it took so long to prove, but rather that so many knowledgeable and supposedly intelligent people refused to accept it for so long. A similar situation applies now. Many professionals and external agencies continue to seek to apply the mechanistic view of urban development to the city, often for a similar reason; it is hard to give up the belief that they, and their sectoral activity, are not at the centre of the urban development universe.

The reality, though, is that the city is a system, and sectors feed into it. This does not prevent them from being a part of another system in their own right; for example, urban water management is part of both the urban system of interactive resource flows and the wider system of regional or global water resources. However, while the Aristotle syndrome continues to dominate development thinking it will remain extremely difficult for Africans to break free of external control over their intellectual space. For they have to contend not only with external control of a flawed academic discourse, which would be challenging enough in its own right, but also with diverse and multiple professional egos all seeking to situate themselves, and their specific specialisation, at the centre of the wider urban discourse. When these factors are further coupled with an insistence, on the part of external agencies, spearheaded by UN-Habitat, that African countries must continue to use a failed urban planning model as the basis for their urban development strategy, then it is not surprising that Africa's urban condition is so dire; and it is easy to see why it is so difficult for African countries to extricate themselves from this disastrous situation and create their own urban development process.

Summarising the externalities blocking urban development in Africa

The exploration of how the urban infrastructure was transferred across to Africa, described earlier in this chapter, supports the findings of Chapter 2. The collapse of the urban infrastructure base was due primarily to a flawed interpretation of both the role and the nature of infrastructure in urban society. This is illustrated by the right-hand side of Table 3.2 in Chapter 3, which summarises the three flawed perceptive interpretations of urban infrastructure. The first is the one that saw infrastructure as a support service for social improvement, rather than a driver of development. The second was that of mistaking engineering for technology, when they are actually quite different. And the third was the failure to understand that urban infrastructure has its own value-based relationship, which is not necessarily the same as that used to define the role of urban planning in society.

In a wider institutional context this already mistaken view of infrastructure was made even more untenable in Africa when it was defined within the organisational framework of the colonial public works department. For unlike the American concept of public works, which is focused on a collective outcome, the colonial interpretation of public works meant something quite different. It was an interpretation that was related to activities, primarily procurement and construction; and the outcome was simply to reinforce the mistaken view that infrastructure and engineering were synonymous. Urban infrastructure failed Africa in a spectacular way and urban planning moved to fill part of the void, which also resulted in a scramble for part of the infrastructure cake by a variety of other emerging line-departmental ministries of national governments. This then reinforced the fragmentation of infrastructure that was already under way under external influence. More critically, it confused an already difficult debate about the wider role of local government.

The final point before we move on relates to the wider issue of how western professionals approach issues of urban development. Once cities mature; and when the infrastructure base is in place, the focus moves towards incremental improvement of urban space and urban spatial relationships. On the one hand this change of focus raises the profile, and the importance, of urban design, which is well suited to this role. On the other hand it encourages increased specialisation, since the focus is on improving the operation and/or performance of systems that already exist. This specialisation is therefore a characteristic of mature societies and, in particular, mature cities. The needs in a rapidly developing country are quite different, requiring professionals with more general skills who can implement a range of initiatives. Imposing the specialist model on developing countries prevents indigenous professionals from building the skills base that they need to take urban development practices to scale, as well as inhibiting the indigenous exploration of local solutions. This imposed model then becomes a critical component of external control over African intellectual space.

Chapter 5

Decentralisation and urban infrastructure

Introduction

The external forces that have been driving urban development in Africa, particularly since the global political transition that began in the late 1980s, have all pushed Africa towards one outcome, which is greater centralisation in government. UN-Habitat (2008) places the responsibility for the failure of African governments to decentralise on a failure of political will in Africa. It is convenient to do so, since it absolves external agencies from any responsibility. Yet it is also misleading, taking the easy option in allocating blame. The real issue, which UN-Habitat fails to explore, is the extent to which decentralisation is prevented, and often reversed, by the need to follow externally imposed development policies and practices.

It is argued here that African governments do seek, actively, to decentralise power, and rightly see the basis for sustainable urban development as being founded upon meaningful decentralisation and the building of strong local government. In their Kigali declaration of 2005, African Ministers of Decentralisation and Local Government stated:

> We now therefore ... recommit ourselves to promote and support decentralisation in Africa through facilitating the formulation of its policy, legislation and implementation, creation of a conducive environment for economic development, management of local resources in an efficient and sustainable manner, and facilitating intergovernmental fiscal transfer.[1]

So if African governments have difficulty in creating effective decentralisation strategies – and they do – it is not through lack of political will; it is simply because they are unable to reconcile the contradictions that are part and parcel of the range of multiple, yet fragmented, external interventions, each with its own agenda, each striving for priority, and all of them dependent for their success on strong central government driving the urban delivery agenda through direct action. It is not a lack of political will but a lack of political freedom that prevents African countries from taking control over their own development. It is for this reason that decentralisation is a critical area of analysis in the exploration of external control over Africa's intellectual space.

Of the many different areas of government, the one that is most affected by decentralisation policy is urban infrastructure, if this term is used collectively to incorporate the range of individual services described in Chapter 3. As a result, the evolution of urban infrastructure in post-colonial Africa is intricately bound up with the wider discourse on decentralisation. The issue in question is how the evolution and the wider discourse impact on each other.

This chapter explores the nature of decentralisation, and its role in creating sustainable local government, with a view to understanding this interaction. It will begin by looking at the way in which external agencies originally interpreted the concept of decentralisation, specifically in an Africa developmental context, with the issue being whether, and to what extent, an external locus of analysis can ever really provide a meaningful understanding of what is happening in another country or region. To address this issue comprehensively requires a re-evaluation of four distinct components of decentralisation: delegation, devolution, deconcentration and deregulation. Each of these will be explored individually in the sections that follow.

Decentralisation is a complex and multifaceted topic. However, by unbundling these different components and exploring each one separately it is possible to see the full extent to which external influence not only has prevented decentralisation from taking place in Africa but has actually been a primary cause of increased centralisation. This understanding of external influence will be taken forward and integrated into the discussion on urban governance in Chapter 11, where it will feed into the exploration of how responsibility for decentralisation can be taken back from the external control and reclaimed by African governments.

The international discourse on decentralisation

Decentralisation's rise to prominence in Africa

Consider this extract from a paper published by the Swiss Development Corporation in 1999:

> Very broadly outlined, the 60s marked a period of projects and of technical cooperation (mainly in Africa, but also in Asia and Latin America). The 70s were a period of regional development or sectoral programs; and the 80s were marked by the importance of macro-economics, rendered indispensable by the weaknesses of national

political developments and the policies of bilateral and multilateral cooperation. The 90s then witnessed a recognition of the importance of managing public affairs well ('good governance', to recall an established neologism), respect for human rights, the role of civil society and the private economy, of participatory development and of decentralization. In other words, in the 90s *the development process was recognized as being primarily a political process which cannot be replaced by external financial flows.* Although the latter are obviously necessary, initially they can also lead to a type of economic development which, although sustainable at first, may remain fragile if not accompanied by inevitable political and social reform in order to achieve lasting development. The Asian crisis surfaced just at the right moment to remind us of this.

Perhaps decentralization is a theme which integrates the entire process, a crossroad conception through which a society project is created. Obviously the contributions found in this edition shed some light on the subject but in no way exhaust it. If they demonstrate the complexity of the matter we will have reached our objective.

(SDC, 1999, pp. 4–5; emphasis in original)

Three years after publication, this 'theme which integrates the entire process' was, to all intents and purposes, dead as a development issue, subsumed by what was perceived, in this analysis, as being one of several constituent parts of decentralisation, namely good governance. Over a period of just a few years, perceptions had changed and roles had been inverted: a component, good governance, had become the new integrative theme, better able to support an Anglo-Saxon, output-orientated development model. In turn, the previously assumed integrative theme, decentralisation, was now nothing more than a footnote in history. This section explores how this inversion came about and discusses some of the implications.

Decentralisation from a political science perspective

The analysis begins with an exploration of the first of three 'perspectives' of decentralisation. It is an academic overview, situated intellectually within the sphere of social and political science. In practice, of course, virtually all discussion of this topic is situated within the political sciences, but some discussions also expand beyond that academic arena; this first analysis is important primarily because it provides a lucid and succinct summary of the topic which, while being situated outside of any specific developmental or sectoral focus, is concerned specifically with sub-Saharan Africa. It is drawn from a report produced for UNRISD[2] by Dele Olowu[3] (2001).

The report begins by defining three forms of decentralisation: devolution, deconcentration and federalism. The first uses the concept of devolved powers in a unitary political system, the second that of delegated powers, while the third uses a mix of the two (depending on the country), but in a federal political structure (Olowu, 2001, p. 2). In looking at how these different systems evolved, in a historical context, Olowu defines four phase of decentralisation in Africa:

- phase 1 (1945–early 1960s)
- phase 2 (early 1960s–late 1970s)
- phase 3 (late 1970s–late 1980s)
- phase 4 (1990s–present[4]).

In phase 1, termed by some the 'golden age' of African decentralisation, the key attributes of local government comprised a tradition of elected councils, a well-defined local tax system, involvement in (social and physical) infrastructure, and involvement in capital investment (Olowu, 2001, p. 4). Phase 2 actually involved a reversal of decentralisation, with power being taken away from the local level and returned to the centre. This was partly due to the belief that central planning provided faster delivery, and partly the politicisation of the nation-state and the creation of a centralised one-party system of government. Internationally, this is a widely accepted conclusion, and we can see a similar analysis in francophone African literature;[5] Chapter 4 of course draws a significantly different conclusion.

Phase 3 was primarily an outcome of structural adjustment and driven by the external development agencies, with the World Bank a major player. Olowu sums this up neatly when he says (of decentralisation) that '[t]he usual pattern was to devolve responsibilities, but not the financial or human resources, to local units' (2001, p. 6). The driver of this phase of decentralisation was an economic rationality, and comprised two parts. The first derived from a series of in-country initiatives to spread responsibility for service delivery. This was taken up and formalised as follows: 'World Bank lending portfolios emphasized the need for its borrowers to utilize opportunities provided by parallel or informal economies and institutions as alternative instruments for the delivery of services' (ibid., p. 7). The second can be summed up by the following paragraph in the report:

A second reason for embracing local governments was that they offered opportunities to develop the local public and private sector economies – an idea premised on the possibility of *separating provision from production* of services. *Provision* deals with such questions as what public goods and services ought to be provided in what quantity and quality, how to finance the production of such goods and services, and how to monitor and regulate the production of such goods and services. On the other hand, *production* is the technical transformation of resources into the delivery of these goods and services. Since many of the justifications for decentralization relate to the provision function and most of the criticisms relate to the production function – i.e. the lack of capacity to perform the production of these services – the separation of these two functions reduces the need for attempting to create large technical capacities in local government. Unfortunately, many decentralization programmes gave local governments the production responsibilities while the central government keeps the provision responsibilities. Furthermore, since the state was in most cases in financial crisis, funding for these decentralized services was sought not from the traditional tax sources or government transfers but from user fees – for basic services like health and education – and also from private sector and non-governmental organizations, including community groups.

(ibid., p. 7; emphasis in original)[6]

Phase 4 of the African decentralization process is described by Olowu as being partly a continuation of phase 3, but then enhanced by 'a search for local institutions that are genuinely participatory and responsible to the local communities' (2001, p. 9).

To this end, Olowu has argued, with validity, that decentralisation is a means and not an end in itself. However, the point of his argument was to move away from the concept of measuring the extent to which decentralisation policies or processes increase the autonomy of decentralised agencies and move to an approach that rather defined the mechanisms used to implement decentralisation. He then tested this approach on five case-study countries which he believes reflect a new type of decentralisation programme,[7] arguing that these mechanisms could then be used to evaluate the effectiveness of decentralisation. These seven mechanisms are:

1   the allocation of responsibilities for services between central and local-level governments, assessed using the principle of subsidiarity;
2   the decentralisation of financing arrangements;
3   the decentralisation of decision-making powers;
4   the management of the personnel of decentralised services, whether by central or by local entities;
5   the enforcement of local government accountability – often very difficult;
6   the involvement of other institutional actors outside the state in the delivery of services;
7   the extent of political competition that is allowed at the local level.

In taking the debate in this direction, it is suggested here that the exploration of decentralisation 'lost the plot', at this point, by shifting the focus away from decentralisation as a core development objective. I shall return to the implications of this later.

An academic analysis with an infrastructure focus

The first analysis was broad and conceptual, with a geographical focus. This is typical of a political sciences debate that generally sees decentralisation as a 'product-independent' concept. There are, of course, cases where researchers cross the boundary between social analysis and practical development, and a paper by Serageldin *et al.* (2000) that looks at 'decentralization and urban infrastructure management capacity' is one of them. It was prepared for UN-Habitat as a background paper for its third *Global Report on Human Settlements*.

Starting from the perspective that infrastructure plays a key role in achieving the core objectives underlying the decentralisation process[8] (a position that of itself dates the analysis to a previous era), the paper argues that

> [d]ecentralization entails fundamental changes to the structure of intergovernmental relationships, involving a shift away from vertical hierarchies to a differentiation of role and the reallocation of among actors operating in the same sector or territory. Political pressure, rather than economic considerations, is driving the pace and degree of devolution.
>
> (Serageldin *et al.*, 2000, p. 1)

From this hopeful beginning the paper then moves to the next section, which looks specifically at the decentralising of infrastructure services, where it makes the following observations:

> The reallocation of functions related to planning and management of infrastructure typically has been guided by the concept of subsidiarity: decisions regarding services should rest with the entity of government closest to the community that is able to deliver these services in a cost effective way while minimizing the externalization of environmental and social costs.
>
> Technological advancements in the infrastructure sector have improved the efficiency of providing services for smaller jurisdictions and market areas [i.e. market segments], thus allowing for a greater degree of decentralization than was possible a few decades ago. This has made it easier for local entities, including private[-sector] operators and NGOs, to participate in the delivery of infrastructure

services. They are now better equipped to respond to community needs, priorities for services, and preferences for technology and service standards, thus creating a more direct link between the incidence of benefits and costs....

The general approach to institutional management in decentralized institutional settings is to unbundle provision in terms of decision-making and management in accordance with the particular characteristics of each service and to allocate responsibilities accordingly.

(Serageldin *et al.*, 2000, p. 2)

Alas for unfulfilled expectations; for in this, the core message of the paper, we see much of the (Anglo-Saxon) thinking that shaped external approaches to urban infrastructure over the next decade. After this, the paper loses its focus and reverts to breadth rather than depth, a weakness embedded in its need to be global in its application. It does have a section dealing with challenges, where it looks at the need to strengthen local government and local initiatives (Serageldin *et al.*, 2000, p. 6), but its main focus is on the potential role of other players outside of government, with specific reference to the private sector and civil society or the community, the latter as both partner and manager. Here, then, can be seen the strengthening of the movement, within the United Nations generally, and UN-Habitat specifically, to shift the role of local development driver away from local government to the private sector and civil society, thereby contributing significantly to the demise of local government in the African development debate.

The demise of the western debate on decentralisation in Africa

There is of course much more material written in the West on decentralisation, both globally and specifically in Africa, coming from major institutions such as the government development agencies, the UNDP and the World Bank, as well as from different academics and research institutions. And there are different levels of intellectual analysis. Thus, the Swiss in particular have had an interest in this subject for many years, because it is the basis on which their own state was built; and a similar situation applies with the Germans. This third review explores some of the material emanating from the Swiss Development Corporation over the years.

When we look at the Swiss and German perspectives on decentralisation, we see how they draw upon the experience of their own country, which is valuable. In the end, though, they all tend to return the discussion to, and focus it around, the group of topics that were covered in the paper by Olowu discussed earlier. The only real difference is that while the Dutch analysis tends to be in the Anglo-Saxon mould – that is, simple, pragmatic and inclined towards the mechanistic – the German or Swiss approaches do tend to reflect a more European style: critical, rational and seeking to ground conceptual constructs in their own realities. In the end, though, neither attempts to situate decentralisation within an African development framework.

That said, there is a point, in the Swiss analysis in particular, where one of the authors, Marco Rossi, who was at the time head of the Policy and Research Section of the SDC, managed to home in on the core issue that is at the heart of this entire decentralisation process in Africa. His insight comes in the introduction to his paper, when he states the following:

> Out of 75 developing countries with more than 5 million inhabitants, we currently find 63 who are taking steps to decentralize. Decentralization is apparently in vogue and is considered by many countries as a highly promising method of solving their many problems and using available potential. In this connection two questions arise: First, is decentralization only a passing fad? And second, can the expectations which are put into all efforts towards achieving decentralization be fulfilled?
>
> Previous experiences with decentralization are just about as varied as its underlying concepts, and seen as a whole they cannot be deemed conclusive. While a whole string of nations (Uganda, Burkina Faso, India/Karnataka, Sri Lanka, Nepal, Bolivia, Honduras, etc.) register encouraging results, in other countries (Ghana, Ivory Coast, Bangladesh, Mozambique, Colombia, etc.) they appear to be less satisfactory. At this point I cannot go into detail on the exact reasons for any success or failure of decentralization in individual countries. *However, in addition to the already presented various decentralization concepts one would certainly have to examine each country's historical inheritance and its culturally determined value system, the government's political intentions, the socioeconomic and legal frameworks, as well as the application concepts which are considered critical for success or failure.* Different studies have shown that measuring the impact of decentralization programs is extremely difficult and that making generalizations can lead to misconceptions. Any past written attempts to assess these complex projects, including their progress and failure, tend to reveal partially divided opinions.
>
> (Rossi, undated; emphasis added)

The second paragraph in this quotation surely goes to the heart of the matter, and to the main conceptual issue of this book, which is control over Africa's intellectual space. When we look at this topic from a western point of view, and in particular the final two sentences in the quotation, we can see why the external analysis ended shortly after this paper was written. It demonstrates clearly that external analysis had gone as far as it could in exploring decentralisation in Africa, *without producing any definitive answers*. And in the section in italics we can see the importance of what Rossi is saying: to take this debate to a deeper level, the locus of the research and analysis would have to move in-country. That, of course, was not part of the western agenda; so at that point the external agencies, whose expectations demand that they are the dominant actor in African research, essentially repackaged decentralisation as part of a 'new' and more wide-ranging exploration of role and relationships, which they call governance. From an external research perspective this may be a reasonable course of action, provided only that we are willing to see research in Africa solely from a western perspective.

In the meantime, there is actually another reality out there (or there would be if it were given the intellectual space to evolve), which is an African reality. African governments have not finished exploring the issue of decentralisation; on the contrary, it is more of a central issue for them than ever before. The fact is that the external debate took this issue as far as it could go when driven from the outside. That was the point at which external actors should have supported the transfer of the locus of debate and exploration into the subcontinent, which is where it really matters. What should have happened then, in a situation where development aid is a partnership, is that they should have picked up on the critical insight indicated in the emphasised sentence of the quotation above, and recognised that the only way to carry this forward was through a transfer of the locus of research from the outside to the inside.

But they didn't, of course, because external agencies have no reason to think, or act, this way. Ultimately they have to face inwards themselves, which for them in their dealings with Africa means looking backwards over their shoulders to their own internal constituency; because that is where they exist, drawing on their own research institutions and their own knowledge base. This lost opportunity is simply one example among many of the failure of external support in Africa, and provides a classic illustration of how the West controls the intellectual space; how this control over intellectual space undermines Africa; and how it then prevents African countries from developing effectively.

From that point onwards, the external exploration of decentralisation was never really able to move forward and eventually petered out, to be replaced by a wider and more inclusive exploration of 'good governance'. The debate on decentralisation in western countries had finally died. The West had supported African countries in their attempts to decentralise, found them wanting after a decade of investing their money in the exercise, had little to show for their investment and decided the time had come to cut their losses and move on. From then on, good governance became the new mantra in the international and western bilateral development agencies.

Yet from an African perspective it is suggested that this debate on decentralisation is far from over; on the contrary, it remains a key development concept. But it has to be Africa's debate, so in the greater scheme of things it is perhaps fortuitous that the West has lost interest. The three sections that follow look at case studies of three elements of decentralisation – delegation, devolution and deconcentration – with the findings highlighting just how important it is to continue this debate in sub-Saharan Africa.

Delegation: exploring the boundaries through the South African experience

Introduction

This first case study looks at delegation as a form of decentralisation, using South Africa as a case study. Chapter 4 highlighted the extent to which urban infrastructure provided the basis for strong local government in the period when South Africa was a dominion, yet showed how easily the apartheid government was able to strip responsibility away from the cities when it chose to do so. This is the inherent weakness of that particular model (of delegation), as the British experience of local government reform after 1974 also demonstrated. In theory, the new South African Constitution of 1996 gave strong legal recognition to local government; and while it modified the previous decentralisation model, it did not change it completely. As a result, what remained was still a model situated broadly within the framework of delegated powers and duties. This section explores how that recognition impacted on local government, and in particular whether it succeeded in strengthening local government or whether the inherent weaknesses of the delegated powers model prevailed.

The powers and duties of local government

The Constitution of the Republic of South Africa (Republic of South Africa, 1996) is widely regarded as one of the most progressive national constitutions in the world. Chapter 7 of that constitution is devoted to the role of local government in society. It is that chapter, and its translation into practice, which is discussed here.

The local government model used in South Africa is derived from the British model of government, albeit adapted to fit into a three-tier structure. The previous chapter touched briefly upon the structure of local government in the apartheid era. With the election of the new African National Congress-led government in 1994, the urban areas were reintegrated, politically at least, and democratic local government introduced.

The most fundamental institutional changes, though, took place at the regional level, as the country sought to rationalise a fragmented geopolitical and spatial patchwork that was the outcome of apartheid. The powers and duties of regional government were clearly defined, and strengthened, as the new government sought to harness that power to integrate the apartheid city and begin to deliver services to the previously disenfranchised urban majority.

In this new, decentralised model, national government devolved powers to regional government, from which level certain powers were then passed down to local government (as described below). The new Constitution strengthened the powers of the lower tiers quite significantly, particularly the powers of the second tier, which in South Africa is termed provincial government, providing each province, for example, with its own constitution. This relationship between national and provincial government was then defined via two schedules of the Constitution. Schedule 4 set out 'Functional Areas of Concurrent National and Provincial Legislative Competence', while Schedule 5 set out 'Functional Areas of Exclusive Provincial Legislative Competence'.

Classifying powers and duties for local government in South Africa is quite complex, in that the system does not fit easily into the division between devolution and delegation, although it owed more to the latter; while the situation was further complicated by the creation of three distinct categories of municipality.[9] This specific discussion will limit itself to the so-called Category A municipalities, which have the greatest powers. A Category A municipality is defined as '[a] municipality that has exclusive municipal executive and legislative authority in its area' (Republic of South Africa, 1996, cl. 151.1).

Unfortunately, the Constitution did not provide the same clear legal definition to local government powers as it gave to provincial government. The powers and functions of municipal government were defined in clause 156, which stated the following:

1   A municipality has executive authority in respect of, and has the right to administer:

    a   the local government matters listed in Part B of Schedule 4 and Part B of Schedule 5; and
    b   any other matter assigned to it by national or provincial legislation.

2   A municipality may make and administer by-laws for the effective administration of the matters which it has the right to administer.
3   Subject to section 151(4), a by-law that conflicts with national or provincial legislation is invalid. If there is a conflict between a by-law and national or provincial legislation that is inoperative because of a

conflict referred to in section 149, the by-law must be regarded as valid for as long as that legislation is inoperative.

4   The national government and provincial governments must assign to a municipality, by agreement and subject to any conditions, the administration of a matter listed in Part A of Schedule 4 or Part A of Schedule 5 which necessarily relates to local government, if:

a   that matter would most effectively be administered locally; and
b   the municipality has the capacity to administer it.

5   A municipality has the right to exercise any power concerning a matter reasonably necessary for, or incidental to, the effective performance of its functions.

At the same time, though, clause 151.3 (Status of Municipalities) states that '[a] municipality has the right to govern, on its own initiative, the local government affairs of its community'; this is 'subject to national and provincial legislation, as provided for in the Constitution' (Republic of South Africa, 1996, cl. 151.1). It is clear from this clause that while a municipality may develop its own powers and duties in accordance with clause 156, these must be approved by provincial or national government, and the only real power devolved to local government is the power to administer. Every other power can be modified, adapted or even challenged, although the legal adjudication of such a challenge would need to take into account the perceived intent of clause 156 of the constitution. While this is a classic example of how the delegation of powers is enacted, it is nonetheless true to say that this local power was fairly extensive, at least in the beginning. This, then, was the situation in the large metropolitan centres, which had the human and financial resources required to manage the extensive range of powers and duties that were within their ambit; and they were able to retain these by formatting them internally prior to submission to provincial government.[10] Where the problem lay in retaining powers, duties and functions was in the smaller secondary towns, which had neither the political clout nor the financial strength to engage with provincial (and national) government in the same way.

Powers and duties in practice: the flaw in the constitutional model

An original, and unique, feature of the South African Constitution is that it situates local government within two spheres of activity, which it terms cooperative government and developmental government. The first is covered by clause 154 of the constitution and the second by clause 153. The first, cooperative government, deals with the relationship between different tiers of government and states that both national and local government 'must support and strengthen the capacity of municipalities to manage their own affairs, to exercise their powers and to perform their functions' (Republic of South Africa, 1996, cl. 154.1).

The second, developmental local government, which is dealt with in clause 153, states that

A municipality must:

a. structure and manage its administration, and budgeting and planning processes to give priority to the basic needs of the community, and to promote the social and economic development of the community; and
b. participate in national and provincial development programmes.

It is the interpretation of clause 153.b that opens the way to a change in the relationship between national and local government, and creates what is arguably the one really major weakness of the Constitution as it applies to local government. An objective of local government is 'to ensure the provision of services to communities in a sustainable manner' (Republic of South Africa, 1996, cl. 152.1(b)). At the same time, in the clause dealing with the establishment of municipalities, the constitution states that '[t]he national government, subject to section 44, and the provincial governments, have the legislative and executive authority to see to the effective performance by municipalities of their functions in respect of matters listed in Schedules 4 and 5, by regulating the exercise by municipalities of their executive authority referred to in section 156(1)' (Republic of South Africa, 1996, cl. 155.7).

What we see here is an attempt to create a constitution to provide the legal status in a system that continues to use delegation to pass powers, duties and functions to local government. The Constitution gives local government rights, but it does not say how those rights translate into legal guarantees for powers, duties and functions – and of course it doesn't; if it did, then they would become devolved powers, duties and functions, and no longer delegated ones. So, although this system is stronger than the British one, in seeking to give a more clearly defined role to local government within a legal framework, it does not address the weaknesses of the delegated powers model, which is open to reinterpretation by central government, as the next section will indicate. In this context it is useful to compare this with the French model of devolved powers, described on pp. 160–61, which demonstrates how meaningful decentralisation, using devolution of powers, duties and functions, has to provide a much clearer and stronger legal framework for local government than is possible under delegation.

Overloading local government: a case study of the water sector

South Africa has made a major commitment to providing water for all its citizens, and overall it is considered to have been successful, although this is still work in progress. The African National Congress (ANC) began to think about a policy of universal access by forming a water and sanitation task group in the period preceding the first democratic elections in 1994, which meant that it was able to move rapidly in providing a strategy once elected. Since then, it has produced a range of policy and strategy documents:

- the Water Supply and Sanitation Policy White Paper (November 1994), DWAF;[11]
- a White Paper on a National Water Policy for South Africa (April 1997), DWAF;
- the Water Services Act 108 of 1997;
- the National Water Act 36 of 1998;
- Norms and Standards in Respect of Tariffs for Water Services (20 July 2001);
- a Draft White Paper on Water Services (October 2002), DWAF;
- a Free Basic Water Implementation Strategy (August 2002) DWAF;
- a Strategic Framework for Water Services: Water Is Life, Sanitation Is Dignity (September 2003), DWAF;
- the National Water Services Regulation Strategy Penultimate Draft (April 2008), DWAF.

These documents are then complemented by further Acts, policies and strategies that apply to the operation of local government.

This case study will use the Strategic Framework document of 2003 to illustrate how this impacts on, and defines the role of, local government. This document opens its preface by stating that

> [t]his Strategic Framework sets out a comprehensive approach with respect to the provision of water services in South Africa, ranging from small community water supply and sanitation schemes in remote rural areas to large regional schemes supplying water and wastewater services to people and industries in our largest urban areas.
>
> (Republic of South Africa, 2003, p. 2)

The Strategic Framework situates itself within the constitutional framework of local government, stating explicitly that '[l]ocal government is responsible for ensuring water services provision' (Republic of South Africa, 2003, p. 10). While this is true, it is actually an indirect responsibility, in that water service provision is actually the responsibility of the water services authority (WSA), and the Strategic Framework defines a WSA as 'any municipality that has the executive authority to provide water services within its area of jurisdiction in terms of the Municipal Structures Act 118 of 1998 or the ministerial authorisations made in terms of this Act' (Republic of South Africa, 2003, p. 11).

This is not merely semantics; the distinction is actually extremely important when viewed from a governance perspective. Within this definition, the relationship is no longer one of cooperative government, between central government (the DWAF) and local government. It is now a relationship between the DWAF and a water services authority. In spite of what the Strategic Framework, and other Acts and White Papers, may say about the freedom of local government, central government has instructed local government how it will structure the provision of water. And going further, not only does central government state that '[t]he primary responsibility for ensuring the provision of water services rests with water services authorities', but it also states that

[m]ore specifically, water services authorities have the following roles and responsibilities:

- **Ensuring access.** They must ensure the realisation of the right of access to water services, particularly basic water services (the first step up the ladder) subject to available resources by seeing that appropriate investments in water services infrastructure are made.
- **Planning.** They must prepare water services development plans to ensure effective, efficient, affordable, economical and sustainable access to water services that promote sustainable livelihoods and economic development (stepping up the ladder).
- **Regulation.** They must regulate water services provision and water services providers within their areas of jurisdiction and within the policy and regulatory frameworks set by DWAF through the enactment of by-laws and the regulation of contracts.
- **Provision.** They must ensure the provision of effective, efficient and sustainable water services (including water conservation and demand management).

Finally, the central government has designated itself (through the DWAF) as the national water services regulator for WSAs, and has produced a National Water Services Regulation Strategy to enforce this relationship. The overall result of these legislative changes is that the municipality has lost its autonomy as an urban local government authority and has become the implementation arm of central government for urban water supply. Quantitative delivery drives the process at the expense of effective management, turning infrastructure into a political tool that is used by central government to strengthen its own constituency at the expense of local accountability and local democracy.

It is possible to dispute this interpretation, of course, by pointing to sections of the report that emphasise the cooperative nature of government and the ongoing relationship between national, provincial and regional governments, but that is not incompatible with what has been stated here; it all depends upon the perspective from which cooperative government is viewed. The reality is clearly stated through the definition of the core objective of this document, provided in the final section of the strategic framework. There the document sets out the five key challenges that inform the support framework. And the first of these is 'establishing and/or developing effective water services institutions'; it is not building effective and sustainable local government.

Outcomes: local government as implementation agency

In 2008, three institutions, each concerned with the extent to which the legal right to water was working in South Africa, came together to carry out an assessment of fifteen municipalities in South Africa and produced a report entitled *Water Services Fault Lines* (COHRE, 2008a). The study analysed, and evaluated, the situation regarding water supply and sanitation in these fifteen municipalities, of varying sizes, and across a socio-economic and geographic spectrum of the country. One of the features that comes across most strongly, particularly in reading the interviews, is *the extent to which those managing the service see themselves as implementing national government policy.* And this is the perceived view of the authors of this report, to the extent that the so-called fault lines – that is, 'the cross-cutting themes that emerged from the interviews and research' (ibid., p. 25) take this role for granted. In fact, their conclusion is that the government should become even more deeply involved in 'micro-managing' delivery, with 'much greater involvement, support and oversight from national government' (ibid., p. 72), as well as much greater regulation. This simply reinforces the point, demonstrated repeatedly throughout this book, that the impact of external (and in South Africa's case even some internal) sector specialists is to remove power from local government, thereby weakening it, and in doing so to effect a recentralising of power back to national government.

The second feature of the study, which is perhaps predictable, given the withdrawal of meaningful powers, duties and functions from small local authorities, relates to the lack of local government capacity. Here the study found that

> [m]ost of the municipalities interviewed expressed the desire to increase their staff capacity, both in terms of numbers and skills. They

are concerned that their failure to attract skilled graduates – especially engineers and technicians, who are vital for the construction, maintenance and repair of water services infrastructure, as well as the treatment and testing of water quality – seriously threatens current and future service delivery.

(COHRE, 2008a, p. 59)

In seeking a solution to deal with this outcome, the study argues that 'if water services are to be prioritised as they should be, additional funding from national government must be made available to ensure the necessary financial, technical and human resources reach the municipal level, where water services delivery occurs' (COHRE, 2008a, p. 61). This begs the question – what are the additional resources to be used for? Are they simply to make local government a more effective delivery agent for central government in this specific sector, or are they to build local government capacity for long-term sustainability? The implication here is clearly that it is the former.

Drawing conclusions from the case study

When viewed from an end-user perspective, and measured by the government's policy commitment, the finding that all that is required to meet delivery targets is more resources and more commitment has logic and validity. In practice it is neither realistic nor achievable, because it fails to address the central question of who will do the work. Here the figures for engineers working in local government tell their own story: local government employed 40 per cent of all civil engineers in South Africa in 1980, but that ratio had fallen to 15 per cent by 2010, with the losses indicated in a report which showed that

[l]ocal government has been particularly hard hit ...
    A census of all local and district municipalities and metros yielded the following statistics:

- Only 45 of the 231 local municipalities have any civil engineers
- Only 25 of the 47 district municipalities have any civil engineers
- Only one civil technician [per municipality]
- Of the 231 local municipalities 42 have only one civil technician
- Of the 47 district municipalities 4 have only one civil technician
- The vacancies that were identified mean *at least 800 to 1200 more civil engineers, technologists and technicians are required in local government alone.*

(Lawless, 2005)[12]

One interesting point to emerge from this study, which was raised by representatives from many of the case-study municipalities, was that of political will. What local government officials are saying here, first and foremost, is that the cause of the problem lies at the centre, and they then attribute the weakness of local government to a failure of political will at the centre. In reality, while this is the perception, it does not have to be the truth. On the contrary, I suggest that the perception is actually defining a symptom, not a cause. The real issue is a structural failure embedded in the delivery-driven model of development. National ministers are faced with a dilemma, which is that meeting targets is an urgent, short-term priority that can only be achieved by pulling local government resources away from management and into delivery to ensure that short-term targets can be met. Building local government capacity is a medium- to long-term process that competes for these limited resources. It is therefore quite clearly self-evident that there are inherent contradictions between these two goals, and that these are fundamentally incompatible.

Ultimately, this contradiction is grounded in the dualistic perceptions of urban infrastructure. The role of local government as an implementing agent of national government is linked directly to the perception that urban infrastructure is a support service. The role of local government as a driver of change is linked to the perception that urban infrastructure has a more central role to play in local government, though it may be going too far to say that it is recognised in this context as a development driver. Over the period since the first democratic elections in 1994, the South African government has moved increasingly to supporting the first interpretation of infrastructure: as a support service. It then seeks to balance this by using planning as its development driver, which it does through the use of integrated development planning (IDP), whereby local government is a driver of spatial (and anticipated social) change. So once again we return to this dichotomy around the role of infrastructure. And since national government does not know how to deal with the contradiction, it is perceived from the local government perspective as lacking political will, whereas in reality it is simply trapped in a conundrum of its own making. In fairness, though, the primary reason why this conundrum exists is due, in large measure, to the use of a delegated model of decentralisation.

It is widely recognised, and fully acknowledged here, that South Africa has one of the most progressive legislative and policy frameworks for water services anywhere in the world, a view supported by the study quoted earlier (COHRE, 2008a, p. 8). Together with Ethiopia, to be discussed in the next chapter, South Africa has a commitment to social equity, and is willing to specify this as a principle underpinning its various urban infrastructure policies, including its water policy; while sustainability is a second principle that underpins all of its (now diverse) infrastructure policies. Seeking to follow these principles through into practice, however, is a different matter. The central issue was clearly identified in the COHRE study, in terms that were clear and unambiguous, with its finding that 'at the municipal level it is cost-recovery, rather than social or developmental benefit, that largely determines water services delivery' (ibid., p. 2).

At the same time, sustainability is also in under threat in the move from policy to implementation. Delivery systems are not sustainable if local government collapses or the technical expertise is no longer available. Thus, the point that emerges most clearly from this study is that there is a strong symbiotic relationship between local government and urban infrastructure, particularly in the smaller towns; and this relationship is only poorly understood. To provide a political and institutional framework that will allow for a better understanding, though, we first need to resolve the issue of how we achieve effective and meaningful decentralisation. The next section looks at the potential of a devolved model to achieve this.

Devolution in a unitary state: the French experience

If delegation represents a weak form of decentralisation, the alternative – political devolution – is clearly a very strong form. The question is, though: is it practical? Political devolution is undoubtedly simpler to achieve in a government with a federal structure, as will be discussed in the next chapter using Ethiopia as a case study. This section focuses on the more challenging context of a unitary state, where the structuring of the relationship between different tiers of government is more complex. Here the French experiment with devolution, which took place after 1990,[13] provides a useful insight into what is required of a unitary state, both conceptually and legally, if it is serious about devolving power to local government.

As Britain was moving from having the most decentralised system of powers, duties and functions in the world to becoming the most centralised state in Europe, France was moving in the opposite direction. The Revolution of 1787, while creating two levels of what the French call local government[14] (the *département* and the *commune*), nonetheless retained power at the centre. The system that was created by the new republic was thus administrative decentralisation rather than political decentralisation. This situation began to change, however, during the global transition of the late 1980s and early 1990s, as the country sought to implement a process of real political decentralisation.

To achieve this, the French used a system of devolution to decentralise powers, duties and functions downwards. This system, which is as valid in a unitary as it is in a federal system, requires that the powers, duties and functions of local government are protected by legal statute. The French system identifies three attributes that attach to lower tiers of government and defined their status. These are that local government has a legal persona, a clearly defined and articulated set of competencies, and a freedom of responsibility for administration. These in turn are underpinned by four key principles:

1   the principle of free administration of local government;
2   the principle of no oversight of one local government over another;[15]
3   the principle of financial autonomy for local government:
4   the principle of central government supervision after the fact.

The issue of what exactly constitutes adequate financial autonomy is difficult to define. In France the imbalance in financial resources between central and local government gives the central government immense political leverage through its greater resource base, particularly in the use of spending for capital investment. By contrast, in Sweden, for example, there is a very high level of financial autonomy arising from a legal requirement to apportion the national budget in predefined percentages across the different tiers of government.

There are two further issues of importance concerning the French system. The first is that the Mayor, while elected locally, is also the local representative of the President of France. At the intermediate level of government (the *région* and the *département*) there is both an elected person at the head of government as well as a person, the Prefect, appointed by the President of the Republic.

The second pertains to the way in which both national and regional spatial planning impact upon the political freedom of local government. Because of the definition, principles and legal basis of local government, planning systems cannot be imposed. At the same time, it is clearly necessary to an integrated planning system that the local level is embedded in, and integrates with, the higher-level spatial plans. This state of affairs is achieved by using a contractual arrangement that situates the one within the other. *Communes* in the large urban centres form *metropoles*, while in other regions *communes* are encouraged to group together to form conurbations. Both of these can then enter into a contract with central government to obtain funding for capital investment and local 'sub-regional' planning developments.

This brief analysis of France would tend to support the view that strong local government is much easier to achieve with a devolved model of decentralisation. This is, of course, a European example. The way that something similar might function in an African context will be explored more fully in the next two chapters, which will discuss decentralised local government in Ethiopia.

Deconcentration: integrating regional and local development

The next component of decentralisation is deconcentration. Both Britain and France are quick to provide 'solutions', as well as experts, to 'assist' Africa in issues of decentralisation and good governance. Yet how do they deal with these complex issues at home? It is useful to look backwards sometimes and see that they do not have any magic solutions in their own countries; on the contrary, they too struggle, both conceptually and practically, with the same complex issues, often with just as much difficulty as do African countries; and they too have their own failures along the way.

Figures 2.1 and 2.2 in Chapter 2 illustrated responses to the global transition phase of international development, which took place in the 1980s and 90s. Over this period, western countries were creating new models of government and new forms of relationship. In contrast, the debate in Africa was still focusing on finding solutions to address the weaknesses of the earlier pre-transitional development era. One important outcome was that the decentralisation debate came to an end just at the point when the impact of regional economic planning was making decentralisation a great deal more complex than it had been previously. In its *State of African Cities* report (UN-Habitat, 2008), UN-Habitat places a major emphasis on regional development and in particular urban growth corridors across all regions in Africa, to the extent of arguing that 'African governments and city managers need to act upon these new realities and view urbanization processes in regional rather than local contexts' (UN-Habitat, 2008, p. 9). It also argues that 'African governments are advised to take more proactive, strategic positions in promoting the role of African cities in the globalized economy' (ibid.). This book has highlighted several times the contradiction in this and other UN-Habitat reports on Africa: between a stated recognition that 75 per cent of Africa's urban population live in secondary towns and the overwhelming emphasis on the major conurbations to define the analytical framework for UN-Habitat's development guidelines. This contradiction distorts many aspects of the debate on African urban development, including the decentralisation debate.

If we focus on the needs of secondary towns, then the distinction between different facets of decentralisation, in particular the balance between devolution and deconcentration, becomes crucial, while even with the larger cities and regional agglomerations the relationship is far more complex than is either evident or acknowledged in this UN-Habitat report. This complexity is also evident if we look at how regional development planning has evolved in France and in England, where we can see much more clearly the impact that the creation of a regional planning framework has on different tiers of government.

France adopted regional development conceptually far earlier than most other countries in the West, beginning this process as far back as the early twentieth century. It was also the major political driving force in creating wider European development strategy. Britain, on the other hand, came late to regional development, and its own process was linked more directly to the global transition of the 1990s. And although it drew on French experience, the way in which the two countries saw the focus of regional development was quite different. Thus, the approach taken by Britain placed the priority focus on economic development, which is directed towards wealth and employment generation. In contrast, that of France is towards more comprehensive 'national spatial planning objectives'. What we see in the UN-Habitat report is the dominating influence of the British concept of regional development; yet this model, as practised in Britain itself, is one of the weakest in its political decentralisation process.

Attempting to write about the planning process in Britain is always difficult, since it is forever in a state of flux, and has been since local government was reformed in 1974. In theory, local government is responsible for local planning while central government has provided what it termed policy statements to 'guide' implementation. Under this system, central government's direct action (until 2010) was limited to ensuring that regional plans were integrated across their boundaries to ensure that they provided linkage and cohesion at the national level. While this may sound fairly innocuous, and even beneficial, with the extensive use of the term 'guidance', it was in practice strongly prescriptive and regulatory. Ironically, this reality was recognised by the incoming Conservative–Liberal Democrat government that came to power following an inconclusive election in May 2010, which in 2011 proceeded to dismantle the entire tier of English regional government.

Immediately prior to that point, local planning processes were 'guided' by a series of 'Planning Policy Statements' (PPS), which had been gradually replacing the previous system of Planning Policy Guidance Notes, with control over the decision-making process being exercised by regional Government Offices (GOs). These GOs were not directly elected; instead, they represented central government in the regions; that is, they were a part of central government and coordinated the activities of the twelve central government departments that had some involvement in local affairs. In this role they constituted 'the primary means by which a wide range of government policies and programmes are delivered in the English regions' (National Archives, 2011c), and as such had a strong influence in ensuring that local plans reflected central government policies and relevant regional strategies.

The system was replaced in 2011 by a new Localism Bill (HM Government, 2010–11) intended to replace deconcentration by a process of decentralisation (HM Government, 2010). Yet in making this change, the British government did not address the need for deconcentration, but instead retreated back to a system of centralised control. The guide presented by the government (ibid.) argues that such is not the intent. However, this argument fails to address the fundamental nature of delegated authority that was discussed in previous chapters, and which remains the legal framework for this legislation. For the reality remains that the relevant government minister (the Communities Secretary) remains all-powerful and ultimately responsible, not only at the level of policy but also at the level of detail.

The outcome represents a further weakening of elected local government in favour of the nebulous term 'community', which is represented by a myriad of local actors. As one critic argued,

> There is a desperate attempt [by the Bill] to delineate what a community is, in the form of wards, parishes and electoral districts. Within these vague boundaries are said to be a multitude of bodies not elected but 'relevant' to the coalition's values: voluntary bodies, community bodies, charities, parishes, 'two or more employees' of a local authority, and 'some other person as might be specified by the secretary of state'.
>
> (Jenkins, 2010)

The critique then goes on to point out that

> [o]f these bodies, only parish councillors are elected. Yet any or all will be free to draw up lists of buildings, including private ones, of community value and demand to take them into community ownership [with the result that]..[t]here is little in the bill to empower democratic localism and much that disempowers it.
>
> (ibid.)

What, then, can African governments learn from this? First, it is quite true, and has to be recognised, that regionalisation (whether within or across national boundaries) is a global phenomenon that will have a major influence on a country's decentralisation strategy. The question is how best to address this phenomenon. Both the British and the French created a fourth tier of government at regional level, the 'regions' in England and the '*régions*' in France. What is interesting in this geopolitical construct, though, is the way in which both initially sought political legitimacy for this fourth tier through referenda. In both cases, however, their citizens rejected the concept: the French in 1969, when the failure led to the fall of the de Gaulle government; the British in 2004 in a pilot referendum in the North-East region. Yet in spite of these defeats, both countries retained this fourth tier. France strengthened the powers of the *régions* during the transition phase, this time by legislation. However, it remains a tier of government little understood by the population as a whole, resulting in very low voter turnout in elections for regional government politicians.

Britain took a different view and constituted regional government by stealth, creating a wide variety of institutions at this level,[16] virtually all of which were lacking in both legitimacy and transparency. The British coalition government of 2010 then decommissioned a number of these, such as the Regional Development Agencies, as well as dismantling the entire tier of regional government offices which has provided for deconcentration of central government at a regional level; and it did so without any form of policy debate. Fortunately for Britain, though, that country is not exposed to the same degree of external analysis as are African countries, and as a result it is able to avoid the level of negative criticism to which African governments are subjected when they create a poor governance model!

A second lesson, which is more directly applicable, is that regionalisation requires a rethink on the nature of the various 'labels' attached to the decentralisation process (e.g. delegation, deconcentration). Simply transferring British ideological constructs about the nature of regional economic development, as UN-Habitat does, will not provide a solution. The real lesson here is that when regional development is introduced into the mélange of multi-tier government, it requires a judicious mix of decentralisation strategies that incorporate both devolution and deconcentration. Taking this further, while deconcentration is accepted as an integral part of a decentralisation strategy, it requires particularly careful analysis if it is to complement, rather than replace, devolution of powers and duties to local government.

Following on from this, the third lesson is that, while regional development clearly has an impact on what happens at a local level, and has to be accommodated, it does not automatically imply a loss of decision-making powers and duties within local government itself. To a large extent the form of government, and the degree of autonomy, at the level of urban local government can continue to be developed using a high degree of decentralised autonomy. However, there needs to be much more thought given to exactly what areas of responsibility are decentralised to what level. Central to this question is a need to move away from the principle of subsidiarity as the basis on which a decision is made regarding the nature and extent of powers to be devolved, and to move across to a decision-making process that is much more strategic in its formulation. This approach will be explored in the chapters on Ethiopia that follow, while a proposal for the secondary cities will be developed in Chapter 11, which is concerned with urban good governance.

Deregulation: the impact of policy on decentralisation

The fourth element of decentralisation is deregulation. Unlike the traditional approach used by external development agencies, which tend to discuss deregulation solely in terms of public–private-sector partnerships, the approach this book takes is to argue that it cannot be separated from the other elements of decentralisation. It is recognised and accepted here that both the private sector and community organisations have an important role to play in local development. However, it is necessary to go beyond simply an exploration of dualities, such as public–private, or public–community, partnerships, and rather to situate these within a wider framework of relationships, since both impact on this wider arena.

This becomes particularly important under conditions where western policies define the direction of development, whether they do so through privatisation, community management or simply delivery-driven development. There is only one way in which we can view this issue of deregulation in a less value-laden context, and that is to move higher up the development ladder to look at the way in which policy formulation impacts on roles and relationships.

The importance of policy for urban infrastructure

The freedom to set, and implement, policy is one of the defining attributes of the nation-state, and consequently it is an important indicator of a country's independence and national sovereignty. Policy provides the framework for future action as well as providing a country with an appropriate and effective development direction – and infrastructure policy is a critical component of that wider policy framework. In parallel, the nature of international politics, with its constant jostling for power and influence, means that the policy arena provides a logical entry point for external countries, and other agencies, wishing to extend their influence over states that may not have the level of knowledge and expertise needed to create independent policy positions, as is often the case in sub-Saharan Africa. In this context, deregulation cannot be separated from a wider discussion of policy formulation.

The basis for policy formulation in most of anglophone Africa has emerged from a specifically British approach, which then raises the question of whether this is in practice the most appropriate for rapidly growing countries. This question is particularly relevant in the case of infrastructure policy, since Africa's current urban condition is closely linked to the adoption of flawed British infrastructure and urban planning models of development. To understand how this specific approach to policy impacts on urban development in Africa, this section looks at exactly how the use of a predefined policy construct, which is based almost entirely on the British approach to infrastructure policy, impacts upon, and limits the freedom of, individual governments in sub-Saharan Africa, particularly with regard to the constraints it places on their ability to decentralise effectively.

The nature of public policy

An Australian review[17] in the early 2000s sought to answer the question 'What is policy?' Defeated in its efforts, the review retreated into a statement from a book entitled *Public Policy in Australia*, which concluded that 'the debate about definitions of policy is largely a futile exercise' (Davis *et al.*, 1993). Fortunately, the discussion here is concerned specifically with that area of policy referred to as public policy, i.e. policy formulated by government, which does create a little space for a more positive outlook on life. None the less, it remains true that '[while] the concept becomes slightly less abstract when the focus is narrowed to the area of public policy … even there the definition is not totally clear and there is no simple answer to the question of what is policy' (Torjman, 2005).

What does this tell us? It is not so much that the nature of policy per se cannot be defined; rather, it is that policy can only situated within a specific worldview (*Weltanschauung*). This is because the way in which we see policy is inextricably linked to the way in which we see the world. In the Canadian view, for example, where there is a mixed French–English cultural heritage, there is a *Weltanschauung* that is influenced by, yet ultimately distinct from, both of these 'parent' cultures. In that culturally mixed marriage, public policy 'seeks to achieve a desired goal that is considered to be in the best interests of all members of society' (Torjman, 2005, p. 3), and thus 'a public policy is a deliberate and (usually) careful decision that provides guidance for addressing selected public concerns' (ibid.). The word 'guidance' is particularly relevant here.

The Anglo-Saxon perception is somewhat different. There the broad definition of policy is 'a deliberate plan of action to guide decisions and achieve rational outcome(s)' (Wikipedia, 2010b), and the various attempts to define public policy follow a similar view, the only difference being that it is government that is making the decision. The British view of policy differs from most continental European views in the way that the former sees little difference between the view of the role of public policy and the view of policy in the wider domain. As a result, this convergence of public policy with more general policy becomes one of the defining elements of the British approach. A second issue then emerges from a common thread that runs through almost all Anglo-Saxon definitions of policy, namely the idea that policy should incorporate, and clearly define, some form of direct action. Thus, we saw, in the earlier definition, that while a plan might 'guide', that same plan is nonetheless 'deliberate'. We see the same thing in British planning policy, described briefly earlier. There again the documents themselves may be termed 'guidelines' but they leave very little individual freedom of scope in their implementation. This is extremely important because, as we will see later, it is this specific action-orientated interpretation of policy that is used by almost all external agencies, NGOs and academics to critique, and judge the efficacy of, African development policy.

If we accept this view that there is no universally accepted definition of policy, then this implies that there is no single 'correct' approach to policy formulation. This in turn means that all policy formulation is situated within a value-based *Weltanschauung*. If that is the case, then surely the implication has to be that African countries should be free to structure policy according to their own perceptions of need – their own *Weltanschauungen*. Such an outcome has radical implications. For when external actors discuss African urban infrastructure policy, for example,[18] or any sectoral policy associated with infrastructure (e.g. sanitation), then two questions immediately arise: on what basis are they judging a country's policy? And how is this linked to their own, specific *Weltanschauung*, their own value system, their own interpretation of what constitutes development or even their own interpretation of what constitutes policy?

Exploring the implications of the Anglo-Saxon interpretation of policy

Public policy, whatever its specific interpretation, is concerned with setting a direction within a specific activity area or sector and then describing how that direction can, or should, be turned into specific actions. Converting this role into practice allows for many different interpretations, which can be explored by creating a continuum embracing the different components, or constructs, as illustrated in Figure 5.1. This continuum needs to take into account the fact that individual constructs at any point on the continuum may contain a mix of both the abstract (conceptual) and the practical.

On one side of this continuum there is the reason for the policy, which could be the expression of a purpose, for example, where the main emphasis is placed upon developing goals and objectives, as well as formulating potential constructs. Abstract or conceptual models also lie at this end of the continuum. From there the continuum moves through more

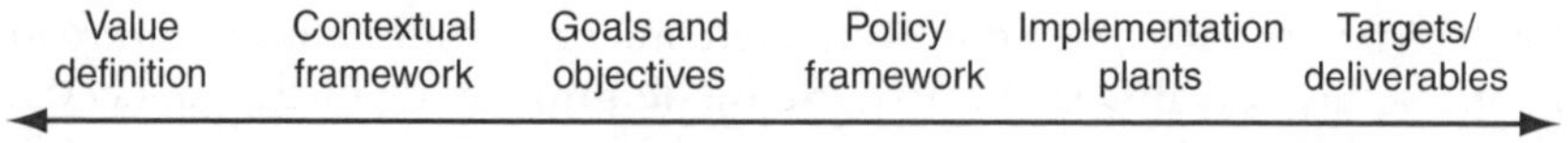

Value definition	Contextual framework	Goals and objectives	Policy framework	Implementation plants	Targets/ deliverables

Figure 5.1 A continuum from values to outcomes.

specific practical objectives, which then follow on through an implementation strategy into specific actions. There is then the complication, with public policy specifically, that the policy needs to be situated within the institutional and legal framework of government. The question then becomes where, on this continuum, does 'policy' begin and where does it end?

The French approach to policy formulation, which is quite distinct from the Anglo-Saxon approach, will generally incorporate either abstract or conceptual models that describe the boundaries of the policy in some way; that is, it will situate the discourse towards the left-hand side of the continuum. Its reason for doing so is linked to the French use of the *problématique* as an analytical tool. The same is equally true of the Ethiopian analysis, which will be discussed in the two chapters that follow. The Anglo-Saxon approach, on the other hand, tends to be strongly action orientated, which means that once the overall goal has been stated, the primary focus of the discourse immediately transfers to a point quite far down the continuum to the right. This focus is characterised by what could be described as the classical Anglo-Saxon view, which defines policy primarily as a product or object, an approach that explains, at least to some degree, why discussions of policy in Britain often use the terms 'policy' and 'strategy' almost interchangeably.

The case study that follows uses the example of the United Kingdom specifically to explore the Anglo-Saxon policy approach. The United Kingdom has been used for two reasons. First, that country, among all those that adopt this Anglo-Saxon approach, takes outcomes-based policy to its most extreme limits of interpretation. Second, that country retains an influential role in anglophone Africa, in terms both of the colonial heritage and of its current position, so that it is often this British policy approach that is used as the benchmark against which African policy is compared. In using this example it is not the intent to make judgemental statements about the British approach to policy as it applies in Britain; that is an internal matter. What this analysis does seek to do is challenge the idea that any specific approach to policy formulation, which has been derived within one country in the context of its own internal *Weltanschauung*, can be exported to other countries as a generic approach.

The failings of an action-orientated policy construct

The case study used to explore this 'action-orientated' policy is energy. Though related to national, rather than urban, infrastructure, it nonetheless provides a valuable insight into an action-orientated infrastructure policy process.

Energy policy in the United Kingdom, like that of all countries within the European Union, is situated within the wider European Energy Policy, produced in 2007 (Commission of the European Communities, 2007). This was a comprehensive policy document that provided a policy framework for member states, within which each state would then develop its own specific policy. In 2009 the British government produced a Renewable Energy Strategy, which committed the government to generating 15 per cent of its energy needs from renewable energy by 2020, the bulk of which (over two-thirds) would be derived from wind energy.

Although (correctly) named a strategy, this document is regularly referred to as a policy, not only by the press but by a range of commentators who might be expected to better understand the distinction – a group that ranges from energy professionals (Newman, 2009), through NGOs and politicians, to business leaders (CBI, 2009). This is the first point, then: that the British approach to policy often confuses policy with strategy, particularly when discussing infrastructure – and this confusion is widespread, extending beyond the energy debate to other important sectors such as water and transport.

Returning to the energy debate, we can start the discussion in August 2009, when Britain set out its strategy for renewable energy. Shortly thereafter the financial magazine *The Economist* noticed that a number of key players in the energy sector were reporting that Britain would face an energy shortfall within four to seven years (*The Economist*, 10 January 2009, p. 79). The article, which was illustrated by a diagram of supply versus demand produced by one of the major energy suppliers in the country, E.ON., generated widespread discussion, with the story being picked up by a number of newspaper articles,[19] even though it had already been confirmed by the head of the National Grid in a newspaper interview the previous year (*The Times*, 2008).

This story tells us a lot about how the British approach to infrastructure policy works, or, perhaps more correctly, does not work. On the one hand there is a statement of intent, which then moves on to the detail of delivery mechanisms. At the same time, there is a recognition among many actors (almost exclusively outside of the government) that the country is lacking, yet has a real need for, meaningful policies in infrastructure delivery, with the term 'policy' being used here to mean a high-level, overarching policy construct, *not* a target-based action plan. In other words, there is a major gap, and an absence of a meaningful discourse, to the left-hand side of the continuum in Figure 5.1. Ironically, this need for a more substantial policy discourse is recognised by the private sector to a greater extent than it is recognised by the government itself. Thus, in an interview with a daily newspaper the head of one of the country's major energy providers neatly summed up the British approach when he described the government's overarching energy policy as too 'event-driven' and lacking a real strategic vision (*Guardian*, 2009). He then went on to say:

There is a need to take [Britain's] energy policy from what I describe as a series of sticking plasters, to a more holistic view with a roadmap of how to get to 2050. Merely setting targets and hoping they are going to be achieved isn't a very clever way to set policy.

(ibid.)

The linkage between policy and privatisation

This discussion leads naturally into the second aspect of policy formulation in Britain, which relates policy to the role of the private sector in society. When a government makes privatisation its overarching development policy, as is the case here, it becomes trapped in a 'catch-22' situation. In the case of energy 'policy', for example, this meant that it was left to the Energy Regulator, Ofgem,[20] to carry out the scenario planning in support of policy formulation,[21] an activity that would normally be an important internal government responsibility. But in the end a Regulator, no matter how powerful, cannot either prescribe or create a policy. The resulting situation was neatly summed up by Dieter Helm, Professor of Energy Policy at the University of Oxford, when he made the following comments in a newspaper interview:

> Britain faces two urgent energy problems. First, we have simply not invested enough in infrastructure to meet future demand for heat and power. There is a yawning capacity gap that, in the next decade, will force prices up for consumers and industry. The second problem is how to mitigate climate change by cutting carbon emissions. The two problems will need more than £200 billion to fix in the next decade ...
>
> Instead of a coherent, integrated policy, we have piecemeal support for particular technologies. Politicians want to be seen to be 'doing something' for the various interested parties — especially for renewables and clean coal. So each gets its own set of supports.
>
> There is a better way. Good energy policy is not rocket science. Instead of the piecemeal approach, coherence and integration are needed...
>
> The bad news comes if we carry on as we are. Present energy policy will be very expensive, especially later in the next decade. As capacity margins tighten, long before the lights go out, prices will rise. Higher prices are the real consequence of inadequate investment.
>
> Britain now needs an energy policy – before, not after, a crisis.
>
> (Timesonline, 2009)

And this is the approach to policy formulation that the major external agencies and donor countries seek to impose on Africa through the use of their aid programmes!

This lack of a coherent approach to policy relates to all the major physical infrastructure services in Britain, and presents the government there with a serious conundrum; for how does a government set policy when it has sold all responsibility for infrastructure, including the entire asset base, to the private sector? By 2010 the British government found itself caught in the policy vacuum, reaping what it had sown in 1987 when, in its rush to transfer assets and operational control to the private sector, it made the privatisation of infrastructure a guiding policy principle. The issue here is not an ideological one, about whether the private sector should be involved in managing infrastructure, or to what extent. Rather, it is simply to point out that this outcome is the result of a flawed understanding of what constitutes infrastructure policy. By making privatisation of infrastructure the primary policy, every action taken thereafter that relates to the infrastructure base is, and has to be, almost by definition, a strategy; and that cannot be right. The situation has to be reversed; and the main lesson that African governments can learn from this mistake is that *if a government is to retain control over its own development, then privatisation of infrastructure cannot be a policy. Instead, privatisation has to be recognised for what it really is: a development strategy.* This is the point at which unintended consequences arise. In this case the use of deregulation as a policy in its own right at best hinders, and at worst prevents, the formation of effective decentralisation strategies.

Policy and decentralisation: the right of a country to define its own policy framework

The dominant focus on output and targets that lies at the heart of external approaches to African development provides the external agencies with immense leverage over African governments, leverage that extends beyond external governments and international development agencies to include external NGOs and academics. The South African case study quoted a study by the western legal NGO COHRE, which also carried out a review on Ghana entitled *A Rights-Based Review of the Legal and Policy Framework of the Ghanaian Water and Sanitation Sector* (COHRE, 2008b). There are both benefits and damaging impacts involved with this type of review. On the one hand, COHRE works in partnership with local NGOs, generally to support challenges raised by those internal NGOs. This approach strengthens civil society in a country, to its long-term benefit. And because the organisation is working within the legal framework of the country concerned, the result is greater objectivity; in this way, it provides an important critique of the current approach to policy formulation.

On the other hand, this legalistic approach also has serious flaws. The use of an external critique is most beneficial when it can be integrated with an internal exploration of indigenous solutions. When the solutions are externally derived, then the external critique simply serves to reinforce external control over the intellectual space. The second flaw lies in the way that findings are interpreted – in this case a legally based analysis that is narrowly focused and mechanistic. Thus, one of its conclusions here was that

> [t]he [legislative and policy] framework [for water and sanitation] does not have a target for universal access to water and sanitation and there is no specific time-bound schedule to achieve equity in access to water supply for peri-urban and urban poor.
>
> (COHRE, 2008b, p. 15)

From an external perspective this may appear to be a reasonable statement, particularly when the situation is viewed from within countries that are fortunate enough to have universal access. If we look back at history, though, it is worth recognising that none of the western countries ever provided this type of detail when they were building their own infrastructure.

This is not because a country does not wish to; but because it is an almost impossible task. Defining goals for delivery and setting up mechanisms to monitor progress is one thing; imposing legally binding targets within timelines, particularly when the goalposts are constantly moving, is something quite different. When a country has an urban growth rate of 4–5 per cent, or more, it will never be possible to give a definitive timescale for achieving legally guaranteed universal access, because the numbers are changing so quickly. Trying to do so is also counter-productive, since defining a physical component, such as a tap or a toilet, as a right is reducing the likelihood of achieving an equally important need, which is to achieve long-term sustainability of operation in the services delivered. Thus, producing a recommendation that requires time-bound obligations to deliver full water and sanitation is actually counter-productive. Many western countries have made obligations to reduce carbon emissions in accordance with the Kyoto Protocol which they are unable to meet, even though they have far greater resources at their disposal than African countries. There is a need to reposition obligations within a framework of sustainable management of delivered systems rather than on a legal statute centred on individual components of those systems.

Ultimately, this whole discussion returns to the role of policy formulation in development and its impact on decentralisation. The British research group WEDC produced a guide for developing countries on what constitutes a good sanitation policy (WEDC, undated) (it applies only to developing countries of course; Britain itself is excluded from the need to have a sustainable sanitation policy). This critique is situated clearly within the British *Weltanschauung*, where the first objective of a 'good policy' should be that it 'provide a clear focus for action by setting clear objectives and targets' (WEDC, undated, p. 2). Yet if the government sets such detailed targets, and then is legally responsible for them (and accountable to a second international group, this time a different NGO, such as COHRE, with a different focus and a different set of interests), who but central government can deliver on this promise? Where does that leave local government? What is the implication for decentralisation? Thus, external control of the intellectual space surrounding the policy process leads inexorably to a weakening of local government and a recentralising of power.

Effective decentralisation means strategic decentralisation

This chapter began by demonstrating that delegation is an inherently weak form of decentralisation and naturally centripetal; that is, its natural outcome is to seek a return to central government control. At the same time, devolution, while providing the only basis for meaningful decentralisation, should be used strategically to achieve defined and agreed development outcomes. This is contrary to the external view, which is based upon the principle of subsidiarity; that is, decentralising powers, duties and functions to local government on the basis of its capacity. Here again, though, we have a western concept, subsidiarity, that was developed to address a specific condition (how to define decentralisation in Europe) but has been translated to a global model without thinking about whether it is even appropriate in a different development arena.

In practice there is a quite different approach that could be used to decide which areas of responsibility should be transferred downwards. This alternative, which is termed here a *strategic approach*, links choice (about which level of government is best positioned to take responsibility for a specific function) to long-term outcomes and the achievement of higher-order goals. Capacity-building then follows to support the chosen tier of government in carrying out that function effectively. Following from this, the most important lesson is that intergovernmental relationships have to be clearly defined, and in particular the powers and duties of local government clarified, *before* looking at deregulation.

Deregulation, whether to the markets or to civil society, then becomes part of a wider, more inclusive development strategy, not a policy. We cannot continue to have western *Weltanschauungen* imposed on other countries as a precondition to their receiving development aid; not only is this morally wrong but the outcome is generally counter-productive. In this specific context (of urban infrastructure), countries that believe local government is the focus of local development activity, for example, should be able to have this recognised as their own *Weltanschauung*. In this context, many African countries place great importance on building sub-municipal structures (e.g. the ward administration system in South Africa, or the kabele administration in Ethiopia), and these are often an integral part of the social and cultural framework that exists across the subcontinent. Seeking to replace sub-municipal government by 'community' control, simply because this is the preferred choice of external agencies, becomes an imposition of external values.

Reformulating the role of decentralisation in urban Africa

This chapter has sought to demonstrate that decentralisation continues to have a tremendously important role to play in creating effective and sustainable urban governance in sub-Saharan Africa, particularly in the secondary towns and cities. At the same time, though, it can generate effective outcomes only if it is driven from the inside. There is a limit to the extent to which this issue can be analysed from the outside, primarily because the topic is so bound up in *Weltanschauung*; or, to use Rossi's analysis, quoted earlier, decentralisation is bound up in a 'country's historical inheritance and its culturally determined value system, the government's political intentions, the socioeconomic and legal frameworks, as well as the application concepts which are considered critical for success or failure'.

External agencies can support this internal process, since it requires both human and financial resources to function. At the same time, it needs to be recognised as a fragile and delicate process, a process that can easily be destabilised. Both this chapter and the previous one have provided a range of different examples where approaches taken by external agencies to a range of urban development issues, while well intended, have had a negative impact at the local level, destabilising and undermining local government and creating a governance framework that has resulted in increased centralisation. Chapter 4 showed how such approaches are linked to the fragmentation and individualisation of urban infrastructure services. Directing the focus for these services towards the individual has the effect of creating a direct linkage between line ministries at central government level and individual citizens, bypassing local government almost completely, while strengthening the role of external actors and agencies, to the extent that these agencies can become shadow local governments themselves.

In this chapter, different examples were provided that led to the same outcome. Here the mechanisms operate through a policy focus on quantitative outcomes, or target-driven development. The imposition of targets, particularly in water and sanitation,[22] requires that these delivery targets form an integral part of a country's policy. This then becomes the expectation of external academics and other analysts, who in turn judge the efficacy of an African policy solely from within the framework of this quite specific British *Weltanschauung*, and effectively 'force' African countries to adopt the British policy approach, in another example of how Africa's intellectual space is colonised.

There are four key issues emerging here. The first is mentioned above; that is, the need for African countries to return to the decentralisation debate and keep it high on their agenda, as they have indicated in their political resolutions, such as that of the Kigali declaration.

The second is a need to be much more strategic in deciding what powers, duties and functions to decentralise, linking this decision much more directly to the development process; and then to be very clear about the mix. To do that, though, there is a need to define the terminology of decentralisation in an African context.

The third is to be able to understand the way in which externally driven initiatives compromise African decentralisation strategies, to the extent that those strategies then become dysfunctional, particularly in the case of target-based delivery.

Finally, there is the whole question of how external interventions, particularly around target-driven initiatives, contribute to the transfer of control over the decentralisation process from internal control to external control, thereby becoming a further contributor to the colonisation of the intellectual space by external actors.

Running through all of these issues is the right of a country to create its own approach to policy formulation. Virtually all external reviews of African development policy – and there are many of them – take as their starting point an assumption that the British approach to policy is the only approach to policy. As a result, they assume a British policy perspective and judge the African policy constructs according to that British policy framework, taking no cognisance of the fact that individual countries may have a different perspective on policy. Other countries acquiesce in this imposition of a British action-orientated policy approach on Africa even when they themselves have a quite different approach to policy formulation in their own country. Such a situation cannot continue and has to change, but it is up to African governments to change it. That is one reason why the Ethiopian case study, discussed over the next two chapters, is so important, because modern-day Ethiopia has evolved largely outside of direct colonial control, and in doing so has created its own indigenous approach to policy formulation.

Chapter 6

Urbanisation in Ethiopia

Introduction

Ethiopia provides a valuable and important case study of urban development in sub-Saharan Africa for several reasons. The first of these stems
from its sovereignty: the country may have been occupied by a western
country for a short period (1935–41), but it was never colonised in the way
that other African countries were. The second lies in its cultural continuity, enabled by having sub-Saharan Africa's only indigenous written language. The third is identity. Ethiopia was one of the first countries in the
world to adopt Christianity as a national religion, which provided social
and cultural definition to the society when political power waned. Finally,
there was geopolitics, with the country having the military power to define
and defend its territory. In the urban context too there are unique features that define the country, the most evident of which is its ambivalence
towards cities and their role in society. On the one hand, there have been
great eras in Ethiopia's history where the city provided the regional locus
of power and influence, as with Axum at the beginning of the first millennium, or Gondar in the middle of the second millennium. At other times,
though, and in total contrast, there have been periods when the monarchy
would move the location of the capital with each reign, leaving the old
space to revert to its previous rural form. Only Harar provided urban continuity, and for much of the time this lay outside of Ethiopian control and
was closed to non-Muslims.

In Ethiopia, then, urbanisation was a phenomenon that ebbed and
flowed; yet at the same time the building of cities remained an important
part of the country's history. As a result, when the country began to open
up to the West in the late nineteenth century there remained a skilled
pool of artisans available to construct the newly emerging urban centres,
such as Dira Dawa and Addis Ababa. This history facilitated the influence
of the French, in particular, who established the first School of Architecture and Urban Planning. Yet while the country absorbed this influence,
the prolongation of a feudal society, followed by a closed totalitarian

dictatorship, prevented the country suffering from the external influences that shaped development elsewhere in Africa in the colonial and post-colonial eras, as described in Chapters 2 and 4.

Because of this unique history, the country's urban development process is quite distinct and specific. It is this specificity that makes Ethiopia important as an African case study, because the outcome was an urban development construct that is situated, clearly and unambiguously, in an urban planning paradigm. Seen from a technological perspective, Ethiopia had an indigenous building technology that allowed it to benefit from, and adapt, European architectural practice; but it lacked the engineering technology base of the Anglo-Saxon countries. This in turn meant that Ethiopia paid only limited attention to infrastructure in its urban development.

This is of immense significance in the context of current thinking about African urban development, because it means that we have here a long history of an approach to urbanisation that corresponds to the desired outcome of the current urban-planning-driven development trajectory being recommended for other African countries by UN-Habitat and other external agencies. In other words, Ethiopia provides the ideal case study for judging the success, or otherwise, of a planning-based approach to urban development.

The Ethiopian experience prior to 2000 illustrates both the strengths and the weaknesses of an urban development model created from the start as an urban planning construct. This model functioned successfully for decades, but in the context of a country that had very low levels of urbanisation, restricted migration and low urban densities. Since the early 1990s, however, the urbanisation rate has been rising and the model has been exposed to a great deal of stress, as planning processes have begun to lag behind the demand for urban land. When it came to power in 1991, the new democratic government established a federal system of government that devolved power not only to the new regional governments but also to the secondary cities.[1] Then, in order to operationalise this decentralised administration, the federal government, in 2003, established a large capacity-building programme.[2] This was deemed necessary in order for these newly created urban government authorities to take up the powers, duties and functions that had been devolved to them under this new constitutional dispensation.

Throughout that process, Ethiopia retained urban planning as the core profession driving urban development. In parallel, though, the government found that if it really wanted to build the capacity of local government, it required a new approach to urban policy that placed infrastructure at the heart of its development programme for the secondary cities.[3] Over time the government, through the Ministry of Works and Urban Development,[4] came to recognise that urban infrastructure was a critical driver of economic development for those cities. It is that process of changing perspectives, and the outcome, that are described here.

My analysis of that experience is based upon direct personal involvement in the programme, and draws upon both direct experience and the input of other people involved in that process. It also draws on the lessons learned in the follow-on to that project as well as from subsequent involvement inside of government, as the programme moved into its implementation phase. The outcomes from all of these indicate that an effective urban infrastructure management strategy is central to the development of a sustainable urban future for sub-Saharan Africa.

This chapter, and the one that follows, constitute the heart of the book, in that they describe African realities and African decision-making at work. In this sense they provide a transition from the past to the future. The developments described here are linked to the way in which Ethiopia evolved politically, as well as the way in which the country is evolving developmentally. This chapter focuses on the political development and is divided into three phases.

The first phase covers the period from the country's early history to 1855. That date is considered the beginning of modern Ethiopia, and the second phase takes up the history at that point, covering the period from 1855 to the beginning of democratic government in 1991. The third phase is that of Ethiopia after 1991. At this point, though, the discussion moves the locus of exploration down from the national stage, via the new regional governments, to the emerging urban centres. The focus here is on decentralisation, and the approach taken by the newly formed federal government towards the management of the urban centres. This part of the chapter also provides the linkage through to Chapter 7 with a description of the eighteen secondary cities that provided the context for the socio-technical case study around which that next chapter is constructed.

Early history from the first century to the mid nineteenth century

Ethiopia is considered to be one of the oldest human-inhabited areas of the world, often being referred to as the cradle of human civilisation; while as a nation it has a lineage of civilisation that can be traced back at least 2,000 years. From an urban perspective several great cities were built during that period but went into subsequent decline, which makes it all the more interesting that there was so little urban evolution in the country's history. Ethiopia's genesis as a nation-state lies in the northern part of modern-day Ethiopia, together with what is now the independent state of Eritrea, and it is there that the early development took place. This was a kingdom commonly known as the Aksumite Empire, an indigenous African empire[5] whose origins can be traced back to the fourth century

BC, and whose power and influence were to reach a peak in the first century, when it occupied an area stretching across northern Ethiopia, northern Sudan, much of Eritrea and across the Red Sea into Yemen and Saudi Arabia. Its capital was Axum, in northern Ethiopia, which at its peak was a bustling metropolis and cultural and economic centre.[6]

Although its power ebbed and flowed, the Aksumite Empire remained a major regional power until the seventh century, when it was finally forced to retreat, first from the Arabian Peninsula and then from the Red Sea region altogether, by the wave of Islamic expansion which characterised that period in history. Axum itself remained and the area around was undefeated, but its power and influence, even within Ethiopia, declined rapidly, until the city fell into disrepair, for reasons that are still not fully understood. And although the empire built other cities, in Sudan and along the Red Sea, there was no significant attempt to build further urban centres within Ethiopia itself. What is known is that, following the fall of the Aksumite Empire, the rulers of Ethiopia abandoned the concept of a permanent capital city and initiated the practice of moving their capital around the country, building predominantly tented cities and living off the land, depleting the natural and agricultural resources of an area and then moving on – a tradition that was to persevere for a thousand years. By the sixteenth century these towns had become more formal in their construction, but were still abandoned when a new site was chosen. It was only with the building of Gondar in the seventeenth century that a new permanent settlement was developed.

Gondar lasted as a city, and as the main urban centre of Ethiopia, for some 200 years, from its founding, around 1635, to 1855, when a new era in Ethiopian history began with the crowning of Tewodros II, the first of the modern monarchs. It was Tewodros II who initiated the process of integrating the country under a single leader, a process that was to be completed by Menelik II thirty years later. At this point the concept of a moving capital was reintroduced and lasted for a further fifty years.

Gondar was subsequently ransacked, and partially destroyed, by a series of Islamic invasions that took place in the 1860s. In looking at Gondar from an urban perspective, three points of interest emerge. The first is that the city was never very large, with a figure of somewhere over 60,000 people quoted as its population during the seventeenth century. So, even under stable conditions urbanisation never became a significant development driver in Ethiopia. The second is that the desire to move back to the old system of a perambulatory seat of government never entirely disappeared from the kingly mindset. Moving was seen as an important aspect of governing – a way of ensuring the territorial integrity of the country. The third relates to the nature of the urban social process. Thus, Levine (1965) refers to the city of Gondar as having 'an orthogenetic pattern of development, as distinguished from a heterogenetic one' (1965, p. 42, n. 42, quoted in Wikipedia, 2010f).[7]

The discussion to date is constructed around the evolution of the Ethiopian state. However, there were also two other components of Ethiopian evolution that impacted on urbanisation, albeit to a more limited extent. The first relates to the strong historical relationship between the monarchy and the church. Wherever the monarchy went, churches were constructed, and while the cities may have been temporary, the churches were often permanent. In addition, numerous other monasteries were also constructed, in keeping with the strong monastic tradition of the Ethiopian Christian Orthodox Church. Many of these churches and monasteries remained, and many formed a potential nucleus for small urban settlements.[8] The buildings also played a role in developing a skills base in masonry construction which laid the foundation for the later creation of a small, but nonetheless significant, architectural heritage, as well as a retained skill in masonry, particularly in the northern part of the country.

The second important feature of Ethiopian life through the period following the decline of Axum was the constant threat, and often the reality, of Muslim invasion. For extensive periods of time, parts of Ethiopia were under Islamic control. However, this of itself was never sufficient to create a widespread urban culture. The one exception is the important Islamic city of Harar. This city, considered to be the fourth most important holy city in Islam, was closed to non-Muslims until 1887, when Menelik II restored central rule (Selamta, 2010). And in this context it was more heterogenetic than Gondar, though this cosmopolitan face was limited primarily to interactions within the wider Islamic world of that time. In the wider context of urbanisation, though, Harar is more a unique example than a wider urban model. It was founded sometime between the seventh and the eleventh centuries and became the centre for the spread of Islamic culture and religion across the Horn of Africa. Yet it remained the only city of significance created in the area of Ethiopia that was under Islamic control. So, while it did not act as a precursor to wider urban development, it was nonetheless to play an important role in the urbanisation that was soon to begin. Together with Gondar, Harar preserved the indigenous skills base and the human resources that would later be needed in the construction of the new capital city, Addis Ababa.

Urban development in Ethiopia, 1855–1991

Political consolidation and regional formation, 1855–1913

The period covered previously was characterised by a division of power and a growth of regional powers structures. Many of these regional leaders were defined as kings (*negus*), and while all recognised the integrity of the wider geographical entity known as Ethiopia, none accepted the overlordship of the others. The period from 1855 to 1913, under the leadership of the Emperors Tewodros II (1855–68), Yohannes IV (1872–89) and Menelik II (1889–1913), was to change that and lay the foundation for the unified state that became modern Ethiopia.[9] Thus, 1855 is the year accepted as the beginning of modern Ethiopia.[10]

That year saw Kassa Haylu depose the last of the so-called Gondarine puppet emperors,[11] following which he was crowned *Negusa Nagast* (King of Kings) under the name Tewodros II. He then moved to consolidate Ethiopia under a single leader, moving first against Tigre, in the north, and then against Shoa/Shewa (the South). From an urban development perspective, though, the major achievement of Tewodros II was to initiate a process of modernisation of the administrative and legal organisation of the country. The effectiveness of this modernisation programme was mixed, as Zewde illustrates in his analysis, which he sums up in the following way:

> Tewodros has been described as 'Ethiopia's first monarch with a concept (however vague) of modernization' (Crummey, 1969, p. 457). Given the breadth of vision and the energy that he brought to the Ethiopian scene, this is a fair assessment. The parenthetical qualification contained in the above characterization is highly appropriate, however. Not only was Tewodros's concept of modernization vague, but his reforms also lacked consistency and method. Ultimately they remained tentative gestures rather than comprehensive programmes of lasting importance. The social and political edifice of the *Zamana Masafent*[12] proved too strong for Tewodros's modernizing efforts. The military and administrative reforms he envisaged were bereft of economic and technological bases.
>
> (Zewde, 2002, p. 31)

These reforms, however 'vague', nonetheless initiated the modernisation process, which was continued under his successor, Yohannes IV, and consolidated under Menelik II. Again from an urban perspective, the most important feature of these reforms was the formal establishment of geographical regions, or districts, which required administrative centres. At the same time, the conservative and traditional nature of the government as a whole, influenced by the trends outlined by Zewde, also had an impact, serving to constrain urban formation. This specific aspect of urban development will be returned to in the later discussion about the current state of secondary cities.

There are three further pieces of the Ethiopian urban evolutionary puzzle that need to be addressed before the full picture can be assembled. The first of these relates to the situation in Shoa, which again is clearly described by Zewde in the following way:

The history of early 19th century Ethiopia would not be complete without a description of the peoples and principalities of the southern half of the country. It was the unification of these two [northern and southern] parts in the second half of the nineteenth century that gave birth to modern Ethiopia. The peoples of Southern Ethiopia had attained varying degrees of social and political organization. The term 'southern' is used here not in the strictly geographical sense, but as a convenient category embracing those states and peoples that did not directly engage in or were peripheral to the imperial politics of Gondar. Their organizations ranged from communal societies to states with powerful kings and elaborate mechanisms for the exercise of authority.

(2002, p. 16)

Second, there was the creation of Addis Ababa as the new capital. Following the tradition that new leaders created a new capital, Menelik settled an area known as Entoto as his new residence, primarily because

[s]electing a capital based on a prophecy or the re-establishment of an old imperial seat was an act that Ethiopian emperors often used to secure their legitimacy. According to oral tradition, Entoto had served as a settlement for the Shewan kings before the establishment of the Gonderine Dynasty.

(Giorghis and Gérard, 2007, p. 30)

However, Entoto was poorly situated, being founded on top of a hill, with a steep climb, and with insufficient resources, particularly wood and water, readily accessible. It was his consort, Queen Taitu, who, shortly after the founding of Entoto, 'moved down to the nearby plain of Finfinne, also known as Filwoha, to bathe in its thermal waters. Addis Ababa, then situated between these sites, came into existence in 1887, when Taitu gave it its Amharic name: Addis Ababa, or New Flower' (Pankhurst, 2007, p. 12).[13]

This move coincided with a change in both local and global geopolitics. Menelik's ascent to the throne created a new capital for the country, while the defeat of the Italians at the Battle of Adwa 'preserved Addis Ababa's status as the capital of the only country on the continent to maintain its independence throughout the European Scramble for Africa' (Pankhurst, 2007). This brought together, for the first time, regional leaders and foreign legations. The new era, occurring around the turn of the twentieth century, fixed the location of Addis Ababa as the long-term capital of the country. What was particularly fortuitous about this move, though, was the location of the new capital, where its position, in the geographical centre, of the country created a balance between the different regions that might well not have been possible if the location had been further north. in Amhara.

Finally, there was the relationship between Ethiopia and the western colonial nations. Following the defeat of the first Italian invasion at Adwa in 1896, Ethiopia was substantively free from the colonial takeover that swept the rest of Africa, though external political pressure continued to be exerted in other ways. At the same time, though, Menelik was extremely interested in, and supported, the introduction of new technologies such as the telegraph and telephone as well as the cinema, roads and bridges, hospitals, schools and hotels, restaurants and bars (Pankhurst, 2007). As a result, the provision of technology provided an alternative route for external influence, with an important example being the Djibouti–Addis Ababa railway, a private venture that began construction in 1897. Planned to pass through Harar, the railway reached a railhead just short of that city, in 1901, where it languished for seven years before being restarted in 1908 and finally reaching Addis Ababa in 1917. This delay led to the creation of a new city to serve the railway, named Dira Dawa. Planned and developed by French *urbanistes*, it was to initiate a long period of French influence in shaping urban planning in Ethiopia in the European tradition, which was to be reinforced by the Italians in their later occupation of the country in 1935.

Overall, the outcome was that, with respect to the western relationship at least, politics and technology were seen as distinct elements. This was quite unlike the situation in anglophone African countries, where technology was a tool of colonialism, creating a symbiotic relationship between politics and development that was to have a damaging long-term impact. As a result, Ethiopia could welcome technology, and see its benefit for development, without confusing this with political control. As a result, the country was able, on the one hand, to maintain its distrust of the colonial powers' political ambitions, while on the other accepting the technology that provided the basis for development – a perspective that continues through to the present time. On the downside, though, it meant that Ethiopia accepted the benefits of technology without ever recognising the fact that this could provide a driver for further development, particularly in the urban centres. Instead, technology was seen as something that enhanced and supported development, with the latter perceived as something that evolved naturally. In this way it reflects the historical British view described in Chapter 3, but for its own reasons. Again, though, as with the British experience, this was to have an interesting, and important, influence on the way that the country was to see infrastructure, and respond to urban development, later.

The unitary state: invasion, restoration and revolution, 1913–91

It is difficult to understand modern-day Ethiopia without understanding the highly centralised nature of the society that existed right through to 1991, first under a strongly autocratic monarch, and then through a military and individual dictatorship. This history also makes the changes that occurred after 1991 all the more remarkable.

When Menelik II died in 1913 he left a country that was stronger and more institutionally unified than it had been for many centuries, as well as having external boundaries which, while not by any means to the liking of the Ethiopian government, were nonetheless internationally recognised – although this recognition did not imply that the country itself was secure. On the contrary, at that point the country's future as an independent state was balanced on a knife edge. On the positive side, Menelik II had foreseen the internal problems, and subsequent external threat, that could occur after his death and had established a ministerial system of government as early as 1907 to provide continuity in policy, as well as naming a successor. None the less, the period from 1913 to 1916 was one of political instability, resulting in a reaction, continuing from 1916 through to 1930, that Zewde describes as one of 'creeping autocracy' (2002, p. 128), followed by 'the emergence of absolutism' from 1930 to 1936 (ibid., 137). This latter phase corresponded with the period between the coronation of Hayle Selassie in 1931 and the invasion by Italy in 1935.

From an urban perspective, the major impact from this period comes from the creation of a new regional structure, shown in Figure 6.1. This illustrated the attempt to create a unitary state and a provincial system of administration based upon forty-two new provinces, which in turn required administrative centres. In addition, the evolution of the traditional north–south trade routes, which was enhanced during this period of increasing political stability, led to the growth of new urban centres, particularly at the junctions. Developmentally, though the main evolution of urban form centred upon the capital, Addis Ababa, influenced strongly by Hayle Selassie's desire to transform the city into a 'modern' capital, a desire influenced by the cities he had seen in his European tour in 1924.

The strong centralising focus of urban development under Hayle Selassie meant that it was the Italians, following their invasion of 1935, who initiated and drove urban improvement outside of the capital, while at the same time continuing the work of building Addis. This improvement was something that they did with great effect, but it was also due, in no small measure, to circumstance and the power of the resistance movement, for, as Zewde makes clear,

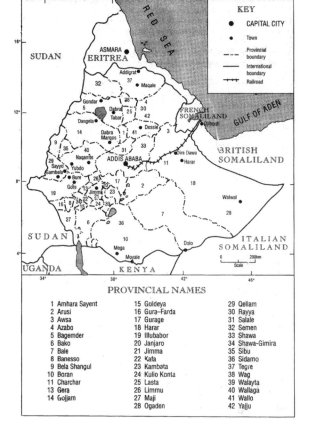

Figure 6.1 Map of Ethiopian regions in 1935 (Zewde, 2002, p. 86).

[b]ecause of the Patriots Resistance Movement during the Italian Occupation,... Italian rule in Ethiopia was largely confined to the towns;
hence it was mainly in the urban centres that the impact of the Occupation was felt. The Italians left a lasting imprint on the architecture of
the capitals of the new governorships, as evidenced by the Italian-built
edifices still visible in such towns as Gondar, Jimma, Harar and Addis
Ababa, not to speak of Asmara and Mogadishu, which had longer spells
of Italian rule. For the capital of their East African empire,[14] Addis
Ababa, the Italians drafted an ambitious master-plan, whose implementation, however was aborted by the collapse of their rule in 1941.

(2002, p. 163)

It was the Italians who left Ethiopia with the legacy of the urban master
plan, although this was an approach supported by the French, who played

a significant role in the post-occupation period in influencing the urban planning system in Ethiopia. This approach to planning was well suited to the centralised and autocratic nature of the state that was a major characteristic from 1930 right through to 1991. However, outside of the capital, and the cities where master plans had been initiated by the Italians, urban planning was a relatively low-key activity. Urban influx was heavily controlled, with the result that most of the growth that did occur took place in Addis Ababa. Thus, it was only in 1987 that the military dictatorship created the National Urban Planning Institute to initiate a comprehensive planning system across the country as a whole.

Urbanisation post-1991: summarising the origins and influences on urban form

At this point it becomes possible to pull together the different threads of Ethiopian history and identify the various forces that were to shape the urbanisation process. And while the French and the Italians undoubtedly had a major influence in shaping Ethiopian approaches to urban planning, this was successful primarily because it aligned with Ethiopia's history of urban development, with its architectural focus. By the 1960s, though, the British influence was becoming more dominant, slowly dislodging the French. So while, overall, it was Ethiopians themselves who took forward and developed their own system of urban planning, they took little from their own indigenous experience, and instead adopted a strong layout-based approach to urban planning that paid little attention to urban form but instead focused strongly on functionality. The result was that, on the one hand, there was a social development process which was quite distinct from that of other African countries, whether francophone, anglophone or lusophone,[15] owing to the absence of racial, and economic, separation. On the other hand, there was an emerging planning process that was, in many ways, similar to that used in the British colonies to create their formal areas.

It is difficult to identify the reasons why a process of this kind arose. When we look at the nature of urban formation from a historical perspective, we can recognise different architectural influences. These come from different points in history and different geographical areas within the country; broadly, though, they can be divided into three categories with respect to origin, namely:

1   indigenous settlement formation and Ethiopia's traditional architectural heritage;
2   the villages created along the trade routes;
3   western-designed and/or western-influenced cities.

In the first category, and on a scale, there were the historic cities: Harar, Gondar and Axum. There were also the churches and Gondarian places that provided urban form. These reflected both indigenous Ethiopian and Islamic tradition.

In the second category were small villages. These would tend to have a wide main road defining the through route, where much of the trade was located, very similar to formations elsewhere in Africa, though driven by indigenous demand. The settlement would then develop behind this main road settlement, with pathways or roads created for local use. This type of urban formation was particularly common in the South, with Shashemane[16] providing a good example. It was settled in 1908 as a small village or *sefer*,[17] at the junction where the road from Adama to the south meets a connecting route to the east, and was awarded municipal status in 1933. While not defining urban form in an architectural sense, these villages nonetheless reflected indigenous social-spatial relationships.

The third category comprised what one might call purpose-built cities; that is, cities in the western mould. Examples here include Dira Dawa, the railhead; the capital, Addis Ababa; Jimma, in the East; and Adama. As was mentioned earlier, Dira Dawa was built by the French in 1902 as a railhead town, with a centre around the railway that was designed in the French colonial style. Addis Ababa was more traditionally Ethiopian. Drawing artisans from Gondar and Harar, and building around core features such as the Emperor's palace, the commercial centre (Arada) and the church, early Addis Ababa provides an interesting example of clustering combining formal and organic growth. Interestingly, the unique nature of these two cities is recognised by their status in the Constitution, where they are defined as chartered cities with their own administration outside the control of regional states.

The Italian invasion replaced French influence by Italian segregated planning. This had a major impact on Addis Ababa and the major regional centres, such as Jimma in western Oromia and Adama, 100 kilometres to the east of Addis Ababa. Unfortunately, this influence was a mixed blessing. On the one hand, it sought to integrate architecture, planning and infrastructure into a single vision of the city. This benefit, unfortunately, was totally negated by the social-political goal of creating a racially segregated city. Its impact was also detrimental to the infrastructure planning, as Giorghis describes in his architectural history of Addis Ababa (Giorghis and Gérard, 2007), where he shows how segregation imposes an artificial transport layout. For example, 'An important problem was channelling the traffic of caravans away from European areas and towards the native quarter' (ibid., p. 146). It also had a wider environmental impact, since '[i]n the attempt to segregate the city, natural landscapes were manipulated' (ibid., p. 148). Finally, though not directly related to desegregation, but reflective of externally imposed intellectual values, '[a] grid plan was superimposed on the organic form of the city', a change that would have a widespread impact on Ethiopian planning through to the present time.

The post-war period saw a rejection of the apartheid city and a return to a more spatially integrated approach to urban development; but the damage was already done, with the indigenous Ethiopian building heritage largely ignored. As Giorghis comments in the foreword to his book,

> When I was a student in the Department of Architecture and Urban Planning [of Addis Ababa University] in the early 1980s, I was disappointed with the lack of information on the history of Ethiopian architecture. If I remember correctly, out of the entire course on the history of architecture, which takes about eight semesters, there only two or, if one were lucky three, lectures, which covered everything from Aksum to Addis Ababa.
>
> (Giorghis and Gérard, 2007, p. 14)

It was only in 1987 that the government of the time established a planning body, the National Urban Planning Institute (NUPI), as a body with an objective that falls clearly within the descriptor that defines an institute as 'a permanent organizational body created for a certain purpose' (Ministry of Federal Affairs, undated) – in this case the development of Ethiopia's emerging urban areas in an ordered and functional manner, as befitted the centralised regime of the Darg. Yet the philosophy of that time was initiated much earlier. This is important when one is exploring the four external forces of influence described in Chapter 1. The nature of political and technical development (and Ethiopia's increasing isolation during the 1980s) meant that the first three forces of influence had little impact, enabling the role of the fourth area of influence (urban planning) to be explored in much greater detail.

If success is judged in terms of the output and implementation of urban plans, then there is no doubt that NUPI proved to be extremely successful. It developed eleven master plans for all of the country's larger urban centres, sixty-two development plans (effectively miniature master plans) and sixteen action plans over the fifteen years of its existence (Ministry of Federal Affairs, undated). Then, with increasing federalism, the government responded. In 2002 it began to hand over the responsibility for plan preparation to the regional governments. With the establishment of a new Federal Ministry of Works and Urban Development in 2006, NUPI was transferred across to that ministry and renamed the Federal Urban Planning Institute, thereby becoming (in theory) an advisory body. It was during this transition period that the country also changed its planning focus from one based upon a master-planning approach to one based on the creation of structure plans. Yet none of these changes was able to keep pace with the rapid urbanisation that was starting to occur.

Looking at the way in which the master-plan approach was carried out and translated into practice by NUPI provides a good indication of the way that urban development was perceived in the country. From the beginning, the urban development construct was silo based, with the core silo being the spatial layout plan. And here Ethiopian planners sought to adopt good western practice. In addition, the growing British influence resulted in a decline in what little French influence remained, linguistically, and a move across to English influence, thereby favouring, among other things, a shift to the Anglo-Saxon approach to planning. Thus, the spatial plan took as its structuring elements a road network hierarchy that was both expensive and highly conservative, and intended to give priority to motorised traffic. A typical example of this hierarchy (which differed slightly across different regions) is provided in Table 6.1.

There was then a second master plan derived from this, which was the drainage master plan. This was intended, primarily, to ensure that all roads were drained; however, the original documents were retained by NUPI, and the cities themselves did not have access to them. The result was that while large, and expensive, masonry drainage channels were constructed along arterial roads, collectors had earth channel drains while local roads had little, if any, drainage. The concept of urban drainage as a wider concept covering all land, and not only roads, did not exist.

Towns covered by NUPI plans also had a master plan for comprehensive water supply, also developed separately and based upon the forecasting of the spatial development plan. The principle was to supply water to a connection to each plot, the intent being that this connection could be extended and a standpipe erected on the property. A water supply could (in theory) only be taken into the house if the house owner received permission.

Finally, sanitation was considered to be an individual responsibility, and we can see here the similarities to the early American model of urban development, with the higher-income Ethiopians (i.e. those that could afford their own house) building large pits below the outbuilding at the rear of the property, covered by a squat pan for defecation. Solid waste management was also considered separately, in the sense that an area of land was allocated to the disposal of solid waste; however, this was not a significant feature of the master plan.

Table 6.1 Example of a road classification system used by NUPI in Ethiopia

Type of road	No. of lanes	Width of lane (m)	Road reserve width (m)
Arterial 1	Dual lane	10.5	42
Arterial 2	Dual lane	9.0	30
Minor arterial	Dual lane	7.0	25
Collector 1	Single lane	11.0	20
Collector 2	Single lane	7.0	15
Local 1	Single lane	6.5	12
Local 2	Single lane	5.0	10

What we can see here is an example of an African country that chose, of its own free will, to adopt a planning approach that draws on, and has strong parallels with, the British planning model described in Chapter 3. In this paradigm the infrastructure has two characteristics. First, to the extent that it was installed at all, it was seen as serving purely a supportive role in an urban development process driven by spatial planning. Second, it was seen as an engineering function. This is clearly evidenced by the approach to the road hierarchy and the drainage and water supply master plans. Across the board, then, we have a model that emerged independently in Africa and set out in exactly the same direction that the majority of other African countries are being encouraged to take now, under the influence of, and pressure from, the major external development agencies (both multi- and bilateral), supported by an array of urban development and planning academics and practitioners. Surely, then, this provides full and complete justification for the current urban development approach being supported by those planners in Africa?

There is no doubt that the urban planning model was successful while the country was able to impose a rigid influx control policy whereby the rate of rural–urban migration could be strictly controlled by authoritarian regimes. It will really be possible to judge whether or not it provides a successful role model only when influx control is removed and the urbanisation rate begins to climb rapidly. What we see emerging, then, is a condition where there is a system in place whereby the government in Ethiopia is still able to influence (i.e. slow) the rate of urban in-migration to a degree; yet this planning model is beginning to collapse. The outcome, however, was not the replacement of the planning model; urban planning remained central to urban development thinking, though primarily because urban planners remain hugely influential in government in Ethiopia and this is the status quo. At the same time, the government recognised the need to look at new ways of exploring the way in which the urbanisation process has been evolving, particularly since 2000, and sought to gain a better understanding of the drivers that underpinned that urban development process, particularly in the secondary cities. In doing so, the first step that it took was to devolve to these cities the primary responsibility for their infrastructure.

Decentralisation and the political geography of modern Ethiopia

When the Darg was finally overthrown, in 1991, this was by an opposition coalition that was rooted in ethnic nationalism; that is, forces that, individually, represented specific ethnic groupings within the country, such as Tigrean, Eritrean, Oromo. This had not always been the only form of opposition. As Guidina states, 'The history of organized politics in

Ethiopia goes back to the early 1960s. From the very beginning there have been two major forces at work, ethnic/regional and multi-ethnic, and the two forces have had a "love–hate relationship" ' (2006, p. 127).

The multi-ethnic opposition had its origins in the student movement, and the two dominant multi-ethnic groupings that emerged from this, MEISON and the EPRP, 'dominated the country's politics in the early days of the Ethiopian revolution' (Gudina, 2006, p. 127). However, this opposition collapsed in the early period of the Darg, in 1976–7 (Zewde, 2002, p. 274), the point at which the leader of the military coup moved from running a 'collective' liberation committee to taking full control as a military dictator. In the ensuing vacuum the ethno-nationalist opposition was then the only group with the resources and the power base to present a serious challenge to the regime.

The implications of this victory by ethno-nationalist forces were profound, and were to define the future political direction of the country. Yet the ensuing political framework also has wider implications and a relevance that extends outside of the country itself. As Turton expresses this,

> The transformation that has taken place in the political structure of Ethiopia since 1991 has been both radical and pioneering. It has been radical because it has introduced the principle of self-determination for federated regional units in a formerly highly centralized and unitary state. It has been pioneering, because Ethiopia has gone further than any other African state, and further than 'almost any state worldwide' (Clapham, 2002, p. 27) in using ethnicity as its fundamental organizing principle. This should make Ethiopia's experiment in ethnic federalism of great potential relevance to the growing debate about the accommodation of ethnic diversity in democratic states. It is an interesting fact, therefore, that the discussion of ethnic federalism in Ethiopia seems to be carried out almost exclusively in an Ethiopian context.
>
> (2006, p. 1)

The primary concern here is the impact of regionalisation on urban growth patterns. However, the latter half of this extended quotation is valuable in providing an example in support of the wider argument made about the external influence of the West on African development. In the end, whatever relevance this unique intellectual exercise in political form and structure might have, it cannot impact significantly, simply because it exists on the periphery of a Eurocentric worldview.

If we return to the urban debate, though, the outcome of the new federal state, termed the Federal Democratic Republic of Ethiopia, was to create ten regions and two chartered 'city administrations' (Addis Ababa and Dira Dawa), with the latter having the status of a city and a regional state. These states and administrations are shown in Figure 6.2.

Figure 6.2 Map of Ethiopian regions in the federal system established after 1991.

From an urban and regional development perspective, the main impact of creating this federal structure was to create secondary cities with a clear regional economic focus, thereby providing (it was hoped) a counter to the dominance of the primate city. The population of the primate city (Addis Ababa) remains an order of magnitude higher than that of the regional capitals. None the less, the latter are beginning to emerge as core urban centres in their own right, and beginning to increase the population differential when compared to other secondary cities.

The regions themselves have been developing at different rates, both economically and institutionally. In seeking to strengthen the capacity of both regional and urban government (termed in this chapter urban local government authorities, ULGAs, which is the official term for urban local government in Ethiopia[18]), the government, working with the World Bank, developed the capacity programme to be described in the sections that follow. In looking at how best to take this programme forward, the government chose to concentrate on the four regions that were considered the most 'developed' institutionally; that is, those best able to implement the programme. The intent was then to use this experience to extend the outcomes and lessons learned to the remaining regions. This choice was also influenced by the urban focus that was a major (though not the only) component of the capacity-building programme, since these four regions contain a large majority of the urban centres in the country. Finally, the study included two other areas, Harari Region and Dira Dawa, since these are also important urban centres in their own right. In total the study encompassed eighteen cities, four from each of the developed regions plus Harar (the capital of Harari State) and Dira Dawa.

The final point in discussing the regional governments of Ethiopia is to look at the balance of powers, duties and functions and how they are allocated between the central (i.e. federal) government and the regional governments. The powers, duties and functions of ULGAs will be discussed later. In his discussion concerning the distribution of legislative authority, Fiseha sums up the situation by stating that

> [t]he Ethiopian Constitution follows the United States and Swiss Constitutions in the formal distribution of powers. According to Article 50 (2) 'the federal government and the states shall have legislative, executive and judicial powers'. Article 51 lists 21 'Powers and Functions of the Federal Government' and is, in principle, similar to the Tenth Amendment of the US Constitution or Article 30 of the Basic Law of the German Constitution. It states that all powers not given expressly to the federal government alone, or concurrently to the federal government and the states, are reserved for the states.
>
> (2006, pp. 138–9)

The majority of (western) external actors, be they international, governments, NGOs or academics, involved with urban development in Ethiopia have little interest in, or even knowledge of, the institutional framework within which they work – a not uncommon situation in sub-Saharan Africa – with the result that externally driven programmes will often ignore this framework altogether. In one point where Fiseha expresses concern about a potential conflict between different parts of the constitution, he states:

> It might appear that, by virtue of the reserve clause [quoted above] any power not mentioned in article 51 belongs to the [Regional] States ... There is, however, a parallel provision of the Constitution which, in the long run might lead to a controversy. The Constitution empowers the federal government to 'formulate and implement the country's policies, strategies and plans in respect of over all [sic] economic social and developmental matters; establish and implement national standards and basic policy criteria for public health, education science and technology'.
>
> (2006, p. 139)

A case study in Chapter 7 will provide one example of this, showing how the Water and Sanitation Program (WSP) exploits this contradiction in the way that it structures the formulation of a national sanitation strategy for Ethiopia. This is not implying purposeful intent, since neither the western employees of the WSP in Ethiopia, nor their consultant, with whom the author interacted over a number of years, had any knowledge whatsoever of the allocation of powers, duties and functions across the different tiers of government. None the less, the effect of its (no doubt well-intentioned) action is (1) to exploit a probably unintended potential contradiction in the Ethiopian Constitution to undermine the power of the regional states; and (2) seriously to undermine the role of local government in Ethiopia by cutting across the powers and duties of that tier of government.

Internally, the Constitution gives responsibility for local government to the regional states. Thus, it is the states that are responsible for the establishment, and formal proclamation, of the urban areas within their geographical boundaries. The project that will be described later, for example, had the regional states as client, even though it was part of a World Bank programme negotiated with the federal government. An interesting outcome of this division of responsibilities is that it leads to a differentiation between policy and strategy which has important implications for urban policy formulation – a problem similar to that discussed in an anglophone context in the previous chapter.

The role of urban infrastructure in urban local government as defined by the urban proclamations of the regional states

Following their establishment, each region decided, individually, and after a consultation process, on the extent of the powers, duties and functions that would be developed to accredited 'urban local government authorities' (ULGAs), based upon a set of agreed aims and objectives. The regions then developed a legal framework that became the city proclamation for that region. This discussion focuses primarily on the four 'developed' regions of Tigray, Amhara, Oromia and the Southern Nations, Nationalities and Peoples Regional State (SNNPRS), though it also incorporates Harar and Dira Dawa where information on these areas has been collected.

The proclamations are broadly similar, though they differ in the detail. Table 6.2 provides an extract that covers the major points.

There are a number of key issues that emerge from this extract that illustrate clearly the expectations that all tiers of government have with regard to the role of infrastructure services. These are:

• The extent to which the responsibility for infrastructure is seen as comprehensive, across all services.

Table 6.2 Summary of local government responsibilities for urban infrastructure

Aims/objectives	Powers and duties	Functions
SNNPRS: • Enhance the economic and social development and the protection of the environment of their respective areas. • Provide or ensure the provision of services in response to the needs of their residents. **Amhara:** • Provide, cause or ensure the efficient and adequate provision of appropriate infrastructure and other services in response to the needs of city residents and service seekers. • Capacitate cities to be free from environmental pollution, to conserve natural resources and to utilise inputs appropriately.	**Tigray:** • Engage in agreements with all levels of government, the private sector and the voluntary sector. To ensure an efficient delivery of services, a city may make an arrangement with the government, engage non-governmental organisations, cooperate with the public, establish public agencies, privatise services or take other measures that circumstances may justify. • A city shall have the authority to determine which option to use for which services and when. • The city council may determine the basic organisational structure of the city government: approve the establishment or annulment of departments, offices, boards, commissions and service delivery options based upon the recommendations of the mayor.	**SNNPRS:** Provide, or ensure the provision of: • environmental services, including the construction and management of city roads, sewerage and drainage lines, parks, gardens and recreation areas, waste disposal, prevention and control of floods, erosion and pollution. • Public utilities, including water, electricity, telephone and transport services. **Amhara:** • Establish service rendering institutions either by itself or in partnership with the private sector in those areas that are key to development activities but the private sector has not been involved in (*sic*). • Regarding the provision of environmental and social services, engage in the construction of roads, except inter-city roads, the provision of road lights, construction of drainages and sewerages. • Regarding economic services, ensure the adequacy of the supply of water, electricity, telephone lines and transport.

- The way in which infrastructure is perceived as central to social and economic development.
- The recognition that much of the infrastructure base is integrated with the environment, and environmental need. This also extends to a recognition of the importance of resource management.
- The absence of any differentiation, in the infrastructure provided, between different socio-economic groups; instead, there is a linkage between the delivery and the collective need.
- The freedom to define appropriate management structures.
- The recognition of the need to involve others, from the private sector, the public sector and civil society, in the delivery and management of infrastructure, and the importance of partnerships.

At the time that the proclamations were issued, they constituted statements of an ideal condition; the reality was somewhat different. At that point the cities had been given responsibility for infrastructure, but the conceptual framework, implicit in the aims, objectives, powers, duties and functions, still perceived infrastructure as a service. What began to change during the study was the underlying perception; whereas initially infrastructure was viewed as a set of individual services supporting a planning process with idealised goals, it came to be recognised as a component of the city in its own right, with a clear social and economic objective. The discussion that follows traces the development of a programme that created an institutional base capable of achieving these ideals, over a period of three to four years; for it to do so, however, a further shift in the perception of infrastructure was required. Situated within this political, social and economic framework, the perception of infrastructure was to change, from its being seen as a service to its being seen as a development driver.

The study of eighteen secondary cities in Ethiopia

The study in context

In 2003, Ethiopia, with support from the World Bank, initiated a three-year project termed 'Capacity Building for Decentralized Service Delivery' (CBDSD). The overall objective of this project was 'to improve service delivery performance by building public sector capacity at the federal, regional and local levels of the country's recently introduced decentralized government system'. This was one of three major projects undertaken by the government, all of which formed part of a 'Decentralized Fiscal Support for Infrastructure' (DFS) programme of the World Bank (undated).

The CBDSD programme had several components (Abbott, 2007), the main one of which was directed specifically at the needs of local government.[19] This was termed 'Restructuring and Empowering Local

Government' (RELG), and its intended function was 'to start and facilitate the process of building local governments that are financially sound and have the ability and incentives to improve service delivery, especially to the poor' (GTZ IS, 2005).

To achieve this outcome, RELG was divided into four subcomponents, termed 'windows', and the exploration of urban infrastructure described here overlapped three of those. Here the primary objective (found within window 2) was to 'support those Regional Governments that have completed (or substantially completed) development of policies, strategies and legislation for decentralized urban local government authorities (ULGAs) to complete those initiatives and operationalize regional policies, strategies and legislation for decentralized ULGAs' (Federal Government of Ethiopia, undated).

At the same time, the study outcomes were also intended to integrate with a second area of reform (window 3), which was concerned with local government restructuring and capacity-building. Finally, the infrastructure component was also directly responsible for a third window (window 4), which was intended to identify and deliver pilot investments for infrastructure rehabilitation.

At first glance this did not appear to be a particularly revolutionary study. On the contrary, it could be seen as a mechanistic exercise to strengthen infrastructure capacity while working within an institutional framework similar to that described in Chapter 3. What emerged, however, was something quite different, because Ethiopia did not follow the standard colonial template described in that chapter. Instead Ethiopia exists within its own *Weltanschauung*, and this would prove to be quite different from anything experienced in other countries, both in the subcontinent and internationally. The outcome was an exploration of infrastructure from a completely new perspective, and the emergence of an infrastructure model that was grounded in the needs, and experience, of the country itself. And while the result of the study was welcomed and warmly accepted by the government of Ethiopia, it was ignored by external agencies because it challenged too many of their established practices and beliefs.

The descriptions analysis and discussions that follow are based upon the unpublished report by Abbott (2007) referenced earlier, supplemented by personal notes on the project. The study was focused on the needs of the secondary cities and therefore excluded Addis Ababa, the capital and the country's primate city, with a population of approximately 3 million inhabitants. In a global context, where the development focus is so strongly directed towards the primate cities, this might appear to be a serious flaw. In practice the reverse is true: it is this exclusion of the primate city that has enabled an in-depth study of secondary cities. This is what makes the project so important in a wider African context.

The project cities

As was mentioned earlier, in order to provide a focus for the CBDSD[20] the study concentrated on eighteen of the country's major cities, with four being chosen from each of the 'developed' regional governments, and two being cities with unique historical and/or developmental circumstances. The final list of cities is shown in Table 6.3. The secondary cities covered a range of populations, from a low of 45,000 to a high approaching 250,000 people (Table 6.3).

The study teams

Infrastructure was one aspect of a wide-ranging study of what could effectively be termed urban governance in Ethiopia's secondary towns. In its entirety the project covered different aspects of urban development, from administration and institutional structures, through spatial planning, housing, economic development and urban financing, to urban infrastructure.

The broad objective of the study was to determine, and document, what each region had done with respect to decentralisation, urban reforms, and restructuring and empowerment of its urban local governments. The process included identifying key issues, priority areas and problems or constraints currently facing the regions as they tried to deepen decentralisation and restructure local government. From this point the study would move to an implementation phase, intended 'to support the Regional Governments in the process of restructuring (in the first instance) the 18 selected ULGAs, in order that they could provide for the effective and

Table 6.3 Population distribution in the eighteen secondary cities in the CBDSD project

City	Population estimate (2005)	City	Population estimate (2005)
Arbaminch (S)	65,000	Bahir Dar (A)	209,000
Awassa (S)	113,000	Dessie (A)	210,000
Dilla (S)	55,000	Gondar (A)	200,000
Sodo (S)	59,000	Kombolcha (A)	65,000
Adama (O)	200,000	Adigrat (T)	100,000
Bishoftu (O)	120,000	Axum (T)	65,000
Jimma (O)	140,000	Mekelle (T)	200,000
Shashemane (O)	120,000	Shire-Endeselassie (T)	45,000
Harar (H)	130,000	Dira Dawa (D)	237,000
CITIES IN STUDY AREA I 'Southern Team'		CITIES IN STUDY AREA 2 'Northern Team'	

Note
S = SNNPRS; O = Oromiya; A = Amhara; T = Tigray; H = Harari; D = Dira Dawa.

efficient delivery of local services, and promote local economic development' (Federal Government of Ethiopia, undated).

With regard to the infrastructure, it was fairly self-evident that this 'support' was perceived as 'engineering' support. In practice, it was to evolve into a major shift in perceptions and understanding, transforming 'engineering' to 'infrastructure' and as a result leading to a significantly enhanced role for infrastructure in the wider urban development process.

The scope of work and the methodology of implementation

The project was allocated to two sets of consultants,[21] who would then carry out separate but parallel studies. The split was defined primarily on geographical and logistics grounds, with the different responsibilities reflected on the two sides of Table 6.1. For convenience these are referred to as the 'Southern Team' (the primary source for much of this discussion) and the 'Northern Team'. From the beginning the two teams took a fundamentally different approach to the project. The government had stipulated a large number of deliverables (over 100 reports were specified for each team), to be presented in written format at different stages during the fifteen-month project timeline. Such a strong emphasis on product output over a short period could only be accomplished at the expense of more in-depth processes; however, this was the route that the government chose.

The two teams structured themselves, and their approach, quite differently. The Southern Team grouped these deliverables and created four sub-teams, covering, broadly:

1   administration and institutional structures;
2   development planning, comprising spatial planning, economic development, land and housing;
3   local government finance; and
4   infrastructure rehabilitation, delivery, operation and financing.

This approach was constructed around a specification by the government that there should be at least four lead specialists,[22] with one for each of the activity areas identified above, all of whom should have extensive experience and a proven track record. The result was a small, cohesive group that operated as a team.

The Northern Team took a different approach, preferring to bring in more specialists to cover the different areas. It identified core staff that would coordinate deliverables, and specialists on short-term assignment. This team also invested heavily in community-based surveys. So, the two approaches were substantially different, and this difference was followed through in the approach to infrastructure. Perhaps because the Southern

Team had a (virtually) full-time infrastructure specialist, and that consultant was given a wide-ranging mandate, greater emphasis was placed on institutional and organisational systems, and on the role of infrastructure in the wider management of local government.

The infrastructure brief

The original brief for the urban 'infrastructure' specialist (actually termed the Municipal Engineer) was clearly defined, to the extent of being prescriptive in respect of output[23] but more flexible in respect of tasks. And because the brief extended across three different programmatic windows, this necessitated two quite diverse terms of reference. The first of these was technically orientated and, as might be expected with a World Bank project, placed a heavy emphasis on the economic aspects of infrastructure delivery. Broadly, this component of the terms of reference stated that the infrastructure specialist (termed a Municipal Engineer)

> will assess the current state of municipal infrastructure in the two regions. He/she will prioritise investment projects, strategize and prepare project proposals for financing under Window 4 of the CBDSD project; (will prepare proposals for at least two reasonable investment projects per region). He/she will help redefine the processes (including revising the Operational Manual for window 4) and assist in building the necessary technical capacity at the local level. In collaboration with other specialists on the team, he/she will carry out studies of service delivery systems, recommend policies and procedures for the two regions, and assist regions in the preparation of service delivery manuals.[24]

The second component of the terms of reference was wider, requesting 'recommendations and implementation strategy/plan for infrastructure delivery and financing', and describing the work as being to 'identify, develop and recommend options for improving infrastructure delivery ... at the municipal level (including identification of options for financing and alternative approaches for production and delivery)'.[25] Finally, the infrastructure services to be incorporated into the study were wide-ranging, moving beyond the infrastructure services described in Chapter 3 (although it included all of these) to incorporate project management, abattoirs and markets. In total, thirteen distinct services were identified.

Beginning the study: the situational analysis

The nature of the situational analysis

The terms of reference demanded that all consultants provide a situational analysis at the end of week 6 of the project. Clearly, this was a very short period of time in which to explore nine ULGAs spread across such a large geographical area, and allowed only a limited amount of contact time for each one. Certainly this approach was unusual; yet it was also remarkably effective. For an infrastructure specialist there is a tendency to move directly into the detail, whether this is a 'taps and toilets' analysis or an institutional assessment. These were included, but when a study involves nine separate ULGAs in such a short period, this demands a use of all senses, not simply the analytical ones. In this exercise, for example, it was only in the sixth ULGA that it was suddenly possible to integrate what had been seen into a 'perception' of just how different Ethiopia was from countries that had been colonised.

This visit constituted what might be termed a first pass in what would be a fifteen-month interaction. As a result, the initial observations concentrated on a more qualitative assessment, which is the outcome described here. And while some broad quantitative data were obtained, the collection of accurate quantitative data would be done later.

In looking at the outcome of this situational analysis, this section is divided into three descriptive elements, covering respectively the Regional Urban Development Bureau, the ULGAs and the overall approach to urban infrastructure management. These are then followed by a summary of the findings and conclusions.

The Regional Urban Development Bureau

The regional body responsible for the ULGAs was termed the Urban Development Bureau. At the same time, other line-functional ministries, such as the Regional Bureaux for Water Resources, also have significant influence in developing the implementation strategy and influencing the powers, duties and functions of the ULGA departments whose activities relate to their specific ministries.

The structure of the various regional bureaux differed across the regional governments. The one shown in the organogram in Figure 6.3 comprised two operational departments, together with a Finance and Management Support Service. The first of these, the Urban Planning and Land Administration Department, had a staff complement of twenty-six people, including that of department head and secretary. It was divided into three teams: a Plan Study and Preparation Team (fifteen persons), a Cadastre Team (five persons) and an Engineering Team (four persons).

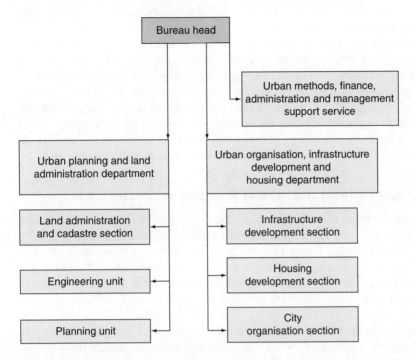

Figure 6.3 Organogram of a regional ministry of works and urban development in 2006.

The last has a team leader, an architect, a civil engineer and a sanitary engineer. At the time of the study, the dominant activity in this Engineering Team was related to building construction. The posts of engineering team leader, civil engineer and sanitary engineer remained vacant throughout the period of the study.

From a developmental perspective, the primary historical focus in Ethiopia had centred on a model in which urban planning was seen as driver of urban development, using master plans to create the spatial framework. The weakness of this planning approach was one of the priorities to be addressed under the new federal system of government, with one outcome being that the regions would take over responsibility for the spatial and economic planning process. As a result, the period beginning around 2002 saw the commissioning of new plans that were a radical departure from the historical master plans. They are better described as integrated structure plans and strategic development documents, and would fit into an internationally recognised structure for the planning process. Using the Adama plan as an example, the studies leading to the generation of these plans were carried out on three levels: the 'urban scope', the 'hinterland' and the 'study region' (GTZ IS, 2005, p. 19).

204 Urbanisation in Ethiopia

The result of this change in approach was evident by the time the study began. Planning, housing and economic development were all in a state of flux. Building on a strong traditional urban planning base, there was a high level of energy among (particularly young) professionals at both regional and urban level, though this was countered in some areas by a strongly conservative planning group that was grounded in the old system. Overall, though, this creative energy was limited to activity areas of spatial planning, economic development and, to a lesser extent, housing; it did not spread to engineering (infrastructure), where the level of understanding, among virtually all of these professionals, was woefully inadequate.

The organisational structure of Ethiopian secondary cities

Because of their diverse histories, the organisational structure of Ethiopian cities can vary quite significantly between regions, although there are also commonalities. Using Oromia National Regional State as an illustration, the Proclamation on Urban Local Government clearly defines the functions of a city. In addition to the 'environmental' and utility services described previously, these include the provision of:

- social services, including education, medical and ambulance services, housing, public notary and vital statistics services, the abattoir service and market service, etc.;[26]
- cultural services, including the promotion of sports and theatres, the establishment of public libraries and museums, etc.;
- protective services, including public security, judicial service, fire control, food and drugs inspection, etc.

A typical example of a management structure for a Grade 1 city is shown in Figure 6.4, with the emphasis here placed on showing the role of the engineering and infrastructure management function in the wider structure.

This organogram indicates the highly compartmentalised structure of the municipal services function. As might be expected in a country where, historically, urban development was grounded in a centralised urban planning paradigm, planning constitutes the major technical activity within the cities, with the largest staff allocation and the greatest depth of expertise, followed closely by housing. Thus, the organisational structure and the institutional capacity to manage spatial and economic development processes were much stronger than those for engineering and infrastructure management.

At the urban level the secondary cities are divided into four or five 'grades', depending upon size. The number of grades, and the size distribution, is a regional decision, so the nature of graded cities may vary between regions. Generally, though, cities are given a grade once their

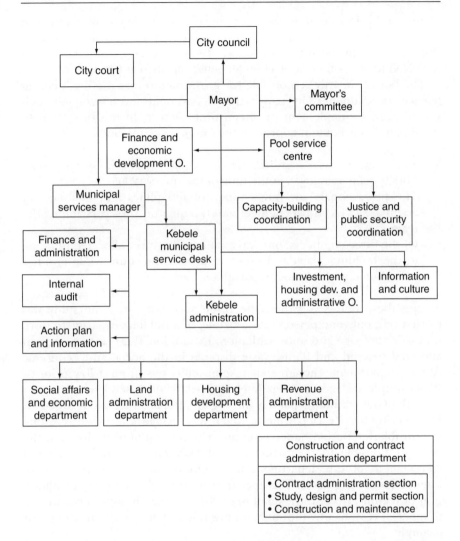

Figure 6.4 Organogram of a Grade I city (excludes education and health) in 2006.

population exceeds 2,000, and Grade 1 cities can start from a population base of 90,000. Below 2,000, urban areas are effectively sub-administrations of the woreda.[27] That said, not all graded cities have autonomy, and some can stay as sub-administrations of their woreda. To gain formal legal status a city must apply for its own proclamation. At the time of the study, those cities having their own proclamations were termed reformed cities.

The region chosen as an example of staffing for infrastructure is the SNNPRS. Other regions may be slightly better with regard to staffing, but the general principles described here regarding the view of infrastructure at the beginning of the study are considered to apply across all regions. Of the four cities in the study, Awassa was the only Grade 1 municipality in the SNNPRS, the other three cities all being classified as Grade 2.

The body primarily responsible for infrastructure was the Engineering Service Department. On paper this department was reasonably well staffed, with a complement of fifteen professionals. In practice, though, the situation was not as it appeared, for a number of reasons:

- Staff numbers were significantly below plan, with only seven professionals being employed at the time of the survey (2005).
- The professionals covered a range of disciplines and included an architect, an electrical engineer and two quantity surveyors among the team.
- Of the three engineers, one was a sanitary engineer allocated full time to the building plans and building permits function, while another contributed to this function part time.

Taking these points together, the result was that when the study was carried out, only one person was available, in a full-time capacity, to work on roads, drainage and some sanitation. In addition, there was one person allocated to solid and liquid waste disposal in the Social and Economic Affairs Department, though that responsibility was given a low priority. Water supply was managed separately and will be discussed later.

In the Grade 2 municipalities the organisational structure included an Engineering Service Department, which was divided into two teams, one responsible for Design Supervision and Contract Administration and the other responsible for Construction and Maintenance. Overall, the full complement of the department was eight people, of whom six were intended to be engineers. This appeared, at first sight, to be a good allocation of technical staff for a small town. In practice, though, there were a number of reasons why the situation was not as it appeared on paper. For example:

- Staff numbers were significantly below plan, with only four professionals being employed in Dilla (two civil engineers, one sanitary engineer and one quantity surveyor). In Arba Minch there was only one professional (a civil engineer). And in Sodo there were only two professionals (both civil engineers).
- Allocation to the building plans and building permits function took priority over roads and drainage in all cities.
- The operating structure was inappropriate. Taking the number of different professions and specialisations and the three levels of management, this made for a fragmented function.

- There was no support for the professionals at a technician level (in drafting work or engineering detail).
- Taking these points together, the result was that only one staff member could reasonably be expected to work on infrastructure. Again solid and liquid waste was the responsibility of the Social and Economic Development, but these services had only a low priority. In Grade 3 and 4 ULGAs there was no engineering capacity.

The institutional structure for engineering and infrastructure management

The situational analysis found that 'infrastructure' management was by far the weakest component of the entire municipal system. When requesting a meeting to discuss infrastructure, the City Manager directed the team to the Construction and Contract Administration Department. In practice this department had a limited involvement in roads and storm-water drainage, and the bulk of the resources were allocated to building plans and permits. In this context the terms 'infrastructure' and 'technical' were perceived to be synonymous, with the term 'technical' in turn being construed as 'building and engineering'. Discussions in this and other departments revealed only a limited understanding of the concept of physical infrastructure. Institutionally, infrastructure management was divided between three operational units: the Construction and Contract Administration Department, the Social and Economic Department and the Water Board.

A more correct description for the first of these, based upon its operational function, would have been a 'Building and Construction' Department. The primary duties were building works, in the form of building plan approval and building permits, and road maintenance. In all the cities visited, a majority of the staff were found to be working on building-related works. In seven of the nine ULGAs, engineering knowledge was limited to basic road pavement and culvert design and basic road maintenance. There was little or no understanding of urban drainage. The department itself was divided into two sections, one for design, construction and contract administration, and one for maintenance. The first of these also dealt with building permits and building plans. From information gathered through personal interviews with staff, it was evident that the greater part of the time was spent on the approval of building plans and building permits, with very little time spent on construction-related activities. On the maintenance side there is one supervisor (of Diploma level or higher) to manage the whole of the road and drainage network. And finally, the Head of Department appeared to spend a large percentage of his time on administration.

The second department was termed 'Social and Economic' (later called a Beautification Section/Department in most regions), which was responsible for 'liquid and solid waste'. The term 'liquid waste' was interpreted as waste pumped from septic tanks. Since the major form of (formal) human waste disposal was the household pit latrine, this meant that sanitation was simply not included as one of the infrastructure services to be managed.

Finally, there was the management of the water supply. Restructuring of the urban water supply sector had been initiated prior to this study by the World Bank, working with the Federal Ministry of Water Resources. The original intent had been to privatise this function, but all attempts to do so had been unsuccessful. At the time this study commenced, the management of water supply was in a complex institutional arrangement that is best summarised by Figure 6.5.

The exact nature of the relationship between the parties was different in the four regions. The example given here is taken from the Southern Region, where the responsibility for managing the ULGA water supply was the responsibility of a water board, the chairperson of which was the Mayor. The Constitution of the SNNPRS (2003) included sections on the powers and duties of the various regional bureaux. Paragraph 28 of the regional Constitution details the powers and duties of the Regional Bureau of Water Resources Development. This paragraph makes clear the power of the Bureau to regulate and control the city water boards in all technical areas pertaining to the extraction and supply of water. It also has the

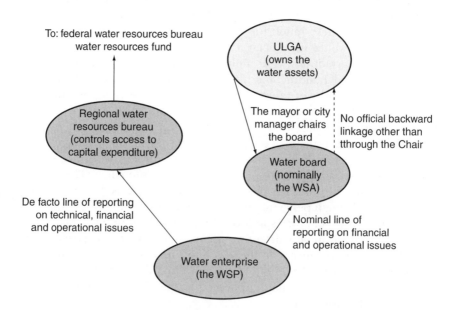

Figure 6.5 Allocation of powers, duties and functions in municipal water supply management.

power to enforce certain operating procedures and practices if it believes these to be in the interests of operational efficiency. Thus, all applications for funding go from the water boards to the Regional Bureau of Water Resources Development, not the Bureau of Urban Development.

Findings, conclusions and outcomes

The findings

The analysis began by looking at findings which were related to specific institutional and technical issues. From an institutional perspective, the main findings were that:

- In every ULGA visited, it was made clear by the administration, based upon surveys they had conducted, that residents placed a range of problems associated with the various infrastructure services high on their list of priorities. These findings were later confirmed by social surveys carried out by the Northern team of consultants. The cities recognised the problems but lacked the knowledge to address these concerns effectively.
- The human resource base was very weak. The engineers who came to the cities were either recent graduates or graduates with one, or at most two, years of experience. Only one of the nine cities visited had more experienced technical staff.
- There was no formal documentation of past activities, which is itself a critical component of institutional knowledge. Engineers came, developed projects, but then took the information away when they left.
- There was an absence of what could be termed 'good management practice'. Thus, there were no records of services, in the form of 'as-built' drawings. In fact, drawings were almost non-existent, as were records, specifications and other basic data. Even basic maintenance schedules were absent. And this absence of drawings meant that it was not possible to 'see' the infrastructure network – again a serious limitation to project planning.
- Too great an emphasis was placed on building plans and permits and too little on physical infrastructure.
- At a conceptual level the use of the term 'infrastructure' was a misnomer. The primary focus across the majority of the services associated with this term was quite clearly on the engineering and building practice. In the environmental services section, responsible for sanitation and solid waste, the focus was on providing a social service.

From a technical perspective, the main findings, which related to individual services, were that:

- Roads had been constructed under the master plans, but their condition had deteriorated almost everywhere. Maintenance was limited to an ad hoc approach based on responses to community complaints; there was no planned maintenance. The engineers who were present recognised the need to adopt a different approach to road design, and were beginning to do so with the use of local materials. On the whole, though, they were simply afraid to do anything that was not in the master plan.
- Drainage was limited in extent, being primarily associated with the small asphalt road network. Elsewhere, poor drainage was the cause of often widespread flooding and affected both individual homes and the public road network. There was no knowledge of urban drainage as a broad concept. Knowledge was limited to road drainage.
- There was no technical understanding of solid waste management practice. On the whole, cities were making a remarkable effort to ensure the removal of solid waste, and a number had instituted community cleaning programmes. But in all cases waste was then placed on open landfill sites.
- Sanitation relied on pit latrines and some septic tanks. Removal of waste was limited and this was taken to the same open landfill site as the solid waste.
- In water supply there was some institutional knowledge, built up primarily by artisans. Given the resource constraints, the existing systems worked remarkably well. However, there was no investment planning, and supply was falling increasingly behind demand as urban growth increased.

Drawing conclusions

There are different ways to interpret these findings, ways that could lead to quite different conclusions. Taking the approach taken in other anglophone African countries, where external influence dominates, sector specialists could see in this situation a justification for their own approach. For example, sanitation specialists could argue that this condition simply demonstrates the need to have a separate line function for sanitation so that this important sector can be developed and funded properly, and would assume that this development and funding could only be done through strong sector specialisation, with a national sanitation strategy and the setting of targets. And ditto for the water managers, and so on. And this was in fact what the external agencies involved with these sectors – the Water and Sanitation Program, the Water Programme of the World Bank and the United Kingdom's Department for International Development, to name just three – were arguing for at a national level.

Yet there is another way of interpreting these findings. The starting point is to ask what the ULGAs want and how they see the role of these infrastructure services in their own city. The answer to this question, which was unanimous, was that they saw all of these services as core ULGA functions. Equally encouraging was that the ULGAs were able to identify and recognise their own shortcomings, attributing these to a lack of understanding of how exactly the management of these various 'infrastructure' services should work. What they did see clearly was that this infrastructure had a central role as a social driver, supporting the needs of their residents, and as an economic driver, essential to future development, even though they were unable to operationalise this vision. In this scenario the answer does not lie in stripping local government of its authority over the various infrastructure services, but rather in building its capacity and knowledge so that it can manage those services more effectively.

To do that, however, and to make it work, we have to answer the question: what capacity is it that we are building? What this study shows is the extent to which this term 'infrastructure' is misunderstood. Certainly this was the case here at the time of this situational analysis: there was little or no understanding of what 'infrastructure' actually meant. It underpinned everything the city was supposed to be responsible for; yet it did not exist! As a result, it was interpreted (in most service areas) as engineering. Even there, though, when we explored these 'engineering' services, there was a complete absence of what might be termed an 'engineering culture'. This lack does actually have some benefits, as Chapter 7 will indicate, but it also has disadvantages, the most important of which is an absence of institutional knowledge on how to manage the physical elements of the urban fabric.

From conclusions to outcomes

It is important, when exploring an urban situation that is in need of improvement, to draw a distinction between *physical conditions* – that is, what exists – and attitudes – that is, how people see their environment. The external agencies working in Africa base their response on the first, when what is actually required is to build on the second. The finding in this study was that, while *physical conditions* were poor, *attitudes and commitment to change* (on the part of ULGA management and staff) were extremely positive. This finding leads to the first important outcome: the government recognised how poor conditions were, and the situational analysis was seen by government as the first step towards improving the situation by supporting local government in its attempt to address this physical deficit. As a result, the work that followed was extremely successful in instituting long-term improvements, because there was political buy-in.

Second, the situation on the ground reflected a lack of institutional knowledge much more than it reflected individual weaknesses (e.g. corruption, or lack of political will); this is a critically important issue when we come to focus on capacity-building. Here, staff at all levels were hugely committed to improving their cities; they simply did not have the knowledge base to do it. This finding is fundamentally at odds with the general view of international agencies and external actors that the inability of cities to manage their infrastructure requires that responsibility be taken away from them and given to others who can (in theory) 'deliver' more effectively.

Following the initial study, the two teams of consultants presented their findings at a workshop, which included a wide audience drawn primarily from federal and regional government but also including key ULGA representatives. With regard to urban infrastructure, the broad findings (summarised above) were accepted, and used to develop the follow-on work. This workshop also resulted in a significant shift in thinking about urban development on the part of government, with both political and administration representatives from all levels recognising infrastructure as a crucial component of urban development.

There is no doubt that this workshop saw a major shift in government perceptions of infrastructure. It did not change its view that urban planning is the primary discipline responsible for urban development. What it did mean, though, was that, within that paradigm, while the government now saw economic planning as the basis for regional economic development, infrastructure was given much greater prominence in building the urban economic base, and recognised as a driver of the internal urban development process. The chapter that follows describes how this new thinking about infrastructure was taken forward into practice.

Chapter 7

From engineering to infrastructure

Changing the urban paradigm

A case study of Ethiopia's secondary cities

This chapter presents a case study that was also a personal journey of exploration and discovery that sought to answer the questions: what exactly is infrastructure; and what role does it play in urban society? The setting covers a broad canvass of eighteen secondary cities spread across a large area of Ethiopia – cities defined in that country by their legal administrative title of urban local government authorities (ULGAs).

When the project began, there were different expectations, depending upon who defined the outcome. For the World Bank, as the funder, the purpose was clear, at least initially: improve the technical management capability of ULGAs as part of a wider capacity-building programme with a strong focus on technical project identification, financial analysis and competitive bidding, using project-based capital investment planning. For the government of Ethiopia, on the other hand, the objective was more holistic: to build the capacity of ULGAs across a range of activity areas, one of which was infrastructure services, in order to meet the needs of urban residents for improved services. For the cities themselves, the objective, at least initially, was to obtain money to spend on 'infrastructure' projects.

This was in many ways a unique opportunity for a consultant. Although there were a large number of defined deliverables, there was also immense potential for innovative thinking about the role and nature of infrastructure in the secondary cities. Table 3.2 in Chapter 3 showed the three major differences between the underpinning rationalities that drove the evolution of urban infrastructure in Britain and the United States respectively in the nineteenth century. Ethiopia followed its own urban development trajectory, described in Chapter 6; and this was quite distinct from that which evolved in other African countries. On the one hand there was the planning paradigm, with infrastructure viewed as a set of supporting services in a wider development process. Included in this was also the idea that urban infrastructure was largely about engineering, though this view was much less pronounced than in the British colonial model, primarily because of the absence of a historical engineering culture. On the other hand, the urban development process itself was grounded in a deep ethos of social equity – a value system that underpins Ethiopian society. Thus, the idea that there should be differential levels of service was quite alien to the developmental culture.

By the time the situational analysis was completed, a number of internal perceptions, and external interpretations of internal perceptions, were changing. The recognition was growing that infrastructure had a wider role in urban society as a driver of economic development. Coupled with this there was a recognition, on the part of mayors and senior managers, supported by the regional bureaux and the federal Ministry (of Works and Urban Development) that infrastructure was central to their management function.

These perceptions provided the support necessary for rethinking the scope of work – not so much in respect of the deliverables, which were fixed, but rather in respect of the approach and resulting content of the deliverables. For the first time in African history there was an opportunity to look at the role and nature of urban infrastructure in the secondary towns of Africa in their own context and from their own perspective. This chapter will describe that process and the outcomes.

Introduction: creating a strategy for the infrastructure study

Chapter 6 described how the 'deliverables' laid out in the terms of reference for the study were defined in terms of a list of anticipated reports, which ranged from strategic analysis, through infrastructure assessments and asset inventories, to project proposals. Given this somewhat mechanistic approach, the challenge was to structure the deliverables in such a way as to create a more integrated and logic-based analytical framework, which would view the deliverables more in terms of a process. This in turn could then be used to explore the wider role of urban infrastructure, create more sustainable systems for delivery and management of that infrastructure, and, at the same time, be used to build local capacity and knowledge. In essence, this entire process became an exploration of the second aspect of Table 3.2: changing engineering to technology, but also going beyond that, transforming an engineering mindset to a much broader vision of urban infrastructure management.

The road map that was developed for this purpose, which was accepted by the government, is shown in Figure 7.1.[1] In exploring this road map the chapter is divided into three sections. Section 1 is concerned with a *technical assessment*, which still remains a necessary prerequisite to a wider exploration; while section 2 provides a *strategic analysis*. This seeming duality reflects the constraints of the programme. However, while this approach may

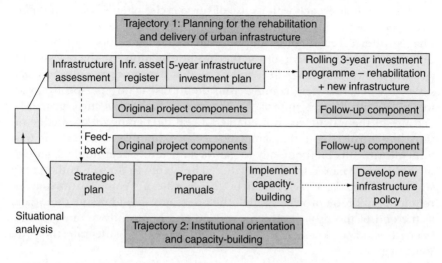

Figure 7.1 The road map for the infrastructure work plan.

initially appear fragmented, it was ultimately beneficial, since it allowed a capacity-building process to evolve based upon the urban reality that existed (section 1), while at the same time enabling a new policy formulation process to evolve as a separate exercise (section 2). Section 3 completes the chapter by presenting findings from the study and drawing conclusions.

The starting point was the situational analysis (described in Chapter 6), which was to be completed in six weeks. After that, the sequence of the work divided into two parallel streams. And while these were intended to be interrelated to some degree, they also followed logical, semi-independent trajectories. Thus, on the one hand there was a common philosophy, whereby the outcome was a set of deliverables 'developed as progressive outputs that facilitate a "learning by doing" process'. This was trajectory 1, and included support for the development of four project proposals (i.e. one per city in the four developed regions). In defining these deliverables, the intention of government was to provide a rehabilitation capacity at city and regional level. These four deliverables were:

1   an infrastructure assessment report;
2   an infrastructure asset inventory;
3   a five-year infrastructure investment plan focusing on rehabilitation of existing infrastructure;
4   pilot project proposals to be prepared by each town.

Thus, the focus of this trajectory was strongly biased towards effective and efficient management of infrastructure – that is, the financial and technical skills base – as might be expected of a World Bank-funded programme.

This overall approach with its use of three cycles of analysis, each going to a deeper level, might be considered unusual, or perhaps even wasteful. The Northern Team, for example, used a different approach, making their visits more intensive and gathering information for the assessment and the asset register together, and using that time to carry out the social surveys. A personal view, coming from the infrastructure perspective, was that the multiple pass approach was actually highly effective, primarily because of the way in which it enabled a real deepening of knowledge of the cities involved. At the same time, it was limiting too, since it was difficult with this methodology to gain a sufficiently deep understanding of the social dynamic within the cities. The ability to do so was the great strength of the approach taken by the Northern Team. Fortunately, a requirement of the project was that the two teams should merge their data at the end of the project, which provided an opportunity to draw on the strengths and weaknesses of the two approaches and integrate them to some degree.

The second trajectory was seen to reflect a broader, more long-term vision, looking more widely at strategy and infrastructure governance, and providing training material to support institutional capacity-building. An important element of the project was the use of interactive workshops for the different levels of government. Foremost among these were the workshops for the ULGAs, which took place at the end of each major activity. What this approach illustrated very clearly was the need to develop a strategic analysis, grounded in process, while pursuing a technical analysis at the same time, and that both are equally necessary.

With this twin-tracking approach in place, an interesting and valuable outcome was an understanding of the way in which these two trajectories cross over and feed into each other in an almost symbiotic way. This is an outcome of an integrated approach which is simply not possible in the mechanistic interpretation of sectoral service delivery. One example was the extent to which understanding the concept of infrastructure as a valuable asset (a nominally technical outcome) turned out to be the key to the entire capacity-building strategy for the city mayors, and managers, as well as the technical staff (a developmental process). For that reason the discussion needs to follow trajectory 1, which relates to the technical assessment, through to its conclusion before moving back to explore the second trajectory, which was concerned with the strategic analysis.

Section 1: the technical assessment

Introduction

This section provides a summary of the technical assessment.[2] The purpose here is to look at the conceptual development of a capacity-building programme, as well as a financial management programme for urban infrastructure in the secondary towns. The typical view of western countries and the international development agencies, which was clearly articulated in earlier chapters, is that infrastructure is unaffordable above an extremely basic level and that small municipal governments cannot manage the level of complexity. This study proved both those assumptions to be incorrect. To demonstrate that conclusion clearly, though, requires a detailed quantitative analysis, which would detract from the flow of the book's wider narrative. Yet if the quantitative analysis is omitted, then this opens the book to the charge that it is no more than a conceptual exercise, which may sound promising but could not possibly work in real life with real infrastructure. To pre-empt this potential criticism the book has included these 'real numbers' on the website that provides supporting material for this book,[3] where an expanded version of the technical assessment described here can be found. This site also provides a second technical analysis that provides information on the infrastructure base of the eighteen project cities as it was in 2006.[4] Moving the technical details in this way allows this analysis to focus on process and the outcomes. Included in this analysis are the infrastructure assessment, the asset inventory process and the financial management process (initially developed on the basis of five-year plans, changing later to three-year rolling programmes).

The infrastructure assessment

The approach

In order to undertake the assessment, the following approach was adopted:

1   A data information template was prepared, with a questionnaire covering quantitative data and qualitative assessment.
2   Interviews were carried out with regional bureau staff and in the cities, with both politicians and officials. Random visits to a range of socio-economic areas were also included, which incorporated discussions with residents.[5] This survey also analysed a wide range of previous reports, including master plans, development plans and strategic planning documents.
3   These data were then analysed. It should be recognised that this was an interim report, so the objective was to gain an overview and focus in on the key issues. This last objective was intended to assess the validity of the findings from the situational analysis, and deepen that analysis. This work would then be taken to a greater level of detail in the Infrastructure Asset Inventory.

The constraints

A critical constraint in preparing this report was the lack of reliable and up-to-date data. Even the most basic data, such as data concerning existing housing stock, population size and yearly investment on infrastructure, were difficult to obtain. Technical data, such as waste per capita (solid waste management), or the extent of leakage in pipes (water supply), were also exceedingly difficult to find. In addition, there were no engineering drawings available, no engineering design data for any of the infrastructure services, and no previous project documentation.

Extent of assessment

Again this report focuses on the six main infrastructure services, comprising:

1 roads;
2 road drainage;
3 street lighting;
4 water supply;
5 solid waste management;
6 sanitation.

The assessment covered the infrastructure base itself, the way it was managed, the way in which it was perceived and the capacity and resources allocated to its operation. A detailed discussion of each of the six major infrastructure services is provided on the website.

The findings

From an institutional perspective the infrastructure assessment confirmed the validity of the findings from the situational analysis. In particular, the assessment highlighted the quite significant difference between the political commitment to decentralise and the practical application of that principle.

From a technical perspective it was clear that the installed infrastructure base was weak and deteriorating. The core issues reflected problems identified across a range of developing countries. Thus, from interviews with staff in the ULGAs it became obvious that sanitation and solid waste were underfunded and that when funding was available to the ULGAs, they tended to prioritise roads, which were seen as more important by the majority of residents. There was only limited understanding, particularly within poorer sections of the community, of the causal relationship between hygiene practices, sanitation and disease.

In thinking about how to take the project forward, the simplest approach would have been to travel a conventional road: recommending variable levels of service; separating both water supply and sanitation from municipal control; moving solid waste management down to a community level – in other words, all the standard approaches that were ingrained from working in an anglophone African environment. And yet ... here was a unique opportunity to work with a government that had given a strong legal mandate for urban infrastructure to the ULGAs, and that wanted ideas and new ways of thinking that could support the implementation of that mandate.

Even at this early stage of the work the experience gained from this study was calling into question two core beliefs that underpin the international institutional approach to urban infrastructure, namely (1) that the core problem of infrastructure delivery is one of individual affordability; and (2) that the situation is best tackled through a mechanistic approach that addresses each infrastructure service separately in what is essentially an engineering analytical exercise. The study highlighted a major difference between, on the one hand, the internal perceptions of the ULGAs, which called for an integrated management approach, and, on the other, the external perceptions of line government departments and external agencies in Addis Ababa, which supported the conventional mechanistic approach. By this point the study had confirmed the initial finding of the situational analysis, namely that the main reason (by far) for the poor state of the infrastructure derived from a lack of institutional knowledge, which was caused, at least in part, by a weak organisational structure and an inherent lack of understanding, on the part of both the city politicians and the senior administrative staff, of the role, and nature, of infrastructure in an urban context. The conclusion was that this state of affairs could best be addressed by integrating urban infrastructure more effectively into the ULGAs and focusing on strengthening capacity to manage this effectively.

This is the inverse of the external view of African urban development. Since the 1980s, many external actors have seen local government as a hindrance and a blockage to effective delivery, as previous chapters have indicated; and in Ethiopia these pressures were also at work. The World Bank (through its water programme) and DFID, the British development agency, were both 'encouraging' (to phrase their actions mildly) the government to separate out water supply, working through the Federal Bureau of Water Resources, while the Water and Sanitation Program was seeking to separate out sanitation, working through the federal Ministry of Health. And all of these organisations gave priority to affordability at the expense of equity. On the other hand, the Ministry of Works and Urban Development was supporting local government in developing its legally proclaimed role, with the focus on building capacity across all infrastructure areas, and in this it was supported by the World Bank[6]-funded CBDSD project and by the German government, working through GTZ (the Gesellschaft für Technische Zusammenarbeit, now called the Deutsche Gesellschaft für Internationale Zusammenarbeit) and the German government-owned development bank KfW.

In terms of the specific findings, it was easier, in the first instance, to address the issue of roads and drainage. These were designed as part of a planning process with no regard to either the capital cost or the long-term financial sustainability; in this context the planning process was divorced from economic reality. And then, having installed this extensive road network, the ULGAs lacked the systems to manage it. As a result, roads were deteriorating at a rapid rate – a situation caused as much by a lack of understanding of the nature of urban storm water as it was by a lack of maintenance. The result was an ongoing decline in infrastructure, with a condition being reached where major rehabilitation was required over much of the infrastructure network.

In sanitation and solid waste the same conclusions applied, though they played themselves out differently. Here there was a lack of understanding about how the individual residents and the administration should relate; that is, where one responsibility ended and another began. External bodies involved with sanitation see sanitation as an individual responsibility, and increasingly a 'right'. If this translates to a 'right' to a toilet, then the approach is naïve at best. Ethiopian cities have simply left the responsibility to provide sanitation to the individual, and the system is constructed around pit latrines.

In newly constructed areas this system was working well, particularly in private, middle-class houses in SNNPRS, where families constructed huge pits below their outbuildings, between 6 and 10 metres deep; but that was not the case everywhere. Some of the cities are built on impermeable soils, and the pits are overflowing. In other cases the assessment found that people were increasingly bringing water (illegally) into their houses and discharging the waste to the pit latrine, thereby changing its biological function and turning it from a dry system into a wet system.[7] In Harar old town, virtually all pits were overflowing and there was insufficient access to empty them with the technology available. And finally, with urban densities increasing rapidly, pit latrine construction was falling behind population growth, meaning that more people had to use the existing toilets. This in turn was raising problems of access. With the growth in sub-letting identified as a major urbanisation trend, owners were beginning to limit tenants' access to their toilets.

All the cities used vacuum tankers to empty pit latrines, but these were in extremely short supply. There was no management plan for sanitation and little understanding of management concepts. There are no clear figures for access to sanitation in the cities. The Ministry of Works and

Urban Development places this at between 50 per cent and 60 per cent in the secondary cities. However, there is no doubt that access is complicated by the tenure system that is emerging. And one important finding of the assessment was that sanitation conditions in the Kabele housing were almost uniformly poor, with many families having to share toilets and a significant number of cases of overflowing latrines.

What this study revealed, then, was an urban construct that was beginning to break down, and seriously in need of re-evaluation. At this point the infrastructure component of the project moved in two directions. The first was to improve the capacity of the city to manage the infrastructure base that existed, which was followed through by the next stage of work associated with building the asset register, with the emphasis on moving towards technical and financial management. The second was to review both technology and institutional relationships, which were both explored through the strategic assessment. All of these findings were taken to a series of workshops, held this time at the regional level, where they were discussed extensively, and where the broad direction for future action, to be described in what follows, was approved.

The infrastructure asset register

The next level of detail in the analysis of urban infrastructure in the nine secondary cities comprised the development of an asset register. The building of financial management capacity was a major objective of the World Bank in this project, in keeping with its own priorities. Hence, the purpose of the first trajectory shown in Figure 7.1 was to develop this capacity through a programme of capital investment in rehabilitation. Capital investment planning (CIP) was therefore seen as the primary mechanism for building the financial management base. The question became one of how best to develop skills in CIP.

The traditional approach, adopted by the Bank, is to use a cost–benefit analysis and/or identify a rate of return on the investment. And this was the approach adopted by the team in the North. However, there are a number of problems with this approach. The first is the need for accurate information, otherwise it follows the maxim garbage in, garbage out – or in this case massaged figures in, positive rate of return out, loan granted. If it is not possible to acquire meaningful data, then the result is meaningless.

The second is that this approach to CIP is often situated in a virtual world far removed from reality, a fact that was clearly demonstrated by a major sanitation and drainage study for one of the larger project cities, which was carried out during the project period by internationally renowned consultants. Over half the study document was devoted to cash-flow analyses, which purported to show how a major sewerage scheme for the city would have a positive rate of return. There were just a few small omissions; for example:

- There were no qualified staff, and no training programmes.
- There was no consideration given to precedent. In reality, the only precedent for such a scheme was in Addis Ababa, where less than 10 per cent of the population is served by waterborne sewerage, and even there the system has a number of serious problems.
- The issue of affordability was glossed over, with assumptions about payment capacity being made without sufficient data.
- The question of how and where people would install toilets and connect to the system was excluded.
- There was no mention of training, either at an individual or an operational level.

The third is that CIP is project-based; that is, it is centred on the viability of an individual project. This is a critical factor in national infrastructure, where large capital investments are required; and it can be used effectively for major projects in cities, such as urban freeways or water treatment plants. However, much of the city is actually constructed at relatively low cost. Here margins of error are larger and there is greater reliance on social benefits, the costing of which is more subjective than with economic benefits.

Finally, it uses resources and skills that are actually quite hard to find in secondary cities. And where they do exist, they draw skills away from other areas such as the technical design and management of the infrastructure base. So, it is not the value of CIP per se which is disputed here; it remains an important tool in deciding the viability of large capital investments. Rather, it is that a conventional CIP approach is inappropriate to the bulk of financial planning applications in secondary cities.

Given the need, clearly articulated in the study, to address capacity-building across a much broader front, a different approach was needed. It was felt that if ULGAs could better understand the value of their infrastructure, they would, in turn, be better equipped to plan and manage that infrastructure; and the way to achieve these goals, which would also lead to financial management, was through the development of a system of asset management. By this term we did not mean simply a mechanistic interpretation of asset management as a financial accounting tool. Rather, it was seen as a way in which to teach the principles of worth and value to the mayors and the city managers. The urban infrastructure base in many secondary towns may be small, yet it still represents the ULGA's greatest asset. Yet as the earlier analyses had indicated, there was no real understanding of the importance, or of the value, of that asset. The answer lay with the creation of a new system of asset management that was constructed specifically to address Ethiopia's urban infrastructure needs.

Building an asset management system

Infrastructure asset management is used almost universally in western countries as a basis for financial management, investment planning and maintenance scheduling. Like so much else, though, when western consultants receive a contract to develop an asset management programme for an African city or country, they take what they consider to be a universal model and transfer it directly to the African context. But these are not universal models; like so much development practice, they are actually western models that western practitioners believe are universal. That is something quite different. As a result, these programmes are rarely successful, and a good concept is lost because of inappropriate application. This is yet another illustration of why Africa needs to build its own models for its own use and its own circumstances if it wishes to create viable and sustainable cities. In Ethiopia the team built an indigenous model and was able to demonstrate its value to the federal government, the regional government and the ULGAs.

The way in which the asset-management-based approach was initiated and implemented was itself the outcome of a process. The concept was put forward in the workshops at the end of the infrastructure assessment and developed initially as a pilot, working with one ULGA that was interested, and willing to commit its staff in support. In this way its applicability as a basic tool of infrastructure management was demonstrated and it could then be followed up in the other ULGAs, thereby demonstrating how it could be taken to scale. This approach to urban development practice was drawn from earlier experience working with communities and organisations on informal settlement upgrading projects in South Africa, which in turn was a lesson learned from the Brazilian approach to upgrading.

Following this process, and having gained a reasonable understanding of the infrastructure base in the nine cities, through the infrastructure assessment, the team began to build a GIS-based map of infrastructure in each city. We were able to obtain GIS-based cadastres for three of the cities, but the rest we constructed from the master plans and updated with our own surveys. In carrying out the work described here, the infrastructure team (comprising one Ethiopian colleague and the author) were given one full-time and one half-time technical assistant. For the rest, the team used their own personal equipment and GIS software; there was no supplementary funding from the Bank, the government or our employer. The reason for mentioning this is because international agencies are reluctant to support the use of GIS at small scale, although they lavish large sums on complex national systems. However, this project was able to demonstrate how such a system can work perfectly well with limited human resource and on a low budget.

In this final phase of the study, the infrastructure team surveyed every road, drain, communal sanitation and solid waste facility and street light across the nine cities. Unfortunately for the water supply, there were no layout plans, so the team used the schematic diagrams of the water network for their initial assessment. One of the most important lessons, which had been demonstrated previously, in earlier work with informal settlements mentioned above, was that it is possible to build a GIS-based infrastructure plan with far less information than is needed for a complete cadastre, yet such a plan will provide accuracy in excess of 90 per cent, a level that is quite sufficient to build a comprehensive asset management plan, at least for the first iteration. The basis of this work is therefore one of incremental improvement, both in knowledge and in accuracy.

With modern technology, every town in Africa, whatever its size, has the information available to build the baseline date required. When this study began, there were no satellite data available, so the project simply used a paper map of a city, which was the only information available. That was placed on a wall and a photo taken of it, and this photo was then used as a raster base for the GIS. Conversion to the vector map (below) was based upon the use of nine control points. Of course it would be far simpler now to access a satellite image using Google Earth, as is illustrated in Figure 7.2, which shows Bishoftu, one of the four project cities in Oromia.

Given this image, the raster information on the maps can be converted to vector-based information suitable for the development of an asset management plan. Figure 7.3 is a diagram of the road layout of the city on the paper map, converted into a vector map. Similar drawings were obtained for drainage and water supply, while communal service points for all services were also added. A database of assets was then drawn up using nodes and points for the linear assets and points for the discrete assets.

Building an asset inventory

The infrastructure evaluation had provided the overview of the urban infrastructure base; this inventory then took that information down to a further level of detail. Information was gathered on quantities and quality for every segment of the database. For the roads and drainage this was extremely detailed, with design data and condition indicators mapped for every segment. For the water supply, few qualitative data were available, since there was insufficient information on the individual system components. And for solid waste and sanitation the data were limited to communal assets. In all cases the survey included movable assets such as vehicles and equipment.

Figure 7.2 Satellite-based map of the road layout in the ULGA of Bishoftu (Google™ Earth, 01 June 2010 ©).

Figure 7.3 Converting the map into a digital vector map.

This exercise of constructing an asset inventory had two outcomes. The first was to provide the appropriate level of detail required for effective technical management of the infrastructure in the future. The second was to provide the information base for the asset management plan to come. The most important lesson learned was in understanding how such a quantity of data could be assembled, in a constructive and beneficial format, with so few resources. This provided the basis for creating a methodology, which could then be taken to scale across all ULGAs. This exercise also demonstrated the critical role played by GIS in building an asset inventory, and further demonstrated that this could also be achieved with limited resources.

Building five-year capital investment plans

The infrastructure asset inventory was extremely valuable to the city leadership, providing them for the first time with a complete 'picture' of their infrastructure. From that point it was a logical progression to the next step, which concerned the establishment of current value, and the cost of refurbishment. That could then provide the basis for an asset management plan. At the same time, it was acknowledged that there is more to asset management planning than this. What was required was a structured approach that is understandable and easy to use and can be replicated annually, i.e. a methodology.

The basis for the methodology was a ten-point asset management plan, the first part of which formed the basis for the infrastructure inventory.[8] Once the inventory had been developed, the next step was to create a cost and value system for the infrastructure. This was done using what are termed unit rates[9] for both new work and for rehabilitation. Here the study used data gathered from recent construction work carried out in the cities, and matched these data with other work from major infrastructure clients (e.g. water resources, roads authorities, Addis Ababa City). Unit rates provide an approximation of cost, generally to within 20 per cent, but as the database is built up the accuracy can be improved to within 10 per cent. Its disadvantage is that the system is susceptible to rapid changes in construction costs, as happens for example in periods of high inflation or when a sudden surge in construction workload increases materials costs and profit margins. And it is no longer favoured by the World Bank, partly because the Bank's major projects require a higher level of accuracy and partly because it does not provide the level of information needed for the conventional, cost–benefit approach to CIP. For use in the secondary cities, however, the project demonstrated that it is a very effective system, allowing cost estimates to be built rapidly and with limited resources, and more effective than the traditional CIP approach. In addition, in situations where data are scarce, accuracy of more than 80 per cent is better than no knowledge at all; it is a figure with which to begin a process, and the objective is to incrementally upgrade accuracy over time as the exercise is repeated annually.

At this point the team ran a series of major workshops.[10] Unlike previous workshops, which were arranged by the regional or federal governments, these focused on the individual ULGAs[11] and extended over three to four days. The first day was given over to a discussion of the methodology and a review of the findings. On day 2 the cities put forward their proposals for rehabilitation. And because some of the services were either extremely limited or in extremely poor condition, this did include some new work. As is generally the case when cities prepare proposals, the extent of the proposed work was significant. So, working in small groups we provided the information for the cities to develop a cost for the work, by using the unit cost list. As might be expected, this was an order of magnitude higher than their estimated budget availability. On examining this information among the group, though, some interesting features emerged. Thus:

- Sanitation and solid waste remained low-priority spending areas, the major focus being on roads and water supply.
- There was a strong desire to increase the amount of asphalt road significantly.
- Water supply was seen as a municipal responsibility, and the mayors in particular saw the water companies as an arm of local government.
- The concept of integrated storm-water management remained elusive, and storm-water drains were seen as being essentially an appendage to the roads.

Overnight, members of the team evaluated the results, allowing day 3 to be devoted to strategic planning and prioritisation. Budgets were revised and the amended budgets submitted. The overall outcome was the production of a series of well-costed and, with the exclusion of asphalt roads, affordable budgets, taking into account the knowledge boundaries of the groups involved. Generally, the ULGA groups responsible for the budgets showed that they had gained the ability to develop goals and objectives and also to be able to analyse the infrastructure, identify weaknesses and define priorities.

Once these tasks had been carried out, the final step in trajectory 1 of the project was to organise a federal workshop bringing together all eighteen project cities and their regional governments, coordinated by the Ministry of Works and Urban Development, at which the five-year plans prepared by the cities were discussed and finalised.

Important outcomes

The process of capacity-building for infrastructure management in the secondary cities was considered by the government to have been a successful one, defined against the initial objectives. The key outcomes of particular relevance to this book are the following:

- The entire process, which covered a period of approximately fifteen months, took the ULGAs from a point where they had an extremely limited understanding of urban infrastructure, even though they were aware (from community feedback) that it was a crucial component of the city, to a point where they had a good working knowledge and were able to make informed decisions about capital investment.
- The bias remained strongly in favour of spending on roads, and particularly high-cost asphalt roads. The main issue that emerged here was not the cost of roads per se, but rather the enormously high burden of fully engineered asphalt roads, designed to support high axle loading at high speeds, yet used in an urban area. The cost of a limited length of asphalt road was shown to take up between one- and two-thirds of the total budget, while the maintenance cost is equally high. These figures demonstrated how this one item was the primary factor keeping the secondary cities from being financially stable and almost self-supporting.
- The importance of sanitation and the need to increase investment in both sanitation and solid waste were emerging as important issues. And while this awareness could be further improved, it was significantly higher than when the project first began. At the same time, it remained constrained by the issues raised after the infrastructure assessment, which related to technology, roles and relationships, particularly those between the ULGA and the individual residents. This issue of what is the 'appropriate' technical response was one that applied, though, across all infrastructure services.
- The most difficult area of infrastructure to portray and indicate the value of was that of urban drainage. All the ULGAs were affected by flooding to a greater or lesser extent, yet the ability to find practical solutions at a reasonable cost remained the greatest challenge of the project, and the only one that was limited in its success.
- Finally, the project, while successful in itself, did raise the issue of continuity and the question of how to convert personal knowledge into institutional knowledge. This issue will be explored further in the next subsection.

The new investment programme and the conversion to a three-year rolling programme

In 2007 the World Bank and the Ethiopian government agreed to develop a new urban development programme to follow up on the CBDSD programme and consolidate the operational systems and structures that had emerged. This new programme, termed the Urban Local Government Development Project (ULGDP), was intended to provide an incentive-driven 'specific purpose grant' that would support improvements in infrastructure and service delivery. This was additional to the fiscal transfers that the government had initiated.

The finance provided by the World Bank would be matched by two local contributions, each amounting to 20 per cent of grant funding, from both the regional government and the ULGA. Excluding Addis Ababa and Dira Dawa, which were allocated specific sums, the allocation between regions was based upon population size. For a medium-sized ULGA this translated into a capital injection of between US$5 million and US$8 million per ULGA, to be spent over a three-year period. Finally, the central government defined a range of activities that would be eligible for funding under this grant, and provided an indicative list of capital investments that would not be eligible.

In a project such as this one, there are a wide range of factors that have to be taken into account, including the definition of social and environmental objectives, procurement procedures, contract formulation and tendering procedures, to name just a few. These will not be discussed here; rather, the discussion has been directed towards the infrastructure planning and decision-making processes at the level of the ULGA, which is the primary focus of the book.

The success of the asset management programme in SNNPRS and Oromia during the earlier CBDSD project led to its widespread adoption by all the regions and project cities. The first step in implementation, therefore, was to roll out the training programme across all eighteen of the project cities. At the same time, an external support programme[12] that was already in place adapted its focus, which up to that point had not included an urban infrastructure component, to incorporate various aspects of infrastructure delivery, including strengthening the capacity of ULGA administrations to prepare what was now a significantly expanded approach to investment planning. Finally, the Ministry of Works and Urban Development made an important shift in its perception of infrastructure investment planning, moving from the five-year planning model, which is not only a rigid investment planning tool but also a static model, to a new model based upon the use of three-year rolling capital investment plans. These provide a much more dynamic and flexible model. This change could not have been operationalised without the foundation of the asset management plan.

In supporting the growth and development of local government, central government has to walk a fine line between two extremes on a continuum. One pole is the government being over-prescriptive, while the other is the government providing insufficient oversight. Providing local authorities with clearly defined powers, duties and functions, devolved and enshrined in a legal statute, as in Ethiopia, provides a framework for this balance, as does having the responsibilities of central government with respect to local government oversight clearly defined.

At the same time, the situation in rapidly growing cities with low levels of capacity is quite different from that of mature cities with a high level of capacity. The ideal in the former situation is to encourage the development of an information base that is primarily beneficial to the ULGA, while at the same time providing the information base for central government to provide an effective monitoring system. That was the approach taken in this project. It resulted in a classification of information with ten elements, which summarised this need:

1   basic geographic and demographic data;
2   income data (income and expenditure profile);
3   capital investment for the past three years;
4   summary of infrastructure development goals and objectives;
5   participatory process – results from community surveys;
6   formulated response to elements (4) and (5) above;
7   the proposed capital investment plan;
8   a three-year rolling programme of investment;
9   an associated maintenance budget (including existing infrastructure);
10 a staffing plan, covering resources and financial implications.[13]

This information is comprehensive, and a ULGA that is able to collect and collate this list emerges with a clear understanding of its infrastructure base and its investment programme, as well as an operational plan. The GTZ Urban Governance Programme, mentioned on p. 220, had support staff in each of the regions involved and was in a position to provide technical assistance to the individual ULGAs in preparing the detailed capital investment proposals, which was being carried out for the first time in this format.

When the process of developing the three-year rolling investment programme was initiated, the detailed support grant information was not available, and in this context the initial proposals did tend to revert to an inflated proposal; that is, one containing elements that could be described as a 'wish-list'.[14] However, with the finalising of the grant, and following a series of reviews and discussions between the federal ministry, regional bureaux and the ULGAs, cities submitted revised proposals that provided the basis for the implementation of the three-year rolling programme of capital investment.

Findings and conclusions

The development of the infrastructure investment programmes for eighteen secondary cities in Ethiopia, described here, was the outcome of a process, illustrated by trajectory 1 in Figure 7.1, that took three years from the beginning of the first situational analysis to the completion and submission of the second draft of large and complex capital investment planning budgets and rolling expenditure programmes. This is a short period in development terms, yet within that period eighteen of Ethiopia's major secondary cities, with a combined population of well over 2 million people, moved from a position where they had virtually no understanding of the infrastructure base, or the role that infrastructure played in urban development, to a point where they could plan and develop major budgets across all infrastructure services. To summarise the findings and conclusions from this part of the study:

1   The greatest challenge in taking this programme forward lies in maintaining the institutional memory and the capacity. How to do so will be discussed further in Chapter 11. That said, this programme, and the follow-on work supported by GTZ, demonstrated clearly that small municipal governments can be empowered, and capacity developed, to manage urban infrastructure in its entirety, provided there is also technical expertise in place.

2   The cities defined the extent of the work to be covered by the investment programme. This was much more extensive than originally intended, yet it derived from how cities saw their responsibilities. The World Bank had sought to limit the activities involved, in particular seeking to omit any spending on water supply (where there was another Bank-funded programme operating through the Federal Ministry of Water Resources) and non-core infrastructure services. By raising their own funding, the ULGAs could overcome this constraint, which only applied to the Bank-funded portion of the investment, and buy using their own resources.

3   Initially, the external grant funding was expected to provide the major portion of the total capital investment funding for the ULGAs. In the final budgets this funding accounted for approximately 25 per cent. The city budgets provided approximately 50 per cent, while the remainder came from different sources (e.g. regional and national funding, private funding and other external funding). Undoubtedly the grant funding programme acted as a major catalyst. Ultimately, though, cities, with the support of regional government, were able to find 70 per cent of the funding themselves, meaning that the original investment from the Bank leveraged an additional 300 per cent of local investment. This was possible because of three factors. The first was due to the

strengthening and reform of the municipal financial management system, which resulted in improved revenue flows and better control of financial planning. The second was due to the success of the infrastructure programme outlined here. And the third was due to the growth of self-confidence within the city administrations.

4   The infrastructure technology, and in particular deciding what is 'appropriate', provided a major constraint on the ULGAs' ability to develop effective infrastructure strategies, and impacted negatively on the capital investment planning process. The reasons will be explored further in the next section, which describes trajectory 2 of the project. However, there were two specific issues that did emerge quite clearly from this study, both of which relate to the roads infrastructure service.

- First, the asset management plan revealed the enormous cost burden placed on poor cities by the expense associated with asphalt roads. A government project running in parallel with this one had been looking at the potential for cobblestone road construction, and during the course of this project it became possible to integrate that work into the wider urban development process. The result was a rapid expansion of the cobblestone road training programme across all the project cities. Starting from a zero base at the beginning of this project, the eighteen cities together had proposals for the construction of 366 kilometres of cobblestone road. I shall not discuss the specific benefits and disadvantages of cobblestone roads. The points of importance, though, are (1) that it is a technology that emerged from within the country; and (2) while the cost is still high, it is only 40 per cent of the cost of an asphalt road yet provides significant job opportunities, and skills training, in labour-based construction.

- The second factor to emerge concerning roads was the issue of proportional cost; that is, the significant cost of roads relative to other infrastructure services such as sanitation and solid waste management, and even urban drainage, resulting in a budget allocation that lacks balance. One of the findings of the wider project was that cities could provide a comprehensive solid waste management service, or a substantive sanitation service, for the same amount of money that it would cost to build 3 to 4 kilometres of asphalt road. By bringing all the infrastructure services together within the ULGA area of responsibility, the budget can be managed more effectively and the ULGA's own budget could easily cover the funding for sanitation and solid waste services in their entirety. The project began the process of reallocation, though it did not go nearly far enough. However, there were also external factors at work here. Sanitation as a whole was the subject of diverse and contradictory approaches, not only within government but also on the part of external agencies. This was emerging as an issue of major importance within the Ministry of Works and Urban Development, though as part of the work covered by trajectory 2. As a result, it will be explored further in the section that follows.

What all of this is telling us is not that we require variable levels of technical service; it is telling us that we need a fundamental rethink of urban infrastructure across the board. This conclusion will be further reinforced in later chapters, and provides the main impetus for writing this book: the need to create a completely new urban infrastructure paradigm for African secondary towns and cities.

Section 2: the strategic analysis

Trajectory 2: an emerging infrastructure strategy

Trajectory 2, shown in Figure 7.1, concerned the development of implementation strategies and institutional structures, and was then followed, later, by policy development. In this section the focus is primarily on the strategy and the policy process. The issue of institutional structures has been discussed briefly in earlier sections, and will be returned to in Chapter 11, which deals with good governance. Institutional relationships, particularly between tiers of government, will be introduced, but again the detailed analysis is incorporated into the later chapter on good governance.

The conceptual approach to this project could best be described as one of 'twin tracking', with the requirements of the two trajectories being quite different. With trajectory 1 the focus was on what was happening at the level of the city through an exploration by the internal dynamic; in essence, this was an exploration of the 'how' of infrastructure practice. Trajectory 2, on the other hand, looked at the city, and in this case its infrastructure, from the outside, in terms of 'what' it should do, primarily in respect of technology, but also institutionally.

Clearly, there are areas of commonality and overlap between the two. However, what this 'twin-tracking' approach did was to enable the same set of issues to be explored from two quite different perspectives; and in spite of initial reservations, this proved in the end to be extremely beneficial. The first trajectory was concerned quite specifically with capacity-building, and in a sense responded to the question: can a city administration in a (relatively) small secondary town be capacitated to manage a wide range of sometimes technically complex infrastructure services?

The second trajectory, on the other hand, was asking a quite different question, namely: can a city be meaningfully empowered to manage that range of infrastructure services? In addition, the second trajectory raised a second question, namely: what technology is most suited to the needs of secondary cities in Ethiopia, enabling them to fulfil their role in providing and maintaining an urban infrastructure base? This latter question needs to be answered if capacity-building is to have a sustainable outcome. And the reality was that, while the work on trajectory 1 was successful in achieving its goals for ULGA capacity-building, to the extent that the World Bank and the federal government created a second, follow-up programme to support more widespread investment in urban infrastructure in the secondary cities, it nonetheless highlighted serious weaknesses in the whole area of infrastructure 'solutions'.

Understanding the actors

Ultimately, technology and management or institutional systems are inter-related, as the previous chapters have indicated. However, the complexity of this interaction makes it useful to explore the two separately, at least up to a point of convergence. This discussion on trajectory 2 will seek to do that, beginning with institutional relationships. In this context the first step in the analysis was to identify key actors.[15] Broadly, these were the following:

- The World Bank, which in the Ethiopian Office included an urban sector specialist managing this programme; a water sector specialist, responsible for the Bank's water programmes; and a transportation sector specialist responsible for (primarily national) roads and transportation. There was also a public finance specialist involved.
- The Water and Sanitation Program, the World Bank proxy organisation working with sanitation, which was located in the World Bank building.
- The German development agencies GTZ, working through the Urban Governance Programme, and KfW, working with the federal Ministry of Works and Urban Development in supporting capacity-building in project management, with the focus on larger urban projects.
- The British development agency DFID, which had seconded a water specialist to support the federal Ministry of Water Resources in water supply.

Within government there were a number of ministries involved with urban development. The wider picture of federal line ministry involvement will be illustrated in Figure 11.4 in Chapter 11. However, the key federal ministries were:

- the Ministry of Works and Urban Development, with separate departments of Capacity Building (responsible for this project), Policy and Planning, Housing and Urban Planning;
- the Ministry of Water Resources, with line responsibility for urban water supply;
- the Ministry of Health, gradually taking responsibility for sanitation;
- the Environmental Protection Authority, situated within the Prime Minister's Office, taking increasing responsibility for solid waste management, initiated through legislation on landfill sites.

In addition, discussions were also held with the federal Ministry of Transport; the Ethiopian (federal) Roads Authority (ERA); EEPCo, the federal electricity parastatal; ETC, the federal telecommunications parastatal; and several departments of the Addis Ababa City Council.

Finally, at regional level there were:

- the regional bureaux of Works and Urban Development;
- the regional bureaux of Water Resources;
- the regional bureaux of Health;
- the regional Rural Roads Authority (RRA) (equivalent in status to a bureau).

Each of these groups approached urban development from its own particular perspective, which is understandable; but also, in many (though not all) cases, with its own predefined agenda, which is perhaps less acceptable. In all the discussions that took place around this issue, though, two major issues emerged. The first was the extent of the sheer lack of understanding that the majority of individuals in these organisations had of relevant issues that lay outside of their own area of expertise. For those in sector-based programmes or institutions, this related to a lack of knowledge and understanding of how local government functioned, and its legally defined role in society. For those in urban specialisations, such as urban planning, it related to the lack of knowledge and understanding of other disciplines in the same urban context, together with a lack of even a basic understanding of the role and nature of urban infrastructure in this wider context. This latter condition also applied to many of the engineers as well.

The second area of discussion relates to infrastructure technology, and its role in urban society. On a personal level I found that working in Ethiopia, after a career working in an Anglo-Saxon urban development *Weltanschauung*, with all the perceptions of what constitute appropriate technical 'solutions' that doing so implies, required a complete change of mindset, as well as a recognition that there are actually other means of urban infrastructure delivery. To some extent the change in this mindset had already started to occur earlier, while I was working on informal settlement upgrading in Cape Town,[16] influenced in that case by working with colleagues in Brazil. However, prior to becoming involved in the Ethiopian project, this had not extended into thinking about infrastructure, other than to express a high level of discomfort with existing practice and approaches. My change of mindset brought home the full extent to which being situated inside the Anglo-Saxon urban development *Weltanschauung* hinders and constrains original thought. When I was working in the secondary cities of Ethiopia, however, in the work that was described under trajectory 1, my thinking changed; suddenly, the contradictions implicit in the current international approach to urban infrastructure delivery became glaringly evident.

From a 'strategic plan' to a strategic assessment

The outputs in trajectory 2 began with the preparation of a 'Strategic Plan'. While building on the experience of Ethiopian practice explored in trajectory 1, and extensive personal experience, this also involved an extensive literature review, covering the UN-Habitat Best Practices library, World Bank projects and a range of academic and web-based literature on practices and experiences from a diverse ranges of sources. From an analysis of all this material, one clear finding emerged: the vast majority of the material originates in Europe and America, and more specifically the United Kingdom. Its genesis then follows one of two routes: either (1) it comes from within western experience and western applications and is then exported, and sometimes 'adapted' for use in African conditions; or (2) it is developed 'for' African conditions. Of course there are actually real 'African' experiences out there, which generally provided the most valuable case studies – an example would be the Ugandan experience in creating an institutional framework for urban water supply in the major cities – but these represent only a tiny fraction of the total. It is not that there is a shortage of new potential solutions in infrastructure technology; rather, it is the lack of indigenous input and expertise that prevents technological solutions being situated in context. This analysis served to confirm, in a very practical way, the findings of Chapter 4.

Eventually an implementation strategy did emerge from this process of intellectual exploration, and was well received by the Ministry; yet it remained constrained, and was still too dependent on these same practices that were being applied elsewhere in Africa, with little success. The next stage of the work sought to integrate some of this practice within the Ethiopian model of social equity, through the production of a series of manuals. And one of these, relating to asset management, did manage to provide a completely different approach designed specifically for Ethiopian use and situated within an Ethiopian operational context. Yet the strategy could not provide ideal solutions, because at that stage there were simply none available, and the time-frame for the project, coupled with the constraints imposed by the large output of deliverables, did not present an opportunity to develop any, a process in any case that was to take two years.

For me personally, what emerged at that stage were more a series of questions about the nature of existing approaches used primarily by international and bilateral agencies. Some of the key questions were:

- Why should the responsibility for water supply stop when water is delivered to a house? After all, water is a resource, not a commodity.
- What happens to water once it has been used, and needs to be discharged, if there is no sewer? Which in turn leads to the wider question: Why is urban water supply so totally separated from urban water resource management as a whole?
- What is the long-term implication of building increasing numbers of pit latrines in urban areas, not just for groundwater but for wider environmental reasons, with urbanisation, and densification, increasing at such a rapid rate? Where is this path taking African cities?
- Is not human waste itself a resource?
- How can we continue to build roads in the way we do when car ownership covers only 5 per cent of the urban population?
- Why are design standards for roads based on vehicular traffic while poor people have to walk on roads that are either incredibly dusty (in the dry season) or very muddy (in the wet season)?
- How much of this urban planning and engineering practice is actually grounded in an African context, and how much of it remains a western export?

There are then a series of broader institutional and philosophical issues, such as:

- Are these western ideas really so good, particularly in a world of rapid climate change?
- Why do western, and western-dominated international, agencies, and professionals, override local culture, and particularly an African belief in human dignity and equity, to impose systems that are socially and culturally inequitable and differentiate rich from poor?
- And the ultimate question, of course: if the Anglo-Saxon capitalist model is clearly beneficial, why does it have to be imposed; why is it not warmly embraced?

Of course, none of these questions is new, and neither is the list comprehensive. A mechanistic response might indicate that each one, taken individually, has an answer. When I was presented with the entire range of questions, though, as happened in the exploration of Ethiopia's secondary cities, it became clear that a mechanistic response is inadequate. These are not simply technical questions, or even social questions; they also raise fundamental moral and ethical issues.

At this point, trajectory 2 moved forward in two ways. On a personal level the questions raised led directly to the writing of this book, which provides an attempt to address them through the creation of a new paradigm grounded in African experience. On a more practical level the report, defined in the terms of reference as a Strategic Plan, was produced. The outcomes of the project described previously, and in particularly those from trajectory 1, had shown that the implementation of infrastructure was less advanced than developments in other urban sectors such as housing, planning and even financial management; and the 'level' of output in the deliverables reflected this discrepancy. So whereas the other study areas within the project were able to produce specific policies and strategies, this was not possible for infrastructure, a situation that was accepted by the Ministry. As a result, the document intended to be a Strategic Plan could best be described as a Strategic Assessment.

The assessment was comprehensive in its coverage of urban infrastructure services and provided twenty-five specific recommendations covering all aspects of infrastructure delivery. At the same time, the Strategic Assessment identified three key issues that impact on policy and strategy development (Abbott, 2006). These were that:

1   There was little, if any, understanding of the strategic, the developmental or even the practical role that physical infrastructure plays in urban development.
2   There are no effective policies or strategies in place to support and develop urban infrastructure. Hence, there can be no follow-through from policy to implementation.
3   The current approach to infrastructure delivery, which is solely project driven, is leading to choices that are not cost-effective. Spending is being misdirected, resulting in an infrastructure that is inappropriate for current needs and unsustainable in the long term.

Following from this, the report identified three 'core areas' on which it was felt the federal government should focus in its support of ULGAs and in furtherance of a sustainable urban infrastructure implementation strategy. These were:

1   *Policy and implementation strategy.* There is a need for clear policies and implementation strategies for urban infrastructure as a whole, with clearly defined aims, goals and objectives.

2   *Organisational structure.* There is a need to create a framework for infrastructure delivery that is delivery driven[17] and that then *continues* to guide and monitor the process.
3   *Financial management of infrastructure.* The approach to the financial management of infrastructure has to be linked more closely with affordability[18] and long-term sustainability.

At this point the assessment was still accepting, albeit reluctantly, the need for a limited form of service-level differentiation, primarily because it could see no other way forward; that is, the thinking was still locked into an Anglo-Saxon infrastructure delivery paradigm. This mindset was to change in the next phase of the work, when more time was available to think through the nature of urban infrastructure more thoroughly and in a context that was more deeply embedded in Ethiopian society.

Towards an integrated urban infrastructure policy

The primary 'client' for the section of the CBDSD programme described here was, collectively, the four regional governments involved, while the federal Ministry of Works and Urban Development played a coordinating role in the overall management of the work and the organisation of the deliverables. However, given the relevance of the findings in the Strategic Plan to federal policy, it was not surprising that the Ministry chose to use these findings as inputs into core policy processes at a federal level, using the three core areas identified above as a guiding framework.

Ethiopia's primary development goal was, and remains, poverty reduction, and its overarching development strategy was contained in its *Plan for Accelerated and Sustained Development to End Poverty* (PASDEP). Within this broader plan, each line ministry would implement one or more programmes which represented that ministry's specific contribution to the achievement of the PASDEP goals. For its part, the Ministry of Works and Urban Development had several inputs, one of which[19] took as its overall goal the need to '[d]evelop the institutional, policy, strategy and legal frameworks that improve the organizational structure and systems of city administrations for the purposes of infrastructure and service delivery'. The purpose of this sub-programme was, in essence, to follow up on the Strategic Assessment and the Final Summary Report described above, to produce definitive outputs.

The work, which was this time carried out from within the Ministry itself, rather than through external consultants, involved nine different activities covering a spectrum from policy and implementation, through institutional change, to education and training, as well as the follow-on support for CIP/Asset Management preparation described under trajectory 1. The majority of these outcomes were operational in nature.

The most radical change, though, was an outcome of trajectory 2, which resulted in a completely new approach to urban infrastructure and its role in a rapidly urbanising society. This outcome was the creation of an Integrated Urban Infrastructure Policy for Ethiopia – a concept that is both original and unique, and that provides the first completely new approach to urban infrastructure delivery in Africa since the end of colonisation.

Exploring an integrated urban infrastructure policy

The work that has been described here led to a range of unanswered questions. At the same time, though, it also led to one very significant conclusion: there was a much greater interaction between the different infrastructure services than was currently acknowledged in western thinking. The purpose of the policy process was to explore these linkages and set out a comprehensive policy document that defined them and that brought all the major infrastructure services into one common framework of analysis and review.

There were four features of this policy that were particularly significant in understanding both the institutional and the developmental role played by urban infrastructure. The first, and perhaps the most significant, was that it enabled a federal policy to be aligned with the legally defined powers, duties and functions of the ULGAs for the first time. This may not appear to be significant at first glance; yet Chapter 5 on decentralisation showed quite clearly the extent to which this inability to link national policy to a defined role for local government contributes to the wider failure of decentralisation strategies in Africa.

The second was the inclusive nature of the policy at a federal level. Thus, the policy sought to identify other ministries and federal institutions involved with local government and integrate them into the policy process. It also sought to ensure that the policy was aligned with other federal policies concerned with urban development, to bring about a wider, and more effective, integration of these policies.

Third, it sought to situate urban infrastructure within a framework of urban governance, placing its delivery and operation at the heart of the government's commitment to the principle, and practice, of good governance. And, fourth, it recognised the need to draw a clear distinction between policy, strategy and implementation. This is, of course, more of a necessity when a federal system of government is operating. At the same time, though, it is also a choice, reflecting an Ethiopian view of the role of policy vis-à-vis strategy and implementation. In taking this approach, the Ethiopian policy provides an alternative to the British policy process discussed in Chapter 5; and in doing so it was able to demonstrate that there is an alternative approach to policy that African governments can use.

They do not have to be reliant on an imported model that is poorly suited to a country undergoing rapid urbanisation.

At the same time, the policy highlighted critical areas that reflect either weaknesses in the knowledge base, or areas where further exploration of the implications is required. This is not a reflection on the government or its policy, which had to be developed within the framework of existing practices and processes as perceived at the time. Rather, by highlighting the weakness it drew attention to the four critical issues that together define the future direction of the African urban debate, as least in so far as it applies to the secondary towns and cities. These areas related to:

1   the nature of the relationship between different tiers of government in relation to urban governance, roles and responsibilities;
2   the technology base for infrastructure delivery;
3   the roles of, and the relationship between, urban planning and urban infrastructure management, in the development of the secondary towns;
4   the role of good governance in policy; particularly the question of whether good governance can, or should, be a policy goal.

Regarding the first of these, the policy provided a list of ministries involved with government and identified the need to achieve consensus in driving the urban infrastructure policy forward. Chapter 5 has already highlighted this as a key area of risk in decentralisation. In addition, it is suggested here that the policy approach was overly idealistic in this regard, in that it failed to take account of the enormous power and influence exerted by external agencies, many of which are unable to cope with the implications of an integrated urban infrastructure policy on their own sectoral power base.

The second point has already been mentioned. The Ethiopian study showed the extent to which urban infrastructure plays a critical and often central role as a driver of economic development in the secondary towns. In addition, it also confirmed the findings of the previous chapters in highlighting the need to find new technological solutions for urban infrastructure which address the current situation: an urbanising society of the twenty-first century faced with resource constraints that simply did not exist in past urbanisation cycles.

The third point relates to the specific relationship between infrastructure and urban planning. The policy sought to situate this emerging interpretation of urban infrastructure: as a key driver of urban development, within an existing planning paradigm that is becoming increasingly anglophone in its construct. The conclusion in Chapter 3 indicated that this goal is not achievable and that the new infrastructure model also requires a rethinking of the existing anglophone planning construct. This study confirmed that conclusion, and questions the current international view that urban planning should provide the basis for urban development in Africa, arguing instead that it is totally inappropriate in its present form and that infrastructure is better able to fulfil this role.

The fourth point, which in many ways is the most important, asks the question: where exactly does good governance fit into the policy process? Urban good governance is central to sustainable development and the principles that have been used to define it are universal; the application, though, is specific, and situated within a value system that is linked to the society within which it operates. The previous approach to decentralisation failed because the locus of intellectual exploration of its role in society was external to Africa. Good governance is in danger of falling into the same trap, with the likelihood that it will result in the same outcome. The question raised here is: if we have a predefined area of action for a policy, which in this case is urban infrastructure, should we not be tailoring urban good governance to that specific application if we want it to be effective? And if that is the case, should we not define, a priori, specific overarching goals, which would then provide a framework for formulating the urban good governance construct?

It was simply not possible to address these four key issues while working to formulate the integrated urban infrastructure policy in Ethiopia; there were simply too many unknowns and too great a time pressure to address them effectively. The fact that they are critical questions affecting the future of urban development, not only in Ethiopia but in Africa generally, and the fact that they need to be debated internally, within African countries, if the secondary towns are to be developed successfully, provided the final motivation for writing this book. And the chapters that follow seek to address these questions. Before we move on, though, the final section will review the findings and the wider conclusions of the Ethiopian study, in order to carry these forward into the ensuing discussion.

Part 3: findings and conclusions

The importance of Ethiopia to Africa

Ethiopia provides arguably the most important case-study experience of an African urban capacity-building programme in recent times. In support of this statement I would suggest that there are six important ways in which Ethiopia differs from other countries in sub-Saharan Africa, when viewed from an urban perspective; and by exploring these differences we can gain a greater understanding of the direction that we need to take to create a sustainable urban future across the subcontinent. These six areas of difference are as follows:

- Ethiopia was never colonised in the way that other countries were. It was invaded, but never subjugated, and played the central role in defeating the invading power on its soil. This provides a unique development perspective because we can see the country as it is, without the colonial overlay that lies like a blanket of mist over so much of the African development landscape.

- The political evolution of modern-day Ethiopia resulted in the country having a delayed response to urban reform. Thus, along with South Africa, it initiated its urban reform process only in the 1990s. This meant that it was able to explore, and learn from, previous experiences elsewhere.

- Its urbanisation process was similarly delayed, so that by the 1990s, when the reform process began, it had one of the lowest levels of urbanisation in the world. It also had an extremely low level of informal settlement activity, as opposed to informal housing, with which it is often confused. This fact enabled the country to explore changes in policy direction to manage future growth rather than extant scenarios.

- The Ethiopian government believes in driving its own development process and resists being dictated to by external agencies. As a result, the framework of external financial support that underpinned the urban capacity-building programme (provided by the World Bank) was supportive rather than prescriptive, albeit under duress. This supportive approach applied as well, though in this case more proactively, to the capacity-building programme provided by the German government (GTZ), which supported capacity-building at both regional and urban government level to implement the reform programme. It also provided the framework for exploring realities, and new ways of thinking around future direction (as opposed to providing predefined and pre-packaged external solutions). This approach was in stark contrast to that followed by the other external development agencies operating in the country.

- The Ethiopian government has a Ministry of Capacity Building, and within many of the line ministries there is a Capacity Building Department or Unit. The funding for the urban programme described here was channelled through such a unit (termed the Urban Development Capacity Building Office, UDCBO) in the federal Ministry of Works and Urban Development. This form of institutional structure, acting outside of professional sectoral line interests, was important in enabling and facilitating an objective study of urbanisation processes.

- Finally, Ethiopia has an ethos of social equity underpinning its development philosophy which is deeply embedded in the society. In spite of economic pressures, the government attempts to ensure that both the spatial structure of the secondary cities and the approach to infrastructure delivery continue to reflect this. This ethos is explicitly stated in the country's Urban Development Policy, which says that '[t]he development [of urban areas] should be able to create [a] situation whereby both rich and poor live together by sharing common infrastructure and social services' (Federal Government of Ethiopia, 2005).

This is not to imply that the programme described here was perfect. The human resource base in particular remains frighteningly low; and this in turn limits the ability of the government to deliver and manage urban infrastructure to best effect. In addition, those driving the urban planning process are finding it difficult to accept the conceptual change from infrastructure as a support service to infrastructure as a development driver. However, even the weaknesses provide important lessons, and three of these in particular provide valuable experiences, identifying core blockages to implementing an effective urban development programme. These blockages are:

- the limitations and weaknesses of the line management approach to government at a national level, particularly the way in which this impacts on local government;
- the approach taken to decentralisation, specifically the allocation of powers duties and functions between sectoral line ministries in federal and regional government and the ULGAs;
- the limitations of an urban development process driven solely by urban planning, reflecting in practice the weakness identified in Chapter 4;
- the narrow focus of the professional knowledge base in applied development areas such as urban planning and infrastructure management, which in turn reflects the inappropriate nature of western professional degrees for providing the knowledge and skills required to provide innovative and creative solutions to the emerging urban development scenario unfolding in Africa.

Building from this, there follow five key findings that highlight specific issues that need to be addressed in going forward. These relate to:

1 the role of infrastructure in urban development;
2 the need to explore the interaction between different infrastructure services;
3 the centrality of social equity;
4 the need to deepen, and strengthen, the indigenous knowledge base;
5 the pressure exerted by external agencies in driving the urban development agenda.

Key finding 1: infrastructure is at the heart of urban development in the secondary cities in Africa

The open political and intellectual space granted to explore the role that infrastructure plays in the development of secondary cities was a significant and important element of the Ethiopian programme, and the result was to demonstrate that urban infrastructure provides the key to successful, and sustainable, urban development, to an extent that is significantly beyond current international thinking.

Historically, Ethiopia has operated within what may be termed a 'planning paradigm', which in turn has driven its approach to urban development. As was illustrated earlier, the country built its cities around master plans. In this development context, infrastructure was seen as a support service and planned within sectoral silos, a process that resulted in a failure to follow planning through to implementation. This was the situation until 2005 and is illustrated by the language of the Urban Development Policy. It is also the trajectory that is currently being followed elsewhere in sub-Saharan Africa under the pressure of external actors, as evidenced by the approach that underpins UN-Habitat's *State of African Cities 2008* report (2008) and the same body's report on urban planning in 2009. In this context, then, the approach taken by Ethiopia up to 2005 represents the logical outcome sought by those, particularly in western academia, who argue for this strong planning-based model to be applied elsewhere in Africa.

However, the way in which the urbanisation study evolved in Ethiopia after 2005 reflects a complete turnaround in thinking about what drives urban development. Planning generally, and development planning in particular, remains the basis for urban development, particularly at a regional level. The view at the beginning of this programme was typical of that described above. Thus, the federal Urban Development Policy of that time did not include infrastructure delivery as either a goal or a principle. In its list of eight core urban development activities it simply lists one of these as the 'supply of land and infrastructure facilities' (Federal Government of Ethiopia, 2005, p. 18). Here we see the classical interpretation of infrastructure as a series of support services.

Three years later the government produced what could be described as its flagship development strategy, the *Plan for Accelerated and Sustained Development to End Poverty* (PASDEP) (MoFED, 2006). As part of its contribution to PASDEP, the Ministry of Works and Urban Development developed two programmes for implementation, which together represented the urban components of the plan. The second of these programmes was the Urban Good Governance Package, and this in turn had a sub-programme on Urban Infrastructure and Service Improvement. In pursuance of this project it was agreed that

[t]he Ministry of Works and Urban Development will, in close consultation with other involved federal bodies, regional and city authorities, draft and then implement a detailed action plan that will put in place, at federal, regional and local levels as appropriate, a clear set of policies, strategies, laws and regulations (or by-laws) for planning, financing, developing, maintaining and managing municipal infrastructure.

(MWUD, 2007)

By 2008, when the government agreed the UDCBP with the World Bank, infrastructure had moved to the heart of the urban development strategy for secondary cities. Thus, by 2010, when the cities had worked with infrastructure development programmes through their capital investment programmes for three years, the government came to the acknowledged viewpoint that infrastructure was the key development driver for the secondary cities, and that, in this regard, a key aim of the government was to implement a sustainable integrated urban infrastructure development and management system in Ethiopia. This in turn led to the second key finding.

Key finding 2: all physical infrastructure services are integral to the urban development process

The inclusion of all aspects of infrastructure management within the ULGA proclamation, as described in Chapter 6, incorporates the concept of total responsibility for infrastructure within a legal framework. This was critical to the further development of an urban infrastructure plan and played a crucial role in building local government capacity. At the same time, it was not possible to achieve the degree of responsibility envisaged, owing to a mismatch of objectives, with the concept of total responsibility being in conflict with the defined goals of individual line ministries involved with specific infrastructure services such as water supply.

From a ULGA perspective this chapter has highlighted how, in the early stages of the CBDSD study, there was a lack of understanding of the role of infrastructure generally in urban development; and this extended to a lack of understanding of how the powers and duties related to urban infrastructure could be operationalised. By the time the follow-on programme (the ULGDP) was initiated, this situation had changed quite dramatically, with there being a much greater knowledge, and understanding, of the role of infrastructure in the functioning of the city.

While the inclusion of all aspects of infrastructure management within the ULGA proclamation embodies the concept of total responsibility (for infrastructure services) within a legal framework, this responsibility was not quite so clearly defined in practice. On the contrary, sector-based federal ministries and their associated regional bureaux were becoming increasingly interventionist across almost the entire range of infrastructure services. This important issue will be discussed further in Chapter 11; here, the focus is on the local government response.

The ULGDP was intended to provide support for urban infrastructure, and as such set out broad guidelines relating to the types of project activities that were eligible for funding. These initially excluded water supply projects, which were funded under a separate programme operated through the Ministry of Water Resources. However, in their capital investment plans all the cities that had water-related investment needs refused to accept this constraint, and included proposals for water schemes in their budget. In discussions around this issue, it became clear that mayors saw water supply as their responsibility. Whatever external actors might argue, based upon technical and economic rationality, the mayors had a very clear understanding of which areas of activity their constituents held them accountable for; and all the major infrastructure services fell into this category.

This reinforces the point that was made in the previous chapter: that there is not only a strong social rationality underpinning local government control over infrastructure delivery in a developing cities context but also a strong political rationality. Taking an infrastructure service away from municipal government has a strong negative impact and impinges upon both of these rationalities. This is not the same as saying municipalities should manage all infrastructure services directly. What the Ethiopian experience tells us – and this provides an interesting contrast with the South African experience discussed in the previous chapter – is that *overall control* of the infrastructure base (as opposed to the operational management of specific infrastructure services) is a prerequisite for political stability at the city level, and a prerequisite for urban good governance.

Key finding 3: socially equitable urban infrastructure is realistic and achievable

The government of Ethiopia is committed to a policy of social equity in service delivery, which, translated into practice, means that everyone is treated equally. This does not imply that all services are designed to the same technical standard; what it means is that differentiation is based upon criteria that relate to the city as a social unit, not upon socio-economic differentiation (i.e. separation at the level of the individual). This is helped, of course, by the simple fact that many areas in the cities comprise a mix of families from different socio-economic groupings. This chapter does not claim that Ethiopia is perfect, and there are numerous situations where inequity exists at a local level, with some poorer settlements on the periphery not having equal access. Yet the fact is that this reflects a lack of capacity; it is not caused by an institutional policy of inequity (i.e. differentiated levels of service).

In comparison, the current policy for delivering urban infrastructure in much of sub-Saharan Africa, which is defined by external actors, links service delivery to individual affordability; that is, poorer people receive a 'lower' level of service than more affluent residents. The reason they do so is due almost entirely to the fact that external governments, development agencies (and staff), development professionals and academics – all those who really control African development – are trapped within the thinking that underpins the four thematic forces of influence described in Chapter 1. The Ethiopian experience indicates that were these decisions to be made in-country, socially equitable solutions could and, if only because of political pressure from below, would actually be found.

There is no doubt – and the study confirmed it – that social equity is intimately bound up with affordability. What the Ethiopian programme showed, though, was that we are interpreting this latter term in the wrong way. Affordability should be defined not at the level of the individual but at the level of the ULGA. By the time this programme was completed, the ULGAs in the eighteen project cities had been able to demonstrate, with real numbers, that they could generate at least 50 per cent of their own funds for their capital investment programmes. Once they realised this, they began to perceive the World Bank grant funding as having overly onerous conditions attached, particularly in respect of procurement and reporting procedures. This in turn resulted in their using their own funding to achieve wider infrastructure coverage while using the World Bank grants for major projects – an ideal response. What this programme illustrated over time was the extent to which ULGA approaches to infrastructure financing are greatly influenced by perceptions and expectations. Thus, if the primary focus is on the external funding support, then the outcome is to create a dependency mentality; on the other hand, if the focus is on the 50 per cent or more of the funding that can be raised internally, with the external funding being supplementary, then the outcome is to build confidence and create a winning mentality.

There are two important provisos to this principle. The first is that there has to be a well-functioning financial management system in place. The CBDSD programme included a study of urban financing, and followed this up with legislation to improve financial management systems and build financial management capacity. Building this capacity has been a priority of the World Bank for several decades now; and this has been shown to be an essential prerequisite to improving both urban governance generally and infrastructure governance specifically. At the same time, though, the Ethiopian project called into question the Bank's approach to capital investment planning, which is based upon achieving a positive rate of return. The approach developed in Ethiopia placed a much greater emphasis, from the beginning, on asset management as the basis for capital investment planning, and limited the need to explore the rate of return to the larger projects. Thus, an asset management system should form the basis for urban infrastructure planning and is sufficient for the internally funded infrastructure, while traditional capital investment planning, based upon a rate of return, whether economic or social, should be limited to large capital-item investments.

The second proviso relates to the technical choices that are made. Ethiopia does not have many high budget reticulation systems. However, having an infrastructure reticulation system in any given service area that has a lower budget than current western systems does not imply a 'lower' level of service. Rather, the work in Ethiopia highlighted the need for a major rethink of technology that is grounded in principles of sustainability from its inception. The way in which such a rethink can be achieved will be explored in detail in Chapters 9 and 10, which will describe a new conceptual framework for sustainable urban infrastructure in Africa.

Key finding 4: long-term sustainability in urban infrastructure management is dependent upon deepening the indigenous knowledge base

This project demonstrated clearly that it is possible to create a sound infrastructure base for secondary cities in an African context; however, maintaining this base is a separate issue. There are a number of initiatives under way to ensure that there is continuity, and the knowledge is institutionalised; and the Urban Governance Programme operated by the German development agency GTZ has contributed significantly to that process. In doing so it highlights the priority need, which is to build capacity. What is often omitted, though, is a second, equally important, need, which is for suitably trained and qualified professionals to actually carry out the work. These are the two areas covered here.

Developing an effective, and ongoing, capacity-building strategy and programmes

The lesson that Ethiopia can provide for international agencies is that capacity-building does work, provided it is targeted correctly. Capacity-building can be seen as a journey through rough terrain. The traveller arrives at a crossroads where the sign has been removed, but fortunately meets a guide who can help to point the way. The journey goes well, but it is only at the end of the journey that the traveller realises she has arrived at the coast, when in fact she wished to visit an inland location. Every journey has valuable lessons, and is an experience in its own right, but the journey is only truly successful if it manages to arrive at the right destination.

One of the most successful examples of capacity-building drawn from this study related to the development of an asset management programme, which underpinned the broader capital investment planning process. This programme was developed locally and tested locally before being expanded, with the full support of the mayors and city managers. It formed the basis of workshops, and one in place was repeated each year during the process of capital investment plan (CIP) preparation. By the end of the fourth cycle, in 2010, the Ethiopian consultant running the training programme was able to report back that

> I would like to express my happiness concerning the change that have come about in the cities toward [the] asset management plan and CIP preparation. Every Mayor in the cities is talking about the importance of asset management. Most of them are also implemented the ten steps and also there is a good beginning on institutionalizing the asset management team to keep its sustainability.[20]

Capacity-building works, and infrastructure provides the best mechanism for developing this local capacity at the city level. For it to be successful, though, there are four preconditions that apply to the approach:

1   The programme has to be developed locally, and it has to begin where people are at, not where external agencies expect them to be.
2   The pilot group has to be chosen with care, using a group that actively wishes to be involved. This in itself takes time and effort.
3   The framework for action has to follow a clearly defined methodology, again linked to local conditions.
4   There has to be continuity in the support programme, with a timeframe of at least five years, and preferably a degree of scaled-down support for another three to five years beyond that.

The first step is widely accepted by those working in local development. The other three emerged from experience gained working with the Brazilians on in informal settlement upgrading, and successfully applied in South Africa in the same area. There is, however, a major problem here, which is that a methodological approach does not sit comfortably in an Anglo-Saxon development framework based on target-setting and physical deliverables. Ultimately, though, it is this approach to capacity-building, with these four steps, that provides the key to success.

Building the professional base

After completion of the CBDSD project, and in the move across the follow-on programme, the Minister of Works and Urban Development asked a simple but extremely important question (paraphrased): Do we have enough professionals, with the right skills mix, to deliver the infrastructure to the cities and then to manage the new urban infrastructure base? This resulted in a study of existing university degrees as well as programmes being taught at the Civil Service College, which had a programme in municipal engineering.

The findings of this study provided a simple answer to the minister's question: there were not enough professionals being trained, and the degree programmes that could supply graduates, such as civil engineering, might be producing good civil engineers, but these graduates were totally unsuited to either delivering or managing urban infrastructure that would meet the needs of the urban areas in Ethiopia. The outcome was the creation of a new degree programme.

An important issue identified by this study was the extent to which external development initiatives, particularly in the area of (both national and local) infrastructure delivery and management, was leading to increased specialisation and sub-specialisation within infrastructure. This was mirroring the western trend of towards moving degree specialisation down from a Master's level to a first (Bachelor's) degree level. Doing so may be appropriate in countries with a well-established and mature infrastructure base. However, it is not necessarily the appropriate system for rapidly growing economies and cities.

The question then became one of where such a programme should be based. The degree programme produced here was situated within a civil engineering framework, which was quite problematic. Infrastructure is about much more than engineering, as too is technology. Engineering skills are used to construct elements of the infrastructure base, but this should never be confused with infrastructure itself. In the Ethiopian case described here, the civil engineering curriculum was all that was immediately available. While Chapter 11 will discuss a more appropriate educational framework, designed specifically for infrastructure management, the Ethiopian curriculum did provide the pilot for that dedicated programme.

The new degree was termed Civil and Urban Engineering, and the core engineering subjects, providing approximately 30 per cent of the total, were similar to those in other countries. However, the applications component, which comprised over 50 per cent of the total curriculum context, was quite different from that of any civil engineering degree programme in a western country, and was designed specifically for Ethiopian conditions. It was this experience, then, that led to the conclusion that the skills needed to manage urban infrastructure do not have to be, and indeed should not be, situated within an engineering framework, but should be quite distinct. What is really needed here is a completely new degree programme that is grounded wholly in African needs and African experience. This need for a new approach to applied degrees, particularly those related to urban development, is equally relevant to Urban Planning, Urban Finance and Urban Management, as well as Infrastructure

Management.[21] This ability to define academic areas within the subcontinent, and break the dependency on western programmatic concepts, is central to both the creation of an indigenous knowledge base in sub-Saharan Africa and the creation of sustainable urban centres. Building such programmes also provides an important prerequisite to taking back control over African intellectual space.

Key finding 5: Ethiopia is under immense pressure from external agencies to conform to their (external) view of what constitutes good urban development practice

When the World Bank agreed to support the programme described here, it was not with the intent of exploring how infrastructure was delivered. The primary objective was to develop local capacity to prepare and operationalise infrastructure 'projects' through a conventional approach to capital investment planning. It is to the credit of the Bank that it continued to support this programme into a second phase, which saw investment channelled into infrastructure with the primary objective of building local government management capacity as an end in itself.

This was an important breakthrough: a recognition that if local government can manage its urban infrastructure base, it can manage virtually anything. At the same time, the Bank was never fully able to internalise, and therefore benefit from, the programme and its findings, primarily because it highlighted contradictions that existed within the internal structure of the Bank itself. For example, the Bank agreed eventually that funding could be extended to water supply projects, provided these complied with the funding mechanism laid down in an agreement between its Water Supply Division and the federal Ministry of Water Resources. Superficially, this provision may appear reasonable; however, it failed to take account of the local exploration of the relationship between the ULGA and the local water boards, which could have made a valuable contribution to the wider debate on how urban water supply is managed. Instead, the Water Supply Division of the Bank continued along the separate path outlined in the previous chapter, which saw water supply as totally independent of place. In addition, the Bank continued to support the urban planning development model and the silo separation that governs sector-based service delivery, thus excluding itself from a potentially valuable learning process. And the issue continued to be perceived by the Water Supply Division as one primarily concerned with technical and financial management skills. This reinforces the findings from Chapter 3 concerning the way that the Bank continues to interpret urban water supply within a narrow economic and technocratic framework.

However, while the approach of the World Bank was contradictory, and indicated a degree of internal confusion about the future direction of urban development policy, it was not nearly as damaging as that of other external agencies and organisations, of which the Water and Sanitation Program (WSP) provided a classic example. This programme had been extremely successful working with the federal Ministry of Health in developing a 'National Sanitation Strategy', which it applied first in rural areas (Federal Democratic Republic of Ethiopia, 2005). The problem arose when it sought to apply that same strategy in urban areas. After attending a WSP workshop in Addis Ababa, the Ministry of Works and Urban Development had long discussions with that body in which it sought to demonstrate how the urban context differed from the rural context; but to no avail. No one in the WSP had any understanding (or even foreknowledge) of the urban proclamations, or what these meant in a federal context. As a result, there were a few minor modifications to the wording of the document, but no significant changes to the approach.

The result was a strategy that cut across the role of local government completely, ignored the proclamations and what they were seeking to achieve, and sought to create a completely new system of management for urban sanitation, driven from central government. For the WSP, local government is no more than another local actor that will be allowed to contribute to the delivery of urban sanitation, provided it complies with a delivery process dictated by the WSP. In adopting this narrow sectoral view, the WSP had the potential to seriously undermine all of the achievements of this project, built over five years, by creating alternative power structures in the cities. Similarly, DFID, with its support in the federal Ministry of Water Resources (and its own agenda), and the World Bank Water Supply Division (in separate actions to those described earlier), performed the same destructive function in the area of water supply. All of these bodies aligned with line ministries at the central level to create national sectoral programmes that (1) cut across and undermine local government; and (2) exacerbate tensions within the different line ministries in the countries concerned, and sow confusion around just who is responsible for what in urban development. The result is a confused and fragmented approach that makes it extremely difficult to achieve a holistic development construct. And when such an approach is developed by a government, as it was in Ethiopia, the actions of these bodies serve continuously to undermine this.

There is then a third external input, which is equally destructive. This derives from a group of external actors, coming from a variety of urban agencies, that have urban development as their major area of focus. As this project developed, it began to attract the attention of a range of agencies, of which there are a sizeable number. These would come to the ministry wanting to become involved in 'supporting the government' in its development efforts, by bringing their expertise. What was interesting, in watching these agencies, is how they wished to 'provide' support and expertise. None of them was interested in asking of the government questions like:

- How do *you* address (a particular facet of) urban development?
- What can *you* teach *us* from your experience?
- How can *we* learn from *you* so that *we* can improve the way *we* work and the service we offer to *you* and to others?

Instead, the drive was to persuade the government to adopt the international practices employed elsewhere in Africa with so little success. This new coterie of intellectual colonialists was coming to tell Ethiopians which development models they must apply based upon this external body of 'experience', after the government had just spent five years carrying out what is arguably one of the most important and valuable urban development initiatives in Africa.

The pressures on the Ethiopian government to conform to the way international agencies believes urban development should happen are enormous; while the fact that Ethiopia has developed one of the most interesting urban capacity-building programmes in Africa is of little interest; after all, this is an African initiative and these agencies were not involved. And it is quite impossible, is it not, to imagine how there could be a successful African initiative, on this scale, without the involvement and support of these organisations? The fact that there can in fact be successful local initiatives without their involvement is of course hugely threatening to these organisations.

In the five years of experience with this project, there was only one international agency (excluding the World Bank from this particular aspect of the discussion) that worked with the government of Ethiopia in helping the Ministry of Works and Urban Development construct its urban capacity-building programme its own way, and was open to exploring whatever findings emerged, while supporting the government in following the approach it chose to take. That agency was GTZ (now renamed GIZ), the German development agency, working through its Urban Governance and Decentralisation Programme and building a combined German–Ethiopian team. The programme was coordinated from within the federal Ministry of Works and Urban Development but operationalised at a regional level. In this way it was able to support government at the point where support was required, and sought to build a meaningful partnership between both staff and institutions.

If there is one lesson to be learned from this experience, one thing that differentiated the German approach from the approach of all other external development agencies, it is this: that the German programme (in good governance) sought to support the Ethiopian government in following the development path that it, the federal government, chose to take with respect to the focus of capacity-building for local government. All the other agencies, including the sectoral arms of the World Bank, were also intent on supporting the Ethiopian government, but with one major difference: that support was conditional and situated within the predefined value system of the agency concerned. Thus, support was provided on the basis that the government followed the development path, and the goals and objectives, that that particular external agency believed to be correct. What these other agencies failed to understand was the lesson that true partnership, like meaningful participation, is not about who decides; it is about who decides who decides, and who decides what is decided. While external agencies decide who decides, and decide what is decided and how, then they will continue to be paternalistic and patronising in their approach to Africa.

From conclusions to outcomes: creating African-based models of urban infrastructure delivery

Infrastructure management is the key to sustainable urban development in Africa's secondary cities. This was the single most important lesson to emerge from the Ethiopian study on decentralisation. Unfortunately, urban development is also the area where external influence over African policy and strategy is strongest and most oppressive (intellectually). The challenge for governments across Africa is to break away from existing schools of thought. Breaking away means, first and foremost, finding an alternative to the dualistic model whereby infrastructure is divided into an economic model providing a service for the rich, which is based upon a maximum level of user convenience; and a social (minimalist) model providing a truly basic level of infrastructure service for the poor. Second, it means facing up to the power of international sectoral organisations, particularly those in water and sanitation, whose internal agendas are the greatest single barrier to effective decentralisation and sustainable urban governance in Africa. While there remains in place an urban infrastructure model that is fundamentally inequitable, and differentiates rich from poor, then there cannot be political stability, and hence there cannot be sustainable development.

These are the externalities, but there are also internal requirements for the African countries themselves. First, the creation of a sustainable urban infrastructure model will only be achieved if there is in place a sound and effective financial management system for local government. Second, there has to be a radical shift away from historical western solutions, which are totally inappropriate for rapidly growing urban centres where the primary challenge is to integrate social development, and social equity, with environmentally sustainable practices.

Third, there are the institutional challenges. Ethiopia has created a theoretically sound federal structure of government that allocates an important developmental role to local government. It was fully recognised that both regional government and the ULGAs were operating in a new area which represented a significant shift from past experience; and this was one reason why the World Bank programmes were established. However, what was not fully realised, either during or indeed after the study, was some of the implications, and particularly those relating to this area of infrastructure delivery. The issue relates to the way in which a decentralised model of government is translated into practice. This relates to, and reinforces, two key points that have been made in previous chapters. The first is that there is a mismatch between central and regional government on the one hand, which both function through sectoral line ministries, and urban government on the other, which operates in a multifunctional, cross-sectoral environment. The second issue relates to the concept of decentralisation, and the need to think more critically around what the Dublin Declaration calls subsidiarity; that is, taking decision-making down to the lowest appropriate level. Both of these issues were explored further in Chapter 5, which discussed decentralisation, and they will be returned to again in Chapter 11, which will discuss a new framework for urban good governance.

The final point, which follows from the above, relates to the political challenges associated with urban good governance. Western countries focus on elective democracy as a critical component of good governance at a national level; yet this element may not be as critical at the level of local government. On the one hand, if the ULGA does not have control of the infrastructure base, as is the case in most countries in Africa (owing to western pressure), then its role in urban development is significantly diminished. Yes, land and housing are also critically important issues, but the group providing infrastructure is the group with power and influence. If this is not local government, then whether there are democratic elections or not becomes less significant because the ULGA is only a side player anyway.

On the other hand, if the local government has responsibility for the overall management of the urban infrastructure base, it is the key player in local development. The priorities then become transparency, so that everyone can see where, why and how decisions are made, and the prevention of corruption. If there is real transparency, then there is meaningful accountability on a level that really matters to people in their everyday life. The existence of accountability does not imply that there should not be elections; these are an important part of a healthy society. If there is real transparency, though, in the way that infrastructure is delivered and managed, then this provides the best basis for democratic debate, with a clearly defined, and locally recognised, accountability; and a real, and tangible, basis for legitimacy.

Chapter 8

Rethinking urban development in Africa

Introduction

This chapter introduces the third part of the book, whose objective is to create a completely new conceptual approach to the development of the secondary towns and cities in sub-Saharan Africa. Ironically, the greatest impediment to the creation of such an approach is not to be found in any of the current assumptions, for example lack of political will, lack of skills, shortage of finance; these are not the core issues. The real blockage derives from the power of western *Weltanschauungen* to stifle indigenous intellectual creativity.

Africa has immense potential to create its own development paradigms that are far more appropriate to the twenty-first century, if only it is given the intellectual space to do so. The objective here is to help liberate this intellectual space by providing a new way of thinking about urban development in general, and urban infrastructure in particular.

Over two hundred years ago the countries of the West, led by the United Kingdom and the United States, both created their own models of urban development. Because the physical outcome was similar – that is, a form of centralised network infrastructure – we tend to assume that the two models are also similar. Nothing could be further from the truth. The technical specialists in the two countries may have interacted and learned lessons from each other, but the wider developmental framework was quite different in the two cases.

The model that was exported to anglophone Africa was the British model. This was unfortunate, to say the least, since it was the wrong choice. That statement is not simply a personal view; the evidence is all around when we see the plight of African towns and cities today. The 'British' model was actually developed in one specific part of Britain: England, which is home to over 80 per cent of the total British population. England was already a densely populated country, one that was geographically constrained. This meant that industrialisation took place without being associated with internal physical expansion. In addition, the country had just recovered from a long war in Europe and was seeking desperately to prevent the seeds of revolution spreading across the English Channel. Together these factors created a unique set of circumstances that provided the rationale for the ensuing approach to urban development, and a unique perception of the role that urban infrastructure plays in development.

The United States was quite different. There, development was inextricably linked to physical expansion; and in this context, physical infrastructure was perceived to have a key role to play in building the nation. At the same time, the country was keen to rid itself of the feudal British system of government, following its successful revolution, and created completely new models of government, together with what we would now term new governance structures. All of this makes the early experience of infrastructure development in the United States far more relevant to the African situation than the British experience.

Chapter 3 presented a comparative analysis of the two countries' (Britain and the United States) approach to urban development in the nineteenth and early twentieth centuries, with a specific focus on how the urban infrastructure base evolved in the two countries. Two quite fundamental differences in approach emerged from this study, which when taken together define two radically different development trajectories. For the past two hundred years the British approach has underpinned international thinking to a much greater degree than the American approach, the only exception being related to public–private-sector partnerships, which were driven by the neo-liberal economic agenda of the 1980s, an agenda that emerged initially in the United States but was quickly adopted by the United Kingdom.

The differences between the British and the American approaches to the development of urban infrastructure can be captured with three aspects of urban infrastructure, the first related to its role, the second to its method of application and the third to its nature or form. With the first, the major difference between the two was that the United States saw infrastructure primarily as a driver of economic development, whereas the British saw infrastructure as a set of services that supported social improvement. With the second, the difference was between a vision that saw infrastructure as being driven by engineering (Britain) and one that saw it primarily as driven by technology (the United States). With the third, the nature or form, the towns and cities of the United States were constantly grappling with, and seeking to integrate, three diverse components: a socio-economic framework, technology and a sustainable system of management. In Britain the unique set of circumstances surrounding urban development at that time meant that the linkage between these components was never at the heart of the debate; instead, the three components were addressed in a much more ad hoc way.

It has become something of a mantra in this book to state that a major reason for Africa's current urban condition derives from using a development model that was developed in a different place and a different time, under a completely different set of circumstances. So why is this chapter revisiting the past? In fact, there is much to be learned from the past; we must simply make sure we are learning the right lessons. This book is arguing that urban development has failed in Africa because it has followed the British infrastructure development model. If we want to create a new model, then one way is to go back and look at what the alternative approach is telling us. That does not mean that we copy it, rather that we learn from it and adapt it to current needs.

As was mentioned at the start, this chapter seeks to build a completely new approach to development, based upon a new way of thinking about urban infrastructure. To do this, it is going back to the early American experience for its building blocks. The rationale for doing so is that we can find in that experience the foundations for successful urban development. These are seen to lie in the interpretations of the two aspects of development described above, namely the role, and the nature, of infrastructure. In this approach the role of infrastructure is seen as being that of a driver of the entire urban development process. At the same time, the form that infrastructure takes is seen as being derived from an interaction between the three components of a value system, technology, and an organisational and management system. Finally, while the United States may have provided these interpretations of infrastructure initially, the way in which these two aspects of infrastructure evolve in the chapters to follow will be situated within an African experience. This approach has been made possible by the outcome of the work in Ethiopia, which validated both of these interpretations and provided the basis for the conceptual framework developed here.

The Anglo-Saxon preference for empirically based solutions

Before we can go forward, we first have to deal with the major blockage described earlier, namely the power of western *Weltanschauungen* to block indigenous intellectual creativity. Lying at the heart of this blockage is the Anglo-Saxon approach to decision-making, which is grounded in a deterministic problem–solution duality. The earlier review of the history of infrastructure showed the extent to which virtually all external approaches to urban development in Africa today are situated in this context, and are essentially reactive: each new development initiative is a response to a past failure and flows directly from a mechanistic attempt to address that failure. To proceed, we first have to change our mindset; and one way to start that process is by showing the extent to which access to intellectual space is blocked by the dominance of that specific way of thinking known as empiricism.

The nature of empiricism

Empiricism (as a philosophy) is 'the doctrine that knowledge derives from experience' (WordNet, 2011). Although developed as a philosophical construct in Vienna in the early twentieth century, where it was known as logical positivism (*Encyclopædia Britannica*, 2008), its roots in Britain go back considerably further, and have led to what is today referred to as classical British empiricism. It is this system of thought that underpins the major Anglo-Saxon *Weltanschauungen* described in this book.

Empiricism is most frequently situated within a conflictual duality, being opposed to a second theory of knowledge referred to as rationalism, and in particular the Intuition/Deduction theory of rationalism. This states that '[s]ome propositions in a particular subject area ... are knowable by us by intuition alone; still others are knowable by being deduced from intuited propositions' (*Stanford Encyclopedia of Philosophy*, 2008). This form of rationalism is an important component of French thinking. The *Stanford Encyclopedia of Philosophy* sets out the two schools of thought as follows:

> Intuition is a form of rational insight. Intellectually grasping a proposition, we just 'see' it to be true in such a way as to form a true, warranted belief in it. Deduction is a process in which we derive conclusions from intuited premises through valid arguments, ones in which the conclusion must be true if the premises are true. We intuit, for example, that the number three is prime and that it is greater than two. We then deduce from this knowledge that there is a prime number greater than two. Intuition and deduction thus provide us with knowledge *a priori*, which is to say knowledge gained independently of sense experience....
>
> Empiricism about a particular subject rejects the corresponding version of the Intuition/Deduction thesis [and other theses of rationality] ... The Empiricism thesis does not entail that we have empirical knowledge. It entails that knowledge can only be gained, *if at all*, by experience.
>
> (*Stanford Encyclopedia of Philosophy*, 2008)

Seen in this light, the British preference for strategy and action-orientated policy becomes self-evident, as does the reluctance to use conceptual models to create policy frameworks or implementation strategies. At the same time, the rationale that has led to the current status, which is based upon a combination of empirical deduction with the British concept of precedence, has clearly failed to lead to self-sustaining solutions. The resulting debate, situated within an exclusive intellectual group and positioned within a geographically externalised locus of discourse, is locked into a mechanistic interpretation of the 'problem' of African development. Coupled with a deterministic view of the future, the result is an intellectual blockage that contributes directly to the continued downward spiral in the African urban condition.

Is the problem of African cities actually a 'problem'?

In the empiricist paradigm there is perceived to be a causal link between the problem and the solution. While this may be a perfectly valid approach when used in a scientific sense, for example, when it comes to the 'problem' of African cities there are no obvious 'solutions' in sight. This begs several questions; for example: (1) Are we diagnosing or interpreting the 'problems' correctly in the first place? (2) Are we asking the right questions? (3) Do we ever go back and question our hypothesis (development constructs)? (4) Have we considered that we ourselves are the reason for the problem? The answer could lie with any one of these, with all of them, or even in a whole different area of exploration. In the end, though, it is largely immaterial, because the real fault lies with the way we approach the issue, with the word 'problem' being one reflection of this. What we are doing is using a mechanistic philosophy to seek solutions based upon what went before. This might suffice if our underlying premise were correct; but it isn't. We continue to build a social improvement model; or a planning model; or a private-sector model; or an individual affordability model – each one a thematic force of influence that dominates the African urban development debates. And as previous chapters indicated, all are based upon a flawed rationality. That is why the current mechanistic approach fails.

To break free of this mechanistic approach, though, we first have to go deeper, and deal with the underlying Anglo-Saxon rationality, which is grounded in the problem–solution duality. In a web search seeking to define the term, we find that the word 'problem' can be applied to a range of needs that vary from the abstract (e.g. 'The problem is that this is not an ideal world'; Technogumption, 2008) to the specific (e.g. 'A problem is a task for a student to perform that typically involves multiple steps'; PSLC Datashop, 2009). In seeking to rationalise the multiplicity of interpretations, Princeton University ended up by defining the term in three distinct, and quite different, ways: (1) as 'a state of difficulty that needs to be resolved'; (2) as 'a question raised for consideration or solution'; or (3) as 'a source of difficulty' (WordNet, 2009). On the other hand, there is another interesting definition of the term 'problem', which differs somewhat from those listed previously, which states that a problem is '*a discrepancy between an existing and a desired state of affairs*' (CRF online, 2009).

It is suggested here that most external agencies would be comfortable allocating one of these definitions to the way that they interpret conditions within their own specific sector, even if they might prefer to use the term 'challenge' these days in place of the term 'problem', viewing this as the

262   Rethinking urban development in Africa

more politically correct. As an example, we can see quite clearly how the last of these definitions, the one in italics, describes the basis for the development of the Millennium Development Goals.

Narrowing this down further, it is argued that there are actually just two of these definitions that can be seen to underpin western thinking about African development. The first is the one highlighted in italics immediately above, and the second is the Princeton definition that a problem is 'a state of difficulty that needs to be resolved'. We can then show how these two play off each other, in a mutually reinforcing way, to explain how external agencies take over African intellectual space.

We begin with the definition that a problem is 'a state of difficulty that needs to be resolved'. This one engages the western social conscience, and ensures that the humanitarian approach based upon social improvement dominates the development debate (as with the MDGs, or the focus on basic needs). It provides a lead-in to the second definition, since it predefines the desired state of affairs. In both cases, however, it is insufficient to simply define the end point, since the achievement of that state of affairs requires a detailed engagement with the means. This is the point at which western interventions become disastrous and counter-productive.

Unlike a statement of an end point, which leaves at least some intellectual space to the recipient, becoming involved with the means requires a framework of action, which in turn requires not simply one or more *Weltanschauungen*, but immersion in a rationality, which is that of Anglo-Saxon empiricism. That is the first step on a slippery slope towards intellectual domination, because once we accept the use of an empiricist construct, then this has to be operationalised. For that we use a mechanistic approach in which we take a complex issue, in this case say the 'failure' of the British urban infrastructure model, and we divide it into many component parts, since the mechanistic construct believes that the whole is the sum of the parts. What do we do, though, when this approach fails, as it has in Africa? We can carry on bumbling, or we can rethink our entire conceptual approach. To take the latter course, however, requires that we change our rationality. The implications of such a change will be described below and operationalised in the chapters that follow.

Turning 'problems' into opportunities: applying the concept of the *'problématique'*

Using the concept of a problématique to define a new reality

While the conceptual relationship of 'problem–solution' has a role in addressing specific issues at a micro level, its use at a macro level acts as a constraint to innovative and holistic thinking, by placing the condition to be explored within an intellectual straitjacket. We can call this thinking inside a box. It does not matter whether this box is a paradigm (as with urban planning) or an ideology (as with privatisation); it still remains a box. If we seek to find new approaches, and new solutions, then we have to think outside of that box. We have to begin to recognise that what we have before us is an opportunity: that is the purpose in developing a *problématique*.

The term *problématique* is a French one,[1] and seeks to apply the French approach, inasmuch as it is possible for someone brought up in an Anglo-Saxon tradition to enter the French mind. As in English, with the word 'problematic', the word *problématique* is used in French both as an adjective and as a noun. Here the concern is with the noun, which in French can be clearly distinguished from the adjective in its meaning.

At its simplest, the term *problématique* is defined by the French *Dictionnaire Hachette* as a '[m]anière méthodique de poser les problèmes' (Hachette Livre, 2007, p. 1307); that is, a methodological approach to exploring a question.[2] Taking this to a deeper level, the interpretation of the term, as used by Calley and Soulé from the University of Bordeaux, given below, provides a useful guideline:

Table B

Original French definition (Lycée Sud Médoc, 2009)	English translation
'Qu'est-ce qu'une problématique?	'What is a 'problématique'?
C'est l'art de poser les bonnes questions nous dit le Robert.[3] Construire une problématique, c'est en fait interroger le sujet. Mais il faut poser des questions pertinentes, qui font débat ...	It is the art of asking the right questions. To construct a *problématique* is to create a framework within which the subject can be interrogated from all angles. But this in turn requires we pose pertinent questions; questions that will stimulate debate and discussion.
La problématique guide la réflexion sur le sujet, ouvre des axes de recherché qui permettent de préciser les différents arguments qui alimenteront la production.'	The *problématique* guides our reflections on the subject; the different axes of exploration which allow us to focus in on the critical issues that will lead to an outcome.'

This exploration of the term *problématique* has three important concepts embedded, when it is applied, in the manner described above, to a developmental situation. First, it identifies the importance of asking the 'right' questions. If there is only one question, as is often the case with a problem-based approach, then the answer is likely to be grounded in empiricism, and to fall back on experience. Second, it emphasises that the topic in question has to be explored from different angles, as well as in an objective way; thus, it becomes important that the questions not only permit, but actually generate, discussion. Third, a *problématique* is not simply a theoretical concept; it can, and should, guide reflection in a way that leads to a clear outcome.

Defining the problématique *for urban infrastructure*

Updating the relational model of infrastructure to the present time

This process begins by adopting the interpretation of the two aspects of infrastructure described earlier: first, that the primary role played by infrastructure in an urban context is that of a development driver; and second, that there is some form of symbiotic relationship between three components of infrastructure: the value system the technology and the management system. In addition, underpinning these three components is a financial model. Going back a hundred years to apply this in an American context, we could adapt Figure 3.1 to provide the relational diagram shown as Figure 8.1. Of course, this is not the reflection of the specific components of the relational model – others would include the private sector, for example – but the broad categorisation is generic.

That is as far as the early American experience can take us; from this point we need to chart a new path. Given the magnitude of global change over the past two hundred years, the challenge then becomes one of identifying what remains relevant to the present time while at the same time adapting the conceptual framework to the modern era. In this exercise there are two major shifts that have taken place since that time which need to be accommodated. The first, described in Chapter 2, is that systems have become far more complex. The second is that the needs, and constraints, of the physical

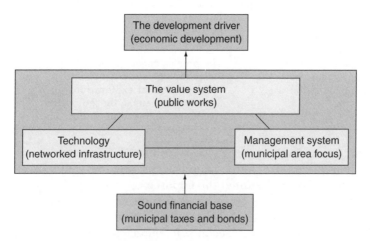

Figure 8.1 A relational model for urban infrastructure (nineteenth-century America).

environment have emerged as critical components of development; and as such they have become central to any discourse on development.

Figure 8.2 shows a modified version of the relational model which has been adapted to current needs.

The first change is that the development drivers have been expanded to address not only the economy but also the social needs of the population and the needs of the environment. The second change is to broaden this concept of a value system. Here it has been renamed to make it a 'value-based surround' – a term intended to portray a broader context for the discourse on values in a society. Finally, the management system has been renamed a regulatory framework, to provide greater scope to explore roles and relationships.

This is a beginning, not an end point. It is an attempt to create a generic model that could be applied to urban infrastructure everywhere. In this way it would provide a frame of reference for discussion that everyone involved with the delivery and management of urban infrastructure could buy into, regardless of their professional or ideological view. At this point it is as close as one can come to being 'value free', enabling it to provide a basis for an exploration of the *problématique*.

Green infrastructure

The generic relational model shown in Figure 8.2 provides a completely new approach to the exploration, and understanding, of urban infrastructure. Its intent is to provide a model that can achieve sustainable urban development across all spheres: economic, social, environmental, political, technical and financial. Such a model we can define as a green urban

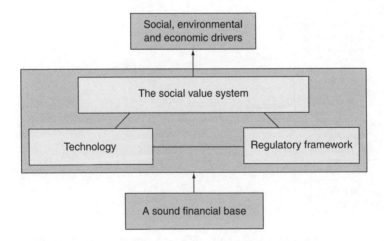

Figure 8.2 A generic relational model for urban infrastructure.

infrastructure model, thereby giving a definition to this otherwise nebulous term. Green urban infrastructure then becomes that infrastructure which can achieve the multiple goals defined here in a balanced way. The implications of this, and the detail, will emerge as the exploration of the *problématique* evolves.

The relational flow diagram for the problématique

The relational model is made up of five major components: the set of development drivers, the financial base and the three components of the infrastructure situated in the middle box (the value-based surround, the technology and the regulatory framework). Breaking them down in this way enables each of them to be explored individually in detail. This analysis begins with the development drivers and the financial base, which are discussed in this chapter. The new conceptual framework, which provides the core relationship in the centre of the diagram (i.e. the three original components of infrastructure), will be discussed in Chapter 9. Chapter 10 will then move to a greater level of detail and explores not only the technology but also the technology systems that emerge from the conceptual framework. Finally, the political regulatory framework will be discussed in Chapter 11.

The order in which these components are explored is critically important, since the outcomes from some will serve as inputs into others. What is required is the sequencing of analysis illustrated diagrammatically in Figure 8.3.

This, then, is as far as we can go with the generic model. It does not provide detailed 'solutions' at this point, but that is not the intent. The

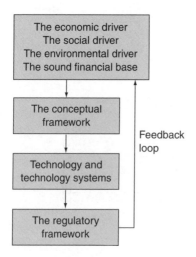

Figure 8.3 The flow diagram linking the different components of the conceptual model.

objective is to provide a framework that everyone can buy into – because from this point onwards we have no choice but to engage with values, which obviously means that views may diverge, or values may differ. Nevertheless, the exploration that follows will seek to remain broadly within a set of universally agreed values; that is, values that the majority of countries have agreed to, as opposed to values defined by a select group of countries and imposed on the rest. In this way the book can build the development construct, while enabling individual countries to adapt this to their own specific value system later.

The three development drivers defining the infrastructure construct

Drivers or imperatives: a question of perspective

The terms 'social', 'economic' and 'environmental' provide three components that are now broadly recognised, in respect of policy at least, as 'the cornerstone of sustainable and equitable development',[3] representing, as they do, the three prime systems of the biosphere, the economy and human society (Robinson and Tinker, 1998). Clearly, though, these so-called prime systems may be perceived and prioritised differently according to needs and perceptions in different countries. In a move to reconcile them, in mutual reinforcement rather than competition, Robinson and Tinker suggested

redefining sustainable development as the reconciliation of three imperatives:

- The ecological imperative to remain within planetary biophysical carrying capacity;
- The economic imperative to ensure and maintain adequate material living standards for all people; and
- The social imperative to provide social structures, including systems of governance, that effectively propagate and sustain the values that people wish to live by.

(1998, p. 22)[4]

This conceptual analysis was developed in Canada, yet it could provide a basis for a broadly acceptable western interpretation. This emergence within a specific western *Weltanschauung* becomes even more obvious as the exploration of their conceptual framework evolves. Even at this point in the discussion, though, the linkage with a *Weltanschauung* is acknowledged, at least implicitly, by the authors when they point out that, in creating this interpretation, 'sustainable development is ... inherently a normative concept, with each of these three imperatives being an ethical statement regarding its respective prime system. All three imperatives are more value laden than objective' (ibid.).

The problem we face is how we work with this form of esoteric exploration in a physical reality of dire poverty. Those quoted above seek to create some form of globally overarching definition, yet openly (and honestly) admit that the imperatives are 'more value laden than objective'. The only way forward under these conditions is to define that point where there is common ground just before the point of departure; and then create our own path forward in a way that suits our purpose most effectively.

That point, unfortunately, comes quite early on. It is the recognition of the three prime systems: the biosphere, the economy and human society. This is also our point of departure, because the term 'imperative' can only apply to a western condition of resource over-utilisation. When we transpose these prime systems to an African urban situation, we need to create a different interpretation, one that can provide a basis for improving conditions in all three prime systems that starts from our current reality. This means driving process from a starting point to an end point. So, whereas western countries are correct to talk in terms of imperatives, African countries have to think in terms of development drivers. The challenge is to define a development driver for each of the three prime systems and then to demonstrate that the three drivers that emerge are not only compatible but mutually supportive. The sections that follow will seek to achieve this outcome, situating each one of the drivers of development in turn within an African *Weltanschauung*: the sustainable development of secondary towns in sub-Saharan Africa.

The overarching goals

The starting point is to create an overarching development goal. Here the specific experience that the book has drawn on is that of Ethiopia, where the exploration of development goals was situated within the framework of an integrated urban infrastructure policy. If we accept the point of commonality as a recognition of the three prime systems, and the point of departure as being the use of development drivers, then we require a policy goal that can guide these. Drawing on experience from the Ethiopian study, one such statement for a development goal, which would encapsulate the three prime systems, could be that:

> **The overall policy goal is to ensure that a country's investment in urban infrastructure is used effectively; that resources are used efficiently; and that resources are allocated in an equitable and sustainable manner.**

The challenge is then to operationalise that policy statement.

Infrastructure: the driver of urban development

Infrastructure drives urban development; that is its purpose and its rationale, the reason for its existence. Furthermore, this is the only interpretation that can address all three prime systems equally. Unfortunately, as was indicated earlier, Africa has been pushed, through events outside of its own control, into a different rationality. During the mid-nineteenth century the United Kingdom created an alternative rationality, one that saw urban infrastructure as a support service which could be used for as part of a policy of social improvement for the working classes through an amelioration of the atrocious physical conditions in which they lived. Of course infrastructure can be used in this way, but that is a limiting conceptualisation of its role and one that actually hinders its evolution and prevents it from being used to its full potential. It worked in Britain (and more specifically in England) because of specific circumstances: a very small, densely populated, yet extremely wealthy and highly industrialised country, with existing towns and an existing urban fabric and industrial base. When applied to a geographically expansive society that occupied a large territory, it could never achieve its wider potential, because it was constrained in a developmental straitjacket. This British specificity is clearly highlighted by Figure 8.4, which shows the full extent to which the industrialisation of the United Kingdom was so much further advanced than that of other countries in the middle of the nineteenth century.

Unfortunately, this was the model that was exported to Africa, where it failed. African governments were blamed for this failure but the real reason lay elsewhere; failure was embedded in the urban infrastructure model they inherited. Africa's current urban condition is a truly unfortunate accident of history.

The country that we need to look to for a solution, if we want to change this African urban condition around, is the United States. And the question we need to answer is: how did America become so powerful so quickly, when we see from this graph that in 1880 its relative level of industrialisation was less than 15 per cent of that for the United Kingdom?

Infrastructure as the driver of economic development

There are a number of factors that contributed to the rapid development, but it is beyond contention that one of them was America's view of infrastructure, at all levels of society, as a driver of economic development. That is where we should have been looking to understand how an urban economy can grow successfully. That is the direction that African countries have to take if they wish to grow in the same way.

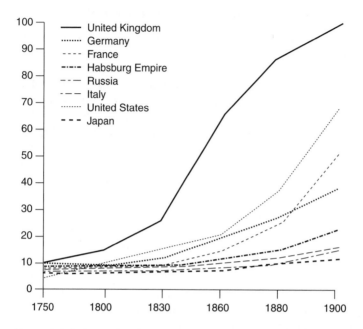

Figure 8.4 Relative levels of industrialisation, 1750–1900 (UK in 1900 = 100). Data taken from P. Bairoch (1982) 'International Industrialization Levels from 1750 to 1980', *Journal of European Economic History* (JEEH), vol. 11, pp. 269–333. Graph available at Wikipedia: http://en.wikipedia. org/wiki/File:Graph_rel_lvl_indz_1750_1900_01.png (accessed 11 April 2011). Downloaded in terms of the GNU Free Documentation Licence.

Africa in the twenty-first century is not, of course, the same as the United States in the eighteenth. That distinction, though, should not change the principle, merely the application. We live in a different world today, but Africa has more potential to adapt to that world than any other continent, simply because it lags the development curve. This is not a problem; it is an opportunity. African countries can learn from the failings of existing models and create new ones; and the secondary towns in particularly are well suited to taking advantage of these new models.

In this world of opportunity, the area with the greatest potential is that of economic development. By starting with a new urban model the secondary towns have the potential to create a truly sustainable green urban economy. That is the primary role of infrastructure as the driver of urban economic development. The experience of building an urban infrastructure model in an African context, one that uses infrastructure as the driver of urban economic development, is to be found in Ethiopia. That provided the seeds but it could not go the whole way, because the knowledge base was simply not there. What the methodology being derived here does is to define our driver, draw upon the lessons of the Ethiopian experience, and create a new technology model.

At this point we have a clearly defined goal: infrastructure as the driver of a new green urban economy. We then have to define the mechanism through which this new economy comes about. At this point we run up against a second inherited weakness of the British infrastructure model, also identified in the comparative review of infrastructure in the United Kingdom and the United States given in Chapter 3. This is the use of an approach to create the physical component of infrastructure that is built around (civil) engineering, rather than technology. This in turn led to the British colonial interpretation of the term 'public works' as being some-thing fundamentally different from the American interpretation of the same term.

The British interpretation of public works is situated within a context of procurement and construction, with its roots in the engineering approach to infrastructure development. This then led to a dominant mind associ-ation linkage between 'public works' and construction. That linkage is now the recognised and accepted one across almost all of sub-Saharan Africa. The International Labour Organization (ILO) also used it to define 'public works programmes' in Africa, and uses these as the basis for a policy of job creation.

The reasons for taking this route are understandable; but it is the wrong route to take in the urban areas. Job creation is linked to construction, which in turn is linked to the engineering interpretation of infrastructure. But infrastructure is not about engineering. The physical basis for infra-structure is technology. And if we want to build a technology base, then our focus is not on job creation per se but on small business development. Thus, infrastructure as a driver of economic development, of the new green urban economy in Africa, has to focus on building and supporting small businesses.

The Ethiopian programme began with a labour-based focus but ended up by focusing on small business development. Masonry drains were con-structed by small private teams. The cobblestone road building pro-gramme was created around the training of both artisans and managers. The federal Ministry of Water Resources funded recently qualified civil engineering graduates to set up as independent consultants in the second-ary towns, providing loans for a vehicle and a computer, and an initial management contract to help them become established. There are bound-less opportunities for small businesses in urban infrastructure. Water systems require pump mechanics and local area managers; while ecolo-gical sanitation opens the potential for a whole new small business area to develop around the use of human 'waste'.

There will continue to be a need for larger companies in some areas, particularly water and energy, but even here there has to be a shift in focus towards much greater subcontracting for local skills development. The economic driver in the secondary towns does not lie with the large international water or construction companies. Instead, it has to be based on the recognition that urban infrastructure can only succeed in driving economic development through a focus on small businesses; urban infrastructure is the economic catalyst that will generate those enterprises.

Infrastructure as the driver of social development

The need to create cities that are socially sustainable has to underpin social development; and sustainable social development means social equity. What history tells us, though, is that social equity is not a natural outcome of development. On the contrary, when natural evolutionary processes are left untouched, the tendency is towards social inequity. This can occur in several ways. First, there is the economic differential that we see in the early history of the United States. Then there is the racial differentiation that was the basis for urban development in the colonies. Third – and this is perhaps the most unusual one – there is the humanitarian approach that is grounded in despair rather than discrimination per se, though the outcome is the same. The basic needs approach and the Millennium Development Goals provide two examples of this last one. This third one is also interesting because we can see a direct linkage between this approach and the original social improvement model created in Britain in the late nineteenth century. In making this connection we can see how these modern interpretations of development are themselves an outcome of this same mistaken development path that resulted from the misunderstanding of the role of infrastructure in urban society.

The movement towards social equity in Europe and America in the early twentieth century was the result of two specific events. The first was emancipation, which gave poor people the vote and the power to demand equal access to infrastructure services. The second was the natural equalising nature of a centralised network infrastructure. These have to be seen together when one is looking at social equity in an urban context. In Africa, western governments and international agencies push the first of these strongly in their interactions with African governments, while at the same time they impose a model of urban development that is fundamentally inequitable; and they appear unable to understand this contradiction. Yet the outcome should be blindingly obvious: while this contradiction exists, urban government in Africa will always be politically unstable; and this instability will continue to impact negatively upon national governments.

What this discussion tells us is that social equity can only be achieved if we strive for it actively. In urban areas this active striving means, first and foremost, creating an equitable urban infrastructure system. When we look at the way that external agencies implement urban development, we can see a huge discrepancy between the use of the term 'social equity', which is expounded as a principle and widely proclaimed, and the practices that those agencies follow, which are generally inequitable. The reason for this dichotomy can be described in one word: affordability. Delivering high levels of service to the urban poor is considered too expensive, and the poor cannot afford them. And since affordability is the basis on which external agencies provide development aid, this takes priority. The answer does not lie in differential levels of service; it lies in rethinking our concept of urban infrastructure. To do this we have to identify social equity as a driver of development.

Infrastructure as the driver of environmental development

Introduction: infrastructure and the physical environment

The role that infrastructure plays in mediating the interaction between people and their physical environment in an urban context is unique; for depending upon the way that infrastructure is used, it may play the role of either hero or villain; and sometimes both at the same time! Like all technology, it may be used or it may be abused. The challenge is to use it in a way that benefits people, and particularly the poor and vulnerable, while integrating its use as closely as possible with natural environmental processes and systems.

The history of modern urban infrastructure began in the late eighteenth century, and the systems expanded rapidly across western countries over the next 150 years. In 1800, at the beginning of this development, the world's total population was 1 billion people, of whom 65 per cent lived in Asia (PRB, 2011). In the eyes of the western explorers and colonists the world outside of Europe (Europe accounted for just 15 per cent of the world's population at that time) appeared to be a place of boundless resources, available for the taking. This had a huge influence on the way that urban infrastructure was perceived, because a key role of infrastructure is to move these resources around. This perception (of vast resources) shaped the way that engineers designed the infrastructure base.

At the same time, this was the era of technology and the industrial revolution, when human ingenuity was perceived as capable of managing nature, to the extent that the British Institution of Civil Engineers was granted a royal charter in 1828. This was to describe the role of the new profession of civil engineering as 'harness[ing] the great forces of nature, for the use of man'.[5] The result, over the next century and a half, was to install a huge networked infrastructure base in the form of what economists terms a 'sunk' asset; that is, it is not readily tradable and, once constructed, it may well have a design life of sixty years or more.

The world we now live in is a quite different world: a world of 7 billion people; a world with ever-diminishing resources; a world of growing climate variability and instability; a world having to come to terms with an atmospheric carbon load accumulated by those same western countries over two centuries or more. The way in which we view this new world, like so much else in life, depends on our perspective. The West caused these problems, yet it is encumbered with billions of dollars in fixed capital investment. The western response, particularly to climate change, is framed within the context of modifying output from this sunk investment to ameliorating the negative impact on the environment, given that it is neither feasible, nor (in their view) affordable to take it all out and start again. In climate change terminology this response is referred to as mitigation. Countries such as China, India, Brazil and South Africa, which are committed to a similar industrialisation path, also have to address this issue of mitigation as a priority. Countries that do not have high levels of fixed capital investment, on the other hand, do not have to follow this route. They are in a position to create new investment that is designed to adapt to the changing global environment. In climate change terminology this is referred to as adaptation. It is a reasonable approach to take when looking at investment at a national level. At the urban level, though, and particularly in the secondary towns, it is not actually the most appropriate strategy. Instead, what we should be looking at here is reconceptualisation.

If we really want to create a green urban economy then we have to move beyond adaptive strategies and build sustainable urban systems from the ground up. The countries of sub-Saharan Africa have a huge opportunity to create a new urban model of development; and the way to achieve this is through the development of a new approach to urban infrastructure that is grounded in the environmental needs of the twenty-first century. Developing such an approach means shaping a new approach to technology: this is the environmental driver of urban development. To do so, the process will need to address three strands of the environmental discourse. These are:

1   the role of urban infrastructure in managing the movement and use of resources;
2   the negative impact of infrastructure on the physical environment;
3   the potential of urban infrastructure to ameliorate extreme climate change-related events through the introduction, up front, of adaptive strategies.

Infrastructure and resources

The exploration of the relationship between infrastructure and resource utilisation in the city operates most effectively within a conceptual framework of urban ecology – more specifically, within the concept that resources have a 'metabolic' function in a city. This is a concept deriving from metabolism in the human body, whereby inputs, in terms of food, are transformed, via different metabolic pathways, to outputs, including waste products. In this context, 'Cities are pivotal sites at which the resource flows "metabolized" by infrastructures[6] are geographically concentrated, and the everyday exchanges between networked infrastructures and natural environments occur' (Monstadt, 2009, p. 1926). Furthermore, and of equal importance, 'Urbanization processes have only become possible because sociotechnical innovations in water supply, sanitation, energy supply, transport, etc., have permitted the extreme acceleration of the urban metabolism.'[7]

This perspective reflects a newly emerging view in the West that seeks to engage with the relationship between the infrastructure base, on the one hand, and the way that resources are used in a city, on the other, resulting in a conceptual framework that has been described as the 'political ecology' of urban infrastructures;[8] before this new view, the focus had been on the resource flows themselves (e.g. water, food, waste). The objective in this new approach is to explore the mediating role that urban infrastructure plays in the movement of these resources; while the use of the term 'political ecology' recognises that infrastructure is by its very nature socio-technical. Finally, this work highlights the importance of understanding the nature of the interrelationships between different infrastructure services, in contrast to the Anglo-Saxon mechanistic approach, '[b]ecause the elements of sociotechnical ensembles have become closely intertwined over time, changing specific elements within a sociotechnical system has consequences for (at least part of) the whole ensemble' (Monstadt, 2009, p. 1928).[9]

The paper quoted here was primarily concerned with existing networked infrastructure in the mature cities of the West. As always, there is much that can be learned from western experience, provided we make sure we are learning the right lessons. Here what are emerging are the first signs that urban infrastructure is actually a critical element of the political ecology of the city in its own right. That understanding then provides support for the concept of infrastructure as a driver of environment development.

Infrastructure and environmental 'management'

As was mentioned in the introduction, urban infrastructure, like much of technology, but perhaps to an even greater extent than most, can be a two-edged sword, providing benefits while at the same time causing damage. This is because networked infrastructures are 'inherently ambivalent [in that] they can be seen both as a vital root cause of many environmental problems and resources shortages and as an important key to solving them' (Monstadt, 2009, p. 1926).

The creation of Agenda 21 at the 1992 Earth Summit in Rio de Janeiro provided the framework for creating more sustainable cities and integrating the needs of the physical environment into urban planning and management processes. The principles underlying Agenda 21 are widely applicable; the challenge lies in their implementation. The development of local Agenda 21 guidelines began with, and addressed the needs of, the mature cities of the West and used the Anglo-Saxon mechanistic approach, which divided the 'environmental' infrastructure services into their component parts. Chapter 4 highlighted how the western development agencies then followed the classic route, applicable across many areas of urban development described previously, of taking this specific approach to the application of an important principle (designed primarily based upon the needs of western cities), converting it into a globally applicable approach through their control of intellectual space and then imposing this as a solution for African cities.

The potential of infrastructure to cause environmental damage has to be recognised, yet in practice the secondary towns in Africa are in a far better position to manage this negative impact, provided they can approach the relationship between infrastructure and the environment in a different way. The biggest environmental problems in urban areas arise from cross-contamination of resource waste streams, which causes pollution of the two major 'lungs' of the city: water and air. Fragmented management has not proved particularly successful in dealing with this issue. The answer lies, rather, in looking afresh at the relationship between resource flows and how crossover pollution occurs; that is, returning to a level of fundamental analysis. African secondary towns and cities can do this because they have a low existing infrastructure base. This 'weakness', as it is perceived by external development agencies, can thus be turned into an opportunity. That approach will be discussed more fully in Chapter 9.

Infrastructure and climate change

Climate change is radically modifying global weather patterns, and the result goes beyond a rise in the global ambient temperature, to an increase in both the frequency and the magnitude of what can be termed extreme weather events, such as floods, drought and hurricanes. Coupled with these changes there is a rise in the mean water level of the oceans, which has major implications for low-lying coastal areas. In 2003, 3 billion people lived within 200 kilometres of a coastline, a figure that is likely to double by 2025 (PRB, 2010); while fourteen of the world's seventeen largest cities, and 40 per cent of cities in the 1–10 million population bracket, are located near coastlines (Tibbetts, 2002).

The majority of extreme events relate in some way to water, and these events have a disproportionate impact on the most vulnerable groups in society (the very poor, the elderly, the infirm). Adaptive strategies can play a significant role in ameliorating the impact of extreme conditions, and infrastructure plays a critical role in this process.

Mediating resource flows: the key to urban environmental sustainability

Africa has a huge opportunity to avoid the mistakes made by western countries in their urbanisation of the past two hundred years. To take advantage of this opportunity, though, requires a new way of thinking about urban resources, and a new way of thinking about urban infra-structure, which mediates the flow of these resources. Chapter 4 high-lighted the extent to which African cities are trapped in a western intellectual pincer movement, with nineteenth-century ideas of network infrastructure on the one side and basic services targeted at individuals on the other, neither of which is either relevant or appropriate to cities that are emerging and growing in the twenty-first century. At the same time, the current approach to urban development in Africa creates an incompatibility between economic development and environmental sustainability.

Following the approach described here means that there is no longer any incompatibility. By creating a system of infrastructure management based upon the overarching concept of urban infrastructure as a mediator of all urban physical resources, we lay the basis for a green urban economy in which economic goals and environmentally sustainable outcomes are mutually reinforcing. In addition, by using the outcome of social equity to drive the wider developmental process, we also achieve the conditions of social sustainability and political stability.

Affordability: the basis for sustainable financial management

One of the biggest mistakes that evolved from the use of an Anglo-Saxon *Weltanschauung* in Africa was the focus on the individual at the expense of the collective. This has nothing to do with the old-style duality of Ameri-can capitalism versus Soviet collectivism. It is about combining the benefits of scale with a communal social development model. The use of a strong, executive-controlled local authority, coupled with accountability, leads to social equity. The argument that equitable systems of infrastructure are unaffordable is flawed, because it is based upon the combination of two externally derived development criteria, both of which have been imposed, not internally generated, and both of which are invalid.

The first is the use of the western infrastructure model based upon maximum user convenience, which takes the most expensive delivery system as its benchmark, with all comparative systems being viewed as factions or elements of this system – for example, a water standpipe is a component of a high-cost water system; a gravel road has the same structural design as a tarred road, but simply lacks the bitumen surfacing. This model completely distorts the economics of urban infrastructure delivery – and always to the detriment of the poor. If we can rethink the way that we perceive infrastructure at a fundamental level, then we can completely change the economics of infrastructure delivery and operation, thereby making it more affordable for towns with lower median levels of income to provide sustainable and equitable infrastructure.

The second seriously flawed development criterion derives from the assumption, dominant in Anglo-Saxon societies, that affordability is an attribute associated primarily with individuals. That is simply not the case. There is another way of viewing affordability, one that sees it as an attribute of the town as a whole.

There are analysts operating within the Anglo-Saxon *Weltanschauung* who have seen this, but their worldview causes them to ignore it and default to the individual linkage. This can be seen clearly in a paper that looked at infrastructure financing, where the author provided a diagram to illustrate the current infrastructure financing challenge in Africa (Figure 8.5). This figure is important, recognising that affordability operates at three levels: central government, local government and the household. It is equally important for its identification of the real 'affordability crunch', which takes place at the level of the local government authority. This was a real opportunity to take the debate on affordability into a new arena. Unfortunately, the paper retreats from doing so, and returns to the convention whereby affordability is linked back to the individual. The justification for this approach is that addressing the 'affordability crunch' at the level of local government is too complex a task, and in any case the responsibility for delivery is moving away from local government to the private sector.

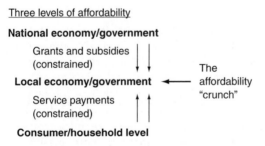

Figure 8.5 The affordability 'crunch' in infrastructure delivery (adapted from Jackson, 1997).

Ultimately, a deeper exploration of this issue of affordability is limited by situating the discussion within an Anglo-Saxon *Weltanschauung*.

What we see here is an example of how a rational analytical process cannot be pursued to its logical conclusion because the outcome is driven by the predefined expectations and solutions that are part of the external *Weltanschauung*. In this case the author argues that the cost of providing conventional infrastructure in African towns will run to billions of dollars if we use conventional western technology. Furthermore, this cost will have to come from the private sector because

> [t]here is widespread recognition that the capital needs of third world countries will not be met from government taxes, donor grants, or DFIs (Development Finance Institutions) such as the DBSA [Development Bank of Southern Africa], but the extra money must come from private sector investors.
>
> (Jackson, 2003)

This paragraph is situated entirely within a value-based preconception, which covers almost the entire range described in this and earlier chapters: individual affordability; private-sector control; specific predefined services levels – all of them are embedded here. And the outcome will be yet another failure, because external agencies are forever seeking to place square pegs in round holes. Yet alternatives are possible, as the Ethiopian study indicated.

Taking urban infrastructure forward as a development driver

Building on the concept of urban infrastructure as the major driver of economic, social and environmental development provides the foundation for a new conceptual model of urban infrastructure delivery and management. It is also the first step in the exploration of the *problématique*. The outcome is a modern vision of infrastructure as the driver of development in the secondary towns, a vision that is built upon three equal and mutually reinforcing pillars:

1   urban infrastructure as the primary driver of a new, green urban economy; achieved through the creation of small businesses;
2   urban infrastructure as the driver of a socially equitable city;
3   urban infrastructure as the driver of the environmentally sustainable city, achieved through the mediation of resource flows.

For these drivers to function successfully we require a financial model that can be integrated with the principles that underlie the different pillars.

Creating such a model means, first and foremost, that we need to transfer our concept of affordability from an attribute that we associate primarily with individuals to an attribute that has to be explored at the level of the ULGA itself. The most effective way to address affordability is to manage it at the locus of the affordability 'crunch'.

Together, these outcomes provide the input to the technology debate. There are no preconceptions concerning what those potential technical solutions might be at this stage; these will emerge from the process inherent in the exploration of the *problématique*, which begins with the next chapter.

Chapter 9

A model for green infrastructure

Rethinking the role of urban infrastructure

The previous chapter initiated the process of constructing a new model of urban development, using urban infrastructure as the main driver of development in the secondary towns. Covering the three spheres of the physical environment, the economy and human society, together with the issue of affordability, this model provided the overarching framework within which urban infrastructure functions. That framework provides the rationale for the green urban infrastructure model that will be developed here. The next step is to understand how the drivers then relate to the central portion of the diagram in Figure 8.3, which is concerned with the three components of urban infrastructure: the value-based surround, the technology and the organisation framework.

Doing so is harder than it appears. For a start, none of these are value free, even technology; instead, all of them operate within some form of value system, which can differ from one society to another. At present the dominant value system is that which is defined primarily by Anglo-Saxon *Weltanschauungen*. Second, we have to deal with a long history of word associations that link a particular term, say water supply, with a specific interpretation of what that term means to us. To escape from the mindset that this creates, we have to move beyond the components themselves to create a new conceptual model, one that allows us to think outside of our existing boxes.

All of us are influenced in the way we see processes of development by our own specific *Weltanschauungen*; and it can be difficult to accept that the solutions that are linked to our own mindset may not be the most appropriate way to support development in another society where the *Weltanschauungen* can be significantly different from our own. As a prelude to this chapter, then, it may be useful to revisit the reason *why* we need such a radical change in mindset, and *why* the current approach to urban development is in serious need of a makeover. So, the next section takes a small detour into an African country, where it eavesdrops on a conversation that took place, behind closed doors, between the Minister of Health and her Permanent Secretary/Director General, on the one side, and a ministerial representative from an unnamed western government, on the other. The purpose of the meeting was to discuss a proposal in which the western government would lead a funding consortium to facilitate the financing of a comprehensive (western-style) sanitation system for the larger secondary cities (those with between 100,000 and 500,000 inhabitants).

A digression into the Minister's office

We join the conversation as the Permanent Secretary is briefing the Minister on the forthcoming meeting with the representative of the western government.

PERMANENT SECRETARY: The representative of the _____ government has arrived to see you.

MINISTER: Remind me, what was it he wanted to talk about this time?

PERMANENT SECRETARY: The provision of sanitation for our major secondary cities, Minister. His government would like to provide aid and consultants to design the sanitation systems.

MINISTER: Very well, call him in.

The western country representative enters at this point. There is a welcome, greetings and general discussions on the weather.

MINISTER: So, you were about to tell us of your own sanitation system?

WESTERN COUNTRY REPRESENTATIVE: Yes indeed, Minister. It is a system with a long history and we are proud to have invented it. Between you and me, it was one of our better inventions, you know. It is really quite ingenious: safe, easy to use, yet technologically advanced.

MINISTER: Please tell us more...

WESTERN COUNTRY REPRESENTATIVE: Well, each home has at least one, generally two, and sometimes as many as four or five units that we call toilets. These are well-designed ceramic pedestals that people can sit on to er, umm, ah, perform their functions. What emerges then falls into a reservoir of water at the base of the pedestal, and a second reservoir, situated above the toilet and connected to the mains water supply, is then used to flush the er, umm, ah, waste, into a drain where it joins all the other fresh water discharged to the drain and is carried kilometres away from the house where it can't possibly do any harm. And there it is treated.

MINISTER: Mmmm, all right; and this treatment: what is its purpose?

WESTERN COUNTRY REPRESENTATIVE: You must understand that the waste water is very dilute but highly polluting, so that treating it requires complex technology and a number of different processes. The concentration of pollutants in the waste is very low, and the highly sophisticated treatment system, which takes place in what we call a wastewater treatment plant, has been designed to remove the polluting component of the waste matter from the water–waste mixture. This makes the resultant liquid safe to discharge back into the river and allows us to use the solid matter (after further moisture reduction) to generate electricity with alternative technologies.

MINISTER: And this is the system you are proposing that we adopt?

WESTERN COUNTRY REPRESENTATIVE: Why yes indeed. A system such as this one is essential for a modern country. Our consultants can generate designs for such systems for all your main secondary towns; we can arrange finance; our engineers can build these systems; and our private utility companies can run them for you. And we can provide all of this with no upfront outlay on your part; it can be done on a pay-as-you-go plan over the next forty years.

There is a short intermission for internal discussion, followed by a resumption of talks.

MINISTER: We've talked this over a little among ourselves, and it certainly sounds most impressive, but it does appear to be rather expensive. What are we going to do if people can't afford it? After all, many of our people living in urban areas are very poor.

WESTERN COUNTRY REPRESENTATIVE: I can understand that, Minister, but we do have a solution for poor people.

MINISTER: I'm very happy to hear that! Please tell us more.

WESTERN COUNTRY REPRESENTATIVE: Oh, it's rather simple really. We get them to dig a hole in the ground and shit into that. Of course, we can't say that – bad form you know, and the press at home wouldn't approve. So we smarten it up a bit and give it a fancy name; we call it a ventilated improved pit latrine. Then everyone's happy.

MINISTER (pondering): Mmm, but that does not appear to be equitable to me.

WESTERN COUNTRY REPRESENTATIVE: Oh, equity is not important, Minister; that's old hat. The point about this system is that it is affordable. That's the key word to remember, Minister – affordable. Affordability is the magic word that you must use to unlock the western funds that you need to meet all your sanitation needs. And think about it: the rich have the ultimate in user convenience, so you will be able to keep them on board politically. And the poor have basic sanitation, so you will be able to keep all your donors, the UN, and all these foreign NGOs happy, and you know what a pain they can be if they get upset. And besides, that's the world we live in – poverty is a reality, and it's not going to go away; so let's just accept that we have it and that there are always going to be two sets of people in the country – rich and poor. That's life!

The conversation comes to an end and the representative leaves. The Minister and her Permanent Secretary are left alone.

PERMANENT SECRETARY: I'm sorry, Minister, but I found that attitude rather patronising. You studied in [name of a western capital city here], didn't you? Is that what they are really like? Or was his attitude reflecting a specific gender bias?

MINISTER: Yes, I received my medical degree from [famous western university here]. And no, they're not really like that, at least most of them aren't. In my personal dealings I always found them polite and charming. And I know they mean well. The problem is they don't really understand what is going on here – the news tends to be rather one-sided – and they can be arrogant, believing they have worked out all the answers long ago. [pause]

Still, to come back to the issue at hand; I'm not strong on the technical side, but let me see if I have got this right. As I understand it, the sanitation system that they propose for those that can afford it works like this. First they withdraw extremely large quantities of water from the river and then, from what my colleague at Water Resources tells me, they treat it to a very high-quality standard at significant cost. They then pump this treated water, at high pressure, into every home, where the individual families use a very small amount of that water for drinking, but significantly more for bathing and cooking. In addition, a substantial quantity of this expensively treated water, which I understand totals in excess of 200 litres per person per day, is then used to flush their urine and faecal matter down the drain, where it joins the remainder of the water brought into the house, which has also been flushed down the drain. [There is a short pause here for reflection.]

You need to help me here, and tell me whether I really have the right gist here. If I understood the representative correctly, what is being proposed is a system whereby a large quantity of water is first drawn from an environment that cannot actually provide it in these quantities in the long term, so it is environmentally unsustainable. The water is then brought into the house, where it is intentionally polluted, to the point where it becomes dangerous to both people and the environment; after which it is thrown away. This 'wastewater' then goes into another set of expensive pipes, where it is carried a great distance to another large plant. There it is treated, again at great expense, to separate the water from the waste that they mixed together in the first place...

No, I give up. Please tell me I have got this wrong; it makes absolutely no sense to me! Surely this can't be the wonderful western technological miracle that the representative was talking about? [The Minister shakes her head, totally baffled.]

PERMANENT SECRETARY: That is what it sounded like to me, Minister, and I have to say that it makes no sense to me either. But to be honest, I am more worried about this idea of theirs for a two-tier system of sanitation, where the rich have the one that is very expensive, and gives them a Mercedes option, while the poor end up with what might be a hygienic system, but at the end of the day is simply a glorified hole in the ground. Apart from the problem of what we do when all these holes are full, there is this critical issue of equity. Our people may be poor, but they are not stupid; they will see that we are intending to give them a second-class service, whatever euphemistic term the representative might use to describe it. Still, at least when he talked of the poor he was willing to be forthright in his use of language! I do worry, though, that this two-tier approach is going to cause a lot of unhappiness, and it's certainly not going to make the job of managing these cities any easier.

MINISTER: I know, but we are in a catch-22 here. We are under immense pressure from everyone, from the [World] Bank, the UN, all these donor countries, NGOs, the foreign press, to provide sanitation quickly. We have to do something, so we will probably have to go along with this system he proposes. If only we had other options; more sustainable and equitable solutions; but there is just no time ... there is just no time ... there is just no time ...

PERMANENT SECRETARY [with a tactful cough]: Minister, you are due in your next meeting; you need to go. Perhaps we can discuss this again later.

MINISTER [coming out of her reverie]: Yes, yes, of course; just remind me again, who are we meeting now?

PERMANENT SECRETARY: It is an inter-ministerial meeting, chaired by the President, with a delegation from the EU. They are here to talk about climate change. Apparently they want to make sure we don't expand our carbon footprint too much and want to help us manage our urban resources better. As part of that process I understand they want to ensure we limit our per capita water consumption to a level that does not exceed 30 per cent of their own...

What this conversation tells us

The above story related primarily to sanitation, but there are equally sombre tales associated with most urban infrastructure services. Its objective is to illustrate that, simply because we have an infrastructure service that people in the West accept, often without question, it is not necessarily the one we would design if we were starting from scratch in the twenty-first century. That is the African dilemma. In many small towns across sub-Saharan Africa, governments are in a position where they could do things differently. Thus, there are huge opportunities to adopt a new approach that can provide their towns with an emerging economic base for further development – towns that are striving towards being socially equitable; and towns that can be environmentally sustainable. Then there is the reality portrayed in the sketch: an approach to urban development that is defined externally and leaves them trapped in a western-imposed duality that is inequitable, unsustainable and lacking the ability to grow its own economy. On the one side is the western urban infrastructure model that provides a high level of service to a privileged minority. On the other side is an underclass made up of the urban poor: second-class citizens for whom only the most basic of services are available.

This book argues that this need not be the only route forward – that there is an alternative which can provide a sustainable urban future with a high level of user convenience for everyone, in a system that is socially equitable and affordable. All that is required to achieve this is a change of mindset, brought about through a change to the way in which we view urban infrastructure. However, such a change cannot be brought about incrementally, because the model currently in use is seriously flawed and dysfunctional. What is needed, and what this chapter provides, is a completely new conceptual model of urban infrastructure, presenting an alternative that is both practical and feasible.

Allowing the development drivers to define the conceptual framework for urban infrastructure

Introduction

The challenge, in a situation such as this one where there is more than one development driver, is to create a harmonious balance between them. Our current difficulty is that when we try to apply western concepts of environmental sustainability, for example, in an Africa context (as with, say, Agenda 21), we end up with a conflictual situation in which the needs of the environment are perceived to conflict with the developmental needs of the poor: the so-called green–brown debate. A similar conflict arises when we try to balance economic and social development, which results in differential service levels. This conflictual interplay arises from placing the focus of development at the level of the individual.

If we want the different economic, social and environmental drivers to be not only mutually compatible but also mutually reinforcing, then we have to move the centre of gravity of the discourse up from the level of the individual to the level of the town or city. In other words, we have to link infrastructure in the first instance to the spatial entity defined by the urban boundary. It is then the environmental driver that is the most critical in shaping the framework for urban infrastructure. And the only way that can be operationalised is by linking the flow of resources to the metabolism of the city as a whole. In following this route we also have to create a model that is capable of integrating both the social driver (equity) and the economic driver (the green economy). That is the basis for green urban infrastructure; and its evolution will be described in the sections that follow.

The concept of the city as a metabolism

The earliest modern work that explored the nature of the city using a biological analogy became known as urban ecology, a concept pioneered by the Chicago School of Urban Sociology in the 1920s. (Vasishth and Sloane, 2002, provide a useful historical discussion of the evolution of this early thinking of the Chicago School.) In this context it sought to apply principles derived from biological science to the explanation of spatial distribution in urban populations. Although no longer used to any significant extent in sociology, the concept of urban ecosystems is still used in a wider sense to explore the impact of people or cities on the ecological system. Thus, the United Nations looked at urban ecology in its Millennium Ecosystem Assessment (Piracha and Marcotullio, 2003), and it has also been used to explore the ecological footprint of a city, for example.

This early analysis began with the concept of linear metabolism, but then became more sophisticated through the inclusion of internally recycled systems, which led to the concept of circular metabolism. Both of these are shown in Figure 9.1.

There are different ways to look at these metabolic flows, though the one that is probably the most commonly applied is that which views them – that is, the resource flows – quantitatively. This approach is strongly favoured in the environmental sciences, particularly by those whose objective is to build an environmental database. This approach, then, seeks to integrate the metabolism of the city with the wider ecosystem through a process of ecosystem analysis, as typified by the work of Piracha and Marcotullio (2003).

This approach is slowly being adapted in the West to integrate infrastructure, but the early attempts remain tentative. One method being used by the University of Newcastle in Britain, for example, is simply to expand the inputs and outputs in Figure 9.1 to provide a more detailed list that can be linked directly to specific infrastructure services. At this point, though, there is a dearth of information, and a large gap in knowledge, as can be seen from the introduction to the university's research programme.

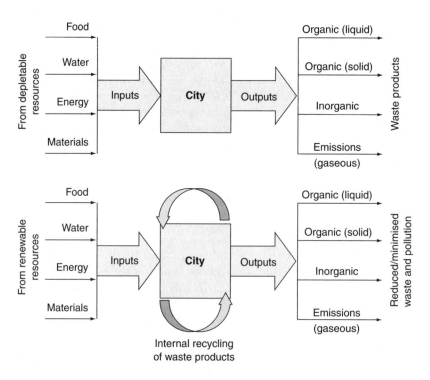

Figure 9.1 The 'metabolism' of cities showing, respectively, linear metabolism cities and circular metabolism cities (adapted from MIT, 2009 and Novotny *et al.*, 2010, p. 273, figure 6.1).

To address these gaps the programme brought together an international team of partners, to tackle the recognised need for greater understanding of the relationship between infrastructure and urban resources, arguing that

> [a]s cities adapt in response to global pressures such as climate change, it is crucial to understand the implications of these adaptations in terms of resource requirements to avoid confounding parallel sustainability initiatives. Whilst the vulnerability of the built environment to climate impacts is to some extent understood, resource flows, such as energy, waste and water within cities are currently poorly-understood and are generally considered in terms of gross inputs and outputs to the urban area. The relationship between urban form, function and these resource flows has only been established from observational evidence e.g. relating population density directly to total transport energy demand. This provides insufficient evidence to appraise, plan and design specific adaptations as it does not account

for crucial properties of the urban system such as land use, human activity, or the topology and attributes of the infrastructure systems that mediate this, and other, relationships (for example, land use and flood risk).

(EPSRC, 2010)

This approach is clearly situated within the context of mature cities with an existing (and fairly inflexible) infrastructure base. As such, its relevance to Africa is limited. There is then a second, somewhat different, approach, which has been developed by a German researcher, Jochen Monstadt (2009), as was discussed initially in Chapter 8. Whereas the Newcastle study reflects a mechanistic approach embedded in British empiricism, Monstadt makes a strong academic argument for an approach that recognises the value of, and need for, more conceptual thinking. This reflects much more the Germanic view of the relationship between infrastructure and resources.

In his paper, which draws upon practical experience in Germany and Switzerland, Monstadt provides direct support for the argument in this book that the role of infrastructure in urban development is seriously undervalued in the Anglo-Saxon approach to urban development, arguing that

[t]he debate on urban sustainability has now been on the research agenda for a number of years. One element that has, however, been undertheorized and empirically understudied is the crucial importance of networked urban infrastructures[1] for the ecological sustainability of cities. These infrastructures mediate resource flows and vitally shape environmental practices and sociotechnical innovation in cities. It is thus argued that we need adequate conceptual approaches which reflect the complex interdependencies between cities, networked infrastructures, and urban ecologies and which broaden our understanding of the ways we can develop, govern, and renew our infrastructures in cities in a sustainable way.

(2009, synopsis)

This interpretation of infrastructure is important for a number of reasons. First, it provides demonstrable, highly reputable academic support for the argument being developed here: that the linking of infrastructure directly to resource use can be a basis for moving towards urban sustainability; and it demonstrates that this argument is being taken seriously in a number of countries in Europe. Second, it strongly supports the position taken here: that there is a need to move beyond the empirical and instead begin to make use of conceptual models.

On the other hand, it is also limited by its geographical focus. The underlying weakness in all of these studies, certainly from an African perspective, is the specific locus of application, which is that of the mature cities of Europe. As a result, any output will remain contextualised within the existing realities of mature cities and the western infrastructure model. None the less, they provide strong intellectual support for the approach taken here, namely that if we are to understand the role of urban infrastructure in the twenty-first century, we have to position infrastructure within a contextual relationship with the use of natural resources. What is required next is to take that thinking outside of the current Eurocentric perspective to a theoretical framework that is constructed around the needs of emerging, rapidly growing towns and cities in the African subcontinent.

Building a new conceptual model of urban infrastructure

It is the recognition that infrastructure *mediates* resource flows through a city that provides the key to this new conceptual framework. Accepting the principle of the city as a metabolism, we can then group resources with a view to facilitating this mediating role of infrastructure, in order to optimise that role. The result is illustrated in Figure 9.2, which shows the flow of resources divided into six distinct groupings. These groupings then define the six primary categories of natural resources.[2] By using the term 'natural resources', this classification excludes financial capital and labour, and focuses the development framework on the infrastructure.

This conceptual model identifies the six primary categories of resource that exist on earth,[3] and it is self-evident that the city draws upon all of these for its growth, development and ongoing functionality. These are:

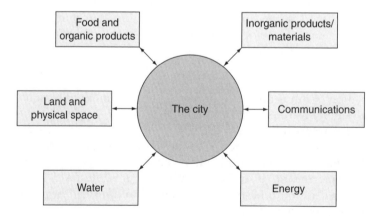

Figure 9.2 The six primary categories of natural resources interacting with the city.

- water;
- energy (including oil and gas found within the earth's surface);
- food and organic products (linked to surface cover in the earth's topsoil);
- inorganic products and materials (coming from the earth's mantle);
- land (differentiated from natural cover) and three-dimensional (physical) space;
- electromagnetic space; that is, the 'non-physical' space, and digital use of that space.

Having identified the major categories of resources, we next need to look at what happens when they cross the boundary from the wider ecosystem into the city. Here the principle of circular metabolism is taken as the starting point. However, this principle is interpreted differently from the way it is shown in Figure 9.1. Instead of a linear throughput with internal recycling, the interpretation explores the city from within a systemic framework of analysis.

The city within the wider global 'ecosystem'

At this point we need to make a small digression. This is because the 'metabolic city' is not the only approach that views the city, as an entity in its own right, from the perspective of environmental sustainability. There is also a second approach, which views the city as an element of a wider ecosystem: the 'eco-city'. This approach is generally represented as a form of city ecology model, of which there are several variants (see Schwirian, 2007, for a view from within the Chicago School). One of these, based upon the concentric zone model, is illustrated in Figure 9.3.

There are two definitive constraining characteristics of the 'eco-city' approach. The first is, once again, a framework of analysis centred on the mature city. The second is its locus of academic exploration, which is situated quite firmly within a dominant urban planning and land-use paradigm (Schwirian, 2007). This carries with it the weaknesses and flaws of that paradigm as described in earlier chapters, the most relevant of which is the misunderstanding of the role that urban infrastructure plays in shaping the urban form; and the dominant perception of infrastructure as being primarily a support service. In addition, the city ecology models took as their starting point the assumption that the infrastructure for mediating resource flows is already in place (i.e. the mature city), and built the model on this basis. The result, quite naturally, is a strong focus on mitigation of environmental impacts. In addition, this use of a mature city allows the model to explore the interaction between the city and the wider ecosystem from a position of relative physical and geospatial stability. The outcome of this starting point is to create much more of a static model.

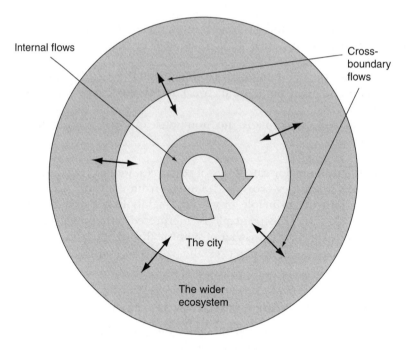

Figure 9.3 Visualising trans-boundary resource flows from an 'eco-city' perspective.

From the perspective of new development, the 'eco-city' model can be used, and is being used, for greenfield sites (or more correctly, perhaps, a brown desert site), but under conditions where the city is being designed to a high level of user convenience, and with a funding model that is based upon a very high unit cost. Thus, it is not exactly a typical real-life scenario that can be applied in the developing world.

Operationalising the green urban infrastructure model

In a city that is growing fast, yet still lacking conventional infrastructure, the most effective approach actually comes from combining the two western models (the metabolic city and eco-city) and then adapting them to the reality of fast-growing towns. The way in which this can be done is through the use of the six categories of resource flows illustrated in Figure 9.2.

By integrating the core concepts underpinning these two basic western models, and exploring them from a systemic perspective, we can create a model that is designed for the African situation. In this model each of the six categories defined in Figure 9.2 emerges as a resources system in its own right, as illustrated in Figure 9.4. These different systems then create an interactive relationship that takes the form of a three-dimensional ecosystemic map. The city itself is a system, but is quite specifically constrained by a geopolitical boundary, which only rarely coincides with natural boundaries. This specific geopolitical, economic and social-spatial system (the city) then interacts with each of the 'systems' defined by the resource categories, whose own boundaries are likely to be quite different from its own, and generally extend much more widely geographically, socially, economically and spatially. Equally, these six major systems are themselves interactive with each other; and together they define a large part of the complete global ecosystem. Of course, this is an illustration for just one city; we then have the cross-linkages between different cities, different independent resource users (e.g. for minerals extraction) and different external sources of pollution – all of which makes for a complex global model. None the less, it is proposed here that we can work with this simplified model to practical benefit at a local level, particularly in the secondary cities.

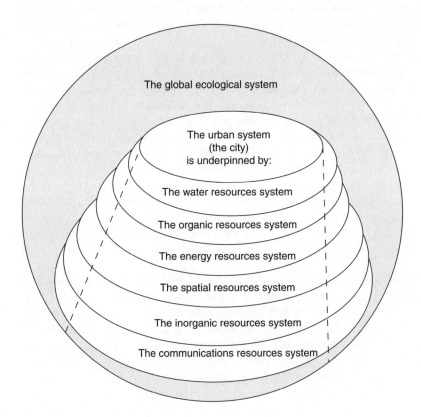

Figure 9.4 Systemic view of the city–ecosystem relationship.

Thus, the key to sustainable urban development in sub-Saharan Africa lies in the integration of the metabolic city and eco-city concepts into a single conceptual model, because each brings important basic concepts to the table. From the metabolic city model, which uses infrastructure to mediate resource flows, we can learn how to manage these resource flows most effectively, and we then have the core environmental driver for urban infrastructure. At the same time, though, we can also learn two important lessons from the eco-city model. The first of these is that protection of the environment (and the ecosystem) is far easier if cross-pollution between the different systemic flows can be avoided in the first place. It is clearly far more cost-effective to retain pollution within its own system, because once pollution crosses a system boundary it becomes much more expensive to redress, and the collateral damage is much higher. The western model of waterborne sewerage is perhaps the classic example of what happens when that principle is either forgotten or overridden.

The second lesson to be learned from the eco-city model is that the more internal recirculation can be incorporated into the urban system, the fewer resources need to be drawn from outside. Thus, the real issue is not simply minimising usage of a resource per se; it is also about minimising *new* usage of that resource. The primary focus in this context is to retain the resources, once imported, within the urban system, by recycling them. Water provides the most obvious example. At this point the primary role of infrastructure within an urban system becomes self-evident: it is to mediate the resource flows between the different external resources systems and the city; to mediate the internal flow of those resources once they enter the city; and to mediate the interaction, and cross-linkages, between those different resources. The detail follows on from this naturally. It is equally self-evident that if we are seeking to achieve a truly sustainable city, then the mediation of the different resources has to be done in a way that is equitable, and treats all urban residents equally, providing all of them with access to the same level of resources. In this way we achieve the symbiotic linkage between environmental sustainability and social equity that has been a major developmental constraint up to this point.

Taken together, these two lessons provide two core principles that underpin the conceptual framework for urban infrastructure. However, on their own they are insufficient, because on their own they can only reflect a mechanistic construct, in which each resource system is viewed separately. This is not the urban reality, but merely a superficial interpretation of reality, which has been made possible in mature cities only because the infrastructure base has already been installed; and pragmatic solutions are required based upon what already exists.

The whole basis of Figure 9.4 is that the city is at one and the same time a system in its own right *and* a physical space, where the different natural resources systems not only come together but also interact. Thus, the very act of laying down a road, for example, interferes with the natural water resources system; using water to take away human 'waste' interferes with both the urban water resources system and the organic resources system; and so it goes on. What is missing from this entire western debate about the city is a core principle that defines the nature of the relation between all these systems, as they come together in an urban context.

It is proposed here that the only way we can achieve real urban sustainability is through recognition that resources can never be taken; they can only be borrowed, and that borrowing creates a debt which has to be repaid. This, then, creates the third core principle of sustainable urban development, which can be defined in the following way:

> *Urban resources draw from different resource systems, where each is important in its own right; yet where each one is also an integral part of the global ecosystem. To ensure long-term sustainability, **resources cannot be taken from one resources system (category) to support action in another system; they can only be borrowed**. This defines all resources as having value. If one resource has to be taken across a boundary for use by another system of resources, then the cost of borrowing has to be calculated and this cost built into the transaction. To achieve real sustainability, the use of any resource has to be recognised as a loan that has to be repaid.*

When this principle is combined with the principles that (1) resource inputs across the urban boundary should be minimised, and (2) that reuse and recycling should be maximised, then we have the three principles of urban sustainability, namely:

1   Resource use within a system should be optimised through recycling and the new input from that resource system into the city should be minimised.
2   Resource use should be retained within its own system and only taken across boundaries when there is no other option.
3   When resources are taken across a system boundary, this transfer should be treated as a loan; that is, the resource taken across the boundary is borrowed, the environmental cost of borrowing the resource should be defined, and the way in which the loan will be repaid should be quantified.

These principles also provide the basis for creating a green urban economy in Africa that can provide a model for the rest of the world. That is, there is only one place in the world where it can still be applied to greatest effect (i.e. without retrofitting), and that is in the countries of sub-Saharan Africa. By learning from the urban development mistakes of the West (of which there are many), Africa can create truly sustainable secondary towns. Thus, its urbanisation process is not a problem at all, but an enormous opportunity.

From theory to practice: expanding the green urban infrastructure model

At this point the underlying concepts and principles have been laid out; and the conceptual model shown in Figure 9.3 can be combined with Figure 9.4 and translated into practice. The next step is to expand each of the categories to encompass the range of urban activities that are associated with each of the individual systems. The result is described, in an illustrated form, in Figure 9.5.

Figure 9.4 provided a theoretical three-dimensional systemic interpretation of the six major categories of resources within the wider global ecosystem. When we physically impose a city on the natural landscape, we are superimposing it on all of these systems. Sometimes this impact is immediate, as with water or land, for example. With other systems the impact

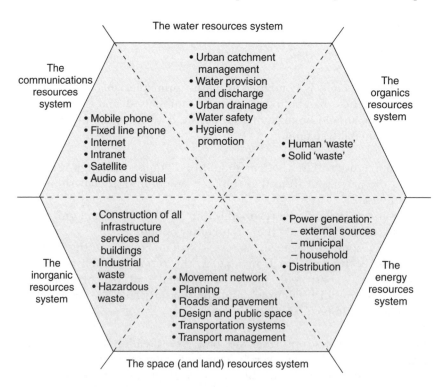

Figure 9.5 Diagrammatic interpretation of Abbott's green urban infrastructure model.

comes subsequently, after we have built and occupied the city, at which point all the systemic flows are potentially interactive.

At a human scale the city is a system in its own right; from a global perspective, though, a small secondary town can be interpreted as a point source. In this interpretation the town brings together the different external systems at a single point, and it is in this context that infrastructure begins to play its environmental role, in mediating the different resource flows within that 'point' of contact, as well as facilitating the interaction between the town and the wider biosphere.

This, then, is the systemic view of the different resource flows, as represented by Figure 9.5. Each system draws from its own external resource base, but each is now interacting with the others in this new urban environment that we have created. The ideal from a sustainability perspective would be to keep the different individual systems separate, but to do so is simply impractical. These are soft boundaries, with the dotted lines separating them indicating this porosity and highlighting how easily cross-contamination occurs. The environmental role of infrastructure in this context is twofold, and hence it carries inherent contradictions. The first is to manage the systems in a way that retains each of them, to the largest possible degree, within their own portion of the hexagon. The second recognises the benefits that can accrue in terms of user convenience from increased interconnectivity across the porous boundary. Thus, the one is seeking to exploit the convenience benefits that come from creating cross-connections, while at the same time the other seeks to limit the cross-connection in support of environmental sustainability; that is the real paradox of urban infrastructure.

Thus, roads, for example, are integral to social interaction and economic development within the city, yet the construction of roads has a huge negative impact in disrupting the natural flow of water across the city. Similarly, mixing water with human waste takes water from its original resource base and pollutes it, while at the same time this same mixing process takes valuable human waste from its own resource system and destroys its value, resulting in a double loss. These examples illustrate the need to adopt the principle of borrowing across resource categories, as described previously. These cross-boundary flows have to be viewed as 'loans'; that is, when a resource is moved from one system to another, this process is viewed as borrowing that resource, thereby creating a 'loan' that has to be repaid. Thus, the cost of the road has to include its destructive impact on the natural water flow; while using water to remove (human and organic) waste from its natural system has to incorporate the cost of that loss.

That is the resource management framework. At the same time, and just to make matters more complicated, the various resource flows have to serve their functional objectives, which are related to the needs of the people living in the urban area. So, we have to incorporate these functional needs, for example the water safety criteria for drinking water, which derive from satisfying social objectives. If we bring these together, then it quickly becomes apparent that, while individual needs have to be met, they have to be met within the wider framework of managing the resource flows collectively. In this context the Anglo-Saxon view of the city, which stresses the centrality of the individual, has to give way to a model whereby these individual needs are still accommodated, but only within a broader framework that integrates people into a systemic construct of the city as a whole (the metabolic city).

In thinking of urban development in an African context, it is important that we continually return to, and stress, the underlying message of history: western infrastructure was constructed using a nineteenth-century model that saw resources as exploitable within a linear view of development (that is, the resources stretched along a line into the future and could continue to be drawn on as and when required). That is not the situation today, where we live in a world that has to be driven by a systemic view of resource use that recognises the finite limits of the resource base. That is the world into which African towns and cities are emerging, and that is the world in which those towns and cities will have to frame their evolution. Now that we have created a conceptual model that describes how this can be achieved, the next step is to explore how this model can be operationalised by adapting our thinking about the nature of technology.

Chapter 10

Green urban infrastructure in practice
Mediating urban resource flows

Introduction

This chapter explores each of the six major resource systems used by the city, as illustrated in Figure 9.5, focusing on the technology component. In each case the starting point is the statement that infrastructure is a driver of development, so that we move away completely from the British model, which views infrastructure as a support service. The objective here is not to look so much at the technology per se but to focus instead on technology systems. In this way we can align technology with resource mediation within each of the six resource systems, these being:

1 the water resources system;
2 the organic resources system;
3 the energy resources system;
4 the space and land resources system;
5 the digital/communications resources system;
6 the inorganic resources system.

Once the technology systems have been defined, the chapter will describe the skills required to manage these technology systems and make proposals for the way that these skills could be developed.

The water resources system

The existing approach, outcome and consequences

The existing approach to the use of urban water resources management is both fragmented and disjointed, reflecting the way it was perceived in the nineteenth century, as described in Chapter 3. There were reasons why this happened, but they were based upon a specific interpretation of events, on cause and effect, and on available technical solutions as they existed at that time. If we were to be faced with the opportunity to begin over again – and African countries have such an opportunity – then we would take a very different approach.

The definitive outcome of that specific interpretative view was a complete separation of water supply from the natural water resources of the town, in a mechanistic, utilitarian view that in a modern context is completely lacking in rationality; it exists purely because that is how it was developed historically. The irony, of course, is that while this may be the reality for mature cities in the West, whose urban water systems were initiated in the eighteenth and nineteenth centuries, it is a ridiculous model for a city being developed in the twenty-first century that is seeking to create a sustainable urban system. It exists simply because western governments, agencies and companies working in the water sector have a vested interest in maintaining it.

The consequences today are self-evident. The world cannot support such a high level of profligate water consumption. In addition, the whole concept of waterborne sewerage and wastewater treatment lies outside the bounds of any logic system, as the previous chapter's conversation in the Minister's office sought to demonstrate. And then, to complete this trilogy of absurdities, the use of impermeable surfaces and 'conventional' urban drainage is equally illogical. These only serve to increase the storm intensity peaks, requiring even larger drains, at ever greater cost – all at a time when climate change is itself resulting in more extreme natural storm events. As a result, where there are problems with flooding, these are compounded further. At the same time, there is also the other extreme of some countries suffering increasingly from droughts, and here the separation of water supply from water resources is also making a bad situation worse, giving too much water needlessly to those who can afford it while the poorer, less fortunate sections of the population have barely enough to stay alive. And in all of this it is western governments and international development agencies that must take responsibility for this nonsensical situation, imposing a separation of urban water supply from urban water resources for their own, purely ideological, reasons.

The countries of sub-Saharan Africa are going to be seriously affected by climate change, and particularly by the rise in the number of extreme water-related events, be they floods, droughts or the rise in sea levels. Yet external agencies, and the western countries that support them, can only offer solutions based on the needs of mature cities, while continuing to impose a flawed vision of urban water management. The privatised urban water supply model has failed to address Africa's needs, while any attempt to address flood risk and drought management is incompatible with the current urban development model based on urban planning, which is simply incapable of dealing with storm water management. The only way forward is to change the way that we perceive water: to recognise that it is part of an integrated system and to work with it accordingly. The question is: why have we not been able to do that previously? As ever, the answer is to be found in the way that approaches to water evolved historically.

Why separate urban water supply from urban water resources?

John Snow's findings, which so clearly demonstrated the linkage between faeces-polluted water and cholera, led Britain to create a water supply system driven by the need to maintain water free of pathogenic organisms; thus, water quality became the conceptual driver behind the structuring of the water industry. The linkage between polluted water and disease led the country to place water quality at the heart of its water supply system, and ensure that the latter was protected from contamination at all costs. It was thus established as a municipal service separate from other infrastructure services, even where it was under the control of the same local authority.

On the sanitary side, the rapidly growing urban areas were already creating storm-water drainage systems to carry the run-off from the growing road network, and it was seen as logical that human waste should be flushed down these same drains to pass the waste into the river system or directly to sea. This was made possible by three specific characteristics of the English landscape.

- Britain's rivers were all relatively short, and no particle dropped into a river took no longer than five days to reach the sea.[1] Thus, it was possible to install rudimentary treatment systems that would remove gross solids and link pollutions to the 'carrying capacity' of the river systems, with the bulk of the purification taking place at sea.
- Water for the major cities, particularly in the Midlands and the North-West – the major industrial locations – drew water from high-rainfall sources quite far from the cities.
- Britain had a temperate climate with year-round rainfall, which meant that storage of water could be limited, as constant replenishment of low-capacity reservoirs could be relied upon. The small rivers and the topography, coupled with the factors mentioned above, made on-river storage uneconomic and impractical, and reservoirs were all constructed off-river.

The specific geographical, topographical and demographic make-up of England meant that it had no need to place the same emphasis on water resources management that Continental countries, with more varied climatic conditions, faced. In addition, in 1989, Britain, to all intents and purposes, gave control of its water resources to the private sector. The change simply accelerated the growth of the private water industry, to the point where there is now a huge investment and huge pressure to maintain the status quo.

The reason why water supply was developed in a specific way in nineteenth-century Britain had its own logic; but Africa is not Britain, and the time is not the nineteenth century. The challenge of the twenty-first century is to balance the needs of people with the needs of the environment. In an urban context such a balance revolves around one core issue: the relationship between the water required for people and the water required to maintain overland flows and aquifer recharge. Viewed in this way, it is self-evident that these are both part of one system. This in turn leads to the logical conclusion that what we are dealing with here is urban water resources management in its totality. The question then becomes one of defining what is meant by urban water resources management.

Defining urban water resources management as integrated and sustainable

As the global urban crisis grows, so more actors are beginning to recognise the importance of managing urban water resources in some way. Yet to date none of them has defined how this should be done. This is partially because they are locked into existing historical constructs, and partially because external agencies continue to support a mechanistic approach to problem-solving. As a result, the limited amount of thinking about the relationship between water supply and water resources management that does exist is concerned with expanding the range of sources in order to maintain the integrity of the existing water supply model.

Idiomatic language would call this a no-brainer. This is not what urban water resources management is about, at least if the objective is to embrace the terms 'integrated' and 'sustainable'. To use these terms and be committed to them, as opposed to using them spuriously for political correctness, urban water resources management has to be explored in its entirety as a system. What is required in turn is a change in conceptual thinking about this core relationship so that instead of seeing water resources as being there to serve water supply (the current mechanistic view), we have to see water supply as being subsumed within the broader context of urban water resources. This is something quite different, because with this as the vision, urban water supply is no longer the outcome; it is simply one component, albeit a very important component, of a broader integrated urban water resources system. Once this vision is accepted, then the historical division between water supply and other components of the urban water cycle can be seen for what it really is: a totally artificial nineteenth-century construct that was never intended to be a global model but was simply designed to address the perceived needs of a particular country at a particular point in time.

Exploring water resources in the context of an urban water catchment

The model in Figure 9.4 in the previous chapter shows the urban as being superimposed on the wider water resources system. In this model, then, the urban water 'catchment' is a part of the wider water catchment, and the principles that underpin integrated water resources management at a national or regional level can be applied equally at a local level within the urban boundary. There have been studies of urban catchment management in sub-Saharan Africa, one of which was a study in Cape Town in 2001 (Abbott Grobicki, 2001). This study was particularly relevant because of the nature of the catchment being studied. Thus:

- It was an urban catchment; that is, the source point for the river system lay within the urban area.
- It was a relatively small catchment, at 80 square kilometres, making it possible to view the entire catchment. It encompassed a variety of land-use types, including formal housing, informal settlements, an airport, agricultural land and industrial areas.
- It provides a mix of natural and artificially created drainage patterns.
- The majority of residents living within the catchment are poor, and the level of personal access to infrastructure services is low.
- The city of Cape Town had historical water quality records covering the previous twenty-five years, which could provide a statistical database.

On one level the study makes depressing reading when viewed from the perspective of water quality and urban ecology, as one might expect. On the other hand, it is able to conclude that urban catchment management is feasible. Overall, Ania Grobicki, who was the primary author of this work, argued that

> [p]erhaps the most important recognition to make in catchment management, especially in the urban context, is that the social and institutional processes should take precedence over purely technical decisions [and that] ... [t]his has been shown over and over again in successful catchment management projects worldwide.
>
> (Abbott Grobicki, 2001, Executive Summary)

On a more specific level, three key points emerge from this study:

1   Land use has to be integrated with the water catchment, and with the management of the water resources as a whole, not the other way around.

2   The management of other resources, particularly those currently classified as 'waste', are critical to the maintenance of the water system, and have to be seen in an integrative way.
3   The financial 'ring-fencing' of water supply and sewerage, and the increased focus on these services as market related, results in the loss of a financial base for catchment management.

The last of these is particularly important. The privatisation of water services, and the narrow British/World Bank view of water supply as a separate institutional arena, makes the achievement of sustainable urban development in Africa virtually impossible to achieve. Taking these conclusions further results in the following exploration of the requirements of integrated urban water resources management for a sustainable and equitable urban future:

- Define how much water we actually need.
- Integrate water supply into urban water resources management.
- Address the impact of cross-system interaction.
- Create a new economic model for water supply management.
- Address the impact of climate change.

Before we explore these issues, though, it is useful to provide a benchmark for the discussion by looking at the economics of conventional urban water supply practice.

The economics of conventional urban water supply

The historical western water supply model established the concept that water was supplied to an individual, which became a deeply ingrained *Weltanschauung* underpinning almost all current thinking. This is a false construct. Like much of the thinking associated with infrastructure, particularly in the areas related to water supply and sanitation, the basis for this concept lies in humanity's rural past, and it is simply the wrong construct for urban society. This is easily demonstrated by looking at the ratio of the amount of water drawn from a modern western supply system, which can vary from 200 to 400 litres per person per day, and the amount of water needed to sustain life, which is just 2 per cent of that figure.

When the western model of water supply, based upon providing what is essentially unlimited access to water that has been treated to a high standard, is applied to poorer urban areas, the outcome is that the poor subsidise the rich. This can be explained by looking at Table 10.1, which shows the cost of providing systems based upon three different design values for per capita consumption. This is a table developed from a South African study in the 1990s (Palmer Development Group, 1994). The actual

Table 10.1 Summary of costs per household for different values of per capita consumption

	Yard	House connections	
		Normal use	High use
Design parameter			
l/ca/day	90	150	300
Relative cost			
Bulk	1,008	1,679	3,359
Connector	322	536	1,073
Internal service	1,143	1,567	2,071
Total	2,472	3,773	6,503

Source: Adapted from Palmer Development Group (1994, p. 21, table 8).

numbers do not reflect current prices, but that is not relevant, since the important point lies in the relationship between the numbers.

These figures were calculated using existing costs from different regions in South Africa, and then attributed to a design scenario where the per capita figure was the design value for the supply network as a whole. This illustrates how high-use networks cost significantly more per capita than low-use networks. Once this network is in place, the fixed cost has to be repaid, regardless of who uses the system. So, the cost for poor people is proportionately much higher. The way around this lack of proportion is to create different levels of service, in which the poorer sections of the population receive a lower level of service, typically accessing water from a communal standpipe, for a reduced cost per kilolitre. But this is false economics, because the cost, as stated earlier, has to be repaid. Variable pricing can deal with this in theory, but only up to a point, since the marginal increase is generally far too small to reflect the real cost; which is exactly why the poor still subsidise the rich. In addition, as the ratio of rich to poor decreases, so fewer and fewer people are required to carry a greater proportion of the cost; but there is simply no way that a small percentage can carry the real cost of such an expensive system, and eventually the financial model simply collapses. Of course the government can subsidise this system, by paying the 'real' cost of the water used by the poor; but since this cost is several times higher than it needs to be, then this simply provides a further subsidy to the rich. Thus, the whole water supply model makes absolutely no sense.

Ethiopia is one of the few countries to recognise this. There, the entire system is designed around providing water to the site (the so-called 'yard-tap' option) for everyone. This system actually works well and does reduce costs significantly, but has two problems. First, those in the higher-income groups are increasingly making illegal connections into their house, resulting in an increase in per capita consumption and contributing to overloading of the design capacity of the network. Second, the international agencies and government supporting Ethiopia's urban water supply are seeking to have the country adopt a more 'conventional' approach, even though such an approach would actually make the situation worse.

How much water do we actually need?

Per capita water consumption varies enormously around the world, from the minimum WHO recommended figure of 50 litres per capita per day to a usage in excess of 400 litres per capita per day in some American cities. The first step in addressing urban water management, then, is to agree a volumetric measure for everyone. The final figure would have to be agreed at an international level, taking into account environmental sustainability needs for the planet as a whole, but at this stage it is possible to make a reasonable estimate. If we recognise that sanitation is part of a different resource group and should not be included in this calculation, then the figure that provides everyone with what they need at an adequate level to live at a reasonable standard is between 80 and 120 litres per person per day.

This figure applies at the *point of use*. However, as the earlier discussion indicated, when we are dealing with an urban system it is the *new input* that is equally, if not more, important. While it may be an ideal, it is not realistic at this stage to design for 100 per cent recycled flow: system losses alone would prevent that. If the goal for urban reuse were set at 75 per cent, then this would reduce the water extracted from the external system to between 20 and 30 litres per person per day. Such a goal then begins to move urban water consumption towards a sustainable future.

If we link this figure to resource flows, then our extraction from the external system for a town with 100,000 residents, based upon a per capita extraction of 30 litres per day, results in a demand of 3,000 kilolitres per day, or approximately 1,100 megalitres per year from the wider urban water resources system. By comparison, in an area with annual rainfall of 600 millimetres per year this total consumption equates to the amount of water that falls in one year on less than 200 hectares of land. The problem we face in the majority of African countries is not a shortage of water; it is the use of an inappropriate and outmoded western model of urban water supply.

Integrating water supply with urban water resource management

Water that is supplied to individuals, or industry, is also fed into the metabolism of the city. Industrial water consumption will be dealt with in a separate section later; this section is concerned with domestic use. The fact that individual consumption incorporates through-flow usage (that is, not all water brought in is consumed) means that water is discharged, and in a form where it has to be polluted. In the current individual model, particularly when there is no sewerage system installed, the responsibility of the water service provider stops at the point of delivery to an individual household.

The integrated urban water model challenges this procedure. In this model the water service provider would take responsibility for the so-called grey water that emerges from a property, and integrate that back into the urban water system. Following the principle that the most financially and environmentally cost-effective way to manage an urban system is to maximise the internal flow (i.e. recycle), the ideal is for the water supply system to operate as close to a closed-loop system as possible. In this context, water leaving a property has to be restored to its inflow quality as close to the point of usage as possible. In this way, water supply is integrated with the generic operational system applicable to all water resource use, which can be illustrated by thinking of recycling as taking place as a series of concentric loops, working from a small neighbourhood system outwards to a collection of neighbourhoods until it reaches the boundary of the urban area itself. In this model the household is a sub-unit of the local area, not the basic spatial unit, a concept that will be explored further in the sections on space and land management. In this context, recycling at the household level is important but is seen as an integral part of the local area water management system, an approach that is quite different from the thinking currently dominating water reuse in mature cities.

Integrating urban drainage with urban water resource management

A city, by its nature, sits on a natural watershed and interferes with the natural drainage pattern. The objective of integrated urban water resources management is to seek to minimise that impact, while at the same time limiting the inverse impact; that is, protecting people and property, as far as possible, from the adverse impact of the extreme storm events that are an integral part of the hydrological cycle.

To a large degree, and for the majority of the time, these require similar measures. The management of extreme weather events will be discussed in a separate section later. The principle of sound management is to return water back to its natural environment as quickly as possible – the principle of a sustainable urban drainage system. A broader systemic approach to integrated urban resource management, however, would go a step further and collect some of the storm water for recycling, together with the grey water discharged from properties, back to source to take the place of fresh water upstream of the treatment plant.

A new economic model for water supply management

When it is applied in an urban system without sewerage, the current economic model for water supply is known as 'cherry-picking'; that is, it takes a component of a wider system that can be isolated from the rest of the system to form the basis of a profitable exercise while leaving the rest of the system financially unsustainable. A useful comparison would be an economic model for the operating cost of a nuclear power station that failed to incorporate the cost of decommissioning.

The resource management model proposed here requires that the water service provider becomes responsible for integrating the grey water – that is, the water discharged from individual premises – back into the urban water cycle. The cost of water would therefore have to include the cost of this reintegration. Such a move would provide the basis for a sustainable model of integrated urban water resources management, particularly when coupled with the introduction of the principle of borrowing across systems, to be described later. At the same time, this should not be viewed as an additional cost. If we look again at Table 10.1, there are two important conclusions that can be drawn regarding the cost of existing network. The first is how much of the cost is attributable to the bulk supply, the concern here. The second is the apparently limited cost differential for what is termed the internal service; that is, the local reticulation component of the network, which will be discussed separately in the next section.

Providing water is expensive, and typically represents over half the total cost. What the integrated resources system described previously does is to switch that cost from extraction and bulk delivery to recycling. Thus, a significant component of the cost of this sustainable system is covered by the funding that would be required in a conventional system to bring water to the city. The total cost of the sustainable system would in most cases be higher, with the difference varying according to individual circumstances. In developing the cost recovery structure, this difference would be accommodated by separating the cost into two components, one of which would be a direct user component and the other a general municipal cost component, with the latter being classified as a 'borrowed resource' and the cost allocated accordingly, as described later.

Changing the economics of local distribution

The study on which Table 10.1 was based used conventional water supply design practice and materials; since that time there have been significant changes in thinking in both of these areas. The Ethiopian experience begins by showing the feasibility of providing the same service to everyone based upon delivery to a site boundary. This can be improved through the use of modern technology to limit the flow to a particular site using modern metering and telemetry. These new techniques do not prevent people from accessing more than the design quantity; their use simply changes the economic model and gives a much more realistic value to water. The design value defines the limit of the municipal responsibility to provide water to all, leaving a number of different options for increasing consumption. What all of these options would have in common, though, would be a shared reflection of the true cost of this additional water, which would be significantly higher than providing the basic design figure.

The second step is to lower the cost of the local distribution system. Advances in materials technology are already helping, but this is just one element. For example, a series of projects carried out in KwaZulu Province, South Africa, demonstrated how significant savings could be made, not only over conventional water supply systems but also over communal standpipes, by converting part of the network to a low-pressure system delivering water at a constant rate to small individual storage tanks situated on each family's site (Nkomo et al., 2004).

In an alternative approach the Asian Development Bank carried out a major study of small piped water networks that explore different management approaches to the delivery of water, using small-scale entrepreneurs effectively working as subcontractors to the main utility operator, looking at how there are actually a range of solutions that different countries can adopt, based upon individual circumstances and culture (Asian Development Bank, 2008). As an example, one approach they quote describes a small network scheme from the Philippines (Asian Development Bank, 2008, p. 19, figure 4). Here there is a main water line operated by the major utility, with water provided to a district meter. This enables the development of a network operational and management system within each district (i.e. beyond the district meter), which can then be varied according to local preference and circumstance.

A similar approach could be used for local distribution in Africa's secondary cities, though with some important differences. First, the system would be designed in this way from the beginning. Second, the primary loop could be smaller, with the subsidiary loops to the districts being larger. And third, the districts themselves would follow topographical, rather than spatial, boundaries, which would integrate the distribution loop with the natural water catchment. An example of how such a system might operate is illustrated graphically in Figure 10.1.

It is not the intent here to go down to a level of detail by exploring the minutiae of different technologies, since it is not the technology per se that is the problem. The real issue is that the use of these alternative local distribution systems, where they do exist, tends to link their application solely to specific urban conditions, most commonly the need to provide

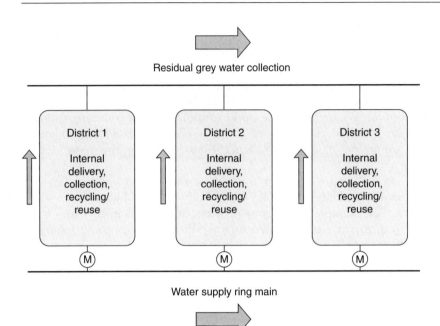

Figure 10.1 Diagrammatic representation of a local area distribution and collection scheme integrating the water supply with the wider urban water resources.

water to poor people, while continuing with conventional models of water supply elsewhere in the town. What is needed is a change in the wider conceptual approach, to a new and sustainable vision that integrates these ideas into a cohesive and comprehensive framework, one that situates water supply within the totality of urban water resources management, at all spatial levels of operation, in a seamless way. That is where the main focus of this discussion lies.

To move to that higher level, though, requires a second, quite fundamental change in mindset. Every single example of alternative systems, including the ones described here, from whatever continent, shares one common trait: every one of them talks of the provision of water to the poor, meaning poor individuals or families. This is where they all go wrong. In an African context the real issue is how to work with 'poor' municipalities or, more accurately and more correctly, municipalities with a low income base. The answer is not to differentiate rich families from poor ones. Nor is it to bring in the private sector as a matter of policy, since doing so simply supports social differentiation. The answer is to provide systems that the local authority can afford, and that are equitable and sustainable. That is why there has to be a fundamental change in mindset and a new way of thinking about urban water resources in a holistic and systemic way.

Invoking the principle of borrowed resources

Water has two key attributes that define its ecological role, namely quality and quantity, and both of these have to be managed or accommodated in a sustainable system. In this context there are two resource systems that have a major impact on the management of the water resources system: the organic resources system and the space and land resources system. Both of these have a deleterious effect on water quality, as well as modifying the hydrological cycle that defines water flows. In both cases the ideal is to manage the impact at source, but it is not always possible to do so. The alternative, where water quality and/or water quantity (i.e. flow) is modified, is to use the third principle of urban resource systems management defined in the previous chapter, namely that of borrowing across resource systems.

In this model, any use of, or interference with, water quality or flow would be defined in respect of a loan of the water resource, and that loan has to be repaid. If quality is affected, the cost of creating that impact, for example by causing pollution of the water, has to incorporate the cost of returning the water to its original quality. That is merely an extension of the 'polluter pays' principle, currently being widely adopted for industry. The same principle should also apply, however, to a disruption of water flow. Thus, the construction of a road should incorporate the full cost of interference with the natural flow. Incorporating the full cost goes beyond simply providing a metre of drain for every metre of road. Instead, it extends to a wider cost of returning that water to its natural environment. Similarly, the construction of a building would have to take into account the impact of a hardened surface on the natural water flow, and the cost of that impact to the system. This concept is recognised already, and is being applied in parts of Germany, where the construction of additional hard surfaces on a property, which lead to additional run-off, carries a charge. The use of the principle that resources taken across system boundaries are borrowed and have to be paid for, coupled with the extension of this principle to internal resource transactions, lays the foundation for a completely new urban resource infrastructure economy as compared with that used at present, provides the basis for green urban economics.

Flood risk and drought management

Drought management is easier to deal with than flood risk in an urban context, since the principles of integrated water resources management described here will contribute significantly to addressing the water shortage. Windhoek, the capital of Namibia, provides an example of a city in a low-rainfall area that has been practising direct recycling of water since the 1970s. And although these practices may not address all the needs of drought-stricken areas, they will minimise the amount of water that needs to be provided from external sources.

Floods provide a much more complex condition, partly because there are different flooding mechanisms and partly because the range of flows is so great. The Associated Programme on Flood Management categorises four types of flooding: local, riverine, flash and coastal, all of which are exacerbated by the impacts of climate change (WMO-GWP, 2008). The first of these, local flooding, is to a large extent caused directly by urban-isation processes, which result in reduced amounts of evapotranspiration, shallow infiltration and deep infiltration, and a concomitant increase in run-off, an increase that can be as great as fivefold (WMO-GWP, 2008, p. 5). The application of the integrated urban water resources management system outlined here would make a significant contribution to ameliorat-ing the impact of local flooding in the majority of cases, the exception being in areas where the natural ground is largely impermeable.

Riverine floods may be affected by rainfall upstream of the urban area, in which case the primary issue will be to ensure the retention, as far as possible, of the natural floodplain. At the same time, riverine floods are also affected by changes in the urban condition, in particular the exten-sive use of piped or channelled drainage systems, which increase peak storm flows.

The Toolbox produced by the Associated Programme on Flood Man-agement provides extensive information on flood management generally, and many of the recommendations in that document (WMO-WP, 2008) would be addressed using the management approach outlined here. The one weakness in that document stems from the difficulty of integrating the recommendations into an urban development model based upon the urban planning paradigm. The reason for this is quite simple: a land-use development model is inherently in conflict with an integrated urban water management model. The alternative, which is the resource-based approach to urban development described here, addresses that conflict by placing integrated urban water resources management at the heart of urban development, with land use being integrated in a sustainable way.

The organic resources system

Introduction

Food security ranks with water security as a primary concern for all coun-tries in Africa; and food security is built on agriculture. Yet the discussion on agriculture tends to exist within a conceptual bubble that situates it almost completely within a sectoral context. In respect of its relationship to the people dependent on its output, this is perceived as a one-way flow: from production to consumption – a perception deriving, like so much else in the world of development practice, from a mechanistic worldview. In reality, of course, agriculture is integral to society as a whole; and improving yields and production areas to meet increasing demand needs to extend far beyond the current narrow debate linking output to fertiliser use. When viewed from a systemic perspective, nutrient flows are part of a much wider life cycle, of which people are an integral part, and it is this wider cycle, in its totality, that we should be exploring in the urban debate. This is what constitutes the organic resources system.

When human beings are reintegrated into the organic resources system, the flow of resources across the urban interface can be seen to have both inputs, primarily in the form of agricultural food products, and outputs, which are generally classified, misleadingly, as waste products. It is the latter that are the main focus here because this is where the major changes in mindset need to occur and where a new approach is required most. In the fragmented and mechanistic western approach the infrastructures most closely associated with this resources system are those described as sanitation and solid waste.

Sanitation: the existing approach, outcome and consequences

The current approach to sanitation is based upon the principle that it revolves around an individual and constitutes a basic need. While true, this is nonetheless an extremely narrow view of sanitation. In its broader context, which is equally, if not more, important in an urban setting, sanitation is a collective output from the city metabolism and an integral part of the wider natural resources system of the planet. It is the failure to recognise this wider role that defines the failure of the western construct. Unfortunately, the wider exploration has been made more difficult through the current interpretation of how best to achieve the Millennium Development Goals. This has encouraged people to conflate and/or confuse the terms 'sanitation' and 'toilet', leading to the view that sanitation for all means a toilet for everyone. This in turn has led to the equally fallacious belief that the best way to achieve the sanitation MDG goals quickly is for the poor majority to build toilets. Within that context, speed and affordability will generally lead such building to the simplest of toilets: the (ventilated improved) pit latrine. In following this route, sanitation provision has been mistakenly assumed to mean also sanitation security; yet this is not the case.

The individual focus that lies at the heart of the current sanitation strategy is a valid rural strategy, but, as this book has constantly sought to demonstrate, that does not make it a valid urban strategy. As a result, the current drive of external agencies and western governments to provide toilets to individuals in order to meet the sanitation goal is not a sustainable solution; and, of even greater concern, nor will it guarantee sanitation security. Instead, urban areas require a totally different strategy. History shows us that the western world has been here before, at the beginning of the nineteenth century; and the discussion of urban infrastructure in Chapter 3 showed where a similar approach led. People built private cesspits, which then took the surplus water from the new water supply systems, resulting in overflowing cesspits and the rapid spread of disease.

The same thing can now be seen occurring across Africa. The study of Ethiopia in Chapter 7 illustrates this. People on higher incomes, with their own houses, and often with tenants, make their own house connections and then discharge the surplus water to the pit latrine – a natural response in the absence of a waterborne sewerage system. A pit latrine, of course, is not a cesspit, and has a greater capacity to absorb water. But equally, its *raison d'être* is based upon its being a 'dry' system. If it remains saturated, then its biological process changes. And even with its greater capacity to pass water into the surrounding soil, it will eventually flood. In Ethiopia the results were visually evident in Harar, the historical walled city of Ethiopia, where physical access for pit emptying is restricted owing to the very narrow streets; and in Sodo, a town that is built on impermeable soil (clay), which limits infiltration. At this point in time the number of overflowing pits may still be limited in number, but it is early days in the construction of urban pit latrines and it is only a matter of time before the urban centres in Africa begin to experience the same problem as did the cities of Europe and America 200 years ago: overflowing pits and the spread of waterborne diseases.

The highly respected Stockholm Environmental Institute described sanitation as '[a] sector which is highly dysfunctional and suffering from limited political leadership at both the local and global levels' (Rosemarin *et al.*, 2008). This statement should not come as a surprise: sanitation is a classic example of too much external intervention driving internal decision-making processes; and there are lots of different external actors out there who wish to be involved. At the same time, the alternative, perhaps surprisingly, does not lie with the construction of large-scale sewerage systems and wastewater treatment plants, which are themselves unsustainable. Rather, the answer lies in a simple change of mindset, from one that sees faecal matter and urine as 'waste' to one recognising that these products are an integral part of the natural resource cycle of life, and as such are essential to the maintenance and sustainability of that resource system.

Disaggregating the term 'water and sanitation' into its component parts is the key to a sustainable urban future

The most misleading and damaging use of word association in 'development-speak' is that linking 'water' and 'sanitation' as 'water and sanitation'. The evolution of urban infrastructure in the United States led to a natural association, quite early on, between the management of water supply and sewerage. Interestingly, though, there was no such association in Britain (prior to 1974), where the two were perceived to be quite distinct and were managed completely independently. There is no such logic in linking the terms 'water' and 'sanitation' in that way. On the contrary, it is much more rational to argue that to use the terms 'water' and 'sanitation' in the same breath is the greatest single obstacle to the achievement of sustainable urban development in Africa. This is because *'water' and 'sanitation' exist within completely different urban resource systems and every attempt should be made to keep them separate.*

The integration of the words 'water' and 'sanitation' arose from the coming together of three divergent development trends. The first was the rising influence of the WHO, promoting health as the key requirement of both water and sanitation in the wake of the breakdown of urban infrastructure delivery in the 1970s. Here the roots can be seen as coming directly from rural practice, as described in Chapter 4. The second was the rise to dominance of the Anglo-Saxon privatisation model of the 1980s, which saw water and sewerage as services to be provided to the individual, thereby reinforcing the existing trend towards sanitation as an individual responsibility, as described above. The third trend was also linked to privatisation, and saw water and sewerage combined in Britain for the first time, when the two were brought under a single management. There was already unified management in the United States, but it was the privatisation drive of the 1980s that made it standard practice, which African countries then had to adopt.

The time has come to rethink that integrated terminology, in an urban context, and to reposition both water and sanitation, returning each of them back to its origins in the wider resources system to which they belong. Doing so will mean dispelling a number of myths about the relationship. One relates to water pollution, where the origins go back directly to the findings of John Snow in the nineteenth century. It is of course true that poor sanitation practices pollute watercourses and groundwater; but then so do run-off from chemically fertilised agricultural land, landfill leachate, industrial effluent and acid mine drainage, to name but a few. Now, though, we have the technology to keep them separate. And yes, people are at risk from touching faecal matter and should wash before eating; but that is an issue of good hygiene, recognised for centuries by both the Jewish and the Muslim faiths. Ethiopian practice too, like Muslim practice, uses the right hand for eating and the left hand for personal cleaning, which also addresses this issue. At the heart of the current linkage between water and sanitation, and a serious problem in creating more open discussions around sanitation options, is a western scatological phobia that has been imposed on other societies that have actually learned to manage human faeces far better than has western culture.

The metabolic city requires a new, and quite different, perspective. Far from being linked, water and sanitation need to be recognised as belonging to different natural resources systems. If they are to be managed effectively and sustainably, their management requires that they should be treated separately, both conceptually and physically. The artificial linkage has to be broken if African cities are to have a sustainable future. Water and sanitation need to be completely delinked, and returned to their own, naturally occurring, resources systems.

Changing the sanitation Weltanschauung

The first step in creating this separation is to show how the myths around sanitation extend far deeper than the artificial water and sanitation construct. These are highlighted in Table 10.2, with the one column outlining

Table 10.2 Comparing the existing sanitation Weltanschauung with the urban reality

Existing, primarily Anglo-Saxon, Weltanschauung	Basis for social equity and environmental sustainability
1 Sanitation is an individual responsibility.	Sanitation is an output from the urban metabolism, and as such is a collective resource.
2 The components of human excretion (faeces and urine) are both waste products.	The components of human excretion are valuable resources, the reuse of which is essential to the long-term sustainability of the planet.
3 Sanitation is an individual right.	On an individual level it is the security of sanitation that is paramount.
4 Sanitation is primarily about toilets.	Sanitation is about metabolic systems, and the role that people play in those systems.
5 Countries must have a single national approach (policy/strategy) for sanitation.	From 1 and 2 above, it is self-evident that there is a need to treat the rural and urban conditions separately.
6 Countries need a stand-alone policy/strategy for sanitation	An urban sanitation policy or strategy has to be integrated with the urban metabolism as a whole, and the wider management of resource flows.

the existing fallacies embedded in the existing western *Weltanschauung*, while the second column describes the reality.

Reintegrating human beings into the organic system

Like all mammals, human beings discharge waste in two components: urine and faeces. This separation is immensely valuable, and indicates the extent to which people are naturally a part of the wider organic system of life. It is the western development model that has lost sight of this and created the current non-sustainable approach to the management of human 'waste', first by mixing urine with faecal matter and then by using water as a transport medium.

Urine and faecal material contribute to the natural cycle in quite different, yet complementary, ways. Faecal matter provides both a carbon (energy) and a soil conditioner, while being high in pathogens. Urine on the other hand provides nutrients but is pathogen-free. The best way of accessing these products is derived from keeping them separate so that each can return the maximum benefit to the natural cycle. This subsection and the one that follows describe the use of urine as a product, with the discussion on faecal matter following on from that.

Studies by the Swedish-based Stockholm Environment Institute have shown that, at a time when farmers around the world are using approximately 175 million tons of synthetically derived urea (nitrogen fertiliser) each year (ICIS, 2010),[2] the western-imposed sanitation systems discharge approximately 50 million tons of fertiliser-equivalent into the atmosphere, waterbodies or pit latrines (Rosemarin *et al.*, 2008, p. 13). And although the world production of chemical fertiliser is expected to match or exceed demand in the short to medium term, the supply of phosphates in particular is likely to peak in the second half of this century.

However, availability is not the critical issue: cost is of much greater significance. When compared to other regions, sub-Saharan Africa (excluding South Africa) currently uses far less fertiliser, at approximately 8 kilograms per hectare, than most other countries (Rosemarin *et al.*, 2008, pp. 13–14). When people talk of the 'Green Revolution' in Asia, which saw a vast increase in rice production over thirty years, they tend to forget that this came at a price, increasing fertiliser use to around 200 kilograms per hectare. In the global competition for synthetic fertiliser that is now emerging, the majority of countries in sub-Saharan Africa are in a very weak position. Yet Africa is also the continent that is most in need of improved agricultural practice. Three-quarters of its farmland is degraded and the subcontinent is losing 30–60 kilograms of nutrients per hectare each year.

Ecological toilets and urine separation

This chapter is concerned with the management of resource infrastructure systems at the city level, rather than at the user interface, which, for the natural resources system, is the toilet. Here there are many technology options available; the objective here is not to discuss these, but simply to clarify the distinction between toilets that separate urine and those that don't, since this is the most critical issue for the overall management of the resources system.

The term 'ecological toilet' describes a user interface that collects the human 'waste' products and retains them in their natural state (i.e. undiluted by an external water supply) so that they can be used subsequently as a fertiliser. In this context the urine and faeces may be mixed or kept separate. When urine separation is built into the toilet (with a separate urinal provided for men), this is often termed a urine diversion dry toilet (UDDT), since it is designed to ensure that the component parts of human excretion, namely faecal matter and urine, are managed separately in the wider resources management system. Like all toilets, ecological units cannot and should not be seen simply as stand-alone 'toilets'. Instead, they need to be recognised for what they really are: an integral part of the wider management system that links people to the wider urban metabolism. Where they differ from flush toilets is in the way that they require people to be involved more directly with the management of their own waste products.

The wider metabolic pathway for resource-based sanitation

The 'toilet', then, is simply one component of a much greater metabolic system. Figure 10.2 shows the full metabolic pathways for the two toilet options described in the previous subsection.

The metabolic pathway is a term used to describe the flow of resources through a system. In this case, food has entered the urban system and results in what has traditionally, though incorrectly, been called waste. Direct consumption results in 'human waste', while product loss results in 'organic waste', which in western societies was mixed historically with other discarded products to generate 'solid waste'. The whole objective of 'waste' separation at source is to be able to reuse or recycle the majority of this waste material.

The national potential of urine as a fertiliser: the case of Ethiopia

Ethiopian imports of mineral fertiliser have been rising rapidly in recent years, from 150,000 tonnes in 2003 to approximately 650,000 tonnes in the

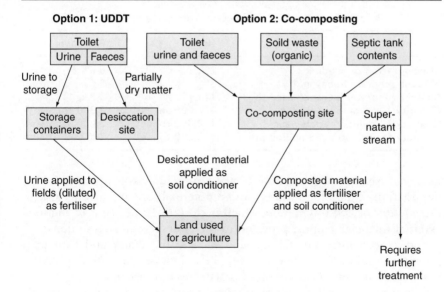

Figure 10.2 The wider metabolic pathway for sanitation.

2006/7 fiscal year. Approximately half of this amount was urea, with the other half being diammonium phosphate (DAP). The cost of urea fell consistently through the 1990s, reaching a low of US$78 in 1999 (IMF, 2001). By 2003, however, the price paid by the government was US$160 per tonne, and this rose to almost US$400 in 2006/7, while the spot price in 2008 was over US$600 per tonne, though it fell back subsequently to the 2006 level. Even at this level, however, the importation of fertiliser cost the government of Ethiopia approximately US$240 million in foreign exchange, which represents almost 5 per cent of the total national expenditure of the country. For countries further into the interior, the cost of fertiliser can be up to twice the cost per tonne used here. Finally, this is the dollar price. Between 2007 and 2011 the dollar exchange rate of the Ethiopian currency declined by over 60%, which means that the local cost of fertilizer increased by an equivalent amount over that four year period.

Agriculture is one of the mainstays of the Ethiopian economy. Table 10.3 shows the potential for benefit to the country and the agricultural sector of replacing imported urea and DAP with urine. These figures are based upon a urine discharge of 1.5 litres per capita per day.

The study of Ethiopia described in Chapter 7 showed that the level of urbanisation in the country was extremely low, at around 15 per cent of the population.[3] Even under those conditions, though, the study of the eighteen secondary towns calculated that the residents of the urban areas (approximate population 3.5 million) discharge the equivalent of over 40,000 tonnes of fertiliser either into the ground or into waterbodies

Table 10.3 Potential for fertiliser production from urine in Ethiopia

Parameter	Urea	Phosphate
Concentration of product	2%	0.6%
Amount generated/person/day	30 g	9 g
Amount generated/person/year	11 kg	3.3 kg
Quantity/1 million people/year	11,000 tonnes	3,300 tonnes
Quantity/10 million people/year	110,000 tonnes	33,000 tonnes
Quantity for Ethiopia (85 million pop.)	935,000 tonnes	280,000 tonnes

(where it causes major pollution) each year. This loss is replaced by the importation of mineral fertiliser, with a potential foreign currency cost to the country of US$160 million, which is close to 10 per cent of the total external financial support provided to the country. Yet even under these circumstances, international agencies such as the Water and Sanitation Program continue to advocate, and often impose, sanitation practices based upon the rapid expansion of pit latrines into urban areas. Quick-fix solutions may satisfy the western social conscience but they will not provide the towns with solutions that are sustainable in the longer term.

That is the situation in Ethiopia. At an even higher level of scale, the Stockholm Environmental Institute calculated that the widespread adoption of ecological sanitation, which is the toilet recovery system, has the potential to satisfy over 100 per cent of the total requirement for nitrogen and 90 per cent of the phosphorus for the entire subcontinent (Rosemarin *et al.*, 2008, figure 23, p. 19).

Finally, the use of urine in place of mineral fertiliser has a further benefit, in addition to its potential for import substitution – and this applies to all urine used in this way, regardless of whether it directly replaces existing mineral fertiliser use or fertilises new areas of land. That benefit is carbon saving and the income from carbon trading. It requires 24 million BTU[4] of natural gas to produce 1 tonne of urea (FETP, 2011). This is equivalent to approximately 678 cubic metres of natural gas, which in turn has a *carbon equivalent* of 332 kilograms. Each tonne of urea generated from urine is therefore worth 0.33 tonnes of carbon credits.

Integrating solid waste management into the organic resources system

Both faecal matter and solid waste can contribute significantly to the natural resources system, as well as having the potential to generate biogas which can be converted into energy. Table 10.4 provides an indication of the potential of both of these products for fertilizer production.

Because of its high pathogen count, faecal matter cannot be applied directly to the land; instead, it has to be treated in some way to destroy

Table 10.4 Potential for fertiliser production from faecal matter and solid waste in Ethiopia

Faecal matter		Solid waste	
Amount/person/day (average)	0.15 kg	Mean (Ethiopian study)	0.8 kg
of which dry matter (at 20%) is	0.03 kg	Organic component (70%)	0.56 kg
Annual production	55 kg	Annual production (organic)	200 kg
Town of 100,000 people	5,500 t	Town of 100,000 people (organic)	20,000 t
Quantity/1 million people/year	55,000 t	Urban population (12 million) (organic)	2.4 Mt
Quantity for Ethiopia (85 million pop.)	4.7 Mt		

pathogens and other harmful constituents. There are three ways in which this treatment can typically be done: by composting, drying (desiccation) or digestion. It is the third of these that produces biogas.

The co-composting process shown in Figure 10.2 incorporates the organic component of solid waste. However, when this is incorporated into the wider natural resources system, particularly in the large towns and cities, there is a further technological option that becomes available, namely that of the biodigester, which can be used for human waste, solid organic waste or a combination of the two. This technology is based upon the principle that under anaerobic conditions, bacteria degrade the organic matter and produce biogas, which is a mixture of methane, carbon dioxide and other gases.

Why ecological sanitation cannot function in the current western urban model

The document from the Stockholm Environmental Institute (SEI) quoted on p. 317, while important and valuable in its message, also illustrates the weakness of the current urban model and why this approach to sanitation has little chance of succeeding in the current western-imposed urban model. The document makes a strong case for the use of urine as a fertiliser and the enormous financial benefits that that would entail, some of which I have already outlined. It then describes the use of toilets at a local level, and the global network to which the SEI belongs[5] is carrying out important and valuable work building a support base for ecological sanitation at an individual level. Where the document falls down is in its failure to link the micro scale to the large scale. The SEI, like almost every western institution working in the field of sanitation, is locked into the existing

Weltanschauung illustrated so clearly in Table 10.1. There is an acknowledgement that the weakness lies at the local institutional level, but a total lack of understanding of how to overcome it. Thus, for example, the document makes the following statement concerning the situation in Uganda:

> An example of how to put these definitions into practice is the case for Uganda. Uganda has well-written national [sanitation] policies, but the challenge becomes more obvious when it comes to implementation in a decentralized governance environment. In general, the major difficulty is in creating an environment in which national policy is implemented at the lowest level of government. It is quite common to find local government offices lacking the technical, managerial, and financial capacity to address the real sanitation needs.
>
> (Rosemarin *et al.*, p. 32)

Need one say more? The real problem does not lie with local government in Uganda, or elsewhere in Africa. The real problem lies with the agencies that seek to promote solutions that were developed in a different time and a different place to address objectives from within a different value system. And while these external bodies make use of the politically correct phraseology, such as 'good governance' or 'decentralisation', the policies and practice they proposed result in the very opposite outcome. In taking this approach they fall into the same trap as all externally based sector specialists, as discussed in Chapter 4: adopting the pre-Copernican view that local government (in fact all government) revolves around their own specialised interest, in this case sanitation.

There only way to scale up the delivery of sanitation in the urban areas is to approach the *problématique* from a systemic perspective: situating the 'solution' within the context of the metabolic city and then creating methodologies that are replicable. Sanitation is not an individual 'problem' or an individual responsibility; it is an integral part of a natural resources system that operates across the city as a whole, and is part of the city metabolism. Only when it is seen in this way will the cities be able to move towards sustainable solutions.

Rethinking alternatives in sanitation

When sanitation is seen in this way, namely as part of a natural resources system, then it has the potential to radically change the way that we view our 'waste products'. This section shows how an integrated resource-based system, moving seamlessly from household to field, provides the framework for the socio-economic model of sanitation against which all other potential delivery systems have to be measured. This framework is not intended to be prescriptive; it does not mean that all cities and countries have to use resource-based sanitation. Countries retain the freedom to choose whatever sanitation option they wish. What acceptance of the inter-relationship between sanitation and the natural resources system does mean is that we change the economic model of sanitation quite radically, and in doing so we change the way that decisions are made about which sanitation option to use. Tables or diagrams such as Figure 4.3, which attempt to demonstrate that pit latrines provide the lowest-cost option, are shown to be based upon false economics which ignore the value of the product completely, and the importance of human waste in the wider global life cycle.

In looking at any alternative, resource-based sanitation, with fertiliser production, has to define the baseline against which other systems should be compared. This is because it is the only option that retains human waste completely within its natural resource system; all 'wet' solutions cross resources systems boundaries. Crossing a systems boundary invokes the principle of borrowing resources. In this case, when water is borrowed to transport human waste, the implication is significant. The closed cycle that is the basis of urban integrated water resources management described in the previous section is broken, to be replaced by a much larger recycling loop that involves much greater expense and much higher water consumption per capita. At the same time, the urine and faecal matter are taken out of their own natural resource system, where they are a valuable product, and used to pollute the water resource system, where they become a significant additional expense. All of this should be factored into the cost of waterborne sewerage, which in turn demands a new green economics approach to sanitation.

Recognising the constraints of ecological sanitation

The use of ecological sanitation requires a systemic approach that will require a major change in mindset. And even when operationalised, this approach may not make urine a full substitute for imported urea, because the two products are different. Chemical urea is granular and in a pure form, which makes transportation relatively cheap. The urea in urine is in a liquid form, at a concentration of 2–2.5%. This means that transportation is an important limiting factor, linking its viable use to within a specific distance from towns and cities, based upon the cost of transport. On the plus side, however, it has a very low marginal cost of production, since it is a by-product of a sanitation system that is required by the cities regardless of this use. From an operational perspective (i.e. excluding the capital cost of individual toilets) it is competitive with externally purchased chemical fertiliser, while freeing the country of the commitment to spend valuable foreign currency reserves. In addition, its production is stable and predictable, and will not suffer from the price volatility of chemical fertilisers.

The system would require the development of a new industry to manage it effectively, which would be managed by small or micro enterprises. The cost of the system is in the transportation of the urine (which is linked to distance), and the storage of the urine on site for prolonged periods. This storage is required partly to ensure that the urine is pathogen-free and partly to match the supply of the product (with a daily output) with the fertiliser spreading period (which is most commonly biannual). While a detailed study would be required to determine the final rates, it is expected that the cost of transportation and storage, calculated for the Ethiopian study, would probably be less than US$100 per tonne equivalent (2007 prices) and would be incurred in local currency. At the same time, the use of this system has a major potential economic benefit locally as well as nationally, providing the basis for a whole new local industry.

Working with indigenous realities

The fact that ecological sanitation is the most effective way to integrate human excreta into the natural organic cycle does not make it the only solution. It should form the basis for the economic model of urban sanitation, as described in the next section, but at the same time there is a need to integrate a sanitation model into the indigenous reality. This need may be a response to cultural concerns about faecal material or it may simply reflect a condition where a number of existing systems already exist. This latter situation will be particularly relevant to larger towns and cities and has to be recognised. The work of Letema *et al.* on the use of mixed sanitation systems in Kampala and Kisumu, Uganda, provides a good example of the need for a practical response to this condition. These authors argue in their conclusion that the

> [s]anitary configuration in Kampala and Kisumu is brought about by different scales, technologies and institutional structures resulting in mixtures. There is a trend towards medium-large-scale public sewerage development in East Africa based on catchments.... The key to sustainable sanitation is to recognize and utilize the co-existence of different sanitation configurations rather than trying to integrate all configurations in a single format of infrastructure management.
>
> (2010, p. 161)

A new economic model for sanitation

Countries should have a choice of sanitation option, and it is not my intent here to argue that ecological sanitation should be imposed. On the contrary, countries should be allowed to choose their own system of sanitation. But is that statement not a contradiction of all that has been said here previously? Actually, no, because the basis of a resource-system derived sanitation model depends for its success not on the choice of technology system per se, but upon the use of a single *economic model*. What is argued for here is a new system of green economics that takes into consideration the full environmental and social cost of alternative sanitation options, and particularly the waterborne sewerage options.

A major financial benefit of resource-based sanitation, when integrated into a resource recovery model that collects urine and faecal material across the entire urban area, is that it provides a cost recovery model that makes urban sanitation affordable to the town. And while this model is not completely self-financing at an individual level, it nonetheless significantly reduces the cost of providing a sanitation system, an extremely important factor in considering how to improve the quality of life of poorer urban residents. That cost can then be reduced further by providing a capital subsidy for the ecological toilet, on the grounds that, like reforestation, it is a critical component of the natural cycle, so that it could be funded as part of the climate change rebate to low-income countries, in which case the operating system would be entirely self-financing.

If such a system is used as the baseline, the economics of providing a waterborne system, and particularly a full, western-style sewerage system, change quite fundamentally. Replacing dry ecological sanitation with a waterborne sanitation option brings additional costs that should be factored into the pricing of these systems:

- the marginal cost of accessing additional water supplies required for flush toilets, which should not be integrated into a unified tariff but calculated separately, and the additional cost added to the per unit cost of waterborne sewerage;
- the loss caused by removing the waste products from the natural system, based upon the price of imported fertiliser;
- the carbon cost of producing the fertiliser that would have been replaced;
- the carbon cost of constructing a wastewater treatment plant;
- the foreign currency premium associated with the importing of both fertiliser and the technical components of the wastewater treatment plant.

The energy resource

Energy in an urban context: why Africa is different from Europe and the United States

The growing acceptance of climate change is radically changing the way in which we view energy supply. For Africa, this enables the opening up of at least one area of infrastructure to a wider debate, since western agencies, which exert so much control over the intellectual space that defines the development debate, are also having to rethink their existing models. The enormous damage that is caused to the environment by the need to burn fossil fuel in order to generate electricity has led to a resurgence in interest in sustainable energy. As a result, things are moving Africa's way for once, since that continent is the best situated to take advantage of indigenous renewable resources. Before we discuss that wider context, though, the *problématique* first requires a more detailed exploration of how energy needs in the mature cities of the West differ from those of the rapidly growing cities in Africa.

Energy uses in an urban area can be broken down into five major categories:

- industrial production;
- transportation;
- commercial and public-sector consumption (bulk users);
- individual consumption (multiple small users);
- home and office consumption for temperature regulation (heating and cooling).

This list immediately illustrates three key differences between mature cities in the West and newly developing secondary cities in Africa. The first is the need for heating and cooling, a major user of energy in western countries that can account for over 50 per cent of general home and office consumptions. Much of the research taking place in western countries regarding energy saving relates to this area of use. Yet such use is negligible in the secondary cities of Africa. That distinction has major implications for the way in which the energy resource is viewed.

The second is in transport. Western countries already have a large road network that represents a huge sunken investment, as well as a large stock of motor vehicles. The majority of the mature cities are now giving ever-increasing importance to public transport models, which (in their usual way) they then seek to sell to Africa as a solution to urban transport problems. Yet the secondary towns in Africa are completely different. They do not have this sunken asset (roads), nor do they have to follow the western models. As a result, they have greater freedom to create new transport models.

The third major difference lies in the industrial model. The West has inherited an old industrial base, which it is seeking to upgrade rapidly. This places the climate change focus on mitigation measure to reduce carbon output. Outside of South Africa, the other countries in the subcontinent do not have this problem. This gives them the freedom to develop adaptive technologies for industry. In this area, as well as in transport, the way that energy is tapped and converted to use will play a major role in defining Africa's future.

The existing approach, outcome and consequences

The increasing intensity of energy exploitation in the modern era began with the industrial revolution and the ability to take the exploitation of fossil fuels to scale. The problem with this system is that the source of the hydrocarbon is fixed by geological processes and was not necessarily to be found close to the point of use where it was needed. Initially, many cities created their own energy generating capacity, though doing so meant transporting the fossil fuel. To benefit from economies of scale, western countries then moved towards developing ever larger, centralised generating stations and using national grids to transport the electricity. In Europe this generally led to the creation of a single state organisation to manage the entire generation and distribution network, a model that was exported to Africa: this defined the initial outcome.

There were thus three separate stages involved in the use of fossil fuel – extraction, conversion and delivery – and sometimes these were managed separately, sometimes together, though in different permutations. In keeping with the privatisation ideology of the 1980s, power generation and distribution were separated to increase competition, and both electricity and gas became commodities to be provided to the 'consumer'. In many African countries the monolithic model used in colonial times remained, however, and as a consequence these countries have not been able to raise the finance needed to expand the system to satisfy demand. Again the western view of this situation is that Africa needs massive investment and that this can only come from the private sector. That view is only partially true. In an urban context the limited amount of energy currently available provides an opportunity for cities to move directly to a model of sustainable energy production.

Power for Africa I: abundant but inaccessible

The subcontinent has enormous hydroelectric power potential that it has barely begun to exploit. Although estimates vary, there is a broad consensus that Africa has at least 1,000 GWh per year of potential hydropower that is financially and technically exploitable (Hydro4Africa, 2011), of which only about 5 per cent is currently used. These numbers are well known and the subject of major studies.[6] However, while hydropower is a major potential resource, the cost of rolling out a programme of dam construction and distribution would be both expensive and time-consuming. Logically it makes sense, in developing this resource, to focus delivery where there will be the greatest economic return, which for Africa means agriculture, and industrial development in the major conurbations. At the same time, though, while there is a great deal of thought about this 'bigger picture', little consideration is given to the secondary towns. In this context the way forward is not simply to wait until the benefits of large-scale, western-style distribution systems finally trickle down; it is to create a separate strategic plan that is designed specifically for those urban areas.

Power for Africa 2: abundant and readily accessible

From household solar panels to thermal generators big enough to power a town, sun power has enjoyed explosive growth around the world. Everywhere, that is, except on the sun-drenched continent of Africa.

(Physorg, 2008)

The per capita consumption of electricity in sub-Saharan African countries is approximately 1 per cent of that in western countries (on average), running at between 2 and 5 watts of generated power per person.[7] Clearly, this low figure reflects low levels of access. Unfortunately, though, it also reflects a second characteristic that is of equal concern, which is ratio of electricity to overall energy consumption. Across the subcontinent as a whole, electricity accounts for only around 2 per cent of total household energy consumption, with by far the greatest contributor to this overall energy demand being fuelwood or charcoal.[8] Switching to solar energy would not only increase access but also facilitate a shift from wood-burning to renewable energy.

From this simple observation it follows that solar energy should provide the basis for sustainable energy production in the secondary towns in sub-Saharan Africa. If we think of the town from a systemic perspective, then we can situate energy use within a conceptual framework of nested 'loops'. The first level of looped energy use is that which takes place internally within the household. Here, the consumption is up to 70 per cent lower than in the West, even in middle-class homes. That is because there is no need for internal central heating, and the amount of heating of water for other purposes is significantly lower. The logic here would be to install a solar panel on every building, whether that building is commercial or individual. This principle extends into the informal sector, to include a 1-square-metre solar panel on every shack. Such panels would provide the basis for energy use at the level of the family.

The second level of looped energy is at the level of the town, or the neighbourhood. This would provide the basis for:

- the intra-urban transport system;
- public and commercial use;

- water resources management;
- supplemented family use.

The necessary energy would be provided by a small solar farm linked to the internal urban energy resources system. The third loop would then expand beyond the town to engage with the wider national or regional grid. The latter would then only be required to provide a base load, thereby eliminating the need for major investments in the bulk distribution network. At this point I shall not discuss who manages what in this system. The issue of roles and relationships will be discussed in the next chapter, and emerges naturally from the logic of the *problématique*.

Adapting the smart grid for Africa

The monolithic national grids served western countries well in building their industrial bases through the nineteenth and twentieth centuries, as well as providing individual users with a high level of user convenience. By the end of the twentieth century, however, this system was in danger of becoming an unmanageable behemoth. Driven primarily by the electrical requirements of digital equipment, demand for electricity is overtaking supply. Yet there are many efficiency gains that could be made in this existing system and would enable that demand to be met without the need for a significant increase in overall supply. The smart grid is seen as the way to provide these efficiency gains.

The smart grid is not one single solution, but rather a combination of technological advances that seeks to apply the benefits of electronic and digital management systems to the electrical grid, thereby making it more flexible and adaptive, and hence more efficient. It is also a recognition that big is not always best. Thus, there is a need to integrate smaller local generators, particularly those utilising renewable energy sources, with the larger, more centralised power generation facilities. Apart from the complexity of this operation, it also raises the technical challenge of merging lots of generating systems that rely on intermittent power sources, such as wind and sun, with baseline (i.e. constant) power sources such as gas or nuclear. To achieve this integration and flexibility, the smart grid draws on hundreds of individual technological advances to make it work. At a broad level, though, there are five key elements of importance:

1   smart meters, also known as advanced metering infrastructure, which enable a connection to be made between the points of use and the points of supply;
2   phasor measurement, which allows the voltage and current to be checked at a local area level almost continuously (e.g. every two to four seconds), thereby monitoring the 'health' of the distribution network;

3   the use of geographical information systems, which provide the visual linkage required to 'see' what is happening where;
4   integrative technologies that allow the intermittent power sources to be integrated seamlessly into the system;
5   large-scale storage systems for electricity.

This development is being accompanied by a major drive to increase insulation in buildings to reduce the demand for heating and cooling.

African national electricity generators, such as ESKOM in South Africa and EEPCo in Ethiopia, are keeping pace with a number of these developments and have been at the forefront in developing operational systems which ensure that poorer people can have access to electricity at a price they can afford. This is, in fact, an area which, along with mobile phones, illustrates the existing capacity of African countries to address the technical challenges posed by infrastructure. It is no coincidence that these are also the two areas where there has not been the proliferation of external 'experts' that has dominated the water sector, or sanitation, a correlation from which Africans can draw their own conclusions.

The land and space resource

A View from the Trees
I recall a television sketch, possibly in the 1970s, in which two comedians[9] dressed as birds perched on a branch of a tree. And as they looked down, they pondered on these creatures that ran the earth. They tended to be rather large, though they came in a variety of shapes and sizes, and they appeared to be metallic. And as with any dominant group, they appeared to have pacified, and taken control over, another species that occupied the planet, enslaving this second species for their own benefit. Thus, this enslaved species looked after them: washing them; feeding them from communal food points; creating paths for them so that they could travel comfortably; and generally looking after their every need. Those creatures that controlled the earth were called Cars and their slaves were called People.

Should African urban space be planned or managed?

Urban development in Africa is situated within a planning paradigm, yet the very term 'urban planning', when used in an African context, is a paradox.[10] On the one hand, an urban plan is intended to shape both form – how the area will develop spatially – and the pattern of land use. On the other hand, for the large majority of African countries at least, there is the reality: that spontaneous land invasion drives an urban process in which the unplanned areas can account for up to 70 per cent of the total. This is the reality that defines the contradiction. This paradox is then compounded by the perceived role of urban infrastructure, which is seen solely as a set of ancillary services that support the planning process.

In spite of this reality, though, the degree programmes in urban planning that are taught in the majority of African universities remain grounded in British planning practice and devote a large proportion of their teaching to the theory of formal spatial relationships, as viewed from the perspective of the mature cities of the West, and particularly through that theory's evolution in Britain. In this planning framework, informality is seen as an anomaly,[11] with the informal settlements being defined as 'slums' – though how a process that accounts for two-thirds of all spatial growth can be defined as an anomaly, or categorised in a derogatory manner, is difficult to reconcile with reality.

Planning seeks to provide spatial relationships with a sense of order or logic, as well as facilitating movement and access. In the Anglo-Saxon system, though, it has another important function, which can often dominate the planning mindset, and that is the legal allocation of property to an individual (or other legal) entity. The outcome of this specific historical evolution has led to a construct whereby land regularisation has become the dominant focus of urban planning in Africa.

There is no question that land is a critical limiting resource in urban development, and that the management of land and space has a central role in that development process. However, these facts do not justify the current western approach to urban development that places land regularisation above all other resource considerations. On the contrary, the analysis in the early chapters of this book argued that this dominant focus on land has hindered the creation of a sustainable urban framework in Africa. If the urban areas are to be sustainable, then this narrow view of land regularisation has to change.

The systemic resource-based approach to urban development radically changes the way in which land is both perceived and managed. First of all, both land and space are considered integral components of a single space–land resource system. This view is already recognised in some planning constructs, such as the one used in Brazil, for example, but not in the British planning model, which differentiates urban planning from urban design. Second, the management of the space–land resource is explored from within the context of all three development drivers. Here the social driver, which actively promotes social equity, requires that priority be given to the social relationship between people and space, and not to the legal relationship between people and land, as is the case with the British model. This viewpoint in turn recognises that it is the infrastructure that will drive the move towards, and achievement of, social equity. Third, the space–land resource is integrated with the wider systemic urban model shown in Figure 9.4. Its integration means ensuring that the space–land management system supports the integrity of the urban water resources system. That provides the framework within which land management needs to be situated and explored. While I recognise that the free market in land will exert enormous pressure in shaping spatial relationships, and that this factor has an impact on economic development, I shall argue that the approach proposed here is resilient enough to accommodate these economic forces, and in doing so reconcile the needs of all three drivers: the economic; the social; and the environmental.

The existing approach, outcome and consequences

There are three dominant features of the current urban development model, which can be described as an urban planning paradigm and are currently being imposed on Africa by the western countries and agencies. The first of these is land regularisation based upon the private ownership and individual cadastre boundaries. The second is the assumption that infrastructure is a support service, not a development driver – and particularly not a driver of economic development. The outcome is to predefine economic development solely in terms of land use. This is a particularly Anglo-Saxon view that is tied to the philosophy that the private sector is the only real driver of development. This third is the design standard for roads, which continue to be defined by the needs of motor vehicles. In fairness, this was an engineering 'solution'. Its original objective was to separate modal users, prioritise the motor vehicle and design a road network that would allow motor vehicles to achieve a high speed safely. The outcome was an engineered hierarchy of roads, designed in such a way as to permit cars to increase speed incrementally.

These three dominant features provided the model for African urban planning and continue to do so. This is evidenced in a paper describing a 'planning-based approach' to informal settlement upgrading in Mwanza, Tanzania, which demonstrates clearly how the primary goal of the upgrading process is land regularisation; that is, the formalising of individual cadastral boundaries. At the same time, the upgrading illustrates the flaws inherent in the planner's view of infrastructure: that it is a support service to planning. The word 'infrastructure' is used no fewer than thirty-four times in the body text of this twenty-five-page paper (Kyessi, 2006), so its importance is clearly recognised; at the end of those twenty-five pages, though, there is still no clear understanding of how infrastructure might best be used to 'support' the upgrading process.

This criticism is not a personal one. Tanzania is at the forefront in producing a new generation of African urban planners seeking to find indigenous solutions to 'problems' of urban areas. The weaknesses described here are not theirs; on the contrary, their work is deserving of recognition and respect. The failure of their approach is endemic to the British urban planning paradigm that provides the conceptual underpinning of their work. The only way to address this failure is through a completely new approach to the management of the urban space–land resource. Such an approach requires us to radically change the way in which we view spatial development in three areas – the management of urban space, social-spatial relationships at the settlement level, and the nature of urban movement networks – all within the context of the wider resources systems development model.

Rethinking the management of urban space

In 1997 the city of Cape Town was in the process of completing its first comprehensive, cadastre-based digital map within a GIS. However, the map was not actually complete, and could not be completed, because the city was not able to integrate the sixty-four then identified informal settlements that existed in the metropolitan area. This brought to mind the situation in Brazil under the military dictatorship, when the government refused to recognise not only the rights but even the existence of the favela dwellers. As a result, maps of the city showed blank spaces where the favelas were situated. It was exploring the way in which these quite diverse circumstances resulted in similar spatial outcomes that led to the idea that these informal settlements could be seen as 'holes' in the formal cadastre (see Figure 10.3), a concept that resulted in a research programme at the

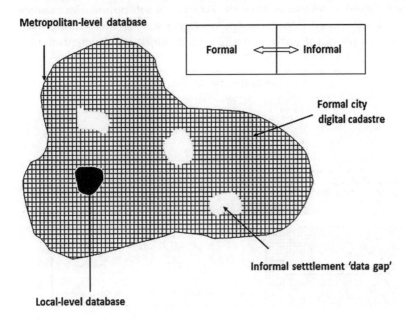

Figure 10.3 Informal settlements as 'holes' in the formal cadastre.

University of Cape Town aimed at creating a 'bi-level' model of the city. This research provided the framework for a new conceptual approach to the city based upon a systemic approach to spatial scale (Figure 10.4).

Initially, the bi-level model sought to situate the database structure for the informal settlements alongside that of the formal city, and this remains a valid construct. However, at the same time as this concept was being developed, a second research programme on informal settlement upgrading was also exploring the nature of what is termed the basic spatial unit (BSU), a spatial unit that provides the building block for the digital map.

In a formal, cadastre-based map, working now within the Anglo-Saxon land management system, the BSU is an individual site or plot of land with a title deed, to which a functional role is allocated (e.g. house, school). The work on informal settlements questioned the underlying assumptions behind this approach and sought to demonstrate the potential of GIS to enable a range of BSUs, more relevant to informal development. An example of how this would work, conceptually, is shown in Figure 10.5.

This then leads to the wider exploration of the role of 'soft' boundaries and opens up huge potential for changing the thinking around urban spatial management in a fast-growing area. It is recognised that the Anglo-Saxon capitalist system, based upon individual title and private ownership, strongly opposes any change in the existing approach on ideological grounds. Equally, the validity of land having a value and being tradable is an important factor to take into consideration. However, when land and space are viewed as resources, then the concept of soft boundaries enables them to be integrated into the wider resources management model in a way that is simply not possible when planning prioritises the creation of a

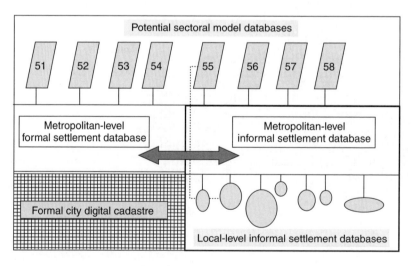

Figure 10.4 The bi-level model developed by Martinez (1999).

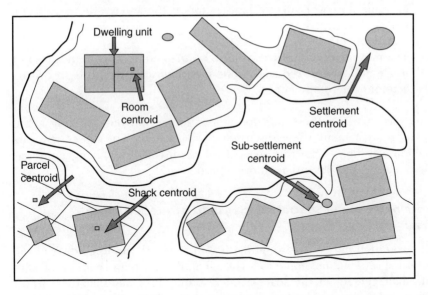

Figure 10.5 Different potential basic spatial units developed for integrating informal settlements into the formal city (Martinez 1999).

cadastral framework that imposes rigidity down to the lowest level of spatial scale.

In parallel with this rigid structuring of both land and space, the existing planning paradigm also sees infrastructure as a support service. Reformulating the role of infrastructure as a development driver, by mediating resource flows and providing the mechanism for achieving social equity, provides the key to changing that perception. When this reformulation is coupled with a recognition that land and space are both limited resources, it transforms the way in which we think about spatial management. Within the context of the broader conceptual shift outlined earlier, there are specific transformations that follow from this and which operate at different spatial scales. These include, but are not necessarily limited to, the following:

- There is a shift at the settlement level that demands greater flexibility, with social-spatial relationships taking priority over regularisation of the cadastre.
- Similarly, at this level the need to provide a sustainable water management plan also takes precedence over artificial boundary definition and formation.
- This flexibility then has to extend upwards to the wider spatial structure of the city, creating a multilevel approach to the basic spatial planning units of the city, with different BSUs operating at different spatial scales.

- Movement network design has to support the water resources system, being integrated into the urban integrated water resources management.
- The movement network also has to be adapted to changes in transport mode and its cost reduced, while retaining its critical role in driving economic development.

The way in which these transformations impact on our thinking about spatial management will be discussed in what follows. The subsequent sub-section will look at how the space–land resource model changes the way that we view, and design, the movement network.

Rethinking social-spatial relationships at the settlement level

The resource infrastructure model is well suited to the upgrading of the informal settlements, home to a large majority of urban residents, and to the management of the space–land resource, in a way that the current urban planning paradigm cannot match. The approach has been developed over a number of years and is based upon experience of some of the major favela upgrading programmes in Brazil, adapted to an African social-spatial context in Cape Town, South Africa.[12] In contrast to the land regularisation model discussed previously, the overriding goal was a collective one: that of retaining the social cohesion of the community in a way that would provide a sustainable urban space.

The approach adopted was based upon the Brazilian concept of a '*plano globale*', a holistic approach to the management of three-dimensional space that incorporates not only the various physical aspects of development (i.e. all the resource systems covered here) but also social and economic development. In this context the resource infrastructure model, with its rationale in the mediation of resource flows, can be integrated in an African approach to urban design that recognises informal settlements as a new urban form. In this way it can achieve a socially and environmentally sustainable outcome because boundaries are soft, reflecting the centrality of social-spatial relationships; while resource flows, both within the settlement and across the settlement boundary, are explored in an integrated, and interactive, way. Land regularisation (urban planning), on the other hand, fails to recognise both the complexity and the diversity of (three-dimensional) space as a social component of informal settlements. Instead, it is the individual cadastre that defines the process; but this does not, and cannot, provide sustainable solutions.

An early outcome of the systemic, resource-based approach result can be seen in two sets of diagrams shown as an example. The first set, Figure 10.6, compares the settlement at the beginning (on the left) to the

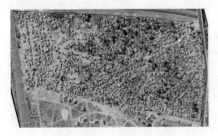
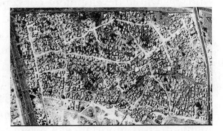

Figures 10.6 The informal settlement of New Rest, Cape Town, before (left) and after (right) phase I of the internal relocation and movement network formation.

situation several months later (on the right) after the community had internally relocated shacks to create a more viable movement network. This constituted the first phase of the project.

The next phase (though operating in parallel with the first) followed the completion of a geotechnical survey and more detailed spatial analysis. The important lesson learned from the Brazilian partnership programme was the importance of dealing with drainage and physical risk first, since this will define the full extent of the relocation. The next pair of figures (Figure 10.7) shows how this was dealt with. The diagram on the left shows the extent of the physical constraints of the site, which were significant, including areas prone to flooding (the darker section); a part of the site built on unstable fill material (the lightly shaded linear section on the left-hand side); and two major servitudes for bulk water supply lines (the lightly shaded linear sections on the right-hand side). Not only were all of these constraints overcome, but they were overcome without a single family having to leave the settlement. A detailed plan of the final proposed site development is shown on the right. This illustrates linkages to the surrounding areas, a local flood management scheme, a small commercial area and a flexible and adaptive movement network. The straight diagonal line follows the servitude, which the community voluntarily turned into a right of way, using it to design a small commercial centre and green space.

Figure 10.7 Site constraints (left) and final development concept (right).

And this whole development concept was created, within the community, without a single move towards land regularisation on the basis of individual title. Instead, the small area boundaries were hardened slowly and incrementally, and it was left to those situated within each sub-area to discuss the type of land relationship they would like. In the diagram on the right the three shaded blocks at the top and to the left give some examples of different types of ownership, including individual site ownership and two different types of communal ownership. This diagram also highlights the importance of urban design in the upgrading process.

At this point those involved with the creation of the broader upgrading concept could have moved on to the next settlement, taking the experience with them and allowing the community leadership to act as envoys for the resulting methodology; leading to rapid scale-up and implementation across the city. At the same time, the internal social-spatial relationships could have been developed further, with the different ownership options described above to be agreed at a local level. That is what makes this approach replicable, scalable and sustainable. Everything was in place, with the project having the full political backing of the community and the city council.

In spite of this, however, the town planners in the city persuaded the council to overturn the project at the last minute, replacing it with a new (top-down) plan where everyone was moved off the site and there was a return to the conventional urban planning paradigm: regularise the land and build formal housing. All the work was lost simply because one professional group was able to impose an ideological construct: the individual cadastre. As a result, the city was still without a replicable upgrading mode eight years later and land regularisation had failed yet again. Meanwhile, within New Rest itself, the social structure of a community had been destroyed to make way for 'orderly development' – an interesting case of history repeating itself.

Integrating the movement network into the space–land resources system

Western countries, particularly in Europe, are undergoing a shift in thinking about the role, nature and function of a city's 'movement network'. None the less, it remains the case that the main access routes continue to provide the basic spatial framework within which the various urban processes involving the movement or reticulation of people, goods and services find spatial form. These structuring elements are at the heart of a city's wider 'structure plan', the successor to the master plan.

Conceptually, the shift from roads to movement network is a critical first step towards a sustainable city. Its limitation at present, though, is the extent to which it remains situated within the wider planning construct of the mature city. It is self-evident that the modal balance of urban transport is changing rapidly, particularly in the West, as the countries of the West seek to counter the impact of climate change, with the adaptive response focusing on four aspects of movement network planning and design. The first is what might be termed the higher-order shift from private to public mass transport, which on the roads will generally mean dedicated or prior-itised bus or tram routes, or, as an alternative, underground trains or ele-vated maglevs or trams. The second involves providing additional space to certain modal forms, such as cycling, that are perceived as beneficial. The third is to introduce traffic-calming measures into the city centres, through mechanisms such as speed humps or chicanes, which slow vehicles down. This approach seeks to provide more of a cohabitation between different modes. And the fourth is pedestrian routes, where vehicles are excluded except for those making deliveries, which are often limited to specific times of day.

These ideas, which are highly relevant to the needs of mature cities, are then provided as the basis for good urban planning and urban manage-ment practice in developing cities. Certainly they have a role, particularly in the large primate cities. That does not imply that they are appropriate in the secondary cities where over two-thirds of the urban population lives, and which are in the process of creating new spatial forms that require their own solutions.

The primary focus on changing modal patterns in the West relates to changes in the geometric layout of the road network and the modal split on that network. Yet geometric design is only one half of road design; the other half is the structural design of the pavement. A road is designed to transmit a heavy point load (from a tyre) in a way that transforms this into a zone of pressure that can be accommodated by the natural ground without distortion. Thus, the higher the point load, the deeper and denser must be the road foundation. There is, then, a second purpose to a road, which is to provide a wearing surface that is smooth enough to accommo-date traffic movement in a way that is comfortable to passengers, and (his-torically) provides an impervious surface that enables water to run off to the side quickly so as to protect the structural integrity of the underlying pavement.

Using costs derived from the Ethiopian study, the cost of a typical urban street designed for conventional motorised vehicles would be split approx-imately 50:50 between the bitumen surface and the underlying structural pavement. Because roads are designed for cars, not people, the first cost saving that is made in the affordability-based levels of service model is removal of the bitumen surface, with the design of the underlying pave-ment surface being modified so that it can continue to serve the needs of cars. Further reductions then come in a reduction of the structural carry-ing capacity until we are left with the most basic level of service: the dirt road, which is nothing more or less than compacted natural ground. At no point in this process are the needs of pedestrians considered to be of paramount interest – hence the comedy sketch outlined at the beginning of this chapter.

In fact, the needs of people are quite different. Their major requirement is a surface that is safe and pleasant to walk on. Satisfying that need requires a radical change from the current engineering and planning mindset, because our current approach results in more than 70 per cent of the movement network being overdesigned yet underutilised roads. The resource infrastructure model uses this reality, together with the fact that up to 95 per cent of people in the secondary towns have walking as their primary mode of transport, to define the management of the space–land resource. There is still a need for vehicle access, but it is significantly less than current design philosophies believe. Similarly, the need to cater for a range of vehicle speeds is simply creating a condition where the poor, yet again, subsidise the rich. By designing a means of movement for people, not cars, we are able to accommodate the primary needs of social equity and environmental sustainability in a way that is simply not possible under the present approach.

The experience of the secondary towns described in previous chapters evolved a new, simplified three-tier system, which comprises:

- Tier 1: inter-city (through) traffic. This would be designed primarily for heavy vehicles.
- Tier 2: internal (circular) movement designed structurally for motorised vehicles (intra-city traffic), but incorporating multimodal use.
- Tier 3: access and internal movement for light modes of transport, which would account for approximately two-thirds of the entire network.

These sections will be described in what follows, beginning with the last one first. In each case, consideration is given not only to the transport needs, but also to the interaction with other resource systems, particularly that of water resources.

Movement network tier 3: prioritising the urban majority

The starting point in designing the physical structure of a movement network is to consider the mode of transport, a subject that is currently undergoing a radical realignment. There are two desired characteristics for the vehicles of the future: that they are lightweight (for maximum efficiency) and that they are non-polluting, which means electric. With private vehicles, at this point in time, these two characteristics are mutually exclusive, owing to the excessive weight of batteries. However, when we look at modes of public transport, particularly for just one to six people, then the situation is quite different: there the two are coming into strong alignment.

This small small-scale transport is a feature of many secondary towns in Africa, and the transformation from traditional to modern is already taking place. Figure 10.8 shows on the left a traditional mode of family transport, the donkey cart, while on the right it shows the donkey cart's current replacement, the petrol-driven rickshaw, bajaj or tuk-tuk, depending on which country you live in.

This, though, is only the beginning, and not the ideal transformation, since we are seeking to move away from fossil fuels; the next step is to transform the drive mechanism. Electricity is the obvious way forward, and here there are two streams of development, both of which have a role: electrically-assisted and electrically-driven vehicles. The first of these derives from the bicycle, and continues to use pedal power, though in this case supplemented by a small electric motor. Two examples are shown in Figure 10.9, illustrating how they can vary in shape and form from the

Figure 10.8 Traditional and petrol-driven family taxis (photos: John Abbott).

Figure 10.9 Electrically-assisted bicycle (photo: John Abbott) and pedal-powered tricycle (photo: Made-in-China.com, 2010).

hi-tech, illustrated by an example from Berlin shown on the left, to the basic, illustrated here by the Chinese example on the right. These vehicles recharge on the move and have the advantage of not requiring an external charge point.

If we move up from this to what is likely to become the more dominant transport form, we find the fully electrically-driven vehicle, of which two examples are shown in Figure 10.10, one battery powered and one solar powered.

The move towards electrically-driven vehicles is restricted, in many secondary towns, by limited access to electricity, which is why the development of a sustainable energy sector is so critical, and so closely linked to the choice of transport modality. Equally important, but given far less consideration, is the potential for changing the movement network itself.

The move towards these small, light, battery-driven or -assisted vehicles is spreading rapidly throughout India and Asia, but the focus is primarily on the large cities, where the road network is already in place. In the secondary cities of Africa, on the other hand, the greatest opportunity cost actually lies in changing the entire design philosophy of the road network. Thus, it is this change of transport modality that makes the shift towards the three-tier movement hierarchy described here possible, and achievable. The 70 per cent of the network that is primarily for pedestrians can also accommodate light vehicles without the need to strengthen the structural pavement significantly, which in turn enables the network to be developed at low cost, as described previously, while still enabling a high quality of surface and a high level of user access. The use of light vehicles also improves the level of user convenience.

Finally, this component of the movement network can be integrated with the water resource system management framework developed on pp. 308–11. Being relatively narrow, adaptable and flexible, this third tier of the network is much easier to integrate into the local level of water

Figure 10.10 Battery-driven family taxi (photo: Bangladesh2day, 2009) and solar powered rickshaw (photo: Greenlaunches.com, 2011).

resources management, particularly if it is designed with a permeable surface that allows storm water to percolate through the surface material into the ground.

Movement network tier 1: the national or regional road through an urban area

The next tier of the network to explore is the national or regional road through the urban area, which takes the inter-urban transport and provides the urban–rural linkage. In Ethiopia a road through an urban area that lies on the national road network is owned by the Ethiopian Roads Authority (ERA), which is also responsible for its maintenance. The same can be true of regional roads, with respect to the various rural (i.e. regional) roads authorities (RRAs). The approach to the *problématique* used here and illustrated in Figure 6.4 shows the roles and relationships as flowing out of the conceptual framework, not driving it. If this approach is applied to the movement network, the issue is not that the major road through the urban area is owned by that central or regional government; that will be explored later. The issue, conceptually, and within the systemic framework, is that this tier of the road network has the greatest impact on the natural terrain, causing the greatest impediment to natural water flows and defining a major, fixed spatial structuring element. It is also part of the 'higher-order' natural resources system, in the sense that it is linked to wider regional or national spatial form. In this context it has to be managed as part of the higher-order system while at the same time being integrated into the city.

These roads are, by the nature of the traffic flows, designed to a higher engineering standard than normal municipal roads and are often significantly more expensive. Thus, they require special design skills and need to be managed separately. In addition, if they were part of the municipal system they would constitute the greatest single cost item on the municipal budget and would be unaffordable. At the same time, they have to be integrated into the urban water resource management system.

There may be one of these roads (in a through-route situation, for example) or several (if the town is located at a major junction, say). To link this tier of the movement network to the wider resource flows, it would need to have its own water resources management plan; and the cost of managing the impact on the urban water resources system would need to be factored into the cost of building and managing that network. This is in line with the principle that resources carried across a system boundary are borrowed. This aspect of design is currently given little recognition. The issue here is not simply that the storm water flowing from this tier 1 network forms part of a 'drainage master plan'; instead, it forms part of the urban integrated water resources plan (UIWRM). In keeping the systemic approach, this tier of the network would have its own water management plan as part of the design process for the road.

Movement network tier 2: internal circulation for motorised vehicles

Clearly, a city has to have a proportion of its network designed for circulating motorised vehicles, and those roads are expensive to build and maintain. Reducing the length of this road network, so that it is limited to less than 30 per cent of the entire network, provides a good starting point; even then, however, this network continues to provide the greatest financial challenge to secondary towns. For example, the Ethiopian study indicated that the cost of 3 kilometres of standard (i.e. 7-metre-wide) asphalt road designed to a high engineering standard and with drains both sides could fund an entire solid waste management system for a town of around 120,000 people, or alternatively a substantial proportion of a sanitation system.

Thus, this second tier provides the most challenging part of the movement network from a design perspective. The first tier is clearly a rigid component of the network, while the third tier is a flexible component associated with settlement formation. The second tier is midway between these, which means that it has two, potentially conflicting, objectives. On the one hand, it retains a spatial rigidity that defines its influence as a structuring element. On the other hand, the way it is managed will strongly influence the success of the UIWRM. The key to reconciling these two potentially conflicting objectives is the use of indigenous materials. This will be described in greater detail on pp. 351–2.

Outcomes: redefining urban planning in an African context

The British urban planning model has failed in Africa, just as did the British urban infrastructure model. This failure does not mean that planning needs to be eliminated, any more than it meant infrastructure needed to be eliminated. What it does mean, though, is that planning in African development needs to be rethought and redefined. The book has argued that urban infrastructure is the primary driver of development in the majority of the secondary towns in Africa.[13] In this role it can be described as an internal driver. When planning is used to shape urban development, it relies on externalities, which in the Anglo-Saxon *Weltanschauung* generally means private-sector investment, to drive economic development. These need not be in conflict; on the contrary, if used correctly they can be mutually reinforcing. To work in this way, though, will require a major shift in mindset.

The urban development model proposed here uses infrastructure as the internal driver of not only economic but also social and environmental development, operating through its role as the mediator of urban resource flows. In this context, planning should be situated where it can do what it does best, which is to guide development processes. Thus, spatial planning has to be more fully integrated with economic planning and moved up to the national and regional governments.

At the level of the urban area there needs to be an equally radical shift in mindset, this time relating to the way in which we view informal settlements. There is a need to recognise that *there are no slums in Africa*; the use of the term 'slum' is a purely western interpretation of how to describe what is happening at the level of the urban settlement. What we are really seeing here is the emergence of a completely new urban form that is quite specific to Africa. Rather than seeing it as a threat, we have to see it as an opportunity. This is the general view. Of course there are exceptions, like Nairobi. There, Chapter 4 highlighted how these settlements are constrained by a specific colonial history (of external land ownership) that effectively prevents meaningful development taking place. The experience of the Cape Town case study mirrors that of Brazil, in demonstrating that informal settlements can be upgraded to reflect the nature of social-spatial relationships in African society. To do this, however, requires professional input. This is not planning, though; it is urban design – not of the western type, but specifically tailored to an African situation. At this level, settlement design works with resource infrastructure management to integrate informal settlements into the wider ecology of the city.

The inorganic resources system

Introduction

The earlier discussion on organic resource flows (pp. 312–25) focused primarily on the outflows, through the exploration of sanitation. The lack of attention to the inputs can be addressed to some degree here, since much of the discussion of the inorganic system will be equally relevant there.

In the wider discussion of resource flows around the city the inorganic resources system is distinct in two ways. The first of these, which is shared with the organic system, relates to the nature of the resource base, which is much more diverse than is the case with water, for example. Furthermore, the city system itself is responsible for only a small fraction of the total incoming resource flow, with the bulk being accounted for by the private sector, either in commercial or manufacturing activities, as well as directly to individuals. The second distinction defines a much wider difference between the organic and inorganic inputs. For whereas the former can be integrated into a process of renewable resource use, inorganic resources are by definition non-renewable, although they may be recoverable and either reusable or capable of being recycled.

These specific features of inorganic resource flows do not necessarily imply that the urban local government authority (ULGA) is without influence in managing them. A major component of inorganic resource consumption is attributable to construction. Here the physical component of the infrastructure required to mediate the various resource flows comprises a significant construction activity in its own right, and this can be influenced directly by the ULGA. In other construction activities the power is indirect, but it is there nonetheless, since all construction plans have to be approved. And finally with manufacturing use, the residual output (waste) can be regulated. This, then, is the framework for the management of the inorganic resources system within the urban boundary.

Addressing sustainability in the Anglo-Saxon construction model

The Anglo-Saxon construction model that has been adopted across anglophone Africa has two distinguishing features. The first is a separation of building works from 'civil engineering' works; while the second is the linear, compartmentalised nature of the process. The latter is described by the project cycle,[14] illustrated in Figure 10.11, within which different groups take responsibility for the various sequential components. This worked well in achieving its original objectives, which gave priority to the central components of design and construction, in an era where these activities were driving economic growth in Britain and the United States; it

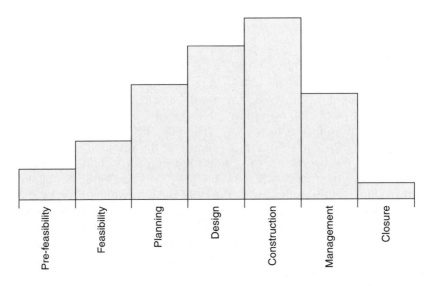

Figure 10.11 The project cycle (weighting allocation by the author).

is much less well suited to a framework of sustainable development, where the compartmentalised linear approach and the range of different actors involved actually impede the transition to a more sustainable use of construction materials.

The Australians were the first to address this fact, primarily within the building sector, with the concept of ecologically sustainable development design, an approach focused initially on building works. In developing a design guide for public buildings that follow this principle (Australian Government, 2007), the approach sought to transform the linear project cycle into a real cycle using principles of life-cycle costing and planning, as indicated in Figure 10.12.

Sebake (2008) explored this and other, similar approaches in a South African context, looking at how the concepts work in practice, arguing that 'very little attention has been given to the difficulties encountered by the built environment professionals, particularly by architects, in the implementation of sustainability principles in the development of building projects'. In the summation of her study, Sebake assembled a table that highlighted the limitations of seeking to apply sustainability concepts into the South African operational project cycle-based work plan developed by SACAP (the South African Council for the Architectural Profession). The table is replicated as Table 10.5.

Of course, all of the elements and constraints highlighted here can be addressed by moving towards a life-cycle approach, as illustrated in Figure 10.12, for example; but that is not the point. The real issue is that this whole approach is not suited to a development framework that needs to

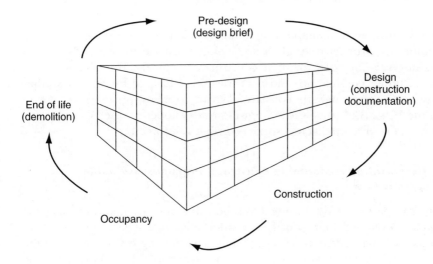

Figure 10.12 The life-cycle costing loop.

Table 10.5 The limitations of current approaches to project sustainability

Stage	Limitations
1 Appraisal and definition of project	a The professional team and contractor are not part of the project at this stage, therefore common sustainability values are not established; and therefore b) the sustainability targets cannot be set.
2 Design concept	c The professional team and contractor are not part of the project at this stage; therefore, the architect develops the concept design.
3 Design definition	d With no sustainability project values and targets set, the sustainability performance of the design cannot be assessed; and e) the comparison of alternative designs may not be explored. f) When the members of the professional team are appointed, the design may undergo major changes as they provide their input.
4 Technical documentation and approvals	g With no sustainability project values, the sustainability aspects may not be captured in the tender documentation, and h) the specification documentation. i) When the contractor is appointed, the design may undergo further changes as the contractor provides input.
5 Contract administration and supervision	j With no integrated design approach or sustainability project values in place, the contractor is left to solely make decisions on the procurement of materials and components.[a]

Source: Sebake (2008, p. 489, table 1.6).

Note
a This last point is attributed by Sebake to: Ngowi (1998).

revolve around sustainability. It is an accident of history, and western countries, particularly Anglo-Saxon countries, have to use and adapt it because it is the basis for their construction industry. It was exported to Africa under colonialism, and countries there have to use it; and so they scrabble to play catch-up, constantly having to follow practices developed in the West. And since the responses are developed in the West, western control over the intellectual space is further reinforced.

Differentiating sustainable construction from sustainable materials flow

Cities in particular do not need to follow that approach, and the systemic model developed here provides an alternative that is far more suited to implementing sustainable development. The starting point is to move the central focus away from sustainable construction. The point was made earlier that building and civil engineering construction were historically separated in British practice. This state of affairs has changed with the growth of construction management as a profession, which has blurred the boundaries. None the less, this is one aspect of historical development that does retain an inherent logic. This is because buildings have a strong individual identity. Infrastructure works, on the other hand, are much more integrated into a systemic framework, particularly in the urban context that is used here.

This distinction becomes important when we recognise that the discussion around the relationship between sustainability and construction actually comprises three distinct streams. These are as follows:

1   Sustainable construction per se. Here the primary focus is centred on buildings, in the manner discussed in the previous section, or on the specific construction activity within the project cycle.
2   Sustainable construction materials and materials flows. This is a specific subset of the wider discussion on sustainable materials flows that also incorporates manufacturing and production.
3   Indigenous materials. This is a different facet of the materials flow debate, which explores the replacement of imported materials by local materials as well as the replacement of inorganic by organic materials.

Within this wider sustainability debate, inorganic resources infrastructure is primarily related to materials flows, and within that to the extended use of indigenous materials, and this should be the primary focus of local government. A separate but nonetheless important issue, related specifically to the disposal of hazardous waste, will be dealt with separately.

A feature of inorganic resource flows, which is shared by some components of the organic resource inflow, is that its use is within other resource systems, meaning that its life-cycle path will pass through another system. This has two implications. First, it focuses the resource sustainability approach strongly around the third principle of urban sustainability described in the previous chapter, namely:

> When resources are taken across a system boundary this should be treated as a loan (that is, the resource taken across the boundary is borrowed); the environmental cost of borrowing the resource should be defined; and the way in which the loan will be repaid should be quantified.

This principle places the onus on the primary functional system to manage resource sustainability for the secondary system. However, a potential conflict of interest between the two resource systems is thereby highlighted, which in turn reflects a weakness in the resource infrastructure management model. This weakness was highlighted in Chapter 8, within the discussion of the 'environmental imperative' that underpins the western approach to urban development. The focus on resources management used here does not implicitly prevent misuse of the wider physical environment. As a result, it is accepted that the resource management model described here will continue to require monitoring for environmental protection – an aspect that will be discussed separately in a later section.

It is not my intent to discuss the detail of sustainable materials flows here; there are many books and papers on this topic, as there are at the level of detail within the other resource infrastructure systems. Instead, the objective here is to establish the overall management framework. The ideas and the approach proposed here are quite fundamentally different from the existing thinking about sustainability. The existing thinking is centred on construction, which is one specific stage in the project cycle and moves outwards from there to other stages, both up front and downstream. This may have relevance to building construction, although the previous discussion highlighted the weaknesses of the focus on the construction phase even there. It is not relevant to infrastructure delivery, though, particularly in the Africa of the twenty-first century. These are nineteenth-century concepts that impede the move towards sustainable development.

The switch to a resources systems approach situates inorganic resources clearly within their own system, thereby enabling the three principles of urban sustainability to apply. From these we can define an operational relationship between this organic resources system and the urban system with which it interacts. Doing so in turn highlights six core elements of the relationship, as follows:

1   Sustainability has to be situated within the materials flow path, rather than the construction phase. Sustainable construction practices are important, and should be adopted, but they support the wider sustainability of materials flows; they do not drive the process.
2   Using the third principle of urban sustainability, it is the operating resource system that is primarily responsible for materials flow into, through and out of the urban system as a whole. This means that the operating resources system 'borrows' the materials, in accordance with this principle, and has the responsibility for reflecting the full and true cost of use of those materials resources.
3   Within that context, those managing the operational resources systems should seek to use indigenous materials in place of imported materials. In a paper on the perception and use of indigenous materials in Nigeria, Adogbo and Kolo (2008) showed just how difficult it is to have indigenous materials use accepted by the construction industry. I would argue here that the reason is linked specifically to the same issue of situating the debate within this phase of the project cycle and its associated industry. If the debate is moved into the operational

resources systems, adoption becomes much simpler, since it is linked directly to improved systems performance, as the next subsection, on cobblestone roads, will demonstrate.

4   Equally, those responsible for the operating resources systems using materials should seek to substitute organic materials for inorganic materials, simply because the former are renewable, and therefore sustainable, while the latter are only reusable, and are therefore continually being depleted.

5   This point leads to the major difference between the inorganic system and other resources systems, namely that the throughput process is linear rather than circular, a fact that invokes what is termed the 'cradle-to-grave' approach, currently associated with the chemical industry and the use of water for industrial purposes. This means simply that materials have to be managed through their entire life cycle, taking into account their disposal and the environmental impact they have at each stage of their life cycle.

6   Finally, while the ULGA has direct responsibility for resource flows through the resources systems, linked directly to the physical aspect of the resources infrastructure, it also has a broader responsibility for ensuring that other users follow the cradle-to-grave approach. This can be done through a regulatory function that relates to the management of the materials flow path through its disposal phase.

Managing own materials

The Ethiopian decentralisation programme described in Chapter 7 developed (among other things) its own approach to asset management, and in doing so demonstrated that this was an effective way to manage a movement network, providing a sustainable basis for both technical and financial management. This system also provided politicians and decision-makers with full knowledge of, and control over, their infrastructure for the first time. And what made this programme successful was the way in which it was developed. This returns to the central theme of this book.

An interesting outcome of this process was the recognition of the full cost of bitumen roads designed to a high engineering standard, with the example of how a complete solid waste management system could be installed for the same cost as 2–3 kilometres of asphalt road. Initially, the government considered banning the use of asphalt completely, though it later recognised that there is still a need for this material on specific types of road. None the less, the debate that took place around this issue led to a major rethink of materials usage in road construction. Working in partnership with the German development agency GTZ, the three tiers of government came together and created a cobblestone road training and development programme.

This move towards cobbled road construction was so successful that within two years it had created a new industry, founded on small businesses, with a level of job creation many times higher than was required for conventional road construction. A substantial part of this industry was run by, and involved, women. By the time the final capital investment programmes were prepared, in April 2008, nine of the eighteen project cities had training programmes in place, while the nineteen cities between them had put forward proposals for over 300 kilometres of cobblestone road. An example of this programme, taken from the city of Dira Dawa, is illustrated in Figure 10.13.

The programme represented an important case study demonstrating the benefits of working with materials flows within a system rather than a sector. The (construction) sector may deliver the roads, but the ULGA requires a parallel capacity-building programme to manage the process. At the same time, the programme also provided important lessons on how further improvements could be made by deeper integration into the systemic approach to management used here. As was highlighted in an internal analysis of the programme, the production of cobblestones by hand is a relatively inefficient use of stone. One cobblestone has surface dimensions (i.e. the dimensions seen on plan after laying) of 10 centimetres square. Assuming 10–12 centimetres depth (the underside cone gives a greater depth overall, but this is different from the volumetric depth), then 1 square metre of cobblestone has a volume of approximately 0.1 cubic metres, producing 0.3 cubic metres (or more) of waste (in the original stone). Thus, planning is needed for the efficient removal of approximately 2,000 cubic metres of waste rock per kilometre of 6-metre-wide road. This, then, has the capacity to create more small business, by using secondary crushers on site to process the 'waste' stone. The latter can then be sold on as other products, resulting in virtually complete use of the original material.

Figure 10.13 Cobbled road construction in Dira Dawa, Ethiopia.

Managing industry within a systemic development framework

Industry retains an important role in urban development, a fact that is fully recognised in this approach. In fact, with this approach the relationship between the industrial sector and the urban area is much clearer than with the existing approach. Many industries are like cities, in that they draw resources from different systems and are situated within a wide range of spatial scales. When constructed as stand-alone units on greenfield sites, they are systems in their own right. When working at a smaller scale, within a city, they are subsystems of the city system. In both cases the same approach applies in respect of the principles of sustainability derived here for urban areas. The only real difference stems from the nature of the waste output, which is wider in scope and can often contain toxic chemicals. This requires a specific approach to the management of industrial waste.

The digital (communications) resources system

Introduction

The digital resources system emerges from the convergence of two technology streams that began and evolved separately: information technology and communications technology. Historically, both have been network based, and it is the merging of the 'networks' that produces the combined system of information and communications technology (ICT). Typically, ICT has been approached mechanistically, in the sense that it is perceived as applications based. Thus, we create individual relationships such as ICT in procurement, in records management or in financial management, budgeting and accounting,[15] for example. This is the IT base. The communications technology, on the other hand, is intrinsically systemic since it operates through the medium of electronic waves, though government licensing procedures seek to package it mechanistically.

ICT, then, is an important advance towards improving efficiency and effectiveness in the management of information. At this point, though, it is a generic tool; that is, it can be applied across many types of organisation, including local government. At the same time, though, local government has a quite specific, and distinctive, characteristic of its own, namely its fixed position in space. Geospatial technology makes use of this to integrate vectors (i.e. points, lines and shapes) with raster images (pixels), within a locational context. This geospatial technology can then be used to create a graphical interface and generate a virtual reality that can mirror the real town, as well as providing a geo-referencing framework for the non-spatial data, and as well as providing a geospatial database that can use digital communications technology to link to both external computer systems and mobile phones. When combined, the systemic city can be portrayed graphically in a condition that is close to real time, providing information as well as data. That is the basis for the digital (communications) resources system defined here.

For many people, particularly in the West, geospatial technology is perceived as a tool or an application, for example the digital map on a computer or the GPS on their mobile phone. In the urban context, though, it is much more than that: it is the framework within which different elements of ICT are truly integrated across disciplines; and it is only the geo-referenced graphical interface that can bring about such integration. The resultant outcome is a different technology mix, one that may not be limited to local government but that does have a specific format within a local authority that does not apply to other organisations, owing to this quite specific geographical construct. The secondary towns in sub-Saharan Africa have an opportunity to leapfrog development in this area of technology by moving directly to this integrated and systemic framework, which is defined here as ICGT: information, communications and geospatial technology.

The application of ICT in government, which applies equally to ICGT, is increasingly linked to the term 'e-governance', which is referred to by UNESCO as 'a set of technology-mediated processes that are changing both the delivery of public services and the broader interactions between citizens and government' (2003). This relationship then interfaces with the next chapter, which will deal with governance generally. That chapter will demonstrate the way in which ICGT influences the construct of good governance at the level of local government. The present chapter is concerned primarily with the socio-technical framework of the ICGT construct.

Data: the basic digital resource

The basic building block for the urban plan used in western countries is the individual site, as defined by a cadastral boundary. This in turn derives from the Anglo-Saxon model that linked the plan to the land registry. This approach has two defining features, when seen from a data management perspective. First, it is a historical construct; that is, it can be traced back to British medieval practice. Second, it is paper based; that is, its use is inextricably linked to the drawing of those boundaries on some form of parchment or paper. In spite of these archaic roots, the land registry continues to be the basis for digital urban mapping, and has been carried over to provide the basis for urban practice in Africa, where it has played a central role in generating urban chaos.

It is not that land registration is not important; it is – but that does not make it the basis for mapping in a new technology. On the contrary, its very nature makes it the last choice that one would make for the core dataset in rapidly growing towns with a low level of human resources. As a system it is rigid and, more importantly, not linked in any way to the natural physical space that is the basis of digital geospatial referencing. In addition, it suffers all the failings of the land regularisation approach to urban development described in the previous chapter.

ICGT provides us with an opportunity to create a system that is grounded in the technology and defined by the nature of the physical space and its associated virtual reality; following which, we can build a relational model accordingly. The key to effective ICGT management in Africa's towns and cities lies in making use of two spatial attributes of this virtual reality, namely the use of soft boundaries and the use of different BSUs for different geospatial scales. We can then use these attributes to provide the structuring elements of the ICGT, to which we will then attach the different blocks of data.

In virtual reality, everything begins with data, and the success of the construct is directly related to the way in which the blocks of data are assembled. If we are trying to model a town in this geospatial environment, then we begin with real features and we attach information to those features first. Viewing this process from the perspective of the city as a system, there are two components of importance: people and features. People, though, move around, so they are not easy to define geospatially, and so we use dwellings as the dominant point source to geo-reference personal data. People are also important because they provide the primary source of income for the city. In respect of features, those of greatest importance, at least economically, are the fixed assets, which not only define the wealth of the city and account for a large proportion of its expenditure, but, equally importantly, incorporate the bulk of the resource infrastructure that mediates the resource flows around the city. In a third group are the natural features, which define the physical environment, followed by the cadastral boundaries, which define the social-economic-political packaging of urban land. In summary, then, the four key geospatial components of the ICGT are:

1   the dwelling, which also creates the spatial linkage for personal data;
2   the fixed asset base;
3   natural features;
4   the detailed cadastre.

The bulk of the non-spatial data are attached to the first two of these, though clearly not all of the data. From a management point of view the component that is most critical is the fixed asset base, which provides the major database for the city's own (i.e. non-personal) data. It will be discussed more fully in a later section that looks at a new financial model for resource-based urban infrastructure management.

Resource management and environmental protection

The earlier exploration of the concept of environmental sustainability, developed in the previous chapter, identified three components to the relationship between infrastructure and the environment. These were:

1   the role of urban infrastructure in managing the movement and use of resources (mediating resource flows);
2   the negative impact of infrastructure on the physical environment;
3   the potential of urban infrastructure to ameliorated extreme climate change related events through the introduction, up front, of adaptive strategies.

The chapter then went on to show that the key relationship was the first of these, which is where the focus of this chapter has been. Focusing on the management of resources ameliorates the negative impact of infrastructure on the physical environment and can also integrate the adaptive measures needed to address the impact of climate change. At the same time, though, there are gaps in this approach, foremost among which is the interaction with the atmosphere. Managing the six resource systems in the way described here will reduce carbon output significantly, and has the potential to create to a carbon-neutral city. Yet there remains a need to monitor outputs and incorporate specific measures to protect the environment. For example, the six resource systems do not include the wider atmosphere, yet clearly there are gaseous outputs (exhaust fumes from cars and trucks, for example; or wood-burning stoves). Similarly, there remain substantial construction works, which will require an environmental impact assessment. So, while this sustainability model, built upon the optimised use of natural resources, will address many of the current environmental sustainability issues, there will still be an important role for environmental protection as a separate regulatory activity.

Creating a new financial management system

The components of the new financial system

The process of developing a new model of urban development for the secondary towns began with the definition of infrastructure as an economic driver of a new, green urban economy. If we are serious about creating such an economy, then we require a fundamental rethink of how we structure investment in urban infrastructure and how we recoup the cost of that investment. The first lesson to learn from the past hundred years of western experience of urban development is that we need to avoid the massive fixed investment associated with the large, centralised infrastructure networks. We may require some major infrastructure works, but the intention should be to keep them to a minimum. In their place we want to create a smaller, cheaper, more flexible infrastructure base for the town. That is the primary objective.

The second objective is cost recovery. There the key is to reallocate costs according to new criteria that affect the way different infrastructure components impact on each other. Linked to this cost reallocation is a need to see the full cost of infrastructure. This is necessary because, in this model, we are dealing with the metabolic city as the primary user, with individuals or families as sub-users. To achieve these objectives, the financing of the urban resource systems model of development, in which infrastructure mediates resource flows, is constructed on three operational pillars:

1   linking the cost structure to the resource flows;
2   an integrated asset management plan;
3   an integrated capital investment plan.

Before looking at these components, though, it is worth recapping on the existing approach.

The weakness of existing financial planning systems

The financial management system for urban infrastructure evolved over time and is neither logical nor coherent, although concepts such as road pricing are seeking to address those deficiences to some degree. Overall, though, the management of roads and their associated drains, which represent the largest single infrastructure investment, is treated simply as a single municipal cost. The result has been described already: a variable level of service that prioritises the small, select group who own cars.

However, the most anomalous situation with regard to skewed and illogical cost recovery models can be found in the water supply network. The current approach separates water supply from water resources, provides water to the household and accepts no responsibility for water after it reaches that point. This system only works because it:

•   serves only the middle class, who can afford to pay for the convenience this system offers, while excluding the poor;
•   undervalues the input cost of its 'product': water;
•   ignores the environmental cost to the water resources system; and
•   isolates one specific part of a larger water cycle that allows the private sector to make a profit, using a practice known as 'cherry-picking'.

The outcome is clearly evident in many western countries. While the private sector benefits from the ability to charge only for the parts of the infrastructure that declare a 'profit', local governments move into debt.

Changing from linear to nested systems

Our objective is to retain the maximum degree of flexibility, and the lowest (life-cycle) cost, in the infrastructure, which means keeping the large fixed assets to a minimum. The way that we begin this process is to create a concept of systemic nesting of infrastructure based upon the variable-scale basic spatial unit (BSU) described on pp. 333–6. This uses the principle of small areas to create the first tier of internal recycling and reuse.

In the water resources system the lowest level of collective system would be the settlement defined by the area BSU, with the first level of reuse or recycling taking place here. The water provider (for that BSU) would be responsible for collecting grey water and either recycling it locally or returning it to the head of the system for treatment. The system would use a variant of that shown in Figure 10.1, except that it would be circular rather than linear, as indicated in this example. This set-up would reduce the length of the primary distributor significantly.

The second system would be organic; it would manage urine, faeces and organic solid waste as a single unit, recycling them back into the agricultural system. This would be an income-generating activity that would be substantially self-funding, being based upon a market cost of fertiliser and a carbon offset.

The energy system would change the current model, which in the West seeks to integrate local generation into large national generation grids, by reversing this relationship. Energy generation would be built from the lowest unit outwards, following the same principle as water recycling. Energy would be based upon sustainable resources, with a solar panel on every roof, while the urban transport and lighting system would be based upon an array serving the urban area, supplemented then by the external grid.

The movement network would be divided into three levels, each of which would be linked to the water resources system. In effect, roads borrow water from that system by interfering with the natural overland flow, and that loan has to be repaid. This repayment could be done by treating each 'level' of the network as a separate cost centre with regard to that loan, and the cost of maintaining that particular level of the movement network would incorporate the cost of repaying the water load; that is, managing the water impacted upon by that level of the network. The two higher levels in this system would have their own financial structure, while the lowest level – the local area – would be integrated with the cost of water resources management within the individual settlements. Large buildings would be treated in the same way as a higher-level road.

The cost of inorganic flow into the urban area would be monitored and a local tax levied, while the wider financial management system would be structured to encourage the use of renewable organic materials for construction.

Once all the systems had been costed, then a charge would be levied as a single item to a family or an individual, although it would have a cost breakdown attached. *In this system, families are not customers, or consumers of products; they are shareholders in the metabolic city, contributing to the mediation of resource flows around that city, and paying a cost for their share of the resources used.* This financial system can be compared to the charge levied to a family occupying an apartment in a block of flats, though clearly on a larger scale. This financial system should not be confused with the old municipal one whereby the cost of 'services' was bundled into one charge. Here there would be a separately identifiable charge for the management of water resources, for example, allocated to the individual family. However, some of the cost of water resources management would also be charged to the owners of the inter-city road network, for example (see p. 343). Overall, the objective is to return to a socially equitable model that is also able to identify the full cost of managing the resource flows in the different resources systems.

A new approach to the allocation of capital and operating costs

The Ethiopian study demonstrated how in excess of 50 per cent of the cost of new infrastructure investment (by coverage) can be funded internally by the local authority from local taxes and charges. The term 'coverage' is important here, since it differentiates small and large capital cost items. Essentially, the local community can pay for the infrastructure in its area, together with a contribution towards the cost of water treatment and electricity generation. The major capital cost items would be funded separately and depending upon their use. The high-order roads, which are part of the regional or national transport network, for example, would be paid for by regional or national government, and the cost of operation would incorporate the management of urban water resources affected by that particular part of the road network. The energy system would be subsidised by funding from the global adaptation fund, since it represents a zero-carbon investment. Similarly, a part of the water treatment plant and the bulk distribution network would also be funded this way since the system is constructed around the optimisation of water use through recycling and reuse.

Water resource flows would be managed sustainably and would therefore be part of the internal community cost at a local level. However, the additional requirements to manage storm-water flows associated with climate change (i.e. extreme weather events) would be funded by funds allocated for this purpose under current and evolving international agreements.

The next step in the restructuring of the entire financial management model is to link the capital investment with the life-cycle cost of the infrastructure base. This linking is done through the asset management planning process.

Asset management: building a replicable methodology

Asset management planning is now a well-established concept that has been evolving in western countries since the early 1990s, reaching a point where it is a core component of the infrastructure asset base. A number of standardised approaches have been developed to support urban infrastructure asset management in these countries. At this point, however, the method has not been applied extensively in the urban areas of sub-Saharan Africa.

There are two reasons why that is the case. The first lies in the difference in the nature of infrastructure delivery. The mature cities of the western countries have built the asset management approach around their primary needs, which are to manage an ageing infrastructure base and provide a financial modality for life-cycle costing. The result is a very technocratic interpretation of asset management. The second reason derives from the fact that the infrastructure in mature cities tends to be well mapped, and accompanied by extensive operational records. So again this existing knowledge base became the basis for the approach to asset management, with the result that those managing the asset base begin with certain assumptions about what exists, which in turn helps to define their own, specific *Weltanschauung*.

The rapidly growing cities of sub-Saharan Africa face a totally different challenge. There the priority is on constructing new infrastructure, and this has to be done with more limited resources and a more limited skills base. At the same time, there is also the value-based, interpretative role of asset management that is specific to the African urban context. In this regard, asset management has two roles that differ from those used in western countries, both of which move asset management out of the specific arena of technical and financial specialists and move it to the heart of the urban community. The first role is linked to Figure 8.2, which illustrated graphically the generic conceptual model for urban infrastructure. There, the element of that diagram most relevant to this discussion is related to the lower block: a sound financial base.

In the western approach the role of asset management in supporting the creation of a sound financial base is quite straightforward, with asset management being a tool, albeit a quite sophisticated one, of financial management.

In an African context, however, the relationship is quite different; and as a result more complex. Here it is the issue of affordability that provides the key to creating a sound financial base. As a consequence, a direct relationship between affordability and asset management, which does not exist in the western model, is created. It is that relationship which is explored here.

To date, two arguments have been made concerning affordability. The first is that it has to be moved from its current position, where it is interpreted at the level of the individual and situated within the framework of the urban system as a whole. Thus, what concerns us is the affordability of the system, not the affordability to individuals within the system. The second argues that simply by moving towards an integrated approach to the management of resource flows through the city, as described for the four resources systems dealt with previously in this chapter, and doing this in a way that meets the requirements of social equity and environmental sustainability, infrastructure is inherently more affordable.

Valid as these arguments may be, the second in particular remains somewhat abstract and theoretical unless it can be operationalised. Doing so is the critical role of asset management: to provide the operational linkage between affordability and the operational framework that comprises the centre block of Figure 8.2. This role was clearly demonstrated in the Ethiopian study, where asset management provided the platform not only for capacity-building but also for the mobilisation of financial resources and the implementation strategy. Without an asset management plan (which extended into the capital investment plan), this entire local government programme in the secondary cities would have been extremely difficult to operationalise.

The second interpretative role of asset management in the context of African urban development relates to its potential to improve good governance at a local level. This potential will be discussed in greater detail in Chapter 11. The key point is that the asset management plan provides an important interface between the local authority and civil society for the dissemination of data and information in a form that is easily understood. This makes it a critical and very important tool in providing accountability and transparency. Those professionals who work in social development may be sceptical of this view of asset management, and with some justification. If asset management is used by engineers and economists purely as a tool of technocratic or financial management, then it will fail. It is only by using it in its social role that it can offer success and provide the means to operationalise a sustainable urban development programme.

The approach that is described here was developed specifically to suit the needs of the secondary cities in Ethiopia, where it evolved as part of the capacity-building programme described in Chapter 7. In that context it was extremely successful and became the basis for all capital investment planning in those towns.

At first glance, asset management can appear to be an overwhelming concept that is simply too big and complex to introduce into an overworked and understaffed small town, but this does not have to be the case. It may not be simple, at least in the beginning, but neither is it especially complex. The key to its success lies in linking it with the flexible BSUs described previously, and introducing it in a phased manner. This is because asset management is a tool that is well suited to incremental development over time.

This concept of phasing relates to the degree of accuracy of information required. The great benefit of asset management is that the process of constructing an asset base can begin with simplified asset inventories and move to more detailed inventories over a period of time, making it an incremental process within, as well as across, the different resource systems. This is possible because asset management can be approached in two ways, using either what is termed a strategic approach, on the one hand, or an operational approach, on the other.

A water reticulation network provides a good example of the first. Here, the assets are buried and information can be difficult to obtain, so the asset value would be assumed, using for example the total cost per linear metre, as opposed a calculating the detailed cost of pipes, fitting and laying. The operational approach, by contrast, builds on a much more detailed knowledge of individual infrastructure items. This approach would be used in developing the asset base for a movement network, for example, where the asset is visible and a much more detailed analysis is possible.

While an operational approach provides the most accurate information, a strategic approach can be used in the first years of construction of the asset base. For linear features such as water mains or roads, one would take the cost per metre of water main (as indicated above) or (for roads) the cost per square metre of road, both as constructed and at current replacement cost. For a building or a drainage retention pond, it would be cost per square metre of surface area. In this way an initial estimate can be obtained. As more information on the specific infrastructure becomes available, through a managed maintenance programme, so the cost can be refined and the asset management system can move gradually across to a detailed operational approach.

The process developed in Ethiopia merged elements of both the strategic and the operational approaches, resulting in a model that was a combination of the two. This approach allows the construction of an asset management plan to begin immediately, based upon whatever knowledge towns have of their existing infrastructure. The methodology is based upon the use of a simple, step-based process. This concept evolved from a process framework with nine elements, which was developed by the Federation of Canadian Municipalities for use in Canada (FCM, 2003), and it was the study of that work which highlighted the extent to which it was situated within a specific value-based surround. Since that time the process itself has become widely accepted in the West, and has subsequently become one of those western models assumed to have global application. In this guise it is applied in an African context[16] and generally fails; yet careful reading of the original guide will clearly demonstrate how it defines its own rationale in a quite specific way that is grounded firmly in a Canadian context (ibid., pp. 5–7).

The original Ethiopian methodology used a ten-step process to develop a comprehensive asset management plan. As the interaction between the asset management process and the wider capital investment planning process evolved over time, though, the relationship was adapted, to produce a modified methodology that is illustrated by Figure 10.14. Here

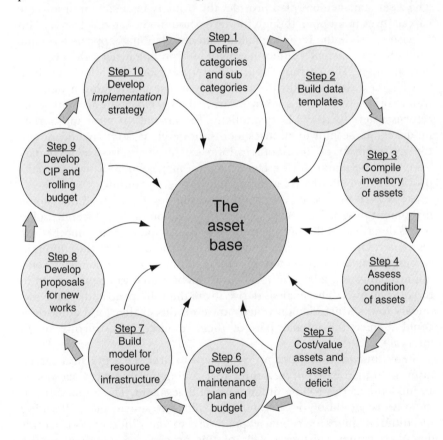

Figure 10.14 The development of an asset management plan.

Note
The ten-step process used here was developed by John Abbott, with support from Fikreyohanes Yadessa. Yadessa created the original loop presentation and Abbott modified that to the current form.

the ten steps remain, but their role changes. The first six steps represent the construction of the asset base, and result in a programme for the sustainable management of that asset base. The last four steps move into the capital investment planning phase, building on this and integrating new work.

Each of the six steps described here makes its own input into the creation of the asset base, as described within the individual circles. While these are self-explanatory, a full description, with examples, can be found on the website supporting the book.[17]

Capital investment planning

The asset management plan provides the primary financial input into the capital investment plan, though this term should be treated with care. This is because, while the term 'capital investment planning' appears to define itself, there are actually different ways of interpreting it, according to need and situation. The current dominant interpretation, which was described in Chapter 7, is essentially project based, and situated within a financial framework defined by a rate of return, albeit taking into account social returns, where these can be quantified. This remains the most appropriate model for large individual investments; however, it is totally unsuited to the vast majority of the resources infrastructures required by secondary towns in sub-Saharan Africa. Here the asset management-based approach provides a far better basis for financial investment planning.

Steps 7–10 in Figure 10.14 summarise the development of the capital investment programme. Step 7 covers the creation of the conceptual plan that is described in the various sections of this chapter, setting out the strategic development of the resource infrastructures for the different resources systems. Step 8 then links these to the different potential financing mechanisms available to local government, which will be described in the next chapter. This analysis derives from the Ethiopian study of the secondary towns which demonstrated how even the smaller local authorities could finance the greater part of their resource infrastructure needs internally.

Step 9 integrates the two previous steps to produce a practical capital investment plan based upon a three-year rolling programme. Finally, step 10 implements this rolling programme of investment. The importance of these two stages also goes beyond the capital investment plan, allocating the different items of capital expenditure to the different cost centres described earlier. Further details of this process are described in the website supporting the book.[18]

Chapter 11

Green infrastructure and urban governance

A few years ago, I attended a meeting of the Global Coalition for Africa (GCA) in Harare, Zimbabwe....

At a certain point in the course of the discussion, the question of good governance in Africa came up. But it came up as a condition of giving aid to African countries. The manner of the discussion and the fact that this was an exchange between African Heads of State and officials from rich countries made me livid with anger.

It reminded me of the social history of Great Britain before the advent of the welfare state. The extremes of individual or family poverty within that country were dealt with through the philanthropy of rich persons to whom such human misery was unbearable. But their charity was given only to those they regarded as the 'deserving poor'. This, in practice, meant that it was given only to those people regarded by the philanthropist as having demonstrated an acceptance of the social and economic status quo – and for as long as they did so.

As the world's powerful nations have not (as yet) accepted the principle of international welfare, they apply the same 'deserving poor' notion to the reality of poverty outside their own countries. 'Aid' and non-commercial credit are regarded not as springing from the principles of human rights or international solidarity, regardless of national borders, but as charity extended as a matter of altruism by richer governments to the less developed and very poor nations. However, the quantity of this 'official' charity being increasingly inadequate to meet the most obvious needs, one of the criteria for a nation being classified as among the world's 'deserving poor' came to be having 'good governance' as defined by the donor community.

And in practice that phrase meant and means those countries having multiparty systems of democracy, economies based on the principle of private ownership and of international free trade and a good record of human rights: again as defined by the industrialised market economy countries of the North. It was in this kind of context that we in Africa first heard about 'good governance'; and this was the manner in which it was brought up at the Harare meeting to which I have referred.

It was this aid-related discussion of good governance, a matter between aid givers and aid seekers, and the arrogant and patronising manner in which it was raised by the aid givers, that discredited the whole subject in the eyes of many of us in Africa and other parts of the South. For used in this manner, good governance sounded like a tool for neo-colonialism. We have therefore tended to despise the concept even as, out of necessity, we try to qualify under it.

I am very far from being alone in rejecting neo-colonialism regardless of the methods adopted to bring it about or to enforce it or to define it! Yet we cannot avoid the fact that a lot of our problems in Africa arise from bad governance. I believe that we need to improve governance everywhere in Africa in order to enable our people to build real freedom and real development for themselves and their countries. And I allowed myself to be persuaded to be a 'convenor' of this Conference on Governance in Africa because I believe that it provides an opportunity for us to understand more about our past political and economic policy mistakes and see how we can improve the management of our affairs as we grope towards the 21st century.[1]

(Julius Nyerere, 1998)

Are concerns about governance in Africa valid?

This chapter is concerned primarily with exploring the nature of the regulatory framework of urban infrastructure. At the same time, though, this is also the point where we can finally engage with that amorphous yet all-embracing topic of urban governance, which will be used as our point of entry into the wider discussion. Internationally, good governance is now recognised as a core principle that should underpin government at all levels, as well as businesses and non-governmental agencies and organisations. At the same time, the translation of good governance from principle to practice is interpretative – with the interpretation being guided by the value system of those performing this task. This was the concern expressed by Julius Nyerere in the 1990s, when looking at governance in an African context. The question now is to what extent that concern is valid today. In other words, who defines the rules of the game?

Let us begin with the idealised view that underpins the western value system. In a speech to the United Nations in 2010 the British Deputy Prime Minister made the following statement: 'Development is, in the end, about freedom.... Development means ensuring that every person has the freedom to take their own life into their own hands and determine their own fate.'[2] This may be a very good soundbite for international consumption, but it also raises important questions about what it means in practice. For who actually interprets these terms; who converts them into real development practices on the ground? Whose ideas do we use for this? Let's look at another speech, by the same person, also in 2010, also in an address to the United Nations; but in a different context. There his message was somewhat different, stating that '[t]he UK Government will fearlessly promote our ideals and interests, while remaining realistic in our approach.'[3]

There we have, neatly encapsulated, the western dichotomy. There is nothing wrong with a country pursuing its own interests, but that country cannot have it both ways. It cannot support the type of freedom espoused in the first speech if every intervention that is made through its aid programme is dependent upon the recipient country accepting its particular interpretation of values, its *Weltanschauungen,* its interpretation of right and wrong. Then this is no longer a discussion about accepting universal values; it has become instead an issue of accepting another country's interpretation of how those values are implemented – something quite different.

The following example illustrates this point when the topic is that of good governance. The two columns shown in Table 11.1 are extracts from two official government websites that provide respective interpretations of good governance as it should be practised by the recipients of their aid – in the donor's view, of course. The one on the left is that of DFID, the British ministry responsible for development aid, while the one on the right is that of GTZ,[4] the German development agency that implements activities, projects and programmes commissioned by the German Federal Ministry for Cooperation and Development (BMZ[5]).

On the side of DFID, the British output-orientated and target-driven approach to policy and strategy, discussed in Chapter 5, is clearly evident; together with the undisputed assumption that this forms the basis for all development everywhere. On the GTZ side the approach is more nuanced, with an attempt to situate GTZ's own input within the value-based surround of other countries. At home, within their own internal spheres of decision-making (i.e. within the United Kingdom and Germany respectively), both have equal validity (i.e. an internalised legitimacy). The problems arise when these values are exported, and imposed, on other countries.

It is suggested that the description from GTZ indicates a genuine attempt to create such a balance, with the use of words such as 'support' and 'promote'. The description from DFID, on the other hand, shows a quite different approach. What we see here is an organisation that is trapped totally within its own value system, providing a classic example of what is meant by a *Weltanschauung.* The use of the word 'must' is on its own sufficient to show how the organisation seeks to impose its value system on others; but there is also the phrase 'need to', and the exploration of how 'DFID uses', which are equally informative. The West places the primary emphasis on individual rights, particularly in Africa, but there are also the rights of governments to independence and sovereignty. The key issue is related to understanding where the balance lies. There was an interesting French study of urban governance that neatly captured this dichotomy when it asked the question 'what particularly qualifies international donors to lay down the rules for the good

Table 11.1 Comparing the British and German government perceptions of good governance in an international development context

DFID	GTZ
'Good governance is based on three things – capability, responsiveness, and accountability. All governments need to be *capable* – to be able to get things done. Does government have the money, the will and the capacity to build wells, provide health services to villagers, offer good education to children and raise taxes to do all these things? When these are absent, countries and their people suffer. 'Governments must *respond* to the aspirations of their citizens through some kind of representative government, and that includes respecting the civil and political rights of their people. 'Governments must also be *accountable*. This means having to explain what you are doing, and answer questions on what you have done. It applies to public officials, to ministers and to governments. 'DFID uses a "country governance analysis" to monitor governance and our partners' commitment to fighting poverty. It is based on discussions with partner governments, civil society and other international partners' (DFID, 2010).	'Good governance implies effective political institutions and the responsible use of political power and management of public resources by the state. Essentially, it is about the interaction between democracy, social welfare and the rule of law ... hence an important activity area for GTZ. GTZ's work in the field of good governance covers the promotion of democracy and rule of law. Human rights play a particular role in this context, especially women's rights. GTZ works in the field of law and justice, helps to fight corruption and promotes the responsible use of public finances. It supports government and administrative reforms, decentralisation and regionalisation of state power and the development of local and municipal government. In doing so, GTZ promotes locally appropriate approaches; it not only cooperates with government institutions but also promotes civil-society actors' (GTZ, 2010a). On local self-government, GTZ proclaims: 'We support structural municipal reforms. In this context we provide advice on organisational development, local political and administrative reforms, and local financial management; [and finally, applying governance to the public sector] ... we support the organisational development of public administrations on the basis of our capacity building approaches' (GTZ, 2010b).

Note
Emphasis has been added by the author.

government of national territories, when it is not their mission and their status precludes them from testing their ideas against reality?' (DgCiD, 2008, p. 53).

Applying good governance in Africa the western way

Like other concepts that have been accepted as universal values, such as freedom, democracy and individual rights, good governance operates at two levels, the one being a statement of principle and the other being its application in practice. The first of these is relatively easy to explore. Thus, one of the most common definitions of the term 'governance' is to say that it describes 'the process of decision-making and the process by which decisions are implemented (or not implemented)' (UN ESCAP, 2009).[6] In this context the term can be applied equally to the public and the private sector. Given that the focus here is concerned primarily with the public sector, a more useful definition, specific to that context, might be that which describes governance as 'the process whereby public institutions conduct public affairs, manage public resources, and guarantee the realization of human rights' (OHCHR, 2011). At a broad level, good governance accomplishes this process 'in a manner essentially free of abuse and corruption, and with due regard for the rule of law' (ibid.). This is a description that can be applied to all countries.

We then come to the exploration of how this concept of governance translates into practice. Here we start to run into problems because governance, like those other universal 'values', can only be operationalised within a specific value system. Perhaps not surprisingly, it is the western countries, and their development agencies, that have defined how this operationalisation works. The first examples, which were subsequently used to create a global model, came from the West. At this point we immediately come up against a dominant characteristic embedded in the Anglo-Saxon hegemony, which has been demonstrated time after time in earlier chapters: the tendency to extrapolate from the specific to the general – to take a developmental construct that works in a specific situation and translate it into a global model. There is of course an enormous amount of 'research' that can be used to demonstrate the validity of this 'model'. However, since all those responsible for deriving this proof operate within the same *Weltanschauungen*, the outcome is not really surprising. This extrapolation from the specific to the general applies here to, in the operationalisation of the principle of good governance.

Good governance is a product of the economic, social and environmental transition of the 1980s and 1990s, described in Chapter 2. In this context it emerges from the transformation of perceptions about the role of government in society. This means that good governance is not, and never can be, 'value-free'. Instead, the way in which it is applied by external agencies, particularly at local level, is influenced by the perceptions those agencies (and, where relevant, their governments) have regarding to the roles and relationships that should operate at different levels of government. Having defined the context, we can fast-forward to 2000, the start of the 'post-transition' phase of international development, and begin with the development of the classic good governance model. This model, which has been adopted by many international agencies internationally to both define and measure good governance, is defined in terms of eight major characteristics, which are illustrated in Figure 11.1.

This diagram formed the basis for defining the characteristics of good governance across the entire United Nations family of organisations, and while there have been some modifications, as we will see later, these are relatively minor and do not alter the fundamental precepts of this model significantly. The same characteristics are taken on board by many external development agencies. Thus, for example, an advertisement by DFID for governance advisers in Africa states that '[c]andidates must demonstrate breadth and depth of knowledge and experience across the eight technical competencies for governance advisors' (*The Economist*, 2009), these competencies being related to the characteristics illustrated in Figure 11.1. And finally, since most African governments have accepted this definition, one must assume that there is buy-in from those governments.

So where do these characteristics come from and what exactly do they mean? The original basis for the principles derives from an OECD[7] study published in 2001, and is based on research that was carried out only within OECD countries. Its purpose at the time was to identify what governments might do to change what the OECD saw to be a situation whereby '[g]overnments are in a crisis of identity, some would say legitimacy, with election turnouts low in many OECD countries and a widespread feeling of disenchantment among citizens with government and the democratic process' (UN ESCAP, 2009). In asking the question 'Can governments do something to change this?' the OECD study concluded that '[w]hat every country needs is more transparency, more consultation and more participation' (ibid.). Furthermore, it was this study which concluded that

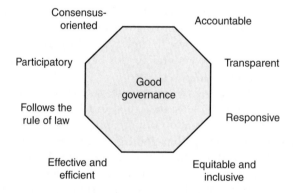

Figure 11.1 The eight characteristics of good governance (UN ESCAP, 2009).

[g]ood governance has 8 major characteristics. It is participatory, consensus oriented, accountable, transparent, responsive, effective and efficient, equitable and inclusive and follows the rule of law. It assures that corruption is minimized, the views of minorities are taken into account and that the voices of the most vulnerable in society are heard in decision-making.

(ibid.)

It was in following up this analysis that the study then developed definitions of the eight characteristics, still used by the majority of external agencies, as follows:

Participation by both men and women is a key cornerstone of good governance. Participation could be either direct or through legitimate intermediate institutions or representatives. It is important to point out that representative democracy does not necessarily mean that the concerns of the most vulnerable in society would be taken into consideration in decision making. Participation needs to be informed and organized. This means freedom of association and expression on the one hand and an organized civil society on the other hand.

Transparency means that decisions taken and their enforcement are done in a manner that follows rules and regulations. It also means that information is freely available and directly accessible to those who will be affected by such decisions and their enforcement. It also means that enough information is provided and that it is provided in easily understandable forms and media.

Effectiveness and efficiency: Good governance means that processes and institutions produce results that meet the needs of society while making the best use of resources at their disposal. The concept of efficiency in the context of good governance also covers the sustainable use of natural resources and the protection of the environment.

Responsiveness: Good governance requires that institutions and processes try to serve all stakeholders within a reasonable timeframe.

Accountability is a key requirement of good governance. Not only governmental institutions but also the private sector and civil society organizations must be accountable to the public and to their institutional stakeholders. Who is accountable to whom varies depending on whether decisions or actions taken are internal or external to an organization or institution. In general an organization or an institution is accountable to those who will be affected by its decisions or actions. Accountability cannot be enforced without transparency and the rule of law.

Consensus orientated: There are several actors and as many view points in a given society. Good governance requires mediation of the different interests in society to reach a broad consensus in society on what is in the best interest of the whole community and how this can be achieved. It also requires a broad and long-term perspective on what is needed for sustainable human development and how to achieve the goals of such development. This can only result from an understanding of the historical, cultural and social contexts of a given society or community.

Equity and inclusiveness: A society's well being depends on ensuring that all its members feel that they have a stake in it and do not feel excluded from the mainstream of society. This requires all groups, but particularly the most vulnerable, have opportunities to improve or maintain their well being.

Rule of law: Good governance requires fair legal frameworks that are enforced impartially. It also requires full protection of human rights, particularly those of minorities. Impartial enforcement of laws requires an independent judiciary and an impartial and incorruptible police force.

(UN ESCAP, 2009)

What is outlined here, then, is a set of principles that form the basis for a relationship between government and society. Accepting that it is written for western countries by western researchers and practitioners, then the description of the specific characteristics may be biased towards a specific culture, although the descriptions could be modified so that they are situated in a different cultural context. With this flexibility of wording taken into consideration, there is a strong case to be made that these characteristics do appear to encapsulate an ideal that could gain universal acceptance. However, that does not imply that they are *interpreted* – that is, put into practice – in the same way in different countries. In particular, the equal weighting that has been given to the characteristics is very specific to the European situation. Thus, the exploration of weighting becomes a central issue when transferring good governance characteristics to rapidly growing societies, particularly at the local level.

Over time, the various UN agencies have sought to provide a more African flavour to these characteristics, as a range of publications from bodies such as UNDP and UN-Habitat demonstrate, for example by introducing an indicator for security. At the same time, UN-Habitat has developed an Urban Governance Index (UGI) as a tool to measure progress in achieving good governance – part of its 'Global Campaign on Urban Governance' (UN-Habitat, 2010). It has also produced its own study of good governance, which sought to tweak these characteristics slightly. Ultimately, though, all of these initiatives continue to be developed using a western, primarily Anglo-Saxon, knowledge resource base that situates the exploration within its own specific *Weltanschauungen*.[8]

Urban infrastructure and the good governance debate

For the past two hundred years, western countries have been the drivers of innovation and modernisation; and there is much that can be learned from their experience. When we explore development in an African context, the book is not suggesting that we ignore this experience; what it is saying is that we have to try to view this experience from a point that sits outside of the western *Weltanschauungen* if we really want to learn the right lessons. And so it is here, with governance: we have to go behind the characteristics that evolved from the analysis and look at the circumstances that provided the analytical framework. If we do so, we can identify at least eight underlying characteristics of western society that influence the way in which the analytical framework was constructed. In the majority of cases the countries concerned had:

1   established democracies;
2   mature economies;
3   an urbanised population with mature cities;
4   a high per capita income base;
5   a social and demographic framework based upon the need to integrate ethnic minorities (immigration);
6   a set of clearly defined roles and relationships that apply to different parts of government;
7   used the principle of subsidiarity as the basis of deciding on which powers, duties and functions to transfer downwards;
8   experienced public disenchantment with the established political system.

It would be useful to carry out a similar exercise for African countries and see how that might change perceptions, particularly at a local level. Some of the African characteristics would be self-evident: the rapid urbanisation; the low per capita income base; weak political structures; a low skills base. In addition, though, there are two characteristics which are central to the discourse, but which are given far too little recognition by external agencies. The first is that, across the board, roles and relationships are far from fixed; on the contrary, for the majority of African countries the establishment of a clear framework of roles and relationships is still work in progress.

The second is a simple recognition that the European concept of subsidiarity is not necessarily valid as a basis for devolving powers, duties and functions. To a large extent there is a correlation between these two points. Thus there is an alternative approach to subsidiarity, proposed in Chapter 5, which entails that African governments devolve powers, duties and functions *strategically* – an approach that would then impact on roles and relationships quite significantly. It would do so because the adoption of a strategic approach to decentralisation would change the core question around, from 'What powers duties and functions can be devolved; that is, what can local governments do (subsidiarity)?' to 'What should local government be doing that will play to its strengths and have the greatest beneficial impact on local development (i.e. defining a strategy)?'

Urban good governance and the three components of infrastructure

This is the point at which we can return to the exploration of the *problématique*. Previous chapters have dealt with the three drivers of development (economic, social, environmental); the financial base and the issue of affordability; the conceptual model defining the technology; and the technology itself. This leaves two remaining components: the value-based surround and the political regulatory framework.

The current (western) approach to urban good governance in Africa tends to conflate these – a natural misconception if a person is grounded in a western *Weltanschauung* within which roles and relationships are clearly defined. However, if we follow the previous line of thinking about a new strategic approach to decentralisation, or even if we simply look at the practical experiences and discussions of previous chapters, then it is evident that the nature of roles and relationships is still evolving, as work in progress. So how does good governance integrate with this condition?

Chapter 2 illustrated the extent to which the freedom to create roles and relationships that are situated within an internal value system is a defining characteristic of sovereignty in a nation-state. That is why we have first to create a model of roles and relationships for a specific development approach, because it is only when we have done so that good governance be explored in a truly African context. At that point the principles and practice of good governance can be used to adapt, modify or even change some specific elements related to either the roles or the relationships, with a view to improving them. If we accept the need to define a set of roles and relationships first, then this translates the three generic components of infrastructure shown in Figure 8.2 into specific components, which are illustrated by Figure 11.2.

This, then, is our starting point: the exploration of a political regulatory framework based upon the creation of a set of roles and relationships. Chapter 2 initiated this discussion when it identified seven sets of key roles and relationships. Building upon the case studies of South Africa (in Chapter 5), and Ethiopia (Chapter 7), this list can be restructured to form a type of hierarchy, which would comprise five levels. These are, in order:

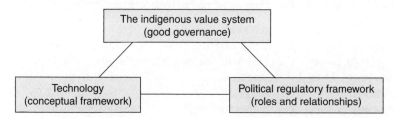

Figure 11.2 The three components of infrastructure in a twenty-first-century context.

1 Defining the role of developmental local government. This is the central issue, and involves allocating powers, duties and functions, and creating a legal framework for local government.
2 Defining the role (and nature) of cooperative local government.
3 Exploring the relationship between central and local government based upon an integration of development and cooperative local government constructs.
4 Defining the role of external actors, particularly the private sector and civil society, and their relationship with local government.
5 Defining the role of external development agencies and other external actors.

Only once these tasks have been achieved can there be a real basis for exploring the application of the principles of urban good governance in an African context. These various components of roles and relationships will be described in the sections that follow.

Level 1: developmental local government

The centrality of local government in urban development

The conceptual model developed in Chapter 9 shows the city as a system in its own right, within which a number of external resource systems come together. The systemic city then uses infrastructure to mediate these different resource flows while at the same time enabling equitable access to these resources for all residents. In this model the role of local government is absolutely critical, and central to the whole process. The systemic city is a metabolic city, and local government is the institution that manages that metabolism. In this way, local government is the guardian of the metabolic city, and as such – as the locus of decision-making – it is the only body that can facilitate the resource flows in an integrated way to achieve sustainable and equitable development.

The role of local government: from subsidiarity to strategic
decentralisation

What I have said so far provides a starting point in seeking to define the role of local government. In this systemic model that role can be seen to have three parts. Thus, local government:

1   is responsible for a healthy metabolic city;
2   facilitates the flow of natural resources; and
3   enables an equitable urban society, which includes equitable access to resources.

And finally, if the local authority is to perform this role, then its function has to be underpinned by a sound financial model and linked to a strategy for economic development.

This, then, provides an alternative to the current western-imposed view that subsidiarity forms the basis for decentralisation of powers and duties described above, and lays a foundation for a strategic approach. It then follows that responsibility for the management of infrastructure resource flows is the key to understanding the role of local government, by defining its primary strategic function, namely: to develop and manage these resources in a sustainable and equitable manner. At the same time, this requires a management of the spatial dimension within which both the residents and the resources function, as well as a management of the finances that underpin the entire system. The outcome can be illustrated by the relationship in Figure 11.3, which shows how managing these three functions provides the linkage between people and the physical environment and lays the foundation for sustainable urban development.

Allocating powers, duties and functions to local government

The powers, duties and functions of local government emerge from the translation of the theoretical model shown in Figure 11.3 into practice. Thus, there are three elements that define the role of the secondary town, and thus determine its powers, duties and functions. These are:

1   urban infrastructure resource management;
2   urban social-spatial management;
3   urban financial management.

Of these, only the third can be described as similar to the function of western local government. The first two are quite different, and specific to an African urban context. This means that they have nothing whatsoever to do with a traditional British urban planning–engineering duality, a

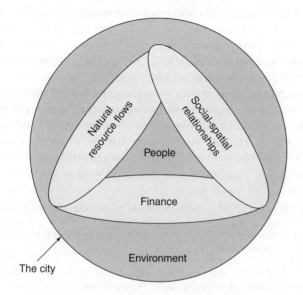

Figure 11.3 The strategic role of local government.

relationship (and terminology) that belongs to a different time and a different culture.

In this new African model, Urban Resource Infrastructure Management becomes a completely new discipline, with its primary responsibility being to manage the mediation of resource flows from the six natural resource systems described in Chapter 9. Similarly, social-spatial management is also a new discipline. It might incorporate some of the elements of the current (British-based) urban planning model, but its primary construct would draw much more from a new African approach to urban design that is grounded in the recognition of informal settlements as an emerging urban form. In this context it would be quite distinct from the British urban planning model, having a much greater focus on the creation of sustainable social-spatial relationships. The nature of these two new disciplines will be described later. The practical elements of the third component of financial management would be similar to the present; however, the model as a whole would change the way in which we visualise the relationship between revenue sources and expenditure flows.

The legal framework of local government

A clearly defined legal framework for local government is the only way to ensure that urban development is sustainable; and this can only be achieved through a process of devolution. The delegation of powers, duties and functions does not provide the degree of stability required to create effective local government, being essentially centripetal; that is, tending constantly to return power back to the centre. And this applies regardless of whether the country has adopted a federal or a unitary form of government at national level, although clearly it is easier to build in at least some checks and balances in a federal system.

There are two elements to the devolution model. The first of these is a set of principles. Here, the principles used in France could form a basis for discussion and development by African countries of their own indigenous system. Their benefit is that they highlight the four key issues of principle associated with devolution of powers to local government. These principles are listed in Table 11.2, together with a brief explanation.

Table 11.2 The principles underpinning devolved local government powers and duties[a]

Principle	Explanation
Principle of free administration of local governments	Elected councils freely administer local governments with regulatory powers to perform their tasks.
Principle of no oversight of one local government over another (follows on from the above)	Since local governments are free to administer their affairs, none may have the power to tell another what to do.
Principle of financial autonomy for local governments	Local governments have resources that they are free to use. Tax revenues and the local governments' own resources from other sources must represent a decisive share of these resources. This means that local governments must not depend on the central government for the majority of their resources.
Principle of central government supervision after the fact	The central government supervises local governments' actions, but this supervision takes place after the fact. Thus, a distinction is made between: • legal supervision to ensure the lawfulness of local governments' actions that are automatically enforceable (local government decisions, regulatory acts, agreements relating to public procurement, etc.); • the need for a higher body, which could be either a court or the Ministry of Finance, to be responsible for conducting the financial audits and legal audits of local governments' budgets, financial statements and financial management.

Note
a This table has been adapted from a French government analysis of some of the main operating principles of decentralisation as described in Ministère des Affaires Etrangères (2006).

Ultimately, these are the principles that differentiate devolved local government from delegated government, yet they are generally overlooked in the literature about decentralisation in Africa, such as that described in Chapter 5. The main impact of this move across to a devolutionary model is to raise the profile of, and the need for, a strong legal framework for local government.

This legal framework, which generally includes a description of powers, duties and functions, is clearly an essential component of devolved government; however, on its own it is inadequate. The description of the Ethiopian case study in Chapter 7 illustrated this well, when it showed how both line ministries and external agencies such as the Water and Sanitation Program can bypass the country's legal framework for urban local government authorities (ULGAs) and simply revert to centralised decision-making. Of course, it would be possible for local government to take this issue to the courts to defend their legal rights, but it is neither practical nor desirable for them to do so. What is required is to first understand, and then define more clearly, the nature of the relationship between central government, line ministries and urban local government more clearly, so as to avoid this deconstruction of the local government reform process happening in the first place. That relationship is encapsulated in the concept of cooperative local government. Building this relationship then becomes the second step in creating a framework for urban good governance.

Level 2: cooperative local government

Introduction

Historically, it is the dysfunctional nature of this relationship (between national and local level) that has been the key stumbling block to effective decentralisation in Africa; yet, ironically, it is also the one area that has never been explored in detail in the literature on decentralisation, at least in its totality. This was the one weakness of the South African constitution and could equally prove to be the point around which decentralisation in Ethiopia fails.

Governments everywhere are changing in a number of ways. Perhaps the most important global shift is characterised by the rising power and influence of the chief executive, be it a president or a prime minister, due in part to the personalisation of international relationships between nation-states, and in part to the changing nature of media coverage, which requires a centralised point of contact to provide a news focus. At the same time, though, there is also a second shift taking place that is less well publicised, namely the shift in power from the legislature to the executive, bringing with it growing power and influence for individual line ministries (and a loss of power and influence for members of parliament). The impact, at least internally, is that the legislature is becoming a collection of individual power centres: a body with many heads, with each of those heads being a minister of a line department. This is particularly problematic for urban government (specifically) and urban governance (generally), since there are so many different line ministries involved, in one way or another, with the management of local government. Defining this relationship between the line ministries and local government in a clear and unambiguous way, then, is not only the key to successful urban development, but also a prerequisite for an effective and realistic urban governance model.

This section has set out the way in which line ministries evolved and shows the fundamental contradictions that exist between the functioning of line ministries and local government. This is not a new phenomenon; on the contrary, the contradiction has always existed, given that line ministries operate within a vertical management system of sector-based silos, while local government traditionally operated a horizontal management system that was cross-sectoral. However, the increasing power of line ministries in the post-independence era, and the fact that line ministries correlate strongly to the United Nations system of internal institutional management, have made the situation worse. The outcome is a primary cause of the failure of decentralisation in Africa.

The growth of line ministries and their impact on urban government

Infrastructure lies at the heart of government, and its influence extends far deeper that is currently recognised. As Chapter 3 indicated, this lack of understanding is due in large part to historical factors, in particular a failure to rationalise the relationship between local government, which is fundamentally cross-sectoral, and national line ministries that are essentially vertical, sector-based management silos. To integrate these two approaches requires a more detailed exploration of the interaction between them than has been the case to date. And the starting point for that analysis goes back to the British colonial model of government.

The political system that Britain established for its colonies and protectorates is generally termed the 'Westminster model'. However, this is something of a misnomer, since it begs the question: which Westminster system? For the true 'Westminster system', which situated control over decision-making with the legislature (Parliament), began to change in 1919 with the formation of the first 'developmental' line department, which heralded a move to line-functional government. Prior to that time, Parliament played a major role in the internal development of the country, and particularly its infrastructure development, with each major work of infrastructure having to gain its own parliamentary Bill before it could proceed. It was only in 1919, following the Great War of 1914–1918, that Britain began to develop line ministries for internal purposes, beginning with the creation of a national Department of Health in that year, extending later into Education, Transport, Housing, and so on. These in turn initiated a slow but steady transfer of responsibility from local government to the new line ministries, which culminated in the removal of the majority of infrastructure services from local government responsibility in the local government reforms of 1974. So while the focus in post-colonial Africa was on the legislature, and the nature of 'democracy', the debate on why many of Africa's political systems and structures failed omitted to take into account the impact caused by the changing relationship between the legislature and the executive, and in particular the growth of executive power at the expense of the legislature. This was not solely an African phenomenon, since it reflected changes already under way in the West as well.

Coupled with this transfer of responsibility, when African countries gained independence they took over a political system that was strongly orientated to managing a rural economy. The colonial administration had set up strong Ministries of Agriculture and Health in particular, and Water Resources was being seen increasingly as important, primarily because of its linkages to irrigation. Little consideration was given to the nature of urban government and the implications of the inherently weak urban management system. When African governments subsequently centralised power, and in doing so effectively destroyed the local government system inherited from the British colonial administration, the change was perceived to be an African failure. Thus, Olowu, for instance, in his analysis of decentralisation, discussed in Chapter 5, talks of the 'golden age' of local government that existed in the immediate post-independence era. However, this book has sought to demonstrate, in its historical analysis, that this is a misinterpretation of events. In reality, the urban construct of that time, grounded as it was in an inequitable two-tier social system, was fundamentally flawed; and it is very difficult to imagine how it might have survived even under more advantageous circumstances. Ultimately, it was a system of urban government that could only have survived by formally institutionalising the exclusion of the urban poor, as South Africa sought to do, albeit along racial lines.

From the 1980s onwards the power of the executive line-functional ministries continued to grow ever stronger, not only in African countries but in developed countries as well. As a result, the World Bank underwent a major restructuring in the 1990s whereby it realigned itself internally to reflect this new sectoral reality, creating the now widespread matrix model of management (with the axes being Regions and Sectors). Yet this centralisation has done little to improve urban governance; on the contrary, the situation continued to deteriorate, and urban systems and structures continued to fail. The World Bank and others argued that this problem could be addressed by bringing in the private sector to manage major components of the urban economy, particularly its infrastructure; but this argument too misread the real issue. For that we have to go back to the root of the problem, which is that the post-colonial institutional and political structures were never designed to cope with strong local government, and have never been adapted to do so. The inherent tensions between central and local government, mentioned at the beginning of this discussion, are brought to the point of complete dysfunctionality in Africa, which is why most attempts to decentralise fail.

The key to understanding Africa's urban condition lies, as it always has done, with the infrastructure. Ethiopia, owing to its history, is less affected than other African countries by the legacy of colonialism. In its decentralisation programme the country has addressed the first two issues covered here, namely the definition of powers, duties and functions; and the creation of a legal framework for local government. What it did not do when it created an integrated urban infrastructure policy, though, was attain a consensus, from other line-functional departments involved with urban infrastructure in one way or another, on how this new set-up might function in practice. It did integrate inter-ministerial consultation into the policy document, and clearly, for the Ministry of Works and Urban Development to have the policy approved in the first place, it had to gain acceptance from the Council of Ministers. However, it is contended here that this is insufficient, particularly given the external forces and institutional actors whose own programmes are based upon individual sector-based interventions in urban areas.

Figure 11.4 serves to illustrate this conundrum. It shows the different line ministries directly involved with some aspect of urban infrastructure management. In Ethiopia the majority of these infrastructure services are still linked to local government; in many other African countries they have been stripped away completely. Even in this diagram, though, the complexity of the interrelationships, and the potential for confusion and inter-ministerial competition for power, is self-evident. This is the central issue that has to be addressed.

UN-Habitat argues that the failure of local government is due to a lack of political will on the part of African governments. This view is strongly contested here. Such a view says more about the failure of UN-Habitat to understand what is really happening with urban development in Africa, particularly in the secondary towns, than it does about African weaknesses. The real reasons why African governments have failed to decentralise effectively become apparent in the above diagram, whose spaghetti-like interconnections speak for themselves.

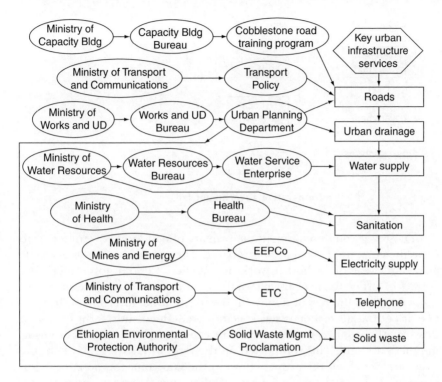

Figure 11.4 The relationship between line-functional national ministries, regional government, local government and urban infrastructure in Ethiopia.

Level 3: exploring the relationship between the different tiers of government

Why developmental local government fails

The failure of developmental government arises from two weaknesses in the existing development paradigm. The first is the use of a delegated model of decentralisation – a form that is essentially centripetal. The second is the use of target-based delivery in infrastructure services, which provides the justification for recentralising power. Reducing relationships to their simplest form, we can think of developmental government in terms of the centre providing an operating framework for local government; and cooperative government as defining the nature of local accountability back to the centre. When we combine target-based delivery with a delegated model, then the effect is either to bypass local government or to turn it into a delivery agent of central government, as is illustrated by Figure 11.5.

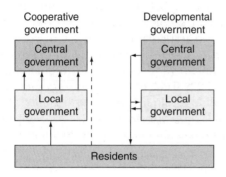

Figure 11.5 Why cooperative government fails.

In target-driven development the primary role of local government is to serve the community by *delivering* services. This appears to be a reasonable goal until we look at how it works in practice. Central government sets targets in order to meet its external commitments. The achievement of those targets is the responsibility (in theory) of local government. In practice, if central government sets specific, predefined short-term targets in this way, then only central government can control the process of ensuring these are met. This is reflected on the right of Figure 11.5, where the heavy arrow defines the primary flow. At the same time, because local government has this theoretical responsibility, then it has to monitor and report on targets. And since there are many line departments involved, all with their own targets, this necessitates a major exercise in information-gathering (the left-hand side of Figure 11.5) which totally overloads the capacity of local government. The result is dysfunctional local government. The main donors who drive this delivery-driven, output-orientated approach to development, such as the British and the Dutch, are very happy, because they can tell their voters how many taps or toilets have been delivered with their aid money. What they don't tell their voters is how the imposition of this approach has made local government dysfunctional and politically unstable; that part of it is an African problem.

Rethinking cooperative government

The dual concept of developmental and cooperative government is excellent, but it can only work properly if it is situated within a systemic framework. The solution lies in redefining the nature of cooperative and developmental local government to provide a more effective power balance. In this new construct, developmental local government should deal with the downward relationship, from the centre, through to the local. From there the relationship between the local authority and the residents should be described within a separate model. Cooperative local government would then focus on the upward relationship, and the responsibility of local government to national government. Here again the responsibility of residents to local government would be defined separately. This integrated local government model is illustrated in Figure 11.6. The role of central government within the two arenas, cooperative and developmental, can then be explored in this light.

Figure 11.5 provides governments in sub-Saharan Africa with a much better understanding of why local governments do not function effectively, even when powers are decentralised. They can then adapt their decentralisation model to one based upon Figure 11.6. In doing so, however, they will also have to address the issue of how central line government ministries relate to local government across a wide front. The key to achieving this outcome emerges from the resources pyramid developed in Chapter 9, since this enables the role of the national line ministries to align the different resource systems more effectively across the urban boundary. To do this we need to progress through the rationale in steps. In the first step we simply take the line ministries as they are, and link them to resource systems, as illustrated (for example) in Table 11.3. However, when we refer this back to Figure 11.4 there may be some rationalisation but overall it remains far from an ideal situation.

The situation can be greatly improved if we use the hexagonal systemic relationship from Figure 9.5 in Chapter 9. Now we have a model that can be integrated into a line ministry system of government quite easily (Figure 11.7). This diagram illustrates how the role of line ministries in the national–local relationship could operate in a systemic framework, and how the use of this approach creates a more rational line-ministerial construct than the one situated within the more mechanistic, reductionist framework of government. The diagram describes

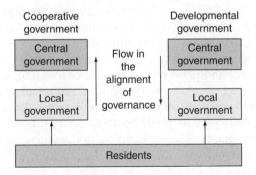

Figure 11.6 Nature of the relationship between cooperative and developmental government.

Table 11.3 The linkage between systems and line ministries

System	Related ministry
The urban system	Ministry of the Environmental Ministry of Finance The Ministry of Economic Development The Environmental Protection Agency
Water resources	Ministry of Water Resources Ministry of Health
Organic resources	Ministry of Agriculture Ministry of Health
Energy resources	Ministry of Energy Resources/Affairs
Spatial resources	Ministry of Economic Planning/Development Ministry of Transport
Inorganic resources	Ministry of Mineral Affairs
Communications resources	Ministry of Telecommunications

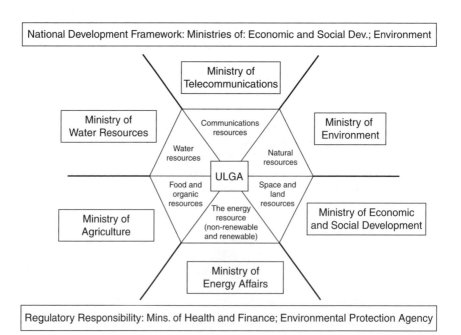

Figure 11.7 Integrating the city into a national government system of line ministries.

three aspects of central government that together provide the operational framework for local government within a cooperative structure. The first, and most important, is the national development policy, which is driven by the Ministry of Economic and Social Development and the Ministry of the Environment. This reflects the extension of the three primary imperatives driving the nation-state, namely the economic development driver (a green urban economy and the creation of small businesses), the social development driver (social equity) and the environmental development driver (sustainability through the mediation of resource flows).

The second aspect of government that emerges from this diagram relates to the way in which line ministries interact. The use of this relational model enables the different line ministries to better understand how their specific sectors interact at the local level. In this context, though, it is important to recognise that, while every system is important, there is a hierarchy of importance, which is reflected in the pyramid in Figure 9.4. The third aspect of government is that of regulation. And here there are three ministries involved: the Ministry of Finance, which monitors fiscal management; the Ministry of Health, which monitors both community and individual health; and the Environmental Protection Agency, which monitors pollution, using this term in its broadest sense.

Now we have a structure (within national government) that is not only fully compatible with the concept of cooperative government shown in Figure 11.6, but also fully compatible with the role of local government defined previously in the discussion around developmental local government. At this point we can return to the discussion on developmental local government and look at how this emerges from Figure 11.7.

Adapting central government to developmental local government

Developmental local government defines the local authority as the government body having the primary responsibility for the management of the development process within its geographical boundary. The challenge then becomes one of creating an interface between central and local government that will facilitate this process while retaining the legal integrity of the local authority. Doing so is almost impossible while each ministry retains a direct influence over the implementation process. Designating one department to have responsibility for local government, as in the Ethiopian example, while providing a solution in principle, has been shown to be impractical. The only way it can be made to work is by providing some kind of forum at the level of central government, which will create a single point of contact while enabling the different line ministries to be adequately informed. Figure 11.8 shows one way of doing this, which highlights the

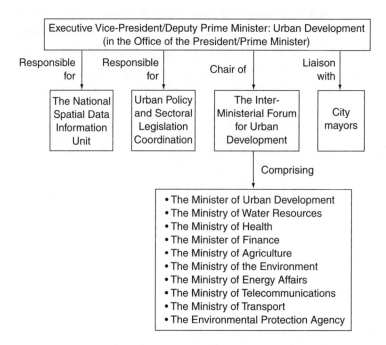

Figure 11.8 A proposed national structure for integrated urban infrastructure management.

different aspects of the interaction between the central and local levels of government. In setting out a specific form of relationship, the intent is not to be prescriptive, but rather to highlight the issues involved in the relationship and thereby provide a basis for wider discussion.

Figure 11.8 is an example of operation in a unitary state. The solution proposed here is based upon a recognition that line ministries (and their ministers) are essentially competitive. Thus, for a unit created within government to be able to rise 'above' this inter-ministerial fray, it has to be situated in the office of the President. If the Vice-President is given the responsibility for urban government (and urban governance), he or she will be a strong executive member of the government, with a clearly defined role.

It can be seen from this diagram that the management of local government involves four different tasks. The first task is that associated with legislation. This includes a responsibility for urban policy, including the infrastructure policy, as well as coordinating strategy and implementation programmes developed at local government level (whether in the urban areas themselves or in regional local government). The second task is to coordinate inter-ministerial action and ensure a unified response at national government level to decisions affecting local government. In this context, each line ministry would be responsible for the wider resource system with which the different elements of the resource base described in Chapter 8 interact.

The third task would be to liaise with the mayors of the different ULGAs. The creation of executive mayors is an integral part of the governance model and would provide a major source of political expertise in the country, and an important feeder route into national politics. The fourth and final task would be to take control of the national spatial data and information unit, which is an essential component of urban development.

The creation of a clear relational model linking central and local government, of which Figure 11.8 is an example, is an essential prerequisite to the creation of an urban good governance system. Without such a model in place, it is difficult to see how urban good governance can ever be achieved.

Level 4: the role of the private sector and civil society

A new conceptual approach to public–private partnerships

For the first time we have a model that integrates economic, social and environmental drivers in a way that is mutually reinforcing rather than conflictual. Creating that integrated framework is the role of government – and a full-time task. Operationalising that framework is the role of other actors who can provide the required specialist skills. It is in this context that public–private partnerships (PPPs) provide the key to sustainable delivery and management of the resource-based urban infrastructure systems. Many previous attempts to achieve successful PPPs in African have failed, but that is because external agencies failed to situate them in an indigenous value system.

Creating successful PPPs for infrastructure delivery at local government level requires that we be able to demonstrate how the three components of urban infrastructure, defined by Figure 11.2, relate to each other. Building small businesses and using locally derived contracts (preferably in an indigenous language) is an important first step in that process. At the same time, though, the needs emerging from the role of infrastructure as a driver of social and environmental development favours the use of specific technological systems. So, we first define our environmental driver, based upon the need to mediate resource flows across all resource systems; ensure that each system provides an equitable outcome to all the residents; and then build our economic delivery and management model. The most appropriate and effective form of public–private partnership will then emerge from this process.

This approach does place a wider social obligation on the private sector. The role of local government in this system is not to manage infrastructure services itself; its role is as the guardian responsible for a healthy metabolic city, through the facilitation of natural resource flows; and the enablement of an equitable urban society. When the private sector becomes involved in managing infrastructure, it takes on an obligation to support local government in performing this role. This is achieved in two ways: support for the broader economic goals of the city, and involvement in a new, integrated financial model for urban infrastructure.

Embedding the private sector in the local economy

The economic driver of urban development is built around the creation of small, medium and micro enterprises (SMMEs) much more than it is around job creation through manual labour. And these enterprises may be either privately formed groups or cooperative groups formed from within civil society, since the systemic approach used here opens up many opportunities for the development of SMMEs through its focus on small, sustainable systems. At the same time, there is also an opportunity for larger private-sector companies to become involved alongside the SMMEs. In entering this market, though, these companies would need to recognise, and accept, that the rules of the game have changed.

In the systemic resource infrastructure model described in Chapter 9, a significant proportion of the work required to build the resource systems can be achieved through small and medium-scale enterprises. Large-scale operators still have a role, particularly in water and energy resources, but roles and relationships have changed. The fact that they will be contributing to the creation of a system, rather than to specific outputs, whether taps or electricity points, will cause the entire financial model to shift. The private-sector operator is no longer outside the system, providing a customer service; instead, it is embedded in the system, responsible for managing the different resource flows across their entire cycle. In this context, public–private-sector partnerships become much more than contractual agreements within regulated markets. In this new system every actor that plays a role in the mediation of resource flows has to accept a shared responsibility for the well-being of the system as a whole, in much the same way that residents of an apartment block have a communal responsibility for the well-being of the apartment building. In this model the choice of large-scale operators of infrastructure services, used in situations where the operation is too large for SMMEs, would be determined by the extent to which they intended to buy into this principle as well as the extent to which they were willing to contribute to the local economy.

This shared responsibility, when coupled with the role of the local authority and the role of central government, then forms the basis for the relationship between the public and private sectors, as well as that between the public sector and civil society. This is a consensual development model which provides the basis for urban good governance. Thus, a large company entering a segment of the resource infrastructure market would have to describe the contribution it would make to the achievement of the economic imperative, namely the creation of SMMEs, and would need to provide a clear development strategy to accomplish that contribution.

Finally, this new approach radically changes the concept of regulation. In this model of cooperative governance the central government ministries provide the regulatory framework. At the same time, though, monitoring of the operation would be the role of sub-municipal government, since this is the group that is closest to the community and equally is the group that experiences the impact on the local environment.

PPPs and urban governance

The creation of a systemic approach to the management of infrastructure resource flows radically changes the nature of PPPs. These are no longer governed by target-based delivery of services to individuals using the classical free-market model. Instead, those involved in one specific system will have to work with the needs of that particular system in their entirety, as described in the previous chapter.

The greatest conceptual shift in thinking occurs in the urban water system. Here water supply is no longer separated from urban water resources; rather, it now becomes an integral part of the wider management of those water resources. On the one hand, this opens up new opportunities for private-sector involvement; at the same time, it draws the private sector into the urban metabolism in a way that is much more intimate than is the case currently. Water supply no longer stops at the door, but flows through (both literally and figuratively) and back into the urban water cycle, where it has to be reintegrated with other water resources.

A similar conceptual shift takes place with other systems. Sanitation and organic waste are part of a cycle of organic flows that have to be integrated with the surrounding agricultural base. Energy is a renewable resource that has to be managed in a way that is much more integrated with the urban area with which it is associated. The management of the social-spatial system draws on new concepts of urban design that are part of the specific African cultural landscape. In each and every case, western models of urban governance fall away, to be replaced by African models that are designed specifically for this new set of systemic relationships. In all of this, Africans are free to explore their own intellectual space and generate their own ideas.

Level 5: the role of external agencies

External agencies would be liberated from their ideological baggage by this new methodological approach. No longer would they need to work at the level of the individual, importing hundreds of consultants in order to reinvent the wheel of individual delivery over and over again. Instead, with the adoption of this development model, the input of development agencies can focus on two generic areas. The first is support for adaptive measures linked to environmental sustainability and climate change. All the systemic flows in this approach are grounded in these: building a new urban sustainability model and at the same time adapting to climate change. For the first time there is a model in place that can support meaningful and equitable internal–external partnerships. The second area of input is in capacity-building. Here the description of the two external interpretations of governance in Table 11.1 becomes important, raising the question: are external agencies there to support or to impose? Capacity-building in this new approach is shaped by internal needs and perceptions, not by external interpretations, and the external agencies will need to adapt accordingly.

Urban good governance: the final piece of the puzzle

Building urban good governance on defined roles and relationships

Creating a coherent and rational model of roles and relationships provides a framework for urban good governance that is grounded in a value system which is indigenous to the country. In this context, good governance becomes a mechanism for monitoring, improving and, where necessary, adapting roles and relationships. Thus, the characteristics become indicators, a shift already envisaged by the UN-Habitat guide described earlier in the chapter. At the same time, though, the use of a strategic approach to decentralisation means that there will be different indicators associated with different roles.

It is not the intent here to become involved in a debate about what might be the most appropriate indicators to use. The purpose rather is to demonstrate how they might be used. For this purpose it is sufficient to use the eight indicators from the OECD model in Figure 11.1 (where they are termed characteristics). The strategic approach to decentralisation described earlier suggests that the focus of local government, and its role in the urban society, rests upon three (interactive) pillars of responsibility, which revolve around the management, respectively, of urban resource flows, social space and urban finance. Each of these will have different priorities across the range of urban good governance indicators, as illustrated in Figure 11.9.

This diagram illustrate that the greatest need in urban financial management, for example, is for *good practices*, which means that, above all else,

Figure 11.9 The three pillars of local government.

it should follow the rule of law. Urban resource infrastructure management, on the other hand, requires *effective and efficient systems*, which correspond to the good governance characteristic of the same name. Finally, the equitable management of urban social space requires *transparent processes*, since this is the area that affects individuals most directly. This way of prioritising does not seek to imply that the specific priority characteristic of the one area only applies to that area; simply that this is likely to be its primary focus.

If we move on to other indicators, arguably the greatest difference between the western approach to good governance and the African approach revolves around the interpretation of social equity. This statement follows from the discussion on this topic in Chapter 8. The primary concern within mature cities generally revolves around the integration of minorities, a need that tends to conflate social equity with social inclusion. In the rapidly growing secondary towns in Africa, both of these are important in their own right. In the development model described here, social equity has been elevated to become a driver of urban development. This then enables social inclusion to be defined as an indicator of good governance that would be used to monitor the achievement of social equity.

E-democracy and e-governance in Africa: the basis for good governance in urban resource infrastructure management

This would leave four further indicators, which respectively monitor accountability, responsiveness, consensus and participation. Again, while in a European context these might be perceived as being of equal weighting, both with each other and with the other four, that is not necessarily the case in a developing urban context. When we look at resources infrastructure management specifically, it is argued here that these four can be grouped within one construct where all can be addressed together, using a single set of data. This grouping would be done through the use of one of the underlying natural resource systems described in the previous chapter, namely that of communications resources.

Spatial information and data management lies at the heart of government. Even prior to the transition to democratic government in South Africa in 2004, the regional administration of North West Province (North West Office of the Premier, 2009) had initiated a programme of spatial data capture and management with the specific purpose of providing information to its residents on all aspects of government activity. And at the heart of this system was something that was called a 'one-stop shop', a depository of Provincial project information spanning all departments, which was made accessible through carefully sited outlets where computers could be accessed by residents.

There is a great deal of scepticism, particularly among external actors, concerning the ability of secondary cities to manage spatial data. However, the Ethiopian project showed how relatively simple it is to collect, collate and disseminate information electronically, using both aerial photography and GIS. In drawing on both South African and Ethiopian experience in this regard, there are two aspects that are particularly relevant to this discussion.

The first is simply a confirmation that knowledge is empowering, and the focus in building urban good governance should be on making information available to residents, particularly concerning the three core activity areas outlined in Figure 11.9. Unfortunately, spatial data management is often used (and perceived) solely as a technocratic tool; if that is the case, then it will in all likelihood fail. The use of GIS in local government, particularly in Africa, is first and foremost a socio-political tool. It empowers local politicians, and, if used as it should (and could) be, it empowers the residents equally.

When spatial data were first recognised as being of value to government in South Africa, in the 1990s, several provinces established the system in the Premier's Office, rather than in a specific line department. The result was remarkable: North-West Province, which was a primarily rural province, rapidly became one of the most advanced in the country in respect of spatial technology management. It did so because, for the first time, the Premier had answers to the key development questions he was being asked continually by residents. Similarly, when a (GIS-based) asset management plan was produced for the city administrations in the secondary cities forming part of the Ethiopian decentralisation project, there was a similar impact, with the mayors being provided with a full picture of their city that they had not previously seen. Those processes not only empower the local leadership but improve accountability and contribute to greater political stability.

Thus, a spatially based information system is a priority need for a secondary town; and this has to be situated within the Mayor's Office so that it provides information, first and foremost, to the city's Chief Executive. This information is then made available to the people at large through the sub-municipal offices. It is this information that provides the basis for judging the effectiveness of urban good governance using the four indicators outlined above, namely accountability, responsiveness, consensus-orientated decision-making and participatory processes. Figure 11.10 illustrates the nature of this relationship.

The primary weakness of spatial data management that prevents a system like the one described above being used is the complexity of the current approach. There are two main reasons. The first relates to the collection of urban spatial data, where the dominant urban planning model prioritises the cadastre – that is, the definition of site boundaries – which in turn is driven by the obsession with land regularisation. This latter requires a detailed and sophisticated management system that in turn requires high accuracy and constant updating. When the city is perceived as a system, this completely changes the way we view data. Using the outcomes described in the previous chapter, the basic spatial unit (BSU) is changed from the individual site to a sub-settlement, which corresponds to the sub-municipal boundary, and the primary focus is on mapping the resource infrastructure. Here the key is to build the infrastructure asset base, through the development of an asset management plan, and from there to build the capital investment plan. Both of these are participatory processes and both result in graphical outputs that are easy for residents

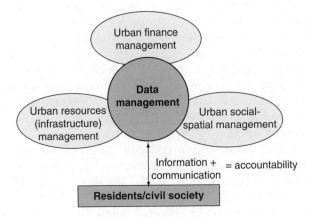

Figure 11.10 From data management to information flow and accountability.

to track and understand. Finally, the use of a soft boundary approach and the use of different BSUs for different levels of spatial scale provide a much better base for local decision-making around space and land management, taking the level of discussion down to the appropriate level, which is the local area, and linking this discussion directly with the sub-government administration.

UNESCO talks about e-governance in terms of e-administration and e-information. While this may be valid, it is also problematic, primarily because the thinking that underpins its construct is situated within the Anglo-Saxon *Weltanschauung*, with its focus on the individual. It is far better, and more effective, to think of data and information flows within the city as a system. In this systemic model there are two sets of flows, one relating to the system and one relating to individuals, and there are then internal and cross-(institutional) boundary flows from the city to the wider civil society. The nature of the relationship between these two is different and they should be treated separately, divided into public and private information, which can be described equally as indirect or direct impact information. The second of these relates directly to the individual or family, for example a title deed, planning permission or an invoice. The first relates to development issues and is the one used here.

The outcome: a new urban development paradigm for a sustainable future

At this point the discussion of all the different aspects of urban infrastructure, first described in Chapter 8, has been concluded, enabling us to bring together and integrate all these into a single conceptual framework for urban development. This process began in Chapter 8 with the generic conceptual model illustrated in Figure 8.2. That chapter then went on to explore the nature of the development drivers and the issue of affordability. Subsequent chapters, including this one, then focused on the three components of urban infrastructure that feature in the central portion of the relational diagram: the value system, the technology (technology systems) and the political regulatory framework (roles and relationships). The outcome was an updated version of this three-component relationship, illustrated by Figure 11.2. Here the basic triangle of interaction is still present, but all of its components have been adapted to the increased complexity of the modern world.

The final step is to pull these various relational diagrams together to create a complete and integrated model for urban development in the secondary towns. The result is the relational model shown in Figure 11.11. This model demonstrates the way in which governance can be seen as a reflection of the value-based surround of society, while at the same time operating within the higher-level value system that defines the social,

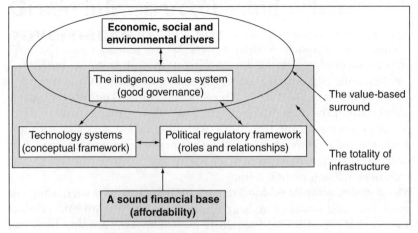

Figure *11.11* The relational model that defines infrastructure.

economic and environmental imperatives that are themselves situated within specific society-related value systems. It is a complex social model that is both varied and dynamic, changing ever more rapidly as the new digital world shortens response times.

Not all (western) specialists in good governance would necessarily support this contention that good governance is an integral part of the value-based surround. Some might argue, for example, that defining roles and relationships is also part of their remit. This book argues that such a point of view would be a specifically western interpretation, directly linked to the needs of a mature and developed society; and that this view cannot be transferred to societies where roles and relationships are still being formulated, and where the urban development model is still evolving. Thus, roles and relationships continue to form the second component of the inner triangular relationship, which is situated within the institutional framework component. Technology, which has been explored within the context of a systemic conceptual model of development, provides the third component.

Everything in this model for development is underpinned by a sound financial base. The urban development model described here returns infrastructure to its roots as a driver of that development process. In this role, when applied to the secondary towns, infrastructure becomes the main, and often the only, driver of economic development. When we integrate this with the role as a driver of social and environmental development, which we do through the linkage of economic development to the green urban economy, then we must rethink our approach to financing. This new approach is then driven by two innovations. The first involves repositioning affordability, moving it upwards from the individual to the metabolic city, which is where the real affordability crunch occurs. This repositioning enables us to achieve social equity. The second is then concerned with providing finance at this level. By creating a metabolic city where infrastructure is the driver of environmental sustainability through its mediation of resource flows, we can generate an integrated model of urban financing that incorporates all the urban resource systems within one financial management system.

When it then comes to funding this system, the Ethiopian study in Chapter 7 showed how well-managed towns can raise a significant portion of their capital needs for infrastructure internally. This funding then has to be supplemented from outside. Working entirely within the framework of a green urban economy means that a significant proportion of the remaining infrastructure investment requirements, particularly that part linked to high-value capital investment, can be integrated directly into global climate adaptation funds.

Finally, all of these changes pave the way for a locational transfer of the locus of knowledge generation. Because the model is specific to an African situation, as opposed to being a variation on a western 'global' model, and because the focus is on the secondary towns, the ability of external actors to control the intellectual space is reduced. This does not mean it will disappear; however, it does allow much greater opportunity and scope for African researchers and decision-makers to reclaim control over their own intellectual space and take back responsibility for their own development of the urban areas.

Chapter 12

Building African cities for a sustainable future

From values to value systems: the new global reality

Values are Universal; Value Systems are Interpretative

An African leader wins 49 per cent of the vote in a national election, assumes power and is considered undemocratic; a British Prime Minister gains a large parliamentary majority having received just 37 per cent of the popular vote and the outcome is considered democratic government. This is not a debate about values; it is a debate about value systems. For whichever group defines the dominant value system not only has immense international political leverage, that group also defines the global development agenda.

It is a commonly expressed western belief that all countries should operate within a framework guided by universal values, of which the most important are democracy and a respect for human rights; and these have been incorporated into the United Nations Charter, to which all member states subscribe. Those same western countries then believe that many countries, through their actions, fail to adopt these 'universal values' to which they have signed up. There are without doubt clear examples of where countries cynically and blatantly abuse these values, even as they continue to pay lip-service to them. Yet there are other cases where the countries in question genuinely believe they are implementing these values, while being accused by western countries of disregarding them. The question is: how does one country decide whether another country commits to these values in practice? To this there is only one answer: their actions are interpreted, partly by a set of rules and laws, but also by a set of (often preconceived) expectations.

When we look at ourselves in a mirror, we may sometimes feel surprised by how different we appear when compared to a photograph; and both of these appearances may be different again to an interpretation of how we look that is given to us by a member of our family or a close friend. Everything that we see around us is interpreted through a lens, and then has to be processed internally by the brain. It is an interpretation of reality, not reality itself.

It is the same with values. We can all sign up to the same set of universal values, but for these to be operationalised they have to be interpreted; and here, each society has its own cultural lens, which can be termed its value system. That value system is an outcome of many factors, from a philosophical interpretation of life itself (be it the nature of humanity, or the interpretation of roles and relationships), through the influence of internal and external social forces, to externalities such as dietary beliefs or the impact of climate and the local physical environment. People in the West may accept this distinction at a superficial level, but they generally find it hard to internalise the full implications, as indeed do all societies when exploring how others see the world. As a result, people who live within a particular society have a tendency to confuse the concept of values as principles with the value system, when in fact they are applying the latter: their own interpretation of how these principles should be applied. This is a perfectly natural response, since we all exist within a value system of one form or another. What makes it problematic is the impact on others when the world moves through a phase where there is a dominant value system coincident with military and economic hegemony. That is the situation that has defined our recent history.

The values of democracy and respect for human rights described earlier can be termed high-level values; that is, they are the core values that provide a frame of reference for action. This framework is then translated into practice through the creation of a set of roles and relationships that define the society. Yet roles and relationships exist on many different levels, a reality that has major implications when one country becomes involved with another on the basis of values. This book has shown that when one country does become involved with another in this way, using values as the basis for its interaction, then it is drawn into every aspect, and every level, of the framework of roles and relationships that operate in that second country. That is the problem with development aid. Values permeate all levels of society. Becoming involved with another country on the basis of values means that there is no area of activity, no level in society, where it is possible to draw the line and disengage.

It is also the core issue in defining western bilateral and multilateral relationships. By using values as the basis for engagement, countries become locked into an engagement with the application of those values at every level of society within the recipient country; yet the way in which that engagement is operationalised stems from a perspective generated within the value system of the donor country. The full implications of this dichotomy have been most strongly felt in sub-Saharan Africa, where the imposition of a dominant external value system has done immeasurable harm.

Africa and the West

The term 'African development' is a paradox: a statement that contradicts itself. For while development may take place on African soil, the ideas and practices that underpin development practice are almost exclusively western. This is most clearly seen in the field of urban development, where virtually every concept, from early colonisation to the present day, has emerged from a western worldview, or *Weltanschauung*, that is embedded in a western value system. The result of this intervention is there for all to see: a subcontinent that suffers from underdevelopment on a large scale.

In looking to find the reasons for this, this book has shown the full extent to which there is a strong correlation between the repeated failure of urban development models in Africa and the external dominance of Africa's intellectual space. It is not suggested that the extent of this intellectual dominance was a deliberate act; nor does the book imply some form of conspiracy theory. The correlation is predicated rather on the recognition that a dominant culture imposes its own value system on the world, and once it has been in power for a sufficiently long period, so that personal experience of the past is lost, this dominant value system comes to be accepted as a universal truth. That is the condition the world finds itself in at the present time. The only reason we can explore the nature of this dominant value system now is because it has begun to collapse, with the slow disintegration, after two hundred years, of British and American military and economic power that enabled these countries to impose Anglo-Saxon economic, social and political hegemony.

When demographics and military might were in their favour, western colonists sought to destroy indigenous populations and the indigenous culture of the countries they occupied. From the numerous tribes of Latin America, through Native North Americans, to the Aborigines of Australia, the list is long and painful. The approach to Africa, though, was different: here the indigenous population was seen as a resource to be exploited as slaves that could be used to fuel western development. The result was a foundation for underdevelopment so well chronicled by Walter Rodney in his book *How Europe Underdeveloped Africa* (1973). Except in Ethiopia, the indigenous people of the subcontinent did not have a written language, and, as a result, almost every piece of knowledge, every perception, that we have of sub-Saharan Africa has been interpreted through a western lens, to an extent that simply does not apply in any other region of the world.

This is the real issue around which the discussion of development in Africa should turn. It is not about whether aid is good or bad. The real issue is that of exploring the impact of a condition whereby one value system dominates another to the extent that the western value system has dominated Africa. We live in the present, and everything we see around us is interpreted through a lens of interpretative perception, which is why the introduction in Chapter 1 went back to history, and the Roman Empire, to see the full impact of cultural domination on this scale. Western domination of Africa exists in every sphere, in everything we do; it is embedded in our psyche and is part of the air that we, as Westerners, breathe. Words and statements of intent alone cannot change that, though they can undoubtedly help. It is only through an understanding, and acceptance, of that reality that we can begin to change the relationship between the West and Africa.

The power of a dominant value system

Aid is the vehicle through which western countries dominate African development, but it is not the driver; for that, we have to move up a level to the philosophy that underpins the concept of donor aid when used in a developmental, rather than in a humanitarian, framework. From a philosophical perspective, 'international development', which defines the basis for the relationship between Africa and the western world, is a purely western construct, situated within a specific value system that is intimately linked to the Judaeo-Christian-humanist worldview. Within this framework, though, is a sub-text. As regards the way in which the construct evolved, the values having the highest level of influence are those of the dominant subculture that is commonly referred to as Anglo-Saxon.

In its original form, the term 'Anglo-Saxon' dates back to the fifth century and refers to the Germanic tribes that invaded Britain during that period. Its current usage, though, reflects a wider meaning: *le monde anglo-saxon* (the Anglo-Saxon world),[1] which was coined by the French to describe a specific socio-economic organisational form and associated culture. This culture was spread through much of the world initially by British colonialism, though it gradually came to be dominated by the United States, as that country evolved into a hegemonic power in the period after 1945.

So why is this dominant subculture so important for Africa today? To begin with, there is the simple fact that embedding a value system in development does not make it a universal truth; it simply reflects one specific cultural interpretation of a relationship. Unfortunately, when one group dominates virtually all the literature on development, this integration of a value system into development is taken for granted, and eventually becomes an assumed truth. The first step in exploring African development is, therefore, to disengage current ideas on development from the notion that they somehow reflect a universal truth.

This disentanglement of interpretation perceptions has been aided in recent years by the re-emergence of China as a world power. This allows us, for the first time, to see how another dominant power approaches its relationship with Africa. Currently, when Westerners look at Chinese involvement in sub-Saharan Africa there is a tendency to home in on, and then criticise, the fact that China continues to trade with countries that the West deems as unsuitable partners, primarily because of the record those countries have on human rights. In taking this view, the West totally misunderstands the Chinese worldview.

The difference between the western and the Chinese worldview, which is so clearly evident in the different approaches to their relationship with Africa, actually revolves around one fundamental question: are values an integral part of a relationship between nation-states? Europeans and Americans would say yes to this question; the Chinese would say no. The first group believes in the universality of values; the other that values are embedded in, and the sole concern of, each country, and hence involvement in another country's value system represents interference in the internal affairs of that country. So, Westerners believe that universal values define a universal value system; the Chinese that value systems are interpretative and distinct.

It is not my intent here to discuss the relative merits or otherwise of different philosophies. I would suggest, though, that the western and Chinese views represent something of a polar duality, and that the reality lies somewhere between these two positions. It has been the intent in this book to show that even though societies have shared values, the perceptions of what constitutes a value system, and what defines core values, are different, and integral to specific societies. Furthermore, these individual value systems are part of a society's sense of existence. As such, they provide a framework for generating, sustaining and applying knowledge. The use of a value system to create this framework is described through the German term *Weltanschauung*.

Every society, then, has its own *Weltanschauung*. The difference is that the western world, and within that the Anglo-Saxon world, through its hegemonic domination of intellectual space, has fallen into the trap common to all dominant cultures: that of believing that its *Weltanschauung* is no longer simply a part of its own culture, but instead represents some form of universal truth. As western control is loosened, though, it becomes possible to see the extent to which this is simply one way of viewing the world, one set of ideas, one interpretation of knowledge.

It is this exploration of the role of values, and the associated *Weltanschauungen*, that provides the starting point for the journey into African development. The point of departure is the recognition that international development is embedded in a specific value system, defined by western countries. This cultural group, which is quite diverse, then has within it a powerful cultural sub-group that has been able to impose its value system on the rest of the world through its political, economic and military dominance – a dominance that has existed now for two hundred years. That dominant subculture is referred to broadly as Anglo-Saxon. An acceptance of this reality, then, opens the way to explore the next important question: to what extent does this imposition of a cultural value system help or hinder other countries in setting out their own path towards development?

There are benefits associated with social and economic domination, particularly in the early stages. Trade in particular is made easier, which in turn provides the basis for wealth generation. Education generally flourishes. People move around more freely and carry ideas – all of which leads to a comforting sense of global security, provided, of course, that one is inside the system. In reality, though, only some of the inherent differences between groups are addressed; the majority are simply suppressed or become dormant. Thus, the difficulties tend to manifest themselves most when domination begins to weaken and the forces holding the hegemonic system in place begin to disintegrate. That is what is happening in the world today, as American global hegemony gives way to a new regionalism. In this context the desire of countries previously trapped within the hegemony against their will begins to manifest itself; which is why it becomes a time of increased risk.

Yet it is also a time of opportunity for many, particularly those oppressed by the impact of cultural hegemony, where this new space opens the way for countries to pursue a more independent path towards development. However, success in achieving this goal during this period of uncertainty requires above all else an understanding of the nature of the dominant value system, and the extent to which it operates, together with an understanding of, and deep belief in, one's own value system.

Acquiring such an understanding is not as easy as it seems. Because the Anglo-Saxon value system is so embedded in the fundamental concept of international development, it has shaped the IMF, the World Bank and all of the UN development agencies, making it extremely difficult for other countries to create an independent development path. Even so, some countries have been better able to exploit this hegemonic collapse than others, often for different reasons. Size and power are clearly important here, as China is able to demonstrate so clearly. So too is a strong indigenous culture that can provide an anchor, allowing countries to hold on to, or rediscover, their own value system even after centuries of occupation and external oppression. Poland provides one example from the early twentieth century, while Vietnam provides a good example today. And finally, language also plays a role, with countries that have a primary language of communication other than English having a natural barrier that limits the power of Anglo-Saxon domination, even when there is a strong historical linkage, as with Brazil, for example.

This, then, is the setting for the exploration of development in sub-Saharan Africa. This exploration is not straightforward, since the panorama that we are viewing resembles an abstract painting more than it does a clear portrait. Simply the fact that large portions of the continent fell under French, Belgian or Portuguese colonial rule, for example, is itself a confusing issue. To simplify the analysis, the focus of the book has been primarily on anglophone Africa, although it can be argued that the Anglo-Saxon dominance of the international development agencies has extended that influence and had a major impact on those other countries, particularly in the period since independence. The original hypothesis of this book rested on the belief that sub-Saharan Africa was particularly vulnerable to external western, and particularly Anglo-Saxon, influence in a way that is unique. In addition, the capacity to benefit from that imposed system was much less than in India, for example, where the country has managed to integrate aspects of its colonial heritage without losing its indigenous identity. Africa on the other hand has been severely damaged by that imposed culture, since the imported model was so fundamentally different from that of the subjugated peoples. The way in which the book has chosen to develop this hypothesis is through an exploration of development, and specifically urban development, since this is where the external impact is strongest and most easily defined.

Value systems, development and decision-making

The way in which development is grounded in a value system is illustrated in Figure 12.1, demonstrating how the linkage between the value system and the decision-making process, explored in the previous section, often passes through a *development construct*, creating a strong interlinkage between the three.

The Chinese believe that decision-making can be divorced from the value system, as was indicated earlier. This separation can work while a relationship is kept at 'arm's length', working at the interface between two societies, something that is possible, up to a point, when the focus of the interaction is trade. Arguably, though, this is because trade can be perceived as being aloof from specific development constructs. So, let's turn to large-scale development (infrastructure) projects, such as those associated with water resources, energy or transport. Again there is an attempt to avoid engaging with the reality of Figure 12.1. None the less, the relationship between values and decision begins to impinge, as the

Figure 12.1 The interrelationship between values, development and decision-making.

international debate on the interrelationship between large dams, development and the environment, for example, illustrates quite clearly. The critical exploration of this relationship, though, comes as development moves closer to people and impacts on their lives more directly. Thus, the reality of this relationship between values, development and decision-making grows as we move downwards through society. The implication is that the current relational model used by the Chinese is actually quite reasonable while the focus of the interaction remains limited to trade. However, the Chinese are now becoming increasingly involved in large-scale infrastructure development. Here the relationship between values and decision-making is going to impinge, but it may still continue to be ignored, possibly. The real impact will come once their involvement begins to move down to a level closer to the local communities, as it must if the current wave of Chinese migration to Africa continues. At that point the Chinese government will have to engage with this question of values, whether it wishes to or not.

When we turn to western countries, we are faced with a situation that is diametrically opposite to the Chinese approach. Here we have a relationship in which development and decision-making are both totally embedded in values. From an internal (western) perspective, Europeans, for example, would argue that their primary concern lies solely with the promotion of core values, in particular human rights and democracy – to which the Americans and the British would probably add the promotion of free-market capitalism. These core values, though, have to be operationalised if they are to have any meaning, and that is the point at which the debate opens up, since the interpretation of these values is situated with a specific *Weltanschauung*, namely the worldview of the country defining the values. It was Henry Kissinger, discussing British foreign policy in the aftermath of the European Napoleonic Wars, who said that '[a] nation will evaluate a [foreign] policy in terms of its domestic legitimization, because it has no other standard of judgment' (1957, p. 328). That is the heart of the matter, and it applies equally, and perhaps even more so, to perceptions of development, where the word 'foreign' could equally well be replaced by the term 'international development'. This would lead to an adaptation of Kissinger's analysis that would read:

> *A nation will evaluate its policy on international development in terms of its domestic legitimisation, because it has no other standard of judgement.*

At this point, western countries might argue that this statement is invalid, since the legitimisation is given by the United Nations through a set of internationally agreed values. That is where the fundamental misconception arises. The values, as principles, may be those with which all members of the United Nations agree. The practice, however, is based upon the indigenous value system, not the international value principles, because principles can only be operationalised through the value system. And it is to those members' own country, their own experience, their own value system that they turn for experiential confirmation of how values translate into practice; that is the basis for domestic legitimisation.

This then leads to the question, whenever the West engages with Africa, of 'Exactly which elements of the value system are we really dealing with?' This question of course dominates the western–Chinese debate, as it does many of the international points of engagement where the countries of the West, and particularly the United States, interface with other nations. However, in the context of African development, this debate is something of a red herring – a diversion from the real, and much more fundamental, issue. The whole construct of international development aid involves donors much deeply in a recipient society than do bilateral trade relations. And in going deeper, the donors tend to become more intimately involved in the recipient country's policies, structures and institutions. At that point the very act of becoming more deeply involved demands an expansion of the broad value system to the local level, thereby integrating sub-national roles and relationships. At this point, where one country is so deeply involved in another, the only rationality it has for making decisions at that level derives from its own experience or, more correctly, its own interpretation of its own experience; that is, its *Weltanschauungen*. This is the tipping point. For each intervention is embedded within its own *Weltanschauung*; and the question is, where does this imposition of these *Weltanschauungen* end?

Why the western value system is so damaging for Africa

The impact of this process was demonstrated in Figure 2.3, which showed the way in which the global political, economic and social transformation that took place in the 1990s entrenched this process of transfer. The result was to expand the internal relationship shown in Figure 12.1 to embrace this western influence. The major changes that took place in the development arena during the 1980s and 1990s were, at heart, changes in value systems; with ultimate success going to the Anglo-Saxon value system. Anglo-Saxon hegemony had reached its pinnacle, a domination of such a magnitude that one historian even called it the end of history (Fukuyama, 1992).

The impact of this change was perhaps rather more prosaic in Africa, but nonetheless powerful. Figure 12.2 takes the linear relationship shown in Figure 12.1 and illustrates how it was used by the West to create a global generic model in its own image. This is seen on the left-hand side of the relational model. However, far from being a global model, this was a specific interpretation of event situated within the Anglo-Saxon value

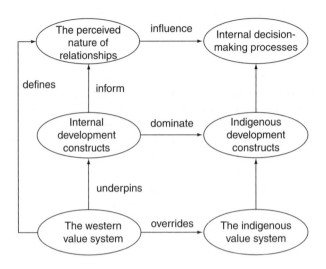

Figure 12.2 The impact of Anglo-Saxon control over the global value system on decision-making in Africa.

system. As a result, it was not universally accepted, but instead was imposed, using a variety of different mechanisms. This gave many developing countries a quite different interpretation of the linear path described in Figure 12.1, which can be illustrated by the path shown on the right-hand side of Figure 12.2.

This construct affected countries differently. In some it caused a backlash that led to physical revolt; in others it caused societies to turn inwards for solutions, rediscovering their own value system and drawing strength from this to build their own models of development, or to redefine their relationship with the West. In this period of rapid global change, though, it was the countries of sub-Saharan Africa, with the partial exception of South Africa, that were most vulnerable to the influence of this external value system. There were a number of reasons why that was the case, as discussed in the book: for example, the prior physical colonisation; the lack of a written language; the exposure to English as a medium; the weak academic and intellectual base; poverty. All of these together defined Africa as being uniquely vulnerable to western influence, thereby enabling the subsequent imposition of the collective Anglo-Saxon *Weltanschauungen* as the basis for defining the subcontinent's development path. The outcome was a colonisation of Africa's intellectual space that has left insufficient room for these countries to drive their own development process.

The period of total dominance described here was of course short-lived. The terrorist attack on New York on 11 September 2001 shattered the illusion of monolithic power. Debilitating wars in Iraq and Afghanistan showed the limits of military power. And the financial crash of 2008 called into question the very basis of the free-market capitalist system. Of course there will be recovery, but the world of Anglo-Saxon hegemony has peaked and a new world order is emerging. The focus on China leads some to define a new global duopoly, but this is not the immediate future. Instead, the world is entering a new regionalism, one that could open the door to a new African dawn. However, this dawn can only come about if African countries can regain control over their intellectual space.

China and Africa: changing the dynamic, but is the West listening?

The growth of Chinese influence in Africa is undoubtedly of immense significance. Some might argue that this growth of influence alone is sufficient to change Africa's relationship with the West; this book would disagree. Growing trade with China provides an immense opportunity, but the Chinese relationship alone will not create the space to free Africa from intellectual colonialism. That freedom can only come through an exploration of Africa's relationship with the West. In some ways, Chinese engagement has actually made this exploration more difficult, for there is now a three-way flow. As Liu Guijan, the Chinese Special Representative for African Affairs, so succinctly phrased it:

> As Africa seeks to position its economies within today's changing competitive landscape, there is a need for increased trilateral cooperation, integrating the interests of China and the Western world in Africa. 'There is a possibility for an alignment of these new emerging interests.... We have different priorities in policy design and different approaches in engaging the African continent. But we have to ensure that cooperation would be a win–win trilateral process that will bring the advantages of the Chinese way of doing things together with the advantages of Western donors so that all African countries will equally benefit.'[2]

From an African perspective this trilateral relationship will not work by playing the one against the other; instead, the relationship has to be based upon partnership. Unfortunately, this is a term that is used too glibly by western governments, without sufficient exploration of what it actually means. For there can be no partnership while one value system continues to dominate another. African countries have to engage with this issue on a fundamental level if they are to change the nature of their relationship with the West.

China's involvement, then, makes this exploration of western control over African intellectual space even more important, because if Africa, as a continent, is to engage with both China and the West as an equal partner, it first has to regain control over its own intellectual space. This book seeks to promote a dialogue between Africa and the West that will help it to do so. By showing the extent to which the western value system dominates the relationship, and the way that western, and specifically the Anglo-Saxon, *Weltanschauungen* play themselves out within that relationship, through control over Africa's intellectual space, and the resultant prescription of Africa's development direction, this book seeks to provide a new basis for a sustainable, long-term relationship between Africa and the West. For it to do that, though, we need to first understand how these *Weltanschauungen* play themselves out in practice.

The application of the Anglo-Saxon value system in Africa

Chapter 1 defined what it termed the four thematic 'forces of influence' that define the approach to urban development in sub-Saharan Africa, which were then explored in greater detail in the chapters that followed. Returning to these forces of influence, having completed the analysis, we can see the extent to which the western value system, and in particular its British derivative, can be seen to drive Africa's development process – primarily through the linkage between the value system and the determination of roles and relationships. This stage of the review summarises the forces of influence at this higher level of decision-making; later, the discussion will return to the impact of these forces of influence as they impact at the level of development practice.

The first external force of influence, the colonial historical context, sets the framework within which governments function. In this context its full impact comes later, with the debate on decentralisation; hence, it will be discussed last. The other three forces of influence each represent a component of the value system that predefines a particular subset of roles and relationships, and in doing so contributes to the disempowerment of African countries, leading to a loss of internal domestic legitimacy and enhancing control over their intellectual space. This is achieved in the following way:

Force of external influence 2: Defining the form and nature of the private sector management model for water supply and other utility infrastructure services. This is concerned with the imposition of the Anglo-Saxon economic model, and the extent to which free-market capitalism predefines both the roles of and the nature of the relationship between the public and the private sectors.

Force of external influence 3: The basic needs approach. This gives clear definition to the individual in its relationship with the State, and is based upon the Anglo-Saxon view of the centrality of the individual in society. At the same time, it operates through a humanitarian interpretation of development that has its roots in the Anglo-Saxon paternalistic view of charity that rose to prominence in the Victorian era. Finally, it draws from this same Anglo-Saxon tradition a specific interpretation of community, seeking to define it as a grouping that can only have legitimacy if it exists outside of formal political structures.

Force of external influence 4: Defining a specific urban planning paradigm. This presents a quite specific interpretation of the relationship people have between one another, governed by control over the structuring of space. In this case it is situated within a specifically British value system that is strongly linked to, and indeed flows from, the economic and social models that underpin the two previous forces of influence. The contributors to the volume edited by Sanyal (2005), among others, have illustrated the extent to which the nature of planning is comparative and situated within a specific culture, termed here a value-based surround, while the specific linkage described here can be seen to have emerged from an 'interdependency of ideology and planning' that was associated particularly with the 1980s Thatcher government in the United Kingdom (Rode, 2006).

Force of external influence 1: The colonial legacy. This of course has many facets and a wide sphere of influence. The one most relevant here is the form and structure of government, which has played a major role in obstructing the process of meaningful decentralisation in Africa. The British parliamentary system imposed two-party, confrontational politics on peoples whose own form of societal decision-making was fundamentally different. This had lasting negative consequences, since it imposed a specific set of roles and relationships at a national political level. The system also introduced a centralised, vertical-silo line government model developed for a rural society, which in turn defined the nature of roles and relationships between politicians and civil servants, again negatively. The most important impact, though, derived from the imposition of the concept of delegated authority, which defines the relationships between central and local government in such a way as to prevent meaningful decentralisation from ever functioning effectively.

These four forces of influence were then supported by control over the knowledge resource base that defined the development agenda in Africa, and ensured that all thinking about development was retained within the western value system. The fact that this arose more by default than intent may rationalise it but does not change the outcome. It is this aspect of the external control that provides the cement holding the four forces of influence in place and ensuring their continuity, since the relationship between intellectual thought and practical application operates within a symbiotic loop.

Finally, as Chapter 4 highlighted, there was one final piece to this jigsaw puzzle, namely the British policy process, which again was imposed on anglophone Africa but has since become dominant elsewhere. Policy formulation provides the basic tool of the nation-state, converting societal goals into practical realities. As a result, the way that this process is applied is itself strongly aligned with the nation's value system. The British approach to policy is strongly empirical and output orientated. The result of being so product or outcomes driven is to make policy reactive rather than proactive, turning it more and more into strategy. In this model there is insufficient space given to the exploration of the *problématique*, which in turn results in lack of questioning of the basic precepts of development. There is also little if any space in this policy process for developing new conceptual frameworks.

The ability of a country to define its own internal roles and relationships is a cornerstone of a nation-state. Together, the forces of influence described here leave African governments with little, if any, latitude to create their own roles and relationships, or even to pursue their historical, indigenous societal form and structure. The result is that African governments have simply no space to manoeuvre; they are caught in an intellectual straitjacket that is controlled by the need for them to conform to the western value system in almost every aspect of their development.

Why Africa is uniquely vulnerable to external influence

To date, this chapter has focused on the nature of external influence and control. What, though, of the other side of the coin? What is the role of the African countries themselves – for surely they play a part in all of the events described here? Unfortunately, the way Africa is viewed by many in the West remains trapped in a paternalistic, and often patronising, framework of analysis. African countries have emerged from an imperial past that stripped them of culture and dignity, while transporting millions of today's Africans' ancestors into slavery. Now they are faced with a new struggle that is of a similar magnitude, this time seeking to free themselves from western domination of their intellectual space.

There are signs that this process of intellectual emancipation is now beginning to happen. However, it would happen a great deal faster if we understood how the mechanisms of control over this intellectual control of Africans' development landscape work. At issue here is the need to understand the full extent to which African countries are vulnerable to the external forces of influence described earlier. Recognising that this is a vulnerability that exists in intellectual space defines the first vulnerability: the lack of critical intellectual mass across much of Africa. This leads on directly to the second area of vulnerability, which is that Africa has been almost entirely dependent upon external agencies to create development models. The outcome is that African countries continue to have a limited indigenous institutional memory from which to extrapolate new ideas. Essentially, there is simply too little absorptive capacity. Finally, there is the underlying problem that the western models of development are themselves deeply flawed, but because of the first two weaknesses, African governments and researchers are simply not in a position to challenge these models. Each of these aspects of vulnerability will be discussed further in what follows.

The lack of critical intellectual mass

The term 'critical mass' was first used to describe the initiation of a chain reaction in nuclear physics. In that context it was defined as 'the smallest mass of a fissionable material that will sustain a nuclear chain reaction at a constant level' (*American Heritage Dictionary*, 2006). However, once defined, it quickly outgrew its scientific roots and was adopted as a concept that could equally be used to describe social phenomena. In this latter context the concept of critical mass explains how there is a need for a minimum number of people in a like group, comprising a minority, to be able to develop themselves and their ideas, and make their ideas heard and accepted by others.

If we look at this concept of critical mass in a social context, it is the United States that provides the most interesting and valuable experience, particularly with regard to the needs of its African-American minority. One of the most lucid and authoritative explorations of this concept was provided by Sandra Day O'Connor, the first female member of the United States Supreme Court. The background was an article in the *Los Angeles Times* in which she invoked 'critical mass' in her justification for holding the concept of 'diversity' as a compelling governmental interest, thereby allowing race to be considered as a factor in admissions decisions. This is explained in the following legal analysis:

> In *Grutter v. Bollinger*, the Supreme Court upheld the University of Michigan's admissions policy, affirming Justice Powell's Bakke diversity rationale. In an opinion written by Justice O'Connor, the Court

held that the Law School had a 'compelling interest in attaining a diverse body', endorsing 'Justice Powell's view that student body diversity is a compelling state interest that can justify the use of race in university admissions.' In reaching this holding, Justice O'Connor discussed the 'critical mass' goal as being distinct from the goal of fulfilling racial quotas. Justice O'Connor's opinion cited to the record of the District Court trial, in which the Law School's Director of Admissions at the time of Grutter's petition testified that the admissions staff was instructed to consider an applicant's race as one of many factors. This was to 'ensure that a critical mass of underrepresented minority students would be reached so as to realize the educational benefits of a diverse student body.' Justice O'Connor also cited the testimony of the Law School's subsequent Director of Admissions, who defined critical mass as 'meaningful representation,' or a number that 'encourages underrepresented minority students to participate in the classroom and not feel isolated.' Finally, Justice O'Connor referred to the testimony of a professor at the Law School, which contended that 'when a critical mass of underrepresented minority students is present, racial stereotypes lose their force because non-minority students learn there is no "minority viewpoint," but rather a variety of viewpoints among minority students.' Justice O'Connor's discussion of the critical mass rationale was significant for how it impacted her justification of the Law School's race-conscious admissions policy.

Critical mass is a tool for achieving diversity, and Justice O'Connor emphasises the benefits of diversity in the school and society in her opinion: 'Numerous studies show that student body diversity promotes learning outcomes, and better prepares students for an increasingly diverse workforce and society, and better prepares them as professionals.... These benefits are not theoretical but real, as major American businesses have made clear that the skills needed in today's increasingly global marketplace can only be developed through exposure to widely diverse people, cultures, ideas, and viewpoints.'

(Law and Letters, 2006)

It is the contention of this book that the same rationale can be applied to the exploration of development constructs in intellectual space generally. In this area, African intellectuals and academics simply do not have the critical mass that is necessary to impinge on the dominant western *Weltanschauungen*. What we are dealing with here is a huge imbalance in intellectual capital, with the stronger side having both a dominant and a domineering value system that it seeks to impose at every level of development, in a context that is itself the outcome of physical colonisation superimposed on previous centuries of oppression. When viewed from within the totality of these actions, past and present, it is argued that *the underlying reason why the majority of countries in sub-Saharan Africa are failing to achieve development lift-off is due to their inability to achieve a critical mass, in terms of academic and intellectual capacity, sufficient to enable them to take control of their own intellectual space and thereby define their own set of roles and relationships best suited to their own societies, which is a prerequisite for taking control over their own development agenda.*

It is for this reason that the book unashamedly uses the term 'colonisation of Africa's intellectual space' to describe the western approach to African development. On the African side, the failure to achieve critical mass is compounded by the second cause, related to absorptive capacity.

Weak adsorptive capacity and a weak institutional memory

Absorptive capacity is a complex and multifaceted topic. None the less, by unbundling the concept a little it is possible to identify the main elements that contribute, of which four are particularly important: the low number of skilled and qualified people; the multiplicity and the fractured nature of these external interventions; the conflicting knowledge base between mature and developing societies; and the rapid fluctuation and rate of change in the externally driven development agenda.

The low skills base

The low skills base aspect has received both attention and recognition in the international media, driven by stories of how the western countries, while desperately keen to limit immigration, are nonetheless happy to take as many doctors and nurses as Africa can produce. While they are doing so, the level of external support for developing universities and boosting graduate numbers remains extremely low on the external development agenda. The problems caused by low graduate numbers can be overcome in theory; the difficulty arises when the other constraints are superimposed.

Multiple interventions and their fractured nature

The best analogy for the current development scenario in Africa is the Tower of Babel, that biblical structure overwhelmed by a cacophony of conflicting voices. In urban development the book has shown how the arena of activity was divided, first by sector and then by agency. The 1980s saw the rise to global prominence of that most famous of American inventions, the consumer, who rapidly took his or her place as the primary target of development. This rise of the consumer led to further fragmentation as development initiatives were moved down to the level of the individual. Chapter 2 showed how the number of external actors involved in Africa rose significantly after the 1980s with the change in the overall approach to development, a move that was further enhanced by the Millennium Development Goals (MDGs). All these changes place an enormous burden on already understaffed governments. There is a constant stream of external donors, ranging in size from the World Bank to the smallest charity, passing through the offices of ministers and their senior staff. When not in meetings, those staff have to prepare ever more complex proposals for development assistance; and when not doing that, they must read the numerous reports that come from this myriad of consultants employed by the external agencies. Finally, this last part is itself made more complex by the conflicting advice given in these reports, which will generally reflect the views and value system of the different commissioning donors. This is Africa's world of information overload. How does a country build an indigenous institutional memory under these circumstances?

Conflicting needs in the knowledge base

It is not only the number of graduates a country produces that matters; it is also the choice of subject. This is not simply a debate about ratios, whether between arts and science or between humanities and engineering, though that is certainly one aspect of the discussion. More critical is the linkage between the nature of education and the phase of development. Using urban development as an example, mature cities, with their installed infrastructure base and housing stock, face a range of issues that can often be addressed most effectively by specialist expertise. Universities in turn can produce specialists on the scale required, because graduate numbers are high and competition strong. When cities are developing rapidly, the best form of expertise is that provided by generalists who can manage a range of interrelated issues.

We are faced with a situation, then, where western countries increasingly fund narrow specialist areas of development, in line with their own needs and their own perceptions of development. African countries are then expected to match these skills by providing graduates with the same profile, which they do in limited numbers by sending their students to western universities to acquire that specialist knowledge. In practice, doing so does not contribute to solutions but simply compounds the problems raised previously.

The rate of change of external priorities

During 2010 the development aid budget of three major western donors was disrupted and underwent quite dramatic change. In the Netherlands the failure to form a government for eight months following an inconclusive election created stasis in the country's ministry responsible for development aid; and when a new government finally emerged, it signalled a significant shift in its external development policy direction. In Sweden the national development agency, SIDA, underwent its biggest internal convulsion in decades as the centre-right government consolidated its hold on power and sought to redefine the basis for Swedish development aid. And in Britain a change of government and a spending review of unprecedented proportions created even more uncertainty in a development agency that already changes its approach to external development programmes more often than most people upgrade their mobile phones. It takes approximately eight years to educate and train a person leaving school to a point where they can accept a high level of responsibility and begin to take decisions. This period probably corresponds quite well with the cyclic change in the development priorities of external agencies as they move from one 'big idea' to the next.

Poor or inappropriate development models

It is this third area of vulnerability that provided the framework of analysis for this book. The existing models of development, and in particularly the urban models relating to infrastructure and planning, are seriously flawed, as is evidenced everywhere by the chronically underdeveloped cities that exist across Africa. The inability of African governments to manage the urbanisation process is blamed for this, but the development models are not African! Virtually every single conceptual idea underpinning African development has come from external agencies, so whose failure is this really? Western control over Africa's intellectual space, working in conjunction with the vulnerabilities described above, locks African countries in a downward spiral. One objective of this book has been to demonstrate the extent to which external control is responsible for this condition of chronic underdevelopment in urban Africa. It is only when we are able to recognise the true extent of the failure of external models that we can even begin to explore alternatives. In creating an alternative model for urban development, as this book has done, the intent is not to impose another external solution; rather, it is to provide a basis for an indigenous debate on urban development that is grounded in African experience and African realities. And this alternative is based upon a complete rethinking of the role that urban infrastructure plays in the emerging secondary towns of Africa in the twenty-first century.

Where urban development went astray: misunderstanding the role of infrastructure in society

To a large degree, urban infrastructure is a victim of its own success. In the late nineteenth century, Britain and the United States used engineering and technology to create a comprehensive urban system that later became known as centralised network infrastructure. This was hugely successful but brought its own problems, primarily because it created a hugely expensive, yet inflexible, fixed asset base. So, although this network may deteriorate, it continues to exist, which in turn has a limiting effect on innovative thinking, encouraging incremental rather than radical change. This makes sense in Europe and America, but has no rationality in places where this network infrastructure is limited or even non-existent in parts, as is the case in many of the secondary towns in Africa. So how do we approach urban infrastructure under these conditions? History shows us that there have been different approaches at different points in time. In each case, though, the approach was part of an incremental, responsive process.

The basic contention of this book is that we have lost our understanding of the role and nature of urban infrastructure, as it relates to the development of a society; because our 'understanding', to the extent that it exists at all, is defined by our current condition, as we perceive it, in the mature cities of the West. The only way that African countries can create sustainable urban development models, particularly in the secondary towns, which is where 70 per cent of their urban population resides, is by rediscovering the true nature of urban infrastructure and its real role in urban society.

A good place to begin the journey of rediscovery is through an understanding of where the original infrastructure model came from. The urban infrastructure base of all western countries today is so ubiquitous (for Westerners, at least) that it is easy to think of this as a global model. Such a view would be incorrect, mistaking the physical reality of network infrastructure for the underlying rationality that drove its initial construction. Chapter 3 compared the way that urban infrastructure evolved in the United Kingdom and the United States respectively. The analysis there found that, while there were commonalities, there were also differences. Three of these differences were so fundamental that the ensuing choice of one over the other is the primary cause of the current African urban condition of underdevelopment. These three differences are illustrated comparatively in Table 3.2, replicated on page 419.

At the beginning of the twentieth century there was a choice of two paths for urban development thinking in the Anglo-Saxon world, each associated with one of the developmental rationalities illustrated in this table, though clearly that choice was to a large extent implicit. Primarily

Table 3.2 The two developmental rationalities underpinning urban infrastructure

The perceptive constructs behind infrastructure	United States	United Kingdom
Its primary role in society	As a driver of development	As a support service in a wider urban development model
The vehicle	Technology	Engineering
The nature or form	Interactive (trinitarian)	Disaggregated

because of Britain's control over the colonies, which enabled it to replicate its model across the world, the British model dominated and became the de facto global model for developing countries, later to be adopted by the multilateral development agencies. This book has demonstrated that this was the wrong choice. Everything – absolutely everything – that has gone wrong in African urban development since that time can be traced back to that one mistake.

The best way to illustrate how this occurred is to track the evolution of the British model of modern urban infrastructure from its origins in the mid nineteenth century in England through its transfer and subsequent collapse in sub-Saharan Africa. Before doing that, however, we need to expand upon the third part of the rationality that relates to the nature or form of infrastructure.

The physical elements of urban infrastructure that we see around us – roads, drains, electricity cables, etc. – have tended to define our understanding of infrastructure. This is understandable, since these services are tangible: we can see and feel them, and they relate directly to our senses. Yet infrastructure is about more than physical components, which we can term 'technology'. The debate about privatisation in the 1980s related to operational systems, while the move towards addressing the needs of the poor in Africa has highlighted the social dimension of infrastructure.

It was the American sociologist Goulet who gave us the first clue to an understanding of a wider interpretation in the 1980s, when he defined three rationalities of development, which he termed technological, political and ethical (Goulet, 1986). When we apply that concept to a historical analysis of American infrastructure in its early evolutionary phase, then we see how that development process presented an ever-changing kaleidoscope of interactions between technology, value systems and management structures. Building on these ideas, we can see infrastructure as being situated within three components: a value-based surround; a technology base, and, if we update the term 'management' to modern times, an organisational framework, as illustrated in Figure 12.3. Goulet argued that

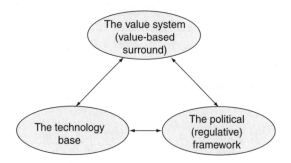

Figure 12.3 The three, interrelated, components of urban infrastructure.

'problems arise because each rationality [of the three described above] approaches the other two in reductionist fashion, seeking to impose its view of goals and procedures on the decision-making process' (1986). To address this inherent conflict, and in support of Goulet's wider argument, the book proposed that the three components that emerged from the historical analysis of infrastructure need to be seen as existing within a trinitarian relationship, where the three components are all part of one wider construct.

However, this was not the historical British approach. If we consider this model specifically, then Figure 12.4 illustrates how the interpretation

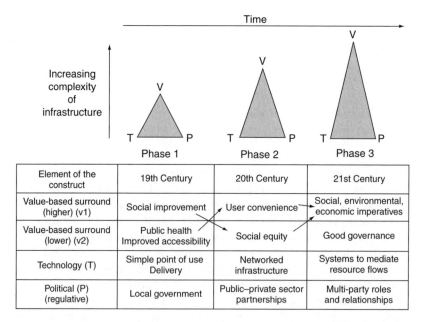

Figure 12.4 The changing nature of the wider infrastructure model over time.

of the three-component infrastructure changed over time. A key point to emerge from Chapter 3 was the extent to which the three components were disaggregated, particularly when compared to the American model, though we need to recognise here that we are talking of relationships that were generally implicit during their own time. That said, it is possible to define these more explicitly from a position of hindsight; and this is what has been done here.

Vertically, the diagram shows the three components of infrastructure. In an attempt to mirror the increasing complexity of infrastructure's role in society over time, the value-based surround (the value system) has been shown as operating on two 'levels', with the lower one nested within the higher one, in a relationship that reflects the societal priorities of the time. Viewed along the horizontal axis, the diagram divides the changes that have taken place into three phases, which correlate roughly to three distinct eras, defined here by the centuries in which they evolved or rose to prominence. It is important to view this diagram systemically rather than from a mechanistic perspective. The three phases shown here do not define distinct and separate conditions, where the one replaces the other. What exists is an evolutionary process in which new priorities and interpretations of society and its needs emerge which either absorb or modify the previous condition. In this way the earlier phases can be seen as nested within the later phases.

Phase 1: the nineteenth century

This first phase illustrates how the early urban development model that applied in Britain was primarily social in nature.[3] The origins of this value-based surround can be traced to two key events in British urban history: the Chadwick Report on the sanitary conditions of the urban poor in 1842, which led to Britain's Public Health Act; and the identification of the causal link between cholera and polluted water, deriving from the work of John Snow in London in the 1850s. While the second played a crucial role in defining Britain's future approach to water supply, it was actually the first that defined the overarching value-based surround. This resulted in the view of urban infrastructure that sees it primarily as providing the mechanism that enables the social improvement of the working classes living in poor areas. This was the dominant concept that underpinned the urban development agenda through the remaining period of the nineteenth century and into the early twentieth century. This social improvement model operated within a framework defined as 'public health', which then defined the parameters for the technology. The outcome was a simple piped system for water supply (which had been evolving since the end of the previous century) and another one for drains (which accommodated both storm water and sewerage).

In the British model the use of the term 'technology' is something of a misnomer. What we have here is better described as a technical approach, where the technical 'solution' exists in a causal framework with the value-based surround, for example insufficient water or poor drains, for which specific solutions were required. This approach had a hugely important impact on the way that infrastructure was perceived in the British model, since it led to a conflation of what are two quite distinct aspects of this wider 'technical' approach: technology and engineering. These are not the same thing at all. In reality, infrastructure is built around technology. In the British model, though, this physical aspect of infrastructure became intimately associated with engineering instead.

Finally, there was the political (regulatory) component. This too was being defined quite simply and clearly, in Britain at least. Using the powers of the Municipal Corporations Act of 1835, local government took responsibility for addressing this social need by taking responsibility for the technical solutions. Interestingly, though, it did so more to protect the autonomy of local government, which would be seriously compromised if central government took this responsibility itself, rather than from a commitment to address the social needs per se. As a result, the entire management system was the causal outcome of an intergovernmental power play.

Phase 2: the twentieth century

The second phase describes the evolution of infrastructure in the twentieth century. The technology that arose to address phase 1 began with simple piped systems, which grew quite rapidly to become more complex networks, whose benefits far exceeded initial expectations. Roads too were improving rapidly, while advances were being made in water treatment, wastewater treatment and solid waste management. As a result, this second phase was actually driven by engineering and technology, though again the main perception was of an engineering development model. This led to the construction of the large networks that could provide a service to every family within the urban area and then beyond into the countryside, the outcome of which was to change the relationship between the three components. In this phase, engineering lost its direct causal relationship with the initial set of social issues, slowly becoming a range of services to the individual – a change that in turn influenced both the social surround and the political regulatory framework.

The spread of networked infrastructure, coupled with other technological improvement that has been mentioned, resulted in the social goals that underpinned the value-based surround, particularly at the lower level, being achieved relatively quickly, and so successfully that they no longer drove the process of infrastructure growth. At the same time, this emerging network infrastructure (i.e. infrastructure's physical component) provided benefits to individuals which, while not totally unforeseen, none-theless exceeded expectations. The outcome was a rapid improvement in quality of life and a new era of leisure and user convenience, which was supported by an exponential growth in individual consumer products. The value system, in Anglo-Saxon countries at least, led to a change of perception of several key infrastructure services, particularly those now defined as utilities, from resources to commodities – the so-called commodification of infrastructure; and this in turn opened up the debate around the respective roles of the public and the private sector. The outcome, in Britain at least, was the transfer of responsibility for many physical infrastructure services to the private sector in a new political dispensation that created a new political regulatory framework.

Phase 3: the twenty-first century

The third phase, which is still unfolding, was initiated in the late twentieth century. It has been driven by a growing awareness of the damaging impact that the western, commodity-driven infrastructure development process that was the outcome of this phase 2 development has had on the physical environment. At the same time, the global economic and political changes also initiated a series of wide-ranging reforms that impacted strongly on the relationship between the value-based surround and the institutional framework. Taken together, the result was a significant shift in the value-based surround, with the most evident result being the rise to prominence of a strong environmental imperative within the value-based surround for the first time.

In parallel, the global changes in the world order that took place in the 1980s and 1990s, described in Chapter 2, brought to the fore the concept of good governance. The driver of this third phase, then, has returned to the value-based surround, which in turn has caused a shift in the nature of the other two components. Institutionally, the first practical response was a renewed focus on decentralisation, based upon the (Eurocentric) principle of subsidiarity, which in turn led to an expansion of societal roles and relationships in the decision-making process. The second practical response, which was to impact most on technology, was local Agenda 21, best described as 'a local-government-led, community-wide, and participatory effort to establish a comprehensive action strategy for environmental protection, economic prosperity and community well-being in the local jurisdiction or area' (GDRC, 2010).

This is the point at which the rigidity imposed by the permanent nature of the physical infrastructure base comes into play. The value-based surround has changed dramatically with the need to address environmental concerns. In this context, major elements within the existing infrastructure base are seen as a blockage to achieving a more sustainable approach.

What was innovative and appreciated fifty years before is now perceived as damaging and detrimental: for example, landfill sites; large storm-water drains; an excess of urban roads built for cars and dangerous to pedestrians. As a consequence, those who designed that earlier infrastructure (the engineers) have lost credibility and the idea that infrastructure might still constitute an important driver of urban development has fallen into disrepute and been abandoned.

The impact of misunderstanding the role of infrastructure on African urban development

Force of influence 1: the colonial legacy

The colonial legacy ensured that all the underlying flaws of the British infrastructure model were transferred to Africa. Inside the colonial urban boundary there was a technical model of infrastructure management that catered for an elite. Outside was a lower level of service delivery that provide a social improvement model to an underclass which was not greatly different from the one that was created in Britain at the end of the nineteenth century. Together, these justified an approach to infrastructure that was based on societal differentiation, initially by race, then later by economic class. This approach totally distorted any attempt to define a wider value system for infrastructure.

It was also a model that saw solutions in engineering terms, through its association with public works (using the British colonial interpretation of this term). This linked infrastructure conceptually to construction and procurement. Finally, it left the political regulation of infrastructure unresolved. The major towns had engineering departments that managed their infrastructure. However, there was no clear relationship between the different tiers of government, while the technical function of municipal government extended beyond infrastructure into a range of other areas. When governments centralised local functions, what they centralised was not so much infrastructure per se but rather a technical function linked to a wider notion of public works; that is, the construction and procurement mentioned earlier. At that point, African governments lost touch with the concept of 'urban infrastructure' as it has been described here, opening the way for the remaining influences to take effect.

Force of influence 2: the private-sector management model for water supply

The British infrastructure model already treated the three components of infrastructure shown in Figure 12.3 as distinct attributes that could be explored individually. The developments of the 1980s simply added a further element of fragmentation by breaking urban infrastructure down into sectors. In looking at the water sector, the exploration of options proposed by the World Bank situated the debate within that component of infrastructure termed the political regulative framework. Treating this as an independent arena of the development discourse, the Bank sought to use the concept of a legal contract to define what it perceived to be a politically neutral relationship. It made no attempt to modify its approach to take account of indigenous values and culture, relying instead on providing a range of partnership 'options' and a regulatory framework. The result, not surprisingly, was that most African countries rejected the whole idea. Unfortunately, it would appear that the real lessons have still not been learned, if a review of the experiences of public–private partnerships for urban water utilities, co-published by the World Bank in 2009 (Marin, 2009), is any guide. As a result, this force of influence remains as strong as it ever was.

Force of influence 3: the basic needs approach

An alternative approach has been to focus on the needs of the urban poor, defining the absolute minimum they need in terms of infrastructure (and other) 'services'. Here, the approach is situated in that component of infrastructure termed the value-based surround. This is a reactive approach, distrustful of 'technical' or 'economic' solutions. Its roots can be traced back to the British Victorian model of social improvement for the economic underclass, developed in the nineteenth century and practised in colonial Africa. As can be seen from Figure 12.4, it focuses on just one specific goal of infrastructure: public health. This is very similar to the approach that failed in the United States in the early phase of urban development there; and it can never be more than a short-term, stopgap solution. In addition, the focus on physical targets required to meet the MDGs can only be achieved by recentralising decision-making and disempowering local government. This is because there has to be a political regulatory framework for infrastructure. It is one of the integral components and it cannot be removed; so, like water running downhill, it has to go somewhere. What this 'force of influence' does is to direct it towards a line ministry within central government.

Force of external influence 4: defining a specific urban planning paradigm

The planning approach that replaced engineering infrastructure has never recorded a major success in sub-Saharan Africa in the thirty years since it took over responsibility for urban development. The analysis of urban planning in Chapter 4 demonstrated the extent to which urban planning, far from being a universally applicable development construct, as, for example, the UN-Habitat global report on planning sustainable cities (UN-Habitat, 2009) would have us believe, is actually reflective of the dominant British developmental *Weltanschauung* within which it originated. The four major weaknesses of this paradigm were described in that chapter: the inability to use conventional planning when the bulk of the land is already settled and informal; the use of the infrastructure model of social improvement; an economic model that relies on externalities to drive urban development, with the emphasis on the formal private sector; and the lack of accountability.

With regard to the secondary towns, the approach is to downscale experiences from theory and the larger centres; but experiences, while they may be scaled up, are far more difficult to scale down, if they can be scaled down at all. At the local level, for example, a paper describing a land regularisation model for informal settlement upgrading in the secondary town of Mwanza illustrates the extent to which this British-based model remains focused almost entirely on the regularisation of individual cadastral boundaries.

Underpinning the forces of influence: control over the knowledge resource base

The last three forces of influence are all supported by a large academic base that has produced numerous papers and reports justifying each of them and arguing for their continuation; yet none of them is particularly successful in reaching even limited goals. The reality is that no one has any solutions that can demonstrate successful outcomes at scale. Only recently have African researchers been able to express themselves within their own value-based surround and their own reality; yet this is where the real, albeit still limited, successes are to be found. Overall, though, this freedom of expression, this ability to explore an African reality from within an African value-based surround, remains extremely constrained by external control over the intellectual space that defines the boundaries of the development discourse.

The importance of the Ethiopian case study

African countries cannot be situated within the western continuum of historical urban development that unfolded during the nineteenth and twentieth centuries. These countries have a totally different situation to deal with, a situation in which they have to address a set of needs that encompass the social, the economic and the environmental all at the same time. And they have to do this with a growing population of mainly poor people, limited financial and skills resources, constraints in how they use external resources, and the impact of climate change. Yet they have to contend with a wide range of external actors cherry-picking small parts of the development arena that have been chosen to suit their own (external) interests: an environmental group there working on landfill sites; a water supply company here working on privatisation; a development agency somewhere else providing a few toilets. Overall, we see here a wasteful mechanistic approach carried to a ridiculous extreme.

What is required here is a major rethink, one that can situate African countries in an intellectual space where they can address all of these sets of needs at the same time. The current urban condition in Africa is not a failing of African countries' own making; it is an outcome of a decision, made almost two hundred years ago, to use a specific interpretation of infrastructure to underpin urban development. That was the wrong decision, not for the country taking it (the United Kingdom) but for countries adopting it. It was never intended as a generic model; it was simply exported as part of a colonising process. Unfortunately, it is not a model that can be adapted to make it better, because the assumptions on which it is based are all totally inappropriate for countries that develop through the formation of new towns in open spaces.

There is only one way to address this condition, which is to create a new development model. To do so, however, requires a new way of viewing the nature of urban infrastructure and its role in urban society. The best way to begin is to go back to the beginning of the modern era of urbanisation. This book has demonstrated that the American interpretative construct of infrastructure, which was the only alternative at that time, could provide a framework for a new direction in urban development that is relevant to Africa today. What is required is to test that construct in an African context.

Chapters 6 and 7 described a project that took place in Ethiopia over a period of approximately five years, which explored the nature and role of infrastructure in a developing society, working with eighteen secondary towns. During that time, every aspect of the developmental rationality that underpinned the early American approach to infrastructure, described in Table 3.2, was shown to be valid. The first clear outcome was the demonstration that urban infrastructure was the major driver of economic development in the secondary towns – a finding that was accepted and endorsed by the government. The second was that engineering is not infrastructure; on the contrary, the engineering interpretation of infrastructure is a major blockage in building technology systems for urban development. A third was the critical importance of a rational political regulative framework to support local government. Although the devolved federal model used in Ethiopia had some weaknesses, it had evolved further than most other African countries in this regard; and there were valuable lessons to learn from both the strengths and the weaknesses.

Fourth was the need to define, and stand by, the principle of social equity, which that country does. Fifth, there was the need for a clear policy framework, which was found in the integrated urban infrastructure policy that the country developed.

At the same time, though (sixth), the potentially damaging role of the external agencies was also in evidence, particularly in support of forces 2 and 3 referred to earlier. Finally, the study provided an important opportunity to study the strengths and weaknesses of an urban development policy that was driven by urban planning. It was a study that led directly to the conclusions about that role that have been expressed here.

This study was far from complete: there were too many gaps, particularly relating to technology systems. Yet it was the experience of Ethiopia that provided the basis for the ideas and the model that emerged in the last part of the book, and which are summarised in what follows. The American concept of infrastructure was important in providing the interpretation of the nature of urban infrastructure and its role in society; but it was Ethiopia that provided the experience which showed that there really is an alternative route to urban development that is socially equitable, environmentally sustainable and capable of driving economic development forward in the secondary towns.

Redefining infrastructure and its role in society

Table 3.2, repeated earlier in this chapter, provides the foundation for a new urban development model. This model gives us three characteristics for urban infrastructure to inform and guide the exploration of the *problématique*. First, infrastructure is a driver of development. Second, it incorporates technology, but technology is something quite different from engineering; thus, infrastructure is not, and never can be, about engineering per se. Third, infrastructure can only be viewed from within a trinitarian, three-component model. The focus at this point is on the third of these characteristics.

The paper by Goulet on the different rationalities in development that was discussed in Chapter 4 explains why we have difficulty understanding this three-component model. Many people have recognised that they are part of the development process, but they have been treated as independent, albeit perhaps interacting, variables. As a result, they have been approached in a reductionist fashion. Goulet argued for a more integrated approach. However, this book takes the nature of that relationship further. To take it further we first go back to explore why it is so difficult to create a single definition of infrastructure. Looking at the various definitions provided in Chapter 3, we can see a commonality of interest, in that each of the definitions focuses on the physical. Yet the three-component model rises above the physical. After all, a dam on its own is not infrastructure;

it is simply a lump of concrete or a mound of earth. Yet engineers believe in dams and define them as infrastructure. The fact is that Goulet's idea of moving beyond reductionist interpretations cannot work, because what we are dealing with is a more complex form of interrelationship than was envisaged in his analysis.

So, if we are to provide a truly universal definition of infrastructure, then we have to build this from first principles. As its starting point in the process, the book would argue that infrastructure was brought into existence to facilitate communal interaction. In this context it exists primarily as a construct of society. Throughout this book the three-component relationship recurs time after time, while Goulet too presents one of the most respected academic arguments in support of it as a fundamental relationship. If we accept infrastructure as a construct of society, then we should be able to find a definition for it by situating it within the framework of the communal interactions that created it in the first place. In modern terminology that means the theory of institutions. Fortunately, this is a field that is becoming more widely understood and is able to provide us with the clear and definitive institutional theory of the American sociologist W. Richard Scott.

It is suggested here that an important aspect of Scott's work, that which was developed originally to explain how organisations function (Scott, 2008), can be applied to the wider society, on the basis that it shows how societies at large formulate their perceptions of communal development processes. Within organisations, Scott defined what he termed 'three pillars of institutions' (ibid., pp. 50–9): the cognitive, the normative and the regulative. Here, the regulative 'regularises' behaviour within an organisation; the normative introduces values and 'norms'; and the cognitive provides 'shared conceptions that constitute the nature of social reality' (ibid., p. 57). Overall, Scott summed up his argument by saying that '[i]nstitutions are comprised of regulative, normative and cultural-cognitive elements that, together with associated activities and resources, provide stability and meaning to social life' (ibid., p. 48).

This book proposes that such a concept can be extrapolated to a wider society and used not only to situate infrastructure in society but also to define it. The comparative relationship is illustrated by Figure 12.5. Here, the cognitive aspect of infrastructure is to be found in the technology. Because infrastructure is something physical, something that we respond to with our cognitive senses, we tend to associate the term 'infrastructure' most directly with technology. The normative aspect of infrastructure is defined by the value-based surround, which explains why infrastructure has to be grounded in a specific value system that links directly to the society involved. Finally, the regulative framework describes the political nature of infrastructure, situating it clearly in a political regulative framework. In this context, confirmation of the validity of these three pillars comes from the way that they are able to integrate with Goulet's own three

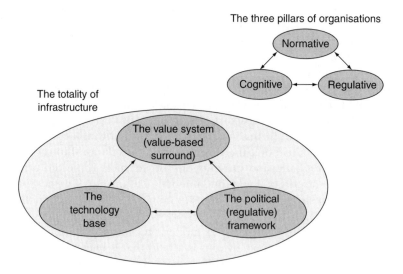

Figure 12.5 The 'three pillars' that together constitute and define infrastructure.

rationalities (the technological, the political and the ethical), while at the same time going beyond them.

We can now create a new *definition* of infrastructure, as follows:

> *Infrastructure is a societal construct made up of three pillars: a value-based surround, a technology base and a political regulative framework.*

This definition then enables us to understand the *nature* of infrastructure, wherein:

> *Infrastructure describes the technology chosen by a society to provide for its developmental needs and the relationship between that technology and its associated political regulatory framework, both of which are defined by a set of social, environmental and economic values termed collectively the value-based surround.*

The third aspect of infrastructure, its *role* in society; is described here in an urban context, though the general principle of managing resource flows applies at all scales. If we move 'downwards' to urban infrastructure, the same overall definition applies. In this urban context

> *The role of infrastructure is focused on mediating the flow of resources that cross the interface between the wider environment and the urban area and circulate within it, in a way that is mutually beneficial to the developmental needs of the urban society and the sustainability needs of the physical environment.*

When the word infrastructure is used in this way we can apply the term 'green', indicating a particular conceptual approach: recognition that the needs of society and the physical environment have to be weighted equally. Hence, green urban infrastructure is infrastructure (as defined above) that balances the needs of society and those of the physical environment in a way that satisfies the needs and requirements of both in equal measure. Applied in an African urban context, green urban infrastructure is infrastructure that satisfies the needs of all urban residents in an equitable way while integrating the urban environment into the wider physical space beyond the urban boundary in a manner that is sustainable.

There is nothing magical or unduly complicated about this term; instead, it flows logically from the definition of infrastructure as a societal construct. When the term is applied in the urban context, there are two outcomes. The first is that green urban infrastructure is a systemic concept; that is, it is about infrastructure systems. This differentiates it from the term 'green technology' – an important distinction. Green technology can, and often will, be a contributory component of green infrastructure, but it cannot of itself define green infrastructure in its totality.

The second outcome is that green urban infrastructure is inextricably linked to the concept of the metabolic city, since its primary role is the mediation of resources in and around the city. This fact defines a two-tier model of infrastructure, with a higher tier mediating urban resources and a secondary tier within that distributing those resources to individuals. Again, an infrastructure system that bypasses this two-tier model and delivers directly to the individual from the source without mediating the resource flow to optimise the environmental requirements of the metabolic city may use green technology but it cannot be green infrastructure. Ultimately, we always return to the concept of green urban infrastructure as that infrastructure which provides a socially equitable and environmentally sustainable system that is in balance.

Building a new urban model for Africa based upon green infrastructure

Once we have a new definition of infrastructure, then we are able to move to the next step, which is a new vision of urban development that is grounded in the needs and realities of sub-Saharan Africa in the twenty-first century. Furthermore, once we have this definition, then we can return to the other aspects of infrastructure that relate to its wider role in society, where infrastructure is the primary driver of urban development.

Arising from an exploration of urban development as a *problématique* (Chapter 8), the book explored each of the three components of infrastructure afresh. The resulting outcome was to replace the three phases of western infrastructure development, as shown in Figure 12.4, with a new unified model that is designed for the African situation in the twenty-first century. This reconstructed the three components of infrastructure to take into account the increased complexity of modern urban society. It was illustrated in the previous chapter as Figure 11.11, and is replicated here for clarification.

The situation in Africa at the present time is that every single element within this model is controlled or determined, at the intellectual and/or conceptual level, by external actors, which makes this model the nexus for exploration if change is to take place. By defining each element clearly and unambiguously, we can provide the mechanism through which control of the intellectual space can pass from these external actors to the internal players in Africa, not only in government but also in business, academia and civil society. The book explored and discussed each of these elements in depth, and the resulting reconstruction of the different components and subcomponents is summarised in what follows.

Economic, social and environmental drivers (Chapter 9)

Economic development continues to be the most important outcome of infrastructure as a driver of the urban development process. What has changed is how the social framework within that economic development is perceived. The objective in an African context is to provide the basis for a new, green urban economy. This can only be successfully achieved,

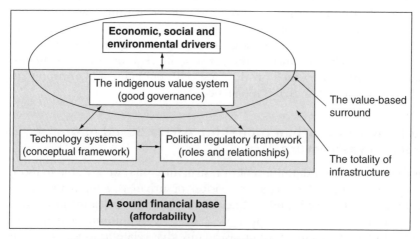

Figure 11.11 The relational model that defines infrastructure.

though, if the process of providing the infrastructure to achieve this goal is structured in such a way as to support the creation, growth and development of small businesses. This is seen to be a more strategic goal than job creation per se because, while it incorporates job creation, it also moves beyond it to focus on the need to build sustainable jobs. This aim defines the role of infrastructure as the *economic driver* of development.

The dominant *social driver* that emerged was the need for social equity to provide the basis for urban development. Physical infrastructure provides the basis for translating this need into reality, and social equity provides the social framework for the infrastructure model and the higher-order value-based surround.

The *environmental driver* seeks actively to achieve sustainability. Infrastructure has both positive and negative impacts on the environment, both of which have to be acknowledged. On the positive side, infrastructure has a major role to play in contributing to sustainable urban development. This derives from its role in mediating the resource flows in and around a city; and it is here that infrastructure becomes crucial to the achievement of environmental sustainability, by mediating resource flows in the most effective way possible. Negatively, infrastructure can be a major contributor to environmental deterioration, particularly air and water pollution, if it is not managed correctly. Correct management requires external monitoring and regulation, through mechanisms such as impact assessment.

In looking at the interrelationship between these three imperatives, the book demonstrated the extent to which they are not only compatible but also mutually reinforcing, provided that the model shown in Figure 11.9 is implemented in its entirety. Under current urban development strategies, though, the opposite is the case, and these three imperatives act in a mutually opposing fashion that leads to a conflictual relationship.

A sound financial base (affordability)

A sound financial base is a prerequisite of sustainable development, and affordability is a critical component of a sound financial base. The current approach to affordability has two major conceptual flaws. The first is to link affordability to the individual, an outcome of situating urban development in an Anglo-Saxon *Weltanschauung*. This book argues that urban development will only become sustainable if affordability is defined at the level of the urban local government authority. At present, the individual-specific interpretation of affordability is the greatest single block to social equity, and that block is instantly reversed if we move to the level of the city to define this indicator.

The applied knowledge base (Chapter 10)

The book has shown repeatedly how the external control of Africa's intellectual space is underpinned by western control over knowledge flows. Creating an indigenous knowledge base is therefore critical, not only to Africans' control over this intellectual space but, more specifically, and critically, their taking of responsibility for defining and managing all of the other elements shown in the model in Figure 11.9. Doing so requires countries to adapt their professional degree programmes in this area to match their own management approach to their own needs.

The indigenous value system (encapsulated within good governance) (Chapter 11)

Good governance provides the basis for the lower tier of the value-based surround. However, good governance is intricately linked to the concept of values, which means that it can, and should, be interpreted from within a specific value system. Here, it is particularly important to recognise that the application of good governance at the level of local government is quite different from its application at the level of national or federal government.

The current approach to good governance is based upon a western model that was developed initially for western needs. The initial work sought to define good governance in terms of eight 'characteristics', defined obviously by western countries, which were given equal weighting, and these continue to play an important role in defining the western approach to good governance in Africa. In discussing this issue, the book supports the view of UN-Habitat that these 'characteristics' should be seen more in terms of indicators that shape good governance, situating each of these within the indigenous value system. In addition, each area of local government activity has a closer defining relationship with some of these than with others, so that all are not equal; they have a variable level of impact, depending upon the activity area.

For infrastructure, which the model proposes should be viewed systemically (as described in the section that follows), the most critical indicator of good government is that its management should be effective and efficient, and the extent to which it meets that criterion becomes the primary indicator of good infrastructure governance. Following from that requirement, the decisions and the outcomes have to be open and accountable.

The political regulatory framework (roles and relationships)

Decentralisation is a concept to which all African governments are fully committed, yet it is rarely achieved. While inability to achieve decentralisation is often blamed on a failure of political will, this book has demonstrated that failure of political will is not the primary cause; rather, it is the lack of clearly defined roles and relationships that is responsible. There are five important aspects to this. The first is decentralisation itself (Chapter 5), which is too often treated as a menu of options. That part of the analysis that focused on delegation as a mechanism for decentralisation demonstrated quite clearly the inadequacy of this approach, showing how it will invariably lead to greater centralisation. Only a model based upon devolved powers supported by a legal statute can provide a firm basis for meaningful decentralisation.

The international academic debate on decentralisation generally refers to the central government as a single entity. The study of Ethiopia, in Chapters 6 and 7, shows the extent to which this interpretation is far from reflecting reality. The relationship between 'central' and local government involves multiple line ministries, each of which has its own perception of how this relationship should function, irrespective of what powers the decentralisation legislation passes to local government. This situation was further explored in Chapter 11, and demonstrates clearly that creating a common position across line ministries is absolutely crucial to the success of decentralisation.

The third aspect of this infrastructure component relates to how decisions should be made about what is devolved. As regards this aspect, the book's findings were that the current approach, which is generally based upon the European concept of subsidiarity, is totally inappropriate for rapidly developing urban centres. Instead, the most effective route should be based upon a strategic assessment that situates local powers, duties and functions clearly within the relationship shown in Figure 11.9. The implications of this finding will be discussed further in the later section on the role of secondary towns (pp. 442–4).

The fourth aspect covers the relationship between the local authority, the private sector and civil society (Chapter 11). This is a major agenda item for external agencies, yet it can only be explored once the first three aspects of the institutional framework have been addressed. Local government partnerships with both the private sector and civil society are crucial to successful urban development. However, if they are to be successful there have to be two prerequisites in place. The first is an indigenous definition of what constitutes these relationships, situated within the value system of the country; and the second is the definition of local government as the key player having both power and influence. If local government is weak, whether institutionally, in respect of its powers and duties, or in its capacity to collect and leverage finance, then neither of these sets of relationships is likely to work. This makes capacity-building the top priority in local development.

The final aspect of the institutional debate links roles and relationships with good governance. Chapter 11 demonstrated clearly the need to differentiate good governance from roles and relationships. It argued that, while good governance may influence roles and relationships, and help them to be adaptive once in place, it cannot drive the formation process. Again the situation in fast-growing cities is radically different from that in the mature cities of the West. Defining role and relationships in the former remains a work in progress, with much work still to be done. Good governance practice may provide valuable inputs, but has to recognise also the need for this exploration to have the intellectual space to embrace a much wider range of issues.

Rethinking the role and function of technology

The final element of the relational model is the technology component of infrastructure, discussed in Chapters 9 and 10. This section summarises the work of Chapter 9. When we look at how the British model evolved (Figure 12.4), the initial phase 1, with its emphasis on public health improvements, could be described as goal orientated. As infrastructure slowly transformed from phase 1 to phase 2, though, the emphasis changed and the management of the urban infrastructure base became much more task orientated. The result was described in Chapter 3: a list of specific tasks which, when taken together, embrace the full range of infra-structure services. While the services are being provided, and particularly when they are provided on the basis of social equity, then it makes sense to bundle the delivery of these services together, and for government to manage the system. Once they have been installed, however, the perspective changes, particularly when viewed from a mechanistic perspective, as was the case in the Anglo-Saxon countries during the 1980s. When free-market capitalist thinking is combined with a mechanistic analysis, this dictates that the logical outcome is to 'unbundle' the services, which by then were commodity services, and repackage them individually.

African countries do not have to follow that route, which is in any case unachievable and unsustainable. The challenge is to find an alternative. The subtext of the technology element in Figure 11.9 was a conceptual framework indicating the need to revisit the role and function of technology at a basic conceptual level if we are to find that alternative. The key to doing so lies in the need to work more effectively with limited and potentially diminishing resources. Once that need is accepted, then the next logical step to view the city itself as a user of resources.

There has been a great deal of research around the nature of the city as a consumer of resources, resulting in the concept of the metabolic city; as well as the city as a part of the wider ecosystem, which results in the concept of the city as an organism, as well as an ecosystem in its own right. Such thinking enables calculations to be made of resource flows and makes it possible to identify where savings might be made, but it has not, as yet, led to significantly improved management models, in part because it tends to ignore the role of infrastructure. When we see infrastructure as the mediator of resource flows, and particularly when we free ourselves from the historical constraints of western mature cities, with their installed network infrastructure base, then we can begin to see infrastructure in a very different light. At that point we begin to gain an understanding of how infrastructure, as the mediator of resources, can be linked to the resources in their wider environmental context: we begin to link infrastructure to resource systems.

The result is a new approach to thinking about resources as a set of overlapping systems, shown in Figure 9.4, reproduced here. The city itself is a system and it interacts with each of these resource systems that constitute part of the wider physical environment, of which six have been identified. As the mediator of resources, this systemic view of the different city–ecosystem interactions provides a framework for the conceptual development of that physical infrastructure designed in such a way as to fulfil this role.

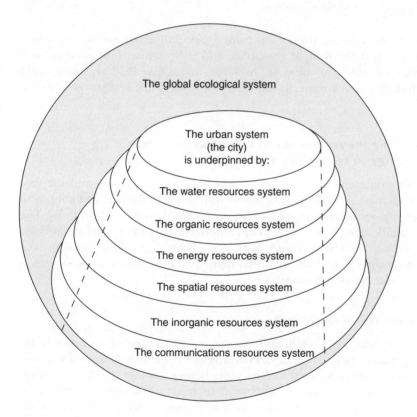

Figure 9.4 Systemic view of the city–ecosystem relationship.

The city interacts with each of these resource systems, but the systems themselves also interact. While existing thinking has focused on quantifying resource flows, this model opens up exploration of the possibilities of managing not only those resource flows but also the interaction between them. The starting point for doing this is to establish some form of operational framework, which has been expressed in this analysis (Chapter 9) as three principles of urban sustainability, as follows:

1   Resource use within a system should be optimised through recycling and the new input from that resource system into the city should be minimised.
2   Resource use should be retained within its own system and only taken across boundaries when there is no other option.
3   When resources are taken across a system boundary, this transfer of resources should be treated as a loan. That is, the resource taken across the boundary is borrowed; the environmental cost of borrowing the resource should be defined, and the way in which the loan will be repaid should be quantified.

The first item in this list derives from existing thinking around the metabolic city and the flow of resources, and is becoming best practice in a number of different areas of resource management. The second and third, though, derive specifically from the conceptual analysis used in the book.

Rethinking the technology of infrastructure: from technology to technology systems

The first outcome of the systemic approach just described, and the first major change in thinking that moves us beyond traditional thinking, is to classify urban infrastructure by systems rather than as a set of tasks. The more challenging outcome is to operationalise the concept. This was done in Chapter 10. The series of brief summaries that follow highlight the major changes in the way we would manage infrastructure once we view it from a systemic perspective.

The water resources system

There are four major changes from the current approach to urban water management. First, when urban water resources is viewed from a systemic perspective there is no differentiation between water supply and other aspects of urban water management, such as urban drainage and grey water containment: all are integrated into a single urban water resources management system. The second is that the integration of different aspects of urban water extends beyond the design into the management. Thus, the operator providing water to the house does not abrogate responsibility at that point, but retains responsibility for the grey water that is discharged, and integrates this with the management of the storm water. The third change is in conceptual thinking. This is no longer about parallel flows reflecting the different water and waste streams. It uses water flow integration at different spatial scales; with each recycle loop nested in the next like one circle within another. The final change relates to the financial model used for water management. In the systemic approach there has to be a single financial system for the management of urban water resources in their entirety.

The organic resources system

The organic resources system has two components. The first reintegrates people back into the organic system, while the second ensures a recycling of incoming organic products back to that same organic system. The biggest change here is psychological, with the recognition that when we see 'water supply' and 'sanitation' from a systemic perspective, we recognise that they are actually quite separate, with each one being a part of its own, quite distinct resources system. If we then follow the principles of urban sustainability described earlier, it follows that they should be treated as separate, since any crossover will significantly impact negatively on both systems. The second major change is in attitudes and perceptions, simply recognising that humans are part of the natural cycle of life, a fact we appreciate when the phrase is used in an animated movie but appear unable to accept in real life. Seven billion people on the planet produce over 70 million tonnes of fertiliser and over 30 million tonnes of phosphorus from their own 'waste' each year, with the first figure being the equivalent of over 40 per cent of total synthetically derived fertiliser used globally. I do not propose to impose ecological sanitation on the world; what incorporating these concepts into development thinking does, though, is to change the economics of urban infrastructure quite radically. The new green economics of urban sanitation have to be built around the reintegration of 'waste' back into the agricultural cycle. Where this is not done, the economic analysis has to incorporate a financial 'loss' in the balance sheet and quantify this.

The energy resources system

The local generation of electricity in western countries was increasingly discouraged from the 1930s onwards, in favour of large centralised generating stations. Now, however, there is growing acceptance of local generation and the use of feed-in tariffs. The World Bank is currently working with African countries to provide a huge increase in bulk power distribution across the continent, drawn from hydropower resources; and certainly there is a role for such an increase. At the same time, Africa has a greater potential for producing energy from the sun than almost any other part of the world. The major shift here, then, is towards a major expansion of locally generated solar power, a major component of which is linked to providing energy to mediate other resource flows. All secondary towns could and should generate their own power from renewable resources to service all the different resources systems in the town.

The space–land resources system

This system encompasses both land and space, and it is where the greatest shift in conceptual thinking has to occur. The current British-derived model of urban planning does not work and cannot work. Planning cannot drive urban development, though it can facilitate it under a predetermined set of conditions, none of which applies in the secondary towns. It is infrastructure that drives urban development, including the movement network; and it is to the infrastructure that we have to look to create a sustainable space–land resources system.

The most obvious shift is in the way that we think about the movement network, changing the focus from cars to people and defining the consequences of this shift – not simply the consequences for layout design but, more critically, those for the structural design of the pavements themselves. One implication is to change the design focus away from a structurally engineered pavement to surface finish and urban landscape. The second shift requires that we understand the extent to which this system is interactive with the water resources system. Currently we define land use taking into account the hydrological constraints imposed by different water-flow regimes. The adoption of the three principles of urban sustainability requires that we instead place the responsibility for, and the cost of, modifying the water flows more directly onto the land and space resource. Again this change creates a quite different economic model, making both land use and the movement network financially responsible for their impact on the natural environment and, in particular, on the urban water resources.

The third implication is to change our thinking about the way that we define land and space, and in particular the way that we use the cadastre, which currently presents a major stumbling block in the search for a more sustainable urban construct. This system was developed in the era of paper-based maps and is also a product of the Anglo-Saxon insistence on the use of individual land ownership as a primary determinant of urban planning. The implication here is a move away from the current approach of land regularisation based upon the individual site cadastre, to a multi-scalar, three-dimensional approach to the management of urban space based upon the security of tenure through the use of a more flexible approach that uses the informal settlements to define our basic spatial unit.

The inorganic resources system

It is the inorganic resources system that is achieving the greatest degree of recognition globally, primarily because it is the system that also links most directly to individual consumption through its use in housing. The changes here are, first, to encourage a movement towards indigenous materials, with a preference for a shift from inorganic materials to sustainably managed organic materials. The second is simply to make the three principles of urban sustainability the basis for managing and pricing inorganic materials consumption.

The communications resources system

The massive expansion of digital telecommunications systems appears to subsume local communications within the global network. The result currently is three distinct threads of communication: between individuals directly; social networking; and (increasingly interactive) websites. Given that the common feature of all of these is shared interests within the communication links, local government faces a specific challenge, since its activity, and its client base, is geographically rather than socially based. E-governance is perceived to be the key to this conundrum, yet the effective use of the communications resource system is seen as the key to indigenous good governance practice in Africa.

A new financial and economic model

The move to resources infrastructure management as the basis for the urban infrastructure base brings with it a need for a new economic and financial model. One aspect of this change has already been mentioned, with the elevation of affordability from the level of the individual to the level of the urban local government authority. The next major change is to link both the economic model and the financing to the individual resources systems. This would mean, for example, that the entire urban water resources system, which includes the water supply, would be considered as a single economic entity. At the same time, the financing would be linked to use. Thus, the higher-order roads, which create rigid corridors that impede water flow, would have to pay for the cost of this impediment, not simply in capital cost (e.g. creating alternative flow paths) but also in the ongoing operational cost.

Although the new urban resources infrastructure is designed to be much more flexible and adaptable than current forms of central networked infrastructure, there remains a capital cost component. This would be managed by a new approach to asset management, an example of which was provided in the Ethiopian study and described in Chapter 10. This is not the economic and technical asset management system used in mature cities. It is a strategic system whose role is to provide the operational linkage between affordability and the resources technology systems.

Finally, the third aspect of the economic and financial model reflects a new approach to capital investment planning that revolves around the asset management plan. This investment plan is used to allocate costs to the different funding centres, drawing on new financial facilities such as the climate adaptation fund.

Secondary towns: an opportunity for a new beginning

The secondary towns provide an enormous opportunity to demonstrate the validity of a new approach to urban development, based upon the adoption of the model I have outlined. In this context the approach would be built around eight critical concepts, which together translate the relational model from Figure 11.9 into practice. These are as follows:

1   Urban infrastructure drives the urban development process through the creation of a green economy, the creation of small businesses, the mediation of urban resource flows and the achievement of social equity.
2   Affordability is defined at an urban local government level, as opposed to an individual level.
3   A clear set of roles and relationships that place local government at the centre of the decision-making process, situating these in an indigenous, not a western, construct need to be adopted.
4   A definition of public–private partnerships and relationships between the public sector and civil society that is built on an indigenous model is needed. This would provide the framework for the private and community sectors to construct and manage the different systems.
5   A systemic approach to the management of resources and resource flows is needed.
6   A methodological approach that provides the basis for replicability, thereby enabling processes to be extended rapidly to other towns, should be adopted.
7   There needs to be fast-tracking of new programmes of university education with degree structures designed locally, to produce professionals with knowledge of the new approach.

8   External support needs to be focused on capacity-building as opposed to physical delivery targets.

At the heart of this model is the systemic approach to the management of resources, which shifts the operation of the infrastructure from the different fragmented elements of Figure 12.3 to the new integrated infrastructure model shown in Figure 11.9. This systemic approach changes the thinking about resources and integrates the social needs of the community with the needs of the physical environment for the first time, while providing a sound economic and financial base from which to operationalise the model.

This discussion has been focused on urban resource infrastructure management as the major driver of development in the secondary towns. At the same time, there are a range of other needs to be addressed if a town is to serve the needs of its residents, for example education. The question then becomes who should be responsible for these other tasks. This book has argued for a fundamental rethinking of this question, and in particular proposes a move away from the European approach based on subsidiarity to a new strategic approach based upon answering the question of how local government creates a structure that best achieves its three imperatives.

The private-sector debate has tended to confuse this issue and overshadow an equally important but less well-defined one, namely the relationship between central, regional and local government – the public–public-sector debate. In today's complex world a good public management system at a local level is one that has a balanced distribution of responsibilities between different public actors as well as a balance between the public and private sectors. In particular, decentralisation has to be balanced with deconcentration, the establishment of local offices for central government ministries. On the basis of its exploration of the nature of local government in different countries, and in particular its analyses of South Africa and Ethiopia, together with its findings from the wider discussion on urban development, this book argues that the most effective strategic role for local government in a fast-growing secondary town is achieved by a focus on physical development, concentrating its capacity and resources there. Social development, including education and health, is best dealt with by central government, through local offices, while the external drivers of economic development, which are the ones most closely aligned with urban planning, are most effectively addressed at a regional level.

In physical development the book has sought to demonstrate the need to change external thinking about its nature and form, situating it much more clearly within the twenty-first century and the needs illustrated in Figure 11.9. What is needed is a rethinking of the role and nature of planning and technology. The outcome is shown in Figure 11.9, replicated here. This diagram shows the three core functions of local government, all of which operate interactively under the control of an executive mayor. These are resources (infrastructure) management, social-spatial management and financial management. Attached to each of these is its core determinant for good governance.

A new strategy for capacity-building

The Ethiopian secondary cities capacity-building programme demonstrated quite clearly the potential of infrastructure as a basis for political and institutional capacity-building. This potential is linked to its three-component construct, which incorporates the value-based surround, technology and the political regulatory framework. In its physical manifestation, infrastructure is real: it can be seen and triggers a cognitive response. It has to be built, and paid for, which requires a balanced judgement about choices and options. And then it has to be managed, which provides the best possible training ground for political and administrative leaders; while the secondary towns provide a level of scale that makes the delivery of infrastructure achievable and the results visible. These facts alone are sufficient justification for an executive mayoral structure to run Africa's towns and cities. The continent is desperately in need of a more effective training ground for young politicians, and managing infrastructure in the secondary towns is the best possible training. Finally, delivering and managing urban infrastructure demands a level of responsibility and maturity that is not found easily anywhere else. It also opens up opportunities for corruption, the exposure to which is an equally important facet of political education.

Figure 11.9 The three pillars of local government.

Political and institutional decision-making, though, does not, and cannot, operate in an intellectual vacuum. To be effective, decision-makers require good professional and technical advice. Thus, the training of the professionals is an equally important part of the process of capacity-building. Chapter 11 showed that the management of the sustainable town is built on three sets of skills, which were illustrated in Figure 11.9: financial management, social-spatial management and resources infrastructure management. By focusing the capacity-building on these three areas of expertise, countries lay the foundation for long-term sustainable development. And all three are equally important; as with a three-legged stool, if one is removed, then the structure collapses.

At the same time, because African countries are in uncharted development territory, they have to build those skills for themselves. Again this was clearly demonstrated in the Ethiopian study, where a completely new degree was established to provide infrastructure managers for the secondary towns. This aspect of capacity-building is absolutely critical. Western countries, with their mature cities, their mature economies and their high level of graduate throughput, have moved towards ever-increasing skills specialisation. Africa's needs are quite different at its stage in the development cycle. Yes, the countries of Africa still require specialists, and they require engineers, but most of all they require managers who are generalists: people who can cover a range of developmental aspects. With regard to the resources infrastructure, the Ethiopian programme showed that it is possible to produce generalists who can manage the full range of resource infrastructure systems in the secondary towns, drawing on the skills of sector specialists at specific points in the development process as and when required. Following this route, it would be possible to produce 10,000 resource infrastructure managers in sub-Saharan Africa in ten years. Now *that* is a meaningful target, with a clearly defined benefit.

From development in Africa to African development: why African countries need to rewrite the rules of engagement

Building the research base may take time, but that does not prevent African countries from instituting change, not only in education but across a range of development activities, and there are many changes that can take immediate effect. This section looks at the major areas where change can be initiated in such a way as to move the centre of gravity of decision-making from western to African capitals. That is the issue discussed here.

At the heart of all decision-making pertaining to development is the value system, and here each country has the right to define its own. When this defining of values is situated within the context of a set of universal values, as agreed by the United Nations, then it should be recognised that each country needs to interpret those values in its own way. Currently, the interpretation is wholly western and driven by western rules. In the new world that is coming, this will have to change. The first level of response, then, is to rewrite the rules of development; and here there are eight key areas where fundamental changes are required. Taken together, these provide the framework that will enable African countries to take back control over the development process and over their own intellectual space.

Differentiate urban policy from rural policy

The argument for differentiating urban and rural development has already been made, and shown to be the most fundamental development shift, underpinning all others. Many rural issues can be addressed successfully using a mechanistic approach, simply because densities are low and the number of people in any one group is small. The urban areas require a collective and systemic approach if development is to be successful. Rural–urban linkages are crucially important to development, yet this need for linkages is not incompatible with the existence of separate rural and urban policies. On the contrary, providing a policy framework using the systems-based model developed here, for example, will actually lead to a better integration of urban, rural and overall regional development strategies, as illustrated by the description of how human and solid waste can be returned back into the natural (organic) resources cycle. This is an important reason why the focus of planning should be moved upwards to the regional and national levels, where economic planning, spatial planning and transportation planning should be integrated. The professional focus on the towns would then be built around resources infrastructure management, while the sub-municipal focus, particularly in the informal settlements, would shift to urban design.

Differentiate primate cities or megacities from secondary towns

Almost all international work carried out to date on cities has focused on megacities. This book provides one of the first major studies to work with the secondary towns, and its findings are clear: secondary towns require their own development framework. The central issue is one of spatial scale and how this impacts on the nature of urban management. It is a relatively straightforward matter to scale up lessons learned at a small spatial scale and adapt them to a larger scale; on the other hand, it is extremely difficult to 'scale down'. UN-Habitat uses a population size of 500,000 people to differentiate the boundary. This figure is questionable; on the basis of practical experience only, I would consider 300,000 as more of a dividing line – but that is open to debate. While this is an area requiring further research, that research would be by way of refining the figures; the principle has been clearly established here that the secondary towns require their own framework of analysis and their own legislative framework.

Generate clear roles and relationships

The right to define roles and relationships is one of the core responsibilities that underpin the nation-state. Chapter 2 highlighted the extent to which influence over the definition and setting of both of these is a critical component of external control of Africa's development agenda. Yet African governments too share responsibility for not grappling with this issue conceptually. Roles and relationships, a phrase that covers everything from inter-ministerial relationships through public–private partnerships to local government responsibilities and the role of civil society, lie at the heart of development. For these to be defined locally, however, they have to be situated within the indigenous value system of the country.

Change the definition of affordability for urban development

The definition of affordability in rural and urban areas is quite different. Individual affordability continues to be a useful indicator of rural development; however, its application in urban areas (a western imposition) is one of the major causes of the failure of urban development in Africa. Affordability remains a major influence in policy formulation, implementation and management. However, affordability has to be measured, and used, at the level of the urban local government authority. Thus, it becomes a collective determinant and not an individual one. Without this change, African cities will never achieve meaningful economic development, social equity, environmental sustainability or political stability.

Return institutional capacity building to the centre of the development process

In development there is a pendulum that swings between building institutional structures and delivering services. Currently that pendulum is at the extreme point in its swing, where it is focused almost wholly on target-driven delivery. This extreme condition may achieve short-term gains but only at the expense of long-term sustainability. By insisting that any development plan has to incorporate a clearly defined institutional model, and that it must be demonstrated how it will achieve long-term sustainability, African governments will immediately move the focus of the development debate from the external priority focus to one that is defined internally.

Take control over the process of policy formulation

The indigenous approach to policy formulation in the majority of African countries differentiates policy from strategy and implementation. Yet external pressure has forced countries to adopt the British approach to policy, which is output orientated. This is not actually policy, as the examination of Britain's own 'policy' approach to infrastructure, described in Chapter 5, clearly demonstrated. This latter approach is action-orientated planning masquerading as policy. African countries need to have the confidence to believe more deeply in their own approach to policy, an approach that is grounded in their own needs and their own societies. Furthermore, the drawing of clear lines of responsibility between policy formulation and the development of implementation strategies is a prerequisite for meaningful decentralisation.

Adopt a systemic approach to urban development

The previous section showed how it was the failure of external agencies to recognise the changing nature of infrastructure, and their attempts to slot infrastructure back into nineteenth- and twentieth-century development constructs, that lie at the heart of the current urban crisis in Africa. These factors are also leading African countries down a road where they will be locked into a long-term condition of being regarded, globally, as second-class societies, with the majority of their urban residents being relegated to the position of second-class citizens.

The only way to avoid that condition, and the only way forward, is to leapfrog these development constructs and move directly to a model that integrates all three of the development phases shown in Figure 12.3. The model described here can achieve that, based upon the integration of economic development, social equity and environmental sustainability.

In this regard the secondary cities do not 'lag behind' those in the West. On the contrary, because they are currently underdeveloped and have not fully installed the physical component of their infrastructure, they are in a much better position to leapfrog immediately to the new infrastructure construct that will drive urban development through the twenty-first century into a more sustainable future.

Take intellectual ownership of the informal settlement debate

UN-Habitat's use of the word 'slum' to describe informal settlements and informal housing, not only in Africa but in developing countries generally, is arguably the most regressive use of terminology in the entire history of modern development. At the same time, the way in which this term is defined provides a classic illustrative example of the mechanistic deductive process that underpins the Anglo-Saxon approach to development. The term 'slum' was used to describe seriously deteriorated housing conditions that became widespread in the inner cities of Britain's industrial towns in the nineteenth century; and that is where it should have remained. It is totally meaningless in any other context.

It is not simply that the use of this term to describe African settlements is misleading: it is both disparaging and denigrating; it destroys self-esteem; and it contributes to the widespread perception of Africa as some form of second-class society. In this way the use of the word 'slum' can be seen as the collective equivalent of, and on a par with, the more obnoxious terms that were used historically to describe, and thereby classify, people of African origin.

To counter this negative view, and for African governments to reclaim the intellectual space around development thinking, it becomes important for African governments to take ownership of their informal settlements and understand what they really are – not what external western actors define them to be. While we continue to define them as slums, then slums they will remain; once we can view them differently, and see them for what they really are, then we are liberated to work creatively in supporting their growth and development. For the reality is that

there are no slums in Africa; only different typologies of settlement formation.

In Latin America there are favelas, barrios, barriadas, to name but a few. In Africa there are informal settlements and bidonvilles. The point here is that they have their own descriptor terminology and we can ascribe whatever interpretation we wish to them. What they all have in common, though, is that each represents an example of a new type of settlement formation. Comparing these to the slums of the working classes in Victorian Britain simply confuses the discussion and detracts from the real issue, which is how we define a sustainable relationship between people and place. If we change our perspective, and see before us newly emerging settlement typologies, then they are no longer problematic, as they were when viewed through a western lens; rather, they are the beginning of a solution: an important step in the way forward towards sustainable urban development. This is much more than an idealised statement; it is one with real practical benefits. To give just one example, it is far easier, and much more cost-effective, to upgrade the majority of informal settlements in a way that is equitable and sustainable than it is to provide a formal cadastre-based development (land regularisation), whether on a new or an occupied site, with a western land development model.

Laying colonial occupation to rest: giving African countries control over their own intellectual space

The need for African countries to situate their policies, processes and practices within a framework of western internal legitimisation – that is, the western value system – is the root cause of the subcontinent's underdevelopment; and that is why the role of the Chinese in Africa is so important and so appreciated (in Africa). Here is a major power, China, that is willing to deal with African countries in a way that enables them to define policy in terms of their own domestic legitimisation. This process in turn provides the space to build self-sufficiency and grow self-respect; and the benefits are visible as African countries begin a move towards development lift-off. Yet still western policy continues to act as a brake on this development, because the majority of western initiatives in Africa, particularly those associated with development aid, continue to be governed by this constraint of having to interpret all development in Africa in terms of a western value system and to judge that development in terms of the degree to which it can internally legitimised within the donor country itself.

Thus, western policy imposes severe constraints on the freedom of action that African countries have to take control over their own development. While this lack of freedom of action is problematic in its own right, the challenges that it poses for African leaders are further compounded by the questionable validity of the western development models that have been imposed. Such is certainly the case in the arena of urban development, where the book has sought to demonstrate the full extent to which western thinking, which has provided the rationality for urban development in Africa, is flawed at a deeply fundamental level.

There are many weaknesses in the western approach to urban development: the inability of centralised network infrastructure to adapt to a world of resource constraints and climate change; the western concept of a small nuclear family coupled with the American concept of individual home ownership on a private site with its own cadastral boundary, as the basis for urban planning; the imposition of free-market capitalism; a poor and inappropriate decentralisation model – to name just a few. Yet underpinning all of these, and the biggest mistake, was the failure of the British urban model to grasp the role that urban infrastructure plays as a driver of development. Africa's current urban condition is not caused by internal failures associated with poor government practices: these are merely the symptoms. The malady itself is an approach to urban development that is constructed around a dysfunctional model. Yes, African governments may have baked the cake; but the recipe had the wrong ingredients from the beginning.

Everything that followed from that first mistake can be seen as an attempt to modify the baking process, never accepting that the real need was to change the ingredients. It was evident from a very early stage that the high-services urban model used in the West could not be applied to Africa: the subcontinent came to the party too late in the day. Rather than looking for alternatives, though, the external response was to abandon the infrastructure model progressively while trying desperately to hold on to the Anglo-Saxon land ownership model – an approach that actually exacerbated rather than relieved the problem. Starting from their own position, where infrastructure services provided them with an extremely high level of service, western countries and their development agencies saw the answer as lying in a progressive reduction in the 'level' or quality of the services provided, until these were reduced to the absolute minimum of basic needs. This was truly a policy approach grounded in despair, one that could only come to pass because decisions were being made for people from the outside. It was also imposing on other countries practices that would never have gained acceptance from their own citizens at home.

At the same time, these same external agencies clung desperately to their narrow view of land regularisation, even while the formation of informal settlements was providing the knowledge that was needed to create a new model of spatial relationships. People living in informal settlements, at least in the countries where they have the freedom to occupy their own internal space, create social-spatial relationships that have an anthropological linkage to traditional form, albeit on a more compressed scale. Instead of learning from this tacit condition, though, western professionals preferred to impose their own views of spatial relationships and in doing so simply made the emerging urban crisis worse. The outcome is the creation of a two-tier society that intentionally differentiates rich from poor. The western-imposed urban development model is turning urban Africa into a global second-class society.

The great irony in all of this is that conditions in Africa's cities and towns do not have to be the way they are. The issue is not high levels of user convenience versus a minimal level of basic needs; that is simply the external view. African towns, and particularly the secondary towns, have the potential to provide a completely new model of urban development that is wholly sustainable, socially equitable and affordable. The only question is one of how to make that model happen. That is the question that has been addressed in this book.

The secondary towns of the twenty-first century are faced with a completely different set of needs and opportunities when compared to those of the West two hundred years ago, a completely different development paradigm. Such is evident with regard to the dominant issues of resources and environment, but it also extends into climate. On the positive side, the dominant need that exists in temperate climates to insulate and warm houses for much of the year does not apply, which reduces the personal energy requirement of households quite significantly. In Africa the major individual energy resource issue to be addressed relates to cooking and the impact this has on natural resource consumption. On the other hand, climate change will impact severely on many African countries, to a greater extent than on countries in temperate climates. What this means is that approaches to urban development are better managed in a collective framework, an approach that is quite different from the strongly individualistic socio-economic and political construct that defines current development practices in Britain and the United States.

In its analysis the book has argued that the most appropriate development model for Africa's secondary towns and cities is one that defines the urban area as a system, with the urban local government authority being seen as the manager responsible for the well-being of that system. Such a model enables both sustainability and affordability to be addressed at the city level, which in turn enables the town or city to function internally on the basis of social equity; it does not imply that the local authority has to run every component of the system itself. On the contrary, this is a development model that supports the involvement of a wider range of actors from both the private and the community-based sectors.

The perception of the secondary town as a system also enables it to interact with other systems, such as the water resources system, and in doing so to integrate itself more successfully into the wider physical environment. The key to success in this approach derives from changing the way in which we see infrastructure and its role in society. Thus, its primary role in the sustainable African city is one of mediating resource flows through and around the urban area, while enabling residents to access those resources as needed. Implicit in this approach is the recognition that land and space are primarily resources and should be treated as such. This recognition then changes our entire frame of reference for land management, which can now be seen as operating within the broader context of three-dimensional spatial management, facilitating the exploration of a new relationship between land and space using indigenous anthropological and societal relational models.

Thus, the key to successful urban development in Africa lies in creating a new urban model that is grounded in indigenous social relationships. African peoples generally live much closer to nature than most Westerners, and as a result are more adaptive in creating a sustainable urban environment. The fact that the social-spatial relationships which emerge differ from those in Britain and the United States should be immaterial to the decision of western governments as to whether they support that development process or not. It is time that western governments and the international agencies stopped seeking to predefine development solutions purely to suit their own *Weltanschauungen*, their own interpretation of the world, which they feel comfortable with, judging the outcomes solely on the basis of their own internal legitimisation processes.

African cities, and particularly the secondary cities, have a unique opportunity to leapfrog two hundred years of unsustainable urban development practice and create a new sustainable future that could be a role model for countries everywhere. All they need is the freedom to take back control over their own intellectual space, the freedom to situate their own development within their own value system, and the freedom to manage their own future. Only then will the last vestiges of western colonialism in Africa finally be laid to rest.

Notes

1 The failure of western intervention in Africa

1 See, for example, Hayter (1971) or Richards (1977).
2 See, for example, Riddell (2007) or Glennie (2009).
3 A writer, academic and broadcaster; see www.kenanmalik.com/top/cv.html (accessed 16 March 2010).
4 By the first century BC, when the Roman Empire entered its major growth phase, the Celts, a people of Indo-European origin who are sometimes described as 'the first Europeans' (see Berresford Ellis, 1998, p. 9), occupied much of Central and Western Europe.
5 The use of this term, which comes from the French concept 'Le monde anglo-saxon', literally the Anglo-Saxon world. See Chapter 12, note 1.
6 Plural *Weltanschauungen.*
7 German is a phonetic language; that is, its pronunciation is consistent with its spelling once you know the rules of pronunciation. Hence '*Weltanschauung*' is pronounced with four syllables, Welt-an-schau-ung.
8 In response to a speech by the British Prime Minister in Pakistan in April 2011, in which he appeared to 'distance himself from the imperial past', the director of the Commonwealth Policy Studies Unit is reported to have responded, 'This is typical of the UK's schizophrenic relationship with former colonies where it is both proud and embarrassed about its past'; while a Labour Member of Parliament's reported response was: 'To say that Britain is a cause of many of the world's ills is naïve. To look back 50-odd years for the problems facing many post-colonial nations adds little to the understanding of the problems they face.' *Daily Telegraph*, 07 April 2011, Politics section: www.telegraph.co.uk/news/politics/david-cameron/8430899/David-Cameron-Britain-caused-many-of-the-worlds-problems.html (accessed 07 April 2011).
9 See, for example, UN-Habitat: www.UN-Habitat.org/categories.asp?catid=374 (accessed 29 September 2009).
10 There are actually many problems with this view, as the book will show later, but this is the most important for now.
11 'Favela' is the Brazilian (Portuguese) term for an urban informal settlement.
12 See the article 'Aid Ironies: A Response to Jeffrey Sachs' in the Huffington Post: www.huffingtonpost.com/dambisa-moyo/aid-ironies-a-response-to_b_207772.html (accessed 01 October 2009).
13 See, for example, the work being done by an association of countries calling themselves the Leading Group on Innovative Financing for Development. www.leadinggroup.org (accessed 28 April 2011).
14 Graça Machel is one of Africa's most eminent political figures and a founder

member of the Elders Group of World Leaders. At the time of writing she was also Chancellor of the University of Cape Town.

15 A recollection from a discussion with Mr Zwane, the leader of the Civic Association in Kwa-Thandeka, Mpumalanga Province, South Africa in 1986; personal notes, unpublished.

16 The population statistics used in this section are drawn from the UN-Habitat report *State of African Cities Report 2008* (UN-Habitat, 2008).

17 A primate city is defined as a city that is at least twice the size of the second largest, combined with a cultural ambience that places it above other cities in the country. Thus, Ethiopia has a primate city, whereas South Africa does not.

2 The evolution of urban development

1 This is explored as a regional event from the interpretative perspective that a specific response was created, primarily by the World Bank, to adapt the events elsewhere to Africa.

2 The follow-on to this discourse on decentralisation, namely good urban governance, will be explored separately in Chapter 11.

3 See, for example, the UN-Habitat *Global Report on Human Settlements 2009: Planning Sustainable Cities*, London: Earthscan.

3 How modern urban infrastructure evolved

1 The term was originally developed in France around 1875 and derived from the combination of 'infra' and 'structure', according to the *Free Dictionary* (2011). Here the meaning of 'infra' is clear, meaning 'below'. The word 'structure', on the other hand, comes from the Latin verb *struere*, meaning 'to put together'. Thus, we tend to interpret it as meaning as something built or constructed (*Free Dictionary*, 'structure'), yet it can also mean a complex system.

2 England is one of four parts of the United Kingdom (Britain). However, it has its own laws pertaining to the way infrastructure is managed, local government functions and planning laws are made, and the word 'England' is used in that context. The terms 'Britain' and 'the United Kingdom' are used interchangeably in referring to the government.

3 This was in Britain. The evolution in the United States was quite different, owing to the more decentralised nature of government, and the greater power of the states and the municipal governments.

4 On 16 February 1923 a Royal Commission had been appointed under the chairmanship of the Earl of Onslow to 'inquire into the existing law and procedure relating to the extensions of county Boroughs and the creation of new County Boroughs in England and Wales, and the effect such extensions or creations on the administration of the Councils of Counties and of non-County Boroughs, Urban Districts and Rural Districts; to investigate the relations between these several local authorities; and generally to make recommendations as to their constitution, areas and functions'. Extract from the Local Government (County Boroughs and Adjustments) Act 1926. See Wikipedia (2009c).

5 The term 'project cycle' is actually a misnomer. In practice it is a linear process that breaks physical development activities down into a number of phases, from conception and feasibility analysis, through planning, design and construction, to operation.

6 Planning for the reform of local government was to begin in 1970 with the establishment of a Royal Commission. The outcome would be the elimination of municipal engineering as it had been understood prior to that point in time.

7 The comprehensive list of responsibilities given by Seeley is reproduced in a background document that can be found at the website www.infrastructuremat-ters.org.

8 The American model was different from both, being something of a hybrid, beginning with standing committees but then evolving into a system with an executive mayor.

9 Bennett phrases it differently, saying, 'In comparison with the USA and with most other OECD countries, the UK urban system has a highly consolidated form of administrative, financial and political control' (2000, p. 67). However, this is simply a polite euphemism, and another way of saying it is that Britain is a highly centralised state.

10 With a population density of approximately 400 persons per square kilometre, England is one of the most densely populated countries in the world (excluding small island states).

11 The term 'trinity' is used here to describe three elements seen as a single, integrated entity.

12 This concept will be discussed in more detail later.

13 The following definition of public works, which was taken from the website of the American Public Works Association in 1997 (in a document dated 1974), has now been superseded by a new definition (www.apwa.net/discover/what_is_public_works, American Public Works Association, accessed 20 October 2011). However, the earlier definition of public works, quoted here, was used consistently until the end of the twentieth century, as can be seen from a reading of the reference.

14 The above definition, and the list that follows, is no longer accessible via the American Public Works Association website (www.awpa.net), where it was found originally.

15 The comprehensive list is reproduced in a background document that can be found at www.infrastructurematters.org.

16 This is the term used in the United States to describe local government.

17 The term 'miasma' comes from the Greek word for pollution, and means a noxious (i.e. poisonous) form of 'bad air'. See Wikipedia (2011b).

18 See, for example, the book by Oliver Cooke (2008).

19 This discussion excludes the utilities of power (electricity supply), which were generally privately owned in the larger cities, though public ownership was common in smaller towns.

20 This specific discussion is concerned with the historical development of infra-structure in Britain and the United States in the nineteenth century. As such, it is exploring infrastructure from within the context of its time, not in the current global context. That discussion, and the subsequent expansion of the model, will take place in a later chapter.

4 Transferring the British infrastructure model to Africa

1 The granting of dominion status to Nigeria in 1954, just six years prior to inde-pendence, came too late to make a significant impact on the development approach, at least from an infrastructure management perspective.

2 This quotation has been extracted from private notes taken during a study of Soweto by the author in 1990.

3 The colonial name for which was Salisbury.

4 This rental system is still active and explains, for example, why Nairobi finds it so difficult to develop meaningful upgrading strategies for its informal settlements.

5 See Carole Rakodi for a good summary of these events, albeit with a liberal economic perspective, in Rakodi (1997b).

6 The Public-Private Infrastructure Advisory Facility.

7 The World Bank creates these proxy organisations, like the PPIAF and the WSP (Water and Sanitation Program), to target specific aspects of development that do not fall within its existing organisational structure, thereby giving the impression that they are entities independent of World Bank orthodoxy. However, while they are free to create their own developmental strategies in theory, the reality is that they cannot stray too far, conceptually, from the World Bank orthodoxy. The head of the organisation may have a degree of independence in setting the development agenda, but would not obtain the position in the first place if he or she did not support the Bank's view intellectually.

8 A Latin phrase that means: 'that which was to have been proved has now been proved'.

9 The discussion here relates specifically to the British model of urban planning, which separates urban planning, urban design and architecture into three different professions.

5 Decentralisation and urban infrastructure

1 Kigali Declaration on Leadership Capacity Building for Decentralised Governance and Poverty Reduction in Sub-Saharan Africa, Kigali, Rwanda, 08 June 2005, prepared by ministers in charge of decentralisation and local government.

2 The United Nations Research Institute for Social Development.

3 Olowu himself is African, but works in a Dutch research institute. Thus, while he may be able to bring some valuable personal insights, he has to situate his analysis, as a social scientist, within the collective academic framework of his peer review group, which is almost exclusively western in make-up.

4 The term' present' should be related to the year of publication, which was 2001.

5 See, for example, Kuengienda (2008).

6 Here Olowu (2001, p. 7) makes reference to work by a number of authors: Barkan et al. (1991); Corkery et al. (1995); Leighton (1996).

7 These countries are Côte d'Ivoire, Ethiopia, Mali, South Africa and Uganda.

8 Reducing disparities among regions; providing flexibility; improving local governance; mobilising private resources; and empowering people.

9 Municipality is the South African term for an urban local government authority.

10 The author was a member of the commission established to review the powers, duties and functions of the City of Cape Town in 1996.

11 The Department of Water Affairs and Forestry, which was restructured in 2009 to become the Department of Water and Environmental Affairs (DWEA).

12 These figures are taken from an extract of the report by its author at www.ally. co.za (accessed 21 May 2010).

13 Here we are concerned with France as a country; which should not be confused with the more controversial view of France as an ex-colonial power.

14 In France, all tiers of government below that of the central government are defined as local government.

15 This principle is specific to the needs of a unitary state and would not apply in a federal system of government, since the powers of local government in the latter would be defined by the regional or state government.

16 These different bodies can be viewed in a background paper prepared for this chapter, which can be found on www.infrastructurematters.org.

17 This review was found in a site that was no longer active, at least in its original format, when visited in 2009: www.ozpolitics.info/guide/phil/policy/ (accessed 25 August 2009). However, since it drew heavily on the work of Davis *et al.* (1993) and this work has been quoted here, and since it is only a passing reference, it has been retained.

18 This is a general point that applies to any area of public policy; its use here is limited to urban infrastructure policy since that is the focus of the wider discussion.

19 See, for example, the *Telegraph*, 'Britain Faces a Blackout – and the Politicians Are to Blame', 02 September 2009; the *Sunday Telegraph*, 'Britain Heading Back to the Dark Ages', 06 September 2009; Timesonline, 'Power Cuts Forecast to Hit UK in Four Years', 10 October 2009.

20 Ofgem is the Office of the Gas and Electricity Markets.

21 Ofgem (2009) 'Project Discovery': 'Project Discovery is Ofgem's investigation into whether or not future security of supply can be delivered by the existing market arrangements over the coming decade': www.ofgem.gov.uk/markets/whlmkts/discovery/Pages/ProjectDiscovery.aspx (accessed 20 April 2011).

22 The use of quantitative deliverables, essentially 'taps and toilets', to individuals.

6 Urbanisation in Ethiopia

1 The word 'city' is used widely in Ethiopia as a generic shorthand term for an urban area that has been given official recognition. The legal term for such an area, though, is 'urban local government authority' (ULGA), a term that will also be used here.

2 Termed Capacity Building for Decentralised Service Delivery (CBDSD).

3 As has already been explained, Ethiopian terminology tends to use the word 'city' for any proclaimed urban centre. It should not be read to indicate any specific property of an urban area, such as size, for example, and is synonymous with the terms 'town' and 'municipality' used elsewhere in the book.

4 Since renamed the Ministry of Urban Development and Construction.

5 The discussion in http://en.wikipedia.org/wiki/Kingdom_of_Aksum quotes the work of the scholar Stuart Munro-Hay and the eminent Ethiopian specialist Richard Pankhurst here as overturning the theory of Conti Rossini that the Aksumite Empire was founded by Semitic-speaking Sabaeans, who crossed the Red Sea from Saudi Arabia (now Yemen).

6 This exploration of Axum is taken from the same Wikipedia discussion, http://en.wikipedia.org/wiki/Kingdom_of_Aksum (accessed 11 February 2010).

7 The concept of orthogenetic and heterogenetic cities was developed by Redfield and Singer (1954).

8 The monasteries, with their traditions of learning and teaching, and the use of a written language, played a critical role in maintaining the social and conceptual integrity of the Ethiopian state over the entire period of its history. It could be argued that it was this tradition, more than any other, that enabled Ethiopia to ward off the numerous Islamic incursions that recurred on a regular basis throughout its history and remain a cohesive state.

9 This was not the final state as we know it today. The resolution of the eastern border with Somalia and the status of Eritrea were to change a number of times over the course of the coming century, while in the South-West the Kingdom of Jimma was only formally absorbed into Ethiopia in 1932.

10 In choosing the time-frame for this part of the discussion, I have drawn on, and would acknowledge, a book by the Ethiopian historian and academic Bahru Zewde entitled *A History of Modern Ethiopia: 1855–1991* (2002).

11 This part of the discussion draws upon the history of Ethiopia to be found at http://en.wikipedia.org/wiki/History_of_Ethiopia (accessed 11 February 2010).

12 The *Zamana Masafent* describes the period prior to Tewodros II. A good summary description is provided on www.ethiopianhistory.com/Era_of_the_ Princes, which explains this period as follows: 'The Era of the Princes, also called Zamana Masafent, was a brief period of history in Ethiopia that lasted from 1769 to 1855. By 1708, the central government was destroyed and the country had split up into three different provinces: Amhara, Shoa, and Tigray. The Amhara region was continually in internal friction and contributed poorly to defending Ethiopia against external enemies. Tigray, on the other hand, played a major role in reinstating an imperial government and hosted a decisive battle at Adwa. On the other hand, Shoa, for the most part, stayed out of the political situations that dealt with the Amhara and Tigray regions. However, Shoan kings did expand their territories southwards and established trade that produce an abundance of coffee and slaves. Ethiopia survived this era in its history because of Tigray and Shoa's gaining steady power.'

13 This description, and the two quotations that follow, were written by Professor Richard Pankhurst in the preface to Giorghis and Gérard (2007).

14 The Italians redrew both the regional and international boundaries where they could, integrating Ethiopia, Eritrea and Italian Somaliland into a single 'empire' of 'Italian East Africa' (Africa Orientale Italiana), which was divided into six major regional divisions (Zewde, 2002, p. 162). They did so with the full approval of, and support from, the other regional European powers, Great Britain and France.

15 Portuguese speaking.

16 Where possible, the cities used as examples are those forming part of this case-study project.

17 Giorghis describes this as follows: 'A *sefer* is an area similar to a military settlement or neighbourhood, which is allocated to a chief of a state dignitary and is distinguished from other similar areas by a buffer zone' (Giorghis and Gérard, 2007, p. 42). The word has no relation to the Hebrew word of the same spelling, meaning 'book'.

18 The government of Ethiopia uses a number terms to describe its urban areas. ULGA is the legal definition. The urban areas are also referred to generally as 'cities' (as mentioned earlier), regardless of their size. Finally, the terms 'municipality' and 'town' are also used in different contexts.

19 The other two components related to Civil Service Reform and Strengthening the Ministry of Capacity Building.

20 Although the CBDSD programme was wide in scope, the abbreviation was used throughout to describe this specific component of the RELG. For that reason, the term CBDSD will continue to be used in all discussions relating to this project.

21 Though managed by international consultants, the teams were expected to comprise local and expatriate professionals in equal numbers.

22 The stipulated requirement was for senior specialists in Local Government/ Municipal Structure Management and Operations; Municipal Finance; Municipal Engineering; and Land, Housing and Urban Development.

23 Of the 100-plus deliverables, over 40 per cent related directly to physical infrastructure services.

24 An extract from the terms of reference provided to the consultant for the 'Southern' cities, unpublished.
25 Extract from the specific terms of reference provided to the author, unpublished.
26 Note that responsibilities in the Education and Health sectors are integrated directly with the wider activities of the regional bureaux in these two areas. Hence, the ULGAs function more as implementing agencies.
27 The woreda is a sub-administration of the regional governments, broadly equivalent to the district in anglophone Africa.

7 From engineering to infrastructure: changing the urban paradigm

1 The diagram shown as Figure 7.1 is slightly different from that presented at the workshop and later incorporated into various reports. The change has been made to better reflect the way in which the CBDSD project was followed up; it does not change the conceptual flow of the original diagram significantly.
2 This chapter draws upon an extensive amount of material collected during the study, which cannot be included here without changing the nature of the book and the flow of the discourse quite significantly. For those who would like to see this background material, it has been collated and can be accessed through the website supporting this book: www.infrastructurematters.org.
3 www.infrastructurematters.org.
4 Further information can also be found on the website of the federal Ministry of Public Works and Construction of the federal government of Ethiopia, known previously (i.e. during the period of the study) as the federal Ministry of Works and Urban Development: www.mwud.gov.et.
5 The parallel team working in the North allocated greater resources to community surveys, which included structured random surveys, and this information was later integrated with, and used to correlate, the work carried out by the Southern team.
6 The World Bank was funding two separate development programmes in Ethiopia at the time, this one in urban development and a separate programme in water supply (both rural and urban), which caused immense confusion in the cities and led to conflicting outcomes.
7 This creates a sanitation scenario that is reminiscent of the early American experience described in Chapter 3.
8 The full details of this plan, together with further information on the development, and management of the urban infrastructure asset management system in Ethiopia can be found at www.infrastructurematters.org.
9 This is an approximation method that describes the cost of work in terms of a linear, square or cubic measure, depending on the type of work. So, for example, a water main or surface drain of a certain size would be defined in Ethiopian birr per metre length, while a road of a certain type would be described in terms of birr per square metre.
10 In addition, there had been a number of local, in-house workshops throughout the contract period.
11 The approach reflects a movement downward from the initial federal workshop, via regional workshops to the level of the ULGA, which in turn is a reflection of the increasing success and effectiveness of the decentralization process.
12 The GTZ (now GIZ) Urban Governance and Decentralisation Programme for Ethiopia will be described in greater detail in Chapter 10, which discusses a framework for urban governance. Details can also be found on the GIZ website: www.gtz.de/en/praxis/6609.htm.

13 More details about the asset management programme can be found on the website for the book: www.infrastructurematters.org.

14 It is worth noting that the ULGAs which had worked with the asset management approach previously provided less inflated figures on the first draft of the CIP than did the ULGAs that had only been introduced to the asset management process at the first national workshop.

15 This section only describes those actors playing a substantive role in urban management as it impacts on urban infrastructure. A number of these, particularly in the international agencies, have different thematic or sectoral programmes. The description of a specialist group or programme, for example within the World Bank, does not imply that this is the only programme within that organisation, or that it is necessarily even its main programmatic activity. Nor does it imply that a specific policy approach which may be discussed here extends beyond the programme in question to a wider policy approach for the agency as a whole.

16 See Chapter 10, pp. 360–4, together with some of the papers and other material produced by the author on this subject, which can be found on the website supporting the book: www.infrastructurematters.org.

17 This is, unfortunately, a much-abused term with different interpretations. Its use here is not that of a target-based approach (i.e. defined quantitative outcomes); rather, it is intended to define the delivery of urban infrastructure systems.

18 At the same time, the study raised the whole question of how affordability should be defined, and at which level (e.g. the individual family or ULGA). This issue will be explored further in Chapter 9.

19 The Urban Infrastructure and Service Improvement Sub-Programme of the federal Ministry of Works and Urban Development.

20 Private communication from Ato Fikreyohannes Yadessa, consultant to the Ministry of Works and Urban Development and Specialist Trainer in Infrastructure Asset Management the Ethiopian way, with minor paraphrasing approved by the writer.

21 The concept of a new degree programme for urban infrastructure management, and proposals for a course structure, are discussed on the book's website: www.infrastructurematters.org.

8 Rethinking urban development in Africa

1 There is a term 'problematic' in English, but it has two meanings, which makes its use in a development context difficult. It is used both as an adjective and as a noun. As an adjective, it is directly linked to the noun 'problem'. As a noun, it is defined as 'expressing or supporting a possibility'. This is extremely vague, and it is this vagueness that, when coupled with its other, better-known use as an adjective based upon the term 'problem', makes it difficult to use in this context.

2 This could be translated as a methodological approach to creating a problem statement. Bearing in mind the earlier discussion associated with the use of the term 'problem' in English, it should be recognised that in French, what appears to be a similar word (*problème*) is not perceived in exactly the same way as 'problem' is in English.

3 This phrase is taken from the title of a book by Schnurr and Hotz (1998).

4 See also Robinson and Tinker (1997).

5 Extract from the Royal Charter establishing the British Institution of Civil Engineers by George IV on 03 June 1828.

6 German researchers use the term 'infrastructures' as the plural form of the noun 'infrastructure'. Anglo-American practice may occasionally do this, but more often uses the term 'infrastructure' as a collective noun (that is, the singular and the plural take the same form).
7 In this sentence, Monstadt (ibid.) is quoting from Harvey (1998).
8 This term 'urban infrastructures' is taken from the paper by Jochen Monstadt (2009) and reflects German usage.
9 Here Monstadt is quoting from Hommels (2005, p. 339).

9 A model for green infrastructure

1 German researchers use the term 'infrastructures' as the plural form of the noun 'infrastructure'. Anglo-American practice may occasionally do this, but more often uses the term infrastructure as a collective noun (that is, the singular and the plural take the same form).
2 The use of the term 'natural resources' has been stretched slightly to incorporate electricity, which would normally be a secondary resource, being a product generated from primary resources.
3 This list of the six primary categories specifically excludes defining any living thing as a resource to be exploited. We may choose, as a species, to use other creatures in this way, and will no doubt continue to do so, or at least a large proportion of the population; but that does not give us the right to define these creatures as a resource in the way that the six major categories are defined.

10 Green urban infrastructure in practice: mediating resource flows

1 This was the origin of the BOD5 standard used for estimating the residual oxygen demand – that is, the 'suffocation potential', as it were – of a wastewater, a good example of how a specific British need translated into an international standard.
2 The figure of 175 million tonnes was the projected figure for 2013 as estimated in 2010.
3 Estimate in 2006.
4 1 million BTU = 1,054,615 GJ (gigajoules) and 1 GJ = $26.8\,m^3$ of natural gas.
5 The Sustainable Sanitation Alliance.
6 See, for example, a report from an African ministerial meeting: *Water for Agriculture and Energy in Africa: The Challenges of Climate Change* (2008) Hydropower Resource Assessment, Sirte, Libya, December 2008: www.sirtewaterandenergy. org/docs/2009/Sirte_2008_BAK_3.pdf (accessed 11 April 2011).
7 Data drawn from *The World Factbook* of the Central Intelligence Agency, quoted in a summary of electricity consumption: http://en.wikipedia.org/wiki/List_of_countries_by_electricity_consumption (accessed 11 April 2011).
8 United Nations Statistics Division, quoted in DESA (1999, p. 2, figure 2).
9 Two British comedians, Peter Cooke and Dudley Moore, if I recall correctly.
10 A paradox is a statement that contradicts itself.
11 An anomaly is a deviation, either from a rule or from what is regarded as the norm.
12 A more detailed analysis of this case study, together with background and supporting material, can be found at the website supporting the book: www.infrastructurematters.org.
13 There will always be exceptions to this, for example when a town is built around an industrial process such as oil drilling; but this will only ever apply to a small minority of secondary towns.

14 This term is itself a contradiction in terms, since there is nothing cyclic about it; it is a purely linear model with clear start and end points.
15 These are three examples of taught course modules taken from UNESCO's *Curriculum Guide on E-Governance for African Government Institutions*, produced by UNESCO and CAFRAD (African Training and Research Centre in Administration for Development), dated 19 December 2007, updated 3 January 2008: http://portal.unesco.org/ci/en/files/25720/11980630809curriculum_guide. pdf/curriculum%2Bguide.pdf (accessed 11 April 2011).
16 See, for example, the development by the Australia South Africa Local Governance Partnership (ASOLGP), *Community Asset Management Guidelines for Provincial and Municipal Staff*, as a good example of taking a western construct and applying locally by 'adapting it to local conditions' but without exploring the underlying social value system: http://devplan.kzntl.gov.za/ASALGP/ Resources/Documents/ASALGPhandbooks/PDF/HB3-intro.pdf.
17 www.infrastructurematters.org.
18 www.infrastructurematters.org.

II Green infrastructure and urban governance

1 This excerpt is drawn from a speech by Julius Nyerere entitled 'Good Governance in Africa', made on 13 October 1998, as transcribed by Ayanda Madyibi: www.marxists.org/subject/africa/nyerere/1998/10/13.htm (accessed 10 October 2010).
2 An extract from the address of the British Deputy Prime Minister, Nick Clegg, to the United Nations Millennium Goals Summit, New York, 23 September 2010, taken from: http://helenduffett.blogspot.com/2010/09/nick-cleggs-speech-at-united-nations.html (accessed 10 October 2010).
3 An extract from the address of the British Deputy Prime Minister, Nick Clegg, to the United Nations General Assembly, New York, 24 September 2010, taken from: www.number10.gov.uk/news/speeches-and-transcripts/2010/09/deputy-pms-speech-to-the-un-general-assembly-55287 (accessed 10 October 2010).
4 GTZ, the Deutsche Gesellshaft für Technische Zusammenarbeit (GTZ) GmbH, was renamed GIZ, the Deutsche Gesellshaft für Internationale Zusammenarbeit (GIZ) GmbH on 01 January 2011.
5 Bundesministerium für wirtschaftliche Zusammenarbeit und Entwicklung.
6 This definition, quoted here from Wikipedia, is the generally accepted definition that can be found in most United Nations publications on the topic: en. wikipedia.org/wiki/Good_governance (accessed 13 October 2009).
7 The Organisation for Economic Co-operation and Development (OECD) was formed with the objective of bringing together the governments of countries committed to democracy and the market economy from around the world to achieve a set of economic goals. It was originally an organisation of high-income countries (plus Turkey). In 2009 it had thirty members, including Mexico, and South Africa was a candidate member. While it has limited additional membership, it is essentially a western club.
8 A strong case in support of this statement is made in the series of analysis that formed part of the French study described previously: DgCiD (2008).

12 Building African cities for a sustainable future

1 A good description, and discussion (in French) of this whole concept of 'le monde anglo-saxon' is provided by Jeremy Jenkins in a Science Po Research Note (Jenkins, 2007).

2 This is an extract from an online article quoting Richard Elliott, Associate Director, Communications Dept. WEF, reporting on the Twentieth World Economic Forum on Africa, Dar es Salaam, Tanzania, 06 May 2010: www.weforum.org/en/media/Latest%20News%20Releases/NR_WEFA10_ChinaAfrica (accessed 25 August 2010). The article has since been taken offline.

3 The situation in the United States was somewhat different, with the additional need to connect the newly emerging towns to the growing national transportation network, which was seen as the driver of the country's economic development.

References

Abbott, J. (2006) *Infrastructure and Service Delivery and Financing: Final Summary Report*, a report prepared on behalf of GTZ-International Services for the Federal Ministry of Works and Urban Development, Government of Ethiopia, June 2006, unpublished.

Abbott, J. (2007) *A Review of the Infrastructure Components of the CBDSD Study*, report prepared for the Ministry of Works and Urban Development, Federal Government of Ethiopia, 30 June 2007.

Abbott Grobicki (2001) *Integrated Catchment Management in an Urban Context: The Great and Little Lotus Rivers*, WRC Report no. 864/1/01, Water Research Commission, Pretoria, South Africa.

Adogbo, K. J. and Kolo, B. A. (2008) 'The Perceptions on the Use of Indigenous Building Materials and Professionals in the Nigerian Building Industry'. *Environmental Technology and Science Journal* (ETSJ) (Nigeria), vol. 3, no. 2: www.abu.edu.ng/publications/2009-06-28-132407_3039.doc (accessed 27 September 2010).

American Heritage Dictionary (2006) 'Critical Mass', *The American Heritage Dictionary of the English Language*, 4th ed., taken from www.answers.com/topic/critical-mass (accessed 14 April 2010).

American Heritage Dictionary (2006) 'Infrastructure', *The American Heritage Dictionary of the English Language*, 4th ed.

Archives Wales (2009) Powys County Archives Office Rural Sanitary Authority Records: arcw.llgc.org.uk/anw/get_collection.php?inst_id=40&coll_id=12080&expand (accessed 24 October 2009).

Asian Development Bank (2008) *In the Pipeline: Water for the Poor: Investing in Small Water Supply Networks*, Asian Development Bank, Mandayulong City, Philippines: www.adb.org/Documents/Books/Water-Pipeline/Water-Pipelines.pdf (accessed 30 April 2011).

Australian Government (2007) *ESD Design Guide: Office and Public Buildings*, 3rd ed., Department of the Environment and Water Resources, Commonwealth of Australia: www.environment.gov.au/sustainability/government/publications/esd-design/pubs/esd-design-guide.pdf (accessed 04 August 2011).

Bakker, K. (2010) *Privatizing Water: Governance Failure and the World's Urban Water Crisis*, Cornell University Press, Ithaca, NY.

Bangladesh2day (2009) 'Electric Rickshaws in Rangpur': www.bangladesh2day.com/newsfinance/2009/August/18/Electric-rickshaws-in-Rangpur.php (accessed 01 September 2010).

Barkan, J. D., McNulty, M. and Ayeni, M. (1991) 'Hometown Voluntary Associations and the Emergence of Civil Society in Western Nigeria', *Journal of Modern
African Studies*, vol. 29, no. 3, pp. 457–80.

Bennett, R. J. (2000) 'Regional and Local Economic Development Policy', in G.
Horváth (ed.) *Regions and Cities in the Global World*, Centre for Regional Studies,
Pécs, Hungary, pp. 58–81.

Berresford Ellis, P. (1998) *The Ancient World of the Celts*, Constable, London.

Bloy, M. (2011) The Peel Web: www.historyhome.co.uk/peel/politics/municip.
htm, update of 06 January 2011 (accessed 09 May 2011).

CBI (2009) 'Energy Policy Too Wind Focused', BBC News article, update of 13 July
2009: http://news.bbc.co.uk/1/hi/8146824.stm (accessed 21 August 2009).

City of Redding (1997) Annual Report 1996/7, City of Redding Department of Public
Works: www.ci.redding.ca.us/pubworks/ar2.htm (accessed 20 October 2011).

Clapham, C. (2002) 'Controlling Space in Ethiopia', in W. James, E. Donham, E.
Kurimoto and A. Triulzi (eds) *Remapping Ethiopia: Socialism and After*, Ohio University Press, Ohio.

COHRE (2008a) *Water Services Fault Lines: An Assessment of South Africa's Water and
Sanitation Provision across 15 Municipalities*, Centre for Housing Rights and Evictions (COHRE), Geneva, Centre for Applied Legal Studies (CALS), Johannesburg, Norwegian Centre for Human Rights (NCHR), Oslo, October 2008.

COHRE (2008b) *A Rights-Based Review of the Legal and Policy Framework of the Ghanaian Water and Sanitation Sector*, Centre for Housing Rights and Evictions
(COHRE), Geneva.

Commission of the European Communities (2007) *An Energy Policy for Europe* {SEC
(2007) 12}, Communication from the Commission to the European Council and
the European Parliament, 10 January 2007: ec.europa.eu/energy/energy_
policy/doc/01_energy_policy_for_europe_en.pdf (accessed 28 April 2011).

Cooke, O. D. (2008) *Rethinking Municipal Privatization*, Routledge, New York.

Corkery, J., Land, A. and Bossuyt, J. (1995) 'The Process of Policy Formulation:
Institutional Path or Institutional Maze', European Centre for Policy Development and Management, Maastricht.

Cornwall Council (2011) 'Sanitary Authorities': www.cornwall.gov.uk/default.
aspx?page=14627 (accessed 09 May 2011).

CRF online (2009) 'Glossary': www.crfonline.org/orc/glossary/p.html (accessed
05 February 2009). This website has since converted to members-only access and
is no longer available for general use.

Crummey, D. (1969) 'Tēwodros as Reformer and Modernizer', *Journal of African
History*, vol. 10, no. 3, pp. 457–69.

Cumings, B. (2010) *Dominion from Sea to Sea: Pacific Ascendency and American Power*,
Yale University Press, New Haven, CT.

Davis, G. Wanna, J., Warhurst, J. and Weller, P. (1993) *Public Policy in Australia*, 2nd
ed, Allen & Unwin, St Leonards, NSW.

Deardorf (2009) *Deardorf's Glossary of International Economics*: www-personal.umich.
edu/~alandear/glossary/i.html (accessed 27 January 2009).

DESA (1999) 'Trends in Consumption and Production: Household Energy Consumption', United Nations Department of Economic and Social Affairs, Discussion Paper no. 6, ST/ESA/1999/DP.6, December, p. 2, figure 2: www.un.org/
esa/sustdev/publications/esa99dp6.pdf (accessed 11 April 2011).

DFID (2010) 'Good Governance': www.dfid.gov.uk/Global-Issues/How-we-fight-Poverty/Government/Good-Governance/ (accessed 22 February 2010; but this page has since been withdrawn).

DgCiD (2008) 'Urban Governance: Questioning a Multiform Paradigm', Summary Report for the Division of Democratic Governance (Directorate for Development Policies in the DgCiD), Ministry of Foreign and European Affairs (MAEE), GEMDEV – AMODEV, January.

Dowden, D. (2009) 'Obama's Direct Line to the Heart of Africa', *The Times* (London), 10 July.

Economist, The (2009) 'Dark Days Ahead', *The Economist* (London), 8 August, pp. 27–9.

Elkind, S. (1999) *Public Works and Public Health: Reflections on Urban Politics and the Environment, 1880–1925*, Public Works Historical Society, Kansas City, MO.

Encyclopædia Britannica (2008) 'Logical Positivism': www.britannica.com/EBchecked/topic/346336/logical-positivism (accessed 02 September 2009).

Encyclopedia of the Nations (2007) 'United States – Local Government': www.nationsencyclopedia.com/Americas/United-States-LOCAL-GOVERNMENT.html (accessed 13 April 2010).

EPSRC (2010) 'Resource Implications of Adaptation of Infrastructure to Global Change', Engineering and Physical Sciences Research Council, ref. EP/H003630/1, 19 November, http://gow.epsrc.ac.uk/ViewGrant.aspx?GrantRef=EP/H003630/1 (accessed 30 April 2011).

FCM (2003) 'Municipal Infrastructure Asset Management: A Best Practice by the National Guide to Sustainable Municipal Infrastructure', November, Federation of Canadian Municipalities.

Federal Democratic Republic of Ethiopia (2005) 'National Hygiene and Sanitation Strategy', Ministry of Health, Federal Democratic Republic of Ethiopia, Addis Ababa: www.wsp.org/wsp/sites/wsp.org/files/publications/622200751450_EthiopiaNationalHygieneAndSanitationStrategyAF.pdf, Water and Sanitation Program, Washington, DC (accessed 20 October 2011).

Federal Government of Ethiopia (2005) 'Urban Development Policy', March, Ministry of Federal Affairs, Addis Ababa.

Federal Government of Ethiopia (undated) *Capacity Building for Decentralized Service Delivery Project, IDA Credit ET-3698: Terms of Reference for Deepening Decentralization in Oromiya National Regional State and Southern Nations, Nationalities and Peoples' Regional State and Restructuring of Selected Local Governments*, Ministry of Federal Affairs.

FETP (2011) 'Case Study: Urea Fertilizer: Import or Produce?', FETP OpenCourse-Ware, Fulbright Economics Teaching Program: www.fetp.edu.vn/short-course/0102/Eco_Management/English/5-Mon-Jan14/4-Urea%20Fertilizer%20Case-English.pdf (accessed 11 May 2011).

Fiseha, A. (2006) 'Theory versus Practice in Ethiopia's Ethnic Federation', in D. Turton (ed.) *Ethnic Federalism: The Ethiopian Experience in Comparative Perspective*, Addis Ababa University Press, Addis Ababa, pp. 131–64.

Fraser, D. (1973) *The Evolution of the Welfare State: A History of Social Policy since the Industrial Revolution*, Macmillan, London.

Free Dictionary (2008) 'Water Supply': www.thefreedictionary.com/water+supply (accessed 27 January 2009).

Free Dictionary (2010) 'Worldview': www.thefreedictionary.com/worldview (accessed 18 March 2010).

Free Dictionary (2011) 'Infrastructure': www.thefreedictionary.com/infrastructure (accessed 27 January 2009).

Fukuyama, F. (1992) *The End of History and the Last Man*, The Free Press, Simon & Schuster, New York.

Gale Encyclopedia of US History (2008) 'Local Government': www.answers.com/topic/local-government (accessed 29 April 2011).

GDRC (2010) 'Local Agenda 21', Global Development Research Centre: www.gdrc.org/uem/la21/la21.html (accessed 07 August 2010).

Gilpin, R. (2002) 'The Rise of American Hegemony', in P. K. O'Brien and A. Clesse (eds) *Britain 1846–1914 and the United States 1945–2001*, Ashgate Publishing Ltd, Aldershot, UK, pp. 165–82: www.mtholyoke.edu/acad/intrel/ipe/gilpin.htm (accessed 28 April 2010).

Giorghis, F. and Gérard, D. (2007) *The City and Its Architectural Heritage: Addis Ababa 1886–1941*, Shama Books, Addis Ababa.

Glatz, F. (2000) 'Question Marks of European History', in G. Horváth (ed.) *Regions and Cities in the Global World: Essays in Honour of György Enyedi*, Centre for Regional Studies, Hungarian Academy of Sciences, Pécs, Hungary, pp. 17–29.

Glennie, J. (2009) *The Trouble with Aid: Why Less Could Mean More for Africa*, Zed Books, London.

Goulet, D. (1986) 'Three Rationalities in Development Decision-Making', *World Development*, vol. 14, no. 2, pp. 301–17.

Greenlaunches.com (2011) 'Solar Powered Auto Rickshaws in India, One Step Closer to Reality': www.greenlaunches.com/transport/solar-powered-auto-rickshaws-in-india-one-step-closer-to-reality.php (accessed 11 May 2011).

Gregory, J. W. (1938) *The Story of the Road: From the Beginning to the Present Day*, Adam and Charles Black, London.

GTZ (2010a) 'Good Governance': www.gtz.de/en/themen/882.htm (accessed 22 February 2010).

GTZ (2010b) www.gtz.de/en/themen/politische-reformen/dezentralisierung-kommunale-selbstverwaltung/2447.htm (accessed 22 February 2010; but this page has since been withdrawn).

GTZ IS (2005) *Situational Analysis and Baseline* [*Study*], ONRS, report prepared for the Ministry of Federal Affairs, Federal Government of Ethiopia.

Guardian (2009) 'E.ON chief Paul Golby strives to generate debate about green goals', *Guardian* (London), 19 June.

Gudina, M. (2006) 'Contradictory Interpretations of Ethiopian History: A Need for a New Consensus', in D. Turton (ed.) *Ethnic Federalism: The Ethiopian Experience in Comparative Perspective*, Addis Ababa University Press, Addis Ababa, pp. 119–30.

Hachette Livre (2007) *Dictionnaire Hachette 2008*, Hachette Livre, Paris.

Hall, D. J. and Lobina, E. (2007) 'From a Private Past to a Public Future? The Problems of Water in England and Wales', Public Services International Research Unit (PSIRU), Business School, University of Greenwich, UK, November.

Hamlin, C. (1992) 'Edwin Chadwick and the Engineers, 1842–1854: Systems and Antisystems in the Pipe-and-Brick Sewers War', *Technology and Culture*, vol. 33, no. 4, pp. 680–709.

Harvey, D. (1998) 'Cities or Urbanization?', *City*, vol. 1, no. 1, pp. 38–61.

Hayter, T. (1971) *Aid and Imperialism*, Pelican, London.

HM Government (2010) 'Decentralisation and the Localism Bill: An Essential Guide, Department for Communities and Local Government: www.communities.gov.uk/documents/localgovernment/pdf/1793908.pdf (accessed 20 October 2011).

HM Government (2010–11) Localism Bill (in progress at the time of publication), see UK Parliament website, http://services.parliament.uk/bills/2010-11/localism.html (accessed 20 October 2011).

Hommels, A. (2005) 'Studying Obduracy in the City: Toward a Productive Fusion between Technology Studies and Urban Studies', *Science, Technology, and Human Values*, vol. 30, no. 3, pp. 325–51.

Hydro4Africa (2011) Home page: http://hydro4africa.net (accessed 11 May 2011).

ICE (undated) 'Municipal Group Scotland', Institution of Civil Engineers (ICE), Scotland: www.ice.org.uk/nearyou/UK-Regions/Scotland/Specialist-Areas/Municipal-Group-Scotland (accessed 21 October 2011).

ICIS (2010) 'Urea Uses and Market Data': www.icis.com/v2/chemicals/9076559/urea/uses.html (accessed 30 August 2010). The figure of 175 million tonnes was the projection for 2013, estimated in 2010.

IMF (2001) *International Financial Statistics Yearbook 2001*, International Monetary Fund, Washington, DC.

IRIN (2011) 'Water: Optimism at World Water Day Conference', a summary article published by IRIN, a service of the UN Office for the Coordination of Humanitarian Affairs: www.irinnews.org/Report.aspx?ReportID=92261 (accessed 23 March 2011).

Jackson, B. M. (1997) 'Private Sector Participation in South Africa's Water Sector: Pressures, Policies and Lessons from Practical Experience', paper presented at a seminar on cost recovery, sustainability and equity in the provision of urban services, Washington, DC, 23 September: www.africanwater.org/ppp_debate2.htm (accessed 14 June 2010).

Jackson, B. M. (2003) 'Financing Municipal Infrastructure in Developing Countries: The Need for Utilities Engineers to Learn New Skills', updated version of a keynote speech prepared for the Annual Congress of the International Federation of Municipal Engineers in November 2003, provided by the author in personal correspondence.

James, C. L. R. (1980) 'The Making of the Caribbean People', in *Spheres of Existence: Selected Writings*, Allison & Busby, London.

Jenkins, J. (2007) 'Peut-on parler d'un modèle anglo-saxon? (Contribution a une histoire de nos préjugés)', Note de Recherche/Working Papers no. 20, Centre de Recherches Politiques de Sciences Po (CEVIPOF), 7 January : www.cevipof.com/fichier/p_publication/476/publication_pdf_ne_20.pdf (accessed 21 October 2011).

Jenkins, S. (2010) 'This Localism Bill Shows Eric Pickles Is Hazel Blears in Supersized Wolf's Clothing', *Guardian* (London), 14 December.

Kay, P. and Kempton, W. (1984) 'What Is the Sapir–Whorf Hypothesis?', *American Anthropologist*, vol. 86, no. 1, pp. 65–79.

Kissinger, H. (1957) *A World Restored: Metternich, Castlereagh and the Problems of Peace, 1812–1822*, Phoenix Press, London.

Kuengienda, M. (2008) *Crise de l'Etat en Afrique et modernité politique en question*, L'Harmattan, Paris.

Kuhn, T. S. (1996) *The Structure of Scientific Revolutions*, 3rd ed., University of Chicago Press, Chicago.

Kyessi, A. G. (2006) 'Participatory Planning in Regularization of Informal Settlements in Mwanza, Tanzania', *Territoriun, Journal of the Institute for Spatial Planning*, Faculty of Geography, University of Belgrade, Serbia and Montenegro, UDC 711.4 (678), June, pp. 56–81.

Law and Letters (2006) 'What Is Critical Mass Theory, and Why Does It Matter?': http://lawandletters.blogspot.com/2006/06/what-is-critical-mass-theory-and-why_06.html, 06 June (accessed 14 April 2010).

Lawless, A. (2005) *Numbers and Needs: Addressing Imbalances in the Civil Engineering Profession*, South African Institution of Civil Engineers, Midrand, South Africa.

Leighton, C. (1996) 'Strategies for Achieving Health Financing Reform in Africa', *World Development*, vol. 24, no. 9, pp. 1511–25.

Letema, S., van Vliet, B. and van Lier, J. B. (2010) 'Reconsidering Urban Sewer and Treatment Facilities in East Africa as Interplay of Flows, Networks and Spaces', in B. Van Vliet, G. Spaargaren and P. Oosterveer (eds) *Social Perspectives on the Sanitation Challenge*, Springer, Dordrecht, Netherlands, pp. 145–62.

Levine, D. N. (1965) *Wax and Gold: Tradition and Innovation in Ethiopian Culture*, University of Chicago Press, Chicago.

Lycée Sud Médoc (2009) 'La Problématique: problématiser le sujet': www.ac-bordeaux.fr/Etablissement/SudMedoc/Tpe_Sm/2002_03/methode/problematique.htm (accessed 28 January 2009).

Machel, G. (2010) 'Stay Out of Africa This Time, Nelson Mandela's Wife Tells Britain', interview with David Smith, Guardian.co.uk, 16 April: www.guardian.co.uk/world/2010/apr/16/big-brother-attitude-africa-zimbabwe-machel (accessed 16 April 2010).

Made-in-China.com (2010) 'Electric Rickshaw': www.made-in-china.com/showroom/sea0067/product-detailnYJEQGmvDxSK/China-Electric-Rickshaw.html (accessed 01 September 2010).

Malik, K. (2002) 'All Cultures Are Not Equal': www.marxists.org/subject/africa/malik/not-equal.htm (accessed 16 March 2010).

Marin, P. (2009) 'Public–Private Partnerships for Urban Water Utilities: A Review of Experiences in Developing Countries', PPIAF (Public Private Infrastructure Advisory Facility); The World Bank, Trends and Policy Options no. 8, February, World Bank, Washington, DC.

Martinez, I. A. (1999) 'The Development of a Bi-level Geographic Information Systems Database Model for Informal Settlement Upgrading', PhD thesis, University of Cape Town.

Meller, H. (1997) *Towns, Plans and Society in Modern Britain*, Cambridge University Press, Cambridge.

Melosi, M. V. (2008) *The Sanitary City: Environmental Services in Urban America from Colonial Times to the Present*, abridged edition, Pittsburgh University Press, Pittsburgh.

Ministère des Affaires Etrangères (2006) 'Spatial Planning and Sustainable Development Policy in France', Direction Générale de la Coopération Internationale et du Développement.

Ministry of Federal Affairs (Federal Government of Ethiopia) (undated) 'Brief Profile of the National Urban Planning Institute': www.nupi.gov.et/nupi.htm#Introduction (accessed 15 February 2010).

MIT (2009) MIT OpenCourseWare's photostream, uploaded 24 February 2009: www. flickr.com/photos/mitopencourseware/3304104122/ (accessed 14 June 2010).

MoFED (2006) *Ethiopia: Building on Progress: A Plan for Accelerated and Sustained Development to End Poverty (PASDEP) (2005/06–2009/10)*, Ministry of Finance and Economic Development (MoFED), Federal Government of Ethiopia, Addis Ababa, September.

Monstadt, J. (2009) 'Conceptualizing the Political Ecology of Urban Infrastructures: Insights from Technology and Urban Studies', *Environment and Planning A*, vol. 41, no. 8, pp. 1924–42.

Moyo, D. (2009) *Dead Aid*, Penguin, London.

MWUD (2007) *Plan for Urban Development and Urban Good Governance*, Ministry of Works and Urban Development, Federal Government of Ethiopia, Addis Ababa, December.

Myers, G. A. (2003) *Verandahs of Power: Colonialism and Space in Urban Africa*, Syracuse University Press, Syracuse, NY.

National Archives (2011a) Public Health Act 1875: www.legislation.gov.uk/ukpga/Vict/38-39/55 (accessed 09 May 2011).

National Archives (2011b) Local Government Act 1929: www.legislation.gov.uk/ukpga/Geo5/19-20/17 (accessed 09 May 2011).

National Archives (2011) http://webarchive.nationalarchives.gov.uk/2010052 8142817/http://www.gos.gov.uk/aboutusnat/, National Archives (United Kingdom), snapshot of 28 May 2010 (accessed 20 October 2011).

Neath Port Talbot (2009) 'History of Roads: Where Did All the Roads Come From?': www.npt.gov.uk/Default.aspx?page=3125 (accessed 26 October 2009).

Newman, N. (2009) 'Britain's Renewable Energy Policy Questioned', *Oxford Prospect*, 08 August: www.oxfordprospect.co.uk/RenewableEnergyPolicyQuestioned. html (accessed 21 August 2009).

Ngowi, A. B. (1998) 'Is Construction a Key to Sustainable Development?', *Building Research and Information*, vol. 26, no. 6, pp. 340–50.

Nilsson, D. (2006) 'A Heritage of Unsustainability? Reviewing the Origin of the Large-Scale Water and Sanitation System in Kampala, Uganda', *Environment and Urbanization*, 18, no. 2, pp. 369–85.

Nkomo, J., Rabie, N., Sussens, H. and Lenehan, A. (2004) 'Low Pressure Yard Tank Systems as an Alternative to Conventional Street Standpipe Systems for Rural Communities', *Proceedings of the 2004 Water Institute of Southern Africa (WISA) Biennial Conference*, Cape Town, 2–6 May: www.ewisa.co.za/literature/files/083.pdf (accessed 26 August 2010).

North West Office of the Premier (2009) Documents, Office of the Premier, North West Provincial Government, Republic of South Africa: www.nwpg.gov.za/Premiers/Office%20of%20the%20Premier/Documents.html (accessed 20 June 2011).

Novotny, V., Ahern, J. and Brown, P. (2010) *Water Centric Sustainable Communities: Planning, Retrofitting and Building the Next Urban Environment*, John Wiley, Hoboken, NJ.

O'Brien, P. K. and Clesse, A. (eds) (2002) *Two Hegemonies: Britain 1846–1914 and the United States 1945–2001*, Ashgate, Aldershot, UK.

OECD (2001) *Citizens as Partners: OECD Handbook on Information, Consultation and Public Participation in Policy-Making*, OECD Publishing, Paris.

OHCHR (2011) 'Good Governance Practices for the Protection of Human Rights' (HR/PUB/07/4), Office of the United Nations High Commissioner for Human Rights: http://www2.ohchr.org/english/issues/development/governance/ (accessed 13 October 2009).

Olowu, D. (2001) 'Decentralization Policies and Practices under Structural Adjustment and Democratization in Africa', Democracy, Governance and Human Rights Programme Policy Paper no. 4, July, United Nations Research Institute for Social Development (UNRISD), Geneva.

Onslow (Earl of) (1925) *First Report of the Royal Commission on Local Government: Relation to the Reform Proposals* (Cmd 2506).

Onslow (Earl of) (1928) *Second Report of the Royal Commission on Local Government: Constitution and Extension of County Boroughs* (Cmd 3213).

Oxford Dictionaries (2011) 'Infrastructure', Oxford University Press: www.oxforddictionaries.com/definition/infrastructure (accessed 09 May 2011).

Palmer Development Group (1994) *Costing of Water Supply Systems*, Water Research Commission, Pretoria, South Africa, May (draft).

Pankhurst, R. (2007) 'Preface', in F. Giorghis and D. Gérard, *The City and Its Architectural Heritage: Addis Ababa 1886–1941*, Shama Books, Addis Ababa.

Physorg (2008) 'Africa Awash in Sunlight, but not Solar Energy': www.physorg.com/news141814134.html, 28 September 2008 (accessed 31 August 2010).

Piracha, A. L. and Marcotullio, P. J. (2003) *Urban Ecosystems Analysis: Identifying Tools and Methods*, United Nations University/Institute of Advanced Studies, Tokyo.

Pitt, M. (2008) 'The Pitt Review: Lessons Learned from the 2007 Floods', Cabinet Office, London.

PRB (2010) 'Ripple Effects: Populations and Coastal Regions', Population Reference Bureau: www.prb.org/Publications/PolicyBriefs/RippleEffectsPopulationandCoastalRegions.aspx, Population Reference Bureau (PRB) article by Liz Creel (accessed 10 June 2010).

PRB (2011) 'World Population Growth 1950 to 2050', Population Reference Bureau: www.prb.org/educators/teachersguides/humanpopulation/populationgrowth.aspx (accessed 10 June 2010).

PSLC DataShop (2009) 'Glossary: Problem': pslcdatashop.web.cmu.edu/help?page=terms#problem (accessed 05 February 2009). PSLC DataShop is a data analysis service for the science learning community.

Rakodi, C. (1997a) 'Global Forces, Urban Change, and Urban Management in Africa', in C. Rakodi (ed.) *The Urban Challenge in Africa: Growth and Management of Its Large Cities*, United Nations University Press, Tokyo, pp. 17–73.

Rakodi, C. (ed.) (1997b) *The Urban Challenge in Africa: Growth and Management of Its Large Cities*, United Nations University Press, Tokyo.

Redfield, R. and Singer, M. B. (1954) 'The Cultural Role of Cities', *Economic Development and Cultural Change*, vol. 3, pp. 53–73.

Republic of South Africa (1996) Constitution of the Republic of South Africa 1996: www.info.gov.za/documents/constitution/1996/index.htm (accessed 15 September 2009).

Republic of South Africa (2003) 'Strategic Framework for Water Services', Ministry of Water Affairs and Forestry, September.

Richards, L. (1977) 'The Context of Foreign Aid: Modern Imperialism', *Review of Radical Political Economics*, vol. 9, no. 4, pp. 43–75.

Riddell, R. (2007) *Does Foreign Aid Really Work?* Oxford University Press, Oxford.

Robbins, P. T. (2007) 'The Reflexive Engineer: Perceptions of Integrated Development', *Journal of International Development*, vol. 19, no. 1, pp. 99–100.

Robinson, J. B. and Tinker, J. (1997) 'Reconciling Ecological, Economic and Social Imperatives: A New Conceptual Framework', in T. Schrecker (ed.) *Surviving Globalism: Social and Environmental Dimensions*, Macmillan, London.

Robinson, J. B. and Tinker, J. (1998) 'Reconciling Ecological, Social, and Economic Imperatives', in J. Schnurr and S. Hotz (eds) *The Cornerstone of Development: Integrating Environmental Social and Economic Policies*, Toronto: IDRC.

Rode, P. (2006) 'City Design – A New Planning Paradigm?', a Discussion Paper of the Cities Programme, London School of Economics: www.urban-age.net.

Rodney, W. (1973) *How Europe Underdeveloped Africa*, Bogle l'Ouverture Publications, London.

Rosemarin, A., Ekane, N. and Caldwell, I. (2008) *Pathways for Sustainable Sanitation in Achieving the Millennium Development Goals*, IWA Publishing/EcoSanRes Programme, Stockholm Environmental Institute, Stockholm.

Rossi, M. (undated) 'Decentralization – Initial Experiences and Expectations of the SDC': www.ciesin.columbia.edu/decentralization/English/General/SDC_initial.pdf (accessed 10 March 2010).

Sanyal, B. (ed.) (2005) *Comparative Planning Cultures*, Routledge, New York.

Schnurr, J. and Hotz, S. (eds) (1998) *The Cornerstone of Development: Integrating Environmental Social and Economic Policies*, Toronto: IDRC.

Schwirian, K. (2007) 'Ecological Models of Urban Form: Concentric Zone Model, the Sector Model, and the Multiple Nuclei Model', *Blackwell Encyclopedia of Sociologyonline*.www.sociologyencyclopedia.com/public/tocnode?id=g9781405124331_yr2010_chunk_g978140512433111_ss1-4 (accessed 18 February 2011).

Scott, W. R. (2008) *Institutions and Organizations: Ideas and Interests*, 3rd ed., Thousand Oaks, CA: Sage.

SDC (1999) *Decentralization and Development*, Swiss Development Corporation Publications, Berne, January, ISBN 3-905398-03-6.

Sebake, T. N. (2008) 'Limitations of Implementing Sustainable Construction Principles in the Conventional South African Design Approach', *Third Built Environment Conference*, Cape Town, 6–8 July, Association of Schools of Construction of Southern Africa: www.asocsa.org/index.html (accessed 27 September 2010).

Seeley, I. H. (1967) *Municipal Engineering Practice*, Macmillan, London.

Selamta (2010) 'Harar', www.selamta.net/harar.htm (accessed 11 February 2010).

Serageldin, M., Kim, S. and Wahba, S. (2000) 'Decentralization and Urban Management' (Final Draft), Background Paper for UNCHS/Habitat Third Global Report on Human Settlements, August, Center for Urban Development Studies, Harvard University Graduate School of Urban Design.

Severn Trent Water (2009) 'History of Water Supply', Severn Trent Water: Education: http://www.stwatereducation.co.uk/server.php?show=nav.36 (accessed 26 October 2011).

SNNPRS (2003) 'The Constitution of the Southern Nations, Nationalities and Peoples Regional Government', Proclamation 64/2003.

Sogreah (undated) 'Infrastructures urbaines': www.sogreah.fr/metiers-fr-5-35-infrastructures+urbaines+vrd.html.

Srivastva, S., Obert, S. and Neilsen, E. (1977) 'Organizational Analysis through

Group Processes: A Theoretical Perspective for Organizational Development', in C. Cooper (ed.) *Organizational Development in the U.K. and the U.S.A.: A Joint Evaluation*, Macmillan, London.

Stanford Encyclopedia of Philosophy (2008) 'Rationalism vs. Empiricism': plato. stanford.edu/entries/rationalism-empiricism/, first published 19 August 2004; substantive revision 6 August 2008 (accessed 02 September 2009).

Stewart, A. P. (1871) 'Royal Sanitary Commission', *British Medical Journal*, vol. 1, no. 535, 1 April, p. 354: www.ncbi.nlm.nih.gov/pmc/articles/PMC2260555/ (accessed 09 May 2011).

Tarr, J. (1984) 'The Evolution of the Urban Infrastructure in the Nineteenth and Twentieth Centuries', in R. Hansen (ed.) *Perspectives on Urban Infrastructure*, prepared for the Committee on National Urban Policy, Commission on Behavioral and Social Sciences and Education, National Research Council, National Academy Press, Washington, DC.

Technogumption (2008) 'Essential Online Advertising Terminology': www.technogumption.com/category/jargon/page/2/ (accessed 12 March 2009).

Tibbetts, J. (2002) 'Coastal Cities: Living on the Edge', *Environmental Health Perspectives*, vol. 110, no. 11, pp. 674–81.

Times, The (2008) 'National Grid Chief Steve Holliday: Blackouts Will Be Common in 7 Years', *The Times* (London), 22 December.

Timesonline (2009) 'Nuclear Alone Won't Keep the Power Flowing', interview with Professor Dieter Helm, University of Oxford, 11 November.

Torjman, S. (2005) *What Is Policy?* Caledon Institute of Social Policy, Toronto, September.

Turton, D. (2006) 'Introduction', in D. Turton (ed.) *Ethnic Federalism: The Ethiopian Experience in Comparative Perspective*, Addis Ababa University Press, Addis Ababa, pp. 1–31.

UN ESCAP (2009) 'What Is Good Governance?', United Nations Economic and Social Commission for Asia and the Pacific: www.unescap.org/pdd/prs/Project-Activities/Ongoing/gg/governance.asp (accessed 13 October 2009).

UNDP (1991) 'Cities, People and Poverty: Urban Development Cooperation for the 1990s', UNDP Strategy Paper, United Nations Development Programme, New York.

UNESCO (2003) 'E-Governance Capacity Building: What Is E-Governance?': http://portal.unesco.org/ci/en/ev.php-URL_ID=12951&URL_DO=DO_TOPIC&URL_SECTION=201.html (accessed 22 September 2010).

UN-Habitat (2008) *The State of African Cities 2008: A Framework for Addressing Urban Challenges in Africa*, United Nations Human Settlements Programme (UN-Habitat), Nairobi.

UN-Habitat (2009) *Global Report on Human Settlements 2009: Planning Sustainable Cities*, United Nations Human Settlements Programme, Earthscan, London.

UN-Habitat (2010) 'Governance': www.unhabitat.org/campaigns/governance (accessed 22 February 2010).

United Nations (2000) *Millennium Declaration of the United Nations General Assembly* (Resolution 55/2), United Nations, New York.

US Department of State (undated) 'Milestones, 1969–1976, OPEC Oil Embargo, 1973–1974', Office of the Historian, US Department of State: http://history.state.gov/milestones/1969-1976/OPEC (accessed 21 October 2011).

Van Ryneveld, M. B. (1995) 'Costs and Affordability of Water Supply and Sanitation Provision in the Urban Areas of South Africa', *Water SA*, vol. 21, no. 1, pp. 1–14.

Vasishth, A. and Sloane, D. C. (2002) 'Returning to Ecology: An Ecosystem Approach to Understanding the City', in M. Dear (ed.) *From Chicago to LA: Making Sense of Urban Theory*, Sage, Thousand Oaks, CA, pp. 343–66.

Warner, S. B. (1987) *The Private City*, revised edition, Pennsylvania University Press, Philadelphia.

Websters Dictionary (1913 edition) 'Water supply', p. 1633, taken from the ARTFL project of the University of Chicago: machaut.uchicago.edu/websters (accessed 27 January 2009).

WEDC (undated) *Sanitation Policy: Why It Is Important and How to Make It Work*, Water, Engineering and Development Centre, Loughborough University, UK.

WHO (2011) 'Trade, Foreign Policy, Diplomacy and Health: Structural Adjustment Programmes (SAPS)', World Health Organization, Geneva: www.who.int/trade/glossary/story084/en/index.html (accessed 09 May 2011).

Wikipedia (2009a) 'History of Local Government in England': http://en.wikipedia.org/wiki/History_of_local_government_in_England (accessed 26 October 2009).

Wikipedia (2009b) 'Margaret Thatcher': http://en.wikipedia.org/wiki/Margaret_Thatcher (accessed 05 October 2009).

Wikipedia (2009c) 'Local Government (County Boroughs and Adjustments) Act 1926': http://en.wikipedia.org/wiki/Local_Government_%28County_Boroughs_and_Adjustments%29_Act_1926 (accessed 24 October 2009).

Wikipedia (2010a) 'Municipal or Urban Engineering': http://en.wikipedia.org/wiki/Municipal_or_urban_engineering, accessed 22 April 2010.

Wikipedia (2010b) 'Policy': http://en.wikipedia.org/wiki/Policy_making (accessed 09 May 2011).

Wikipedia (2010c) 'World view', http://en.wikipedia.org/wiki/World_view (accessed 15 February 2010).

Wikipedia (2010d) 'Benjamin Lee Whorf': http://en.wikipedia.org/wiki/Benjamin_Whorf, accessed 15 February 2010.

Wikipedia (2010e) 'Paradigm': http://en.wikipedia.org/wiki/Paradigm (accessed 15 February 2010).

Wikipedia (2010f) 'Gondar': http://en.wikipedia.org/wiki/Gondar (accessed 11 February 2010).

Wikipedia (2011a) 'Empiricism': http://en.wikipedia.org/wiki/Empiricism (accessed 11 May 2011).

Wikipedia (2011b) 'Miasma': http://en.wikipedia.org/wiki/Miasma_theory (accessed 08 April 2011).

WMO-GWP (2008) 'Urban Flood Risk Management: A Tool for Integrated Flood Management', Associated Programme on Flood Management, World Meteorological Organization, Geneva, and the Global Water Partnership, Stockholm, Version 1.0, March.

WordNet (2009) 'Problem': http://wordnetweb.princeton.edu/perl/webwn?s=problem (accessed 05 February 2009). WordNet is a lexical database for English developed by the Cognitive Science Laboratory at Princeton University.

WordNet (2011) 'Empiricism': http://wordnetweb.princeton.edu/perl/webwn?s=empiricism (accessed 26 October 2011).

World Bank (1990) *World Development Report 1990: Poverty*, Oxford University Press, Oxford.

World Bank (2004) *World Development Report 2004: Making Services Work for Poor People*, World Bank, Washington, DC.

World Bank (undated) 'Ethiopia: Decentralized Fiscal Support for Infrastructure (DFS) Program': http://siteresources.worldbank.org/ETHIOPIAEXTN/Resources/DFS_note.doc (accessed 20 January 2010).

Zewde, B. (2002) *A History of Modern Ethiopia: 1855–1991*, 2nd ed., Addis Ababa University Press, Addis Ababa.

Index

Page numbers in *italics* denote tables, those in **bold** denote figures.